# a
# People's
# History
## of
# Detroit

MARK JAY + PHILIP CONKLIN

# a People's History of Detroit

Duke University Press   Durham and London   2020

Library of Congress Cataloging-in-Publication Data
Names: Jay, Mark, author. | Conklin, Philip, author.
Title: A people's history of Detroit / Mark Jay, Philip Conklin.
Description: Durham : Duke University Press, 2020. | Includes bibliographical references
   and index.
Identifiers: LCCN 2019033498 (print) | LCCN 2019033499 (ebook)
ISBN 9781478007883 (hardcover)
ISBN 9781478008347 (paperback)
ISBN 9781478009351 (ebook)
Subjects: LCSH: Detroit (Mich.)—Economic conditions. | Detroit (Mich.)—Social conditions. |
   Detroit (Mich.)—History. | Urban renewal—Michigan—Detroit—History. | Community
   development—Michigan—Detroit—History.
Classification: LCC HC108.D6 J39 2020 (print) | LCC HC108.D6 (ebook) | DDC 977.4/34—dc23
LC record available at https://lccn.loc.gov/2019033498
LC ebook record available at https://lccn.loc.gov/2019033499

Cover art: Workers on strike at the General Motors factory, around 1945–46.
Photo by Keystone-France/Gamma-Keystone, courtesy Getty Images.

To our loving partners,   **MINNE + KATRINA**

We see that this whole society exists and rests upon workers, and that this whole society controlled by this ruling clique is parasitic, vulturistic, cannibalistic, and it's sucking and destroying the life of workers, and we have to stop it because it's evil.

KENNETH COCKREL, LEAGUE OF REVOLUTIONARY BLACK WORKERS, 1970

# Contents

# Acknowledgments

I WOULD LIKE to first thank my family. Mom, Dad, Abbey, Hannah, Grandma, Deb, George, and the Roys: thanks for the unconditional love and support. I also want to express my deep gratitude to Aranye Fradenburg Joy, who gave me my mind back. I should also acknowledge Simonetta Falasca-Zamponi, Chris McAuley, Kevin Anderson, Jon Cruz, and William I. Robinson, who advised me throughout the process of writing this book. Thanks especially to Simonetta for her warmth, indulgence, and skepticism; to Kevin for his endless knowledge of all things Marx; and to Chris, who was always there to talk and who was always down for a reading group. A further thanks to Olivier Teernstra, for all the conversations and metaphysical speculations; to Raihan Ahmed, my companion in all things philosophy and football; and to Kevin Chamow, my dear, iconoclastic friend, whose novel *The Two Hundred Dollar Day* is a constant source of inspiration. A further shout out to all the people in Detroit and Santa Barbara who kept me going these past years: Buzz (RIP), One Be Lo, Don DeLillo, David Feldman, Ashwin Bajaj, Virginia Hotchkiss, Salvador Rangel, Jamella Gow, Hoai-An Nguyen, Laura Halcomb, Joel Feigin, Isaac Miller, Aaron Handelsman, Dominic Iseli-Smith, Kelvin Parker-Bell, Darren Reese-Brown, and all the youth locked up at Lincoln Center. Finally, I'd like to thank the Feilers—love you, Sid.
—*Mark*

WHILE WRITING THIS BOOK I was working at the Inn Season Cafe in Royal Oak. I'd like to thank my coworkers for making it a warm and convivial place to be, especially my guys Rob Streit and Beau Lukas.

My experiences living in Detroit and Hamtramck inform much of the contemporary analysis in this book. I'd like to thank all the people who, knowingly or not, influenced my thinking about the city, and politics in general. I'd like to also thank the librarians of Hamtramck for dealing with all my MELcat requests and renewals (and for being lax on the late fees).

And, of course, a big thank you to my parents, my brothers, and all my friends and extended family for their support, encouragement, and inspiration throughout the years.

—*Philip*

WE FEEL DEEP GRATITUDE to all the editors and staff at Duke University Press, who were a joy to work with. Thanks in particular to Gisela Fosado, who believed in this project from the beginning. We also want to thank our two anonymous reviewers, whose incisive critiques and suggestions for further reading both humbled and motivated us. Sections of the book draw upon articles that we've written in *Race and Class, Monthly Review, Social Justice, Jacobin, Historical Materialism,* and the *Berkeley Journal of Sociology*; thank you to the editors of these publications for shaping our ideas, and for helping to publicize the oppression, exploitation, and political struggles that continue to occur in Detroit and beyond.

We also want to acknowledge Jerome Scott, whose insights were essential to our understanding of the League of Revolutionary Black Workers, and revolutionary politics more generally.

Finally, we'd like to thank David Harvey, whom we've never met but who provoked us years ago when he complained that the scope of academic studies was ever diminishing, and that nowadays few scholars were prepared to "really go for it." This book is our attempt to really go for it.

# Marx in Detroit

Here, man, oh man, it's a dream. Anything can be created in Detroit. —**DAN GILBERT**, chairman of Quicken Loans, Inc., quoted in Ben Austen, "The Post-Post-Apocalyptic Detroit," 2014

The state does not want us to have water. —**EMMA FOGLE**, seventy-four-year-old retired Ford worker and current Highland Park resident, quoted in Ryan Felton, "Not just Detroit," 2015

The story of Detroit has passed even beyond the realm of cliché. Epitome of the American Dream, Arsenal of Democracy, Poster Child of the Urban Crisis, Most Violent City in America, and now the Comeback City—Detroit has long been a canvas for our collective fantasies.[1] Detroit, it's been said, is the soul of America; as its fortunes rise and fall, so do those of the country. In the popular imagination, Detroit is a sort of "funhouse mirror" of twentieth-century America, which at once reflects and magnifies the ups and downs of a tumultuous history.[2] Motown, some have said, is "the starting line of the world's imagination."[3] The cradle of modern manufacturing, the hub of global industry, and "the birthplace of the American middle class"—the Motor City was in the first half of the twentieth century the ostensible apex of Western capitalism, a city that could seemingly provide for the needs of all.[4] But deindustrialization and the hollowing out of urban cores that plagued the nation in the postwar years was particularly devastating to Detroit. According to the popular narrative, the riot of 1967—the most violent in a season of urban riots across the nation— was the final straw, as the explosion of racial tension inaugurated forty years of decline. In the late twentieth century, Detroit's "hyper-crisis" became a shorthand for the collapse of urban America, culminating in 2013 in the largest municipal bankruptcy in U.S. history.[5] By that time the city's population had declined from its 1950 peak of 1.8 million to less than 700,000, and its white population had dropped from more than 1.5 million to less than 100,000. Once the industrial center of the world, Detroit now leads the United States in rates of unemployment and poverty. "Ruin porn" photographers have found in the fallen Motor City a panorama of industrial decay unmatched almost anywhere.

But hope remains. Detroit, they say, has shown time and time again that it can bounce back from anything.

"We hit rock bottom," former mayor Dave Bing admitted.[6] But rest assured: "Detroit was down . . . but not out."[7] Thanks to the city's "infectious, survivalist spirit" and "entrepreneurial, roll-up-your-sleeves energy," Motown has become "America's great comeback story."[8] Since the completion of its bankruptcy, Detroit's motto—"We hope for better things; it will rise from the ashes"—rings throughout the city, as resilient long-timers and eager newcomers "turn emptiness into opportunity."[9] "Artists, entrepreneurs and young people" are "converting vacant lots into urban farms and abandoned buildings into cafes and museums."[10] The flurry of reinvestment has turned the "new Detroit" into "America's most ambitious renovation project."[11] National media outlets laud the fallen city's revival: the *New York Times* declares that there is a "new spirit and promise" in "post-post-apocalyptic Detroit."[12] An *Economist* article about Detroit's bankruptcy titled "A Phoenix Emerges" opens with the line, "There is an exciting feeling of a new beginning."[13] The *Washington Post* speculates that Detroit will be the greatest turnaround story in American history.[14] *The Atlantic* proclaims, "The signs are everywhere: 'Opportunity Detroit.'"[15] *Detroit: Comeback City*, a History Channel documentary produced by the Detroit-born hip-hop star Big Sean, tells the story of "a city of ruins that is now on the cusp of an exciting rebirth."[16]

As the city's mayor Mike Duggan put it in 2016, "The goal is to create a city where we're a center of invention and entrepreneurialism, like we were in the early nineteen-hundreds."[17] And indeed it seems Detroit has finally passed through the gauntlet of deindustrialization and successfully remade itself in the image of twenty-first-century urbanism—as a hub for tourism, white-collar industry, and high-end consumption. Recently ranked second on *Lonely Planet*'s list of best cities in the world to visit, and called "the most exciting city in America right now" by the *New York Times*, Detroit is "transform[ing] itself from a punchline to a cool-cat destination."[18] "The food scene is making it a must-visit," declares *Food Network*.[19] "Something remarkable is happening here," reports the *Toronto Star*. Detroit is "coming back better, stronger, artier."[20] One giddy *New York Times* travel writer visiting Detroit imagined himself "on a Disney ride. *See the future American City being built before your eyes!*"[21]

But despite the very real changes transforming the city, the euphoria is far from universal. Flouting the media's triumphalism surrounding Detroit's "revival," one publication, citing high rates of crime and poverty and a poor job market, rated Motown the worst U.S. city to live in in 2018.[22] Even the *New York Times*, one of the main champions of Detroit's revival, asserts that "The real story is a tale of two cities."[23] While billions are invested in the roughly seven-square-mile area of Greater Downtown, many neighborhoods throughout the rest of the city's 130 square miles languish, prompting local activists speaking in front of the United Nations to take up the 1951 declaration of the Civil Rights Congress: "We charge genocide!"[24]

Even *Forbes* wonders, "How could you keep Detroit's boom from replicating America's economic divide?"[25] Many see Detroit re-creating the problems faced by other cities that have experienced gentrification. While the largely poor, black residents on the city's outskirts continue to suffer from underemployment, crime, and austerity, the more affluent, disproportionately white newcomers have created a Downtown playground of consumption and luxury cut off from the reality of the rest of the city: "Today, the sidewalks of [Dan] Gilbertville are packed with millennials taking a break from beach volleyball to sip craft beer and nibble on artisanal pickles."[26] It's no wonder that the city's poorer residents, having endured forty years of immiseration and dispossession, feel alienated by Detroit's glittering "recovery." As Coleman A. Young Jr., son of Detroit's first black mayor, put it during his 2017 mayoral campaign, "If you can't afford to participate in any of the things that are going on downtown, what does it mean to you? If you can't afford your house? Can't afford your water bill? Can't afford car insurance?"[27]

In April 2018 the University of Michigan's Population Studies Center released a survey about Detroiters' attitudes toward the city's changes. The findings are revealing: "Asked about who benefits most from downtown and Midtown investments, more believed it was non-residents (38 percent) than city residents (20 percent); white people (47 percent) as opposed to black people (2 percent); and wealthier people (70 percent) over poorer people (2 percent)." "The negativism is a little starker than we thought," concluded Jeffrey Morenoff, the director of the Center.[28]

Despite its highly contested nature, Detroit's recovery is nonetheless happening and is considered by most outside commentators to be, on the whole, broadly beneficial. Even Alan Mallach, author of *The Divided City*, which details the inequality of Detroit's revitalization, concludes that "the basic revival trajectory is positive."[29] The prevailing sentiment holds that it's not a question of *if* but *when* the Downtown boom will reverberate through the neighborhoods. And many participants and outsiders alike hope that the changes transforming Detroit will have an impact not only on the city itself but on the country and the world at large. "Detroit is a city that hit rock bottom that is bringing you back," said former CIA director and U.S. Army General David Petraeus on a recent visit to the city. "The question is: how to do that for the entire country?"[30] Similarly *Forbes* sees in the Motor City's revival "a blueprint that could work across the country."[31] JPMorgan Chase sees in Detroit a "model . . . that can be replicated in other places."[32]

In the current political moment, when the currency of nostalgia helped propel right-wing billionaire Donald Trump to the presidency, the prevailing logic seems to be that if we can make Detroit great again, perhaps we can do the same for the whole country.

But what's at stake is more than just questions of economics; Detroit is also the soul of the country. "Americans love a good comeback story," *Lonely Planet* explains, "and Detroit is writing a mighty one. How the city navigates the tricky path to recovery remains to be seen, but we're pulling for the underdog."[33] The *Detroit Free Press* asserts, "Not just the nation—but the world—is rooting for the city."[34]

It becomes clear that what's at stake in the city's fortunes is not just whether its recovery happens but how its recovery will be *made to mean*. Acknowledging the importance of positively framing Detroit's revival, the city government recently became the first in the United States to hire a "chief storyteller."[35] While ideological struggles take place everywhere, they seem somehow more intense in Detroit. What does it mean to live in Detroit? How should new residents comport themselves? What is the best way to think about the city's political-economic transformation?

Kenneth Cockrel, a longtime Detroit lawyer, activist, and socialist politician, has laid out some of the stakes of Detroit's redevelopment:

> We've come a long way in our city, from a few years back being regarded
> as the murder capital of the world, to a city that is now seen as the model
> to which you go if you're interested in urban revitalization. Urban revitalization that is essentially keyed to an elaborate combination of schemes that
> marry the public sector and its powers of licensing, taxation, regulation,

zoning and so on—marries those powers and subordinates those powers to the interests of enhancing the profit-making potential of various private entrepreneurs. We do it with tax abatements, we do it with tax increment financing, we do it with bond schemes . . . or [by appealing to] the upscale, educated, affluent young types who "really can make a contribution" to the tax base, being brought back to *eat quiche* while the poor are taxed out of their homes.[36]

Lest we are tempted to take seriously claims of newness surrounding the most recent round of redevelopment to hit Detroit, we should note that *these words were spoken in 1979*. Cockrel, who died young in 1989, did not live to see Detroit's current renaissance. He was responding to the efforts since the Great Rebellion of 1967 to remake Detroit along principles of "economic growth," an effort spearheaded by a cadre of public and private elites known as New Detroit, Inc. This group attempted to revitalize the city and quell future unrest through economic development, the most visible legacy of which is the Renaissance Center in Downtown.

As the following pages will show, nothing much about the New Detroit is in fact very new. The incredible inflow of capital and the physical transformation of certain areas of the city to which the national media has responded so jubilantly represents, rather, the success of specific strategies that have been ongoing for at least half a century and the continuation of a deeper capitalist logic that has shaped the Motor City since the birth of the automobile industry that made its name. It is worth dwelling on the fact that the revitalization efforts that appeared so successful in 1979 are today remembered as utter failures: this should serve as a warning of the ephemerality of the newest New Detroit, and indeed of every capitalist success story.

## Theoretical Framework

Capital never solves its crisis tendencies, it merely moves them around. —DAVID HARVEY, "The Enigma of Capital and the Crisis This Time," 2010

I would rather return to the dioramas, whose brutal and enormous magic has the power to impose on me a useful illusion. I would rather go to the theater and feast my eyes on the scenery, in which I find my dearest dreams artistically expressed and tragically concentrated. These things, because they are false, are infinitely closer to the truth. —CHARLES BAUDELAIRE, 1859, quoted in Walter Benjamin, *The Arcades Project*

This project began as a two-person reading group at Colombo's Coney Island in Southwest Detroit, itself an outgrowth of our work on *The Periphery*, a literary and political journal we and our partners, Mallika Roy and Katrina Santos, founded in 2014. With this reading group we were attempting to understand what we were living amid—most of all, the twin spectacles of Downtown boosterism and the high-profile SWAT raids that mostly targeted petty criminals, weed dealers, and unemployed people in poor neighborhoods suffering from intensive austerity (we were immediately confronted by the injustice and hypocrisy of these raids when a friend of ours, a pregnant mother, was arrested and touted by the local media as a criminal, when her only charge was a late payment on a ticket for possessing a gram of marijuana a year prior). At first we examined the city's bankruptcy, but this was clearly an event—a coup—laden with history. Nor did the concept of *racism* or *neoliberalism* seem to fully get to the root of things. So we went back to the Great Rebellion of 1967. But how can one understand an uprising if one fails to understand the material conditions and the political consciousness of the people who took to the streets? So we went further back, to the post–World War II era, only to discover that, for most Detroiters, this supposed golden age was far from golden: it was instead a time of intense economic instability, harsh work conditions, and racial violence. Finally, we decided to start with the era of Ford and the International Workers of the World, and to begin unraveling the contradictions from there.

A few years later this book resulted: it is an attempt to understand the contemporary situation in Detroit by offering a particular kind of history. This is not a comprehensive history.[37] Rather, what we are attempting to do here is excavate the city's past in a way that brings to light the underlying logic of processes that continue to this day. To be sure, this book aims to correct many of the myths that pervade scholarly and popular understandings of Detroit's past. But a deeper motivation is to contextualize the present situation: we insist that in order to make sense of the dramatic shifts occurring in contemporary Detroit, one needs to have a broad understanding of the central tensions and contradictions that have driven the city's development over the past century. This requires an analysis of the broader system of capitalism, in which Detroit is embedded. In short, to understand what is happening in Detroit, one needs to understand how capitalism works.[38]

Capitalism, as defined by Black Studies Professor Christopher McAuley, is a system of "managed commodity production for profit by workers who do not own the means of production."[39] It is the first type of society in which people acquire the overwhelming bulk of their goods on the market and in which, in order to survive, most people have to seek out a capitalist who can profitably dispose of their labor. Without a serious analysis of how this capitalist economy works—how jobs and resources are allocated, how exploitation and inequality are contested, justified, and institutionalized—one cannot fully understand the conditions of day-to-day life in Detroit, or most anywhere else.

As the title of this book suggests, we have a deep appreciation of the radical historian Howard Zinn's classic work, *A People's History of the United States*, which highlights the oppression and political struggles that have shaped this country since its genocidal birth. However, we feel that in order to give a true "people's history" one must do more than condemn the malevolence of those in power and celebrate the activists who have struggled for justice; one must also come to terms with the social system in which these people lived. In our case, this means confronting the logic of capital.

Unfortunately, however, even the most critical accounts of Detroit generally take the logic of capital for granted. To a certain extent, this is understandable. "Capital," Hardt and Negri write, "functions as an impersonal form of domination that imposes laws of its own, economic laws that structure social life and make hierarchies and subordinations seem natural and necessary." It is easy to take for granted "the basic elements of capitalist society—the power of property concentrated in the hands of the few, the need for the majority to sell their labor-power to maintain themselves, the exclusion of large portions of the global population even from these circuits of exploitation, and so forth."[40]

In the scholarly literature on Detroit, one reads often about inequality, exploitation, unemployment, dispossession, and the like. But very rarely do authors analyze how these sorts of injustices are integral to the functioning of capitalism. Emblematic is the highly acclaimed *Origins of the Urban Crisis* by the historian Thomas Sugrue, probably the most widely read book on the history of Detroit. The work is an excellent piece of scholarship that documents how racial discrimination in housing and employment in the post–World War II era led to the outbreak of the Great Rebellion in 1967. The larger point is that the so-called Urban Crisis of the mid-1960s (involving deindustrialization, ghettoization of black communities, rising crime, and urban uprisings) did not just spring from the moral deficiencies of urban communities, and Sugrue's book, published in 1996, is a corrective to conservative ideologies, which claim that urban rebellions were a result of black criminality and entitlement fostered by liberal social programs. But by restricting his scope to a fifteen-year period (1945–1960) and focusing mainly on two issues (housing and employment), Sugrue's work remains basically at the level of the *symptom*. It is our contention that the origin of the urban crisis is not housing and employment discrimination in the years after World War II, though these were certainly a proximate cause; the origin of the urban crisis is the system of capitalism, which dispossesses and alienates the majority of the people to enrich a small class of owners. Despite myriad studies of specific time periods or aspects of Detroit's past and present, there has not yet been a book which attempts to coalesce the city's modern history into a structural critique of the political economic system that we all live under. To correct this gap in the scholarly literature and popular understanding, we have turned to Marx—who remains the premier theorist of capitalism—as well as the myriad Detroit activists who were influenced by, and attempted to practice a politics based on, Marxism.

In an essay titled "Marx in Detroit," which appeared as a postscript to his 1966 work, *Operai e capitale*, the Italian Marxist philosopher Mario Tronti argued that, though the ideological influence of Marxism had been greater in Europe, Asia, and Latin America, it was in the United States, and in Detroit in particular, that social relations were "objectively Marxian": "For at least half a century, up to the post–Second World War period, Marx could be read [in the United States] in the reality of the struggles and of the responses provoked by the demands of the struggles. This does not mean that Marx's books provide us with an interpretation of American labor struggles. Rather, it means that these struggles provide us with a key for an accurate interpretation of Marx's most advanced texts . . . *Capital* and the *Grundrisse*."[41]

Following Tronti, we claim that not only does Marx help us to understand Detroit but that Detroit helps us to understand Marx. In *Capital*, Marx suggests that the "secret of profit-making" is not to be looked for in the "noisy" marketplace but in the "hidden abodes" of the workplaces where capitalists exploit laborers and extract profits from their sweat and blood. When we look inside Detroit's gargantuan factories, we find vivid, devastating examples of the processes Marx theorized: workers treated as raw commodities by huge monopoly firms, systems of production that turn each worker into an "appendage of the machine," militant worker struggles against degrading and dangerous workplace conditions, the constant reproduction of an unemployed "reserve army of labor," and on and on. In short, as the backbone of U.S. industry and the center of industrial unionism, Detroit presents a distilled version of the process of class struggle Marx theorized. Marx and Engels also suggested that the perpetual need for higher profits "chases the bourgeoisie over the entire surface of the globe"; in Detroit we see a vivid portrait of what society looks like when the factory owners leave but the system of capitalism remains.[42]

It comes as little surprise, then, that Marxism has had a significant ideological influence on thinkers, politicians, and workers throughout Detroit's history, as the following pages will show. To take just one example, consider these words spoken by Jerome Scott, a member of the League of Revolutionary Black Workers

(LRBW), a radical group that led struggles against economic exploitation and racial oppression in Detroit's plants in the late 1960s and early 1970s (soon after the publication of Tronti's essay): "Marxism—Marxism-Leninism—[w]as the theory that related most closely to our lives. Mind you, we were production workers. Marxism was written for workers."[43] The League and other militant groups launched a series of strikes in the 1960s and 1970s that drew the attention of leftist workers in Italy's auto industry: in the words of the renowned scholar-activist Paolo Virno, "Fighting at FIAT of Turin, we were thinking of Detroit, not Cuba or Algiers."[44]

But while Detroit's past is full of attempts to build organized worker movements to combat exploitation and inequality, the city's history also demonstrates the difficulty of realizing Marx and Engels's famous vision: "Working men of all countries, unite!" In their actions, Detroit workers frequently demonstrated that they disagreed with the notion that in joining such a unified anticapitalist movement, they had "nothing to lose but their chains."[45] The divisive politics of the Motor City shows the validity of the Marxist philosopher Alberto Toscano's claim that "any kind of 'class unity' or 'solidarity' is a very precarious product of political work and not some underlying and secure ground which is merely obfuscated by capitalist brainwashing, liberal ideology, or indeed, 'identity politics.'"[46] Racism, sexism, ethnic divisions, political factionalism, generational differences, tensions related to place and geography (urban vs. suburban workers; workers of one nation against another), occupational differences (skilled vs. unskilled workers; workers of one industry vs. another)—these are just some of the tensions and contradictions that influenced and, to varying degrees, undermined, attempts at working-class solidarity, and they play a central part in the story of Detroit's political, economic, and cultural development.

This highlights the distinction Marx made between a class *in itself* and a class *for itself*. Capitalism separates people into different classes, regardless of each individual's understanding of their position in society. The primary distinction between people is a structural one: there is the ownership class, which controls the means of production, and the working class, composed of those who are separated from the means of production and forced to sell their labor power in order to earn their livelihoods. Regardless of this objective relation, class consciousness is never spontaneous or self-evident but is always forged and continually re-created in the face of the various divisions among workers. But however implacable the subjective differences among workers may appear, this structural relation joins workers together. Furthermore, capitalism is necessarily organized such that the vast majority of people are workers. This is a *people's* history of Detroit because it is oriented toward the majority, the workers, and our aim is to explicate the class relation which dispossessed these workers of the wealth that they produced in the city of Detroit.

Throughout this book we will see divisions among the working class, and we will see attempts to bridge these divisions and pursue a politics based on the common interests of workers *as workers*. In recomposing the history of Detroit from the perspective of its workers, we hope to contribute to such a political project, to the transformation of the working class from a class *in itself* to a class *for itself*.

Before proceeding with our historical analysis, let us further elaborate on our theoretical framework. Our history of Detroit is guided by the dialectical relationship between two concepts: creative destruction and mythology.

## Creative Destruction

Marx and Engels famously wrote in the *Manifesto of the Communist Party*, "Constant revolutionising of production, uninterrupted disturbance of all social conditions, everlasting uncertainty and agitation distinguish the bourgeois epoch from all earlier ones."[47] Building off of Marx and Engels's work, Joseph Schumpeter wrote in his classic work from 1942, *Capitalism, Socialism and Democracy*, "The essential fact about capitalism is the perennial gale of Creative Destruction." With this phrase Schumpeter meant to emphasize the destruction that is *inherent* to capitalism, a system that "incessantly revolutionizes the economic structure from within, incessantly destroying the old one, incessantly creating a new one."[48]

"Obsolescence is the very hallmark of progress," declared Henry Ford II in the early 1950s. "The faster we obsolete products, machines, and antiquated ways of working, the faster we raise our living standards and our national wealth."[49] In capitalism, one of the only things that doesn't seem to become obsolete is the process of obsolescence itself.

This process of creative destruction has particular importance when it comes to the built environment. In the words of the Marxist geographer David Harvey, "Capitalism perpetually seeks to create a geographical landscape to facilitate its activities at one point in time only to have to destroy it and build a wholly different landscape at a later point in time to accommodate its perpetual thirst for endless capital accumulation."[50]

In contemporary Detroit, the destruction of the old to make way for the new is particularly acute. The problematic phrase *New Detroit*, which has become a shorthand among those in the know for everything that's wrong with

Detroit's comeback, is nonetheless plastered on billboards and buildings, recited by CEOs, and used unironically by suburbanites flooding Greater Downtown. Detroit is being re-everything: revitalized, rebuilt, reborn, renewed, refurbished, revamped, restored, redeveloped. It is a "blank slate," an "investor's playground."[51] Detroit's derelict landscape, an "American Acropolis," is marketed as its greatest asset.[52] Here, where the obliteration of social forms and built environments has been more exaggerated than perhaps anywhere else in the country, capitalism's destructive capacity is cause for national celebration at the same time as it has ravaged the lives of hundreds of thousands of Detroiters.

In *All That Is Solid Melts into Air*, the Marxist theorist Marshall Berman captures the full implications of creative destruction:

> "All that is solid"—from the clothes on our backs to the looms and mills that weave them, to the men and women who work the machines, to the houses and neighborhoods the workers live in, to the firms and corporations that exploit the workers, to the towns and cities and whole regions and even nations that embrace them all—all these are made to be broken tomorrow, smashed or shredded or pulverized or dissolved, so they can be recycled or replaced next week, and the whole process can go on again and again, hopefully forever, in ever more profitable forms. The pathos of all bourgeois monuments is that their material strength and solidity actually count for nothing and carry no weight at all, that they are blown away like frail reeds by the very forces of capitalist development that they celebrate. Even the most beautiful and impressive bourgeois buildings and public works are disposable, capitalized for fast depreciation and planned to be obsolete, closer in their social functions to tents and encampments than to "Egyptian pyramids, Roman aqueducts, Gothic cathedrals." If we look behind the sober scenes that the members of our bourgeoisie create, and see the way they really work and act, we see that these solid citizens would tear down the world if it paid.[53]

## Mythologies

It is clear, however, that capitalism is not always experienced as an antagonistic and exploitative system that runs on destruction. If it were, then the only way to achieve social order would be naked coercion. And while there has always been a heavy dose of coercion—from the police, the military, and private forces, as well as from "the silent compulsion of economic relations" that force people to sell their labor in order to survive—much of the acquiescence to capitalism can be explained another way.[54] According to John Watson, a Detroit radical, "It is through the control of knowledge that the ruling class maintains its power. The struggle over the control of knowledge is a political struggle."[55] And as Roland Barthes puts it in his seminal work, *Mythologies*:

> Myth does not deny things, on the contrary, its function is to talk about them; simply, it purifies them, it makes them innocent, it gives them a natural and eternal justification. . . . In passing from history to nature, myth acts economically: it abolishes the complexity of human acts, it gives them the simplicity of essences, it does away with all dialectics, with any going back beyond what is immediately visible, it organizes a world which is without contradictions because it is without depth, a world wide open and wallowing in the evident, it establishes a blissful clarity: things appear to mean something by themselves.[56]

As well as the destruction of the built environment and the social conditions it creates, the reproduction of capitalism entails the reproduction of mythologies, the obfuscation of its social relations. In capitalism the sphere of production is separated in space and time from the spheres of distribution and consumption. This makes it impossible to immediately see the social processes that determine the coordinates of our day-to-day existence—especially in today's era of globalization. Our social relations are shrouded in darkness. As Marx pointed out in his discussion of commodity fetishism, a basic condition of capitalism is that people are constantly forced to mistake surface appearances for underlying social relations.[57]

Myth—"ideology in narrative form"—is the necessary complement to capitalism's inherent opaqueness and innate tendency for creative destruction. Myths allow the exploitation and social dislocations inherent in this political-economic system to be signified and smoothed over.[58] Paraphrasing Baudelaire, we can say that although the myths that sustain capitalism are in a sense false, they also reveal a deeper truth about the brutality and lack of transparency of capitalist social relations: *capitalism needs myths in order to survive.*[59]

As novelist Leonard Michaels has written, in contemporary capitalism there is an "unprecedented dedication to illusions far more powerful than any religious myth. . . . Thousands dedicate their lives to sustaining mass fantasies in politics, news, advertising, public relation, movies, the stock market, etc."[60] While this elite-driven dedication to illusion is certainly a huge aspect of contemporary society, it is also true that myths are not to be understood simply as top-down propagandizing. Nor are they pure fiction. Rather, myths can take hold only if, in some real way, they resonate with people's everyday lives: a myth provides "a veiled, unclear representation of the truth. . . . Unless it awoke some echo in [people], they would never accept it."[61] Myths are so powerful because they appear valid; they do not materialize out of thin air but instead manipulate surface-level appearances into narratives that allow people to locate the apparent causes of social disruptions without implicating their true origins: capitalism's structural dynamics.

Throughout this book we tend to deploy the term *mythology* in a specific and explicitly political way: we seek to shed light on the ideologies that have masked capitalism's destructive tendencies and shifted the blame for social dislocations onto discrete, identifiable groups: black people, criminals, immigrants, greedy unions, communists, "outside agitators," and the like. The point, however, is not simply to condemn myths and mythmakers. We must also explain why, at different historical conjunctures, different mythologies prevailed in and about Detroit, and in this way to break the hold that myths have on history.[62]

Much of the power of myths comes from the sense of security they provide. Unmoored by the whirlwind of creative destruction, people can grab hold of myths—stories that provide easy answers to complex and disturbing political-economic dynamics. Myths tell stories that map on to our desires about how the world ought to be rather than how it actually is. A critical look at Detroit's past also reveals that political programs that present a positive, emancipatory vision for society can similarly capture people's imaginations and catalyze collective action to reshape society. The prevalence of myths, therefore, can be understood only alongside the formation and repression of political movements that advocate radical social alternatives. Repression, however, is rarely presented as such in the popular discourse, and so analyzing the myths that justify state violence is another important aspect of our history.

We are aware that some might view our narrative as yet another myth; this is inevitable. But following Bruce Lincoln, we insist that an essential difference between our narrative and many of those that we criticize is that ours will be *footnoted*.[63] The myths that legitimate and naturalize capitalism tend to depend for their persuasive power on what they obscure; our narrative, on the other hand, will be as transparent as possible to the reader.

## The Organization of the Book

In the chapters to come, we structure our history around the interplay between creative destruction and mythologization. In deploying these concepts, our aim is not to give a complete or exhaustive analysis of social relations during the past hundred-plus years; rather, the concepts are a sort of guide we use to orient the reader through the city's turbulent past.

Chapter 1 is in many ways the heart of the book. Here we provide an in-depth analysis of the political and economic dynamics at work in contemporary Detroit. We aim to cut through the hype and clearly spell out the investments, policies, and political struggles that are shaping the city's revitalization. We argue that the disparity between investment Downtown and dispossession in the neighborhoods that has produced the "Two Detroits" consensus in fact represents two components of a dialectical unity: redevelopment and austerity are not distinct processes but *two elements of the same process of uneven development*. New Detroit is not a tale of two cities but a tale of one city that is being massively and unequally adjusted to accommodate the pursuit of wealth, an adjustment that took place partially through the consolidation of Detroit's debt during its bankruptcy proceedings. An extended analysis of this situation leads us to a consideration of contemporary policing strategies: "broken windows" and paramilitary raids. These tactics, we argue, are part of a broader political project to coercively manage and contain poor and underemployed workers—the very Detroiters who have been excluded from the city's revitalization. This is a discussion that will be taken up in later chapters.

Chapter 2 dissects the birth of Detroit as the world's industrial center, from Ford's famous "Five Dollar Day" through the post–World War II era. These were the supposed glory days of Detroit, a popular assumption on which Detroit's later decline is predicated. For most workers, however, these years were characterized by brutal work conditions, immiseration, and intensive class struggle. Workers increasingly suffered during the Great Depression as unemployment skyrocketed, working conditions worsened, and prison populations ballooned. Only World War II would bring Detroit out of depression. The war created millions of jobs, but the military economy had pernicious effects. First, the growing power of workers resulting from the increased demand for labor was curbed by a "no-strike pledge" between unions and auto companies forged behind the backs of rank-and-file workers, which paved the way for further union capitulation after the war and alienated many workers from the labor movement. Second, high demand for labor during the war brought large numbers of black workers into production for the first time, and, as competition over scarce resources intensified throughout the 1940s and 1950s, so too did racial violence. After the war, companies increasingly moved their operations outside the city limits, and the social dislocations caused by automation, deindustrialization, and suburbanization came to be legitimated by mythologies of greedy unions, communist agitation, and black criminality. Economic instability, violent crime, punishing working conditions, and racist police brutality became the order of the day in Detroit's so-called golden age.

Chapter 3 explores the radical movements that grew out of this nexus and their eventual combustion in the Great Rebellion of 1967. The strategies of liberal reformists and the mainstream of the civil rights movement, we argue, excluded and alienated many working-class Detroiters, fomenting a more militant approach to struggles over exploitation and oppression. Although the uprising in 1967 is commonly referred to as a race riot, when we situate it in the context of the efflorescence of radical political activity in the 1960s it becomes clear that it was a political uprising. And though national troops were able to reestablish order after five days of fighting, the contradictions and conflicts that had caused the uprising would continue to animate Detroit's political landscape in the years to come.

Chapter 4 is a detailed examination of two radical organizations active after the Rebellion: the League of Revolutionary Black Workers and the Black Panther Party for Self-Defense (BPP). While these groups tried to channel the energy of the uprising into a political movement against injustice and inequality, elites on the New Detroit Committee advocated a different response to the Rebellion: they hoped to quell urban unrest with an economic redevelopment program eerily similar to what is happening in Downtown Detroit today. The militancy of the LRBW and the BPP put them in conflict with these elites, and both groups were subjected to violent repression. We consider the effects of this repression: the straightforward elimination of political threats through imprisonment and assassination, the attendant hollowing-out of working-class communities and a weakening of their capacity to resist the state, and the consolidation of a punitive approach to the problems of underemployment and dissent, eventually leading to the phenomenon of mass incarceration. Crucially, the repression of the most radical elements of the black working class was accompanied by the recognition of formal racial equality and the progressive incorporation of many African Americans into the political machinery—a process we call the dialectic of repression and integration.

In chapter 5 we explore how this dialectic played out against the backdrop of economic crisis and the rise of the now hegemonic regime known as neoliberalism. In short, if the period after the Great Rebellion was characterized by the conflict between revolutionary forces calling for a refashioning of Detroit's political economy on the one hand, and repressive state forces allied with corporate interests vying for a continuation of capitalist accumulation on the other, the period from 1974 to the present marks the victory of the latter camp. From the long tenure of Coleman Young through to Detroit's bankruptcy in 2013, the dialectic that characterized Detroit politics involved criminalization of the poor, draconian austerity, and attempts to redirect global capital flows back toward the Motor City. The current moment in Detroit represents a continuation of the first two of these terms and the success of the third.

# 1

## A Tale of
## One City

Ultimately, the market is going to determine what happens to Detroit. Look at the history of capital: it destroys an area, reduces the prices of the property, and then flows back in because a lot of money can be made. And that's what's gonna happen. —RON GLOTTA, Detroit-based lawyer and activist, early 1990s, quoted in Robert H. Mast, *Detroit Lives*

Wish you bought gold in '06? You'll wish you bought Detroit in '12. . . . Detroit has bottomed out, so now, there's nothing but upside. —JOHN LINKNER, Dan Gilbert's business partner, 2012, "Wish You Bought Gold in '06? You'll Wish You Bought Detroit in '12," *Forbes*

### Investor's Playground

Money is pouring into Detroit, transforming the city's topography before one's eyes. More than $9 billion was invested in Downtown real estate developments from 2006 to 2014.[1] During that time, but especially since the city's bankruptcy, this seven-square-mile area has operated essentially as one massive construction site. The signs of redevelopment are inescapable—Motown is getting a wholesale façade renovation. Skyscrapers that for years stood vacant are studded with scaffolds. At every turn construction blocks roads and sidewalks. The hum and shriek of machinery cloud the air, and gargantuan implements carve out mounds of earth. Cranes swing like puppeteers over the skyline as husks of new buildings rise from steel beams. Laying track for the QLine, a recently completed streetcar that crawls for three miles along Woodward Avenue, reduced Detroit's main thoroughfare to two lanes for the better part of three years. Art Deco high-rises are converted into office buildings, which serve as the headquarters for a growing number of white-collar firms from around the globe (including Quicken Loans, MSX International, and Blue Cross Blue Shield). Abandoned industrial buildings are restored as luxury lofts. New parking lots are paved by the dozen. Restaurants and shops open at a breakneck pace. National chains flock to the Motor City (Nike, Shake Shack, Under Armour, Whole Foods, Warby Parker, Bonobos, and many others), plastering Downtown streets with logos and slogans.

Much of Detroit's redevelopment bears the hallmark of two local billionaires: Mike Ilitch and Dan Gilbert.

Ilitch, who passed away in 2017 with a personal net worth of more than $6 billion, was, with his wife, Marian, the founder of Little Caesars Pizza and the owner of the Detroit Tigers, the Detroit Red Wings, and Motor City Casino Hotel. Ilitch had acquired one hundred acres of real estate in the Greater Downtown area over the past few decades, and for many years his immense personal wealth allowed him to hoard these properties in anticipation of lucrative development opportunities. In 2013, as the Ilitch organization was set to begin a massive development project in the heart of Greater Downtown, the city sold him thirty-nine parcels of land surrounding those he already owned, all for the price of one dollar.[2] Ilitch Holdings, Inc., the umbrella company of the Ilitch business empire, is now headed by Mike's son Chris Ilitch, and through their company Olympia Development the Ilitch family continues to have an outsized influence on Detroit's "renaissance."

Gilbert, whose personal net worth was $6.6 billion in 2018, is the owner of the Cleveland Cavaliers as well as the chairman and founder of Quicken Loans, the largest retail mortgage lender in the United States, and Rock Ventures, a holding company for more than one hundred of Gilbert's businesses which employs seventeen thousand people, making it Detroit's leading employer.[3] Since 2006 Gilbert has invested over $5 billion in the city, buying up around a hundred buildings in the Downtown area. As with Ilitch, many of these properties were sold to him by the city government, several for just one dollar. Gilbert now effectively owns more than half of Downtown Detroit, an area of more than 13 million square feet. The scale of his investment has led many to depict Gilbert as the city's savior. ABC Detroit named him "Newsmaker of the Year" in 2013; the *Atlantic* wondered if he was "Detroit's New Superhero"; and the *New York Times* called him a "missionary" on a "quest to remake the Motor

City."[4] In 2014 a United Way billboard near Downtown showed a picture of a young white boy and had the following caption: "The next Dan Gilbert. The Detroit of tomorrow starts with a donation today."[5]

With Gilbert and the Ilitch family in the lead, new developments in Detroit break ground at a frantic pace. Among ongoing and recently completed projects, perhaps the most dramatic is the District Detroit, a project led by Ilitch-owned Olympia Development, in partnership with the city, which aims to create a contiguous fifty-block sports and entertainment district connecting Downtown and Midtown. The centerpiece is Little Caesars Arena, completed in fall 2017 at a cost of $863 million, a sprawling state-of-the-art facility that serves as the home of the Detroit Red Wings and the Detroit Pistons, hosts concerts and events year-round, and houses myriad restaurants, shops, and a Google office. In addition to bringing the Pistons back into the city (they had played in the suburb Auburn Hills since 1989), making Detroit the only city in the country with four professional sports teams in its Downtown, the Ilitches will also build a new practice facility and corporate headquarters for the team in the New Center area just north of Midtown. While the five residential neighborhoods around Little Caesars Arena promised by Olympia have yet to materialize, the company has built the Mike Ilitch School of Business for Wayne State University next door to the arena and undertaken a $150 million expansion of Little Caesars world headquarters a few blocks away.[6] According to Olympia, the District is responsible for $4.2 billion in new investment—$1.4 billion invested by the company itself and another $2.4 billion in outside investments "catalyzed" by the company—430,000 square feet of new office space, $18 million in infrastructure improvements, and 120,000 square feet of shopping and dining in the area.[7]

Gilbert's real estate company Bedrock has invested in an array of projects spanning Greater Downtown. At the time of writing, four projects in the works Downtown have been the subject of much media attention: redevelopment of the Hudson's department store site into a 1.4-million-square-foot "city within a city" which, at 912 feet, will be the tallest building in Michigan and will include retail, residential, offices, and seven hundred underground parking spaces; renovation of the thirty-eight-story Book Tower and thirteen-story Book Building into another mixed-use development; the Monroe Blocks development, a multisite project including a thirty-five-story office tower and 482 residential units; and a massive addition to One Campus Martius, a large office complex in the heart of Downtown. Totaling $2.1 billion, these four projects are expected to add 3.2 million square feet of office, residential, and retail space to Downtown, along with two thousand parking spaces.[8] Bedrock also collaborated with the luxury Detroit-based leather company Shinola on a 130-room hotel Downtown that opened in late 2018. Just northeast of Downtown, Bedrock has undertaken a redevelopment of the historic Brush Park neighborhood between Midtown and Eastern Market, a twenty-four-block area which until recently consisted mainly of vacant lots speckled with dilapidated Victorian mansions. Bedrock has two huge developments underway in this area: City Modern, an eight-acre development that aims to renovate existing properties in the area in addition to constructing a range of new mixed-use and residential properties, adding four hundred residential units along with retail, offices, and public spaces to the area; and the Brewster-Douglass redevelopment, a $300 million project that will bring nine hundred residential units, 3.2 acres of public space, and sixty thousand feet of retail to the former site of a public housing project whose four towers were demolished by the city in 2014.[9]

One Gilbert-led development is perhaps more emblematic of the situation in contemporary Detroit than others. In March 2018 Gilbert came to a tentative agreement with Wayne County to redevelop a site not far from Brush Park, where the construction of a criminal justice center had stalled in 2013 due to cost overruns. The so-called fail jail, a potent and visible allegory for the city's economic woes and alleged municipal mismanagement, was transferred to Gilbert's company, which plans to build a $1 billion mixed-use commercial development on the site. In exchange, Rock Ventures, in a private-public partnership with the county, agreed to build a $533 million criminal justice complex at a site further from Downtown, to include a new courthouse, administrative offices, juvenile detention facility, and 2,280-bed jail.[10] As we'll see in the rest of this chapter, the simultaneous construction of a commercial complex and a criminal justice center represents two sides of the same process of Detroit's redevelopment.

While they may be the biggest players in Detroit's redevelopment, Gilbert and the Ilitch family are far from the only major investors. On the near northeast side, the former Packard Automotive Plant is being restored by the Spanish-born developer Fernando Palazuelo, whose past redevelopment projects span from Lima to Barcelona and Nepal. Palazuelo's company Arte Express bought portions of the industrial campus in the 2013 tax foreclosure auction, and ground broke on the project in 2017. Once considered the most modern automobile manufacturing facility in the world, the Packard Plant slowly deteriorated after Packard went out of business in the late 1950s, and the sprawling facility has long served as one of the most notorious symbols of the city's decline, as well as a popular site for Hollywood movie crews shooting apocalyptic action sequences. The forty-five-acre plant is now being billed as "the largest renovation project in North America," a four-phase project expected to take fifteen years to complete, bringing offices, retail, artists' lofts, gallery and event space, a recreation center, and much more to the former factory.[11]

Three miles north of the Detroit River, up Woodward Avenue, redevelopment of the New Center neighborhood is dominated by a company called the Platform, a partnership between Peter Cummings, a real estate mogul whose company Ram Realty Services has developed and managed properties in the southeastern United States for thirty-eight years, and Dietrich Knoer, a German-born businessman who moved to Detroit in 2013 to "explore a new opportunity in real estate." The pair formed the Platform in 2015, after Cummings came together with the New York–based real estate firm HFZ and the metro Detroit real estate firm Redico—where Knoer was chief investment officer—to purchase the historic Fisher and Albert Kahn buildings on West Grand Boulevard at the Wayne County tax foreclosure auction for $12.2 million. Since then, along with a proposed $100 million renovation of those historic landmarks, the Platform has taken on numerous high-profile developments in the area. These include new construction of 234 residential units and a 28,300-square-foot grocery store on a parking lot adjacent to the Fisher building; the Boulevard at Third and Grand, a 231-unit mixed-use residential and retail building just down the street from the Fisher and Kahn buildings; a $30 million high-end condo development called Cass and York featuring "a rooftop deck with a swimming pool and a club house, a common garden, a bike storage room, big windows with skyline views, two-story penthouses, and a 24-hour concierge in the lobby"; Baltimore Station, a block south of Grand Boulevard on Woodward, where a two-phase project of renovation and new construction will bring 161 new residential units as well as retail space; renovation of an abandoned Wayne State University building into office, gallery, and retail space; and, a few blocks east of Woodward on Grand Boulevard, the conversion of the nine-story Chroma building into a "creative center" featuring retail, event, and gallery space, part of an effort to "catalyze historic Milwaukee Junction as Detroit's preeminent neighborhood for the creative class."[12] The Platform is also involved in the Pistons' corporate headquarters and practice facility being built in the neighborhood, a partnership between the Pistons and Henry Ford Health Systems, which is also in the midst of a three-hundred-acre, $155 million expansion of Henry Ford Hospital on Grand Boulevard near the Fisher building, a development that will include a six-story glass pavilion and a skyway across the six-lane boulevard.[13] Nearby, the German developers Optima Aegidius Group have purchased four former industrial buildings, which they plan to convert into lofts and retail space.[14]

Activity abounds also along Detroit's riverfront. Led by the nonprofit Detroit Riverfront Conservancy, expansion to the east and west will extend the current riverwalk over four miles along Detroit's southern edge. On the West Riverfront, a park designed by New York–based Michael Van Valkenburgh Associates—an internationally renowned firm that designed Brooklyn Bridge Park in New York City and Maggie Daley Park in Chicago—will transform a twenty-two-acre space into a public park featuring "a tree-lined promenade, a cove with a beach for swimming, a large performance shell, a stone isle for wildlife, and areas for play, nature, and relaxation."[15] On the East Riverfront ground broke in 2018 on a 3.2-acre "urban beach" with parks, playscapes, retail space, and a floating barge serving food and drinks. Other developments in this area will add parks, greenways connecting the riverwalk to other parts of the city, streetscape improvements, and rehabilitation of old warehouses into mixed-use buildings, restaurants, and residential.[16]

Suffice it to say that the scale of development occurring in Detroit's main commercial corridor is dramatic. Less tangible but perhaps even more powerful is the *feeling* of resurgence that has captured the city and captivated the world. No one describes the mood of redevelopment better than its official boosters. The Detroit Metro Convention and Visitors Bureau released a video in early 2018 that typifies the energy and ideology of the engineers of Detroit's renaissance. The centerpiece of a larger marketing campaign with the catchphrase "It's GO Time," the video's narration is worth quoting in full: "They say history repeats itself. Motown. The Motor City. Detroit's had its time on top. And now, with hard work, and people who believe that never gave up, our time has come again. Because right now, in Detroit, it's Revival time. Envision time. Dinner time. Game time. Show time. Move-in time. And now's the time to experience all the things you've heard about Detroit for yourself. It's time to see it. Taste it. Hear it. Feel it. Witness it. And believe it. This is Detroit. And we're here to tell you: it's GO time."[17]

This video contains many of the themes of Detroit's economic resurgence. First is the projection into the past of an idyllic period of prosperity, followed by a period of decline, and now the resurrection of prosperity (and, presumably, the end of history repeating itself). Second is the mythic depiction of Detroiters as hard-working, blue-collar, gritty, and perpetually optimistic. And finally, the focus on Detroit as a destination for tourism and entertainment. After years of deterioration, this video tells us, Detroit is finally getting its restitution, as economic revival is carried out on behalf of those plucky Detroiters who stood by their city through it all.

Nothing captures the confluence of the economic and ideological currents of Detroit's renaissance better than Ford Motor Company's recent purchase of Michigan Central Station. Built in the same year that we begin our history of Detroit, 1913, the eighteen-story train station was designed by the same architect who designed New York's Grand Central Station, and at the time of its construction was the tallest train station in the world and a visible symbol of Detroit's burgeoning industrial power. Closed in 1988, the abandoned train station has for decades served as the most iconic "ruin porn" landmark in a city full of them. Appearing in every cable-news video montage of Detroit's decay, a mecca for urban spelunkers, the subject of myriad investigative reports, the go-to backdrop for Hollywood action films looking to "paint a cinematic picture of post-apocalyptic urban decay," and a taunting eyesore looming over Detroit's hippest, most gentrified neighborhood (Corktown), the train station underwent a series of demolition false starts and failed rehabilitation attempts before Ford finally purchased the towering husk in June 2018.[18] Now, in an almost too perfect metaphor for the current remaking of Detroit, Ford plans to turn the train station and its surrounding area into a 1.2-million-square-foot "innovation hub" geared toward "mobility solutions that will shape the future of transportation."[19] So a city whose fortunes were built on the auto industry, and whose degeneration followed its abandonment by that industry, is now, in the throes of its rebirth, becoming a hub for the transportation industry of the future.

The symbolic significance of the Motor City's most iconic car company purchasing the international emblem of Rust Belt decay in the midst of the "greatest turnaround story" in the annals of urban revitalization was not lost on anyone. "The symbolism here is huge," reports *Curbed Detroit*. But much more than symbolism is at stake: "Let's keep dreaming big. Michigan Central Station is being revived—anything is possible."[20] Speaking at a press conference announcing Ford's vision for the area, Bill Ford, the company's executive chairman and great-grandson of founder Henry, invoked the company's long history in the Motor City and the significance of their purchase of the station today. "[One hundred] years after Henry Ford's assembly line revolutionized industry, we're reimagining mobility," he explained. As the center of this effort, the station will become "a beacon of development, possibility, and opportunity once again."[21]

Ford's purchase of the train station has for many also signaled a milestone in Detroit's recovery. As a *Detroit Free Press* columnist put it, quoting Winston Churchill, the deal marks "the end of the beginning" of the city's rebirth. "Ford's act of faith in Detroit's future with the enormous investment it will bring signals a new era. Victory no longer seems so remote. The issue is no longer in doubt." After some rough years, "progress in Detroit development will become the norm, not the exception. From now on, redevelopment will occur as the natural and expected outcome in a city once again on the move." With comparisons to the first moon landing and World War II, the author claims that, having solved "the toughest of all Detroit's redevelopment puzzles," the city is on a conveyor belt to prosperity—all thanks to a company that has supported Detroit from the beginning: "The Fords have *been there* for Detroit."[22] Shortly after purchasing the train station, Ford projected in story-high letters the city's official motto: "Speramus meliora; resurget cineribus"—We hope for better things; it will rise from the ashes.[23] (Less noted in the triumphalist media narrative was the fact that a primary focus of this "innovation hub" will be driverless cars, which is a particularly ominous development in Michigan, where, in 2018, upward of 100,000 people worked as drivers.[24])

It's difficult to overstate the degree to which all this investment has transformed Greater Downtown Detroit. Depictions of Detroit as a ghost town are exaggerated and overplayed, but no one can deny that the level of activity currently animating the city core is an exponential increase from even five years ago. It is a qualitative as well as quantitative metamorphosis. The city's white population has increased more than 25 percent since 2010, with the majority of the newcomers settling in the Greater Downtown area, where, between 2011 and 2016, white residency increased by 66 percent while black residency decreased by 5 percent.[25] A hum of energy shivers through streets where once foot traffic was scarce. Yuppies walk their labradoodles. Spandex-clad joggers run in place at street corners with earbuds in, waiting for the light to change. Suburbanites, tourists, and hipsters rub shoulders with office workers on lunch breaks. Visible signs of poverty make way for privately commissioned street art. Newcomers to the city lounge in the manufactured beach in the center of Downtown, surrounded by bars and food trucks. In the words of Olympia Development CEO Tom Wilson, "Just come down and enjoy a *new* Detroit."[26]

## The Gentrification Blues

These transformations have not come without significant growing pains, and debate rages over who really benefits from Detroit's renaissance. The problems associated with urban redevelopment in Detroit mirror those of other cities that have experienced similar processes, problems that usually go under the heading of "gentrification." In her celebrated poem "Just Say Hi! (The Gentrification Blues)," Marsha Music bemoans how the city's black residents have become "urban background, just a haze," and exhorts white newcomers to "say Hi!" to black Detroiters.[27] A local planning consultant and sociologist, Meagan Elliott, has put forward a similar message, advocating that we use the term *cultural displacement* instead of *gentrification*: "When I ask [longtime residents] what can (new residents) do to soften [tensions], one person said, 'Have them take a test, like immigrants do.' . . . To come in without that context or understanding is one of the most damaging things that happens over and over again."[28]

This type of critique of gentrification has become widespread and is particularly pertinent in Detroit; it is an overwhelmingly black city, but if you walk around Downtown, you see a preponderance of white faces. In 2017 Dan Gilbert launched an advertising campaign for a new development with the slogan "See Detroit As We Do" overlaying a mostly white crowd. Predictably this led many to speak out against Gilbert and decry how gentrification made black people "invisible."[29] The racial dynamics in high-profile gentrifying neighborhoods like Brooklyn are similar, leading the film director Spike Lee to complain that formerly black neighborhoods now look like the "Westminster Dog Show" and causing the *New York Amsterdam News* to equate gentrification with "ethnic cleansing."[30]

For a full understanding of gentrification these types of racial and cultural critiques must be accompanied by an understanding of the political-economic logic driving this phenomenon. Gentrification's highly visible racialized impacts do not account for all of its causes or manifestations. As Alan Mallach has pointed out, in the United States "predominantly African American neighborhoods are less, not more, likely to experience gentrification than largely white, working-class neighborhoods."[31] Moreover gentrification is not simply an American phenomenon: poor people are being displaced and disempowered in gentrifying cities from Amsterdam to Lisbon, Cape Town, Buenos Aires, Mexico City, San Francisco, Beijing, Pittsburgh, and beyond.[32] As Neil Smith presciently observed in 2002, gentrification has become a "global urban strategy." Increasingly, urban areas feature

> whole new complexes of recreation, consumption, production, and pleasure, as well as residence. Gentrification as urban strategy weaves global financial markets together with large- and medium-sized real-estate developers, local merchants, and property agents with brand-name retailers, all lubricated by city and local governments for whom beneficent social outcomes are now assumed to derive from the market rather than from its regulation. Most crucially, real-estate development

becomes a centerpiece of the city's *productive* economy, an end in itself, justified by appeals to jobs, taxes, and tourism. In ways that could hardly have been envisaged in the 1960s, the construction of new gentrification complexes in central cities across the world has become an increasingly unassailable capital accumulation strategy for competing urban economies.[33]

This is all part of what David Harvey has identified as a shift from the "managerial" to the "entrepreneurial" city.[34] In the face of budgetary shortfalls caused by federal neglect and capital flight, city governments attempt to raise revenues by *marketing* themselves as attractive places for global capitalists to invest in and for middle- and upper-class residents to "live, work, and play" in.[35] Gilbert has openly praised the Detroit government for its attempt to "curate and package our region in a way that has never been done before."[36]

"Come discover the opportunity that is called 'Detroit,'" Gilbert raved in a 2017 letter urging Amazon to establish its second headquarters in Detroit, where the corporate behemoth was promised cheap real estate, low taxes, a business-friendly government, and a vibrant atmosphere to lure potential employees.[37] That the $4 billion Detroit pledged to Amazon was not enough to attract the company indicates that there are many other locales with similarly lavish incentives. And as cities compete against one another for increasingly mobile capital, branding becomes an integral strategy to lure business investment as well as consumer spending. Detroit's destitution and poverty, as well as its history as a blue-collar industrial center, have become the main nodes of the city's image: Detroit is "gritty," "authentic," "resilient." We see this in the many poverty tours that have popped up around the city in recent years, in Chrysler's "Imported from Detroit" marketing campaign, and in the success of the "Detroit Hustles Harder" clothing line.[38]

Attracting physical redevelopment has thus become the preeminent urban strategy. As urban theorist Samuel Stein has written, whereas a century ago industrial capital was the "dominant force in urban politics," today it is "real estate capital": "Global real estate is now worth $217 trillion, 36 times the value of all the gold ever mined. It makes up 60 percent of the world's assets." Growing investment in real estate is linked to the problem of industrial "overcapacity," which according to *Business Insider* is "ruining our economy." In short, as wages stagnate and wealth inequality rises, industrial firms have the capacity to produce far more commodities than the market can consume, and thus capitalists look elsewhere for profitable ways to invest their surplus cash. "Real estate," Stein writes, "becomes the latest stop on what geographer Cindi Katz calls 'vagabond' capitalism's eternal search for profitability. . . . In 2016, a record 37 percent of home sales were made to absentee investors."[39]

All this investment puts upward pressure on property value and rents; wages, meanwhile, remain stagnant. As a result, "there is not a single county in the country where a full-time minimum wage worker can afford the average two-bedroom apartment." In black and Latino neighborhoods, the percentage of income put toward housing is particularly high: 44 percent and 48 percent, respectively.[40]

In Detroit, home values and rents in gentrifying areas have more than doubled since 2010. So too have Downtown rents. Throughout Greater Downtown, upscale condos, ranging from middle-income, two-bedroom units starting at $275,000 to multimillion-dollar luxury units, have proliferated. Griswold Apartments, a rent-subsidized building housing mostly low-income seniors, has been transformed into the Albert, where one-bedroom apartments rent for $1,400 to $2,500 per month and where the owners aim to make the residents "feel like they're living in a five star hotel."[41] At Gilbert's David Scott Building one-bedroom apartments cost between $1,920 and $2,100 a month. Detroit's revitalization means that, increasingly, the Detroit skyline is owned by companies like Triton, which, according to its website, has a "private equity portfolio with combined sales of around €11.5 billion." Triton recently opened Water's Edge apartments, "an upscale apartment community on the Detroit River with a private marina and two private lakes."[42]

As investors move in, thousands of working-class Detroiters have been displaced. Some of this displacement is attributable to the foreclosure crisis and to general cost-of-living increases, but many Detroiters have been coerced into leaving their homes and neighborhoods by more forceful means. In April 2013, for example, low-income residents in over two hundred apartment units in Cass Corridor (now referred to as Midtown) received a notice "saying that they had to move out within thirty days." As these residents were being evicted, two other large Downtown apartments were taken over by international developers; the residents of these buildings, who were Section 8 (low-income, state-assisted) renters, were ordered to vacate the property.[43] This process is ongoing. In October 2018 low-income residents of Park Avenue were told to move out; one resident remarked, "As one of the last affordable places to live, this is displacing many poor and low-wage working people."[44]

Political elites purport to address problems of displacement by stipulating that a certain percentage of new housing projects must be "affordable." But what's affordable in affordable housing initiatives is based not just on the

FIGURE 1.1. A group of Detroiters sit on a Downtown sidewalk in front of a construction site for a new luxury hotel built by the Shinola leather company. A few minutes after this photo was taken, this area was cleared by private security and Detroit police. Photo © Philip Conklin, 2016.

median income of Detroit residents ($25,764) but on the median income of the metro Detroit region ($68,000), meaning, according to activists, "all of the newly developed affordable housing built in Detroit still isn't actually affordable to most Detroiters."[45]

Gentrification, then, represents much more than cultural incompetence; it is a necessary element of urban political economy in contemporary capitalist society. The racialized components of real estate investment are a symptom of structural processes that do not always manifest in racial terms. As well as calling into question the utility of the term *gentrification*, this suggests that in order to curb the displacement attending to urban development, we must go well beyond acculturating newcomers and being friendly to our neighbors, and address the root of the problem: the creative destruction wreaked upon cities, and in particular their most vulnerable residents, by the whims of highly mobile real estate capital.

## A Disaster Zone

We got a hell of a job out here to deal with. We're dealing with emergency managers; they never existed before in this country. We're dealing with the fact that people don't understand that these suckers don't care if they have water or not, because if you are not a part of their production, they don't need you no more. —**MARIAN KRAMER** of the League of Revolutionary Black Workers and the National Welfare Rights Union, "Marian Kramer," *League of Revolutionary Black Workers: A Media Project with the League of Revolutionary Black Workers,* 2015

Economists fret that Detroit, in the absence of the manufacturing economy that built it, no longer has any reason to be. —**BEN AUSTEN**, "The Post-Post-Apocalyptic Detroit," 2014

Even more illuminating of the logic underlying Detroit's recent transformations is another set of processes occurring in the peripheral regions on the city's East and West Sides, colloquially known as "the neighborhoods." Across the city, *only 53 percent of working-age Detroiters were formally employed at any point in 2013.*[46] But as the *Detroit News* reported in August 2015, the situation is even more dire on the East and West Sides: "Roughly half of the city's population lives west of Woodward Avenue—more than 335,000 people. But across that vast stretch of Detroit, there are only 30,500 jobs—less than one job for every 10 people. Similarly jobs-poor areas abound on the city's east side. That compares to the 64,000 jobs from Midtown to downtown, where just about 18,000 people live (Detroiters hold about 27 percent of the Midtown-downtown jobs). All told, the city has a little more than 200 jobs for every 1,000 people, well below St. Louis' 613, Cleveland's 481 . . . and Baltimore's 391."[47]

Many people living in these "jobs-poor" areas struggle to make enough money to survive. Many depend entirely on their friends and family. Some panhandle. Others sell bottles of water, DVDs, cigarettes, or drugs or engage in other criminalized hustles. In 2013 a few of our friends from the East Side who had been recently released from incarceration supported themselves by taking two buses to get to the suburb of Southfield, where they then waited in line for hours at a plasma donation center. Including the rides there and back, it was a ten-hour day, and they typically earned around $50 for their donation. When one of us went with them to CSL Plasma, the place was so overcrowded with Detroiters that the line stretched outside onto the sidewalk.

As investment in the metro area increases, some new jobs are created. But the question is: What kinds of jobs? Many people on the periphery take the bus to night jobs as dishwashers and line cooks at restaurants in the suburbs, and increasingly in Downtown and Midtown, jobs that are low-wage, monotonous, and physically taxing. Or they travel to the several warehouses that

Amazon has recently opened in the metro area. Employees inside these behemoths have become increasingly vocal in denouncing their work conditions. Mohamed Hassan, one of the workers who took part in a recent strike in an Amazon warehouse in Minnesota, said, "The pace of work is inhumane. Everyone feels continuously threatened by the system." Many workers have decried the company's union-busting tactics, as well as productivity standards that force people to stay on their feet all day long and leave no time for bathroom breaks, leaving many to urinate in bottles or trash cans. One recent undercover reporter described "employees collapsing at work, suffering panic attacks, pulling muscles and more." As was the case in the early days of Ford, work conditions are so grueling and degrading that worker turnover has become a huge issue for Amazon.[48]

Other Detroiters make their way to day labor companies such as PeopleReady, just east of Downtown. Companies like these have "spread like wildfire" in recent decades, becoming "a ubiquitous presence in poor, predominantly urban communities across the country." As the sociologist Gretchen Purser has noted in her incredible ethnographic work, day labor companies heavily recruit formerly incarcerated workers and give them one-day labor contracts: "jobs without a tomorrow." Often these companies partner directly with parole officers, as well as "re-entry" and social service organizations. Purser concludes that the 70 million or so U.S. workers who have a criminal record are not merely "excluded" from the economy; they are relegated to "its bottom-most segments in what has recently been referred to as the 'gloves-off economy,' where jobs are precarious, working conditions are perilous, violations of labor laws are pervasive, and wages are paltry."[49]

Workers' ability to resist degrading and low-paying jobs decreased further in 2014, when Michigan became a right-to-work state, meaning that mandatory unionization is no longer legal. (This has not, however, stopped workers from taking action: a strike campaign by the Service Employees Local 1 won 1,700 local janitors a $15 wage, and the UNITE HERE Local 24 workers' month-long picket line at the Downtown Westin Book Cadillac hotel won improvements in work conditions and pay, then released this message: "[We] proved that even in a right-to-work state, when working people stand in solidarity, we win.")[50]

The fact that many Detroiters are still out of work, and that an outsized portion of the jobs that recent investment has created are low-wage, helps explain why in early 2019, after years of so-called revitalization, *WalletHub* concluded that due to its incredibly high rates of poverty for children (55 percent) and adults (32 percent), "Detroit is the neediest city in America."[51] Kurt Metzger, director of *Data Driven Detroit*, comes to a similarly bleak conclusion: "the economy is not moving folks out of poverty."[52]

And while it is true that adult poverty rates have declined slightly in recent years, it remains unclear whether this decline is attributable to actual poverty alleviation or to the fact that many of the poorest Detroiters have been forced out of the city—both by police and by the sheer scale of the dispossessions that have occurred in recent years, mostly in the city's East and West Sides. These dispossessions have been so sweeping that local activists have labeled them "genocidal."[53] Three main processes are at work here: water shutoffs, home foreclosures, and school closings.

WATER SHUTOFFS

Between 2010 and 2018 the Detroit water department issued around 143,000 shutoff notices, directly affecting *more than 40 percent of the city's residents*. To be subject to shutoff, water customers need be only sixty days behind on their payments or have $150 of unpaid bills. Despite the outcry of neighborhood organizations and the intervention of the United Nations, the shutoffs have continued up to the time of writing (summer 2019). In March 2018 the city council approved a $7.8 million contract for Homrich Wrecking to continue water shutoffs through 2021.[54]

From 2006 to 2016 water rates in Detroit increased 120 percent, and the average monthly water bill in the city was nearly double the national average. Then, in 2017, the Board of Water Commissioners approved another rate increase. Meanwhile the Detroit city government has spent billions of dollars budgeted for the Water and Sewage Department to repay its creditors, mainly Wall Street banks; in 2011 "the agency spent $537 million that had been earmarked for repairs paying off interest-rate swaps to major banks."[55] The city has offered a payment plan for residents, but some see it as a scam, since it requires payments up to $200 per month. Residents who have turned to "illegal water hook-ups" have been aggressively prosecuted for the felony of "malicious destruction of utility property."[56]

As we will see, water shutoffs are part of the city's debt-restructuring program implemented by its emergency manager, Kevyn Orr, and the pattern of shutoffs demonstrates how Detroit is being remade in the interests of corporations over those of residents. Though city officials have presented them as a straightforward response to delinquent water bills, the shutoffs evidence a clear pro-business bias. In 2015 residential properties owed the city $26 million in outstanding water bills, compared to $41 million owed by commercial properties; however, residential accounts were four times more likely to be disconnected than commercial accounts.[57]

In 2014 We the People of Detroit Community Research Collective interviewed hundreds of residents on the city's periphery, where the shutoffs were concentrated. They concluded, "Nearly 30 percent of our contacts had been shut-off, which seems incredibly high. We even talked to someone whose house had been shut-off for a 38 cent unpaid water bill. Fifty percent of the people were on some sort of payment plan. Only 30 percent of the households reported that every one there was healthy. So 70 percent had health issues. Forty-four percent of homes had multiple medical issues."[58] Dehydration and problems related to sanitation have become critical issues. Studies have also shown that water-borne diseases were more likely to occur on Detroit blocks that had experienced a water shutoff. Residents in the Detroit area are currently being ravaged by the worst Hepatitis A outbreak in the United States.[59]

Activists have responded to the shutoffs in various ways. Marian Kramer, a longtime Detroit activist and a cofounder of Michigan Welfare Rights (the local section of the National Welfare Rights Union), was arrested along with eight other members of the Homrich 9 for blocking trucks that were being sent to conduct water shutoffs.[60] Other activists have set up emergency water stations and distributed water bottles throughout the areas hit hardest by the shutoffs. However, as Valerie Vande Panne of *In These Times* has reported, some residents don't want to admit that their water has been turned off, for fear that Child Protective Services will take their children away. Some parents without water even keep their children from attending school, worried that they'll tell their teacher that there is no water at home.[61]

The Detroit Water Brigade, an organization committed to "bringing an end to the water crisis," has aptly summed up the situation: "This is a disaster zone—and immediate relief and preparation is needed."[62]

## HOME FORECLOSURES

In 2017 the myriad organizations attempting to combat homeowners' violent dispossession—such as the Detroit People's Platform, the United Community Housing Coalition, the Moratorium Now! Coalition, Detroit Eviction Defense, the Coalition to Stop Unconstitutional Property Tax, and the Detroit Black Youth Project—organized a public forum. There, Wayne State University law professor Bernadette Atuahene reported that "between 2011 and 2015, one in four properties in Detroit was foreclosed on for unpaid property taxes by the Wayne County treasurer, a number not seen since the 1930's depression. When you combine the effect of tax foreclosures with the 65,000 mortgage bank foreclosures that also took place, Detroit has approximately one-third fewer occupied homes now than ten years ago."[63]

According to a 2009 report by the city's Planning and Development Department, during the subprime mortgage crisis Detroit had the highest home foreclosure rate among the nation's one hundred largest metropolitan areas. Though Michigan law requires municipalities to reassess real estate values every five years, the city of Detroit did not do so once between 1995 and 2015, with the consequence that after the housing crash, as the market value of homes plummeted, Detroiters were still expected to make payments at inflated pre-crash rates. Some estimates hold that 85 percent of homes in Detroit were taxed at overassessed rates during this time, many at rates that violated the state constitution. In some neighborhoods the disparity is so stark that one year of property taxes can amount to more than the market value of the home. A recent University of Chicago study found that, between 2011 and 2015, 10 percent of Detroit's tax foreclosures were "caused by inflated property assessments." By 2014 fully 47 percent of Detroit homeowners were underwater on their mortgages.[64]

The way the government deals with unpaid property taxes has further exacerbated the crisis. In fact, the procedures appear as nothing short of a coordinated effort to dispossess Detroit residents of their homes. According to a state law passed in 2000, when property taxes are not paid to the city of Detroit, the debt gets passed on to Wayne County. The county then charges 18 percent interest on these delinquent taxes—that is, interest charged, after the recession, on property tax assessments that in many cases were already unconstitutionally inflated. If these payments are delinquent for three years, the law mandates that Wayne County foreclose the home and put it up for auction. The Wayne County treasurer's home foreclosure auction, according to the *New York Times*, has become "one of the world's largest real estate auctions."[65] Since 2002 one in three Detroit properties has been put up for sale under this system.[66]

Although many Detroiters would have legally qualified for "poverty tax exemptions," the city made it too difficult for residents to learn about, and qualify for, these exemptions. This was the subject of a lawsuit, filed against the city by the ACLU, which was settled in July 2018 mandating that Detroit create a more streamlined and user-friendly exemption application process.[67] Meanwhile federal money sent to Michigan to aid struggling homeowners was routinely redirected toward razing abandoned houses. In the summer of 2016, for example, the Michigan state government received $188 million in federal funds as part of the Helping Hardest Hit Homeowners program; only one-quarter of the money went to support homeowners under threat of foreclosure, and the rest was reserved for "blight removal."[68] The city's demolition program is the subject of an ongoing FBI investigation, after demolition costs spiked 60 percent in 2015 under the Duggan administration.[69]

There is a brutal irony to the fact that Gilbert, the owner of a mortgage lending company, rose to prominence in Detroit in the aftermath of the sub-prime mortgage crisis. Quicken Loans closed an enormous $353 million in the years preceding the crisis; during this time nearly 75 percent of new mortgage loans in Detroit were considered subprime. One report found that "Quicken corporate management pushed its employees to falsify borrowers' incomes on loan applications and to push overpriced deals on desperate or unwary home-owners. Employees reported being bullied and pressured into illegal acts." In 2017 homeowners won an $11 million class action lawsuit against Quicken for its "unconscionable" and "truly egregious" predatory practices, which included artificially inflating home values without carrying out genuine ap-praisals. Nationwide 70 percent of homes that received subprime mortgages from Quicken between 2002 and 2008 were foreclosed on within three years. "Quicken directly carried out 1,058 foreclosures in Detroit, 52% of which were on subprime loans."[70]

Gilbert is not alone in profiting from the foreclosure crisis. Wayne County has required that homes purchased at the foreclosure auction be paid off in full within twenty-four hours, keeping most Detroiters, who don't have thousands of dollars in disposable cash, from reacquiring their homes. Instead real estate speculators have pounced: in 2013 twelve investors bought more than a hun-dred homes *each*, many with plans to leave them vacant until their property value appreciates.[71] Wayne County itself also benefits from this system. From 2010 to 2017 the county's general fund received $456 million from property tax foreclosures. This direct transfer of wealth from the most disadvantaged sections of Detroit's population is integral to the county's financial stability; investigative reports have concluded that "the county now relies on property owners' misfortune to balance its budget."[72] The same process has been at work in Ferguson, Missouri, where in 2014 a series of uprisings occurred after the police killed an unarmed black man, Michael Brown. Fueling black residents' anger was the fact that fines levied almost exclusively against the city's poor population accounted for one-fifth of all revenues in 2013. Robin D. G. Kelley has called this process "revenue by primitive accumulation."[73]

The United Community Housing Coalition (UCHC) has responded to this vulturism by purchasing hundreds of foreclosed homes and attempting to hold them until the original owner can repay the purchase price. However, as the *Free Press* has reported, this remains the exception to the rule: "Many of the most prolific auction bidders are not homeowners looking to plant roots but speculators who 'rent' houses back to owners who lost them, using predatory schemes that often lead to new evictions and cycles of instability. Or, as is more common, the speculators just sit on them."[74] There's some hope that the worst of the foreclosure crisis in Detroit is over. After peaking in 2015 at 24,793, the number of occupied homes for sale in the foreclosure auction decreased to 2,715 in 2018. Additionally the Make It a Home program, launched in 2018 as a partnership between UCHC and the city, which allows the city to divert some homes from entering the auction and then sell them back to the owners, may make it easier for some Detroiters to hold onto their homes. However, the reasons to be optimistic remain shaky at best. Tax foreclosures have decreased, but with one-third of all homes already affected by the foreclosure crisis, one wonders whether this is simply an indication that the transfer of homeowner-ship out of the hands of poor Detroiters and into the hands of investors has been largely completed. Likewise there is no plan in place to offer restitution to the homeowners who have been preyed upon by lenders, overtaxed by the city, charged interest, and foreclosed on and evicted by the county—in short, the damage has already been done. In this context it is also important to note that the state-mandated tax foreclosure auction was itself intended as an urban renewal strategy to "reactivate abandoned spaces and spark new ownership." In the Fitzgerald neighborhood, the dispossession caused by the foreclosure crisis has become the node of another round of urban renewal intended to "revital-ize" "abandoned" lots and "leverage" new investments. That is, the very same properties that were wrested from poor Detroiters are being shifted into pri-vate hands, with the help of local government, to be redeveloped by investors and rented back to the community: so-called community investment. And so the cycle continues.[75]

## SCHOOL CLOSURES

In the past twenty years, more than two-thirds of Detroit Public Schools (DPS) have been closed. As has been the case with the water shutoffs and home fore-closures, the school closures have disproportionately affected residents of the city's peripheral regions.

In 1999 the state of Michigan placed DPS under emergency management, which lasted more or less continuously up to 2016. At the time of the first state takeover, DPS had a $100 million budget surplus and 168,000 enrolled students. After sixteen years of emergency management by the state, the district was $3.4 billion in debt, enrollment had fallen to 47,000, and the state had closed a staggering 195 Detroit schools, leaving only 93 open. As a majority of the schools were closed, forcing students to seek other options, and the district lost 70 percent of its students, the decline in enrollment was tautologically used as a reason to close more schools. The drop in DPS enrollment is tied to two developments in public education in Michigan in the 1990s. In 1993–94 the state eliminated all property taxes devoted to schools, tying funding instead to enrollment.[76] At the same time, new measures were adopted allowing districts to recruit students from outside their boundaries, which made Michigan one of the most permissive states for charter schools. Increasingly students no longer served by DPS are attending charter schools and schools in districts outside of Detroit. Charter schools, which as of 2014–15 had as many as or more students than DPS, have been the most harmful to Detroit students. Eighty percent of charter schools in Michigan are for-profit entities, and charter schools cost the state $1 billion annually. Charters generally offer no bus transportation, no services for special education students, and spend $2,000 less per student than public schools; they have not shown significant improvement in educational outcomes (which are measured largely by standardized test scores). Furthermore, as Julia Putnam, the principal of the James and Grace Lee Boggs School, has warned, the public debate as to whether charter schools increase or decrease test scores often obscures a critical fact: judging schools based on test performance is itself problematic, and it has the result of "incentivizing or tempting [charter] schools to push out kids who are poor because it really hurts their scores."[77]

Despite these facts, deregulation, privatization, and "school choice" remain the order of the day in Michigan, and in the country as a whole. Arne Duncan, President Obama's secretary of education, has said, "I think the best thing that happened to the education system in New Orleans was Hurricane Katrina," referring to the transition to charter schools in the city following the natural disaster. Duncan has now deemed Detroit to be "Ground Zero for education in this country." Even more alarming are the policies of President Trump's secretary of education, Betsy DeVos, a billionaire Michigan native who comes from one of the most powerful families in the state; her husband, Dick DeVos, is heir to the $6 billion Amway fortune and ran for governor in 2006. One of the key funders of the 1993–94 pro-charter legislation, DeVos has essentially worked to end public schools, promoting for-profit education, vouchers for parochial schools, and limitations on the power of teachers' unions. As one teacher-activist, Julie McIntyre, has written, "Supporters of charter schools often argue that when the administration is freed from the restrictions of union contracts, it can retain high-quality teachers. However, in many cases the model focuses on hiring the cheapest (least experienced) teachers to work many more hours than public school teachers are contracted to work."[78]

There has been some pushback to this kind of draconian educational reform. In 2013, for instance, teachers at Cesar Chavez Academy, a charter that serves two thousand students in Detroit, formed a union. (Ironically, the Academy, named after a legendary union leader, attempted to intimidate the union members and has consistently negotiated with them in bad faith.)[79] Another group, MIStudentsDream, has organized around issues of social justice. But by and large DeVos's vision for public schooling is being realized in Detroit. In March 2016 new state legislation split DPS into two districts: Detroit Public Schools became a shell district tasked solely with managing the district's debt, and in that capacity its funds will be directed mostly to Wall Street banks; a new district, Detroit Public Schools Community District (DPSCD), was created to actually run the schools. The legislation includes strict financial oversight of the new district by the state; a loosening of academic qualifications (Detroit is now the only city in Michigan that allows the regular hiring of uncertified teachers); antistrike measures to curb the power of teachers, who closed DPS for two days in May 2016 in a massive "sick-out" after the legislation was passed; a new law requiring the state to shut down all schools that land in the bottom 5 percent of state rankings for three years and, crucially, no measures for the city to regulate charter schools. With the public education system in Detroit hollowed out to almost nothing, and the city's residents on the hook to pay back billions of dollars of debt racked up while DPS was under state control, Attorney General Bill Schuette announced in September 2016 that twenty-seven more DPS schools were slated to be closed by the state in the next year. Thanks to political and community pressure, an agreement between DPSCD and the state has saved these schools from closure for now; they will instead be entered into a partnership program with the state to improve their performance. But this is only a temporary, remedial measure, similar to other "improvement plans" that most schools on this list already had to adopt in recent years. With the state law requiring the lowest-performing schools to close still in place, the future of Detroit's schools remains tenuous. Indeed, this same state law requires that the city's already scrutinized schools be given a letter grade based on student performance, with schools who get multiple F's in danger of being shuttered by the state.[80]

As across the country, student scores on standardized tests are the basis of a school's performance rating. One result of this obsession with standardized testing is that "critical thinking" goes by the wayside, which according to Marian Kramer is no accident: "we know that capitalists don't want us to think."[81] Another effect, as Alex Vitale points out, is that the emphasis on high-stakes exams creates a "pressure-cooker atmosphere" that facilitates the school-to-prison-pipeline: "States that rely heavily on high-stakes tests tend to shift teaching toward . . . rote learning; this drives out creativity and individualized learning, which contributes to discipline problems as students grow uninterested or resentful. Schools too often respond to this dynamic by adopting ever more restrictive and punitive disciplinary systems. As a result, suspension, arrests, and expulsions increase, driving students out of school and into the criminal justice system. In this environment, teacher morale declines and dropout rates increase."[82] In Detroit, an ex-police chief runs the city's "public schools' force"—"the only full-service police agency in the state offering constant service to schools."[83]

Even though Detroit may be an extreme case, by and large, what is happening to the city's most impoverished students has happened across Michigan: low-income students account for more than half of Michigan's students, but per-pupil funding for these students fell 60 percent from 1995 to 2015.[84] The same thing is occurring throughout the United States. For Julie McIntyre, market-based education "reform" is "a meticulously designed machine built to dismantle public education over the next several decades." "Public schools," she writes,

> are being intentionally underfunded and dismantled. Over the past ten years, teachers have been forced to follow scripts and rigid pacing guidelines, practices that contradict research about culturally relevant, responsive and inquiry-based teaching as methods to improve student achievement. . . . As public school teachers and students are pushed to failure, private interests will swoop in to provide alternative solutions and reap significant profits. Districts have shifted from elected school boards to mayoral or gubernatorial control, business leaders have orchestrated the shuttering of public schools and their replacement by charter schools, and seasoned, unionized teachers have been pitted against the bright-eyed Teach for America corps members and "superman" charter school leaders.[85]

Charter schools are disproportionately staffed by young teachers, who, in the absence of union protections, are pressured to "sign flexible, risky contracts," and then are expected to use their own creativity, enthusiasm, and desire for social justice to make up for budget cutbacks. In Detroit, educational nonprofits like City Year (where we both worked in 2012–13) and Teach for America (which came to Detroit in 2010) have permeated the school system. Despite the lofty rhetoric of these organizations, they are a constituent element of market-based educational reform. Underpaid "corps members" are instructed not to worry about the politics of the education system: labor conditions, the focus on high-stakes tests, the profit model, the slashing of employee pay and benefits, the motivations of corporate sponsors, the heavy police presence inside schools, and so on. Focusing on these political factors, nonprofit leaders insist, is a "distraction" from the real work of helping under-served students. To be sure, nonprofit workers are generally well intentioned. But all too often they function as a cover for processes of dispossession, exploitation, and union-busting.[86]

## One Detroit

We're hired by the citizens and the people of the state of Michigan and our responsibility is to give them great customer service. —FORMER GOVERNOR RICK SNYDER OF MICHIGAN, "State of the State Speech," 2013

I can cut somebody's throat and leave them to bleed out in the gutter with the best of them. —DETROIT'S EMERGENCY MANAGER KEVYN ORR, quoted in Shea Howell, "Asking Questions," 2013

It's hard to imagine a starker juxtaposition. While local and national media praise a "new spirit and promise," community activists cry "genocide."

The disparity between what's happening in the Greater Downtown area and what's happening in the peripheral neighborhoods is widely acknowledged. The idea that there are "two Detroits" has permeated public discourse, becoming an inescapable aspect of everyday life and of politics. Coleman A. Young Jr., who ran against Mike Duggan in the 2017 mayoral race, based his campaign on the Two Detroits thesis, to which Duggan's subsequent slogan, "One Detroit. For all of us," is a direct response. Residents old and new push back against the violence inherent in the term *New Detroit*, which erases the already existing residents and institutions. The disparity that characterizes the city is recognized as well by the city government and certain private developers in their efforts to bring redevelopment to some of these peripheral neighborhoods. Many of those moving to the city are active in social justice issues and aware of the dislocation and cultural displacement that gentrification entails. This stance is even embedded to a degree in the ethos of the business community; it's common for businesses to donate a percentage of profits to charitable organizations, promote workforce development, and the like. And donations from corporate philanthropies have a big hand in the Motor City's revival. Complicating the issue is the fact that gentrification is not always experienced negatively by those it affects, particularly home and business owners, leading many residents to welcome the changes coming to the city. Those attending the festivals and events that have accompanied Detroit's revival are an economically and racially diverse group, spanning the city's population. And to those who can afford to remain in the city, the cosmetic and infrastructure improvements that accompany gentrification can be preferable to what they experienced before. As one Detroiter put it, "I hear talk about gentrification, but many times that's just redevelopment. If redevelopment means I can drive down 6 Mile in the winter without worrying about it being an ice rink, then give me redevelopment."[87]

What's missing from all of this is a recognition of the necessity of both of these poles—investment and dispossession—to the process as a whole. The problem is continually framed along these lines: How can the development going on in Detroit be more equitably spread across the entire city, and not just Downtown? But Downtown development and dispossession on the periphery are not two separate processes; they are *two elements of the same process of uneven development*. The corporate revival can't be divorced from immiseration. These are mutually constitutive processes, wherein the city is remade into a center of investment and profit-making—at the direct expense of the poor and working class. *In short, the problem is not that there are two Detroits but that there is one Detroit, and it is part of a class society*. Detroit has become a standing testament to Marx's "absolute general law of capitalist accumulation," according to which wealth accumulates at one pole of society in direct proportion to the accumulation of poverty and misery at the other.[88]

If one considers Downtown and the neighborhoods as a *unity*, the extent to which the city's poorest residents have subsidized Detroit's "renaissance" becomes clear. First of all, redevelopment has been able to flourish because of the vast amount of vacant land and buildings and rock-bottom real estate prices in the city. Investors and new high-income residents scoop up this real estate, giving further impetus to the city's redevelopment; the more businesses and high-income residents that move to the city, the more Detroit becomes a good investment for other potential investors. Detroit is often considered a blank slate, and developers are congratulated for building something where there was nothing. But for a proper analysis we must think historically. As will be explained in later chapters, manufacturers and the white middle class fled Detroit precipitously after World War II, leaving huge portions of the city vacant. The businesses that left bore none of the cost of this abandonment—in fact, thanks to state-subsidized suburbanization, they profited from it—but those Detroiters who couldn't afford to leave had to endure the social and economic costs of this devastation. Now this devalorized real estate is scooped up by investors at bargain-basement prices, and the fact of its abandonment by the previous generation of investors is erased from historical memory.[89]

We have elaborated the extent to which development is uneven spatially, in the disparity between the torrent of investment Downtown and the dispossessions in peripheral neighborhoods. A few more examples drive this point home. First, consider Detroit Future City (DFC), which published its "Strategic Framework" in 2013. The DFC was the product of a private-public partnership managed by the Detroit Economic Growth Corporation and became an independent nonprofit in 2015. It presents the "Strategic Framework" as a fifty-year "blueprint for Detroit's future." Mayor Duggan's chief economic advisor has called it his "bible."[90]

In order to arrive at a future that is "aspirational" as well as "just and equitable," the DFC explicitly advocates a program of service cuts and blight removal in the city's impoverished neighborhoods. This, it argues, will free up needed resources which can then be diverted toward more "viable" gentrifying areas. In short, the DFC plainly articulates the plan to revitalize the city by shifting the costs of its fiscal crisis onto Detroit's poorest residents. According to Dave Bing, the mayor at the time, relocating people is "absolutely" part of the city's plan: "There is just too much land and too many expenses for us to continue to manage the city as we have in the past. . . . There are tough decisions that are going to have to be made." Despite Bing's comments, there is no general plan for relocating residents. The DFC stresses that no residents will be forced to move; however, it is apparent that without key services—street lighting, trash collection, public transportation, and so on—the residents will not be able to stay.[91]

Meanwhile, elites complain that the city has too much empty land, and also that there are not enough parking spaces near Downtown. As many activists have pointed out, since the completion of the Little Caesars Arena, the Ilitches' investments have been confined mainly to catalyzing new parking lots—over twenty acres of them.[92] Gilbert himself owns more than seventeen thousand parking spaces. But according to the managing CEO of Gilbert's Bedrock Detroit, a major obstacle to the city's revitalization is the "strong need for additional parking options."[93] The geographical unevenness is stark: on the one hand, political elites have depicted Detroit as "abandoned," "thinly populated," and in need of "downsizing" so as to justify vast service cuts in peripheral neighborhoods; on the other hand, with the help of public subsidies, billionaires continue to build parking lots to increase their concentration of wealth in a few gentrifying neighborhoods.

Another example of uneven development is provided by the QLine street-car system, which Gilbert spearheaded. Initially conceived as part of a larger regional transit network, in its final form the QLine ended up covering only a three-mile stretch of Woodward Avenue spanning Downtown and Midtown. Largely a symbolic gesture to investors, the QLine serves more to encourage investment and facilitate tourism than to effectively transport residents; it is sleeker, but also slower and less frequent than the Woodward bus which covers the same area. Although it was mostly privately funded, the state and federal government spent $47 million on the QLine. Meanwhile at least 25 percent of Detroiters live without a car and rely on the city's underfunded bus system to get around.[94]

Inequality and unevenness can also be witnessed in the major subsidies given to Detroit's capitalist class. This happens indirectly, as when public services are shut off in the periphery while public funds are redirected toward schemes to lure investment downtown. It also happens more explicitly: for instance, when, in the midst of contributing to the city's blight and its residents' foreclosures, Gilbert received $200 million in subsidies to keep his companies in Detroit, after threatening to move them to Cleveland, essentially compelling Detroiters to subsidize their own foreclosure crisis.[95] A week after Detroit declared bankruptcy, city officials announced that the public would cover more than half the cost of the $450 million Little Caesars Arena. And, as mentioned, thirty-nine parcels of land for the arena and the surrounding District Detroit were sold to the team's billionaire owner, Mike Ilitch, for just one dollar—without the parcels ever being appraised.[96] These charitable dealings with moneyed interests stand in stark contrast to the aggressive enforcement of unpaid residential water bills and delinquent property taxes, pursued in the name of austerity by the same city government.

Proponents of these deals bristle at the contention that billionaires are gifted money from public funds, pointing out that Detroit doesn't simply write developers a check; rather, developments are subsidized through complex tax-capture arrangements, in which the developer collects tax revenues which would otherwise go into public coffers. Their argument is that developers are receiving only money that would not exist without them. But this is erroneous. In 2017 a new set of "transformational brownfield" bills passed in the Michigan legislature, greatly increasing the amount of public money available to developers. Named after their biggest sponsor, the so-called Gilbert bills are explicitly designed to facilitate real estate developments in Detroit. After the passage of these bills, four of Gilbert's developments Downtown—the Hudson site project, Monroe Blocks, Book Tower, and One Campus Martius—were approved for $681 million in tax incentives. Typically, the brownfield concept is a relatively straightforward redevelopment strategy, opposed by few politicians on either side of the aisle, wherein private developers can capture property taxes from developments they build on polluted land. But the situation in Detroit is different. Under these new regulations, the brownfield designation has been expanded to include blighted, foreclosed, and dangerous property. In other words, the types of investments that qualify for public subsidization have increased dramatically. Further, developers are allowed to capture not only property taxes but income taxes for employees who end up working at the redeveloped sites, income taxes for construction workers who build the sites, state sales taxes for construction materials needed to build the sites, and income taxes of residents who live in the buildings.[97]

Where is the benefit for the city if all the newly generated tax revenues go back into the pockets of developers? Claims about "catalyzing" investments and creating "investor confidence" are nebulous at best; it seems the main thing investors have to be confident about is that *a closed circuit has been created wherein all potential public benefit from new developments remains in private hands.* The alleged number of jobs created in these developments is almost always inflated, and municipalities remain opaque about reporting the actual number of jobs created by subsidized developments. A report by the Mackinac Center for Public Policy concludes that of the 434 projects of the Michigan Economic Growth Authority (MEGA), which received subsidies on the basis of projected job creation, only 10 met or exceeded their expected job counts. That's a paltry 2.3 percent. The Michigan Economic Development Corporation, which oversees MEGA, predicted that the projects would produce 122,785 jobs; only 13,941 actually materialized.[98]

This points to the fact that capital profits from Detroit's impoverishment not only directly, by purchasing cheap and abundant land and putting to work cheap and abundant labor, but also indirectly, through an ideological manipulation of Detroit's poverty into a branding strategy that depicts investment as socially conscious. That is, the decrepit state of the neighborhoods, its abandonment by industry, and the poverty of its residents allow developers to portray their business activities as a form of philanthropy. Instead of being revealed as sheer profiteering, investment is painted as charity; recall, for instance, the *New York Times* labeling Gilbert the city's "savior."

"Bringing jobs to the neighborhood," "reactivating public spaces," "investing in communities" are just so many euphemisms for the pursuit of profit. Whether the developers themselves believe these maxims is beside the point; the fact is they are investing in Detroit because cheap real estate can be purchased and turned into lucrative investments. That these activities can be portrayed as charitable is one more way that capital has benefited from Detroit's impoverishment.

When ground broke on the Hudson's development downtown, protesters showed up to decry the fact that the billionaire's project was subsidized by residents of a city with a 40 percent poverty rate. Gilbert responded that they were not being "rational": without such subsidies, he said, investors will move their capital elsewhere.[99] The same thing has been going on for decades. In the early 1980s, Kenneth Cockrel, then a socialist city council member, criticized Mayor Coleman Young for gifting hundreds of millions of dollars to General Motors in a bid to have the company relocate a factory to Detroit. Young's response is telling: GM, he reminded Cockrel, "ain't running no . . . welfare program."[100] Nearly forty years later, political elites and corporate media outlets continue to argue that if the city is to truly come back, it must lower taxes, further deregulate business, and increase corporate subsidies.[101] Most ironically, as Representative Rashida Tlaib of Detroit points out, the supporters of public subsidies for private development "use economic recession and recovery as an excuse to not collect 100 percent of property, sales, and income tax produced by these for-profit, large-scale developments. Depleted public coffers will not be filled by giving away more public funds. . . . In a city where residents cannot easily access land and are losing their property at alarming rates . . . our resources and public lands are being turned into commodities to be brokered."[102]

In Detroit, as in the rest of the world, the working class has in recent years had to endure austerity measures as a means to pay for public debt. After the global financial crisis of 2007–9, bailouts from local U.S. governments to financial institutions amounted to a staggering $20 trillion, turning private debt into public debt. To pay for these bailouts, governments shifted to austerity programs. The working class paid for the profit recovery through layoffs, wage cuts, reduced work hours, and slashed social services. In the political scientist and activist David McNally's words, "When one U.S. economist observes that we have today 'a statistical recovery and a human recession' . . . we need to add, as one California teacher put it to me, that there is a statistical recovery *because* there is a human recession."[103]

A final example of the inequality and unevenness that underpins Detroit's revitalization is the city's recent bankruptcy, which was completed in 2014. The previous year Governor Rick Snyder appointed a corporate lawyer named Kevyn Orr as Detroit's emergency manager, and in mid-2013 Orr declared bankruptcy on the city's behalf, its estimated $18 billion debt making it the largest municipal bankruptcy in U.S. history. A law that greatly expanded the powers of emergency managers had been passed in Michigan in 2011, was struck down by voters in a referendum in 2012, and was finally pushed through the legislature later that year in a revised form which rendered it immune to referendum. Under this law, Orr—a nonelected official in a position voters had rejected—was given autocratic power to restructure nearly all aspects of city government. The end result was a reduced payout for Detroit's creditors at the cost of an austerity plan for city residents and increased influence and power for corporations in the city. Historian and Detroit scholar Scott Kurashige explains, "Detroit's bankruptcy functioned as a hostile municipal takeover by financiers commissioned by the governor and emergency manager to reinvent Detroit on the basis of corporate restructuring principles."[104]

The result of Detroit's bankruptcy came to be known as the "Grand Bargain." In reality, it is the same breed of austerity plan that has gutted fiscally strapped governments across the globe. Social services, pensions, and public utilities are eliminated or privatized, while business-friendly policies are implemented to make Detroit more attractive to investors. The plan includes a reduction in payments to current pensioners to between 74 and 96 percent of the original; an end to cost-of-living increases, meaning that these deflated pensions will also decrease in value as inflation increases; and a 90 percent reduction in retirees' health care benefits (which Orr estimated were actually more valuable than the pensions themselves). Banks took a significantly reduced payout on their loans—due largely to sustained efforts by the Moratorium Now! Coalition and other activists who protested throughout the bankruptcy and resisted Orr's most draconian recommendations (which included an 86 percent cut to retirees' pensions). But corporate interests were compensated by other means. Several banks who were "the biggest losers on paper . . . received access to Downtown Detroit land and property rights that could prove to be far more valuable in the future." Detroit taxpayers were billed more than $164 million for the services of the consultants and lawyers who negotiated the deal, including a bill for $1 million to guard against excessive spending, and a bill for tens of thousands of dollars from the lead firm Jones Day for reviewing their fees with the examiner.[105]

The post-bankruptcy restructuring of Detroit also involves a push to increase revenues and reduce expenses in order to make the city viable in the future. This involves selling off public assets, deregulating industry, and further pushing costs onto poor Detroiters. From his penthouse suite, Orr—whom the *Washington Post* deemed "the man who is trying to save Detroit"—privatized the city's trash collection services and threatened to sell its entire water system to a private company before mandating the creation of a regional authority to take control of the water system, which already serves the entire metropolitan region.[106] The initiation of water shutoffs by the Detroit Water and Sewerage Department (DWSD) was a response to suburban communities' concerns that city residents do not pay their water bills; convinced that DWSD was coming under fiscal control, the Great Lakes Water Authority was created in 2014, transferring control of Detroit's water system outside the city. Residents will feel the push for revenue in other ways as well, with fines and fees expected to be raised for services like buses and parking. The bankruptcy plan also included "reinvestment initiatives," which Orr was particularly "hopeful" would secure Detroit's future. The two largest sums were for "blight removal" ($460 million) and "public safety" ($230 million), of which two-thirds will be devoted to policing.[107]

A consensus soon emerged among political elites and national news outlets that Detroiters got a fair deal. The austerity program that the bankruptcy prescribed was inevitable—nothing more than a commonsense response to the city's history of profligacy. Ex-mayor Bing claimed that the roots of the city's fiscal crisis lay in its residents' "entitlement problem." Emergency Manager Orr lectured, "For a long time the city was dumb, lazy, happy, and rich." These claims were echoed in the national press. The *New York Times* wrote that the city's fiscal crisis followed "a trail of missteps, of trimming too little, too late. . . . Now the chickens have come home to roost." The *Economist* likened Detroit's government to an alcoholic and hoped the bankruptcy would sober the city up. The Cato Institute depicted the bankruptcy as a long overdue solution to self-inflicted wounds: "Detroit is a model of tax-and-spend liberalism. The city's per-capita tax burden is the highest in Michigan. . . . The city's own choices, not free markets and limited government, are really responsible for Detroit's failure."[108] Georgia's Republican senator Newt Gingrich fantasized about turning the city into a tax-free zone.[109] It was widely agreed by corporate and political elites that the sweeping cuts already made by the city were not large enough to address the fiscal crisis.

The idea that fiscal crises in the public sector are caused by overindulgent welfare policies, greedy unions, and bloated state bureaucracies is not novel; in fact, it has become something of a commonplace in recent decades as austerity programs have been implemented around the world. This has particularly been the case in the wake of the 2007–8 financial crisis: "As unemployment and home foreclosures continued to rise, social state restructuring and public service cutbacks were (re)presented as overriding imperatives for fiscal restoration and debt recovery. . . . In this curiously familiar 'new normal,' the costs of restructuring and insecurity are being revisited, once again, upon the poor, along with cutbacks in entitlement programs and public spending."[110]

It is particularly foreboding that this narrative of overentitlement can gain traction in Detroit, where rates of poverty, child poverty, and unemployment are the highest of any large U.S. city. Moreover, as we will detail further in chapter 5, by the time the city was declared bankrupt, residents had already suffered decades of crushing austerity. Between 1990 and 2013, for instance, the city's municipal workforce was *halved*. And from 2008–13 half the city's parks were closed. Meanwhile the welfare state has been gutted. In 1991 Governor John Engler, citing the need for austerity, ended general assistance, eliminating welfare for eighty thousand people. Then, in 2011, as people in Michigan were reeling from the effects of the economic crisis, state lawmakers passed a law to limit people to only four years of cash assistance. Between 2007 and 2013 the number of people in Michigan receiving cash assistance was cut in half, and in 2014 Governor Rick Snyder responded to outlandish claims that welfare recipients were lavishly spending their assistance on drugs and in casinos and strip clubs by introducing mandatory drug tests for some welfare recipients; the program failed to detect any drug users.[111]

Despite, or rather because of these cuts, elites see in Detroit a model case of urban governance, one that is replicable in deindustrialized cities across the nation. This too is part of a broader trend. As elites attempt to make cities around the world more propitious to investment, they rely on cosmopolitan technocrats to create "portable policy paradigms" that can be adopted from one place to the next. As Orr was appointed, Moody's Investors Services announced that Detroit's bankruptcy could "change how other distressed cities approach their pension and debt obligations" and that "bankruptcy may become more appealing to other stressed local governments if Detroit succeeds in lowering pension benefits and discharges most of its general obligation debt."[112] Indeed there are striking similarities between Detroit's corporate restructuring and the recently imposed economic "recoveries" in impoverished and debt-ridden places like New Orleans, Greece, and Puerto Rico (where debt restructuring was carried out by some of the *same people* who administered Detroit's bankruptcy).[113] In all of these places, economic issues are presented as too important to be discussed democratically by local residents, who are depicted as ignorant or self-serving, thus opening space for elite technocrats to administer sweeping austerity.[114]

Throughout Michigan, corporate tyranny is ascendant. Startlingly, around half of black Michiganders have been subject to emergency management this last decade.[115] The situation in Flint is particular dire. There, a series of emergency managers worked with corporate elites to shift the city to a poisoned water source and subsequently to cover up the fact that the water had lead in it, resulting in a devastating health crisis. The official death toll from Flint's criminally poisoned water is twelve, though health officials indicate that the actual number of fatalities is more likely in the hundreds.[116]

In Detroit, and throughout Michigan, activists have attempted to combat this sort of heinous corporate rule. The 2017 town hall meeting "Real Detroiters Speak Out" featured 150 activists who "spoke on and heard about the role of the banks, global corporations and political comprador elites in perpetuating the superexploitation of the majority African-American, working-class and poor residents who have been totally left out of the so-called rebirth of Detroit."[117] This meeting helped build momentum for the 2018 Conference to Defeat Austerity in Detroit. In advance of the 2018 Demonstration to Defend Detroit's Neighborhoods, the Moratorium Now! Coalition—which has spearheaded efforts to resist processes of dispossession—issued a statement summing up the criticisms of many local activists:

> The Detroit "comeback" has bypassed Detroit neighborhoods. While billionaires receive massive tax breaks and taxpayer funds to finance their private projects in 7.2 square miles of central Detroit, the rest of the city, about 133 square miles, continues to face the largest wave of home foreclosures since the 1930s, while thousands of families face water shutoffs. Meanwhile, toxic waste is dumped into the Detroit Sewer System in one of the city's poorest neighborhoods, where sewer backups spread the toxic materials into residents' basements and streets. Air quality in some neighborhoods is so bad that Detroit experiences the highest asthma rates in Michigan! . . . Meanwhile, the city's rulers have diverted the federal Hardest Hit Funds to tear down homes instead of keeping families in their homes.[118]

## Neighborhood Revitalization

In the past few years there have been increasing attempts on the part of the city, nonprofit agencies, and private developers to address the oft-cited problem that the city's "'comeback' has bypassed Detroit neighborhoods." The Fitzgerald Neighborhood Revitalization project is the clearest example of how local leaders are attempting to bypass the radical critiques of local activists and come up with a solution to problems of inequality and geographic unevenness that *leaves unchallenged the basic tenets of capital accumulation.*

The Fitzgerald neighborhood lies about ten miles to the northwest of Downtown, far from the burgeoning entertainment district and the plethora of new mixed-use developments. The project's focus is the roughly quarter-square-mile area bordered by McNichols Road to the north, Puritan Avenue to the south, Marygrove College to the west, and University of Detroit–Mercy to the east. Situated within the larger Livernois-McNichols area, which Mayor Mike Duggan proclaimed his "number one neighborhood revitalization priority," the Fitzgerald revitalization zone is a residential area which, like similar areas on the city's East and West Sides, has been hollowed out by disinvestment and depopulation.[119]

As Alan Mallach asserts, "gentrifying areas are rarely the most distressed areas of a city," and the existing assets of the Fitzgerald neighborhood are at least as important as its vacancy and potential for improvement in the city's decision to focus its efforts here.[120] The area is close to two higher education institutions and the Livernois commercial corridor, one of the few areas of the city experiencing the kind of retail renaissance confined mainly to Greater Downtown. Nearby are several historically high-income neighborhoods, the University District, Sherwood Forest, and Palmer Park—where stately rehabbed mansions are selling for anywhere from $200,000 to more than $800,000. (The city's median home price was $37,000 in 2018.)[121] These surrounding resources all make the Fitzgerald neighborhood a prime site for revitalization.

The array of actors and the types of approaches to the neighborhood's revitalization are perhaps even more indicative of the structure of contemporary urban development than the larger-scale, billionaire-funded projects concentrated near Downtown. A dizzying ensemble of public, private, nonprofit, and quasi-public institutions and individuals, in interlocking and overlapping relationships (referred to in development-speak as "braided investments" and "multisector teams"), have come together to effect the neighborhood's revival. We have done our best to try to make the Fitzgerald project as transparent as possible, but as the reader will surely notice, wading through all the acronyms, jargon, and cobbled-together entities isn't easy, which raises serious questions about the democratic accountability of these sort of opaque investment schemes.

The Fitzgerald project is led by the City of Detroit, in partnership with the Fitz Forward development team, composed of the Platform and Century Partners, a real estate development group formed in 2015 by two young entrepreneurs who relocated to the city from New York to try to "fill the gaps" in Detroit's resurgence by investing in "neighborhood revitalization" and "wealth-building" among the city's black population. Together the city and Fitz Forward hope to "instigate catalytic local neighborhood development and launch a new paradigm for how inclusive development can be successfully implemented within urban ecosystems."[122] The project involves rehabilitating 115 vacant homes into a mix of for-sale and rental properties, landscaping 192 vacant lots, creating a two-acre park to serve as a community hub, and linking different parts of the neighborhood together through greenways. This effort is situated explicitly as an alternative to the kinds of developments happening in Downtown and Midtown, with references to "residential stabilization," "community engagement," and the needs of "existing residents" recurring throughout the official literature. Demolition will be as limited as possible, and no new structures will be built; instead the neighborhood's existing houses and vacant lots will be transformed into "productive" community assets, "preserving the character" of the neighborhood while "increasing density" and walkability. Fitz Forward is also partnering with local workforce development nonprofits and urban agriculture nonprofits like Greening of Detroit, which will turn some of the vacant lots into community gardens.

In order to carry out the reactivation of vacant lots and "abandoned" homes, the city has requested the transfer of 373 parcels of land owned by the Detroit Land Bank Authority (DLBA), a public institution "dedicated to returning Detroit's vacant, abandoned, and foreclosed property to productive use." DLBA is currently Detroit's largest landowner, controlling about 100,000 parcels in the city, which also makes it the largest land bank in the country (seven times the size of the second largest).[123] The land bank was formed out of the rubble of the subprime mortgage crisis as a centralized repository for the increasing amount of publicly controlled land in the city. Its mission to turn Detroit's vast amount of vacant and blighted land to "productive use" involves selling vacant lots (homeowners can buy empty lots adjacent to their property for $100); auctioning houses online; selling a select few "rehabbed and ready" homes, with renovations subsidized by Quicken Loans; assembling parcels for development projects; and demolishing blighted structures, which between 2010 and 2017 was funded with about $380 million in federal funding through the Hardest Hit Fund.[124] The activities of the DLBA have ramped up significantly since the beginning of Mayor Duggan's first term in 2014, when it controlled a mere seven hundred parcels, and because of the institution's massive land holdings—it currently owns 68 percent of the city's 43,576 vacant homes—it plays an enormous role in redevelopment projects across the city.[125] Of the 373 parcels the DLBA owns in the Fitzgerald neighborhood, 323 will be transferred to the developers behind Fitz Forward, to be either rehabilitated and put on the market or demolished and turned into "productive landscapes." The city will receive the remaining 50 parcels, which it will convert into new greenways and public spaces.

In projects like this one commentators see implications far beyond the city itself: "If Detroit can make a land bank work on this scale, it would provide a replicable model for other large cities."[126] Indeed local institutions are not the only ones involved in the Fitzgerald project. The larger Livernois-McNichols area surrounding the Fitzgerald neighborhood is one of the sites selected for Reimagining the Civic Commons, a program in which four national philanthropies—the John S. and James L. Knight Foundation, the JPB Foundation, the Kresge Foundation, and the Rockefeller Foundation—pooled $20 million to distribute among five cities: Akron, Chicago, Detroit, Memphis, and Philadelphia. Socioeconomic mixing, civic engagement, environmental sustainability, and value creation are the four pillars of this program, and the Fitzgerald neighborhood revitalization is the centerpiece of these efforts in Detroit. The expected impact of these efforts is far-reaching. Reimagining the Civic Commons declares, "Detroit is creating a new model of community development with civic assets at its heart, and has learned lessons with implications for cities far outside its borders."[127] According to Detroit's design director, "The lessons we've learned in Fitzgerald over the past year and a half . . . will create more engaged, equitable and thriving neighborhoods across Detroit—and even across the country."[128]

The Fitzgerald revitalization is only one aspect of a much larger effort undertaken by Mayor Duggan since he took office in 2014 promising to spread the benefits of redevelopment across the city's population. His office crusades under the slogan "One city. For all of us." In his first year in office he launched the Strategic Neighborhood Fund (SNF), an effort to coordinate investments in neighborhoods where market conditions make traditional investments impossible. The SNF is a partnership between the city and Invest Detroit, a federally certified Community Development Financial Institution that uses a mix of public and private funding to finance development in low-income and underserved communities and brings "partnerships and philanthropic resources together to catalyze growth in Detroit by supporting real estate and business projects that struggle to find traditional financing."[129] Livernois-McNichols was one of the first three neighborhoods selected for the SNF, which expanded to ten neighborhoods in 2018 under SNF 2.0. This initiative is funded through a mix of city money ($59 million), philanthropic donations ($56 million), and state financing ($15 million). It's centered on four principles: "park improvements, streetscape improvements, commercial corridor development, and affordable single-family home stabilization."[130] That last effort is also supported by the Affordable Housing Leverage Fund, a partnership between the City of Detroit Housing and Revitalization Department, the Michigan State Housing and Development Authority, and the Detroit office of the Local Initiatives Support Corporation, a national Community Development Financial Institution formed by the Ford Foundation in 1979 that "connects communities with resources" by pooling funds from government agencies, banks, philanthropies, and private companies and using them to finance community development projects. The $250 million Affordable Housing Leverage Fund in Detroit is directed toward the preservation of the quality and affordability of existing housing stock and the construction of new housing affordable to people "across a range of incomes," all in the same neighborhoods targeted by the Strategic Neighborhood Fund, as well as Greater Downtown. However, it's important to reiterate that "affordable" housing "isn't actually affordable to most Detroiters."[131]

Various local nonprofits, philanthropies, and community-minded developers are entwined in these braided redevelopment initiatives. Revitalization of the Livernois-McNichols area is to a large extent coordinated by the Live6 Alliance. (McNichols Avenue is the official name for 6 Mile Road, the name residents generally use.) Live6, a nonprofit organization that coordinates development efforts in the area, acting as a "conduit" between the community and various other local and national institutions. These include Motor City Re-Store, a façade improvement program launched in 2017 as a partnership between the City of Detroit, the Detroit Economic Growth Corporation, the Economic Development Corporation of the City of Detroit, and the U.S. Department of Housing and Urban Development, in which local businesses receive matching grants for improving their storefronts. Live6 also works with Motor City Match, another partnership created by these four entities. Motor City Match is a $500,000 quarterly grant program that seeks to develop small businesses in Detroit by pairing local and national businesses with the "best available real estate" in the city, as well as providing loans and business planning and counseling to new businesses and businesses relocating to Detroit.[132]

This is only a partial snapshot of efforts to redevelop Detroit without the unevenness and displacement that usually attend the process of gentrification. What we can see from this sketch is the extent to which—in contrast to the relatively straightforward, federally funded urban programs of the New Deal and Great Society eras—urban development is today effected by an incredibly complex web of public, quasi-public, philanthropic, and private institutions at local and national levels. This approach, which has its roots in the "progrowth coalitions" that sought to quell urban unrest with economic development starting in the late 1960s, has arguably reached its apogee in contemporary Detroit, where a line can be traced from a new coffee shop in a "turnaround" neighborhood all the way to the federal government by way of local and national nonprofits, city and state governments, the largest philanthropies in the country, and a menagerie of financial institutions.[133] The architects of these braided, multisector redevelopment processes refer to their work as "filling the gaps," and, indeed, in a situation where private investment is not economically rational or feasible on its own, and where government funds are insufficient to provide for the needs of city residents, this concatenation of actors and funding sources is necessary if redevelopment is going to occur at all.

In fact, the same is true of the developments in Greater Downtown that opened this chapter. Dan Gilbert and the Ilitch family would not be reconstructing the center city into a mecca for tourism, entertainment, and white-collar industry without the intervention of the city government. The logic of contemporary urban development necessitates that nearly all the real estate investment activities in Downtown Detroit are publicly subsidized. While tax breaks for billionaires in the poorest city in the country appear heinous, those who argue that without these subsidies redevelopment would not be occurring at all are, within the framework of the "entrepreneurial city," correct. Fierce competition for highly mobile capital creates a situation where cities are forced to fall over one another to offer the highest subsidies to increasingly fickle transnational corporations. This is vividly demonstrated by the inter-city contest for Amazon's HQ2 in 2018, in which urban governments across the country competed to provide the company with the most generous package of tax breaks and business friendly conditions, a competition which threw Downtown Detroit's boosters into a marketing frenzy for several months. Amazon's subsequent abandonment of one of their selected sites in New York City (which Governor Andrew Cuomo called "the greatest tragedy that [he has] seen since [he has] been in government") demonstrates the volatility of this profit-driven logic, and the precarious position faced by cities forced to conform to such logic.[134]

The *New York Times* has recently written, "There are no real assurances that gains will be spread democratically across the city, or that city planning and public resources will serve the needs of everyday Detroiters. But the hope is that private individuals will keep the greater good in mind." Local elites have heralded the spread of "mini Gilberts" and "black Dan Gilberts" who will invest in more socially conscious ways.[135] However, despite the city's efforts to employ strategies consonant with the necessities of capitalist development *and* with principles of inclusion, equality, and community engagement, there is every reason to believe that the negative aspects of revitalization are not aberrations that can be solved with smarter and more inclusive investments. Rather, as the previous sections demonstrated, inequality is hard-wired into the functioning of the capitalist city. Well intentioned as these efforts may be, as long as they leave unquestioned the logic of capital accumulation they can at best only ameliorate the deprivations caused by this system. More often, such efforts work hand in hand with these deprivations. The form of neighborhood revitalization being practiced in Detroit is, for example, perfectly consonant with the city's austerity plan. The neighborhoods targeted for investment are in every case those with already existing assets like colleges, hospitals, active commercial corridors, relatively high rates of occupancy, and cultural institutions. As such, their reinvigoration leaves unquestioned the concomitant disavowal of the most impoverished and derelict neighborhoods advocated by Mayor Bing and the DFC, which considers such neighborhoods, and thus the residents who occupy them, not "viable" in the process of Detroit's recovery.

But the inability of the neighborhood revitalization framework to overcome capitalism's destructive tendencies becomes even more obvious when we consider that capitalist development is uneven not only spatially, but also temporally. Simply put, Detroit could not be redeveloped if it had not already been disemboweled. The only reason the Fitzgerald neighborhood can be "revitalized" is that it was leveled through another public-private partnership in the recent past; mortgage lenders, Wall Street financiers, the City of Detroit, and Wayne County worked together to dispossess vulnerable populations from their homes, a process which has now come under the misnomer of "abandonment." Without this underdevelopment, there could be no redevelopment.

And while the former glory of Detroit is omnipresent in the zeitgeist of the city's renaissance, historical memory stops short of a recognition that the lows of Detroit's past could also be replicated in the future. But where mythology obfuscates this possibility, real-time events prove an irrefutable reminder.

In February 2019 Fiat Chrysler Automobiles (FCA) announced plans to invest $1.6 billion to convert old factories on the East Side of Detroit into new production facilities, which would constitute "the first new auto assembly plant in Detroit in a generation." Michigan's governor Gretchen Whitmer proclaimed, "It's been a long time since we've seen an investment this big and transformative," with Mayor Duggan adding that the deal is a "once-in-a-generational chance to change the economic fortunes of thousands of Detroiters."[136] The constituencies of these politicians will, as a result, heavily subsidize the new plants built by FCA, a company that was created as part of Chrysler's $12.5 billion federal bailout after the 2007–9 financial crisis.[137] Detroit residents' forced contribution will be a full 200 acres of land, assembled by the Duggan administration's aggressive land bank authority, gifted to FCA for nothing other than the promise of future jobs and so-called economic development. On top of this,

FCA will receive up to $270 million in various incentives and tax abatements, of which at least $34 million would otherwise have gone toward school funding.[138]

The deal is reminiscent of GM's controversial Poletown Plant, built through a similar process of land acquisition and tax incentives in the early 1980s, which destroyed a thriving neighborhood in the process. Mayor Duggan himself compared the current deal to Coleman Young's infamous one.

In late 2018 GM announced that it would be closing the Poletown Plant, along with several others of its factories, in order to downsize the company's workforce and maintain profitability. The nearby city of Hamtramck (which is completely within the city of Detroit), will be left in a "major financial crisis" without the revenue from the factory.[139]

The new plants being built by FCA in Detroit face, then, an unfortunate but predictable future. Whether, as in the Amazon HQ2 fiasco in Long Island, the deal falls through, leaving the city and its taxpayers in the lurch, or whether, as in the Poletown Plant's slow demise, the years simply render it obsolete, this momentous deal will eventually go down as another failure piled on the trash heap of capitalism's history.

But where it cannot rely on the passage of time, capitalism turns to more coercive mechanisms to push through its vision for society. We now turn to the police's role in facilitating capital accumulation in contemporary Detroit.

## Policing the New Detroit

The officers had real, real long rifles. It was like the army or something on Jefferson [Avenue]. Like an invasion. —**MARCO FREEMAN**, resident of Detroit's East Side, quoted in Mark Jay, "Policing the Poor in Detroit," 2017

Over the past few years there has been much emphasis on the need to address Detroit's crime problem. In his report to the state government, Emergency Manager Orr claimed that the crime problem in Detroit is "endemic" and is a primary obstacle to the city's revitalization. A Michigan Radio story titled "How Is Crime Hindering the Comeback of Detroit?" is indicative of the liberal media's coverage of crime in contemporary Detroit.[140]

The appointment of James Craig as chief of the Detroit Police Department (DPD) in 2013, and the department's subsequent implementation of broken-windows tactics, have been viewed by the local and national media as a long overdue response to this crime problem. The broken-windows theory holds that punishing even the smallest crimes—such as loitering, panhandling, and graffiti—is necessary to create the atmosphere of lawfulness that will prevent more serious crimes from being committed. This strategy, which includes zero-tolerance policies and stop-and-frisk tactics, was famously implemented in New York City in the 1990s by Mayor Rudolph Giuliani and Police Commissioner William Bratton (although, as we will see, stop-and-frisk first emerged in the 1960s to combat black political militancy). Chief Craig served under Bratton when he brought the broken-windows policy to Los Angeles in 2002. In 2013 the city of Detroit paid $600,000 to the Manhattan Institute and undisclosed fees to the Bratton Group for their help facilitating DPD's adoption of broken-windows tactics.[141]

It is true that, for the past several decades, Detroit's reported crime rates, including violent crime rates, have consistently been among the highest for large U.S. cities; this is understandable when we consider the high rates of poverty and unemployment, as well as the city's dramatic demographic shifts. But it is also clear that broken-windows tactics, and anticrime measures more generally, have served a broader purpose: they have simultaneously helped to *administer and legitimate* the social order required for the city's revitalization to take place. To get a sense of what we mean by this, let us take a closer look at the social effects of these anticrime measures, again contrasting Greater Downtown and the neighborhoods on the city's deeply impoverished East and West Sides.

## POLICING GREATER DOWNTOWN

As displacement increases in the Downtown area, the dislocated residents are generally depicted as the unfortunate, though inevitable, casualties of Detroit's comeback. At other times, however, the displaced are presented as criminals impeding the progress of gentrification. A 2016 *Detroit News* article headlined "Revival of Detroit's Cass Corridor Crowds Out Criminals" begins, "In the rebranded Cass Corridor, police say hipsters are crowding out the criminals. But the drug dealers who have permeated the neighborhood for years aren't going down without a fight." The article goes on to quote DPD Captain Darin Szilagy: "The revitalization of the Cass Corridor has left very little territory for drug dealers. . . . The little that's left has become valuable territory, and that's led to some violence. You have your OGs (original gangsters) who go back to the 1980s, and they're fighting with the younger guys who are trying to move in. . . . This is where these dealers have operated for years, and they want to hold on to it." In the same article, Lyke Thompson, director of Wayne State University's Center for Urban Studies, offers a similar version of the story: "Gentrification . . . affects criminals, too. . . . It's been happening all over the country. . . . You see development, and when you have a strong foundation of investment, that brings more law enforcement and people who are more likely to report crimes. *And the criminals are forced to go elsewhere*."[142]

We can see here how the subtle narrative gloss is performed wherein those Detroiters pushed aside by revitalization are rebranded as undeserving criminals. There is no room in analyses like this one for contradictions, complexity, or history; it paints a simple conflict between police—stewards of Detroit's economic recovery and, thus, representatives of the common good—and bad guys: "drug dealers," "OGs," "criminals." This sort of mythologization has hardened into a kind of political common sense: in 2016 the city spent $547 per capita on police; that same year, per capita spending on food stamps in Michigan was less than $21.[143]

The city's homeless population has been similarly criminalized. According to Mark Jacobs, director of Heart 2 Hart, a Detroit homeless outreach organization, there were around 20,000 homeless people in the city in recent years but only 1,900 shelter beds—enough for less than 10 percent of the homeless population. Mayor Duggan recently promised to reduce the number of people "wandering" and "begging" near Downtown. A 2013 ACLU report details that, Downtown, homeless people are "being approached and harassed by police, not necessarily for anything they're doing, but just because of the way that they look. . . . Often they're being dropped off late at night in neighborhoods that they don't know. Police often take any money they have out of their pockets and force them to walk back to Detroit, with no guarantee of any safety."[144] This process is ongoing. In February 2019, for example, Detroit police "wiped out" two makeshift camps Downtown that had been used by homeless people for decades. According to *Metro Times* and WXYZ Detroit, the city cleared the areas as part of a larger effort to "keep the city clean" and place the city's homeless population in shelters. In the middle of a winter that saw temperatures drop to −30 degrees Fahrenheit, and on the brink of an ice storm that closed schools and froze infrastructure across the metropolitan region, police seized all the belongings of the camps' residents and forced them to move elsewhere. One sixty-six-year-old homeless man had his wallet and ID taken as part of a "clean sweep" in which officers confiscated the accumulated belongings of Detroit's most vulnerable population as they tried to survive the winter: coats, hats, gloves, blankets, sleeping bags, tents, and sleeping mats.[145]

Making matters worse, the United Community Housing Coalition, one of the main local organizations that works with displaced Detroiters, lost 40 percent of its government funding in the summer of 2019.[146] In the absence of any plans for employment, public works, or large-scale affordable housing programs, homelessness is generally treated as a security problem. Nationally

FIGURE 1.2. Two private security guards patrolling Downtown stop to talk to a couple of residents. Photo © Philip Conklin, 2016.

the trend is the same: more than 15 percent of new arrestees report being homeless during the year of their arrest. In a recent Los Angeles city budget, $87 million of the $100 million devoted to the problem of homelessness was allocated to the police.[147] In Detroit, according to Police Chief Anthony Holt, the message from police to panhandlers is clear: "We don't want you to move from Woodward and Warren to Woodward and Selden. We want you to stop the behavior." But in the city with one of the highest unemployment rates in the nation, it is unclear what alternatives could allow them to "stop the behavior."[148]

As the political scientist Cedric Johnson reminds us, "Aggressive policing is central to urban real-estate development and the tourism-entertainment sector growth, both of which serve as central economic drivers in the contemporary landscape."[149] In Detroit this policing is bolstered by a variety of private security firms. Dan Gilbert employs private guards from a wide range of companies who are "trained to spot potential trouble and to deter thieves, drug dealers, muggers and even aggressive panhandlers." These guards are typically paid just above minimum wage: "Security contractors have been reluctant to

FIGURE 1.3. Police officers question a man sitting on a sidewalk in Hamtramck.
Photo © Philip Conklin, 2016.

significantly raise wages because they are under competitive pressure to keep
costs low." Detroit police officers are in radio communication with guards from
the multiple security firms that Gilbert employs, and they work in concert to
remove these human "broken windows" from the Greater Downtown area.[150]

Gilbert has also installed a multimillion-dollar surveillance system of over
three hundred cameras that captures most of what happens in Downtown.
And all of it is seen by Gilbert's security staff, who monitor the live feeds
twenty-four hours a day from a Downtown "command center." In 2015 *Motor
City Muckraker* reported that Gilbert's surveillance team was illegally installing
cameras throughout Downtown on buildings Gilbert did not even own. Gilbert denied the accusations, calling his critics "lying venom filled wannabes"
and "dirty scum," but the story was corroborated by local business owners.[151]

Detroit is not the only city whose downtown area is patrolled by a panoply
of private and public security forces. The number of private security guards in
the United States is rising rapidly, and it is estimated that by 2020, there will
be 1.2 million private guards employed, roughly the same number of full-time

police officers in the country. These private security forces, however, have not replaced police so much as collaborated with them, amplifying their power and helping them to implement strategies such as broken windows.[152]

Downtown security has also been bolstered by Wayne State University's Urban Safety Project, a partnership with AmeriCorps, a national nonprofit organization. The project's motto is "Come together in a community effort to secure and beautify!" The program is "designed to build a culture of neighborly communication . . . in order to reduce crime." AmeriCorps members are given such tasks as "taking surveys, talking to residents, boarding up houses, organizing community meetings." They become the eyes and the ears of the police, passing along information about criminal threats to promote neighborhood beautification. This program is consistent with the broader logic of community policing, a logic characterized not by a reduction of police authority but a *diffusion* of police authority throughout society.

POLICING THE PERIPHERY

From 2013 to 2015 the DPD carried out a series of seventeen paramilitary police raids under the moniker Operation Restore Order. Presented by the department and local media as a way to combat the city's "most problematic" and "crime-riddled" areas, the raids invariably targeted the same impoverished neighborhoods on the city's periphery most impacted by water shutoffs, home foreclosures, and school closings.[153]

The DPD has allocated resources to these expensive paramilitary raids— which killed seven-year-old Aiyana Stanley-Jones in 2010—even as more immediate community needs go unmet. In 2013 Emergency Manager Orr estimated that the police's average response time to emergency calls was fifty-eight minutes.[154] Five years later the *Motor City Muckraker* reported that the response time was still among the slowest in the country: "In 2018, police averaged nearly 40 minutes to respond to priority one and two calls, the most urgent crimes, from burglaries and armed robberies to homicides and kidnappings." Nevertheless, as part of the city's recent austerity, DPD's ranks have been cut around 25 percent.[155]

Police Chief Craig has defended the deployment of SWAT teams, claiming they were used only in extreme situations: "[In] fortified locations . . . where there are heavy armaments, who better to send inside that location to execute a search warrant other than special response teams of SWAT units? . . . When we have to address an active shooter situation or barricaded suspect, I think the community would applaud us coming in with an armored vehicle, not only to keep our officers safe, but to keep our community safe."[156] However,

FIGURE 1.4. A police SWAT team on a raid detain several Detroiters. © 2014 Karpov.

as Ryan Felton has reported, the evidence from the seventeen raids that composed Operation Restore Order tells a different story. Over the course of the operation, police made over a thousand arrests, but these yielded little in the way of prosecutions. Wayne County's prosecutor Kym Worthy admitted, "Our office simply has not received an influx of cases from these raids."[157] Despite Chief Craig's claim that paramilitary units are deployed only in "active shooter situations," these SWAT raids were little more than routine, low-level drug busts: police seized three hundred kilograms of narcotics throughout the raids, 99 percent of which was marijuana, a drug that Detroiters voted to decriminalize in 2012 and that was legalized for recreational use in Michigan in 2018.

Across the country the pattern is the same. In recent years, there have been around fifty thousand SWAT raids annually in the United States, up from three thousand in the early 1980s. Almost all are in poor neighborhoods. Although

FIGURE 1.5. Militarized officers prepare to enter a Detroit home. © 2014 Karpov.

SWAT teams emerged in the late 1960s to combat the Black Panther Party, nowadays they are mostly deployed for drug searches in the country's poorest neighborhoods, predominantly communities of color—and in at least one-third of cases these searches yield no drugs. During the past few decades, spending on police across the United States has increased by 445 percent. Much of this has gone toward militarization, with more than $400 million spent each year on military-grade equipment, compared to $1 million in 1990. Between 2006 and 2014 the military donated 128,000 items of equipment to Michigan police departments alone. These include "17 Mine Resistant Ambush Protected Vehicles . . . built to counter roadside bombs; 1,795 M16 rifles, the U.S. military's combat weapon of choice; 696 M14 rifles; 530 bayonet and scabbards; 165 utility trucks; 32 12-gauge, riot-type shotguns; nine grenade launchers; and three observation helicopters."[158]

The militarism of Detroit's police extends beyond its equipment and tactics; it permeates the mind-set of many of its officers, who often treat

| KEY |
| --- |

——————  Borders of the City of Detroit (excluding the separate municipalities of Highland Park and Hamtramck, indicated by the white space in the center of the map).

· · · · · · ·  Outline of Greater Downtown Detroit.

– – –  Borders of the three zip codes in which the most foreclosures took place between 2005-2014. Within these three zip codes, at least 26,107 foreclosures occurred during this 10-year span.

☆  Locations of paramilitary police raids launched between 2013 and 2015 as part of Operation Restore Order (including the raids that killed Aiyana Stanley-Jones [2010] and Terrance Kellom [2015]).

▬  Census block groups that endured the most water shutoffs between January 2015 and February 2016. Within each of these block groups, at least 15 properties and at most hundreds of properties lost access to water.

FIGURE 1.6. Map of water shutoffs, home foreclosures, and paramilitary police raids in Detroit. Sources: We the People Community Research Collective; *Detroit News*; City-data.com; 7.2 SQ MI. Image © Mallika Roy.

"disorderly" Detroit citizens as enemy combatants. In August 2017, for instance, Damon Grimes, a fifteen-year-old black youth, was riding his ATV through Detroit's East Side and "popped a wheelie." When police attempted to apprehend Grimes for his reckless driving, he fled and police followed, shouting, "Don't run from the state police, you'll get fucked up!" When Grimes slowed down, State Trooper Mark Bessner tased him, causing Grimes to crash his vehicle. Although Grimes died soon after the crash, Bessner insisted that he had "no sympathy at all for [that kind of] bullshit."[159] In another incident in October of that year, two DPD officers, Ronald Cadez and Stephen Heid, were involved in a high-speed chase that led to the death of another black youth, nineteen-year-old Jerry Bradford Jr. The officers reached speeds of 75 miles per hour during the chase, which they initiated in violation of police protocol, failing to turn on their lights and sirens or notify Dispatch that they were involved in the chase. The officers eventually "disengaged" and later learned that the teen had hit another car and smashed into a tree, causing his fatal injuries. Detroit police are allowed to chase a suspect only if they believe the suspect has committed a felony, but no reason was given for this chase. Chief Craig explained that police officers "operate on hunches."[160]

This type of violent policing is justified by a mentality that views marginalized Detroit residents as, first and foremost, security threats. This ideology is so deep-rooted that, throughout Operation Restore Order, whenever no criminal activity was found at the site of a raid, the media reported that the suspects "got away" or that they managed to hide their criminal activity or even that they were "tipped off" by others in their criminal network. Therefore, the reasoning went, more raids would be required. The paranoid logic at work here is eerily reminiscent of the argument Stalin used to justify his purges of seemingly innocent members from the communist bureaucracy: "The best proof of people's guilt is the lack of all proof. For if there is no proof, it must be because they have hidden it; and if they have hidden it, then they must be guilty."[161] To take just one example, here is the transcript of ABC Detroit's report on the operation's final raid:

REPORTER JONATHAN CARLSON: The Detroit Police Department is getting good at these organized crackdowns. . . . On this snowy March morning they were at it again, this time hitting this home, which *the chief says was a drug den.*

JAMES CRAIG: It was an active narcotics location based on what we're finding.

REPORTER CARLSON: But in this case *the suspects got away*. Could be the *bad guys* know this is becoming more common. . . . When the accused drug dealers get home, they'll find a rude awakening, and a casualty.

JAMES CRAIG: There was a large-sized pitbull inside that the [Special Response Team] officers had to put down. He became aggressive during the entry. They fired two shots.

REPORTER CARLSON: This was the seventeenth Operation Restore Order. Every now and then the SWAT vehicle rolls into trouble spots in *a show of force*. It's *to put wrongdoers on notice*, and to let residents know the department means business. . . .

JAMES CRAIG: This is about making this city safe, and we have to sustain it.

REPORTER CARLSON: And the chief says when he rolls into one of these busts now, the people say, "We know you were coming, but we didn't know you were coming today." A sign that the message is getting across.[162]

Though Operation Restore Order ended in 2015, paramilitary raids in the city have continued. In the summer of 2016 officers raided an alleged drug house on the East Side. According to the residents—a pregnant woman and her fiancé—the police did not announce their presence until they shot their way through the front door, killing the couple's dog and lodging a bullet at head height in the living room wall. Immediately after searching the home, the police issued a statement that drugs had been found. The residents, however, insisted that the police discovered nothing illegal. Their claim is corroborated by the fact that no arrests were made, and no tickets related to drugs were issued. A few months later, on September 27, 2016, a team of DPD officers, Michigan State security personnel, and U.S. Drug Enforcement Administration (DEA) agents raided a West Side home as part of a collaborative "undercover narcotics operation." According to the *Detroit News*, "What police believed was a barricaded gunman situation . . . turned up nothing after they searched a home." The alleged criminal was not in the house; in fact, a DEA agent involved in the operation admitted that it was unknown whether the suspect had ever been there. A forty-one-year-old disabled woman was, however, present during the raid and "was safely removed."[163]

Despite the often arbitrary violence associated with paramilitary raids, these police tactics do enjoy some support among poor Detroiters. Throughout Operation Restore Order, black residents in the city's periphery were consistently shown on the news cheering on the officers as they pursued mostly black low-level drug offenders.[164] While this depiction is partially a product of the media's pro-police predilection, it also reflects the reality that many Detroiters do in fact support police tactics that target the city's poorest residents. ABC's coverage of a SWAT raid in 2014 provides a vivid example of this attitude:

REPORTER JULIE BANOVIC: Many of the homes being raided are tips from neighbors, who fear they are living next to drugs like this home on the West Side. One of the adults being questioned buried her head in her hands.

CHIEF CRAIG: We have three adults out front that are detained and we'll continue with our investigation.

REPORTER BANOVIC: Someone in the home tried to get rid of the marijuana by throwing the bag out a second-story window. But police find it. Relieved, neighbors show their gratitude to Chief Craig. Sadly there are three small children in this home, so Child Protective Services will be coming by. When we go to the next home, police check tennis shoes for hidden drugs. . . . The three young adults who lived here were detained on the front lawn. Again, neighbors show their appreciation.

RESIDENT: Thank y'all.

REPORTER BANOVIC: But police could not find the marijuana everyone could smell and had to let the adults go.[165]

When an older black resident thanked Craig for launching the SWAT operation, another reporter asked him what he wanted to tell his younger neighbors: "Get a job," he yelled. "To all them, get a damn job!" That the rate of unemployment in this particular West Side neighborhood is among the highest anywhere in the United States went unmentioned in the news report.[166]

Anyone who spends time in Detroit's peripheral neighborhoods is likely to notice a number of signs for community crime patrols. As Jackson Bartlett has demonstrated in his compelling ethnographic work, these patrols are generally led by black residents who are caught between understanding crime as a "symptom" of poverty and as a straightforward problem of "personal responsibility." Members of these patrols tend to be middle-class, and though they are often uneasy about the nature of police violence and its racial overtones, in the absence of substantive social programs, a "moral" interpretation of crime generally prevails, one that treats crime as a behavioral issue. The result is that deep-rooted socioeconomic problems are treated as crime problems and are dealt with by the police, courts, and prisons.[167]

This dynamic is not unique to Detroit: according to one study covering the first decade of the twenty-first century, 73 percent of white Americans, as well as 64 percent of black Americans, felt that the criminal justice system dealt with criminals "not harshly enough."[168] This was after a half-century of mass incarceration, in which the number of people in prison, in jail, or on probation or parole increased from less than 800,000 in 1965 to more than 7 million.[169] The number of Michigan state prisoners increased from 8,000 in the early 1970s to around 41,000 in 2016; by the latter year, 25,000 Detroiters were under some form of punitive state control, including several thousand who must wear electronic collars. (This form of control, increasingly marketed throughout the United States as a cheap and humane alternative to imprisonment, has increased 70 percent in the past two decades and is now a $6 billion industry.)[170]

As we will see in the chapters to come, mass incarceration has been used to manage the poorest and most recalcitrant members of the working class.[171] A 2018 report from the People's Policy Project comes to significant conclusions about who, exactly, mass incarceration has targeted. The report's author, Nathaniel Lewis, divides the U.S. population into five quintiles, based on people's "household income during adolescence, their current household income, their education, their current assets, and whether they own a home or not." Lewis also breaks down the "probability of ever being jailed"; the "probability of being jailed after arrest"; "the probability of being jailed more than a month"; and the "probability of being jailed more than a year." The conclusion is that, "for all four incarceration outcomes, being lower class rather than middle or upper class makes a massive difference. Being black rather than white makes a modest difference that is statistically insignificant for all outcomes except one: the probability of being in jail or prison for more than a year. And even in that case, whites in the lowest class group are more likely to be incarcerated than blacks in the second-to-lowest class group."[172] This maps onto the Yale law professor James Forman Jr.'s finding that, "while the lifetime risk of incarceration skyrocketed for African American male high school dropouts with the advent of mass incarceration, it actually decreased slightly for black men with some college education."[173]

The black political elites who governed Detroit from 1974 to 2013 all advocated aggressive anticrime measures against the poorest Detroiters. (Coleman Young, the city's first black mayor, said in his famous 1974 inaugural address, "I issue forward a warning now to all dope pushers, to all ripoff artists, to all muggers: It's time to leave Detroit.") And Detroit was no outlier: "an absolute majority of African-American [congressional] representatives voted in favor of each of the major federal crime bills" of the past half-century.[174] These politicians, the historian Touré Reed writes, were "pressured not just by the federal government, but by *black* constituencies in high-crime neighborhoods in cities rocked by deindustrialization."[175] Thus when Mike Duggan, the city's first white mayor in forty years, supports aggressive anticrime measures, he is part of a long lineage, and, on this issue, he generally has the support of a good segment of the black population.

## A Very Real Terror Squad

The security industry downtown is growing because there's more people downtown. People were not downtown. Businesses were leaving. But now businesses are coming back. —JAMES HARRIS, manager at Securitas, a private security firm, quoted in JC Reindl, "Detroit's rebound brings surge in downtown security jobs," 2018

In *The Fabrication of Social Order*, Mark Neocleous traces the historical origins of the institution and concept of police, arguing that as capitalism developed, "the police mandate was to fabricate an order of wage labor and administer the class of poverty."[176] Crime prevention as such has never been the purpose of police; rather the role of police in capitalist society is the maintenance of *good order*, and disciplining the working classes to the regime of wage labor is integral to this process. It is telling that the series of raids carried out by DPD from 2013 to 2015 was called Operation Restore *Order*. The massive amount of investment occurring in Detroit has created many new low-wage service-sector jobs. Retail, restaurant, janitorial, construction, and other poorly paid positions will necessarily have to be filled by Detroit's laboring poor. Certainly, high levels of crime are a pressing social and political issue in the city, and one that disproportionately affects the city's poorest residents, hence the support for paramilitary police raids among the city's poor; but this should not lead us to believe that the raids are a straightforward response to crime. Though Detroit's crime problem has plagued the city for decades, a spectacle on the order of paramilitary police raids becomes especially important now that reinvestment is occurring.[177] These raids thus have a dual effect. First, they coerce those on the receiving end to accept the capitalist order: *either find a job or leave the city*. Second, to all employed residents, potential gentrifiers, and investors, the raids offer a message of reassurance: *Don't worry! The crime problem is being dealt with head-on. Detroit is a safe place to live, work, and play!*

In *Capital*, Marx suggested that, absent a unified working-class resistance, the "silent compulsion of economic relations" would force people to work on capital's terms. And indeed, in the contemporary United States, where 46 percent of Americans don't have enough money to cover a $400 emergency expense, sheer poverty certainly does a lot to motivate people to work low-paying, degrading jobs.[178] But there are also significant forms of *extra-economic force* compelling workers to take whatever jobs they can find, even if the pay is bad and the work is dangerous and alienating. As we have seen, impoverished people face an aggressive criminal justice system that punishes them harshly for any missteps. Additionally, as we write, the Trump administration is implementing plans to introduce mandatory work requirements for a broader array of social programs, including food stamps, housing, and Medicaid. As Tracie McMillan has reported, "The combined budgets of the public programs currently targeted for work requirements—food assistance, health care, and housing—total $704 billion."[179] Thus the *threat* that Operation Restore Order conveys to poor people is expanding throughout society: either accept whatever jobs are on offer, or you will be locked in a cage or shackled with an electronic collar or suffer sheer destitution and homelessness.[180]

As we mentioned in the introduction, and as we will detail in the chapters to come, attempts to revitalize Downtown and lure big businesses and high-income workers to Detroit go back at least a half-century, to the efforts of New Detroit, Inc. in the wake of the Great Rebellion. So it is unsurprising that our critique of DPD has precedents throughout these decades. To take just one example: a 1973 pamphlet released by the Detroit activist group From the Ground Up has eerie parallels to the contemporary situation. The pamphlet criticized Stop the Robberies, Enjoy Safe Streets, more commonly known as STRESS, a DPD "decoy" unit operating mostly in Cass Corridor (today's Midtown), which, on the thin pretext of targeting robbers, killed twenty Detroiters between 1971 and 1973.[181] From the Ground Up insisted that Downtown developments such as the Renaissance Center would "be life-giving only for those entrepreneurs whose investments of substantial sums of wealth will reap even greater profits" and that, against the background of mass poverty and uneven development, "the function of STRESS as a tool of those in power becomes clear. The intimidation of the black community, the fostering of racial tension and division, the ostensible effort to 'make the streets safe' in the center, all represent an attempt to perpetuate the existing structure of society. . . . 'Street crime' will continue as long as society is organized for the profit of the few at the expense of the many." The pamphlet goes on to paraphrase Kenneth Cockrel's critique of STRESS, a critique that in many ways echoes contemporary critiques of DPD's paramilitary raids: "STRESS must be viewed not only as a very real terror squad operating outside the law, but also as an integral part, a conscious program, of the city's power structure. As such, STRESS is a concrete example of the brutality, criminality, and racism which maintains the present structure and its priorities."[182]

DPD's prominent role in maintaining and legitimating a deeply unequal and unjust Detroit is nothing new. What is new is that more money than ever is pouring into Downtown Detroit, and the police force tasked with securing the city's revitalization is now headed by a black police chief and is composed of mostly black officers.

The relationship between the criminal justice system and the city's power structure becomes clearer when we consider two current examples. First, the Detroit Police Department has access to Gilbert's private panopticon and works with his private security staff to monitor the Downtown area during events like professional sports games and protests.[183]

Second, in 2014 two Detroit activists, Dale Lucka and Antonio Cosme, painted the words "Free the Water" on the Highland Park water tower. Next to these words they painted a large black-power fist. The artists were part of a collective that joined thousands of Detroiters in resisting mass water shutoffs. Soon after they painted the tower, the two men were arrested by Highland Park police and faced felony charges. The protesters were accused of "malicious destruction of property" as well as trespassing at a "key facility," a post-9/11 law that is punishable by three to four years in prison. Cosme said in an interview with Democracy Now!, "The criminalization of artists is part of a larger war on public space. It's coinciding with a war on public good. And privatization is being implemented on our public schools, on our water, our health care."[184]

Perhaps the most ominous sign of this "war on public space" is DPD's use of facial recognition technology. As Steve Neavling has reported in the *Metro Times*, "In July 2017, the city signed a three-year, $1 million contract with DataWorks, a facial-recognition vendor that offers 'real-time video surveillance' and a system that 'provides screening and monitoring of live video streams.'" Since then, DPD has "been using the face-scanning system for nearly two years without public input or a policy approved by the Detroit Board of Police Commissioners." As part of Project Green Light, a government initiative to expand surveillance throughout the city, the face-scanning system "enables police to identify and track residents captured on hundreds of private and public high-definition cameras installed at parks, schools, immigration centers, gas stations, churches, abortion clinics, hotels, apartments, fast-food restaurants, and addiction treatment centers. Police can identify people at any time using databases containing hundreds of thousands of photos, including mug shots, driver's licenses, and images scraped from social media." Combined with Gilbert's private panopticon, Detroit's surveillance system has become one of the most pervasive and invasive in all the country; and if the city's elites get their way, Detroit may well follow in the footsteps of China, where the Communist Party watches over everyone with the help of all-pervasive security cameras that are attached with microphones.[185]

When, in the summer of 2019, the public was finally made aware of this clandestine, dystopic police program, there was significant backlash. A coalition of 12 civil rights groups, for instance, have called on the city to end the "flawed and dangerous" program. But, as of our writing, DPD has not budged. At a public Police Commissioner's meeting on July 11, the publicly elected police commissioner Willie Burton repeatedly criticized the program's secrecy and called for a public ballot initiative so that Detroiters could vote on facial-recognition technology; as a result, *Burton was arrested on the spot.* Congresswoman Rashida Tlaib has also been a vocal critic of the program. "With little to no input," she said at a May 22 hearing, "the city of Detroit created one of the nation's most pervasive and sophisticated surveillance networks with real-time facial-recognition technology. Policing our communities has become more militarized and flawed. Now we have for-profit companies pushing so-called technology that has never been tested in communities of color, let alone been studied enough to conclude that it makes our communities safer." When Tlaib called on Police Chief Craig to terminate the "bullshit" facial-surveillance program, Craig responded that "nobody ever talks about the victims in these cases. I would offer a word of caution to the congresswoman about using that kind of language in referring to technology that gives these grieving families closure." Craig went on to say that, at a meeting with relatives of crime-victims, "when I mentioned facial recognition technology, they cheered."[186]

The implementation of this draconian police program points to a larger dynamic in the city's so-called revitalization. Detroit's "comeback" leaves hundreds of thousands of Detroiters mired in poverty and unemployment. While the city government has not proposed any serious policies to address this problem, it continues to find new ways to criminalize the most vulnerable Detroiters, and to mythologize them as an immoral group of people that represent a dangerous threat to working Detroiters. In the end, this is simply a cheap way of managing poverty, and the ultimate goal here is to use the police to ensure that investors, consumers, and homeowners feel safe in the New Detroit.

## The Myth and Reality of Detroit's Renaissance

What we can see from all this is the contradictory unity of dispossession and investment, privation and luxury, austerity and revitalization in contemporary Detroit. As Samuel Stein has written, "A planner's mission is to imagine a better world, but their day-to-day work involves producing a more profitable one."[187] While efforts to equalize the benefits of redevelopment may be well intentioned, what should be clear by now is that, so long as the profit motive reigns supreme, inequality and unevenness will be integral to Detroit's revitalization.

The situation becomes more understandable when viewed through the framework of creative destruction and mythologies. Capitalism continually destroys the landscape it creates in order to make way for a new regime of accumulation. What's happening now in Detroit is not new or unique; it is the contemporary iteration of the transition that most manufacturing cities have undergone as they transform from an industrial to a postindustrial economy. What is unique about Detroit is the amount of time this transition has taken and the immensity of the disinvestment and poverty it has incurred in the meantime. After a series of false starts beginning in the late 1960s, Detroit has finally succeeded in becoming what various scholars have called the "corporate," "progrowth," or "entrepreneurial" city, one whose political economy is centered around corporate headquarters, "meds and eds," tourism, consumption, and entertainment. Despite the confidence of investors, city planners, and new residents, we can't be sure how long this success will last. The only thing we can be sure of is that at some point the postindustrial landscape, like the industrial one that preceded it, will eventually become obsolete and will have to be destroyed to make way for a new landscape that fits whatever follows in its wake. As long as capital perpetuates itself, it will perpetuate this process of creative destruction.

We contend that this inherently destructive process continues to engender itself and retain legitimacy through the concomitant process of mythologization, which redirects and obfuscates capitalism's destructive tendencies, allowing people to make sense of the contradictions swirling around them without pointing to their structural causes. The primary mythology sustaining the creative destruction of contemporary Detroit is the one we've disputed throughout this chapter—that redevelopment can be equalized across the city, if only two conditions are met: if poor people behave in a more moral and less criminal fashion, and if business owners invest in more socially responsible ways.

Mythologies, in our sense of the term, are not simply tales of propaganda constructed in the boardrooms of the elite or decreed by fiat from on high;

rather they are often the spontaneous result of political and ideological struggle and are utilized both by those in power, who need mythologies to legitimate their rule, as well as by those without power, who need them to make sense of their situation. This is perfectly evident in Detroit today. The engineers of Detroit's renaissance need to portray their efforts in a way that makes them appear benevolent, for if they appeared to the public as supporters of an avaricious scheme to siphon profits from the city's impoverished residents, they would have a much harder time achieving their goals. And so the pursuit of profit is cloaked in a language of "job creation," "community investment," and variations on the theme of "walkable, mixed-income urban neighborhoods." New residents, at least those aware of the negative impacts and connotations of gentrification, likewise wish to absolve themselves of directly or indirectly displacing current residents. And so a portion of profits are donated to charity, small businesses are patronized, and inclusive development is supported in spirit, if not in practice. Long-time residents, meanwhile, who seek to make sense of their neighborhood's deterioration, often take refuge in mythologies that blame their lazy and criminal neighbors. This way, relatively well-off Detroiters can believe that they succeeded because of their hard work and ingenuity, while those who languish do so because of individual failings. In this way, the system of capitalism, which necessarily produces a class of poor, unemployed workers, is absolved.

This is not to say that any of these claims or actions are disingenuous—just the opposite. In order for mythologies to be effective, they must resonate with real conflicts and anxieties and satisfy actual needs and desires. For this reason, mythologies go hand in hand with political struggles. The attempts by contemporary activist groups in Detroit—We the People of Detroit, the Moratorium Now! Coalition, Detroit Eviction Defense, the Michigan Welfare Rights Organization, and many others—to demonstrate the connection between the "two Detroits" necessarily confront the mythologies that legitimate Detroit's revitalization. The question is, which vision of the city's present and future will resonate most deeply with Detroiters: one that justifies the profiteering of capitalist elites, or one that advocates for a more equitable distribution of the city's resources?

We situate our work as a complement to these struggles, as an ideological challenge to the prevailing mythologies of Detroit's renaissance. To borrow from Marxist philosopher Massimiliano Tomba, whereas mythologies distort the past and present capitalist social relations "as something that cannot be transcended," Marxist history "reopens, in the moment of a current struggle, the possibility of beginning another history, alternative to the course of capitalist modernisation."[188] Reconceptualizing how we think of Detroit's past is part and parcel of this struggle toward building a more humane future.

# 2

# Fordism and the
## So-Called
# Golden Years

c. 1913–1960

The wretchedness of the worker is in inverse proportion to the power and magnitude of his production. —**KARL MARX**, *Economic and Philosophic Manuscripts of 1844*

The intellectual—be he scientist, engineer or writer—may think Automation means the elimination of heavy labor. The production worker sees it as the elimination of the laborer. Not being in a factory, the intellectual may think that the Worker in Automation is being turned into a technician. The production worker, however, knows this simple truth: when he is not thrown into unemployment, he is subjected to the inhuman speed of the machine. —Detroit autoworker and labor organizer **SIMON OWENS** (aka Charles Denby), *Workers Battle Automation*, 1960

Donald Trump was elected president in 2016 promising to "make America great again," continuing the far right's legacy of the strategic deployment of nostalgia to manipulate people's discontent with the present and uncertainty about the future. Before its recent decline, so the story goes, America was a land of wealth and opportunity, and with the right set of policies this prosperity can be resurrected. The same sort of nostalgia for a mythic past animates the discourse around contemporary Detroit. The best-selling author David Maraniss's *Once in a Great City: A Detroit Story* capitalizes on this nostalgia in its tale of Detroit's "glory days," when the city was, as the *New York Times* explains, "a symbol not of urban decline and Rust Belt blight, but of high hopes and youthful dreams."[1]

This near-ubiquitous nostalgia for Detroit's "glory days," which underlies the contemporary spirit of "comeback," remains operative because of its tangential relationship to the truth. As the center of the auto industry, the city once flourished; as the "arsenal of democracy," it boomed with war production; and as the nation's foremost "union town," Detroit boasted high wages and benefits for its autoworkers during the postwar period. Barthes writes that "myth is speech *stolen and restored*. Only, speech which is restored is no longer quite that which was stolen: when it was brought back, it was not put exactly in its place."[2] Mythology, in this sense, is often a historical action; it relies on a certain temporal distance from the events it describes, a gap within which its distortions evaporate, leaving a sedimented gloss over the reality of the past.

Nowhere is this more evident than in the legend that surrounds Henry Ford, the most impactful individual in the making of the Motor City. The changes that the Ford Motor Company wrought on the auto industry in the early 1900s transformed not only the city itself but the entire modern industrial process and our conception of work. His influence was so great that the era of mass industrial production bears his name: Fordism. Ford himself has become an emblem of the American ideals of hard work, individualism, and pick-yourself-up-by-your-bootstraps resourcefulness, and his mark is a constant presence in Detroit today, so ubiquitous and naturalized that it becomes almost invisible. The most potent memorialization of Ford is the museum complex based in nearby Dearborn called The Henry Ford, encompassing three campuses. The first is Greenfield Village, a sort of living museum of early American life where "300 years of American perseverance serve as a living reminder that anything is possible," which includes working farms, a replica of a traditional Main Street, and demonstrations of traditional crafts.[3] Second is the Rouge Factory Tour, touted as "America's greatest manufacturing experience," where guests can view the workings of a real automotive factory and have "awe-inspiring encounters with America's celebrated manufacturing past, present, and future."[4] And finally, at the Henry Ford Museum of American Innovation visitors step "into a world where past innovations fuel the imagination of generations to come. A vibrant exploration of genius in all its forms," the museum "allows you to experience the strides of America's greatest minds."[5]

The Henry Ford presents a mythological image of Ford: the name itself, with the simple introduction of "The," turns the man into a concept, a monolith representing the tenets of "innovation, resourcefulness, and ingenuity," the three "key words" of the museum's mission statement.[6] The museum is explicitly historical; Ford was a collector of antiques and Americana, and the museum was founded on his personal collection. Of his original project Ford stated, "When we are through, we shall have reproduced American life as lived; and that, I think, is the best way of preserving at least a part of our history and tradition."[7] At The Henry Ford, visitors are presented with an image of America's history and ideals *frozen* in time. You are invited to "try your hand at working on an assembly line. . . . See how Henry Ford revolutionized modern manufacturing. . . . In this hands-on activity, you'll work with other guests to assemble a miniature wooden Model T using the station and moving assembly line methods."[8] But these historical exhibits serve, paradoxically, to evacuate history, replacing it instead with rigid, nostalgic *images* that, separated from their original context, only veil the complex and contradictory processes which they envelop.

What's missing from the mythological nostalgia for Detroit's glory days is the intensity of the class struggle during these years, a constant and violent conflict that pitted the *builders* of Detroit's prosperity, its workers, against the *owners* of that prosperity, the auto companies. A Marxist theoretical framework makes the situation perfectly legible. Capitalism reproduces a dialectical relationship between labor and capital; where capital thrives, labor is immiserated. The prosperity that allowed business to flourish and some members of the working class to achieve a structurally superior position to others is the same mechanism by which the majority of the working class was intensely exploited and eventually made entirely redundant to the production process. As Marx suggests, "Accumulation of wealth at one pole is . . . at the same time accumulation of misery, agony of toil, slavery, ignorance, brutality, mental degradation, at the opposite pole."[9]

From the Fordist regime, which made Detroit the center of global manufacturing through the creation of a "new human product," to the "boom years" of the postwar period, when the prosperity of the auto industry was built on the coordinated debilitation of the labor movement, the mythological story of Detroit's former glory can be told only by eliminating the violence and contestation that was always embedded within it. In short, the wealth of Detroit was built on the blood, sweat, and exploitation of its workers.

## Ford's House of Terror (1913–1940)

You can tell Herr Ford that I am a great admirer of his. I shall do my best to put his theories into practice. . . . I regard Henry Ford as my inspiration. —ADOLF HITLER, quoted in A. James Rudin, "The Dark Legacy of Henry Ford's Anti-Semitism," 2014.

The modern industrial age can be said to have begun in 1913, when Henry Ford opened a new production facility on 160 acres in Highland Park, then a small farming community just north of Detroit proper. The Crystal Palace, so called for its façade of windows, contained the world's first moving assembly line and was designed as a model of a new form of labor organization known as "scientific management." Under this system, work was broken down into highly specialized, minutely timed individual tasks which a worker would perform ceaselessly and without variation. Such methods had been undertaken by industrial employers in the United States since the turn of the century, including by Ford at his Piquette Avenue plant in Detroit, but the Highland Park factory represented a wholesale implementation of this philosophy. Taylorization—named after the father of scientific management, Frederick Taylor—led to an unprecedented shift in the scale of production and the nature of work in the U.S. auto industry, and Ford's enthusiastic adoption of its principles led to his company's meteoric rise: beginning as one of hundreds of small automobile manufacturers in 1903, by 1914 Ford's share of the automobile market was nearly 50 percent.[10]

Ford's legacy as the founder of modern manufacturing is the result not of his genius as an innovator or engineer but of his reorganization of the industrial labor process. The earliest cars, Ford's included, were produced slowly, at immobile workstations, with a minimum of standardization, and by the cooperation of various skilled craftsmen: metal finishers, upholsterers, machinists, woodworkers, and others.[11] As David Montgomery has documented, in the mid- to late 1800s, craft workers in the United States generally managed themselves and the "helpers" that worked under them. These workers were well-organized and self-sufficient, and they typically set the pace for their own productive labor. Workers' monopoly on the know-how required for their particular task gave them a significant degree of power and autonomy; there was thus relatively little need or capacity for surveillance within the workplace.[12] This is not to say that this was an idyllic time for most working people, or that market pressures played no role in orienting work relations. But it was drastically different from the production regime that succeeded it.

In order to understand the radical shift in working conditions that took place at the turn of the twentieth century, it is helpful to turn to Marx's crucial distinction between the *formal* and the *real* subsumption of labor under capital. Under *formal* subsumption, which is characteristic of earlier stages of capitalist development, workers collaborate to produce commodities for market exchange, and the profit from this exchange accrues to a small group of capitalist owners; the capitalist, however, "does not intervene in the process of production itself, which proceeds in its traditional fashion, as it always had done."[13] In contrast, under *real* subsumption, in addition to claiming the profits, capitalists take over the labor process itself, and workers generally lose control over their laboring activity.[14]

Control over production was a point of struggle between workers and capitalists from the beginning of the auto industry, expressed in the distinction between a closed shop, one controlled by workers and "closed" to management's influence, where only union members could be hired, and an open shop, one where employers intervened directly in the work process by hiring nonunion (and thus cheaper) labor, introducing new machinery, and speeding up production.[15] While workers formed unions to attempt to limit capital to the *formal* subsumption of labor, capitalists formed organizations like the Employers' Association of Detroit to further the *real* subsumption of their employees' labor. Taylor's theory addressed the needs of these capitalist organizations, based as it was on the complaint that in most workplaces "the shop is really run by the workmen and not by the bosses." His solution was to take control of the work process from the laborers and put it in the hands of management, "classifying, tabulating and reducing this knowledge to rules, laws and formula" according to "the laws of science."[16] In short, "All possible brainwork should be removed from the shop and centered in the planning or laying-out department."[17]

In other words, deskilling workers was one of the primary goals of the Fordist-Taylorist labor revolution. Removing "brainwork" from daily operations and putting control of knowledge in the hands of the bosses removed the workers' main source of bargaining power. Complex tasks performed by craftsmen with accumulated years of experience were replaced by a simple series of movements performed by an unskilled worker requiring little to no training. By the early 1920s, nearly 50 percent of Ford's jobs required only one day's training, and a full 85 percent required under two weeks to learn.[18] With control of production thus firmly situated in the minds of management, the Taylorist factory owner was free to implement new machinery, speed up production, and otherwise command the bodies and motions of his workers, each one identical to the other, now at the mercy of an increasingly mechanized and automated pace of work.[19]

Marx wrote that the real subsumption of labor "transforms the situations of the various agents of production . . . [so that] a complete (and constantly repeated) revolution takes place in the mode of production." This revolution can be seen not only in the increased efficiency and output of the auto companies but also in the scaling up of their workforce: in the mid-1800s Detroit's largest employer, Michigan Central Railroad, had around 200 paid workers;

by the early 1930s the River Rouge complex, Ford's successor to the Crystal Palace, employed more than 100,000. In Michigan's auto industry, this scaling up was possible only because companies like Ford, Packard, Buick, Olds, and Cadillac were financed by elites who had made incredible profits in the timber, copper, and railroad industries.[20] Smaller, family-owned operations struggled to compete, and more and more people had to work as wage laborers for large capitalists in order to survive: from 1880 to 1930 the percentage of U.S. workers who were wage or salary employees increased from 62 to 77, and the percentage of workers who were self-employed decreased from 37 to 20.[21]

The Fordist-Taylorist reorganization facilitated a dramatic rise in productivity and efficiency. Between 1910 and 1914 Ford reduced the time for assembling the Model T from seven hours to ninety minutes. While 10,600 Model Ts were sold in all of 1909, 16,000 were sold *per month* by 1913, and in 1924 Ford's factories produced 7,000 autos *per day*. From 1908 to the early 1920s the price of the Model T dropped from $850 to $290. The success of this vehicle was due to its design as a mass-market product, suitable for every potential customer, standardized to be exactly alike and easily replicable. (Ford famously commented that customers could choose any color they liked, so long as it was black.)[22] The quantitative shifts engendered by the manufacturing of the Model T also corresponded to a shift in the quality of work: while one in three workers at Ford were skilled craftsmen in 1910, that ratio was only one in five by 1917, significantly weakening the strength of craft unions and thus further eroding the laborers' control of their work.[23]

Deskilling workers was part of a broader strategy for increasing productivity at Ford. Coercion and surveillance inside the plants, facilitated by management's increasing control of the shop floor, was also integral to this boom. Foremen "had a raised desk in the centre of their work area from which to monitor the shop floor and also to remind their supervisees that they were being watched. . . . Supervisors had the power to enforce a range of petty rules, all designed to embody corporate control over the worker's body: bans on talking, singing, whistling or smoking."[24] Writing at the time, Lenin saw Fordism as little more than a tactic to "suck" more surplus value from the worker: "And if he dies young? Well, there are many others waiting at the gate!"[25]

These workers waiting at the gate were in fact an integral part of this system, for soon after Ford opened the Crystal Palace a major problem emerged: no one wanted to work at the new Taylorized factory for very long. In 1913 so many workers left Ford—either ill, wounded, or full of hatred for their bosses— that Ford had to hire four workers for every waged position.[26] The cost of this turnover forced the realization upon Ford that he had to pay more attention to the "human element of production." His solution, in 1914, was to introduce the Five Dollar Day, widely considered as the moment the manufacturing middle class was born.[27] This momentous event, however, was not as straightforward as it is remembered today. As Ford himself stressed, the Five Dollar Day did not represent a simple increase in wages. Only half of the $5 was guaranteed as wages; the other half was a contingent profit-sharing plan, dependent on worker behavior and actions both inside and outside the plant. As Stephen Meyer III has written:

> The essence of the Ford Five Dollar Day and Profit-Sharing Plan was the use of profits to alter and to control the lives and the behavior of the Ford workers. . . . Money alone was not enough to induce workers to speed up machinery. It was simply a key to open the door to the source of the labor problems. It allowed Ford sociological investigators to enter the homes of Ford workers and to gather information on their values and styles of life. And, with this information, the investigators used the monetary incentive to change what they considered inefficient aspects of working-class life and culture.[28]

For the Italian Marxist Antonio Gramsci, Fordism represented "the biggest collective effort to date to create . . . a new type of man."[29] Just as the Model T was designed to be exactly like every other Model T, Ford's workers were disciplined into being like every other Ford worker. The company's Sociological Department implemented this employee standardization, conducting "character investigations" on nearly every employee in order to determine whether they would qualify for their profit shares. Investigators evaluated workers' sexuality, financial responsibility, and religious attitudes, deeming at least 40 percent of the workers ineligible for the Five Dollar Day. The Department also institutionalized Ford's patriarchal ideals: a worker whose wife worked outside the home was also disqualified from receiving the full $5.[30]

Part of Ford's attempt to create an undifferentiated mass of workers was a special program to socialize foreign-born and nonwhite workers. By the early 1910s three out of four Detroiters were either immigrants or children of immigrants; they came mostly from Southern and Eastern Europe, fleeing poverty, dispossession, and political and religious persecution. For these workers, Ford—a notorious bigot and eventual Nazi supporter—created the Americanization program, with the stated goal of creating a new "human product." According to the program's *Ford Guide*, "yellow races" were "half civilized," and black people "came from Africa where they lived like other

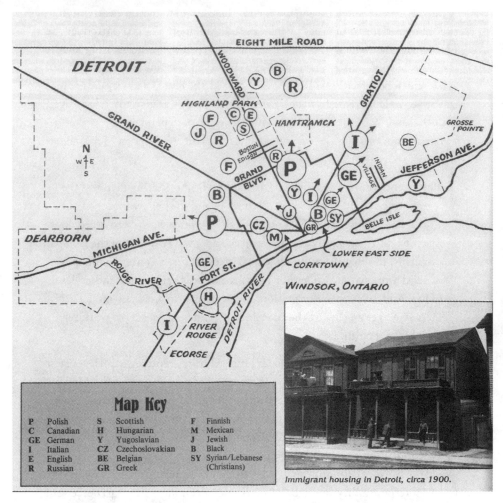

*Immigrant housing in Detroit, circa 1900.*

FIGURE 2.1. Map of Detroit, circa 1900. Source: Babson et al., *Working Detroit*, 26; Burton Collection, Detroit Public Library.

animals in the jungle. White men brought them to America and made them civilized."[31]

Paternalistic, brutal, and racist though they were, Ford's policies had the immediate effect that he desired. Worker turnover, as high as 370 percent in 1913, decreased to 16 percent in 1915.[32] But Ford's dream of creating a Procrustean bed on which his workers could be made to fit the demands of industrial production would soon prove to be unrealizable. The contradictions of capitalism were too pronounced to be remedied by any of Ford's technical fixes.

## Wobblies, Reds, and Goon Squads

Another major reason for Ford's introduction of the Five Dollar Day was the specter of class struggle. Workers did more than quit in frustration with the new industrial regime: many of them were organizing to resist the dehumanizing and humiliating conditions at auto factories across the city, posing a significant problem for Detroit's industrial elite.

Although less than 10 percent of Detroit's workforce was unionized in 1911, there is a rich history of worker struggles in Detroit before the days of Ford. Strikes, such as the General Strike on Labor Day in 1886, won such concessions as shorter workdays and more control over the shop floor. Detroit's business elites, however, fought tirelessly to keep Detroit an open-shop town, depicting unions as "criminal conspiracies" against the rights of private ownership. Owners hired spies to infiltrate workers' organizations, and the police were routinely called upon to escort foreign-born strikebreakers past picket lines.[33]

Worker militancy began to intensify in the early 1910s. In 1912 the International Workers of the World (IWW), colloquially known as the Wobblies, entered the fray. Some three thousand Ford workers would gather around during their lunch breaks to listen to the IWW organizer Matilda Rabinowitz, who advocated direct action to "burst the shell of capitalist government." In response, Ford outlawed outdoor lunches and had Rabinowitz and other Wobblies arrested. In 1913 thousands of Studebaker workers walked off the job in the first major autoworkers' strike in Detroit's history; led by the IWW, they marched across the city, attempting to initiate an industrywide strike. The police attacked and dispersed the crowd and arrested the strike's organizers.[34]

The IWW and its short-lived efforts at insurgency—the organization's Detroit chapter dissolved shortly after the mass strike of 1913—was one of many attempts to organize the Motor City's industrial workforce.[35] In the late 1910s the socialist-led Auto Workers Union had forty thousand members in Detroit alone. At the time, more than half of Detroit's workers were employed in the auto industry, making the autoworkers' movement Detroit's central political problem. As Zaragosa Vargas has noted, "Because of the peculiar nature of mass production, 'a minutely divided, closely timed, mechanized process,' the auto industry was analogous to a huge synchronized machine—a disruption of any sort would shut it down completely."[36]

In the context of growing militancy the nation experienced its first "Red Scare," a campaign by the federal government to repress workers' resistance. As millions of American industrial workers displayed their solidarity with the Russian Revolution of 1917, and many more identified with the countries that the United States was fighting in World War I, the Espionage Act of 1917 and the Sedition Act of 1918 were passed, mandating severe punishment for any person who "shall willfully utter, print, write, or publish disloyal, profane, scurrilous, or abusive language about the government of the United States." During these years the entire IWW leadership was arrested, as was Eugene Debs, the presidential candidate of the Socialist Party. In the 1919–20 Palmer Raids (in which the future FBI head J. Edgar Hoover took part), the government rounded up six thousand "radicals" and exiled one thousand foreign-born socialists.[37] During the First World War, the American Protective League, a private organization that was officially sanctioned by the U.S. government, conducted thirty thousand investigations in Detroit alone, aimed at rooting out radical workers. Publications like the *Michigan Socialist* were outlawed; socialist meetings were banned; and carrying a red flag became illegal in the state.[38] Nativist ideologies were rampant, and immigrant workers found themselves in a vulnerable position; many of them left the city, including most of the 100,000 Mexicans in the metro area.[39]

This coincided with the first great migration of African Americans to the northern United States. More than one million left the Jim Crow South in the 1910s and 1920s, and Detroit's black population increased from less than 6,000 in 1910 to more than 120,000 in 1930. The causes for this migration include mechanization of agriculture, which left many black farmhands out of work; crop and bank failures; and the everyday terrors of the Jim Crow South.[40] Additionally, in the midst of the Red Scare, the federal government limited immigration from southern and eastern Europe, causing northern industries to become more reliant on black migrants. Indeed "much of the mobilization of the migration was orchestrated in the boardrooms of northern industrial enterprises."[41] Black workers were often deployed as strikebreakers and private guards and functioned as a cheap labor pool used to keep wages down.[42] These workers were forced to work what Abdul Alkalimat and others have referred to as "shit work"—the worst paid, most degrading, and most dangerous work. In the auto industry, blacks were largely confined to jobs as production assistants, janitors, and foundry workers.[43]

African Americans were also forced to live in the segregated Black Bottom neighborhood, which contained the city's worst housing stock, often owned by predatory absentee landlords.[44] The relegation of black Americans to inner-city ghettos was a nationwide process, facilitated by an alliance between business interests and the police. The Code of Ethics of Detroit's realtors' association told salesmen not to sell to "members of any race or nationality . . . whose presence will be detrimental to property values," restricting the growing black population to the ghetto, "with police playing the role of both containment and pacification."[45] Chances for integration were hampered in 1923, when the Michigan State Supreme Court ruled that racially restrictive provisions in the sale of homes were legal.[46] When Ossian Sweet, a black doctor, moved his family into a white neighborhood, white supremacist groups attacked the house, and the police failed to protect Sweet and his family. In the ensuing confrontation, a white person was killed; subsequently all eleven black people in Sweet's household were arrested and held without bail on the charge of murder; all were eventually acquitted.[47]

Blacks organized themselves against this terror and oppression by joining the union movement, as well as forming "church groups, women's clubs, Black veterans' groups, community organizations . . . and political clubs."[48] Numerous black newspapers were formed during this time, including the pro-labor *Michigan Chronicle*. The Garveyite movement, which stressed black self-determination and advocated for black business development, also grew rapidly in Detroit as it offered a refuge for many black workers who were stripped of dignity inside and outside of the factory. (Garvey, however, was frequently criticized by black socialists such as A. Philip Randolph for his uncritical stance toward capitalism and class divisions within black America.)[49]

The Detroit Police Department expanded its operations significantly in the 1920s, largely to repress workplace strikes and contain the influx of black migrants. At the time, Detroit was also home to many white-supremacist groups. In the 1920s Michigan had the largest Ku Klux Klan membership of any state, and at least thirty-two thousand members lived in Detroit. (Nationally, KKK membership exceeded two million in the early 1920s.) In 1924 the KKK's candidate for mayor won Detroit's popular vote; he was disqualified only on the technicality that, as a write-in candidate, his name was frequently misspelled on the ballot. The police, whose membership often overlapped with the KKK's, deployed violent containment strategies to keep black workers in their designated place: in the first eight months of 1925, Detroit cops shot fifty-five black Detroiters. As the *Detroit Independent*, one of the city's black newspapers, wrote at the time, more black men were "shot down in the streets [of Detroit] without a reasonable excuse than [had] been lynched in the entire South, during the same period."[50] The Black Legion, a splinter group of the KKK, had a chapter in Highland Park with as many as thirty thousand members in the mid-1930s, including a former mayor. Blacks were not the only target of the Legion: Jews, Catholics, and communists were also condemned by the Legion for violating the sanctity of a pure Detroit. Police estimated that Black Legion members committed as many as fifty murders, including the bombing of union headquarters and the slaying of prominent communist organizers. At the time, to be a radical activist, particularly a black activist, was a very dangerous proposition.[51]

Police worked hand in hand with the auto companies to contain worker dissent. By the mid-1920s, when Ford shifted operations from Highland Park to the River Rouge complex in Dearborn, creating the world's largest factory, the company had taken a more direct and violent approach to the problem of worker behavior. The Five Dollar Day was dropped in 1921, and with wages soon falling below the industry average, direct repression became the preferred form of labor management. The Sociological Department was replaced by the Service Department, headed by Harry Bennett, who soon "assembled the world's largest private army, and established the most extensive and efficient espionage system in American industry."[52] Bennett recruited mainly former boxers, gangsters, and ex-convicts to staff this security force, which "body-searched workers, patrolled washrooms and interrogated anyone suspected of union activity."[53] At the same time the number of foremen in Ford's factories doubled, creating a "penitentiary atmosphere" for workers.[54] Along with major auto companies such as General Motors, Dodge Motors, Studebaker, and Packard, Ford worked with the Employers' Association of Detroit, which hired labor spies and blacklisted workers suspected of union activity. In the case of any union mobilization, the Association had a roster of forty-four thousand strikebreakers.[55]

## The Great Depression

The production boom that this type of coercion facilitated was historically unprecedented. Worker productivity in Detroit's auto industry had increased 1,000 percent in just two decades. The heavy capital outlays required to keep up with Ford's production techniques—sprawling factories, moving assembly lines, cutting-edge machinery, and a massive workforce—drove most of the country's small manufacturers out of business, resulting in a remarkable *centralization* of capital. In 1908 there were 253 auto producers in the United States; by 1929 that number was 44, with just three companies—Ford, General Motors, and Chrysler—accounting for 80 percent of industry output. This centralization of capital led to a drastic increase in wealth inequality.[56]

The oligarchic auto industry was the motor of both the local and the national economy. Car production consumed more than 50 percent of the steel produced in the United States, 75 percent of the glass and rubber, and 20 percent of the nickel and tin.[57] Particularly in Detroit, few jobs were not in some way dependent on the auto industry.[58]

Competing firms, in all types of industries linked to the auto boom, were being forced by the coercive laws of competition to make a choice: either invest in new machinery and rationalize production or lose market share. All this led to an unprecedented construction bonanza that included factories, railway tracks to move the product, and houses to shelter the swelling industrial labor force. In Detroit a dramatic building boom also transformed the Downtown skyline in the years before 1929, leading a contemporary publication to enthuse, "Detroit has crowded more than three-quarters of a century of achievement . . . into a short space of two decades."[59] But a problem was brewing, one that would eventually bring the system crashing down. The real incomes of 90 percent of U.S. workers *declined* in the Roaring '20s. Who, then, was buying all these new cars and other consumer goods?[60]

In volume 3 of *Capital*, Marx illuminates a central contradiction of capitalism: "The more productivity develops, the more it comes into conflict with the narrow basis on which the relations of consumption rest."[61] Eventually consumption *always* lags behind production for the simple reason that if the workers were paid enough money to buy all the products they produced, there would be no profit. This gap is widened by the downward pressure on wages that the "coercive laws of competition" exert; these laws dictate that firms with the cheapest costs of production can generally undersell and outcompete other firms. That the working class as a whole doesn't have the disposable income to purchase all the products it produces is a contradiction that can *never be resolved within capitalism*; it can only be displaced in time (through credit) and space (through the conquest of foreign markets).[62]

In the 1920s Detroit factories were producing cars at a rate that far exceeded the capacity of consumers to purchase them; the same was true in industries across the country. But Wall Street remained optimistic: even as corporate profits declined, stock prices (shares of those profits) were increasing.[63] In late October 1929, however, the gap between productive capacity and consumption became too wide, and the house of cards came crashing down.[64] Investment stopped. People were laid off en masse. Within a few years auto production in Detroit fell 75 percent. Even as the crisis deepened, however, the Big Three firms "thrived": "Ford and Chrysler endured only two modestly unprofitable years while General Motors recorded no losses at all, with profits surpassing the 1928 record as early as 1936. This was accomplished by . . . massive permanent layoffs, 50 percent reductions in annual pay for those remaining, and unprecedented speed-ups, while at the same time maintaining the pace of product and process innovation."[65] The extent to which workers were asked to shoulder the load of the crisis is revealed in one Chaplinesque anecdote: as a result of Ford's speed-up campaign, one worker's job entailed operating two drill presses, one in each hand.[66]

The destitution and misery that workers faced is hard to overstate. By the end of 1930, 150,000 Detroiters were out of work. Across the United States, the unemployment rate reached 25 percent. A quarter of U.S. children were malnourished. Millions lost their homes. "Homeless armies wandered the country on freight trains; one railroad official testified that the number of train-hoppers caught by his company ballooned from 14,000 in 1929 to 186,000 in 1931." There were 568 suicides in Detroit in 1931, five times the number in 1927.[67]

## The Spirit of 1937

In 1930 Detroiters elected Frank Murphy, a liberal, pro-labor candidate for mayor who promised to combat the "financial dictators" who were responsible for the city's immiseration. Although Murphy enjoyed wide support across the city, his big ambitions were curtailed by harsh economic realities and a budgetary shortfall. Part of the problem was that Ford had deliberately set up his major factories outside of city limits (in Dearborn and Highland Park) to avoid paying taxes to the Detroit government, despite the fact that as many as 35 percent of relief recipients in the city were Ford employees. As Detroit's tax revenue sagged, Ford stuck to his policy of never donating to local relief groups, claiming that "self-help is the only means of combating the economic depression."[68] Reminiscent of the 2013 bankruptcy, the banks that loaned Detroit the money to maintain its social services in the face of these revenue shortfalls demanded an austerity program in exchange, including a reduction in the city's welfare expenditures and cutting the wages of thirty-five thousand municipal employees. And, as in contemporary Detroit, a huge percentage of the city's revenue was redirected toward repaying its creditors: in 1932, whereas 7 percent of the city's revenue went to relief efforts, 43 percent went to banks, half for interest payments.[69]

In 1933 Franklin Delano Roosevelt, a close associate of Murphy, was elected president promising to create a "New Deal." Henry Ford and many other of Detroit's industrial tycoons were opposed to Roosevelt's (and Murphy's) support for increased government intervention into the market. When Roosevelt traveled to one of Ford's factories in Detroit, Ford refused to meet with him, claiming Roosevelt was advancing Soviet-style policies.[70] But many enlightened members of the capitalist class realized that more government intervention was needed to right the economy and restore a semblance of order. Furthermore, Roosevelt was no socialist. The president himself called relief

FIGURE 2.2 An Unemployed Council protests in Downtown Detroit in 1932.
Sources: Babson et al., *Working Detroit*, 57; *Detroit News*.

"repugnant to the American ideals of self-reliance." His programs alleviated some sections of the working class's worst suffering but brought the country nowhere close to recovery. The New Deal's Civilian Works Administration, for example, provided enough jobs for only 40 percent of the 10 million unemployed workers who applied. The Social Security Act excluded all farm and domestic workers, with the result that, in 1933, 11.4 million white workers and 3.5 million black workers were left in the lurch.[71] Piven and Cloward insist that resistance to a more robust welfare state was "not only a reflection of harshly individualistic American attitudes. They were also a reflection of American economic realities. Work and self-reliance meant grueling toil at low wages for many people. So long as that was so, the dole could not be dispensed permissively for fear some would choose it over work."[72]

As immiseration spread and jobless workers were forced to steal in order to survive, the state responded with mass arrests. Between 1925 and 1939 the U.S. incarceration rate increased 73 percent. As George Rusche, an affiliate of the Frankfurt School, wrote at the time, the imprisonment boom was part of a campaign to displace blame from the economic system onto "immigrants and Negroes."[73] In 1936 black people accounted for 4 percent of Michigan's total population but 20 percent of its prison population.[74]

As prisons grew overcrowded (some stuffed to 300 percent of their capacity), a series of prison revolts broke out in the metro Detroit area and across the country. Rusche wrote, "There is a shortage of beds; the air, calculated carefully per head in the narrow cells, is consumed excessively. . . . The sanitary facilities are becoming pestilential. . . . Under these conditions a hell is created."[75] The growing number of prison riots and escape attempts caused an international scandal, and prison officials were warned to be hypervigilant in preventing any further upheavals. So when a fire broke out in a prison in Columbus, Ohio, in April 1930, prison guards suspected it was a ploy of the prisoners and responded by securing the gates with "machine gun emplacements." By the time the guards realized that the fire was no ruse and attempted to put it out, it was too late: 322 prisoners in the overcrowded prison had burned to death. This story was front-page news in Germany.[76]

To combat widespread immiseration, the U.S. Communist Party (CPUSA) organized Unemployed Councils to block evictions, restore disconnected utilities, and protest social deterioration. A year after the National Hunger March, the head of the CPUSA in Detroit organized the Ford Hunger March. On March 7, 1932, three thousand workers marched on the city's employment office. Their demands were relief payments, employment, the right to unionize, and an end to discrimination in Ford's factories. The DPD, Dearborn police, and Michigan state troopers attacked the crowd and a fight broke out in which the police killed five people. Although no police officers were killed, the *Detroit Free Press* blamed the deaths on the "red mob" that was led by "chronic agitators." The night of the march, officers used the violence as a pretext to raid the homes of many well-known communists and union organizers. Days later thirty thousand people marched in solidarity during the funeral procession of the murdered protesters.[77]

As around the country, Depression-era protests were often multiracial, which deeply worried local elites. Ford, for example, had long understood the danger of black activism. In 1923 his newspaper characterized the civil rights movement as "the Jewish attempt to Bolshevize the Negro." That same year, the Ford Service Department hired a black ex-cop, Donald J. Marshall, to run the black Service Department. One Department operative wrote, "If a colored man would give any back talk in his employment office, Marshall would take him out in the back room somewhere and . . . beat the very last daylights out of him."

Ford is often praised for being the first among the major auto companies to hire a representative number of black workers, but it is important to note that in the 1930s, more than 99 percent of black Ford workers were confined to the Rouge factory. According to University of Kansas professor Elizabeth Esch, Ford's strategy was a contingency plan: in case white workers initiated a mass strike, he could rely on black workers to maintain production. Ford had long used divide-and-conquer strategies, pitting various ethnic and racial groups against one another inside the plant. He gave financial contributions to a select few churches that he knew to be politically conservative, and used these churches as employment agencies to find loyal black workers and strike-breakers. (Reverend Charles Hill was outstanding in his efforts to encourage blacks to resist this unholy alliance and join the union movement.) When A. Philip Randolph, the black socialist leader of the Brotherhood of Sleeping Car Porters, came to speak at a black church in Detroit, Ford issued a threat to all his black workers that whoever attended Randolph's speech would be fired—and many were.[78]

It was not only capitalists who supported racial divisions within the working class. The American Federation of Labor (AFL) clung to its policy of racial seg-regation, even though that policy had undermined one of the union's largest strikes, the steelworkers' strike of 1919, when tens of thousands of black workers crossed a picket line rather than stand in solidarity with a racist organization. But thanks largely to the work of black leaders like Hubert Harrison, Cyril Briggs, and the African Blood Brotherhood, the Communist Party increas-ingly worked to organize black workers. The 1930 Comintern—an interna-tional organization that met to advance global communism—stressed the im-portance of the "Black Question." By 1931 there were over one thousand black members in the CPUSA.[79]

In 1935 the United Auto Workers (UAW) was formed as part of the Commit-tee for Industrial Organization (CIO), a radical sector within the increasingly conservative AFL, and began consolidating all the radical workers' groups in and around Detroit. The UAW had a distinct faction linked to the CPUSA, which organized the UAW's campaign for a thirty-hour workweek and worked closely with the National Negro Congress, a left-wing organization formed in 1936, to unionize newly arrived black laborers. In 1935 the executive council of the AFL warned of the growing leftist influence in union movement: "If the

Communists succeed in their efforts it means no more or less than the dissolution or destruction of our movement." The *Detroit Free Press* added, "The responsible leaders of American labor cannot be hoodwinked into believing that the seizure of their movement by Communists would bring in the new millennium." The Black Legion murdered UAW secretary George Marchuk, and the militia is suspected of being behind the deaths of other UAW organizers who were murdered during the 1930s.[80]

Despite such repression, in 1936–37 the UAW led a historic series of sit-down strikes. As opposed to the walkout, during which workers would leave the plant and picket outside the gates to try to keep strikebreakers out, in the sit-down strike workers occupied the factories and locked themselves in. This tactic was adapted from one used by capital *against* workers; in 1933, when fifteen thousand autoworkers struck in Detroit, plant owners set up barracks so that the strikebreakers could live in the factories to ensure uninterrupted production.[81] Workers put this strategy to use with the help of small businesses and women-led groups that supplied striking workers with food and other necessities, and sit-down strikes soon spread throughout the city and across industries, as workers in Detroit's department stores, lunch counters, and hotels all sat down. The labor historian Steve Babson writes, "The sitdowns welded workers of diverse skills, nationalities, races and religions into a powerfully unified movement."[82]

These sit-down strikes, which essentially codified the labor movement as a force in twentieth-century American politics, were successful thanks to concurrent developments in the country's political life. In particular, as the labor historian Nelson Lichtenstein explains, the union movement seemed to offer a solution to two of the most pressing political problems of the 1930s, underconsumption and industrial democracy, both of which grew out of the contradictions which had culminated in the Great Depression. As we've seen, the Depression was caused by overproduction and a highly regressive distribution of wealth that put the new consumer products (especially automobiles) that were now driving the economy out of the reach of most workers. To solve this problem, "a broad upward shift in working-class purchasing power was essential," and the union movement seemed the only institution capable of achieving this "American standard of living" for all workers.[83] On top of this, unions were the institution that seemed capable of bridging the gap between the rights discourse prevalent in American society with the culture of autocracy and obedience of the parochial industrial workplace. Many of the new unionists were African Americans, Mexican Americans, or from European immigrant families, and the union movement's promise of "industrial democracy" offered them a sense of citizenship they were denied in civil society.[84]

This popular upsurge, garnering legitimacy from the anti-business senti-ment engendered by the Depression, was given institutional expression by the politicians of the New Deal. The 1935 Wagner Act, named for Senator Robert Wagner, was a "Magna Carta" for the labor movement, designed to put in place a permanent set of mechanisms by which the labor movement could organize itself and resolve its grievances with management. The Act gave workers the right to strike, boycott, picket, and, crucially, select their own union by majority vote, which the companies would now by law be forced to recognize as the sole collective bargaining agent of its workers. The next year the American public voiced its approval for the New Deal coalition and its poli-cies by reelecting President Roosevelt in a historic landslide victory. It was this wave of popular support and institutional authority that the UAW rode on its path to official recognition during the sit-down crusade.

The longest and most influential of the sit-down strikes was the 1936–37 occupation of General Motors in Flint, Michigan. This strike, which was cata-lyzed largely by communist and socialist organizers, lasted forty-four days.[85] In a tactic that the League of Revolutionary Black Workers would emulate thirty years later, UAW organizers targeted specific "mother plants"—plants that produced *all* of an essential part needed for GM cars. By targeting these plants, striking workers were able to shut down production at all GM plants within three days. As in Detroit's Great Rebellion thirty years later, the Na-tional Guard was called in to help the police repress the workers, who refused to capitulate even in the face of bullets, tear gas, and vomit gas.[86]

After the strike, GM was forced to legally recognize the UAW as the sole bargaining agent for all of its workers, and Chrysler soon followed. But GM also moved much of its production from the Flint plant to upstate New York, an early example of what labor historian Beverly Silver describes as a "spatial fix," one of industrial capital's main strategies for escaping militant labor. And this fix set an important precedent: in the decades to come, the Big Three firms fled southeastern Michigan precipitously, in an effort to escape the strong workers' movement.[87]

But the sit-down movement was too strong for most capitalists to simply repress or evade. In March 1937 Detroit's leading newspaper declared, "Revolu-tion is here." Babson explains:

The sitdown wave spread through virtually every industry in the city. Four hotels, including two of the downtown's largest, were occupied. So were at least 15 major auto plants (including Chrysler), and 25 smaller parts plants; a dozen industrial laundries; three department stores and

FIGURE 2.3. Strike at Dodge Main in 1937. Sources: Babson, *Working Detroit*, 80; United Auto Workers.

over a dozen shoe and clothing stores; all the city's major cigar plants; five trucking and garage companies; nine lumber yards; at least three printing plants; ten meat-packing plants, bakeries and other food processors; warehouses, restaurants, coal yards, bottlers, and over a dozen miscellaneous manufacturers. . . . Even non-employees sat down. On March 11, 35 relief participants occupied the Fort Street welfare office.[88]

Reactionary forces opposed the sit-down wave through mythologization and outright repression: city elites consistently blamed worker militancy on "outsiders"; the House Un-American Activities Committee had hearings on the "communist conspiracy" behind the sit-downs; and the National Guard was routinely brought in to retake the occupied buildings. Nonetheless, radical unions were winning recognition across the city and across the country. More than 2 million U.S. workers participated in a strike between September 1936 and June 1937, and CIO membership increased to 3.7 million.[89]

Ford was the last of the Big Three to hold out against unionization. His strategy was outright coercion. Almost 10 percent of Ford's ninety thousand Rouge employees were secretly working for the Service Department. Harry Bennett, who by then had taken over the day-to-day management of Ford's enterprise due to Henry's health problems, ruled with an iron fist. The Service Department continued to recruit from gang members, bouncers, boxers, and convicts; while Bennett was on the board of the Michigan Prison Commission, from 1935 to 1937, "convicts were paroled to the Ford Motor Company at a rate of approximately five a week."[90] Bennett used the three thousand members of the Service Department to brutalize any and all workers suspected of union activity. In 1937, at the Battle of the Overpass, the Department violently attacked UAW activists, including future UAW President Walter Reuther (then of the Socialist Party), who were leafleting during a shift change. In the next four years, Ford fired four thousand workers for suspected union activity. But workers withstood this repression, in no small part thanks to the National Negro Congress, which helped the UAW organize black workers. In the decisive walkout of 1941—which finally forced Ford to recognize the UAW—Bennett deployed black workers to attack the picket lines and to work as strikebreakers in a deliberate attempt to foment a race riot. But this divide-and-conquer strategy failed when the majority of the 16,000 black workers stood in solidarity with their white co-workers.[91]

In the context of pervasive racial violence, a deepening penal crisis, rampant unemployment, militant workers' movements, and economic stagnation, many in power realized that the state needed to take a much more active role in managing the capitalist market. But attempts to manage the crisis, notably the New Deal, proved insufficient to remedy the country's faltering economy. By the late 1930s, Detroit's auto companies were still producing fewer cars than they had in 1929. In Detroit 135,000 people were still unemployed (including 80 percent of the UAW's 250,000 members), and the national unemployment rate was 15 percent. Meanwhile factories across the country had more productive capacity than their owners knew what to do with; as factories and machines stood empty and unused, there was simply no way, within capitalist logic, to connect this surplus capacity with the mass of unemployed workers.

It would take a war to pull American capitalism out of this crisis: as historians Jefferson Cowie and Nick Salvatore write, "*The* major reallocation of the American division of wealth was, in fact, not the New Deal, but the Second World War."[92]

## The War Years

In late 1940, with the Second World War raging in Europe, President Roosevelt gave a speech titled "The Great Arsenal of Democracy." A year before the attack on Pearl Harbor, the speech was an announcement of the country's material and ideological support of the Allies in their fight against the Axis powers. After warning of the direness of the situation in Europe and the Nazi project to conquer the world, Roosevelt decried the possibility of U.S. complacency, rousing the nation to the cause of Great Britain and "Democracy's fight against world conquest." Though not engaged militarily, American support would come in the form of "sending every ounce and every ton of munitions and supplies that we can" to our allies across the ocean. Every industry, Roosevelt proclaimed, no matter its peacetime function, "must yield, and will gladly yield, to our primary and compelling purpose." Asking for sacrifice from workers, managers, and executives, Roosevelt urged, "The nation expects our defense industries to continue operation without interruption by strikes or lockouts. It expects and insists that management and workers will reconcile their differences by voluntary or legal means, to continue to produce the supplies that are so sorely needed." The stakes were nothing less than "the defense of our civilization and . . . the building of a better civilization in the future."[93]

Before entering the war militarily, the United States was involved in the war economically. And the war was hugely productive for the economy, finally pulling the country out of the Depression. Nationally the war effort helped create 17 million jobs. The task of armament fell primarily to the industrial cities of the North, and Detroit in particular became the arsenal within the "Arsenal of Democracy." Factories were converted wholesale to produce military equipment. (From 1942 to 1945 no autos were produced in the Motor City.) General Motors and Ford Motor Company were, respectively, the first and third highest-producing companies of military equipment for the war effort in the country. The number of unemployed workers in the city declined from 135,000 in 1940 to 4,000 in 1943. As thousands of Detroit's workers joined the armed forces, demand for labor in the military economy was so high that women were recruited to work in the plants in record numbers: there were 260,000 women earning a wage in Detroit in 1943, up from 44,000 a few years earlier. And for the first time, black women were drawn into the industrial workforce: the number of black women employed by Chrysler increased from zero to 5,000 between 1941 and 1945; as around the country, black women were relegated to the lowest-paying industrial jobs and were routinely subject to racist attacks and sexual assaults.[94]

Even before the U.S. declared war on Japan, UAW leaders, and in particular Walter Reuther, had sought to use defense mobilization as a way to build goodwill for the union movement among the populace and consolidate labor's position in the political life of the country. While it enjoyed tremendous popular support, the 1936–37 union upsurge was the product of a temporary and tenuous coalition of forces. The incredible growth of union membership after the sit-downs belies what Lichtenstein calls the "surprising weakness of the union forces."[95] A small group of radicals had been responsible for the GM sit-down, with the mass of workers supporting the union only after the strike had succeeded. Further, the strikers were victorious not because of pro-union sentiment among workers but because the corporation was temporarily denied recourse to the police power of the state thanks to the pro-union governor Frank Murphy's hesitancy to deploy the militia after the 1936 election demonstrated the population's support of workers' rights to bargain. However, this window of political opportunity was a brief one, and the future of the UAW was by no means assured. The nascent union was in shambles by 1938, faced with an economic slowdown and the power of the corporations they were up against. Divisions within the movement mirrored those in the broader polity, and reactionary forces hemmed in the union on all sides. Faced with this situation, Reuther latched on to the war production effort as the means to bolster the union's position and popularity, first by proposing a plan to pool the industry's unused industrial capacity to produce military equipment, and then, after the U.S. entered the conflict, by ensuring labor's complete cooperation with defense mobilization.[96]

Immediately after the attack on Pearl Harbor on December 7, 1941, union leaders rushed to show their support for the war effort by calling off strikes and pledging peaceful labor relations, fulfilling President Roosevelt's entreaty. On December 9 the president of the AFL issued a statement: "Labor knows its duty. It will do its duty, and more." In the following days, meetings between the government, industry, and labor leaders produced an agreement that would ensure uninterrupted production during the war. President Roosevelt codified the agreement as follows:

1    There shall be no strikes or lockouts.
2    All disputes shall be settled by peaceful means.

3   The President shall set up a proper War Labor Board to handle these disputes.[97]

This War Labor Board would be filled with union representatives who had nearly unanimously agreed to these conditions. As Martin Glaberman, a prominent Detroit Marxist and former autoworker, writes in his hallmark work, *Wartime Strikes*, "One of the interesting aspects of the adoption of the no-strike pledge was that no union bothered to consult its membership in advance, and very few bothered to consult afterward."[98] Indeed, the no-strike pledge was anathema to workers' interests. Though the pledge was predicated on the notion of "equality of sacrifice" on the part of labor and management, in reality workers bore the brunt, with union brass ignoring their members' immediate interests in exchange for a more secure place at the bargaining table, sowing the seeds for the accommodationist posture of the UAW after the war.[99]

In exchange for a no-strike pledge, federal military contracts were almost exclusively given to firms that employed unionized workers. (The government gave contracts mostly to big businesses, largely excluding small businesses from the wartime boom, and concentrating employment in large industrial enterprises.) As a result, unions were given carte blanche to register all laborers that worked in the war effort, increasing union membership and filling union coffers. These unionized workers were forbidden from quitting during the duration of their contract, a rule that benefited unions by securing their membership, and benefited capital and the state by mitigating work stoppages. This arrangement facilitated the largest growth in union membership in U.S. history: by 1946 more than two-thirds of manufacturing workers were represented by unions.[100]

The booming war industry caused a high demand for labor, creating a contradictory situation for workers. On the one hand, work was plentiful and salaries were relatively high; on the other hand, the ability of workers to resist the demands of management was severely limited. This was due both to the no-strike pledge and to the popular call for patriotism and sacrifice, which fell primarily on workers. Many workers, despite the strike ban, initiated wildcat strikes—strikes not authorized by the union—but when they did, they faced resistance from all quarters of society. One worker at a plant in Hamtramck, a municipality inside Detroit, explained the media's reaction to striking workers: "We were allies of Hirohito and next to Pearl Harbor, we were responsible for the rest of the troubles of the country."[101] Echoing this sentiment, General George Marshall, the army's chief of staff, called wartime strikes "the damndest crime ever committed against America."[102]

Industry and the government fed into this mythology by claiming that the actions of striking workers were the result of a small group of "outside" radicals sowing dissent for its own sake. One future Michigan governor, George Romney, an auto industry representative during the war years, claimed, "The manpower problem exists principally because the desire of the majority of workers to do more work and get this war over with is being thwarted by an unrestrained militant minority group."[103] In his "Arsenal of Democracy" speech, President Roosevelt provides a potent example of the way mythological language can create these types of divisions: "The evil forces which have crushed and undermined and corrupted so many others are already within our own gates. Your government knows much about them and every day is ferreting them out. . . . They seek to stir up suspicion and dissension, to cause internal strife. They try to turn capital against labor, and vice versa. . . . These trouble-breeders have but one purpose. It is to divide our people, to divide them into hostile groups and to destroy our unity."[104]

Declarations of patriotism and anticommunism obscured another reason for the crackdown on labor at this time. Not since before the Great Depression had there been a significant labor shortage. In other words, "this was the first time in anyone's memory that workers had the means to exert considerable pressure for improved wages. That, in fact, is why the government rushed to freeze wages at a ridiculously low level."[105] The relatively favorable conditions brought about by the war—nearly full employment and unrelenting demand for the goods of war—put labor in a better position to negotiate than it had had in a long time. It's no coincidence that severe limitations on labor's primary bargaining tool—the strike—were put in place at this time, precisely when wages were capped by federal decree and the president and industry leaders were demonizing struggling workers as the enemies of democracy and freedom. If patriotism were all that was at stake, then the companies themselves would have been forced to sacrifice for the war effort as well, but as one GM worker explained, "The corporations were showing no sense of patriotism or loyalty and were contributing nothing. All the sacrifices were on the part of the workers."[106]

The differential treatment of labor and capital during this period is stark. To control labor and ensure continuous production, the federal government took an increasingly direct role in the management of capital-labor relations. In addition to what we've already seen—the no-strike pledge, the regulation of wages by the government instead of through collective bargaining, and the intervention of the War Labor Board in labor disputes—Congress passed the Smith-Connally Act in 1943, which gave the federal government the power to seize any "essential" factory or mine during a strike and force workers back on the job. Workers who promoted a strike were subject to imprisonment and a $5,000 fine.[107] At the same time, the federal government was subsidizing private plant construction to an astonishing degree, with new factories disproportionately located in suburbs (such as Ford's Willow Run bomber facility, between Detroit and Ann Arbor), further curbing the power of organized labor and accelerating unemployment in central cities in the postwar years.[108] Between 1940 and 1944 GM built $900 million in new factory capacity, almost all of it paid for by the federal government. During the war corporate profits rose from $9 billion in 1940 to $24 billion in 1944. On top of this, the government promised to rebate most of the taxes on these profits after the war. As Secretary of War Henry Stimson wrote at the time in his wartime diary, "If you are going to try and go to war in a capitalist country, you have got to let business make money out of the process, or business won't work."[109]

Despite widespread pressure from their employers, the government, the public, and union leadership, many workers continued the battle against capital. In addition to low wages, horrible work conditions were a major factor. *In Michigan, one workplace death, five amputations, and one hundred serious injuries occurred per day in 1944.* Between 1943 and 1944 four million American workers took part in 8,708 wildcats. In early 1944 Detroit workers averaged a dozen strikes per week, making the Motor City the leading center of workplace worker militancy. A local union president in Detroit, describing the rush to contain strikes during the war, said, "It was like a fireman with a water bucket running around trying to put fires out." Wildcat strikes continued to increase in number throughout the war.[110]

In response, striking workers faced direct coercion. The military was often brought in to stabilize factory operations. "Military officers in uniform were present in all of the war production plants during the war and they regularly intervened in strikes and potential strikes. In other words, the reality of the war and the role of the government were concretely present to workers who went on strike or who threatened to go on strike."[111]

Mythologies smooth over contradictions to make the world legible, simple, and palatable. Wartime strikes in Detroit presented a series of contradictions. This is clearly seen at the UAW's 1944 convention, when workers rejected all proposals on the no-strike pledge: to uphold it, to slightly modify its terms, or to rescind it entirely. During this time a majority of union members were violating the no-strike pledge through wildcats and other actions; despite this, in a referendum on the no-strike pledge union members voted 2 to 1 to uphold the strike ban, and two-thirds of the membership failed to even mail in their ballots. This result shows that the connection between patriotism and the passivity of labor was not as simple as the government, the press, and corporate elites made it out to be. Workers, it turned out, could support the war, understand their sacrifices as a contribution to the war and an affirmation of patriotism, and *at the same time* oppose the blatant profiteering of their employers and the federal government's intervention in their relations with management.[112] The mythology that overlay these inconsistencies allowed the situation to *work*; that is, it facilitated the accumulation of capital (letting business "make money out of the process," as Stimson explained) during the war, while providing an accompanying ideology that cast those who would challenge the production of profit from the sweat and sacrifice of workers as "un-American," "unpatriotic," or "outside communist agitators." It allowed for profit-making, the exploitation of labor, and the containment of dissent.

Mythology also facilitates concrete repression when the mythology itself isn't enough to resolve ambiguities in public feeling. In other words, the mythology here casts labor organization and collective bargaining as unpatriotic and criminal. This mythology itself is not enough to convince the striking workers and any who support the actions of the workers, despite the slander of the press. But the mythology justifies the repression of the workers who fail to accept the mythology. With striking or otherwise disobedient workers equated with Hitler and the enemies of freedom, the government was free to administer the full force of its repressive apparatus, with the military intervening in situations where the indirect influence of government—through legislation, ideological pressure, and bureaucratic procedure—was insufficient.

## The Postwar Regime

We shall solve the city problem by leaving the city. —HENRY FORD, quoted in Amy Kenyon, "Detroit's Road to Ruin," 2013

The postwar period is remembered as Detroit's Golden Years, a time of almost magical prosperity, when well-paying and dependable auto manufacturing jobs were available to everyone; when ascendance to the middle class—in the form of homeownership facilitated by steady work in the auto industry—was within reach for almost all Detroiters; when "Motown ruled the airwaves"; when liberal governance and the civil rights movement seemed to promise a slow but unwavering surge toward racial equality. "In the postwar years," a *New York Times* article stated in 2017, "Detroit became the epitome of the American dream."[113]

As we know, myths are not without their material foundations, and this period in Detroit was indeed one of comparative affluence. Detroit was the center of the globally dominant U.S. auto industry, and in the context of a booming postwar national economy, many in the working class enjoyed a rising standard of living: between 1939 and 1959 real median family incomes in the United States doubled.[114] In Detroit these gains were largely thanks to the success of the UAW, which during the immediate postwar period earned significant wage and benefits gains for its members, while becoming institutionalized within the city's factories. This period in Detroit coincided with global economic trends: "The world economy had never seen anything like the Great Boom of 1948–73. For a full quarter-century the dominant economies surged ever forward, generating jobs, robust profits, and rising incomes year after year. These were the golden years of western capitalism."[115] To understand Detroit in this period it is necessary to keep in mind this broader context. The United States emerged from World War II as the leader of the capitalist world, dominating global politics throughout the Golden Years. America's military was the strongest in the world: it had hundreds of bases across the world and carried in its arsenal the nuclear weapons that had just killed more than 100,000 people in Japan. In the economic arena, the United States also towered above the rest: at war's end, U.S.-based production accounted for more than half of global production. Using its influence to globalize trade and finance, the United States also supplied Europe and Japan with the physical capital, commodities, and cash to rebuild their economies. In addition, the combination of imperialist machinations and co-opted liberation movements opened space for capital expansion in the Global South, as previously undeveloped countries became repositories for Western capital.[116]

The myth of the Golden Years is twofold. First, this period mythologizes the Great Boom as the capitalist norm, with the attendant assumption that the conditions of this period could be permanently resurrected. In this framework, the period from 1973 to the present is viewed as a "long downturn" or "long crisis." Yet, as Thomas Piketty has famously documented, the reduction in inequality following World War II was an *exception* to the general rule of capitalism, a system that tends toward widening inequalities.[117] Second is the myth that these years were golden at all. Despite increasing aggregate wages, this period in Detroit was marked by pervasive unemployment, intense class struggle, volatile racial strife, and the permanent relocation of auto manufacturing jobs outside of the city. Throughout the 1950s unemployment in the auto industry frequently exceeded 10 percent, and between 1947 and 1963 the city lost 134,000 manufacturing jobs.[118] As the labor historian Daniel J. Clark has provocatively written, "The very concept of 'autoworkers' is problematic. There was no consistent body of people who could be classified as autoworkers during these years. Instead, people periodically entered and left auto work, often with little control over the timing."[119]

The actions of workers themselves at the time should disabuse us of the myth of the stable, prosperous autoworker. In the immediate postwar years, the labor movement reached a crescendo when over four million workers participated in a nationwide strike to demand higher wages. Between this labor militancy, widespread unemployment, and hostile race relations, the transition to a stable postwar regime of capital accumulation was far from guaranteed. While the United States was the dominant military, economic, and political power across the globe at war's end, the transition to peacetime production was not a matter of resuming business as usual; it was just as impossible to continue producing military equipment as to return to pre-Depression standards.

The principle of creative destruction posits that capitalism must continually revolutionize itself in order to survive. Nowhere is this clearer than in the history of Detroit after World War II. The massive investments in factories and other infrastructure that had facilitated capital accumulation during Detroit's industrial buildup became obstacles to the growth of capital in the postwar period. Auto companies were turning to automation and other new production processes to reduce costs and increase efficiency, and if capital was to expand in Detroit, it would either have to rebuild within the city—which was experiencing a shortage of land for new plants—or move elsewhere. Detroit was also home to one of the most organized and militant industrial labor forces in the world, a group that commanded high wages and could exert considerable control over the production process. These two problems together—the strength of the labor movement and the obsolescence of the city's industrial base—formed the basis of Detroit's deindustrialization after World War II.[120]

What resulted was a dispersal of manufacturing and people and a concerted effort by capitalists and the state to limit the power of unions, coinciding with a coordinated Red Scare that limited the scope and appeal of leftist politics, both within the labor movement and in society at large. These two strategies fed into one another: as industry increasingly fled the city, rising unemployment meant unions had less power to control production; with unions unable to control the shop floor, companies were free to automate, speed up, and otherwise control work processes. Dispersal of people—suburbanization—also curbed union power by separating the working class and investing them in the new values of middle-class consumption (two-car garages, TV sets, and all the rest of it), facilitated by rising union wages, rather than in worker solidarity and collective well-being.

The specific strategies involved were, crucially, a direct outgrowth of the war: the push for uninterrupted production; the construction of highways (originally conceived as a military strategy), which facilitated the flight of industry outside the city; the use of the military to mediate the class struggle; and the Cold War ideology that justified the purging of leftist union elements at the same time that it legitimated the new role of the United States as a global policeman ensuring security and encouraging free trade. The creative destruction that fashioned the new postwar regime was accompanied by a powerful set of mythologies that smoothed out its contradictions, involving an amalgamation of anticommunist hysteria, racism, and a patriotic belief in the American Dream.

## Purging the Parlor Pinks and the Treaty of Detroit

Q: When did you become a member of the Communist Party?

A: I never became a member of the Communist Party.

Q: If you are, as you say, a loyal American, why do you persist in denying that you were a member of the Communist Party?

—Transcript of QUESTIONING FROM THE U.S. LOYALTY PROGRAM in the 1950s, quoted in Neocleous, *Critique of Security*, 2008

Soviet agents are coming into the U.S. disguised as Jewish rabbis. —Detroit Police CHIEF HARRY TOY, quoted in Babson, *Working Detroit*, 1984

This is the context in which the Cold War materialized. The United States and the Soviet Union had emerged from World War II as the two global superpowers. With the temporary alliance against Nazi Germany dissolved, the countries embarked on a long ideological and military struggle for global preeminence, producing a powerful mythology that shaped global politics throughout the second half of the twentieth century—the Cold War ideology of a division between the good guys and the bad guys, totalitarianism and liberty, communism and democracy, an ideology that proved extremely useful for repressing resistance movements. As we saw from the Red Scare during the First World War, demonizing anticapitalist political movements did not originate in the post–World War II era, but McCarthyism and the Cold War, which pitted the United States against communist forces at home and across the globe, took these tactics to new heights and profoundly impacted American political policy and popular mentality for years to come.

The Cold War was synonymous with the postwar economic expansion, as the Us versus Them mythology became the justification for American economic and military imperialism. During this time the Marshall Plan sent billions of dollars to American allies around the world, much of it earmarked for the purchase of U.S. commodities. Though the Marshall Plan is usually characterized as a magnanimous attempt to rescue war-devastated European economies, Mark Neocleous makes the critical point that, "excluding Germany, no country was actually on the verge of collapse. There were no bank crashes, very few bankruptcies and the evidence of a slowdown in industrial production is unconvincing. . . . By late-1946 production had roughly equalled pre-war levels in all countries except Germany."[121] The primary goal of the Marshall Plan, and U.S. foreign policy in general during this time, was to support "economic security as a means of maintaining political order against the threat of communism." As Neocleous has provocatively written, *the Soviet Union was a side issue.* American national security advisors at the time recognized that the military capacity of the USSR was "limited and weak" and that the country posed no military threat to the United States; rather, the global specter of communism posed a *political and economic threat* to the order of private property. According to NSC-68, an important National Security document from this time, "Even if there were no Soviet Union we would face the problem of the free society, accentuated many fold in this industrial age, of reconciling order, security, the need for participation, with the requirements of freedom."[122]

For all its ephemerality, the Cold War was profoundly violent. The American National Security doctrine adopted at this time, which has survived fully intact into the twenty-first century, established a sort of good cop/bad cop duality: the humanitarian good cop sends money to countries around the world in the name of freedom and democracy, while the authoritarian bad cop violently disrupts and reorders the affairs of countries that express a form of politics opposed to the capitalist notion of order. One CIA official estimated in 1991 that overt or covert operations carried out in the name of security had resulted in a *minimum of six million deaths* in Korea, Vietnam, Indonesia, Cambodia, Nicaragua, and Angola, among many other places.[123]

The same anticommunist ideology that was justifying U.S. economic imperialism the world over was used domestically to destroy unions and repress dissidence. At home, the Cold War spawned McCarthyism, the Hollywood blacklist—which targeted entertainment industry workers with leftist politics—and many other repressive policies. As former FBI director William

Sullivan stated, Cold War tactics "were brought home against any organization against which we were targeted. We did not differentiate. This is a rough, tough business."[124]

The scope of the Red Scare was broad, reaching from the halls of the federal government into the banalities of daily life. Echoing the Sedition Act and Espionage Act of the World War I era, in 1949 fifteen states passed "anti-subversion laws," and in Michigan the writing or uttering of "subversive words" became punishable by life in prison. Detroit's city council banned the Communist Party's newspaper, the *Daily Worker*, and some council members attempted to paint over Diego Rivera's murals in the Detroit Institute of Arts because of Rivera's communist politics. Even the NAACP was listed as a "Communist-Front" group. From 1947 to 1956 the U.S. government undertook "loyalty screenings" to root out left-leaning workers, leading to the firing or resignation of seven thousand federal employees. In 1952 the line between the police and the military, and between domestic and foreign operations, was further blurred when President Truman formed the National Security Agency (NSA), an integral component of the larger "containment" doctrine associated with the Cold War. The NSA was tasked with monitoring subversive activity both in the United States and abroad, helping the government to dismantle and discredit radical union activities throughout the 1950s.[125]

The fate of unions, however, was far from decided in 1945. Indeed the postwar era is often remembered as the height of the labor movement. Building on membership gains and cooperation with management during the war, the UAW in the immediate postwar years became an institutionalized component of the auto industry. Some ten years after the Big Three first recognized the union, collective bargaining had won its membership significant wage and benefit increases. With the UAW leading the charge, between 1945 and 1955 the average weekly wage of Detroit's industrial workers rose to $98, compared to a national average of $75, which was 40 percent higher in real wages than at war's end. The UAW also led the way in winning such benefits as company-financed pensions, sick pay, health plans, life insurance, and paid vacations. The backdrop for this was a flourishing auto industry: in 1949 auto sales surged to 5 million, finally breaking the record set in 1929, and in 1955—after a partial conversion to military production during the Korean War—sales soared past 8 million.[126]

But such numbers leave us with a distorted and impartial picture. These gains were won only after a period of intense struggle immediately following the war, when national prosperity was far from assured. The wage increases and benefits finally earned in the late 1940s and early 1950s came at the cost of increasing coordination between the union and the auto companies, the alienation of the rank and file from union leaders, management control at the point of production, and the evisceration of leftist elements from unions.

The sunny picture of auto work, and of postwar prosperity in general, is belied by the massive wave of postwar strikes in the auto industry and beyond. Workers did not soon forget the sacrifices they had made during the war years, and with the return to civilian production many were defiant that these sacrifices should be compensated. The weekly wages of nonwar workers declined 10 percent in the first months after the war; war workers, meanwhile, saw their wages drop 31 percent. According to a government study, these wages were inadequate to maintain prewar living standards. Strikes began within days of the war's end. In September 1945, the month of Japan's surrender, the number of days lost to strikes doubled. In October it doubled again. Oil workers, miners, lumber workers, longshoremen, truck drivers, machinists, textile workers, and others struck before the end of 1945. By early 1946 more than 1.5 million U.S. workers were striking. The months that followed, according to the U.S. Bureau of Labor Statistics, constituted "the most concentrated period of labor-management strife in the country's history." Throughout 1946 over 4.5 million workers went on strike; the average duration was four times that of wartime strikes. This was as close to a sustained national labor strike as the United States ever came.[127]

The UAW rank-and-file membership played a huge role in catalyzing these strikes. In November 1945, 225,000 GM workers walked off the job in a nationwide strike. Three days after the war's end the UAW had requested from the company a 30 percent pay increase without an increase in prices (to stave off inflation). GM countered with a 10 percent cost-of-living increase and said its prices were none of the union's business. When workers requested the company defend its claim that it couldn't afford to raise wages, the company refused to open its books, and workers responded by striking. They were soon joined by other industrial workers: "On January 15, 1946, 174,000 electrical workers struck. The next day, 93,000 meatpackers walked out. On January 21, 750,000 steel workers struck, the largest strike in United States history. . . . On April 1, 340,000 soft-coal miners struck, causing a nationwide brown-out. A nationwide railroad strike by engineers and train men over work-rule changes on May 23 brought 'an almost complete shutdown of the nation's commerce.'" Using wartime emergency powers, the federal government stepped in to settle these disputes. The U.S. Army and Navy were deployed to seize railroads, mines, oil refineries, and factories occupied by striking workers. President Truman later wrote, "We used the weapons that we had at hand in order to fight a rebellion against the government."[128]

Even when the military wasn't called in, the government generally sided with management in these disputes. When GM workers refused the president's request to go back to work, Truman established a neutral fact-finding board: it concluded that GM could afford a 19.5-cent hourly wage increase (17.5 percent) without raising prices. The company rejected these findings, and workers remained on strike, despite the UAW's acceptance of the deal, which amounted to little more than half of their initial demand. Soon, however, workers in other industries accepted similar deals; wages were increased, but so were prices, essentially nullifying wage gains. And despite the findings of its fact-finding board in the GM strike, the federal government pushed workers to accept this compromise in industry after industry; where workers refused, the military was waiting in the wings. When striking railroad workers refused the government's order to go back to work, Truman threatened to draft them and call in the army; when coal miners refused to end their strike, Truman fined their union $3.5 million.[129]

Eventually, with workers across industries accepting similar deals, even GM's militant UAW membership was forced to capitulate, finally accepting an 18-cent-per-hour wage increase, with no mention of prices.[130] The high wages so often referenced as a benchmark of postwar worker prosperity were achieved only after the postwar strikes were quashed and this pattern had been established: wage increases were granted, but companies were allowed to raise prices, meaning that the cost of these wage increases were passed onto workers themselves in the form of inflation—in other words, their pay increased, but this increased pay bought the same amount of goods. At the same time, unions became more bureaucratic, and relations with management more regularized. Between 1949 and 1955 many UAW members voted to have union dues deducted directly from their paychecks (which Ford had done since 1941); under this system, instead of union stewards going from member to member to wrangle union dues, the companies delivered huge sums deducted from paychecks directly to the union treasury. In addition, the cooperation between corporate executives and union leaders—behind the backs of the rank and file—which had established the no-strike pledge during the war set the stage for further cooperation in the postwar period. The relationship had proven valuable for both parties: "the greatest growth of union membership in American history came in this period," and the War Labor Board declared, "It is in the interests of management, these companies have found, to cooperate with the unions for the maintenance of a more stable, responsible leadership."[131]

Because of these and other policies, the leadership of the UAW had by this time alienated many workers. During the strike wave of World War II and the postwar period, workers had demonstrated that, through coordination and solidarity, they had the potential to paralyze not just one corporation or industry but the entire country. Nevertheless union leadership had continually worked to mitigate the militancy and the power of their members. When UAW leadership consented to the firing of twenty-six workers who led an unauthorized wildcat strike in a Ford factory during the war, it lost the trust and respect of much of the rank and file. Union leaders were also amenable to demands like GM's in 1946 for "responsibility for uninterrupted production." Ninety percent of the labor contracts signed by unions in 1945 and 1946 pledged *no strikes* by 1947. Such submission went straight to the top: the presidents of the AFL and CIO signed a "Charter of Industrial Peace" with the president of the Chamber of Commerce in 1945.[132]

In general, workers went on strike during and after the war against the wishes of their unions. The historian Jeremy Brecher concludes, "The unions were unable to prevent the post-war strike wave, but by leading it they managed to keep it under control."[133] The anxiety of business and union leaders was to a large extent justified, as the projected postwar boom failed to immediately materialize: though industry experts forecast the production of 6 million passenger cars in the first year after the war, the total was less than 400,000 eight months after Japan's surrender. Widespread strikes had resulted in "shortages of crucial materials such as coal, iron, steel, copper, aluminum, and glass." In response, workers were generally laid off until corporations could profitably secure all the means of production they required. Employment during this time was "sporadic," and most Detroiters suffered: "Corner grocery stores extended credit when possible, medical bills went unpaid, and rent, mortgage payments, and utility bills piled up." Things were particularly dire for women, who were laid off en masse after the war: 259,000 women worked in Detroit's factories in 1943, as compared to only 67,000 in 1946, and 88,000 by the mid-1950s. These layoffs reinforced a system of patriarchy in which many women were made dependent on a male breadwinner. Meanwhile the Michigan Unemployment Compensation Commission exacerbated the situation for all workers by "ruling that no one on strike, or who was laid off because of it, was eligible for unemployment benefits." As late as the end of 1948, "no one in the industry thought that the postwar boom had arrived."[134]

The problems of a sluggish economy and the militancy of workers fused with the nation's Red Scare in the Taft-Hartley Act of 1947. This aggressive antilabor legislation, passed by the newly elected Republican Congress, outlawed sympathy strikes, wildcat strikes, mass picketing, and "secondary" boycotts against stores selling nonunion goods. It allowed states to pass right-to-work laws, which facilitated capital flight to nonunion areas and gave workers the option to opt out of the union, meaning they could refuse to pay dues even while enjoying the benefits of collective bargaining. The act also forced union officials to sign affidavits guaranteeing that they had no contact with the CPUSA, and those who refused lost the protection of federal labor law.[135]

Taft-Hartley exploited the tension within the working class by blaming striking workers—depicted as unpatriotic agitators—for the hardships of the postwar economy. The act facilitated a sharp decline in the Communist Party's membership, from 80,000 members in the early 1940s to 10,000 by 1957. (The decline was also due to the Party's support for Stalin, which alienated many workers.) This is when Walter Reuther consolidated power in the UAW. He used the act to remove from the union all "parlor pinks," a derogatory term for workers with communist sympathies. According to the legendary labor organizer and Marxist theorist James Boggs, Reuther "pushed aside all the militants and radicals who in sitdown strikes and during the war had built the UAW into a model for the CIO." As well as weakening or eliminating the most radical elements of the union movement, Taft-Hartley also facilitated an absolute decline in the number of unionized workers in the United States, which decreased from 5.2 million in 1945 to 3.7 million in 1950.[136]

As Nelson Lichtenstein has noted, despite widespread worker interest, Reuther abandoned plans for a separate labor party during this time, limiting union efforts instead to the pursuit of a "private welfare regime." In sum, Reutherism

> tied its fate more closely to that of the industry and increasingly subordinated the endemic shop-floor struggle over working conditions and production standards to the UAW's national bargaining program. As a union political-economic strategy, Reutherism moved from a demand for structural changes in the management of the auto industry and by implication in the political economy as a whole, to negotiation of an increasingly privatized welfare program that left unchallenged essential power relationships in the industry. . . . The defeat or expulsion of the Communists from within its own ranks had the practical effect of robbing these new unions of their oppositional character and welding them even more closely to the Democratic Party[137]

The history of the National Negro Labor Council (NNLC) exemplifies the postwar repression of leftist worker movements. The NNLC, whose executive secretary was a future Detroit mayor, Coleman Young, was formed in 1951 from unions that had been expelled from the CIO for retaining communists.

The Council led struggles demanding that "fair practices" clauses be inserted into union contracts that would protect the rights of women and nonwhite workers. In 1954 the House Un-American Activities Committee denounced the NNLC as "pro-communist." The NNLC's efforts also met stiff resistance from the conservative leadership of the UAW. When NNLC president William Hood circulated a petition urging Detroit workers to support "fair practices" clauses, the UAW International labeled Hood's petition "Communist-inspired" and forbade UAW workers from signing. In 1956, due largely to pressure from the state, corporations, and unions, the NNLC folded.[138]

Despite the restrictions imposed by Taft-Hartley, workers continued to fight for improved conditions. Refusing to lower car prices, auto companies competed with each other mainly by lowering their production costs. This led to a dramatic intensification of factory operations and numerous strikes over work conditions. In 1949 workers took part in a strike against production speedups at the Ford Rouge plant. The strike, which lasted twenty-four days, involved "including strikers' families, at least a quarter million Detroiters." A few months later a 104-day strike took place at Chrysler. Workers protested work conditions and demanded (and eventually won) a pension plan similar to what had been recently won at Ford. During this time the ranks of Detroit's unemployed neared 200,000; profits, meanwhile, were high, and Detroit's auto leaders declared the situation "tremendously successful." On the brink of starvation, striking and laid-off workers sought alternative incomes: in February 1949 thousands of unemployed workers waited in the cold to be among the eight hundred workers chosen by the Department of Public Works to work as a snow shoveler. One official described it as "the biggest line since the depression."[139]

Desperate to avoid more work stoppages, GM in 1950 agreed with the UAW on a five-year contract. In exchange for a no-strike promise and handing over to capital control of the shop floor, UAW workers were granted pensions, unemployment benefits, and annual cost-of-living increases. *Fortune Magazine* coined the deal the "Treaty of Detroit," noting that "GM may have paid a billion for the peace, but it got a bargain. General Motors has regained control over one of the crucial management functions . . . long range scheduling of production, model changes, and tool and plant investment."[140] Similar deals were soon signed with Ford and Chrysler.

"In the early forties," Lichtenstein writes, "Ford's recognition of the UAW touched off a virtual revolution on the shop floor. Workers ignored petty shop rules that regulated smoking, eating, and talking, unpopular foremen were forced out of their departments, production standards were set only after checking with the department committeemen."[141] However, with the Treaty of Detroit, higher-ups in the UAW gave back control of the shop floor to the owners in return for monetary gains. But even these proved illusory, as the gains assured on paper were undermined by job instability and generalized economic insecurity.[142] Though there were booms and busts in Detroit's auto industry throughout the 1950s, the booms (in 1953 and 1955) were short-lived, and the busts were devastating: in 1952, due mostly to automation and materials shortages in the auto industry, 10 percent of *all the unemployment in the United States* was in metro Detroit. Automation was a large factor in such widespread unemployment. In addition to the machinery that replaced unskilled labor, the constant pressure of automation drove smaller automakers out of business and put their workers out of a job. "The economics of automation," Dodge's president explained, "are harsh, but simple: automate or die." In addition to driving their smaller competitors out of business through their investments in technology and advertising, Big Three firms also became more "vertically integrated," meaning that they made more of their parts in-house, causing many local suppliers to lay off their workers and close up shop.[143]

During this time the charged situation brought about by the Red Scare produced a mythical discourse that blamed the city's socioeconomic problems on a range of scapegoats: unions, white southern migrants, old workers, women workers, and black workers. George Romney, the American Motors Corporation president and future governor of Michigan, said unions were the country's "number one problem" and called union president Walter Reuther "the most dangerous man in Detroit." The Detroit Board of Commerce questioned how many of the unemployed were "actual citizens" of the Motor City, and suggested migrant workers should leave. For their part, old workers were seen by many younger Detroiters as having an unfair monopoly on the city's stable jobs, and there were insistent calls to overturn systems of workplace seniority and enforce a retirement age. Working women, meanwhile, were frequently reminded that their natural place was in the home, not competing in a crowded labor market with men. And impoverished black workers were consistently depicted as the source of the city's social ills, particularly the increasing number of property crimes occurring throughout the city.[144]

In 1955 the conservative AFL union merged with the CIO (a union federation that included the UAW), and Reuther's UAW renewed the Treaty for another three years. The first day after the contract was signed, 134,000 GM workers struck in protest, and so did 114,000 out of 140,000 Ford workers. These workers were dismissed in the media as greedy and pessimistic; the Free Press called the strike the "revolt of the victors." However, the "disastrous" economic years of 1956 and 1957, and the mass layoffs and speed-ups that followed, undermine the idea that the workers were the true "victors."[145]

The government's Red Scare, the purging of radicals from the union, the capitulation of union leadership, and the UAW's ensuing loss of control at the point of production produced the results that the auto companies desired: during the first eight years of the Treaty of Detroit, work stoppages declined dramatically, and worker productivity on Ford's assembly lines increased 25 percent. As similar contracts were signed between management and unions across the country, investment in plant and equipment drastically outpaced total wage expenditures. Between 1953 and 1957 plant and equipment expenditure increased 37 percent.[146] During these same years, three major Detroit plants closed down, total employment in Michigan's auto industry decreased 27 percent, and total manufacturing employment in Michigan fell 15 percent.[147]

In 1958 the UAW signed another deal with the Big Three that won retirement benefits for older workers but did little to address working conditions. James Boggs explains:

> When the 1958 contract was finally signed, there were few workers in the plant who did not realize they had returned to fully company-controlled plants. Time-study men and work layout specialists roamed the plants like sniffing bloodhounds, spying, taking pictures, watching over the workers' shoulders, while the shamed union representatives hid behind pillars or in toilets. . . . Today the workers are doing in eight hours the actual physical work they used to do in twelve. At 6:30, a half hour before the day shift begins, you see workers setting up their operations so that they will not fall behind during the hours for which they are paid. They are afraid to go to the toilet, to get a drink of water, to take time off to go to the funeral of a relative. If they refuse to work overtime, they are written up and sent home.[148]

In addition to allowing for stricter management control inside the plants, the Treaty of Detroit also facilitated rising rates of unemployment.[149] In 1949 the father of cybernetics, Norbert Wiener of the Massachusetts Institute of Technology, wrote to Reuther warning of the potentially disastrous social effects of automation, which he feared would lead to "the factory without employees."[150] Despite such warnings, Reuther's UAW never seriously combated the problem of automation. As late as the 1960s Reuther imagined that a collaboration between workers, unions, corporations, and technology could achieve full employment.[151] Against Reuther's mythological optimism, Boggs, in his classic work, *The American Revolution: Pages from a Negro Worker's Notebook*, presciently wrote:

> Automation replaces men. This of course is nothing new. What is new is that now, unlike most earlier periods, the displaced men have nowhere to go. . . . As automation spreads, it will intensify the crises of capitalism and sharpen the conflicts among the various sections of the population, particularly between those working and those not working, those paying taxes and those not paying taxes. Out of this conflict will grow a counter-revolutionary movement made up of those from all social layers who resent the continued cost to them of maintaining these expendables but who are determined to maintain the system that creates and multiplies the number of expendables.[152]

As the number of these "expendables" grew, Ford decided that it was more cost-effective to pay some workers overtime than to pay for the training and benefits of new workers, and he instituted a compulsory fifty-four-hour work week in his Lincoln-Mercury plants. Compulsory overtime soon became standard practice at all Big Three factories.[153] Black workers were generally the last to be hired and the first to be fired and were made to work in the least-skilled, most dangerous positions. Therefore, as the percentage of unskilled laborers in the U.S. workforce *decreased from 36 percent in 1910 to 5 percent in 1962*, young black workers were disproportionately hurt (though tens of thousands of white workers were discarded by Detroit's auto industry during these years as well).[154] Meanwhile, the city's east side, where blacks were mostly concentrated, lost more than 70,000 jobs between 1954 and 1960.[155] Across the U.S., *nearly one in four young people of color were unemployed in 1960*.[156]

### Race, Class, and Suburbanization

The communist purges of the Cold War era weakened the militancy of unions, allowing industry to take greater control of the production process and subsequently automate jobs and flee outside the city to more business-friendly areas with less organized labor forces. In Detroit and beyond, reactionary forces also conflated the spectre of communism with another ideological challenge to the ruling order—that of racial integration. Progressive causes in general, and the civil rights movement in particular, became easy fodder for those seeking to uncover "subversive" activities threatening the "American way of life." The Chairman of Washington state's inquisition claimed, "If someone insists there is discrimination against Negroes in this country, there is every reason to believe that person is a Communist." Picketers outside a church in Detroit in the 1950s made the same connection between racial integration and left politics: "Race mixing is communism in action," one sign declared.[157]

It's no coincidence that labor organization and civil rights for black Americans were often conflated during the Red Scare. Just as anti-communism in the union movement allowed capital to wrest control of the shop floor from unions and flee the city, so too did the racialization of the working class facilitate the economic reorganization of the postwar era.

The deindustrialization of U.S. cities, however, began much earlier, in the period between 1910 and 1920. The inauguration of modern manufacturing at Ford's Crystal Palace in 1913 also marked the beginning of suburbanization in Detroit; at the time Ford moved there from his Piquette Avenue Plant in Detroit, Highland Park was a small farming community far from the bustle of the city center. Less than fifteen years later Ford moved even further away, to the western suburb of Dearborn. This pattern can be seen across the industrial cities of the Northeast and Midwest. John Mollenkopf locates the transition from the industrial to the postindustrial city around 1920. From this time, manufacturing relocated away from the cloistered, multi-level, labor-intensive facilities in urban cores to sprawling, horizontal, increasingly mechanized factories in the outlying, undeveloped regions of metropolitan areas. We've outlined already the two primary reasons for this shift: to escape organized labor, and to meet capitalism's need to continually revolutionize the means of production (creative destruction). And, as we saw in the first chapter, the industrial city would eventually become the corporate city, with manufacturing replaced by corporate offices, administrative buildings, hospitals, and universities.[158]

But this transition did not happen quickly or on its own. "Urban blight" was already a national political issue in the early 1930s. Broke city governments and bankrupt businesses couldn't afford infrastructure improvements or new investments during the Depression, and with the dispersive tendencies of manufacturing already operative from the 1910s, city cores had significantly deteriorated by the beginning of World War II. The war accelerated these processes dramatically. The War Production Board (WPB), which directed the use of government funds in private plant construction, was largely separated from other federal agencies and dominated by business leaders. "Leaders of the largest industrial corporations could thus use government financing to reconstruct the private sector's capital base along new and more desirable lines" by moving out of the city. Detroit received the largest absolute amount of plant investment from the WPB, whose efforts nationally amounted to a *doubling* of U.S. industrial capacity. "The war-created facilities," according to the WPB's summary report, "represent the greatest increment to manufacturing capital recorded in modern industrial history."[159]

This was a continuation of the more direct role the federal government had taken in managing the economy since the Depression, when it had initiated massive public programs to address unemployment and blight. After the war the government likewise took an outsize role in the process of suburbanization, through federally backed mortgages, highway and school construction, and the urban renewal efforts that sought to replace slum housing and deteriorated manufacturing facilities with the institutions of the corporate city.

Each aspect of this process was thoroughly racialized. Black Americans were by and large excluded from suburban homeownership by government policy and everyday practice; subsequently barred from the benefits of suburban manufacturing employment and wealth building through homeownership; confined to substandard central city housing, which became the target of slum clearance during urban renewal; and then blamed for the social problems that resulted from these dislocations.

Racial enmity was prominent and widespread in World War II–era Detroit. The city's black population increased by sixty thousand during the war. Expecting to find work in the booming war industry, blacks faced persistent patterns of discrimination in employment and housing. Many of Detroit's workers blamed southern black migrants—as well as "hillbillies" and "white trash" from Appalachia—for overcrowding the city's job markets, and workplace discrimination was constant. Even when stable work was available, there were nowhere near enough houses to shelter the growing population. Wartime restrictions on nonmilitary construction put a freeze on most housing construction in the 1940s—and as black Detroiters were barred from 85 percent of the city's housing, their situation was particularly dire.[160]

In 1941 the Sojourner Truth housing projects were built in Northeast Detroit, primarily to house poor black Detroiters. On February 28, 1942, the day the first black tenants were scheduled to move in, 1,200 white picketers greeted them. Many tenants, who had already paid their first month's rent, were determined to move in nonetheless. According to the *Free Press*, police fired "three volleys of tear gas . . . when a truckload of Negroes crossed the 'no man's land' that police were trying to preserve and were bombarded with bricks and white pickets who swarmed over the truck." In the next few days of violence, 104 people were arrested, all but two of them black. It would take another month and a half of fighting and picketing before the first black residents could peaceably enter their legal address.[161]

In response to the economic exclusions and degradations faced by black workers, A. Philip Randolph organized a March on Washington movement in 1941. The specter of 100,000 black men and women marching on the U.S. capital forced FDR to sign Executive Order 8802, prohibiting racial discrimination in the war industries. Despite this legal intervention, however, "there were still limits in upgrading, in the separation of production jobs by departments, and in relative exclusion from certain corporations and certain plants." Black workers were thus more limited in their ability to resist degrading work conditions. While white workers, in a situation of relative labor shortage, could be reasonably assured of gaining employment at another plant if they were fired for striking, black workers did not have the same easy access to new jobs. Many black workers therefore supported the militant stance of Randolph, who the CPUSA had labeled a proto-fascist for his unwillingness to support the strike ban. This was a point at which the Communist Party drew away many black workers.[162]

Even where blacks were able to make gains on the job, they faced the racist attitudes of many white workers. A wave of hate strikes occurred in Detroit and across the United States in 1941 and 1942 as a result of the federal government's mandate to integrate war plants. In 1943 twenty-five thousand white workers at Packard walked off the job in protest of the promotion of three black men. Unlike in the wildcat strikes mentioned earlier, the police were not on hand to break up these strikes.[163]

A couple of weeks after the hate strike, a fight broke out between black and white Detroiters at Belle Isle, a huge island park in the Detroit River. The next day a series of violent confrontations erupted throughout the city. The white residents, with the help of the DPD, were the aggressors in what came to be called the Race Riot of 1943. Michigan's Governor Harry Kelly declared martial law, and six thousand U.S. troops were summoned to Detroit to enforce a 10:00 p.m. curfew. Officers ordered black bystanders to "run and not look back" and shot several people in the back as they ran away, killing seventeen black people and not a single white person. All in all, thirty-four people were killed, twenty-five of them black; 85 percent of the 1,800 people arrested were black. The National Advisory Commission on Civil Disorders called this "the bloodiest riot in the U.S. in a span of two decades." This sort of state violence is a significant reason why many black leaders, from Ida B. Wells to Malcolm X and Robert F. Williams, have historically opposed attempts to disarm black Americans.[164]

A picture taken from the riot, published in *Collier's* magazine, with a readership of over 2.5 million, had given rise to an international scandal: the image showed two police officers holding down a black man as a white man approached

FIGURE 2.4. "A Colored Man Is Held by Unconcerned Detroit Cops While a White Man Slaps His Face," 1943. Sources: Murakawa, *The First Civil Right*, 33; Associated Press; "Race Riots Coming," *Collier's*, September 18, 1943, 11.

and slapped him in the face. In the aftermath of the riot, Thurgood Marshall referred to the Detroit police as the U.S. version of the Gestapo. Police attacks on black people were nothing new in the U.S., but at the time, the country was engaged in a world war that was ostensibly against totalitarian governments, and the hypocrisy of the U.S. government's attempts to portray itself as a just global policeman was there for all the world to see.[165]

Local and national elites mythologized this contradiction by shifting the blame for the riots onto communists and blacks. Detroit's Mayor Edward Jeffries—who had campaigned on a promise to stop the "Negro Flood"— claimed that "Negro hoodlums" were to blame. The head of FDR's Civil Rights Section said that the "rioting and looting are outstanding examples of Negro hoodlumism and wanton murder." The Michigan Governor's Committee on the Causes of the Detroit Race Riot blamed Randolph, even though he was nowhere near Michigan at the time, for inspiring in black Detroiters a "disregard for law, order and judicial process in seeking the racial equality to which they are entitled." The Committee also blamed the strife on the influx of southern black migrants who exhibited a propensity toward violence and lawless behavior that the city's black leadership had encouraged by instilling in new Detroiters the unrealistic expectation of equal rights in the North.[166]

Hate strikes, riots, public housing protests, mythological distortions—such was the situation of race relations in Detroit during the war. In the postwar period, racial violence and discrimination hardened into ideological commonplace and bureaucratic procedure.

Between 1947 and 1958 the Big Three auto companies built twenty-five new factories in southeast Michigan—none of them in Detroit. "From almost every angle," the Marxist theorist Chris Wright concludes, "moving industry out of the cities benefited businesses."[167] In the suburbs capitalists found cheap land, low taxes, business-friendly governments, and a relatively docile workforce. Managers of new suburban plants in California in 1946 testified that "their employees are more loyal, more cooperative, more productive workers than those they have had in the big cities."[168] The relocation of manufacturing outside the city fed into the escalating housing crisis. When 100,000 migrants arrived in Detroit in the early 1950s at the onset of the Korean War—mostly with unrealized hopes that Detroit would again be a major center of wartime production—they found themselves in an incredibly precarious situation: "Housing experts had concluded that there was virtually nothing available in the city for persons of low or average income. Only one-tenth of 1 percent of rental units in metro Detroit were open, and those commanded rents . . . well beyond the range of autoworkers." By 1952 the number of homeless far exceeded the capacity of the city's three shelters. And for those who could find housing, 250,000 lived in substandard units, "defined as 'dilapidated' or without indoor toilets, bathtubs, or running water."[169]

Federal housing policy assured that black Detroiters would stay confined to blighted, rundown housing stock in the center city, while whites fled to newly constructed homes in the suburbs. In the late 1940s 90 percent of housing in Detroit was off-limits to blacks.[170] The two federal programs supporting homeownership—the Federal Housing Authority and the Home Owner Loan Corporation—both developed systems that strongly favored "racially homogenous" neighborhoods. The federal home loan agency's official guidelines for underwriting mortgages were set forth in the *Underwriters Manual*, which outlined color-coded areas where lending was most likely to succeed. Areas that were largely black or mixed were outlined in red—hence "redlining"—making them essentially ineligible for public or private loans. The result was that less than 1 percent of federally guaranteed and subsidized mortgages in the United States between 1935 and the early 1960s went to nonwhites. Less well known than redlining practices are the *specifically suburban biases of these federal housing policies*. The *Underwriters Manual* also "made it difficult to get an insured loan for already-built housing, and certain construction guidelines—such as requiring a certain amount of distance between the house and the street—forced people to move to newly constructed housing in the suburbs instead of purchasing in the cities." This essentially forced prospective homeowners "to purchase new buildings instead of existing housing stock." Moreover an assortment of federal subsidies and tax credits made it so that "it was often cheaper to buy in the suburbs, including purchasing one or two cars, than to rent equivalent housing in the city."[171]

As well as federal policy, the spontaneous organization of homeowners in Detroit limited the housing options available to working-class blacks. Homeowners throughout Detroit fiercely resisted public housing projects being built in their area. It was not only racial animosity that fueled such actions; an economic logic underlay them as well. "Better-off blacks," writes Thomas Sugrue, "like their white counterparts, often sought to . . . ensure the exclusiveness of their neighborhoods."[172] Developers and real estate agencies frequently exploited the situation by engaging in blockbusting—moving one or two black families into the neighborhood, then working to rouse paranoia about a coming "Negro invasion." The blockbusting realtors would then buy up the homes of fleeing whites at below-market value and sell them to blacks at inflated prices.

Touré Reed argues that "white homeowners resisted integration . . . not simply because they did not like African Americans, but because they wanted to protect their investment."[173] Certainly blockbusting real estate agents and federal housing policy tied home values to race in a way that operated independently of individual homeowners' prejudice. But while racist housing policies and the like are partially explained by the desire of homeowners to "protect their investment," the prejudice and outright violence faced by black residents and workers go well beyond the logic of economic rationality. In 1948, for example, more than half of the city's restaurants practiced racial segregation. And throughout the postwar era, blacks who attempted to move into "white" neighborhoods often faced violence from vigilante groups like the KKK, as well as from white homeowners' organizations, which sometimes terrorized black families moving into their neighborhoods for months on end.[174]

Suburban homeownership also gave rise to worker conservatism. As David Harvey points out, mortgage debt was crucial here: "Debt-encumbered homeowners do not go on strike."[175] The housing issue was so inherently conservative-leaning that even union members who supported integration on the shop floor often believed in residential segregation. "They should have equal opportunities," one white worker said of blacks, "and . . . as we become better educated we will have less prejudice. And we should have less. But I don't want to live next to them."[176] The isolating and consumerist lifestyle in suburbia also proved to be anathema to collective politics: "Where before union members often lived in or near the same neighborhood as their factory and union hall, now a growing number were scattered throughout the metropolitan area, making the round trip to union meetings a matter of some inconvenience."[177] Long commutes meant that people's work lives and social lives were even more divorced. The home became "a self-sustaining microcosm in which the outside world only entered via electronic media such as radio, television and eventually the computer. . . . At the same time, the yard provided a fenced-off replacement for parks and playgrounds and other public facilities in which nature might be experienced collectively."[178]

Suburbanization inscribed the racial division of the working class into the landscape of metro Detroit. Between 1950 and 1960 Detroit's white population decreased by more than 350,000 while its black population increased by more than 180,000. As late as 1970, in Detroit's three largest suburbs, out of nearly 400,000 total residents, *only 186 were black*. And metro Detroit continues to bear the marks of this bout of creative destruction: the region remains one of the most segregated in the United States.[179]

The other side of suburbanization was urban renewal, which sought to address slum conditions in center cities across the industrial belt as part of a larger strategy to transform urban cores into centers of corporate and administrative activities. In city after city, controversy attended these efforts, as initiatives ostensibly intended to ameliorate the living conditions of a city's poorest residents—who were almost always black—instead became land grabs for big business, subsidized by local and federal governments, which eliminated slums in favor of high-end developments. In Detroit the center of this process was Black Bottom.

In the late 1940s, 140,000 black Detroiters lived in Black Bottom, a neighborhood on the city's lower East Side. Together with its commercial district, Paradise Valley, this area was in many ways the city's cultural hub. Known as the Harlem of the Midwest, Black Bottom was "the birthplace of the Nation of Islam, the former center of the largest concentration of Black-owned businesses in the country, the home of the religious and cultural institutions that nurtured the rise of the Motown sound."[180] By the postwar period it was also the city's worst slum district. Over half the structures had been built before 1900, and many lacked indoor plumbing, meaning residents had to rely on outdoor latrines. Migration during and after the war exacerbated the neighborhood's endemic overcrowding. As Black Bottom was adjacent to the Downtown commercial center, it became the focus of the Detroit version of urban renewal.[181]

In 1946 Downtown business interests proposed an urban renewal program called the Detroit Plan, under which the city government would buy and demolish slum property, and then, instead of building public housing, sell it to private real estate developers. These private developers would then, supposedly, build low- to moderate-income housing in the area. The plan was decried by CIO leaders and several city council members as a scheme to swindle taxpayers and subsidize private developers. Nevertheless the city began condemning slum property in 1947 and 1948. In 1952 the Michigan Supreme Court gave legal sanction to these efforts when it ruled that cities could sell land to private developers at subsidized rates. Mayor Albert Cobo—elected in 1949 over the CIO-backed liberal candidate George Edwards, thanks to overwhelming support among whites in the city's outlying wards, including many union members—proceeded to bulldoze seven hundred buildings in Black Bottom, displacing nearly two thousand black families. Soon the same fate befell other aging areas around the city core.[182]

As the black studies professor David Goldberg has pointed out, many black Detroiters initially supported plans for slum clearance and hoped that urban renewal programs would lead to improved living conditions. This support was short-lived, however, as urban renewal displaced thousands of black families and eliminated far more affordable housing than it created. "Rather than improving neighborhoods and providing affordable, updated, and sound housing," Goldberg writes, "urban renewal displaced Black Bottom residents and the institutions they had built, making way for middle- and upper-income housing while also creating a buffer between the city's poorest residents and a newly expanded central business district, medical and cultural centers, and the university district."[183]

This dispossession should be seen in a national context, as decaying urban cores became a central political problem across the country. A 1953 study by the Twentieth Century Fund concluded, "No matter in what city we may be, we see broad areas of deterioration. . . . Old buildings are rarely replaced and old districts rarely renewed to their former vitality."[184] The 1949 Federal Housing Act, which addressed this problem, was gutted by a conservative Congress. As a result, instead of constructing public housing, the 1949 Act provided the tools for local business and political elites to use federal funds and the rallying cry of "urban renewal" to clear low-income residential districts and replace them with private developments and public infrastructure.[185] Robert Moses in New York City was a pioneer in this regard, using federal largesse to, in his own words, take a "meat axe" to the Bronx in order to make way for a highway project that linked New York City to its surrounding suburbs.[186] Several years earlier, by including a few rundown tenements that were home to fewer than three hundred residents, Moses had used federal urban development legislation to take control of two square blocks of thriving commercial land in Manhattan, and with $26 million in federal assistance he built an exhibition center, a parking structure, and a luxury housing development at the site.[187] In 1947 Illinois passed the Blighted Areas Redevelopment Act and the Restoration Act, allowing the city of Chicago to use eminent domain to acquire slum areas and sell them to developers at subsidized rates. The city subsequently cleared hundreds of acres of slums to make room for middle-class housing complexes which inflated rents by as much as 600 percent. During his twenty-year tenure Mayor Richard J. Daley used this precedent to demolish low-income inner-city neighborhoods to make way for highways, administrative buildings, skyscrapers, and high-end housing.[188] The scale of destruction involved in this process led many contemporary commentators to make comparisons to the violence of war: one organization in San Francisco battling urban renewal declared that the city's efforts constituted "not a *war on poverty* but rather a *war on the poor*."[189] Summing up the situation across the country, the Urban Planning Professor Rachel Weber writes, "Urban renewal pulverized [the] inner city in the middle of the century, funneling billions of federal dollars into costly downtown commercial projects, highways, and sanitized streetscapes. Between 1949 and 1965, one million people, mostly low-income, were evicted in the name of eliminating and containing blight."[190]

The same was true of Detroit, where large swaths of Black Bottom, including the famous Hastings Street, were eventually replaced by highways or high-end neighborhoods like Lafayette Park, which remains one of the wealthiest areas in Detroit. Highway construction under Cobo alone destroyed twenty thousand homes. In Detroit as elsewhere, slum removal generally equaled "negro removal." The majority of all housing aid granted to the city by the Federal Housing Act of 1949 was directed toward slum clearance and subsidizing high-end urban renewal projects, dislocating up to half of Detroit's black population. For Cobo, who promised voters that he would stop the "Negro invasion" of white neighborhoods, this was "the price of progress."[191] Meanwhile, as Detroit's public housing program was destroyed, Cobo—who owned the Cobo Realty Company—"stacked the Detroit Housing Commission with people from real estate and construction industries, both of which helped to ensure that Detroit's urban renewal favored private developers at the expense of the city's poorest residents."[192]

New "affordable" high-rise buildings were built, but thousands of the poorest and most marginalized Detroiters were pushed into dilapidated units owned by slumlords, or simply rendered homeless as the city's housing market faced an "acute shortage." The Detroit Urban League decried "the staggering magnitude of the relocation program," and in the early 1960s Detroit's city council debated what to do about the growing homeless population. In 1962 city council member Mel Ravitz came up with an idea: "Why can't we control and designate a specific area for them, before we find the effects of a new Skid Row appearing throughout the city?" The "specific area" that the council settled on was Cass Corridor (today's Midtown), and police soon shifted homeless residents into this area.[193]

Capital develops unevenly across space and time, and as we saw in chapter 1, a new process of urban renewal is now occurring in the same area that was designated to contain residents dislocated by a previous urban renewal project, causing this group to be dislocated again. We can see the relevance of Engels's insight: "The Bourgeoisie has only one method of settling the housing question. . . . The infamous holes and cellars in which the capitalist mode of production confines our workers night after night are not abolished; they are merely shifted elsewhere."[194] Here the power of mythological thinking is on full display. The *Detroit News* article that details the postwar history of dislocation of black workers and the creation of Cass Corridor as a ghetto to contain them is the same article referenced in chapter 1, titled, "Revival of Detroit's Cass Corridor Crowds Out Criminals." That is, even after noting the violent history of dispossession *in the past*, the article naturalizes those same processes in the present, by branding those who are being dispossessed today as criminals. Mythological thinking always creates a strong barrier between history and the present. While the systemic nature of past injustices may be acknowledged, the same implicit claim is always made: between then and now, *progress* has occurred.

### "What about the Negro Crime Rate?"

Despite its brutal outcome, urban renewal was directed toward a very real and pressing problem: the deterioration of inner cities, particularly their low-income neighborhoods. But as we've seen, the poor quality of housing stock was only a pretense to clear the land for the institutions of the corporate city. In order to carry through the seizure of these slum neighborhoods and their replacement by commercial centers, middle-class housing, and highways, city governments needed a justification. What eventually coalesced was a mythology that equated the decayed inner-city neighborhoods with the people who lived in them. Planners depicted these areas as decrepit not only physically but morally and culturally as well. Disinvestment was conflated with social deterioration to create a picture of a pathologized population: not only was the neighborhood "blighted," but so were its people. The dispossessions that had already affected these neighborhoods were then used to justify their flattening, as statistics on crime, disease, and vice were lined up to paint a picture of a population in ruins, ignoring the strong elements of community life in these neighborhoods (churches, social clubs, ethnic institutions, and cultural landmarks often animated the neighborhoods targeted for urban renewal). This is especially apparent in the case of Black Bottom, which, despite the dereliction of its infrastructure, was a thriving commercial and cultural hub for Detroit's black community.[195]

John Mollenkopf writes, "Renewal planners and administrators faced a difficult bind: on the one hand, all the political and economic incentives pointed toward supplanting a 'blighting' population and its 'blighting' land uses with a higher-status population. On the other hand, they could not acknowledge to those about to be displaced, or perhaps even to themselves, that they were engaging in highly regressive social engineering."[196] In this context, one particular metric of social dislocation became more efficacious than others in the containment of "blighting" populations: crime.

While black workers were devastated by unemployment and state-sponsored dispossession, they were also increasingly criminalized. This was just the beginning of the "counterrevolution" Boggs had presaged, in which privileged sectors of the working class would rebel against having to pay taxes to support an immoral class of "expendables." Hyperaggressive police kept poor blacks away from more "respectable" Detroiters, and they also disciplined black youth to the needs of the capitalist labor market, closing off any attempts to make money outside of the wage labor system. As John Hersey, author of *The Algiers Motel Incident*, writes, black youth in Detroit "for the most part . . . [had] no foreseeable future except among the hustlers and minor racketeers. For the most part, they are cynical, hostile, frustrated, and angry against a system they feel has included them out."[197] It was the activity of these "hustlers and minor racketeers"—in Marx's terms, the lumpenproletariat—that was most intensely targeted by police. In 1951 Truman signed into law the Boggs Act, which established a two-year mandatory minimum for first-time marijuana possession. Five years later the Narcotics Control Act increased these mandatory minimums and ratcheted up federal funding for police work that targeted narcotics-related crime. From 1950 to 1965 the number of drug offenders in federal prisons nearly doubled. In 1955 Detroit, though blacks made up only 20 percent of Detroit's population, they constituted 89 percent of the drug arrests.[198]

The criminalization of the surplus population was justified much as it is today: by condemning the behavior of a racialized "underclass." A 1957 article published in the *Detroit Free Press*, titled "What about the Negro Crime Rate?," notes that black Detroiters accounted for 49 percent of arrests in the previous year. The article asserts, however, that racial statistics belie the true nature of the situation. But the other factors contributing to the statistical disproportion the author mentions are perhaps even more telling. Citing sociologists, he claims that "it is environment, not race, that results in the disproportion of arrests." This leads him to conclude:

> Whatever the basis for the arrest record, it is disturbing to *law-abiding* Negroes. They make up the great majority of the race in the community. What about the large part of the aggressive crime involving Negroes? Most of it is directed against other Negroes and occurs in the city's poorest quarters. *Blind passion often is at the basis of the act.* Dr. Lyle W. Shannon, University of Wisconsin criminologist teaching this year at Wayne State University, stresses *environmental factors*: "The middle-class Negro probably does a better job of being a citizen because he is so conscious of his responsibility to the community."[199]

Environmental factors, not race alone, have produced a stratum of the urban poor alienated from the norms of civilized society and from the "respectable" elements of the racial group: such notions of a pathologized and nihilistic community are the basis of "underclass" discourse that remains operative up to the present. The idea of the underclass skirts structural explanations in favor of tautological "descriptions of associations," producing a narrative of a self-regenerating layer of society beyond the reach of political intervention.[200] Crucially, the *Free Press* article produces a litany of factors—poverty, unemployment, substandard housing, educational deficiencies—that, in some amorphous way, produce "Negro crime." But this assemblage produces not an explanation, but an *image* of crime; we know very well what crime looks like, and the factors which somehow produce it, but we remain in the dark about the procedural connection between *environment* and *criminal*. The article repeats the implicit claim, identified by the political scientist Adolph Reed Jr., that "dealing with the problem of an underclass depicted as almost ferally alien requires the black elite's intermediary role as socializing agents and role models."[201]

In the years to come, as the city's economic problems deepened, violent crime soared, and Detroit's homicide rate was nearly triple the national average. This problem was treated above all as a problem of lawlessness in the city's black ghettos. In 1957 a Republican named Louis Miriani, whose UAW-endorsed mayoral campaign centered on his promise to wage a war on "Negro crime," won in a landslide election.[202]

In December 1960, within a few weeks of each other, two young white women were murdered, and black men were the suspects in both cases. In response, Mayor Miriani declared, "The time has now been reached to realize this thing is not spasmodic. It is an outbreak that will continue and we've got to use strong measures to abate it and stop it." The *Detroit News* went so far as to offer a $5,000 reward for information leading to the arrest of the "vicious killer" of "pretty" Marilyn Donahue. The police responded with what the *Free Press* called "an all-out war on crime." Within a week more than 1,500 black Detroiters were arrested and questioned. According to Buddy Battle, a black UAW organizer at the time, the police targeted "any Negro standing on the corner, coming out of the house to get in his car, going to the church, going into a store, coming out of a store, going into a nightclub or coming out of a nightclub."[203] A coalition of black pastors responded by partnering with the Michigan Corrections Commission to launch a "crusade on crime." Reverend Dr. McNeil said, "We will want to give every assistance to the police to enforce the law and to encourage our own people to view their responsibilities with civic maturity."[204]

At the same time, however, a radical movement led by black workers was emerging to contest the state's attempts to "police the crisis." These workers challenged more than aggressive police tactics, taking aim at the city's power structure, eventually helping to catalyze the city's Great Rebellion in 1967. It is to the efforts of these militant workers that we turn in the next chapter.

# 3

# The Conditions
## of the
# Great Rebellion

We learned from Detroit to go to the cities. —**GENERAL VÕ NGUYÊN GIÁP** of the Vietnam People's Army, 1968, quoted in Jay and Leavell, "Material Conditions of Detroit's Great Rebellion"

The Great Rebellion of 1967 is considered by people across the political spectrum to be foundational to the ensuing decline of Detroit. Across five days of armed conflict, forty-three people were killed and over one thousand were injured in the bloodiest uprising of a summer of urban rebellions across the country. The city commemorated the fiftieth anniversary of the Rebellion in the summer of 2017, and commentary on the conflagration and the ensuing fifty years of history show that the meaning of this seminal event is still highly contentious. Whether to refer to it as a "riot" or a "rebellion," whether it was provoked by a small group of radicals or represented the will of the majority, whether it was a cause or a consequence of the city's downfall—these and other debates continue to animate the struggle over the signification of Detroit's largest civil uprising. In short, the Great Rebellion has become a prime site of analysis for mythmaking.

There are two aspects to the mythologization that surrounds the Rebellion. The first is that both liberals and conservatives tend to obscure the political-economic coordinates of the uprising. Conservatives tend to ignore material conditions altogether and blame the "riot" on the irrational, irresponsible be-havior of the rioters themselves. Emblematic is the attitude of the organizer of Mayor Jerome Cavanagh's 1967 "secret riot-spy network." Participants in riots tend to come from what he describes as the "no-winner" crowd: "A typi-cal 'no-winner' . . . is hostile, angry and frustrated. 'He believes that if he can't have what he wants he will destroy. He's childish and doesn't know any better.'"[1] Liberals, on the other hand, tend to blame discriminatory policies and the racist attitudes of white citizens and police. This attitude does not stop them from viewing such outbreaks of violence as irresponsible and misguided. The *Washington Post*, for example, described Detroit's uprising as "the greatest tragedy of all the long succession of Negro ghetto outbursts."[2] To take a more recent example, during the uprisings in Baltimore that followed the killing of an unarmed black man, Freddie Gray, by the police, David Simon, creator of the celebrated HBO series *The Wire*, wrote, "This, now, in the streets, is an af-front to that man's memory and a diminution of the absolute moral lesson that underlies his unnecessary death. If you can't seek redress and demand reform without a brick in your hand, you risk losing this moment for all of us in Baltimore. Turn around. Go home."[3] Both the liberal and the conservative positions obscure the material conditions of the uprisings, preferring to cast them in mythic terms, as winner/loser, moral/immoral, and so on. Whether one views those protesting as simply bitter and opportunistic or as righteous but misguided, casting the issue in individual, ethical terms directs attention away from the structural issues that caused the uprising in the first place. Such a framework also papers over the fact that our political-economic system makes it exceedingly difficult, if not structurally impossible, for the protesters to collectively seek legal, peaceful redress for their demands. Embedded in the call for responsibility on the part of protesters is an insistence that only demands made through the formal and regularized political process are legiti-mate, ignoring the fact that eruptions of this sort tend to arise out of the ex-clusion of certain elements of the populace from this process or its failure to address specific issues. The truth is, throughout U.S. history and up through the violent uprising in Ferguson, Missouri, where Mike Brown was killed by police in 2014, riots have in fact often been catalysts for social change: under the national and international spotlight that violent protests produce, politi-cians have been forced to implement reforms they might otherwise have forgone.[4]

The second way that the Great Rebellion, and similar uprisings, are my-thologized is by obfuscating or erasing the importance of all of the organizing efforts that helped to catalyze the uprising. Throughout the 1960s political organizers facilitated reading groups, distributed pamphlets, and gave speeches that helped to raise workers' political consciousness. Organizers also created networks for militants and hosted workshops in political education and military strategy. By ignoring the activism in the lead-up to the Rebellion, one easily falls into the trap of thinking that when things get bad enough, uprisings happen "all by themselves."[5]

In this chapter we give an account of the macro-level causes of the Rebellion and how they informed the praxis of radical leaders on the ground in Detroit. We highlight the processes of creative destruction that devastated workers in general, and black workers in particular, and how militant groups of workers attempted to resist these processes. We look at the myths that shifted the blame for social turmoil onto the militants themselves, as well as the police tactics used to repress political dissidence and restore bourgeois order. Finally, we give a detailed account of the Rebellion itself and how the state repressed and mythologized this event.

### The Civil Rights Movement and Its Discontents

In order to understand the turbulent politics and radical imagination operative during this time period, let us first return to the contradiction between capitalism's capacity to produce and its capacity to consume, a contradiction that the intensive automation in the auto industry during the Treaty of Detroit brought into stark relief. This antagonism is well illustrated by a fabled conversation between Walter Reuther and Henry Ford II. "Walter, how are you going to get those robots to pay your union dues?" asked Ford. Reuther responded, "How are you going to get them to buy your cars?"[6]

This contradiction was further heightened by competition in the global market. In 1950 U.S.-based firms' share of global car production was more than 80 percent; by 1961 that figure was 48.5 percent, as firms in Western Europe and Japan (subsidized by U.S. dollars, courtesy of the Marshall Plan) made a dent in the global auto market with sleeker, more energy-efficient models. To defend their market share, U.S. firms continued to automate (worker productivity increased around 50 percent between the end of World War II and 1960), churning out more and more cars. Nearly 58 million cars were produced and sold by U.S.-based auto firms in the 1950s, one new vehicle for every three Americans, the elderly and infants included. In that decade GM spent more money on advertising than any other company in the world. But even as the booming advertising industry played up the novelty of each newer model, there was clearly a limit to consumers' willingness and capacity to purchase more cars.[7]

At the same time, in the U.S. South, automation was causing demand for black farm labor to plummet. Between 1940 and 1960 the percentage of black workers employed as farm hands decreased from 32 to 8. Detroit's black population more than tripled between 1940 and 1960 as many of these newly superfluous farm workers made their way to Detroit. This population was exploding just as the city's employment opportunities were shrinking: between 1947 and 1963 Detroit lost 134,000 manufacturing jobs. As these economic problems deepened, and police tactics to deal with underemployed black workers became more aggressive, the civil rights movement entered its most radical phase.[8]

The rise of civil rights protests in the South, after the Supreme Court's *Brown v. Board of Education* ruling ended legal segregation, catalyzed political activity in the urban centers of the North, and in the late 1950s and early 1960s there were sustained efforts to fight for civil rights within a legalistic, nonviolent framework in Detroit. In 1961 Jerome Cavanagh, a liberal candidate who ran on a platform of racial integration, was elected mayor of Detroit. The Trade Union Leadership Council (TULC), a liberal-black coalition formed by UAW workers in 1957, was influential in turning out the black vote for Cavanagh. This was the first time in the postwar era that the majority of black voters had been on the winning side of a mayoral election, and the result, according to legendary Detroit activist Grace Lee Boggs, was that blacks got "a taste of their political power."[9]

In the early 1960s the newly elected liberal administration in Washington would prove responsive to the wave of activism in the South and the urban North. During this period a wealth of new federal urban programs provided new funding resources for local activists and politicians. The Great Society, as it would come to be known, attempted to revitalize the urban program delivery system developed during the New Deal era, which had generated conflicts during the urban renewal projects of the conservative 1950s. In 1960 forty-four federal grant programs sent about $4 billion annually to the big cities; by the end of the Great Society, there were over five hundred federal grant programs distributing $14 billion to cities, which rose to $26.8 billion in 1974.[10] As well as providing novel funding to cities, the legislative initiatives of the Great Society increased the role of the federal government in local politics and tied the health of cities directly to federal funding—a relationship that would have drastic consequences in the decades to come, when this funding was drastically reduced.

TULC organized support for President Lyndon Johnson's War on Poverty and successfully lobbied him to select Detroit for his Model Cities program, which provided Detroit with $360 million in federal antipoverty aid in the mid-1960s. TULC also successfully fought for more black employment in the skilled trades, as well as more black representation in local government and in local universities: Mayor Cavanagh placed several prominent black figures in key positions, and Wayne State University's black enrollment increased to 2,500, more than in the Big Ten and Ivy League schools combined. TULC also helped organize the larger than expected 200,000-person turnout for the 1963 March for Freedom, in which Martin Luther King Jr. walked hand in hand with Mayor Cavanagh, Governor George Romney, and UAW president Walter Reuther along Woodward Avenue before delivering the day's keynote speech. The partnership between TULC and the liberal establishment led *Harper's* magazine to claim that Cavanagh's administration was helping to "build a bridge over the river of hate" between the government and the black community.[11]

But this bridge was unable to address the city's endemic economic problems, problems that particularly devastated black members of the working class. According to Dan Georgakas and Marvin Surkin, Chrysler's Dodge Main plant represented typical demographics: "99 percent of all general foremen were white, 95 percent of all foremen were white, 100 percent of all superintendents were white, 90 percent of all skilled tradesmen were white, and 90 percent of all skilled apprentices were white." In fact, due largely to capital flight, automation, and the vulnerable position black workers occupied in the labor market, the disparity in incomes between black and white families *increased* between 1950 and 1965. Furthermore, black youth unemployment in the United States *increased* from 16 percent in 1954 to 26 percent between 1956 and 1965; this figure was nearly 33 percent in Detroit and grew to 50 percent for high school dropouts.[12]

Structural economic issues ensured that the War on Poverty in general, and policies of integration in particular, would do little to ameliorate the daily living conditions of working-class black Detroiters.[13] Partly this was due to a lack of funding. Although Detroit was consistently lauded as one of the country's most exemplary and progressive "model cities," "had the city distributed its entire antipoverty budget . . . among the city's poor, each would have received only $60."[14] Even so, the funding managed to reach only a small portion of those in need: of the 360,000 Detroiters living below the poverty line in 1967, only 70,000 received aid through the War on Poverty.[15] In addition to poor funding, there was the issue of how the social programs were designed. Cowie and Salvatore explain, "Unlike the New Deal's focus on creating jobs directly . . . the 'war on poverty' programs emphasized helping individuals to reform themselves so as to gain better access to the job market—mostly through job training and educational assistance. The tacit assumption of Great Society policymakers was that in the midst of the greatest economic boom in American history, unemployment was not a structural problem but a personal one."[16] This individualistic approach went hand-in-hand with liberal attempts to divorce race and class as they emphasized the "distinctiveness of African American poverty." As Touré Reed has stressed, the Johnson administration attributed "high rates of black poverty in the early 1960s to the unique challenges African Americans faced in the form of racial discrimination and blacks' related soft and hard skills deficits." As a result, War on Poverty programs "like Job Corps and Community Action Programs emphasized provision of job training and cultural tutelage to impoverished minority youth rather than public works."[17]

It should be no surprise, then, that the War on Poverty failed to address Detroit's deep-rooted structural problems. Programs like Head Start, for instance, helped many poor Detroiters but could do little to address the overarching problems in the city's education system: the high school dropout rate at Detroit's overcrowded, underfunded schools remained above 50 percent. Additionally, when the housing programs funded by President Johnson's Model Cities were exhausted, only 758 low-income units had been built, doing little to alleviate the housing shortage that left the vast majority of Detroit's black residents in substandard housing. The housing situation in Detroit shines a light on the growing class division within the city's black population. On the one hand, by 1967 the percentage of African Americans who were homeowners grew from 39 to 48, giving Detroit the highest percentage of black homeownership in the country. On the other hand, many poorer blacks struggled to find adequate shelter: around 26,000 dwellings were demolished in 1960–67, replaced with only 15,500 housing units, most of which were for middle- and high-income residents. As the union activist Mike Kerwin notes, by the late 1960s, the Housing and Urban Development Committee, headed by George Romney, "just ran hog-wild. It was corrupt. Everybody was raking money out of it: real estate agents, insurance people, rehabilitation people, inspectors, appraisers."[18] David Goldberg writes, "Legal and political struggles for open housing in the city's outskirts or suburbs did little to address the realities and problems faced daily by poor and working-class Blacks," who confronted "living conditions that were often worse than those that residents had experienced prior to urban renewal." Absentee slumlords collected rent while failing to make repairs, often in the hopes that allowing their properties to deteriorate would qualify them for lucrative urban renewal projects. The results were horrendous: "Residents' complaints ran the gamut from falling plaster, rotted beams, exposed hot wires, septic cellars, lack of hot water, broken plumbing and furnaces, leaky roofs, and broken windows to rat, roach and bedbug infestation and bites."[19] To combat such conditions local activists formed more than fifty tenants' rights organizations in Detroit in the mid-1960s. These groups launched rent strikes and held demonstrations to combat these predations. Landlords initially responded by making some minor repairs, as well as evicting housing activists or driving up their rent.[20]

Another problem was that the liberal gains of the civil rights era did little to curb processes of criminalization and police brutality: by 1967, 82 percent of black Detroiters felt DPD used excessive force; at the time, blacks amounted to 35 percent of Detroit's population but less than 5 percent of its police force.[21] Police Commissioner Ray Girardin admitted that the way many Detroit cops dealt with African Americans was "to hit them on the side of the head."[22] Widick writes of the city's nonviolent civil rights movement, "Closer examination showed that most of the gains benefited the Negro middle class."[23]

The perceived and real limitations of liberal integrationism, or the failure of what Robin D. G. Kelley calls "Black Bourgeois reformism," spawned a "generation of black radicals whose dissatisfaction with the civil rights movement's strategy of nonviolent passive resistance drew them closer to Malcolm X and Third World liberation movements."[24] World historical transformations occurring at the same time as the civil rights movement changed the way many viewed the black struggle in the United States. The same year of the Supreme Court's *Brown* decision the Viet Minh defeated the French military, ending French colonial rule and bringing communists to power in North Vietnam. In Africa, the Kenyan Freedom Army—which became known as the Mau Mau in the Western press—waged war against the British colonial army. The following year a historic conference in Bandung, Indonesia, brought together representatives from twenty-nine African and Asian nations with the goal of combating colonialism and increasing cooperation among oppressed peoples.[25] Combined with the conservatism of trade unions following the regularization of capital-labor relations in the postwar period, these developments led to a growing consciousness that the agent of revolutionary change was no longer the mass industrial worker but rather the colonized, the unemployed, and the dispossessed. Activists increasingly viewed black Americans as a colony and related their struggles to those of the colonized peoples of developing countries.

Disaffection with Communist Party politics was another important node of this transition. "Every time a Negro would pick up a piece of Communist literature," claimed Frank Marquart, a white autoworker and union organizer in the 1930s, "he would always find something that pertained to the problems of the Negro."[26] But the Party's policies and bureaucracy alienated many black workers during World War II and in the postwar years, when traditional left orthodoxy failed, in the eyes of many, to account for the social and economic changes facing society. In 1944 the prominent black novelist and social critic Richard Wright published his scathing indictment of the Communist Party, "I Tried to Be a Communist," and Claudia Jones denounced the Party's paternalistic attitude toward black women workers. James Boggs argued that although the Communist Party was an important factor in raising workers' consciousness on the shop floor, it often had a condescending and racist attitude toward black workers.[27] Perhaps the most well known African American novel, Ralph Ellison's *Invisible Man*, published in 1952, dramatizes the Party's inability to recognize the individual humanity of black members, treating them instead as part of an undifferentiated mass. As Harold Cruse, author of *The Crisis of the Negro Intellectual*, wrote, "American Marxists cannot 'see' the Negro at all unless he is storming the barricades, either in the present or in history." Such a stance, Cruse explained, led communist organizers to wrongly view blacks as "a people without classes or differing class interests."[28] A former Communist Party member, Cruse defected over frustration with the Party's failure to account for the changing nature of class struggle. Critiquing the stale social theory of Party bureaucrats, he asked why it was assumed "that everything in society is subject to the processes of change except the historical role of the working class in advanced capitalist nations."[29]

In the context of black workers' alienation from "old left" dogma and the rise of anticolonial movements abroad, the Johnson-Forest Tendency germinated in Detroit. Founded in 1941, the Tendency originally formed within the Trotskyist Workers Party, later joining the Socialist Workers Party in 1947, and finally forming an independent organization called Correspondence. The group took its name from its two founders, the Trinidadian Marxist C. L. R. James, author of *The Black Jacobins* (who used the pseudonym J. R. Johnson), and the Ukrainian Marxist Raya Dunayevskaya, a former secretary of Leon Trotsky (who published under the name Freddie Forest). The third principal member was the Chinese American activist Grace Lee, a Bryn Mawr–trained philosophy PhD who married the autoworker James Boggs after he joined the group. The Tendency also included notable scholars and activists such as Martin Glaberman, Simon Owens, and George Rawick. In the group's early years they made a major contribution to Marxist theorization when Grace Lee Boggs produced the first-ever English translation of Marx's now famous 1844 *Economic and Philosophic Manuscripts*. The group also published a range of theoretical books and pamphlets on worker self-activity and Communist Party politics, such as *The American Worker* (1947), *State Capitalism and World Revolution* (1950), and *Facing Reality* (1958).[30]

The first issue of the *Correspondence* newspaper came out in 1953, and it soon claimed a regular readership of as many as four thousand people, one hundred of them contributing regular pieces to the paper. As Stephen M. Ward writes, *Correspondence* was committed to "affirming the role of the working class as the agent of revolutionary change; rejecting the concept of the vanguard party and instead celebrating the self-activity of spontaneous mobilization of the working class; and standing in full opposition to all forms of bureaucratic control."[31] Inside the plants, *Correspondence* activists attempted to lead a "revolt against Reuther." Simon Owens distributed pamphlets like *Workers Battle Automation* hoping to catalyze worker resistance to speed-ups and unemployment.[32] The initiatives of *Correspondence* were influential throughout European leftist circles, who looked to Detroit's working class for tactical guidance and ideological inspiration.

In his 1948 essay "The Revolutionary Answer to the Negro Problem in the USA," C.L.R. James described the "immense revolutionary potentiality" of black Americans, in whom the "readiness to destroy" bourgeois society existed "to a degree greater than in any other section of the population in the United States."[33] Arguing that the struggle against capital was still fundamental, James cautioned against subordinating the civil rights movement to trade unionism or left politics. Though the group had split by 1962 over ideological differences, James Boggs expressed a similar sentiment in his seminal and widely read work of 1963, *The American Revolution: Pages from a Negro Worker's Notebook*: "American Marxists have tended to fall into the trap of thinking of the Negroes as Negroes, i.e., in race terms, when in fact the Negroes have been and are today the most oppressed and submerged sections of the workers. . . . The Negro struggle in the United States is not just a race struggle. . . . The goal of the classless society is precisely what has been and is today at the heart of the Negro struggle."[34] Boggs concluded that "the black masses were bypassing workers as the force most prepared or able to disrupt society." In the years to come, the Boggses championed the Black Power movement, but also criticized Black Power leaders who "would rather keep the concept vague than grapple with the systematic analysis of American capitalism out of which the concept of Black Power has developed."[35]

In the mid-1960s the black nationalist Reverend Albert Cleage of the Shrine of the Black Madonna in Detroit laid out a Christian variant of revolutionary black nationalism: "With the emergence of the nationalist movements of the world's colored majority, the historic truth is finally beginning to emerge—that Jesus was the non-white leader of a non-white people struggling for national liberation against the rule of a white nation, Rome."[36] Cleage consistently drew large audiences for his polemical sermons, railing against white supremacy and condemning TULC's "Uncle Tomism."[37] In a well-attended memorial meeting for Malcolm X at Detroit's Socialist Forum, Cleage captured the changing tenor of the black struggle: "When you were just begging the white man to give you something, you didn't need organization. All you needed was a kneeling pad so that you could kneel down and look humble. But if you want power, you have got to organize to get it—you have got to have political power, you have got to have economic power."[38] Throughout the 1960s Cleage worked with a range of activists who shared a radical vision for the black movement in Detroit. Cleage organized a "Do Not Buy Where You Cannot Work" campaign and organized boycotts of racist businesses throughout Detroit. He also worked with Richard and Milton Henry, who were close friends of Malcolm X, and the Boggses to organize the Group on Advanced Leadership, a socialist, black nationalist organization formed in 1962.

A few months after the civil rights leader Medgar Evers was assassinated by a white supremacist in Mississippi, the Group on Advanced Leadership organized the 1963 Northern Negro Grass Roots Leadership Conference at King Solomon Baptist Church in Detroit, a formative event in the history of the Black Power movement. There Malcolm X, whose nickname was "Detroit Red" and who had briefly worked in Detroit's Lincoln-Mercury Plant, delivered his famous "Message to the Grass Roots" speech. Offering a scathing critique of mainstream civil rights leaders, he told his Detroit audience, "Whoever heard of a revolution where they lock arms, singing 'We Shall Overcome'? You don't do that in a revolution. You don't do any singing, you're too busy swinging."[39] Exposing what he saw as the conservative dynamics underlying the civil rights movement, Malcolm X portrayed the 1963 March on Washington as "an effort to subdue the groundswell of dissent while consolidating support for Kennedy's proposed civil rights reforms."[40] Due to his relationship with Detroit's radical activist network, Malcolm X returned to Detroit the following year to deliver another influential speech, "The Ballot or the Bullet." "I am not anti-white," he insisted. "I am antiexploitation, antioppression."[41]

In addition to their own organizational work, Cleage and James and Grace Lee Boggs served as mentors to a new generation of black activists. In 1963 students at Wayne State University—including many future leaders of the Dodge Revolutionary Union Movement, such as John Watson, Luke Tripp, and General Baker—formed Uhuru, a black Marxist-Leninist organization. Uhuru—Swahili for "freedom"—helped found the Freedom Now Party, a black-leftist political party led by the Boggses, Cleage, and Harold Cruse. Members of Uhuru also attended the Socialist Workers Party's Friday Night Socialist Forum. The activists formed reading groups to discuss the works of Marx, Lenin, Mao, Malcolm X, Frantz Fanon, C. L. R. James, and Che Guevara. Uhuru members also studied the writings of Robert F. Williams, which had been published in *Correspondence*. Williams had served in the U.S. Marines and labored as a factory worker in Detroit before he went to Monroe, North Carolina, and became president of the local NAACP chapter. In the late 1950s he formed black armed self-defense groups, and when the KKK attacked the organizer of a local campaign to desegregate the public pools, Williams and others returned fire and succeeded in running the white supremacists off. Williams's tactics helped reduce the incidences of racial violence across Monroe, where he stayed until 1961, when he was threatened by a violent lynch mob. He found asylum in Cuba, where he soon met with Mao Zedong. Following their meeting, Mao wrote, "The evil system of colonialism and imperialism grew up along with the enslavement of Negroes, and it will surely come to its end with the thorough emancipation of the black people."[42]

In 1964 Williams published an influential essay titled "The Potential of a Minority Revolution" in which he gave specific suggestions for building a "poor man's arsenal": "Gasoline fire bombs (Molotov cocktails), lye or acid bombs (made by injecting lye or acid in the metal end of light bulbs) can be used extensively. During the night hours such weapons, thrown from roof tops, will make the streets impossible for racist cops to patrol. Hand grenades, bazookas, light mortars, rocketlaunchers, machine guns and ammunition can be bought clandestinely from servicemen, anxious to make a fast dollar."[43]

In 1964 the Progressive Labor Movement invited several Uhuru leaders on a trip to Cuba, where they met with Williams, Fidel Castro, and Che Guevara to discuss revolutionary tactics. General Baker, a future leader of the League of Revolutionary Black Workers, remembers, "It was a laboratory of revolutionary fervor."[44] Ernest Allen, a friend of Huey Newton and leader of the Revolutionary Action Movement (RAM) in Oakland, was also in Cuba at the time. As a result of the meetings, Allen and the cadre of Uhuru activists committed themselves to applying "'Marxism-Leninism Mao Tse-tung thought' to the conditions of black people." Once back in Oakland, Allen soon recruited Bobby Seale, the future cofounder of the Black Panther Party for Self-Defense, into RAM. In Detroit James Boggs was elected RAM's ideological chairman, and he and Grace Lee Boggs helped organize RAM's journal, *Black America*. According to a former Black Panther member, Ahmad Rahman, Detroit's RAM activists became "the underground, military wing of the black liberation struggle for which Malcolm X's Organization of Afro-American Unity was to be the aboveground vehicle."[45] RAM had links with the Afro-American Student Movement, which published a journal, *Black Vanguard*, edited by John Watson, a future leader of the Dodge Revolutionary Union Movement, which was distributed throughout the city's factories.[46]

Around the United States, the struggle was becoming increasingly violent. In 1964 the Student Nonviolent Coordinating Committee launched its Mississippi voter registration campaign, and white supremacist groups responded by bombing forty homes, burning thirty-five black churches, and murdering six people. That year also saw urban uprisings in Harlem, Chicago, Philadelphia, and several other cities. In February 1965 Malcolm X was assassinated. A few months later residents of the Watts neighborhood in Los Angeles took part in what *CBS Reports* called a "virtual civil insurrection probably unmatched since [the Civil War]." During the Watts rebellion, LAPD Chief William H. Parker said, "This situation is very much like fighting the Viet Cong. . . . We haven't the slightest idea when this can be brought under control." Days of armed struggle resulted in 3,952 arrests and more than $40 million in property damage. Thirty-four people were killed, nearly all of them black, and most of them by the police.[47] To make sense of this insurrection, it is helpful to consider the political-economic context: between 1963 and 1965 the LAPD killed sixty black people, and twenty-eight factories had left the local area.[48] When Martin Luther King Jr. traveled to Watts to organize the rebels into a nonviolent movement, his speech was interrupted and ridiculed by an angry crowd. King's friend and fellow nonviolent activist Dick Gregory attempted to intervene, borrowing a bullhorn from the police and shouting at the rebels, "Go home!" A protester subsequently shot Gregory in the leg.[49]

Following Watts, President Johnson addressed the nation with these words: "A rioter with a Molotov cocktail in his hands is not fighting for civil rights any more than a Klansman with a sheet on his back and a mask on his face. They are both more or less what the law declares them: lawbreakers, destroyers of constitutional rights and liberties, and ultimately destroyers of a free America. They must be exposed and they must be dealt with."[50] The president's statement bears an eerie resemblance to an earlier statement by King: "Lawlessness, looting and violence cannot be condoned whether used by the racist or the reckless of any color."[51]

## Stop-and-Frisk Comes to Detroit

The state responded to this upsurge in militancy by bolstering its police forces. Following the Watts uprising, the LAPD introduced stop-and-frisk tactics in the black neighborhoods that launched the rebellion. That same year, President Johnson passed the Law Enforcement Assistance Act, launching his War on Crime, which would run parallel to his War on Poverty.[52] At the same time, Mayor Cavanagh proceeded to modernize and enlarge the DPD as part of his own "war on crime." Cavanagh said that the government must "show to those who break the law that you are an enemy. Show to those who respect the law that you are a friend."[53] As part of this effort, he expanded DPD's Red Squad. Tasked with monitoring and infiltrating radical groups, the squad grew in size from six to seventy members from 1958 to 1970. The mayor also proposed a "stop and frisk law." According to the *Free Press*, "The law would empower a policeman to stop any person he reasonably suspects is committing, has committed, or is about to commit a felony or high misdemeanor. . . . It would also allow the policeman to search the person for a dangerous weapon if the policeman 'reasonably suspects' he is in danger."[54] In 1965 DPD also introduced tactical mobile units, "an elite corps trained to deal with civil disturbances." The high-crime areas being targeted by an enlarged and modernized DPD were poor areas with high concentrations of black residents.[55]

Antipolice sentiment had already been running high in Detroit's black community after a police officer killed Cynthia Scott in 1963. Following Scott's death—she was shot three times, twice in the back, having allegedly slashed an officer on the hand—the *Free Press* titled their ensuing article "Police Kill Woman in Vice Case" and labeled Scott a prostitute and a "188-pound former wrestler." A mass protest ensued, with as many as five thousand Detroiters marching on police headquarters, chanting, "Stop killer cops!" The city prosecutor, however, declared the officers' actions justified.[56]

On the night of August 9, 1966, police officers attempted to arrest three black youth who were "loitering" on the sidewalk.[57] A crowd estimated at one hundred people responded to the arrests on Kercheval Street by attacking private property and throwing rocks at the tactical mobile units. For three nights Detroiters, armed with rocks and Molotov cocktails, clashed with police. Eventually the police arrested fifty-five people, most on charges of "inciting to riot" and "conspiracy to disturb the public peace." Those arrested included General Baker and Glanton Dowdell, future organizers in the League of Revolutionary Black Workers.[58] In an article titled "Lessons Learned from City's Racial Violence," the *Free Press* concluded that at Kercheval Street "Detroit experienced a sharp, violent and potentially explosive disturbance. It didn't explode, and that, too, is significant. Detroit learned that when an illegal outbreak occurred, police and other community agencies moved quickly to contain it and defuse it. The police have had the youth movement under almost constant surveillance."[59] In short, rather than address the root causes of social unrest—poverty, unemployment, poor housing, violent and racist policing—members of Detroit's power structure were confident that they could effectively contain the crisis by policing it.

In response, activists began patrolling the police officers and monitoring their activity. "Join the black guards" slogans could be found throughout Detroit. Two months after the Kercheval clash, on October 30, the *Free Press* published a brief article titled "Negro Check on Police Is Criticized": "A predominantly Negro political group said Saturday that plans to recruit Negroes to police Detroit policemen were considered 'ill-considered and ill-advised.' The community and Labor Political Action Coalition (CALPAC) issued the statement after a militant inner-city civil rights group told of plans to form 'black panther patrols.' The unarmed patrols will record all incidents of police brutality."[60]

As black militancy grew, elites propagated a myth that blamed these militants for the city's increasing crime rates. In late 1966, for example, thirteen Black Panthers were arrested and interrogated after a sixty-one-year-old grocer was murdered. In their front-page story on the arrests, the *Free Press* called the Panthers "an alleged terrorist gang." Three men were charged with first-degree murder, and "police said a waiver would be sought on a 15-year-old, said to have served as the lookout during the holdup, so that he might be tried as an adult with the others."[61]

Compare this with the criminal justice system's treatment of white Detroiters. In the summer of 1967 a group of white men killed Danny Thomas, a black war veteran and former Ford employee, at River Rouge Park. Thomas was murdered after attempting to defend his pregnant wife, whom the men raped, causing her to have a miscarriage. Initially Detroit's major newspapers attempted to silence the story, and Thomas's murder was covered only by the *Michigan Chronicle*. As political pressure mounted, several days after the attack the *Free Press* published a muted story of the killing—burying it on the paper's third page, behind a cover story about a blind puppy that white homeowners took in.[62] The police immediately released five of the men detained for killing Thomas. Only one person was charged with the murder, and he was eventually acquitted. At that time, in Detroit, no white person had ever been successfully prosecuted for the murder of a black person.[63]

That same week, in a series of police raids, sixteen Revolutionary Action Movement members in New York were rounded up and arrested on trumped-up charges. The police action came on the heels of a *Life* magazine exposé on RAM, which claimed that the "Peking based group" was "impressively well read in revolutionary literature—from Marat and Lenin to Mao, Che Guevara and Frantz Fanon." All charges were subsequently dropped.[64]

A week later, on July 1, Vivian Williams was murdered. The *Free Press* buried the story on the eleventh page. In the fifty-four-word report on the murder, the paper did not mention that Williams was black, nor that multiple witnesses claimed that Williams had been killed by a white police officer who had had repeated, hostile run-ins with her.

Both Danny Thomas and Vivian Williams lived in the deeply impoverished Twelfth Street neighborhood, where the Great Rebellion would begin. The demographics of this West Side neighborhood had changed dramatically in recent decades: 99 percent of the residents were white in 1940, and only 4 percent were white by 1960. Many of the incoming black residents had moved into the area after Black Bottom was razed.[65]

On July 20, a week after a black-led insurgency in Newark, New Jersey, in which twenty-three people were killed, Mayor Cavanagh's Summer Task Force began a riot simulation in the Twelfth Street neighborhood. Public officials were tested on their ability to respond to a "mock riot." According to the designer of the Early Warning System, "things look good."[66]

## The Great Rebellion

In the city's factories, it was mostly blacks who worked the late shifts—shifts that often lasted until three in the morning. As bars were officially closed at this time, "blind pigs"—unlicensed, after-hours drinking and gambling establishments—were the only places where workers could congregate and unwind after their shifts ended. Police raids were common at blind pigs, a source of anger among black workers. On Saturday night, July 22, a group of black Detroiters went to a blind pig in the Twelfth Street neighborhood to celebrate the safe return of two GIs from their tours in Vietnam.[67] At around 3:30 a.m. police used a sledgehammer to break into the establishment. Officers poured in, arresting eighty people and throwing them into paddy wagons. When people protested the aggressive manner in which the arrests were being made, officers raised their batons and told them, "If you stay where you are, no one will get hurt." According to the sergeant who led the raid, "The real trouble didn't start until we started to leave with the last wagonload, and we couldn't get our cars out. By the time we pulled away, more bottles and bricks were coming. A lot of the windows were broken out in one of the cars."[68] One black youth, thought to be a Ford employee, incited people to fight back against the police with cries of "Black Power!" It wasn't long before people began "looting the stores that siphoned their money out of the community, burning the slums to which economic exploitation and housing discrimination confined them, and fighting the police force which harassed and often brutalized them."[69]

Initially the police response was tentative, due to fears that a strong repressive response would escalate matters and provoke more violence. This hesitancy came under sharp criticism from business owners, middle-class residents, and political elites. Nor was it only whites who complained. The executive secretary of Detroit's branch of the NAACP worried about the "restrained" police response, and the black president of the 12th St. Businessmen's Association blamed the riot's escalation on the police's initial failure to use fire power to stop looters.[70]

Just as Martin Luther King Jr. was brought in to try to defuse the violent uprising in Watts, John Conyers, a black U.S. representative from Michigan, came to Detroit. He drove around Detroit with Hubert Locke, a black assistant police commissioner, asking people to leave the streets. On Sunday afternoon he stood on a car on Twelfth Street with a police bullhorn, but the crowd shouted him down. A black man called out, "Why are you defending the cops and the establishment? You're just as bad as they are!" The crowd even began throwing bottles at the congressman, who later offered this explanation for his inability to quell the crowd: "They're alienated from us. We don't speak their language. We throw $100 dinners and some of these people don't see $100 in a month."[71]

Rebels meanwhile grew in numbers, and "molotov cocktails, guns, stones, bricks, and bottles were used against police," who were outnumbered and overwhelmed.[72] Attacks on private property intensified on Sunday afternoon. The fires of arsonists spread rapidly amid the dilapidated slum housing, and the Detroit Fire Department, one of the lowest funded per capita in the country, was powerless to contain the conflagrations. A total of 531 fires were lit on Sunday.[73]

At 4:20 p.m. Mayor Cavanagh called in the National Guard. A few hours later the mayor instated a 9:00 p.m. curfew, declaring a state of emergency. He then ordered all the city's gas stations to close, following reports that they were selling gasoline in "buckets and bottles" to rebels. Governor Romney commented that there was so much combat, "it looked like the city had been bombed on the West Side." By day's end, police had arrested at least 1,030 people. DPD had suffered twenty-eight injuries, compared to two hundred injured residents. Several were shot, including two black men: Robert Boyd, who was in critical condition after a security guard shot him in an alley just west of Twelfth Street, and Clinton Pryor, who was killed by a National Guardsman. Two black men, Willie Hunter and Price Williams, had died from asphyxiation inside a burning building, and a white woman, Sheren George, was killed by a crowd of black men. Overnight another eight thousand National Guardsmen were summoned; they were instructed to "shoot to kill if fired upon, and to shoot any person seen looting." Romney announced, "Fleeing felons are subject to being shot at."[74]

Violence escalated on Monday, July 24. As Hubert Locke writes, "By midnight on the second day of the riot veteran police officers were convinced they were engaged in the worst encounter in urban guerilla warfare ever witnessed in the United States in the 20th century."[75] The Fire Department was alerted to 617 alarms on Monday, triple the number of the previous day. Fire Chief Quinlan believed arsonists employed "a divide-and-conquer-strategy. They set a fire in one area, and when the firemen get there the guys who started them are several blocks away starting another." Some calls were "merely traps to lure the Fire Fighters into ambush to be sniped at." Firefighters were "pelted with rocks, bottles, and cement."[76]

Attacks on private property were largely targeted. Black-owned stores displaying "Soul Brother" signs were generally left alone. At other stores rebels burned credit records, freeing residents of crippling debt. Some also targeted pawn shops with guns, stealing 2,500 rifles for their war chest. "African Americans," Ahmad Rahman writes, "had attacked few civilian white Detroiters. Instead, the black rebels directed their wrath almost exclusively against the most visible symbols of capitalism and racism: first, property, and second, the firefighters and policeman who protected it."[77]

By day's end, seventeen uprising-related deaths had occurred, the highest of any day that week; this included seven black looters killed by state forces, one black man killed by a black private security guard, and another two looters—one black, one white—killed by the same white business owner. In all, 2,931 people, mostly black, were arrested for riot-related activities.[78] The *Free Press* blamed the violence on looters who erupted in an "orgy of pillage": "As the looting spread, so did the conviction that this riot had less to do with race than with color TV sets, less with Black Power than with something for nothing."[79] President Johnson added, "Pillage and looting and arson have nothing to do with civil rights. I know that with few exceptions the citizens of Detroit . . . deplore and condemn these criminal acts." For his part, the editor of the *Michigan Chronicle*, a black-owned weekly, chastised DPD's "permissiveness" in handling the looters: "This was the time firm action should have been taken, to nip this thing in the bud. . . . A firm hand would have chased these people away."[80] Taking a similar line, TULC leaders blamed the "riot" on a "relatively small number of hoodlums and hatemongers" whose actions threatened to "destroy years of effort to build community," a "proud" effort

FIGURE 3.1. Twelfth Street during the first day of the Great Rebellion.
Sources: Fine, *Violence in the Model City*; *Detroit News*.

that yielded "substantial progress." Martin Luther King Jr., Roy Wilkins of the NAACP, Whitney Young of the Urban League, and A. Philip Randolph soon issued a joint statement arguing that "riots had proved highly ineffective, disruptive, and highly damaging to the Negro population, the civil rights cause, and the entire nation."[81]

Late on Monday night, President Johnson invoked the Insurrection Act of 1807 to order 4,700 army paratroopers into Detroit to deal with the looters committing crimes in Detroit. (Of these, 2,750 paratroopers were stationed throughout five East Side high schools—and as we saw in the first chapter, this police presence has continued in Detroit's schools to this day.[82]) It was only after consistent appeals from local leaders that the troopers were ordered in. Even UAW leader Walter Reuther and African American congressman Charles Diggs Jr. called the White House asking for military intervention.[83] The media also played a role in fostering local and national support for military intervention. In her PhD dissertation on the media framing of the 1967 uprising, Casandra E. Ulbrich concludes, "Blacks were clearly described as the aggressors, and

FIGURE 3.2. Detroit children celebrating during the Great Rebellion.
Source: Locke, *The Detroit Riot of 1967.*

white business owners were depicted as the targets or victims of the aggressors. Language pertaining to those who died as a result of the uprising also tended to follow the notion that blacks were the aggressors and that many who died did so as a result of their own actions."[84]

Tuesday morning, according to Hubert Locke, was "the most intense period of the riot," "a total state of war." At the Ford Hospital on the West Side, sniper fire hemmed in forty officers and Guardsmen. Tanks were brought in to clear the streets where the most violent resistance was taking place. The 82nd and 101st Airborne divisions engaged in firefighting with snipers whom the *Free Press* described as "terrorists." Officers acknowledged that the resistance "look[ed] organized." The *Free Press* reported, "Negro snipers turned 140 square blocks north of West Grand Blvd. into a bloody battlefield for three hours last night, temporarily routing police and national guardsmen.... Tanks thundered through the streets and heavy machine guns clattered.... The scene was incredible. It was as though the Viet Cong had infiltrated the riot blackened streets.... Since the Negroes know their battleground best, they were out to make it the kind of war they could fight."[85]

FIGURE 3.3. The National Guard patrols Linwood Avenue on July 23, 1967.
Sources: Fine, *Violence in the Model City*; *Detroit News*.

On Tuesday another thousand-plus people were arrested, and the official
death toll rose to twenty-five, including one police officer and one firefighter.
That day Richard and Milton Henry, representatives from the Malcolm X Society, which had worked closely with RAM in the buildup to the Rebellion,
sent a telegram to Mayor Cavanagh, Governor Romney, and the White House
claiming they would work toward "a cessation of all hostilities by insurrectionists" if the government would meet the following demands: the withdrawal of
federal troops, "amnesty to all insurrectionists," giving residents the right to
veto urban renewal programs, funds for "community-owned businesses and
cooperatives," and community control over the school board.[86] It seems unlikely that the Henrys had the capacity to control the militants, but the telegram does speak to the fact that many local activists saw the insurrection as a

FIGURE 3.4. The U.S. Army patrols Detroit during the Great Rebellion in a tank with the words "Mission Impossible" written on it. Sources: Fine, *Violence in the Model City*; *Detroit News*.

fundamentally political event, not the "orgy of pillage" that the media described. As in Watts, rather than countenance any political demands, "a 'dragnet' process was evoked in which the ordinary canons of evidence necessary to arrest and the normal constraints of limited police manpower were largely ignored in an all-out effort to clear the streets." Police targeted activists for arrest, and the courts refused bail to 98 percent of arrestees until the uprising ended. Judge George Crockett Jr., a progressive African American, stood out in his refusal to set high bail to keep arrestees locked up.[87]

Prison conditions were brutal, and lack of facilities forced many prisoners to remain in police buses for upward of thirty hours. Prisoners were even kept in Belle Isle, earning the park the nickname "Bellekatraz." "Hundreds of those arrested were forced to spend several days in an underground garage that lacked toilets. Police inflicted sexual abuse and brutality on prisoners, with many requiring hospitalization following 'interrogations.'"[88] One prisoner, while being interrogated, "had his skull cracked open, and was thrown back in the cell. He was taken to a hospital only when other arrestees complained that he was bleeding to death." A female prisoner was forced to strip, photographed nude, and then raped by a police officer. In solidarity with the rapist, police officers took off their badges and taped over their license plates, making it "virtually impossible" to identify the officer who committed the rape.[89]

Throughout Tuesday officers and Guardsmen frequently fired into apartment complexes in which militants were believed to be hiding. Among the casualties of such a tactic was Tonya Blanding, a four-year-old black girl who died when an army tank fired into her apartment building. The "flash" the tank was firing at was later confirmed to be from Tonya's uncle, who was lighting a cigarette. According to a resident of the building, police "just started shooting and shooting. . . . We yelled to them that we had children in there, but it didn't do no good. They said there was a sniper in our building. We told him there wasn't nobody in there but families with children, but they shot in anyway." Remarkably, though the *Free Press* acknowledged that the flash that police were responding to was nothing but the flame from a cigarette lighter, the newspaper still titled the article "A Sniper Was Under Fire, but a 4-Year-Old Girl Died." A fifty-one-year-old white women was similarly killed by indiscriminate tank fire. Also on Tuesday, State Representative Arthur Law of Pontiac killed a black "hoodlum" who was looting a grocery store. Law was quoted in the *Free Press* as saying, "The only answer is a double-barreled approach. The police and National Guard must shoot to kill and the courts must back them up by giving maximum sentences on all offenses."[90]

By Wednesday night the military had finally succeeded in quelling the Rebellion, and the *Free Press* reported that things were "nearly back to normal." But even after the city's streets were largely cleared of militants, the paratroopers remained. "Most Detroiters know why. [President] Johnson was using them as a buffer to prevent the revolt from spreading further east, to neighborhoods like Grosse Pointe where Henry Ford and others of the city's ruling class lived."[91]

By Thursday morning the reported death toll was thirty-six. This included one black youth whom police told to run away, after which they fatally shot him in the back—the same tactic police officers had used in 1943. The most heinous state violence occurred at the Algiers Motel, where officers converged in response to alleged gunfire—which turned out to be a toy gun. The police killed three unarmed black men; nine others, seven black men and two white women, were viciously beaten and forced to endure hours of what can only be described as kidnapping and torture.[92]

On Thursday the state police began to leave, and by Friday there was only one gun battle between rebels and police. In the days that followed, the National Guard slowly pulled out of the city, curfews were lifted, and almost all businesses were open.

As the historian Sidney Fine writes, "It required a total of about seventeen thousand men drawn from the army, the Michigan National Guard, the State Police, and the Detroit Police Department to quell the Detroit riot." State forces fired over 150,000 rounds of ammunition; there were so many empty shells lying throughout the streets that people used them for necklaces. In all, forty-three people were killed, thirty-three of them black, at least twenty-nine of them killed by state forces. About 7,200 people were arrested—more than double the amount in the Watts uprising—64 percent for looting and 14 percent for curfew violations. Twenty-six people were charged with sniping, and 552 buildings had been damaged or destroyed.[93]

Though the uprising was black-led, thousands of poor white workers, many of them southern migrants, took part: 12 percent of those arrested were white, and whites committed 27 percent of the arsons. Many of these white workers were part of the National Committee for Democratic Action, an organization within the UAW that called on the union "to return to the militant and united action which was once the strength of the rank and file in the 1930s."[94] General Baker insists that what makes Detroit's Rebellion unique was not simply its scale—it was the largest uprising in the United States since the Civil War—but also its integrated character: "The first person that was killed in the Detroit Rebellion was a white worker that was looting a store down in Trumbull. When they carried me to Ionia, I had two white guys on my [prison] bus that was arrested for sniping."[95] Recognition of white participation in the Great Rebellion would prove to impact the organizing strategies of groups, like the League of Revolutionary Black Workers, which formed in its wake.[96]

## The Consequences of State Repression

The state's response to the uprising had important political consequences that would reverberate throughout the era of mass incarceration. Mass arrests were used to quell urban militancy, causing the rate at which new inmates entered the prison system in the late 1960s and early 1970s to increase faster than at any time since the Great Depression.[97] As the scholar-activist Dan Berger writes, "Although these arrests resulted only in brief incarcerations, they were dry runs in dedicating massive state resources to widespread imprisonment. As the economy began its postindustrial turn, elites changed these urban uprisings into experiments in detaining large numbers of people."[98]

National and local media outlets justified the repression by describing it as a necessary response to combat lawlessness. Emblematic is *Time* magazine's account: "If there is one point that has been proved repeatedly over four summers of ghetto riots it is that when the police abandon the street, the crowd takes it over, and the crowd can swiftly become a mob. It happened in Watts, in Boston's Roxbury District, in Newark, and in blood and fire in Detroit."[99]

When considering the militarization of the police in the United States, it is important to remember that during the uprising in Detroit, as in insurgencies across the country, the police and National Guard proved incapable of restoring order on their own. One member of Mayor Cavanagh's staff complained that the National Guard had "no more training for this kind of situation than a good group of Boy Scouts."[100] One Guardsman described them as "lost boys in the big town carrying guns."[101] Fine suggests that the chaotic and often racially motivated violence of the police and National Guard should be characterized as "a riot of police against blacks." It was not uncommon to hear Guardsmen—almost all of whom were white—saying things like "I'm gonna shoot anything that moves and that is black." And on multiple occasions police themselves were reported to be looting, "filling a paddy wagon with goods taken from a store."[102] As Rodney Stark points out in *Police Riots*, the army's discipline stood in stark contrast to the police and Guardsmen's wanton violence and ineptitude: "These dramatic and critical differences seem to have stemmed from discipline. The paratroopers had it. The police and guardsmen did not. The army ordered the lights back on and troopers to show themselves as conspicuously as possible; the police and the guardsmen continued shooting out all lights and crouched fearfully in the darkness. The troopers were ordered to hold their fire, and did so. The police and guardsmen shot wildly and often at one another."[103]

It was the army's superior ability to repress the uprising that justified and catalyzed the militarization of U.S. police forces in Detroit and across the country in the wake of the urban rebellions of the late 1960s and early 1970s. In the years to come, the U.S. military, which had over a thousand military bases around the world at the time of the Great Rebellion, would increasingly occupy U.S. cities like Detroit to pacify political militancy, giving credence to the Black Panthers' equation of the police with a foreign army of occupation.[104]

## Post-Rebellion Consciousness

One poll taken soon after what it called the "July Insurrection" found that 56 percent of black respondents characterized the events in Detroit as a "rebellion or revolution," compared to only 19 percent who called them "riots." The role of unemployed people and of industrial workers in the uprising stands out: surveys reveal that 30 percent of those who took part in the Rebellion were jobless and that 40 percent of the arrestees at one Detroit prison were employed at Detroit's Big Three auto companies. Worker absenteeism was so high for several days during the uprising that production had come to a near standstill.[105]

The 120 social scientists who were originally hired by the U.S. government to investigate the causes of the country's uprisings concluded, "A truly revolutionary spirit has begun to take hold . . . an unwillingness to compromise or wait any longer, to risk death rather than have their people continue in a subordinate status." The team that composed the report was subsequently fired and their insights removed from the final version of the Kerner Report, an influential document that serves as the government's official public account of the urban uprisings.[106]

In the aftermath of the Great Rebellion, black activists who would soon organize the League of Revolutionary Black Workers launched the *Inner City Voice* newspaper. The first issue contained these words: "We are still working too hard, getting paid too little, living in bad housing, sending our kids to substandard schools, paying too much for groceries and treated like dogs by the police. We still don't own anything and don't control anything. . . . In other words, we are still being systematically exploited by the system, and still have the responsibility to break the back of that system. . . . Think about it brother, things ain't hardly getting better. The Revolution must continue."[107]

On the other end of the political spectrum, Governor Romney declared, "Violation of law to secure needed social and economic improvement cannot be countenanced. . . . No American has the right to break the law." Romney said that he would use any means necessary to "stop lawlessness and violence" and pledged to support "responsible" black leaders to help reestablish peace.[108]

The opposition between the governor's sentiment and that expressed by the *Inner City Voice* could not have been more stark. And it was the contradiction between them—efforts to restore bourgeois order on the one hand, and efforts to subvert the political-economic system on the other—that would define the years to come.

# 4

# Revolutionaries
### and
# Counterrevolutionaries

The biggest lesson that we learned out of the rebellion was that when they established curfew, if you got sick you couldn't go to the hospital, if you got hungry you couldn't go to get no food, but if you had a badge from Chrysler, Ford or General Motors, you would get through the police line, the National Guard line, and the army line to take your butt to work. We learned a fundamental lesson out of that, that the only place that black people had any value in the society was at the point of production. And that's why we turned our efforts to organizing in the factories, and within a year's time after the Detroit Rebellion, DRUM was born. —GENERAL BAKER of the League of Revolutionary Black Workers, "General Baker Speaks!" 2010

The Negro youth and moderates must be made to understand that if they succumb to revolutionary teaching, they will be dead revolutionaries. —FBI director J. EDGAR HOOVER (year unknown), quoted in Bloom and Martin, *Black against Empire*

In July 2017 *Detroit* was released to widespread critical acclaim. Directed by the Academy Award–winning director Kathryn Bigelow, the film restages the city's 1967 uprising. *Detroit* is "harrowing, relentless, and intensely angry," declared the *New Statesman*. "As it should be." The filmmakers decided that the fiftieth anniversary of the Great Rebellion was the perfect occasion for *Detroit's* release, and advertisements for the film papered Detroit while the city commemorated the uprising. In deciding whether to take on the project, Bigelow thought, "Am I the perfect person to tell this story? No. However, I'm able to tell this story, and it's been 50 years since it's been told. . . . I always feel that the purpose of art is to agitate for change, but you can't change anything if you're not aware of it. . . . With the events unfolding today, the story needed to see the light of day. My hope is that a dialogue comes out of this film that can begin to humanize a situation that often feels very abstract."[1]

*Detroit* opens with a stage-setting voice-over: after black workers' Great Migration north, a second great migration occurred, when racist whites abandoned cities, "taking jobs and money with them." As we have seen, deindustrialization, suburbanization, and ghettoization are impossible to understand without taking into consideration the broader political and economic landscape. But in Bigelow's depiction, white racism is the transhistorical scourge. This simplification allows Bigelow to turn the deeply rooted urban rebellion into a race riot, a violent spectacle to be staged with a $34 million budget.

Bigelow obscures not only the political causes of the uprising but also the political content of the uprising itself. The myriad radical political organizations and leaders that helped galvanize Detroit's uprising are entirely absent from the film. Militant autoworkers, so central to the Rebellion, are likewise erased; insofar as they appear in the film, autoworkers appear only at work, often discovering that their sons, who they wish were "smarter than that," have foolishly joined in the uprising. And white workers, who took part in the uprising in significant numbers, are nowhere to be found in Bigelow's drama. Instead of a political uprising, we are left with a picture of enraged, despairing black men looting the city, a picture not dissimilar from that offered by the media at the time in their attempts to discredit the uprising as an "orgy of pillage."

The word *rebellion* sometimes gets thrown around in progressive circles. It's often used to describe and romanticize any event with political determinants that entails mass resistance. But, as Grace Lee Boggs has written, there is a qualitative difference between a rebellion that is simply a negative reaction, a tearing down, and a rebellion that creates space to reshape and overcome the thing one is rebelling against. Rebellions can pave the way to revolutionary politics only when people have assumed "the role of subject in the precarious adventure of transforming and re-creating the world. They are not just denouncing but also announcing a new positive." Detroit's rebellion encompasses the *positive* vision for a new type of society that animated the radical organizations that proliferated in Detroit, both before and after the rebellion.[2]

The radical imaginary that animated many in Detroit at the time is obscured in the debate about Bigelow's merits as a white woman. This is clear from the appraisal given the film by Dr. Michael Eric Dyson, a Detroit native and one of the country's most prominent black political commentators (whom Bigelow consulted while making *Detroit*): "This is a white woman telling the truth as much as she can on film about racial injustice in America. That will resonate very powerfully with white folks. What better way to use your white privilege than to undermine it, raise questions about it, leverage it on behalf of black and brown people who usually don't have a voice in the matter at all."[3]

Obscuring the political-economic coordinates of the Rebellion in favor of a straightforward story of racial enmity and oppression is nothing new. In 1968 the National Advisory Commission on Civil Disorders, known as the Kerner Commission, issued a seminal report on the country's recent "racial uprisings." Adolph Reed Jr. comments:

> The report concluded with more than seventy pages of specific, mainly social-democratic recommendations for national policy action to prevent future disturbances. Those were by and large ignored, even in popular discussion. Instead, the report's most meaningful and lasting impact on American politics resulted from its generic diagnosis that "white racism" was the ultimate source of the manifold inequalities and disparities the report catalogued and its prognosis that "the nation is rapidly moving toward two increasingly separate Americas . . . a white society principally located in suburbs, in smaller central cities, and in the peripheral parts of large central cities; and a Negro society largely concentrated within large central cities."[4]

In other words, the dominant interpretation of the Kerner Report was to divorce race from class and obscure the complex material causes of the urban uprisings. The conclusion that "white racism is essentially responsible for the explosive mixture which has been accumulating in our cities since the end of World War II" had far-ranging effects on politics in the post–civil rights era. If uprisings were caused primarily by racism, then they required a racial solution: more black politicians, police officers, college graduates, and so on. By pushing political-economic causes to the background, it became easy to ignore the recommendations of black leaders like Coretta Scott King, Bayard Rustin, and A. Philip Randolph, who were calling at the time for full employment.[5]

Meanwhile the Kerner Commission's call for more "training, planning, adequate intelligence systems, and knowledge of the ghetto community" was widely heeded, and the new multiracial political elite sought tighter control over the exploited and alienated populations who were responsible for the uprisings.[6] As the black political establishment became more and more entrenched and black membership in the middle class grew, conditions for black workers, and the working class more generally, worsened dramatically, with unemployment and incarceration rising in tandem.

In this chapter we analyze the post-Rebellion years in Detroit, focusing on the activity of two radical groups that tried to subvert the power structure from below, the Black Panthers and the League of Revolutionary Black Workers, and on the corporate and political elites who attempted to navigate their way out of the crisis through a combination of repression, co-optation, and mythologization.

## The Scope of the Crisis

In the late 1960s the future of the American and, indeed, the global political-economic system was far from assured. The U.S. economy was stalling. Workers were taking to the streets. The Black Power movement was at its height, its most militant adherents calling for the black nation's secession from the white supremacist United States. Antiwar mobilizations were calling into question the imperialism that underpinned American domination. A counterculture movement was patently rejecting the value system that capitalists like Henry Ford had worked so hard to inculcate. During this time, elites and radicals both realized that things could not go on as they had. Their combative attempts to actualize their political visions helped to define this era of social turmoil and radical possibility. Before we examine how the capitalist class managed to gain the upper hand and escape this crisis, let us take a closer look at what, exactly, the crisis entailed.

Western capitalism's hegemony in the world system was under serious threat in the late 1960s from surging liberation movements in Cuba, Algeria, Poland, Vietnam, Mexico, Congo, South Africa, Palestine, Uruguay, Brazil, Jamaica, and Northern Ireland, among other places. In May 1968 "an assault on the culture and superstructure of late capitalism" was mounted across Europe, Japan, Mexico City, and Jamaica, as workers and students occupied universities, factories, and public squares.[7] The anti-imperialist movement had also become a formidable force within the United States. Hundreds of thousands of protesters marched on Washington, denouncing the war in Vietnam. Martin Luther King Jr., increasingly influenced by the socialist leader Eugene Debs, criticized the war in his famous "Beyond Vietnam" speech, in which he made the link between "poverty, racism and militarism." A couple of years later the

North Vietnamese government made the same connection, offering to release American prisoners of war if the United States released arrested Black Panthers. By then there was also an open revolt of U.S. ground troops in Vietnam against the war effort.[8]

In response to King's assassination in April 1968, there were uprisings in over one hundred U.S. cities. In Detroit thousands took to the streets in protest, and the National Guard was again called in to restore order. In 1969 there were major anti-establishment protests at three hundred U.S. universities, one-quarter of them involving strikes and building takeovers.[9]

This wave of mass discontent was particularly worrying for U.S. elites given that it was occurring just as U.S. companies were losing their dominance in the world market. In 1953, 30 percent of global exports came from U.S. producers; by 1966 (the first year in decades that the profit rate fell) that figure was just 16 percent. The United States soon faced its first postwar trade deficit and would have to go further and further into debt to finance the disastrous Vietnam War, as well as the social programs that working-class radicals were struggling for.[10]

It was in this contradictory, tumultuous historical moment that the League of Revolutionary Black Workers was born.

## The League of Revolutionary Black Workers

Exploitation and oppression are part of the same coin, part of that monster that is standing on our chest, and you can't eliminate one without the other. —JEROME SCOTT, "A Media Project with the League of Revolutionary Black Workers"

Labour cannot emancipate itself in the white skin where in the black it is branded. —KARL MARX, *Capital*

In the words of Manning Marable, "The League was in many respects the most significant expression of black radical thought and activism in the 1960s." While several book-length studies of the LRBW already exist, recent and ongoing efforts shed new light on this seminal organization. A recent oral history media project contains interviews with dozens of League members, and their stories force scholars and activists to reconsider the group's history.[11] Furthermore, Jerome Scott and Walda Katz-Fishman are in the process of publishing a book about the League, written in collaboration with many other former members.[12] All we aim to do here is situate some of this radical history within our broader narrative.

The *Inner City Voice* (*ICV*), "Detroit's Black Community Newspaper," printed an average of ten thousand copies per issue in its first year. The radical paper was edited by John Watson, a former member of Uhuru and the Student Nonviolent Coordinating Committee (SNCC). As Watson reported in an interview in 1968 with *Radical America*, "The people who created [*ICV*] were Marxist-Leninists, revolutionary socialists. . . . We have our office in a large building with our own coffee house and with our own school, teaching black history and now courses in Marxism-Leninism." Influenced by Lenin's pamphlet *Where to Begin?*, *ICV* attempted to build a newspaper that "organizes the division of labor among revolutionaries."[13]

When Watson was asked about his reaction to Black Power leader Stokely Carmichael's insistence that "socialism and communism was not for black people," he called the claim "bullshit": "To say socialism or communism is irrelevant is foolish and we oppose this. . . . When Stokely is attacking socialism he is attacking us. How can socialism be irrelevant? We don't understand that."[14]

Interest in a Marxist position grew as General Baker and other workers at the Dodge Main plant organized interest in *ICV*. Nine months after the army had evacuated Detroit, when Dodge attempted to speed up the production line, four thousand workers, led by a group of white women, shut down the plant in the first wildcat strike in over a decade. One major catalyst for the strike was the organizing of workers affiliated with *ICV*, who, after the strike, renamed themselves the Dodge Revolutionary Union Movement (DRUM). The strike, which cut Chrysler production by 1,900 automobiles, resulted in the firing of twenty-six workers.[15] The *Detroit Free Press* condemned the strike and described DRUM as "seeking to force Chrysler to adopt an employment policy of reverse Jim Crow. One of the leaders of the DRUM movement, fired by the illegal strike activity was General Baker . . . a Negro racist."[16]

Working-class support for the wildcat, however, forced Dodge to rehire the workers; almost immediately they led black workers in another three-day wildcat strike, again violating the union contract. The strikes mobilized support from black industrial workers across Detroit, whose numbers grew 21 percent between 1967 and 1969 as the Detroit Board of Commerce initiated a hiring campaign for minority workers as a concession to defuse the tensions that had exploded in the Great Rebellion. Inspired by DRUM, workers throughout the city and around the United States formed their own Revolutionary Union Movements—not only factory workers but also postal employees, newspaper workers, and other service workers.[17]

According to Luke Tripp, a DRUM organizer, while the consciousness of the young radicals had grown out of their involvement in civil rights protests, they spurned the integrationist character of the mainstream of the movement: "Most of us who were Black did not subscribe to the philosophy of nonviolence nor to the belief that racism and social inequality could be abolished within a capitalist system." Echoing the sentiments of C. L. R. James and James Boggs, Tripp writes, "We believed that organized Black workers, more than any other segment of our community, constituted the force with the greatest power to pressure the ruling capitalist class for social change." DRUM consciously positioned itself in opposition not only to the company and the union but to the black middle class and black political elites. Six months after the formation of DRUM, the National Urban League held a banquet in Detroit where they presented awards to Ford, GM, and Chrysler for their "pioneer efforts in furthering the concept of equal opportunity." Black workers showed up with picket signs to disrupt the gala, which they characterized as "the farce of the year." Earlier that week DRUM had organized a public rally to further their organizing efforts. Tripp recalls, "Prior to the rally, raffle tickets were sold. The selling of raffle tickets, in addition to providing money, served to inform community people about the struggle of Black workers. The first prize offered was a new M-1 Rifle, the second prize was a new shotgun, and the third prize was a bag of groceries."[18]

Within two years of the Great Rebellion, the city's various RUMs had led dozens of wildcat strikes and coalesced into the League of Revolutionary Black Workers, with a central staff of eighty and over one thousand members. The *Michigan Chronicle* noted at the time, "No matter what the actual number of DRUM members, many other black auto workers knew this mess for what it was and while they may not be DRUM members, they sure as hell support some of the DRUM goals."[19]

The disaffection of black workers from the union and from auto work in general was a direct result of the UAW's tactic since the Treaty of Detroit: negotiate for wage increases and fringe benefits and cede full control of the shop floor to the corporation. Despite the production boom of the 1960s, when "jobs were more plentiful than at any time since World War II," auto work was so dangerous and degrading that, as in the years before Ford's Five Dollar Day, worker turnover was tremendous: throughout the 1960s the majority of unskilled new hires quit within one year. Between 1960 and 1965 the auto industry had to hire over 1.5 million workers to fill just 250,000 jobs. Worker absenteeism was at 5 percent during the decade, double the rate of the 1950s, and climbed as high as 20 percent in some factories on Mondays and Fridays. This coincided with a generation shift among workers, with the old guard who had participated in the historic sit-down strikes of the 1930s and lived through the Depression replaced by younger workers with little experience in unions. All this contributed to a state of affairs in which "factory workers in general, and Detroit's in particular, were becoming increasingly unhappy with their jobs." In addition to absenteeism, disciplinary issues were rife in the auto plants, with young workers increasingly defiant toward factory discipline and the monotony of their jobs.[20]

The racist policies of corporations, and of the UAW, also catalyzed support for the League. Despite its ostensibly progressive record on racial issues, the UAW had marginalized black workers to the extent that its acronym took on a new meaning for many: "You Ain't White."[21] The League repeatedly took the UAW to task for its failure to protect the lives and livelihoods of black workers. These criticisms were often unsparing: in an *ICV* edition published days after Walter Reuther's death in a plane crash, the League characterized the former UAW president as a "reactionary conservative leader" and a "friend of the auto barons" who failed to raise "any struggle against the racism that existed in his own union or in the plants where Blacks constituted a majority."[22] According to LRBW member Jerome Scott, the League's militant stance "humiliated" UAW higher-ups, who thought of themselves as progressives.[23]

To contextualize the League's harsh denunciations of the UAW, one need only look at conditions inside the plants. A big reason for the League's support among even moderate black workers was the UAW's refusal to challenge the Big Three over the horrendous safety conditions in Detroit's auto plants. After the Treaty of Detroit in 1958, a chilling dialectic took effect: worker productivity soared in concert with workplace accidents. Reported accidents increased 30 percent between 1958 and 1970.[24] A 1973 report found that *significantly more people died each year inside U.S. factories than on the battle-fields in Vietnam.* The report "estimated 65 on-the-job deaths per day among auto workers, for a total of some 16,000 annually. Approximately half of these deaths were from heart attacks. There were also 63,000 cases of disabling diseases and about 1,700,000 cases of lost or impaired hearing. These statistics did not include many long-term illnesses endemic to foundry workers and others exposed to poisonous chemicals and gases, nor did they include deaths and injuries made by accident."[25] These 16,000 deaths pale in comparison to the toll of industrial diseases, which the Public Health Service estimated took 100,000 lives each year. Foundry workers, machinists, and coarse-metal finishers had a significantly greater chance of having fatal heart disease and lung disease than other workers. These were the jobs that Detroit's black workers were primarily assigned.[26]

Indeed black workers bore the brunt of exploitation during this time. According to Tripp, "Generally, as the proportion of Black workers grew in the factory, the working conditions tended to deteriorate. Tasks that had been performed by two White workers were assigned to one Black worker. Black workers characterized this as niggermation."[27]

The factory with the most League membership was Chrysler's Eldon plant, where 70 percent of the workforce was black and the majority of the work was "machining metal parts." Among the four thousand workers at the plant, three thousand injuries occurred each year that were serious enough to warrant examination by workmen's compensation lawyers.[28] On May 26, 1970, Gary Thompson, a black twenty-two-year-old Vietnam veteran was killed when his jitney overturned and crushed him. Less than two weeks earlier, Mamie Williams, a fifty-one-year-old woman, despite being ordered to stay home by her doctor, was told to return to work or risk being fired and losing all the benefits she'd gained from twenty-six years of employment at Chrysler; the next week she passed out on the line and died shortly thereafter.[29] Two months later, on July 15, James Johnson, a black worker, came to work and killed two foremen and a machine operator. He was represented in court by the League's cofounder Kenneth Cockrel, who went on the offensive, declaring, "We'll have to put Chrysler on trial for damages to this man caused by his working conditions."[30] Cockrel then took the jury to Eldon to see the inhumane conditions under which Johnson had spent years laboring. The jury ruled that the work conditions were so awful that they had caused Johnson to suffer the psychological breakdown that led him to kill the three men; Johnson was sent to a state hospital, and Chrysler was ordered to pay him $75 in benefits every week.[31]

The League situated its critique of these conditions within the broader economic context. From the end of the war to 1969, "wages had increased by 25 percent, while profits went up 77 percent, dividends 60 percent, personal corporate incomes 80 percent, and undistributed corporate profits 93 percent."[32] While the exploitation of black workers stood out, the LRBW understood that their condition could not be separated from the class dynamics of capitalism. Jerome Scott has summed up the League's position on the relationship between racism and class exploitation:

> There was a high level of racial discrimination in the plant and [LRBW members] recognized that. But that wasn't the motivating force. The motivating force was more of a mixture of, "Alright, they treat us like dogs. But not just because we're black. They're treating these white folks like dogs, too." They put us in the worst jobs, so we understand that they have this racial overtone. But the real content is that they're making a ton of money off of us. And that exploitation is true for us and it's true for everybody else that works in this plant.[33]

Another LRBW member, Leah Rogers, insists, "It wasn't just a black thing, even though the name of the organization was the League of Revolutionary Black Workers. It had to be involved with coalescing with people across national lines or racial lines." The role of white Detroiters in the Great Rebellion had convinced many within the League that white workers could participate in the revolutionary struggle.[34] The League's legal team was multiracial, and the League's activism put them in contact with a number of radical organizations. As Mike Hamlin, a member of the League's Executive Committee, recalls, Detroit was at the vanguard of revolutionary activity in the late 1960s and early 1970s: "Everyone who was a leftist came to Detroit because we were drawing workers to Marxism." A list of white-led organizations that worked alongside the League in Detroit includes the International Socialists, Students for a Democratic Society, the Revolutionary Communist Party, the Socialist Workers Party, the white-led United National Caucus (which had formed within the UAW to challenge the union's racist and pro-business policies), People Against Racism, Fredy Perlman's Detroit printing cooperative, and the Motor City Labor League (which was instrumental in getting the Marxist lawyer Chuck Ravitz elected as the judge of Detroit's Recorders Court in 1972), among others. These groups were active inside Detroit's factories or on Wayne State's campus, many with their own newspapers.[35] According to John Williams, also a member of the Executive Committee, the League's position in relation to these groups was that "the black worker in and of itself played a pivotal role, and Marx spoke to [that role] when he told the white workers, 'yeah, there's nothing you can do as long as your black worker is in chains.'"[36] Attempts at racial solidarity saw mixed results and were undoubtedly complicated by the ascendancy of white supremacist groups throughout Detroit in the post-Rebellion years: the neo-Nazi group Breakthrough, for instance, set up a picket line at Grosse Pointe High School to protest a speech there by King in July 1967.[37]

The reactionary potential of white workers was of course apparent in the late 1960s in Detroit, and across the country, as politicians stoked racial fears and mobilized nativist sentiments among the white electorate. In the 1968 Democratic Primary in Michigan, the far-right, openly racist candidate George Wallace received the most votes, running, as John Watson put it, on a "populist, fascist" campaign that portrayed bankers and fat cats "in an alliance with the niggers" against white workers.[38] Nevertheless, while the League's program was based on the principle that blacks were the vanguard, and black workers the "vanguard within the vanguard," of the struggle against capitalism, they remained committed to the elimination of oppression and exploitation among the working class as a whole.

The League's efforts were not limited to struggles inside the factory. The Black Student United Front, formed under the tutelage of the League, used tactics such as walkouts and building occupations to fight a school system they viewed as illegitimate. In one memorable action, 150,000 Detroit students "made Malcolm X's birthday a holiday by conducting a successful walkout." Furthermore, many of the League's female activists were formerly active in the West Central Organization, which organized Detroit neighborhoods targeted for urban renewal. Sheila Murphy Cockrel remembers that the Organization "took on issues like land use policies, how landlords took care of rental property, police-community relations—that whole set of local, daily-life issues."[39] Women activists were instrumental in shifting the League's energy and resources to these community struggles. Marian Kramer of the League recalls, "One faction said that the focus should be in the plants, at the point of production. I said, 'Yes, but all those men got to come back into the community; they live somewhere. We've got to be organizing both places.'"[40] Women also fought against the male supremacist attitudes prevalent among men in the League. They formed the Black Women's Committee to organize the wives of men fired for wildcat strikes and combat male dominance in League leadership. In Ilene Baker's words, the women were initially seen as "handmaids." However, Kramer insists, although they were frequently "shit upon," women eventually emerged from their "second class status" within the League to become leaders of the organization.[41]

The League was able to publicize its multifaceted struggles by creating a broad communications network. As Chris Robé has pointed out, due to innovations like offset printing, which "allowed for easy and cheap printing[,] . . . 1967 to 1973 marks the explosion of the underground press within the United States."[42] The League was at the cutting edge of this trend, operating its own bookshop and printing shop. In addition, John Watson was elected editor of Wayne State University's newspaper, the *South End*, which had a daily distribution estimated at eighteen thousand. The direction the *South End* took under Watson is evident from the masthead he adopted for the paper: "One class-conscious worker is worth 100 students." Struggles on Wayne State's campus soon resulted in the creation of the Black Studies Center in 1970 at Wayne State University.[43]

In 1969 James Forman, formerly of SNCC and the Black Panthers, joined the League. Money from his "Black Manifesto"—which called on religious organizations to give reparations to "support things like a Black publishing company, a Black workers' strike fund and a land bank"—helped finance the League's 1970 film, *Finally Got the News*.[44] In the film, a collaboration between the League and a white film collective, Newsreel, Kenneth Cockrel delivers an eloquent and devastating critique of capitalist exploitation and imperialism, which, as it captures the tenor and force of the League's ideological orientation, is worth quoting at length:

[Capitalists] give you little bullshit amounts of money for working—wages and so forth—and then they steal all that shit back from you, in terms of the way he got his other thing set up, his whole credit gimmick society, man—consumer credit: buy shit, buy shit on credit. He gives you a little bit of shit to cool your ass out, and then steals all that shit back, with shit called *interest*: the price of money. Motherfuckers are non-producing, non-existing . . . motherfuckers who deal with paper. There's a cat who will stand up and say to you he's in "mining." And he sits in an office, man, on the 199th floor in some motherfucking building on Wall Street, and he's in "mining." And he has papers, certificates, which are embroidered and shit, you know, stocks, bonds, debentures, obligations, you know. He's in "mining." And he's sitting up on Wall Street and his fingernails ain't been dirty in his motherfucking life. He went to Phillips Andover or Exeter. He went to Harvard, he went to Yale, he went to the Wharton School of Business, and he's in "mining"? And the motherfuckers who deal with intangibles are the motherfuckers who are rewarded in this society. The more abstract and intangible your shit is, i.e. stocks—what is a stock? A stock certificate is evidence of ownership in something that's real. *Ownership*. He owns and controls and therefore receives, you know, the "benefit from." That's what they call profit. He fucking with stuff in Bolivia, he fucking with shit in Chile. He's Kennecott. He's Anaconda. He's United Fruit. He's in "mining." He's in what? He ain't never in his life produced shit. Investment bankers, stockbrokers, insurance men—it's motherfuckers who don't do nothing.

At the time of the film, despite decades of automation and capital flight, black industrial workers were still central to the engine of capital accumulation. In 1970, though the Big Three's market share was declining, General Motors, Ford, and Chrysler were each among the world's five largest manufacturing companies. By 1968 black workers constituted a majority in the production departments of these megacompanies.[45] The Eldon Avenue plant *produced all of Chrysler's axles*, so shutting down Eldon was tantamount to shutting down Chrysler's operations.[46] The strategic position of black workers in the production process was the basis for Watson's claim in *Finally Got the News*: "There are certain groups which could just stop work tomorrow, and it might cause some kind of minor disruption in terms of the overall running of the society. But there are certain other groups, that if they stopped working tomorrow, the whole system is going to cease to function."

Although *Finally Got the News* never achieved a wide release in the United States, it did help to spread the League's message to an international audience. The film was released just as the "hot autumn" of industrial strikes in Italy was coming to an end, and Watson was invited to lecture to workers there and to introduce *Finally Got the News* at the Pesaro Film Festival to.[47]

But while the film allowed the League to spread its ideological vision, the production of *Finally Got the News* also brought to light key contradictions within the organization. In keeping with its Leninist approach, the League's Executive Committee dealt with the organization's strategic concerns. Only two of the seven members of the Committee, however, were factory workers or organizers, and none of them were women. This hierarchical structure allowed the Committee to become somewhat alienated from the rank and file. Many of the college-educated members on the Committee thought it vital to engage in an ideological campaign to popularize and justify League tactics. Leaders like Watson and Cockrel saw the film as a tool of propaganda that would facilitate the creation of a nationwide organization, Black Workers Congress (BWC), which they felt was necessary to more effectively combat the national corporations they were challenging. Toward this end, Black Star Productions was formed under Watson to create further films. But as Dan Georgakas pointed out at the time, many rank-and-file members "were concerned with the kinds of problems the [Black] Panthers had encountered in trying to expand nationally. The unifying factor was a feeling that there should be more factory work and less media activity."[48] These and other tensions would eventually hasten the decline of the League.

## Repression and the Collapse of the League

They are applying a sticks and carrots policy on us. First they beat us with sticks . . . and then with carrots. —SERBIAN APHORISM

In a *South End* article from 1969, Luke Tripp, a member of the League's Executive Committee, characterized elites' response to League activism as "the honky's carrot and stick policy": "with one hand" elites promoted advancement opportunities for individual African Americans, while "the other hand threatens the community with the stick (the police force)."[49]

In terms of the carrot, the LRBW lost momentum precisely because of the reforms it won within the factories and the UAW. Executive Committee member

General Baker suggests, "The UAW and Chrysler Corporation had made some fundamental changes to try to alleviate the contradictions we'd talked about, but they'd never give us credit for it. Chrysler created an urban affairs department. . . . Walter Reuther came and offered to help us take over Local 3. Minorities began to get elected in local plants. There was a new Black vice-president at Dodge Main. They upgraded a lot more Blacks in staff positions."[50]

David Goldberg has shown that activists in the struggle for tenants' rights were similarly co-opted and integrated into the "power structure." These struggles were particularly acute in units owned by the Goodman Brothers, the city's most infamous slumlords. According to the *Inner City Voice*, Goodman Bros. units "are overpopulated with gigantic rats, cinches (bed bugs) and roaches."[51] With help from the West Central Organization and activists in the League, the United Tenants for Collective Action (UTCA) organized tenants' councils and rent strikes in six Goodman Bros. properties. Goodman soon decided that it would be too costly to make the repairs that tenants were demanding, and so they "agreed to turn over to the UTCA the management and control of seventeen of [their] apartment buildings, most of them in the 12th Street area." Goodman stipulated that they would still earn 25 percent of the units' income. The League's General Baker and Marian Kramer suggested UTCA reject the deal, arguing that Goodman would still profit while activists did all the day-to-day work to maintain and improve the apartments. Nonetheless UTCA leaders agreed to the deal, seeing it as an opportunity to gain the local ownership integral to Black Power politics. But as Goldberg notes, the UTCA struggled to maintain its contradictory position as both landlords and tenants' rights organizers, especially as the government funds that the organization relied on dried up. As a result, the organization "quickly sought to turn a profit to satisfy lenders, all but abandoning its political activism and grassroots origins."[52]

Where the carrot was not enough, the stick was always poised to strike. Many of the League's most successful organizers were fired from Detroit's plants because of their role in organizing strikes. Even more effective in disciplining the organization was the police. As Cockrel puts it in *Finally Got the News*, "When Chrysler is attacked . . . it pushes a buzzer and gets the Hamtramck Police Department. The whole city structure goes into action. At Ford, you are dealing with Dearborn. The fact that we closed down Dodge Main, the basic assembly plant for Chrysler operations in this entire country, means we got a response. We got police. We got injunctions from the courts." A familiar mythology, one that portrayed the radical workers as criminals and communist extremists, legitimated this repression. After the first DRUM strikes, the international office of the UAW sent a letter to all UAW members describing the

League as the "voice of a worldwide propaganda network" and claiming that "Negro members are too intelligent to permit themselves to be used as pawns by an outside group of extremists who want to divide us and create chaos." Emil Mazey, a social-democratic leader of the UAW, "gave an interview to the press describing the League as a 'black peril' which was worse than the 'red peril' of the 1930s." With the full support of the *Free Press*, Chrysler obtained an injunction illegalizing DRUM protests in front of the Dodge Main plant.[53]

The League also faced repression in its struggles outside the plants. In 1969 Wayne State University went so far as to suspend operations of the *South End* until Watson was removed as editor. Even Reuther took part in the campaign to remove Watson.[54] Moreover, in response to the student militancy spearheaded by the League's Black Student United Front, Judge James Lincoln instituted more punitive measures in his court. As the *sole* judge in Detroit's juvenile court, Lincoln was an influential figure in the criminal justice system, handling nearly 1 percent of the *nation*'s delinquency and neglect cases between 1960 and 1977 and becoming president of the National Council of Juvenile Court Judges in 1971. In 1968 he "issued a memorandum calling for the arrest of juveniles found loitering around schools."[55] By 1969 police officers were permanently stationed in the city's high schools.[56] As Michael Stauch Jr. has written in his dissertation on Detroit's punitive turn, "with the onset of militant, collective struggles led by African American youth in Northern cities, juvenile delinquency became increasingly racialized. Juvenile penology, in turn, lost the thrust to treat young people as 'maladjusted' individuals, and began to see them as 'case-hardened' criminals acting en masse as gangs."[57]

The League and its affiliates may have had more resources to withstand this multifaceted repression had it won any of its union elections against the UAW, but in elections at Dodge Main and Eldon, the police, the company, and the UAW national headquarters worked in concert to rig the votes against the League's popular candidates: at the request of the UAW, the union's ballot boxes were held overnight in police stations.[58] True, the League had alienated many workers with its denunciations of "Polish Pigs" and "Peckerwood Honkies," as well as its characterizations of the UAW and TULC as "Uncle Tom's Cabin." But it seems that, in a fair election, the League would have had enough support to beat the UAW in at least a couple of plants.[59]

After these losses, however, the League lacked the financial resources to provide for workers fired for strike activities, as well as to deal with pressure from the criminal justice system. Some of this pressure was strictly financial: cars that had bumper stickers supporting the League were constantly being ticketed. Other forms of pressure were more violent. As Cockrel put it, "They tried to destroy our organization. They tried to kill leaders like General Baker and Chuck Wooten. Most all of the members of our central staff had to go to trial sometime in the year of 1969."[60] Baker recalls that the League was "under such harassment and intimidation by the police, FBI, Internal Revenue Service, that personally I never did think we were going to live very long. We had too many close calls. Fred Lyles . . . was head of the United Tenants Union and was shot and paralyzed right after the Dodge strike. We thought the shot basically was aimed for me. . . . You didn't sleep the same place most nights. You just tried to build whatever organizational strength you could and educate as many workers as you could to try to keep the struggle on course."[61]

This pressure intensified conflicts about the Executive Committee's decision to spend money on films and speaking tours. Initially the Committee responded to criticisms by purging dissident members, but things eventually came to a head at a heated meeting between the Executive Committee and the rank and file.[62] According to Jerome Scott, FBI infiltrators intensified these tensions at the meeting, which ended in the collapse of the League.[63]

One group split off to join the Black Workers Congress, which never became more than "a scheme for possible unification, a promise without fulfillment." The majority of the rank and file, however, "retreated" into political education. Marian Kramer suggests, "The split was a good thing for us, because it made us understand that we needed an education to go to the next level. We had just about won every reform in the factory that had to be won."[64] These members embarked on more than a year of daily study of Marxist texts. Alonzo Chandler remembers, "The basic thing that we grasped out of that educational period, whether we were studying Lenin or Mao-Tse-Tung or Marx or whatever . . . was the deep-rootedness of economics in all of this . . . economics based on a money system that doesn't just use money as a means of exchange, but uses money to manipulate people."[65] These workers eventually merged with the California-based Communist League, a multiracial organization that catalyzed wildcat strikes throughout the early and mid-1970s.[66] When these activists led a wildcat strike in 1973 at Ford's Mack Avenue plant, the police and the UAW's own "goon squad" teamed up to violently break the strike. Afterward a police officer told UAW officials, "I'm glad we're on the same side."[67]

The League was also undercut by capital's increasing capacity to relocate away from militant workers. Following the production boom of the early 1960s, manufacturing employment in Detroit decreased 27 percent between 1967 and 1977. The recalcitrance of workers in the face of automation and dangerous working conditions was a major factor in this process. Nationally there were 5,200 strikes per year between 1967 and 1974, making this period "the most sustained period of wildcat strikes in history." In 1968 the number of strikes in Michigan's industries set a postwar record, and in 1970 "strike-related production losses . . . surpassed anything in Michigan's history." As one League worker at the Eldon plant put it, "[Chrysler will] have to move the factory or let us have it." Corporations generally chose the former response.[68]

## Detroit's Black Panther Party

While some folks might think it was nonviolent marching and singing that spurred the integration of the big city police departments, those of us who were there know that it was the white cops' fear of getting shot. —TONY NORMAN of Detroit's Black Panther Party for Self-Defense, quoted in Rahman, "Marching Blind," 2009

*This section is dedicated to the late Ahmad A. Rahman: revolutionary, political prisoner, and educator.*

Whereas in most cities across the United States the Black Panther Party for Self-Defense (BPP) was the most prominent black Marxist organization, in Detroit this was not the case, as the League dominated the city's leftist scene during the late 1960s and early 1970s. As Jerome Scott recalls, the League placed some of its members into the Panthers' ranks to keep tabs on the group. Both groups wanted to create a "black Bolshevik" vanguard party, but they clashed on the question of tactics. At the 1970 antirepression conference in Detroit, Cockrel criticized the Panthers for supporting reckless tactics like fighting the police and then having to spend all their resources on court battles. A bigger source of contention, James Geschwender writes, was that many in the League "believed that the Oakland-based Black Panther Party was moving in the wrong direction by concentrating on organizing lumpen elements of the Black community. The League did not believe that a successful movement could be based upon the lumpen, as they lacked a potential source of power. The League believed that Black workers were the most promising base for a successful Black movement because of the potential power derived from the ability to disrupt industrial production."[69]

Whatever one thinks of these criticisms, it cannot be denied that the Panthers were seminal in their willingness to organize the criminalized "surplus population"—in Marxist terminology, the "lumpenproletariat." Leftists had long recognized that crime and criminalization were political-economic symptoms, but they were not willing or able to organize the criminalized population into a potent political force. The first group to do so was the Nation of Islam, a black nationalist group founded in Detroit during the Great Depression.

While serving a stint in a federal penitentiary in 1945 for resisting the draft, Nation leader Elijah Muhammad realized that mainstream civil rights organizations "had no programs to recruit and to transform the most oppressed members of the race: convicts, dope addicts, pimps, young delinquents, prostitutes, criminals, and the permanently unemployed." After shifting its efforts to these groups in the postwar period, the Nation experienced a dramatic upsurge in membership, from a low of about 1,000 in 1945 to between 65,000 and 100,000 in 1960. In 1957 four thousand people filled Detroit's Temple of Islam to listen to an address by Malcolm X, which included a call for the "little man in the street . . . to take matters into his own hands."[70]

The Black Panther Party attempted to organize these same strata into a revolutionary force. As BPP cofounder Bobby Seale wrote, "Marx and Lenin would probably turn over in their graves if they could see the lumpen proletariat Afro-Americans putting together the ideology of the Black Panther Party. Both Marx and Engels used to say that the lumpen proletariat wouldn't do anything for the revolution. But today, in a modern technological society, with the CIA, FBI, electronic surveillance and cops armed and equipped for overkill, here are black Americans demanding our constitutional rights, and demanding that our basic desires and needs be fulfilled, thus becoming the vanguard of the revolution, despite all attempts to totally wipe us out."[71]

The Panthers issued a ten-point list that included, among other things, a program for combating poverty, racism, militarism, and police violence. Point 7 states: "We believe we can end police brutality in our black community by organizing black self-defense groups that are dedicated to defending our black community from racist police oppression and brutality." This resonated with working-class blacks throughout urban America, who had been subjected to police brutality and repression in their communities for years as the state attempted to mythologize political-economic issues as problems of "criminality."[72]

The Panthers became famous for their armed confrontations with the police. But state repression soon caused the group to shift to a strategy of "community control" centered on "survival programs": "The Free Breakfast Program, the People's Free Food Program, The Intercommunal Youth Institute, the Legal Aid Education Program, the Free Busing to Prisons Program, the Free Commissary for Prisoners Program, the People's Free Shoe Program, the People's Free Clothing Program, the People's Free Medical Research Health Clinic, the People's Sickle Cell Anemia Research Foundation, the People's Free Ambulance Service, the People's Free Dental Program, the People's Free Optometry Program, the People's Free Plumbing and Maintenance Program, and the Community Housing Program."[73]

These community programs were well received by working people of all races in Detroit and across the country. As Panther leader Carlton Yearwood said, "When we provide free breakfasts for poor kids, we provide them for poor whites and poor blacks."[74] Like the League, the BPP developed a willingness to collaborate with radical white organizations. BPP leader Kathleen Cleaver saw the Panthers as "the vector of communication between the most important vortexes of black and white radicalism in America."[75]

In May 1968, the same month as the DRUM wildcat at Dodge Main, the Detroit chapter of the Black Panther Party was officially born. In addition to combating police, by 1969 the BPP operated a free health clinic, offered a free rodent extermination service, and was serving free breakfast to Detroit children at three locations, two on the city's West Side and one on the East Side.[76] The Panthers' plan was to emphasize nonviolent aspects of their program in the hopes of winning community support and avoiding the police repression that had been visited upon Panther chapters throughout the country. State violence, however, proved able to quash even these efforts.[77]

## Repression of the Black Panther Party

The universal appeal of the Panthers' community programs was what most worried FBI director J. Edgar Hoover, who oversaw the Bureau's Counterintelligence Program (COINTELPRO). The program began in 1956, with a plan to "increase factionalism, cause disruption and win defections" inside the Communist Party USA, whose membership declined from eighty-five thousand in 1942 to fewer than three thousand by the late 1960s. According to the 1975 Congressional Church Committee, throughout the 1960s and early 1970s, the government launched "a secret war against those citizens it consider[ed] threats to the established order."[78] During the 1960s COINTELPRO took aim at the student New Left, the Socialist Workers Party, Martin Luther King Jr., and Black Power radicals. By the end of the decade the program's main goal was preventing the rise of a revolutionary black movement. The primary target became the Panthers, a group that Hoover declared to be the "greatest threat to the internal security of the country" in 1969. The FBI launched 233 operations against the Panthers, including raids, infiltration, and assassinations of BPP leaders.[79]

The government treated *all* aspects of BPP's operations as security threats, even the Breakfast for Children program, as a memo that Hoover wrote to an FBI operative on June 1969 reveals:

One of our primary aims in counterintelligence as it concerns the [Black Panther Party] is to keep this group isolated from the moderate black and white community which may support it. This is most emphatically pointed out in their Breakfast for Children Program, where they are actively soliciting and receiving support from uninformed whites and moderate blacks. . . . You state that the Bureau under the [Counterintelligence Program] should not attack programs of community interest such as the [Black Panther Party] "Breakfast for Children." You state this because many prominent "humanitarians," both white and black, are interested in the program as well as churches which are actively supporting it. You have obviously missed the point.[80]

In the ensuing months, the FBI distributed leaflets in communities warning that the BPP's breakfast programs were serving "poisoned food" to children. On September 8, 1969, police raided the Breakfast for Children program in Watts, California. In Detroit, the FBI went to absurd ends to sabotage the Party's newspaper, the *Black Panther*, the sales of which helped fund Party operations. According to an FBI memo, in 1970 Detroit FBI agents doused a shipment of the newspaper with "a solution capable of duplicating a scent of the most foul smelling feces available."[81] The execution of this mission rendered thousands of newspapers "unsaleable." This is not the only tactic police used to undermine the *Black Panther*, a newspaper with a weekly circulation of 139,000 in 1970 that consistently called police officers "Pigs" and documented incidents of police brutality in Detroit. According to Rahman:

> The *Black Panther* had become an increasingly ubiquitous symbol of black power's transgression of place, and the police department worked daily to disrupt its sales. Numerous Panthers and community workers selling the paper reported being stopped, arrested, beaten, and charged with either assaulting the officers who beat them or resisting arrest. One legal investigator noted on August 10, 1970, "17 year old [Black Panther] girl was ticketed for littering, witnesses said melee ensued & girl hit with blackjack." On August 25, 1970, Patrolmen Caldwell "bust[ed five] newspaper salesmen on Woodward & State for interfering with pedestrian traffic. . . . A woman tried to help & was beaten by Ptr. Colbert." By October, police had issued twenty-four tickets to paper-selling Panthers for "impeding the pedestrian flow of traffic" on just one Detroit Street.[82]

Armed confrontations were increasingly commonplace as Detroiters attempted to counter police violence. In spring 1969 the Republic of New Afrika, a black Nationalist group leading a campaign for $400 billion in reparations from the U.S. government, hosted a meeting at New Bethel Church in Detroit. Police presence outside the meeting was heavy, and as Republic members filed out of the church, a shootout ensued in which one officer was killed, another was injured, and four Republic members were wounded. The police proceeded to arrest 142 people in the church, including many children, for murder.[83] In another legal victory that proved disturbing to both liberal and conservative elites, the League's Kenneth Cockrel successfully defended and won acquittal for the two black activists who were charged with the police killings. In court, the Marxist lawyer acknowledged that the defendants killed the officers, but he attacked the legitimacy of the police, which he painted as a corrupt, racist organization that functioned as a tool of oppression.[84] As in the trial of James Johnson, Cockrel's ability to go from the defensive to the offensive—in the first case, putting Chrysler on trial, and in the second, putting the whole system of criminal justice on trial—demonstrated the willingness of working-class Detroiters to accommodate a structural critique of capitalist social relations rather than capitulate to mythological thinking.[85] This was further proven by the election of Cockrel's law partner Justin "Chuck" Ravitz as judge of Detroit's criminal court in 1972, largely thanks to the groundswell of public support generated through these high-profile cases. At the time the openly Marxist Ravitz was called the "first radical judge in the U.S." by the *New York Times*.[86]

Where mythologies failed to take hold, however, the state's punitive arm was there to administer the necessary repression. The police used the New Bethel incident as a pretext to raid and destroy the BPP headquarters. A few weeks later more BPP members were arrested, some on the charge of robbing a prostitute whom the police had observed donating her money to the Panthers, others on the charge of robbing local black businesses, many of whom had likewise donated to the BPP and actively denied the police's charges. All charges were dropped, but not before much of the BPP's time and money were tied up in court proceedings.[87] Across the nation, police harassment was a constant theme, as "police used petty laws, like unlawful use of bullhorn or loitering, to harass the Panthers."[88] The many arrests drained the Panthers' resources: between 1968 and 1969, 739 members were arrested, at a cost of $4.9 million in bail.[89]

In the summer of 1969 someone shot a bullet through the head of nineteen-year-old Michael Baynham during a BPP meeting and fled before anyone could confirm who had done it. The *Free Press* did not report on the incident; the police immediately labeled the death a suicide and closed the case. BPP leaders understood that the group had been infiltrated, as this death was no anomaly:

state authorities killed twenty-seven BPP members during 1969 alone. This number included Fred Hampton, chairman of the Party's chapter in Chicago. In a planned assassination, state operatives drugged Hampton then shot him in the head while he slept next to his pregnant partner.[90]

By this time, Geronimo Pratt, the BPP's deputy minister of defense and a decorated veteran of the Vietnam War, had organized the Panthers into a formidable force, with military capacities that included sandbag fortifications, underground tunnels, and sizable arms caches. It proved difficult for local police departments to overpower the Panthers, and this led to the first-ever SWAT raid, in 1969, which targeted the BPP's LA headquarters. During this four-hour shootout, police fired five thousand rounds of ammunition and prepared to detonate dynamite on the roof. Internal memos reveal that the FBI intended to "neutralize Pratt as an effective BPP functionary." In 1970 he was arrested on trumped-up murder charges. Like so many others during this time, Pratt became a political prisoner, serving twenty-seven years behind bars, eight of which were spent in solitary confinement, before the charges were vacated.[91]

At the same time, the widespread implementation of "stop-and-frisk" tactics gave police officers the discretion to harass any and all street-level political activity. In the words of one member of the Detroit chapter of the Black Panther Party, these tactics allowed the Panthers to become the police's "punching bags."[92]

As state repression accelerated, in Detroit and elsewhere, efforts to check this violence through legal means were blocked. In Detroit the police successfully resisted activists' attempts to institute a citizen review board. The leader of Detroit's Police Officers' Association said that all critics of police were "part of a nefarious plot by those who would like our form of government overthrown." In May 1970 the *Free Press* reported that the Detroit chapter of the NAACP had filed twenty-four separate charges of police brutality against the Black Panthers; each of these charges was subsequently dismissed.[93] All this made it clear to Detroit Panthers that the legal system would not protect them from the police. And so, after BPP leader Malik McClure's mother's home was raided, the underground military wing of the BPP, led by several soldiers recently back from Vietnam, accelerated its operations.[94]

In the summer of 1970 a black teenager was shot in the *back of the head* by a police officer. The officer claimed the boy attacked him with a broomstick, and he faced no criminal investigation. In response, BPP member Lawrence White attacked and wounded two police officers. The police then raided White's home, and a ten-hour shootout ensued. When White, a former marine, finally surrendered, DPD officers "nearly beat him to death."[95]

On October 24 tensions rose even higher when a police officer assaulted a salesman of the *Black Panther*. A fight broke out in which a Panther killed a black police officer. According to the *Free Press*, that night paramilitary officers laid "siege" to BPP headquarters: one hundred officers in armored personnel carriers swarmed the address and initiated a shootout. This firefight lasted nineteen hours. As Judge Ravitz put it, "This could have been the showdown—a holocaust. It could have been 1967 again, and more." But largely thanks to Nadine Brown of the *Michigan Chronicle*, an activist who mediated the conflict, fifteen BPP members eventually surrendered without losing their lives. All fifteen were charged with murder and conspiracy to murder. Each was eventually acquitted of all charges, but, as was the case with the League, the legal fees and the time and energy required to wage battles in court drained the Panthers.[96]

By the early 1970s state repression had led to the Panthers' undoing. The arrests that these operations produced, the deaths they caused, the mistrust and paranoia that pervaded the organization because of widespread infiltration and use of informants, the intraparty divisions insidiously fomented by Hoover and his staff—all this led to the Panthers' collapse.[97]

### The Dialectic of Repression and Integration

The decline of the League and the BPP occurred in the context of the decline of myriad other movements of the time: the Black Power struggle, the antiwar movement, student rebellions, and anticolonial struggles, among others.[98] In particular, the internal divisions that eventually contributed to the dissolution of the League are indicative of larger trends within black political development in the late 1960s and early 1970s. The similarities and differences between the problems of the League and those of other organizations shed light on the transformation in black radicalism during a time of increasing incorporation of blacks into the American political apparatus in the aftermath of the civil rights reforms of the mid-1960s.

The efflorescence of Black Power lasted from 1966 to 1974. This period witnessed various and wide-ranging attempts to harness and weld together the myriad forces of black political life—the grassroots energy of the black populace, the organizational skills and national esteem of old guard civil rights leaders, the militancy of young activists, the influence of the growing class of black politicians, along with artists and intellectuals—into a movement capable of defining and implementing a political program for black people. These efforts resulted in several national Black Power conferences and black political conventions, produced various attempts to create an independent black political party, contributed to the election of black public officials across the country, and led to historic protests against international imperialism. Affirmations of black cultural values and attempts to ameliorate the specific problems faced by black people served as a powerful salve against racial discrimination and marginalization, and for many the new black political class represented an unprecedented embodiment of the public will in the country's highest institutions.

Many of these initiatives were also stymied by the drive for racial unity in the face of ideological diversity. While many in these movements recognized the reality of contradictions and variance among black people, the predominant reasoning held that these differences should be subordinated to ethnic unification. The League's avowedly interracial, class-oriented political program was a notable departure from this prevailing tendency of Black Power discourse, particularly from "the momentary hegemony of nationalist activists within early seventies black political culture," which called on blacks to "close ranks" and deal with their internal debates "behind closed doors." According to Cedric Johnson, this "repressive tendency . . . hinders the development of open, principled debate," and such a framework essentially shuttled black political development into the familiar framework of ethnic pluralist politics. According to this framework, which often relied on a misreading of American political history, white ethnic political incorporation had occurred thanks to the strength of ethnic solidarity.[99]

In the eyes of Dr. Nathaniel Wright Jr., chairman of the 1967 Black Power conference in Newark, New Jersey, "Black Power was essentially the fulfillment of the deferred process of black assimilation into American political, cultural, and economic institutions."[100] In the context of black politics in the postsegregation era, the drive for racial unity led to the idea of a singular black political subject, which allowed newly incorporated black politicians to claim to represent the authentic will of the black masses and use their authority in that capacity to implement policies which were often detrimental to their working-class black constituencies.

Between 1964 and 1971 the number of elected black officials increased from 100 to 1,860.[101] By 1974 there were 104 black mayors, many of them elected in cities that had just experienced rebellions.[102] This occurred alongside a dramatic uptick of government employment for black college graduates, which allowed many middle-class blacks to find employment even as the industrial economy stagnated: "By 1970 the government employed 57 percent of all black male college graduates, and 72 percent of all black female college graduates." Many of the newly elected officials deployed progressive-sounding rhetoric but advanced economic programs that mostly benefited their middle- and upper-class constituents. As Johnson has written, "Although Black Power evocations of Third World revolution and armed struggle carried an air of militancy, the real and imagined threat posed by Black Power activists helped to enhance the leverage of more moderate leadership elements, facilitating integration and patronage linkages that delivered to them urban political control and expanded the ranks of the black professional-managerial stratum. The threat of black militancy, either in the form of armed Panther patrols or the phantom black sniper evoked by public authorities amid urban rioting, facilitated elite brokerage dynamics and political integration."[103]

Black people were incorporated into the political structure of cities at a time when the economy of those cities was transforming from one based on manufacturing to one based on white collar industry, tourism, and high-end consumption. According to the political scientist Adolph Reed Jr., the "pro-growth" politics of the "corporate city" brought black politicians into the fold of the ruling class at the same time as it necessarily dispossessed the working classes of those cities, especially in later years when the federal funds that such politics relied on were cut. As such, newly elected black mayors and city councilors had little choice but to administer a political program that was detrimental to most of the base that got them elected, a politics based around wooing corporations and real estate developers through tax breaks and subsidies, securitizing downtown from poor residents in order to facilitate consumption by the wealthier classes, and eventually presiding over highly regressive austerity programs.[104]

Many Black Power advocates at the time were aware of the potential for such dynamics. Of the 1967 Newark Conference, Julius Hobson, an activist with the Congress of Racial Equality, noted, "The general consensus of this gathering was that we need to transfer the economic power wielded by white men in the Black ghettoes of America to Black men."[105] Further, in the early 1970s it had become evident to many black nationalists that black political incorporation had failed to ameliorate the condition of poor blacks. Notable in this respect is Amiri Baraka. One of the most prominent public figures of the Black Power moment, Baraka had been instrumental in organizing the Black Power conferences, in marshalling the coalition that would lead to the election of Kenneth Gibson as the first black mayor of Newark, and in organizing efforts to create an independent black political party. In the mid-1970s Baraka shed his hardline nationalist stance for its apparent shortcomings, adopting in its stead "Marxism-Leninism–Mao Tse-Tung thought." In 1974 he explained, "Those of us who were still determined to serve the people began to understand that merely putting Black faces in high places, without changing the fundamental nature of the system itself, served to make that system more dangerous, since for the masses of us . . . the hardship, exploitation and oppression continued."[106] Echoing Baraka's sentiments, many cultural nationalists and Black Power organizations adopted an overtly Marxist ideological posture around this time, causing vitriolic denunciations from their former allies, who saw Marx primarily as a "white" thinker.

The Marxist-nationalist schism proved to be a death knell for the temporary unity that had been achieved among the sundry ideological factions of black political life. The rise of ideological conflicts led both camps to privilege ideological education over populist political strategies. The mid-1970s gave rise to a proliferation of local study groups, of both the nationalist and Marxist variety, which, according to Johnson, "despite their progressive veneer . . . were equally grounded in undemocratic pedagogy that maintained status hierarchy." While the brokerage dynamics of the black political conventions are more obvious (the Congressional Black Caucus, for example, explicitly sought to serve as the "legitimate spokesman on national issues" for the black population), the emphasis on ideological expertise, with its implicit privileging of intellectuals over workers, revealed a "muted elitism within black radical discourse."[107] The contention that ideological clarity must be achieved before struggles can be carried out understandably undermined the kind of grassroots mobilizations which had characterized the civil rights and Black Power movements. As such, each side in the sectarian split receded from popular struggles in the years to come.

The history of the League of Revolutionary Black Workers flows as well through these broader contours. Certainly charges of elitism could be leveled against members of the League's Executive Committee, as only two of the seven were factory workers. The split among the members of the Committee which led to the League's dissolution in 1971 was to a large extent precipitated by this hierarchical structure, consequent charges of elitism, and the conflict over the importance of ideology versus on-the-ground organizing. According to Georgakas's and Surkin's account of the split, "The in-plant people charged that the BWC wing liked to be with 'bourgeois' people and with white folks more than they liked to be with black workers. Cockrel was cited for having what was termed an arrogant and authoritarian attitude toward comrades. Watson was charged with having become a dreamer who let transoceanic trips and filmmaking fantasies replace his former vision of a worker-led American revolution."[108]

The tendency toward a top-down, ideologically stringent structure is evident also before the split, as in a *South End* article by Luke Tripp in which the

Executive Committee member declared that political education should "cultivate a firm and correct political orientation, an industrious and pure style of work, and flexible strategy and tactics."[109] It's important to note as well that James Forman's membership in the League was understood by some members to have caused the split. As a nationally recognized organizer with a history in SNCC, Forman personified the elite-driven, ideological orientation that alienated much of the rank and file. "Above all," Forman wrote, "I wage the ideological struggle—the drive for political education."[110]

Such a framework should not serve, however, as a totalizing schema. Both factions after the split could be said to have retreated into ideology: the BWC focused its efforts on a broad-based, national-level ideological campaign to try to draw workers and other organizations to their cause, while those who joined with the Communist League formed intensive Marxist study groups. It must be remembered, however, that the strength of the LRBW's political education, its ability to make Marxism appeal to workers, constituted a large part of its operational force and appeal to leftist organizations around the world. "One of the significant contributions I think the League made," said member Wiley Rogers, "was to implant the idea of analysis and study within the working class."[111] In the case of the LRBW, rather than revolutionary posturing or sectarianism, Marxist ideology was a practical means of understanding and responding to the material conditions faced by workers. Jerome Scott recalls searching for a way to analyze the situation: "We ended up with Marxism, Marxism-Leninism as the theory that related most closely to our lives. And mind you we were production workers, and Marxism was written for workers."[112] John Taylor, a white worker associated with League members at the Eldon Avenue plant, explained, "The first time I read the *Communist Manifesto* was late 1969. I thought, 'This is far out. They are talking about this plant.'"[113] The alliance of intellectuals, workers, and community activists, and the cross-fertilization between them, was an integral part of the League's power.

In fact neither political incorporation nor ideological dogmatism fully accounts for the subsequent history of the League. The privileging of filmmaking, propagandizing efforts, and the attempt to spread the League's vision to cities across the country may well have undermined its ability to address worker struggles. However, the economic situation was undoubtedly more impactful in this regard, as 1973 saw the unwinding of the Great Boom, the permanent elimination of most manufacturing jobs from the urban centers of the northern United States, and thus the elimination of the conditions that had produced industrial trade-unionism. The study circles of the Communist

League, which became the Communist Labor Party, were in part a response to changing conditions. Losing their intellectual wing, General Baker recalls, "became the basis for [them] to become tolerant of the educational process": "We withdrew totally from all participation in mass activity and began the tedious process of struggling with a Marxist education. . . . The more you learned the more conservative you became in choice of tactics." For Baker, this process was integral in transforming the working class, in Marxist terms, from a class *in itself* to a class *for itself*: "Objectively, the working class is already revolutionary. They've gotta do *something* to get the necessities of life. What *we've* got to do is help the working class develop the intellectual capacity to understand what's happening."[114]

Baker ran unsuccessfully for state legislature on the Communist Labor Party ticket in 1976 and on the Democratic Party ticket in 1978, on his second attempt coming in second out of a field of nine. Ken Cockrel was elected to city council in 1978, where he served until 1982 and, true to his militant rhetoric, did not in his short tenure capitulate or back down from his Marxist perspective, usually casting the lone dissenting vote on matters of economic development, corporate tax breaks, and other issues that continue to plague the city.[115] These forays into the formal political process do not constitute "incorporation" so much as an attempt to bring radical politics to the electoral level. While these efforts were clearly unsuccessful in bringing about the revolutionary transformation at the heart of the League's program, neither did former members come to preside over neoliberal austerity programs and paramilitary policing regimes; rather, they continued, in various capacities, to challenge them, which we'll see throughout the rest of this book.

Where the carrot of integration of moderate black leadership into political office failed to quell the challenge of black radicalism, the stick of repression was there to administer the necessary excess of force. Nowhere is the dialectic of integration and repression more evident than the official stance of the FBI's COINTELPRO, which, despite being officially disbanded, continued to inform the ideological and programmatic elements of subsequent initiatives throughout the early 1970s. FBI memos and documents relating to the early 1970s national black political conventions reveal a general strategy of targeting "black extremists" for repression while legitimating and protecting "the pursuit of black political goals through conventional channels." Johnson writes, "The Bureau's policy of selective targeting was allegedly intended to protect 'legitimate political activities' among blacks. In promoting moderate forms of black politics, state investigatory activities worked hand in hand with other state maneuvers like the community action programs and the War on Poverty initiative to shape black political life in a more conservative direction."[116] It is to this conservative direction that we now turn.

## Controlling "Revolutionary Attitudes"

I met Marx, Lenin, Trotsky, Engels, and Mao when I entered prison and they redeemed me. For the first four years, I studied nothing but economics and military ideas. I met black guerrillas, George "Big Jake" Lewis, and James Carr, W. L. Nolen, Bill Christmas, Torry Gibson, and many, many others. We attempted to transform the black criminal mentality into a black revolutionary mentality. As a result, each of us has been subjected to years of the most vicious reactionary violence by the state. Our mortality rate is almost what you would expect to find in a history of Dachau. —GEORGE JACKSON, *Soledad Brother*, 1970

During the late 1960s and early 1970s, as governments violently cracked down on radical movements throughout the United States, the rate at which new inmates were thrown into prison increased more rapidly than at any time in the twentieth century, eclipsing even the rate during the penal crisis of the Great Depression.[117] Loïc Wacquant, a prominent sociologist at UC Berkeley, expressed a common myth when he wrote that the prison boom that has occurred in the United States in the past fifty years was "contrary to all expectations." In fact, as the state accelerated its violent crackdown of radical organizations, many within these organizations foresaw the imminence of mass incarceration. At the same time that the French philosopher Michel Foucault, in his widely celebrated *Discipline and Punish*, wrote that the "widespread, badly integrated confinement of the classical age" was coming to an end and that "the specificity of the role of the prison and its role as link are losing something of their purpose," Black Panther leader Assata Shakur accurately predicted the exact opposite: "In the next five years, something like three hundred prisons are in the planning stages. This government has the intention of throwing more and more people in prison."[118]

As underemployed blacks were thrown in prison en masse, leaders like George Jackson of the BPP organized prisoners as part of the Panthers' general strategy of turning the lumpenproletariat into a revolutionary force. *The number of prison uprisings increased from five in 1968 to forty-eight in 1971.*[119] Jackson wrote at the time, "Only the prison movement has shown any promise of cutting across the ideological, racial and cultural barricades that have blocked the natural coalition of left-wing forces at all times in the past." Indeed although the majority of rebelling prisoners were black, Jackson insisted on the uprisings' socialist character: "If a man wants to relate to my blackness, fine, but I would prefer he relate to me on the basis of my status as a soldier in the

WORLD revolution."[120] The state's response to the increasing number of prisoner uprisings was to turn prisons into sites of "low-intensity warfare."[121]

The most famous uprising was in Attica, the maximum-security prison in New York where the most recalcitrant prisoners were sent. On September 19, 1971, a couple weeks after Jackson had been assassinated in San Quentin Prison, 1,300 prisoners took control of Attica. On national television, the prisoners made demands such as "adequate food, water, and shelter," "effective drug treatment," an "inmate education system," and "amnesty from physical, mental, and legal reprisals." In response, Governor Nelson Rockefeller ordered police and National Guardsmen to quash the uprising, which they did, but only after killing twenty-nine prisoners and ten of the guards who had been taken hostage.[122]

The national media initially blamed the deaths on the Attica rebels. The *New York Times* suggested that "the deaths of these persons by knives . . . reflect a barbarism wholly alien to civilized society. Prisoners slashed the throats of utterly helpless unarmed guards."[123] But days later an autopsy revealed that the prisoners had not killed a single person; the raiding officers had killed all thirty-nine men.[124]

Soon after the uprising, Rockefeller allocated $4 million to Attica to enhance the security apparatuses at the prison and search out new sites for a "maxi-maxi prison" to place militant prisoners.[125] The narrative was clear: Attica had not been a political uprising but a riot by lawless criminals and communist agitators. As Dan Berger has shown, this narrative legitimated the state's authoritarian response: this is when supermax prisons were built to lock up the country's most recalcitrant prisoners, keeping them in solitary confinement for twenty-two to twenty-three hours a day.[126]

As the prison warden of Marion, the nation's first supermax prison, explained in 1973, "The purpose of the Marion control unit is to control revolutionary attitudes in the prison system and in society at large."[127] In the mid-1960s Marion was the only supermax prison in the country; by 1997 there were more than fifty-five.[128] The Marion model of "indefinite lockdown and limited access to the outside, brutal segregation and random attacks . . . has become the dominant model of prison in America."[129]

In these supermax prisons, which cost between $30 million and 75 million to construct, "physical contact is limited to being touched through security doors by correctional officers while being put in restraints or having restraints removed. Most verbal communication occurs through intercom systems."[130] These prisons offer "virtually no educational" programs, and the books available for reading are extremely limited. Supermaxes are set up so that never again will a prisoner like George Jackson have the chance to be "redeemed" by revolutionary literature.[131] Had he served his prison sentence in a supermax, Malcolm X would surely not have been a member of a prison debate team that beat MIT's debate team.[132]

## Law and Order

In Detroit and around this country, the authoritarian response *inside* prisons paralleled an authoritarian response *outside*. Police funding offers one barometer of this process: between 1962 and 1977 local government spending on police increased from around $2 billion to $9 billion. In 1970 there was one paramilitary police unit in the United States; five years later there were five hundred, and Detroit and most major cities had their own paramilitary unit.[133] To understand this shift, let us take a closer look at the way political elites managed and mythologized social turmoil in the late 1960s.

As Marxist criminologists Morton Wenger and Thomas Bonomo observe, "The loss of confidence in the ability of a particular form of the capitalist state to handle its own social contradictions can as easily lead to a shift of allegiance by the socially insecure masses to a more proactive and brutal capitalist regime."[134] This is precisely what happened in the late 1960s. Richard Nixon won the 1968 presidential election with an appeal that included the claim that the "crime problem" would be solved "not [by] quadrupling the funds for 'any governmental war on poverty,' but convicting more criminals." The counterrevolution that James Boggs had predicted just a few years earlier was taking shape. The liberal War on Poverty had already demonstrated that it was unable to restore corporate profitability and quell widespread dissent—and so the War on Crime was ratcheted up.[135]

In Detroit, liberal elites were under attack for their inability to restore law and order. Predating the contemporary "New Detroit" revitalization efforts by almost fifty years, in the wake of the Rebellion, liberal elites had assembled the New Detroit Committee (NDC), a coalition of union higher-ups, community leaders, political elites, members of the black middle class, and corporate CEOs. The NDC, the "backbone of any liberal attempt to improve conditions in the Motor City and regain political legitimacy after 1967," sought to quell the city's tensions via urban renewal and racial redistribution, promising to invest millions in downtown development and community programs. As Judge Crockett recalls, NDC's primary concern was "to sort of quiet things down" after the Rebellion.[136] The historian and Detroit native Heather Ann Thompson writes that, at the outset, the NDC operated under the assumption that "black militants were relatively minor figures" who "posed a long-term threat" only if civil rights issues continued to be ignored by the state.[137] The NDC therefore was prepared to "listen to, and even to fund, black radicals." New Deal funding was thus channeled to radical programs that included the Community Patrol Corps, which emulated the Black Panthers' famous police patrols. Teens in "all-black uniforms" patrolled the city and monitored instances of police brutality.[138] By supporting such programs, liberals signaled their attempts to fund, and thereby politically integrate and co-opt, local dissidents.[139] This incorporation strategy didn't always work, as, for example, when Detroit's Federation for Self-Determination, an organization made up of local activists such as Cockrel, Grace Lee Boggs, and Reverend Cleage, turned down a $100,000 NDC grant which stipulated that the money was not to be used for "political" purposes. Rejecting the money, Cleage said, "We will not accept white supervision and control."[140]

Whereas activists complained that NDC proposals were both inadequate and mostly about co-optation, many conservative elites feared that NDC's contacts with local militants would facilitate a revolution. Heather Ann Thompson points out that in the span of a couple of years, "'marginal' black radicals had managed to take over the media of key liberal institutions such as Wayne State University, and were encouraging black students to take over the very schools that liberal School Board members were trying to integrate. Worse yet, black radicals had joined with whites in the call for an all-out urban revolution."[141]

In 1969 Wayne County Sheriff Roman Gribbs stepped in to mediate this situation with an iron fist. Gribbs was elected mayor of Detroit having run a campaign that centered on the promise to end liberal permissiveness, create an elite police unit to deal with civil disturbances, and wage an "all-out fight against crime in the streets."[142]

As we have seen, the crime panic of the late 1960s did have important roots in reality—the reality of increasing crime rates. Nationally, reported street crime *quadrupled* between 1959 and 1971, and rates of violent crime and homicide doubled between the early 1960s and early 1970s.[143] Detroit's population decreased by 300,000 between 1950 and 1970; during these years the white population nearly halved, while the black population more than doubled. (These two racial groups made up 98 percent of Detroit's population in 1970.)[144] In 1970, the year that Gribbs took office, there were more than twenty-three thousand reported robberies. The city's homicide rate more than *tripled* between 1960 and 1970.[145] As many as two-thirds of these murders were linked to the drug trade.[146] This was the time of a devastating heroin epidemic, one with roots in the Vietnam War: 30 percent of U.S. soldiers used heroin during their time in Vietnam, and heroin was imported into the country at cheap rates during and after the war.[147] "One journalist cited as many as fifty thousand heroin addicts on [Detroit's] streets, spending over a million dollars a day to feed their habits."[148] By the time Gribbs took office "an army of drug addicts lived in the remains of 15,000 inner-city houses abandoned for an urban renewal project which never materialized."[149]

When one considers the problems of deindustrialization, along with Detroit's dramatic demographic shifts, racial tensions, and widespread unemployment, the rising crime rate is a tragic and foreseeable outcome.[150] Liberal critics of mass incarceration tend to obscure the reality of crime, arguing that rising crime rates were an invention white elites used to justify a regressive program of racial discrimination. There is truth to these sentiments, as racial disparities in the criminal justice system more than attest to. To deny the reality of violent crime, however, shifts the focus away from the political-economic causes of crime like deindustrialization and the gutting of the welfare state, issues that also disproportionately affect minority populations. Such interpretive moves make invisible the support of poor people and minorities for anticrime members, as, for example, the black activists in New York City who campaigned for Governor Rockefeller's draconian drug laws in the late 1960s.[151]

Both the League of Revolutionary Black Workers and the Black Panthers developed alternative strategies to explain and combat the country's crime issue. While League leaders acknowledged that crime and heroin addiction were real problems, they viewed the country's moral panic as an elite-driven strategy to obfuscate the class struggle. As Watson says in *Finally Got the News*:

> There's a lot of confusion amongst white people in this country, amongst white workers in this country, about who the enemy is. The same contradictions of overproduction . . . are prevalent within the white working class, but because of the immense resources of propaganda, publicity . . . white people tend to get a little bit confused about who the enemy is. You take a look at white workers in Flint for instance, in the automobile industry, who are pretty hard pressed because the Buick plant up there is whipping their ass. . . . But who do they think the enemy is? . . . Crime on the streets is the problem.

BPP founder Huey Newton said that most criminals were simply "illegitimate capitalists"; like Watson, he understood that although white workers and black workers occupied similar "objective" positions in the economic structure, the racialized, law-and-order narrative of urban crisis made it so that white workers would "feel more and more that it's a race contradiction rather than a class contradiction." The Panthers' "survival programs" sought to address the roots of crime and immiseration by providing impoverished residents with food, shelter, health care, and political education.[152]

When police harassment made sales of the *Black Panther* a less tenable source of income, Panthers began robbing Detroit's drug houses, both to earn money and as an attempt to address the interrelated problems of drugs and violent crime. BPP member Ahmad Rahman recalls, "Drug-related crime began to wreak havoc in Black neighborhoods nationwide, diluting calls for community control as citizens turned to the police for relief. Many black people began to shift to the political 'right.' . . . Calls for community control of police, became calls for the police—and more prisons."[153]

After a botched raid on a "drug den" that resulted in one death, Rahman was captured by police.

> When his case went to trial Rahman discovered that the Panther Party superior he and the other young comrades took orders from was an FBI informant and the dope house break-in was part of a COINTELPRO designed to capture "the four most active and productive Panthers in the area—Rahman and his three co-defendants." Rahman, who was nowhere near the murder when it occurred, pled not guilty. The other three pled guilty [and] were found guilty of felony murder. The shooter in the case served only 12 years and was set free, but for Rahman, who fought to prove his innocence, it would be more than two decades before Gov. John Engler commuted his sentence.[154]

There are two points worth stressing here. First, it was only after radical working-class groups like the Panthers and the League were brought down that the punitive strategy of mass incarceration could be implemented in poor neighborhoods without meeting violent resistance. The second, related point, is that the war on crime was actually part and parcel of the repression of these radical groups (the very groups that were attempting to combat the causes of crime). During these years *crime* operated as a signifier that demonized political resistance and collapsed the social causes of the urban crisis into an individualized, moral problem—a perfect example of the process of mythologization. Law and order, rather than progressive social change, could then "resolve" the crisis.[155]

As already mentioned the Kerner Report called for more "training, planning, adequate intelligence systems, and knowledge of the ghetto community."[156] The Omnibus Crime Control and Safe Streets Act of 1968 dedicated $1 billion per year to bolstering U.S. police forces with "computers, helicopters, body armor, military-grade weapons, SWAT teams, shoulder radios, and paramilitary training."[157] Many of the strategies that police adopted to control working-class militancy at home had their precedents in counterinsurgency tactics used by U.S. forces to quell communist movements abroad. During the Cold War, the Office of Public Safety had worked closely with the CIA to train police in South Vietnam, Iran, Uruguay, Argentina, and Brazil. As scholar-activist Alex Vitale writes, upon their return to the United States, imperial officers "moved into law enforcement, including the Drug Enforcement Agency (DEA), FBI, and numerous local and state police forces." The director of the Office of Public Safety, Byron Engle, testified before the Kerner Commission, "In working with the police in various countries we have acquired a great deal of experience in dealing with violence ranging from demonstrations and riots to guerilla warfare."[158]

By January 1971 the new, highly militarized police unit that Gribbs promised was instituted; it was called Stop the Robberies, Enjoy Safe Streets (STRESS). STRESS was a local—and particularly brutal—iteration of a national trend to bolster police departments against the threat of "guerilla warfare."[159] According to the *Detroit News* article unveiling the program, in a tactic borrowed from police in New York City and the Bay Area, "decoy units" would be sent undercover in "high-crime" areas to play-act as vulnerable citizens, resembling

old women, old men, businessmen, grocery clerks and gas station attendants. . . . They will be prime bait for robbers who prey on such people. And they will be armed and ready. . . . The disguised men will work in teams so that the one being used as a decoy will never be out of sight of one or more of his buddies. . . . "We are going to look like people who live and work in Detroit," said [District Inspector] Smith. "We are going to make ourselves the victims of crime, rather than other members of the community."[160]

In the 1971 police murdered an unarmed black Detroiter named Clarence Manning Jr. As part of a decoy operation, a STRESS officer disguised as an intoxicated hippie had provoked Manning, and when Manning approached him, several STRESS officers jumped out of their hiding spots and killed him.[161] This murderous behavior was all too common. Within six months of its unveiling, STRESS, which was composed of one hundred officers, most of them white, made forty-six arrests *daily* using this entrapment technique. In this period, STRESS fatally shot fifteen citizens, thirteen of them black.[162] These STRESS killings were the primary reason why DPD had the highest rate of per capita civilian killings of all U.S. police departments in 1971—four times the rate in New York City.[163]

FIGURE 4.1. Cartoon mocking the brutality of the decoy tactics used by STRESS. Source: Schultz, *Detroit under STRESS*, 3.

" Let's not get involved - he might be a STRESS officer going about his job. "

In September 1971 five thousand protesters marched in Detroit demanding an end to STRESS and condemning the murders of the Attica rebels. Cockrel announced, "STRESS will be abolished. We're going to show them discipline the man never knew existed in the black community."[164] He and radical groups like From the Ground Up presented STRESS as a "tool of those in power" used to intimidate and terrorize impoverished black Detroiters, and decried the increasing "utilization in the domestic law enforcement scene of new terminology, operating techniques, weaponry and equipment produced from the 'test fields' of counter-insurgency activity abroad." From the Ground Up insisted, "We, the people of Detroit, need to confront the divisions brought about by the unjust and criminal distribution of wealth and control of life resources."[165]

A 1973 poll found that 65 percent of black Detroiters disapproved and 78 percent of white Detroiters approved of STRESS.[166] Many wealthier members of the black community, however, supported STRESS—signaling a growing class cleavage within the black community. Days after the 1971 protest, the *Detroit News* published an article titled "Black Leaders Support STRESS."[167] Black business organizations and black homeowners' associations threw their support behind STRESS. The city's main black newspaper, the *Michigan Chronicle*, published an article titled "STRESS Protest Shows Blacks Short on Foresight":

> The biggest issue in Detroit for the past four years has been crime in the streets. In recent months more aggressive enforcement, plus participation by citizens, has lessened the problem somewhat. . . . The civil

FIGURE 4.2. Nathaniel Johnson, witness to the STRESS murder of Clarence Manning Jr., standing with his lawyer, Kenneth Cockrel (right). After spending months in jail following his run-in with STRESS officers, Johnson was acquitted of the erroneous charge of armed robbery. Source: Schultz, *Detroit under STRESS*, p. 20.

disturbances of 1967 should remind black people not to attempt to destroy something they can't replace. There is no merit in biting the hand that feeds you. It is understandable that many blacks harbor resentment against police because of past atrocities. But when one of these idle, nonproductive, soap box pork choppers calls a policeman "pig" while at the same time sucking on a barbecue bone, his thinking faculties are not together.[168]

This support persisted in spite of the fact that in their first thirty months of operation, STRESS units launched an estimated five hundred raids without search warrants. During one of these raids in 1972, STRESS officers murdered a Wayne County sheriff's deputy in what was believed to be an inner-police-department battle over control of the city's drug trafficking. As Surkin and Georgakas write, after a fatal shootout involving three black militants,

"Commissioner Nichols went on television describing [the three men] as 'mad-dog killers.' In the weeks which followed, STRESS put the black neighborhoods under martial law in the most massive and ruthless police manhunt in Detroit history. Hundreds of black families had their doors literally broken down and their lives threatened by groups of white men in plain clothes who had no search warrants and often did not bother to identify themselves. Eventually, 56 fully documented cases of illegal procedure were brought against the department. One totally innocent man, Durwood Forshee, could make no complaint because he was dead."[169]

It was not until the city's first black mayor, Coleman Young, came into office in 1974 that the rogue police unit responsible for the deaths of at least twenty Detroit citizens was finally retired. But the demise of STRESS—which Young described as an "execution squad"—did not spell the end of aggressive anticrime measures. In fact the opposite was true: criminalization would only intensify as black liberals took control of Detroit's political establishment.[170]

### Race, Crime, and the 1973 Mayoral Election

Already the big question in cities like Detroit is whether a way can be found for these outsiders to live before they kill off those of us who are still working. How long can we leave them hanging out in the streets ready to knock the brains out of those still working in order to get a little spending money?—JAMES BOGGS, *American Revolution*, 1963

A long record of community activism, buoyed by a string of remarkable legal victories, led many to believe that Kenneth Cockrel was a viable candidate in the 1973 mayoral elections. But after considering a run, Cockrel decided against it, on the grounds the time was not yet ripe to seek revolutionary struggle inside mainstream political institutions (though by the late 1970s Cockrel changed his mind and successfully ran for city council).[171]

With Cockrel on the sidelines, the election pitted John Nichols, the city's hard-nosed white police commissioner, against Coleman Young, a black state senator with a long history of labor organizing.[172] Nichols ran on a straightforward law-and-order platform. But, as Stauch Jr. has documented, Young "made a powerful case as a more viable law-and-order candidate than the city's own Police Commissioner." In a speech one month before the election, Young declared Detroit to be the nation's "murder capital" and claimed that Nichols had allowed the city's crime problem to accelerate during his tenure as police commissioner. Young distributed campaign flyers that read, "Can YOU live with Detroit's Crime Rates?" and "JOHN NICHOLS DID NOT DO THE JOB!"[173]

Young proposed a program of "law and order, with justice." He said he would integrate and reform the police department, making it a "people's police department," while at the same time launching a broad initiative to stamp out criminals and defend the rights of crime victims. Rather than perpetuate the dragnet approach, which had drawn the ire of many in the black community, Young promised a "community policing" approach that would allow citizens to work closely with police in order to more precisely target criminals. In a speech to the Detroit Economic Club, Young promised to launch "more intensive undercover investigations" and to institute harsher laws for drug traffickers.[174] He would help actualize Henry Ford II's goal of making Downtown Detroit a "safe spot" to invest in. The black state senator further ingratiated himself with business leaders by insisting that the black community would stand behind his administration, whereas if Nichols was elected mayor, it would only fuel racial polarization and social unrest. "Who better than a black mayor," Young asked, "can deal with the dudes on Dexter, on Livernois, and start turning things around?"[175]

Race proved central to the election. In an incredibly close final tally, Young eventually triumphed by securing 92 percent of the black vote, whereas Nichols took 91 percent of the white vote. In his famous inaugural address, Young declared:

> I recognize the economic problem as a basic one, but there is also the problem of crime, which is not unrelated to poverty and unemployment, and so I say that we must attack both of these problems vigorously at the same time. The Police Department alone cannot rid this city of crime. The police must have the respect and cooperation of our citizens. But they must earn that respect by extending to our citizens cooperation and respect. We must build a new people-oriented Police Department, and then you and they can help us to drive the criminals from the streets. I issue a forward warning now to all dope pushers, to all ripoff artists, to all muggers: It's time to leave Detroit; hit Eight Mile Road. And I don't give a damn if they are black or white, or if they wear Superfly suits or blue uniforms with silver badges: Hit the Road.[176]

At Young's inaugural celebration, black leaders shared the platform with the new mayor and supported him in his crusade against crime. U.S. District Court judge Damon Keith, for example, a former civil rights activist, challenged Young to "lead a revolt of the people of this community for justice and against crime" by "ridding this city, root and branch, of the criminals who are committing murders, rapes, and assaults on the people of this city."[177] One

*Detroit News* reporter wrote, "The best-intentioned, strongest civil libertarian, most white mayor of Detroit . . . would have felt uncomfortable saying what Young and Keith said about crime."[178]

The support for Young's law-and-order campaign highlights the dialectic of repression and integration taking shape at the time. In the context of systematic violence against poor black Americans—from pervasive unemployment to state brutality and the systematic repression of dissident movements—a better regime of racial representation would be necessary if capitalism was going to legitimate itself in urban America. But as we will see in the next chapter, the integration of many middle-class black Americans into the political establishment occurred alongside, and was inextricably linked to, a deterioration in living standards among the poorer segments of the working class—a deterioration that continues to this day.

# 5

# Post-Fordism
## and
# Mass Incarceration

c. 1974–2013

The more a ruling class is able to assimilate the foremost minds of a ruled class, the more stable and dangerous becomes its rule. —**KARL MARX**, *Capital*, vol. 3

Automation got rid of half of the working force, and the half that's working won't say shit. —**GENERAL BAKER**, early 1990s, quoted in Mast, *Detroit Lives*

In the minds of many metro Detroiters, Coleman Young is synonymous with Detroit's decline. During Young's twenty-year tenure (1974–94) the condition of the city steadily deteriorated, making Young an easy scapegoat, as is exemplified in the cheap assessment of Harvard University's Glaeser and Shleifer: "In his 24 years as mayor, Detroit's Coleman Young drove white residents and businesses out of the city."[1] Young personifies to a great degree the racial divide, both real and perceived, between the city and the suburbs which grew in the post–World War II years. In his inaugural address, his admonition to criminals and dope addicts to "hit Eight Mile Road," were understood by many suburbanites as an attack—he wanted not to solve Detroit's problems but to foist them onto the suburbs. Not only is this type of thinking deliberately obfuscating, but it totally eliminates the material causes of Detroit's decline (including its connection to the more prosperous suburbs), blaming them instead on the supposed reverse racism of the city's first black mayor. In the early 1990s Sheila Murphy Cockrel, widow of Ken Cockrel, summed up the mythological view of many suburban whites: "'Detroit would be OK but for the Blacks taking over.' That's a comfortable analysis for people to make about the last thirty-five to forty years' worth of economic history in this city."[2]

In order to properly assess Young's reign, we need to keep some context in mind. By the time black politicians were beginning to gain some power, urban centers were already experiencing structural crises that limited the scope of their actions. "With relatively few exceptions," Manning Marable writes, "the black mayors and councillors were caught in an unenviable position, between black constituents with high expectations, a massive fiscal debt, a deteriorating industrial and commercial base, and an alienated and fearful white constituency."[3]

For David Goldberg, the way elites co-opted Detroit's tenants' rights struggles is symbolic of the dilemmas and contradictions facing black politicians in the post-Rebellion era:

> The approach of Goodman Bros. to Black grassroots organizing against slum conditions mirrored in various ways the broader approach taken as Blacks mobilized for political power, self-determination, and community control during the late 1960s and 1970s. When confronted with grievances resulting from negligence and racial exploitation, whites ceded certain aspects of outward political and economic control of cities like Detroit. In the process, they absolved themselves of being held responsible for the failures that their actions or privilege had ensured. By co-opting and manipulating calls for community control and Black power, companies like Goodman Bros.—and on the national stage, the Johnson and Nixon administrations—effectively inaugurated what soon became a policy of benign neglect, leaving Black politicians, businesspeople, and activists to take the fall for their inability to overcome externally institutionalized racial limitations and obstacles to collective Black economic and political development.[4]

It is clear, then, that Young was certainly not responsible for the decline of Detroit, whose industrial economy had been in the process of disappearing for almost thirty years by the time Young took office. Nonetheless Mayor Young did have some room for political maneuver, and the policies of his administration were instrumental in determining how the effects of this decline would play out. As Cockrel, now a city councilor, put it in 1979, Young's administration was composed mostly of "fake leaders" who were "not up to the fight" of taking on the political and corporate elites who were holding the city hostage. Indeed, Young, a former socialist, had long "made his peace with capitalism" by the time he became mayor. He cozied up to multinational corporations, giving them lavish gifts at the expense of social spending. Meanwhile, as rates of poverty and unemployment grew, Young's willingness to criminalize the most disadvantaged sections of the black working class was "central to the growth of mass incarceration in Detroit."[5]

The series of black mayors who followed Young—Archer, Kilpatrick, Cockrel Jr., and Bing—largely followed in his footsteps, attempting to revitalize Detroit through a combination of corporate subsidies, Downtown development, criminalization, and austerity. However, we should be careful about framing such policies, as the media so often tends to do, as the result of moral failings, corruption, or incompetence. As Adolph Reed Jr. has written, the issue is "not that black regimes are led by inept, uncaring, or mean-spirited elitists; in fact, black elected officials tend to be somewhat more attentive and liberal than their white counterparts in their attitudes about social welfare issues." The problem is rather that black urban regimes (those led by black mayors and majority black city councils) operate "in a local political culture and system dominated hegemonically by the imperatives of the very 'growth machine' that is the engine of black marginalization."[6]

The economic policies of these regimes certainly did benefit some of their constituents, leading to a growing class division *within* black America: "The percentage of African-Americans making at least $75,000 more than doubled from 1970 to 2014, to 21 percent. Those making $100,000 or more nearly quadrupled, to 13 percent (in contrast, white Americans saw a less impressive increase, from 11 to 26 percent)."[7] In Detroit these gains came as "legal" segregation ended, and many upwardly mobile African Americans took the opportunity to join the white residents who left the Motor City for the suburbs. This created a vicious spiral: as people left, their absence gutted the city's tax base and further isolated the city's poorest residents; as things worsened, those who could afford it often left, perpetuating the cycle.

This context tends to be obscured in mythical accounts of Detroit's demise. For example, a prominent *New York Times* feature on Detroit's bankruptcy begins, "In a matter of decades, Detroit went from one of America's most prosperous cities to one of its most distressed. Here is a look at how the collapse of this metropolis—battered by financial missteps, racial tensions and leadership lapses—culminated in insurmountable debt that led the city to file for bankruptcy." Focusing on five categories—"reliance on a single industry," "racial tensions," "shortcomings of leadership," "lack of an efficient transit system," and "impact of poverty"—the feature is a paragon of mythological history. As we have seen, Detroit's "decline" is the result of the contradictions of a capital accumulation process stretching back at least to the beginning of the twentieth century, not just "a matter of decades."[8] Moreover, to isolate certain features of the destructive socioeconomic system—which at certain times caused "prosperity" and at others "distress"—is misleading. Certainly if another industry shared prominence in Detroit, if political leadership had made different decisions, if racial tensions had been less pronounced, things may have turned out better for the Motor City. However, the causes of Detroit's decline put forward by the *Times* and others are in fact *symptoms* of underlying political-economic issues: What were the causes of racial tensions? Why was there so much poverty? Why did capital flee the Motor City? What constrained the city's leadership? Which powerful groups blocked the city from obtaining an "efficient transit system"?

Any genuine attempt to answer these questions brings us beyond matters of policy failures and irrational actions and forces us to confront the troubling dynamics of capitalism.

### Early Tests for the People's Police Department

After the right-wing reaction set in, everybody was happy that they had a Black mayor. The Black middle classes were bought off with jobs and favors. The more radical elements were told, 'Thanks for your help in getting us here, but we don't need you now.' A lot of us were jettisoned. I know of so many people who weren't able to get employment, and were hounded and jailed.
—**GENE CUNNINGHAM**, Detroit activist and politician, early 1990s, quoted in *Detroit Lives*

It did not take long for Young's "law and order, with justice" political program to be put to the test.[9] Just weeks after the November election, a group of black men kidnapped and murdered two black children. Mayor-elect Young responded that the black community had a "collective responsibility to put an end to such senseless and terrible crime." Local black leaders echoed this message. "Blacks who perpetrate crimes against their own people," said former SNCC member Larry Nevels, "are not our brothers, they are the enemy." Barry Hankerson, a member of the grassroots organization United Black Coalition, called for an "all-out war on crime." "In the past," the *New York Times* noted, the Coalition "had bitterly accused the police department. . . . This time, the coalition rallied to the side of the police."[10]

In support of this war on crime the federal government gave $441,000 to Detroit for its "mini-station program," which placed police officers downtown and throughout the city in "high-crime areas." In addition to this program,

Young immediately set about integrating the police department. In the wake of this integration, the scholar-activist Herb Boyd wrote in the *Black Scholar,* "The increased number of minority officers has vastly improved police-community relations and has definitely reduced the number of civilian complaints brought against the police. . . . With a black officer on the scene of an arrest, especially the arrest of a black suspect, the likelihood of excessive force and brutality are minimized."[11]

In late July 1975 Young's police department faced its most serious test when Andrew Chinarian, a white bar owner, killed Obie Wynn, a young black man, in the alley behind Chinarian's bar. Chinarian was picked up by police and soon released on a $500 bond; when news of his release spread, black people throughout the local area took to the streets in violence. In the ensuing days the "worst racial confrontation to strike Detroit" since the 1967 Rebellion broke out. In the midst of this violent unrest, Marian Pyszko, a local factory worker and Holocaust survivor, unwittingly drove through the area, and several black youth pulled him out of his car and bludgeoned him to death with a piece of concrete. The police proceeded to lay down a dragnet, making more than a hundred arrests but quickly releasing all but five suspects—the so-called Livernois Five—who would eventually be tried for Pyszko's murder.[12]

Young's first attempt to control the black residents who took to the streets was to go to the area in person. But when he refused the group's demands that Chinarian's bar be burned down, someone threw a brick at him. His next move was to tell his police commissioner to deploy as many black and female officers as possible to the area.[13] In another effort to put a "friendly face" on state attempts to restore order, Young actively recruited community "peacekeepers," volunteers who came mostly from local civil rights organizations, to patrol and restore order in the Livernois area.[14]

Not all political organizations, however, were so easily recruited to support this law-and-order response. Radical groups like the Revolutionary Socialist League and the Communist Labor Party (formed by Communist League activists) supported the protesters and gave legal aid to the Livernois Five. Kenneth Cockrel represented one of the accused men in court and got him released.[15] More common among the black establishment, however, was the opinion of the black activist and journalist Nadine Brown. In an editorial for the *Michigan Chronicle* she claimed, "All blacks and any other people need to do now is get behind the mayor's program to move this city ahead. Putting roadblocks in his way is like cutting one's own throat."[16] Michael Stauch Jr. sums up the response of black leaders to the violent unrest: "During and after the Livernois disturbance, civic, community and church leaders organized parishioners to work with police against the young men and women involved in the Livernois disturbance. . . . For upwardly mobile members of the black community, Young's election signaled the culmination of the goals of the Civil Rights and Black Power movements and therefore the end of militant street action against ensconced power relations."[17]

Although city authorities eventually succeeded in pacifying the Livernois area, their response did little to address the conditions that had led to the disturbance. And indeed the following summer the issues of crime and violent unrest resurfaced again in spectacular fashion. At a summer concert at Cobo Hall, hundreds of poor black youths descended on the mostly white crowd, assaulting and stealing from many among them and attacking the Downtown commercial center. Witnesses reported that the youth chanted at the concertgoers, "We want what you've got." Mayor Young's immediate response was again to dispatch as many black officers as possible to restore order in the area. Forty-seven people were arrested.[18]

After the Cobo Hall incident Young recalled 450 laid-off police officers, instituted a citywide 10:00 p.m. curfew for people seventeen years old and younger, and dispatched a "police gang squad" to "crack down" on youth gangs and to arrest anyone violating the curfew near Downtown. Young called for an "all-out war on juveniles responsible for the increase in crime." "I want the pimps, prostitutes, gangs and youth rovers off the streets," he added. In response to Young's call to action, the city council amended the city's stop-and-frisk policy, giving police legal sanction "to take any suspicious person, at any age, who failed to produce adequate identification into the precinct station." This stop-and-frisk policy would become permanent. The *Detroit News* printed a list of alleged gang members, justifying the decision to do so by claiming, "This is war. . . . The *News* will continue to identify youngsters at war against the city."[19] One such identified youth visited the newspaper to insist that the root of the crime problem was the city's bleak economic situation. "If they give me a job," he said, "we'll guarantee no more of this fighting." But rather than providing jobs for the city's youth, business leaders were increasingly determined to keep them away from Downtown. The "mini-riot" at Cobo Hall was front-page news in the *Free Press*, and it ran alongside the headline "Merchants Say Crime Is Ruining Business."

Black leaders were unequivocal in their support for Young's "all-out war" on crime. The president of Detroit's branch of the NAACP pledged that his group would "do everything in its power to support an all-out drive against the lawlessness that is prevailing." Urban League president Francis Kornegay went so far as to call for a return to STRESS tactics to bring the city's criminals to heel. The prominent black UAW leader Robert Battle signaled the union's intention to aid in the "fight against street gangs." Moreover, weeks after the Cobo incident, civil rights groups organized a March against Crime. Thereafter these groups formed the Coalition to Resist Crime, which combined with business groups to "mobilize civil rights tactics against the perceived crime wave gripping the city." Evidencing the growing moral and class division within black America, the article announcing the Coalition stated, "Coalition is taking aim at crime; Blacks see rights gains lost to thugs."[20] Court of Appeals Judge Vincent Brennan soon added his stern voice to the fray, demanding "adequate police protection" for the city's key commercial areas and calling for juvenile offenders to be treated in the legal system as adults. "I don't buy this so-called mythical age of 16," the judge declared. "We've got hardened criminals in this city who are only 13."[21]

Michigan soon passed the 650-Lifer Law, an adaptation of New York's draconian Rockefeller Drug Laws, which called for *life imprisonment* for the distribution or possession of 650 grams or more of any Schedule I or II opiate. A few years later, when the police arrested forty-one members from the YBI gang that had cornered the city's heroin trade, the courts opted for a harsh punitive response. One Michigan judge stated during the proceedings, "Whether rehabilitation is even a goal of our current penal system is an open question."[22]

As Young launched his war on crime, the Pulitzer Prize–winning author Studs Terkel visited Detroit and reported, "There's a new attitude in the city. . . . The police are no longer looked upon as a foreign army of occupation. . . . It reflects a new respect between the people and the police."[23] To be sure, police brutality had decreased significantly with the end of STRESS and the integration of DPD, and local animosity toward the police seemed to decline. But while this new era of post-rebellion civil harmony was being hailed, *the prison population simultaneously ballooned*: in Young's first decade in office, the number of Michiganders in state prison increased from 8,630 to 14,658.[24] As black mayors were elected across urban America, the situation was similar: between 1971 and 1981 the national unemployment rate doubled and the prison population in the United States increased by 45 percent.[25]

In Detroit those caught up in the penal dragnet faced brutal conditions in the state's lock-down facilities. Cockrel and his law partner, Chuck Ravitz, drew attention to the conditions in Wayne County Jail in a lawsuit in the early 1970s. Citing common instances of vermin infestation and faulty plumbing and electricity, the radical lawyers asserted, "Conditions in the jail rob [inmates] in many instances of their right to a fair trial, because the inmate may be induced to plead guilty to charges against him in order to get out of Wayne County jail."[26]

But most political elites were concerned with the victims of street crime, not of state violence. By this time, Detroit was the nation's "murder capital," with much of the violence linked to the heroin trade, in which DPD was largely complicit. One muckraking journalist reported at the time that "as many as 200 Detroit policemen [were] involved in city-wide heroin corruption" by extorting and protecting the city's main dealers.[27]

Though Young and the black community worked together to clean up the city's police department and dismantle the heroin trade, chastising drug dealers and corrupt cops alike, no amount of police reform or moralizing could address the deeper socioeconomic causes of crime and addiction. As we've seen, during his inaugural address Young recognized that crime is "not unrelated to poverty and unemployment" and promised to attack the causes of the latter. But his attempts to do so were thwarted.

In 1977 Young published the Moving Detroit Forward plan, a revitalization program centered on the development of a sleek Downtown commercial center, rehabilitated housing, incentives for industrial capital to come to Detroit, and an enhanced police force. Young requested $2.57 billion from the federal government to enact his plan. But Washington—which, following the collapse of the War on Poverty, began cutting back on social aid to cities—allocated Detroit *less than one-third of what Young requested*. Meanwhile the mayor's attempts to create a transport system that united the suburbs with the city were blocked. In response, Young issued a statement: "Our problems have not been caused by local mismanagement, but rather by national economic trends aggravated by Federal neglect and policies which have favored the suburbs at the expense of the city. For twenty years, suburban growth has been subsidized by the Federal government at the expense of the cities through policies, which gave the suburbs cheap roads, housing, water, and other developmental necessities. This allowed them to meet market demands for the replacement of aging central city housing and precluded its construction of the inner-city."[28]

## The Revolution from Above

Raising unemployment was an extremely desirable way of reducing the strength of the working classes—if you like, that what was engineered there in Marxist terms was a crisis in capitalism which re-created a reserve army of labor, and has allowed the capitalists to make high profits ever since. —ALAN BUDD, economic advisor to British prime minister Margaret Thatcher, 1992, quoted in Trilling, "A Nightmare Experience"

In order to make sense of the policies of Coleman Young and other black politicians in the 1970s, and the role that the federal government played in shaping these policies, we need to examine the broader crisis of global capitalism. Young was elected the same year that the Great Boom of the post–World War II years—which saw unprecedented and sustained rates of growth for twenty-five years across the capitalist world—began its explosive unwinding. The mid-1970s economic crisis was at its core a crisis of declining profitability and overaccumulation. As capitalists were investing more and more money into machinery in order to outproduce other capitalists, the capacity to produce commodities outpaced the capacity to consume them—not least because people thrown out of work by automation lacked purchasing power. For large U.S. companies, the crisis was all the more acute now that companies in Germany and Japan (whose economic growth the United States supported after the war so as to combat communism) were outcompeting them on the international market.[29] At the same time, rising wages and protests in industrial centers around the world ate into profits and kept corporations from investing. These contradictions would bring the world economy crashing down. Between 1974 and 1976, "industrial output dropped 10 percent in the Global North. The American stock market lost half its value and the world system was rocked by the two biggest bank failures since the Depression, as Franklin National in the U.S. and Bankhaus Herstatt in Germany both collapsed. With recessionary forces kicking in, businesses rapidly cut back and layoffs mounted. The number of people officially unemployed in the major capitalist countries nearly doubled from eight to fifteen million."[30]

According to Keynesian orthodoxy, when capitalists don't invest, governments should. And so governments everywhere pumped money into the economy at the first sign of recession in 1971. But the expanded money supply caused inflation to soar: the relative value of the dollar to gold went from $35 an ounce in 1971 to $800 an ounce in 1979.[31] In general, as inflation rose, producers hiked up commodity prices in an effort to maintain profitability. And as governments continued to try to spend their way out of the crisis, essentially printing money to pay their way, a vicious spiral was created.

This problem was exacerbated by the 1973–74 oil crisis, which saw oil prices quadruple. (As the Marxist scholar-activist Vijay Prashad has shown, OPEC's decision to raise prices was a response to rising commodity prices, as well as a tactic to weaken the stranglehold Western countries had over the economies of the oil-producing nations.) As oil prices went up, demand for autos declined; U.S. auto production fell 29 percent during the embargo.[32]

The result of all this was *stagflation*: economic stagnation combined with high rates of inflation. One of the most significant effects of this situation was the consignment of a significant portion of the working class to *permanent unemployment*. In the U.S., black workers were hit hardest: "The recessions of 1969–1970 and 1973–1975 forced at least 550,000 black workers permanently out of the job market. . . . By 1978, only 10.8 million out of 18.1 million black persons over 14 years of age could find employment."[33] Meanwhile federal policy facilitated a massive influx of migrant workers, with the result that the foreign-born population of the United States increased around 50 percent from 1970 to 1980. In Detroit alone, the Hispanic population increased around 400 percent between 1940 and 1980. These workers were thus thrust into competition with underemployed black workers.

The economic crisis led to declining tax revenue for municipalities across the country. With New York City on the brink of bankruptcy, a financial coup occurred, one with deep parallels to Detroit's recent bankruptcy. David Harvey suggests:

> It was a kind of major experiment, in which the investment bankers took over the budgetary structure of the city. It was a financial coup as opposed to a military coup. And they then ran the city the way they wanted to do it and the principle they arrived at was that New York City revenues should be earmarked so that the bondholders were paid off first and then whatever was left over would go to the city budget. The result of that was that the city had to lay off a lot workers, had to cut back on municipal expenditures, had to close schools and hospital services, and also had to make user charges on an institution like CUNY (City University of New York), which up until that point was tuition-free. What the bankers did was to discipline the city along ways which I think they didn't have a full theory for, but they discovered neoliberalism through their practice. And after they had discovered it, they said, ah yes, this is the way in which we should go in general. And of course this then became the way that Reagan went and then it became, if you like, the standard way the International Monetary Fund starts to discipline countries that run into debt around the world.[34]

In 1979 Paul Volcker, chairman of the Federal Reserve, declared, "The American standard of living must decline."[35] This heralded an offensive against the working classes and the Global South that would restore corporate profits at the expense of social spending, decreased wages, broken unions, and impoverishment for a majority of the country (a process now known as neoliberalism).[36] The offensive was mythologized as a war against laxity and laziness. Americans had for too long been complacent, the story went, expecting that standards of living would keep rising no matter how hard they worked, and liberal governments had exacerbated things with lavish social programs that scared off investment.

In 1980 Volcker spiked interest rates to 20 percent.[37] This caused a dramatic shrinking of the economy, as high interest rates made it exceedingly expensive to borrow money, thus stalling investment and driving down prices. Small businesses and homes, which largely run on credit, were hamstrung by the increased price of money: from 1977 to 1981, the rate of small business failure and personal bankruptcies nearly tripled.[38]

In 1970 the Nixon administration had considered a similar monetary policy. However, "the political costs of sustaining a serious anti-inflationary policy . . . quickly proved unacceptable."[39] Given the intensity of social protest taking place in 1970, this hesitancy makes sense; to manufacture an economic crisis at that point would have been to risk social revolution. However, a decade later, with radical groups decimated by state repression, the gambit was able to succeed. But the remaining vestiges of working-class resistance still had to be quashed. With that in mind, Reagan recomposed the National Labor Relations Board. He appointed Donald Dotson as chairman, a man who once claimed that "unionized labor relations have been the major contributors to the decline and failure of once-healthy industries" and have facilitated the "destruction of individual freedom." Between 1975 and 1984 unions in the United States lost 4 million workers, and the percentage of the labor force that was unionized decreased from 29 to 19. By the end of 1982 public employees, whose unions had grown in tandem with the postwar welfare state, as well as "truckers, steelworkers, meatpackers, and workers in the trucking, airline, rubber and agricultural-implement industry *had all agreed to major concessions.*"[40]

The Volcker Shock and the attack on unions had a decisive effect on the resolution of the 1979–82 auto crisis, which had led the Big Three to lay off 300,000 workers in 1980 alone. (In total, the United States lost 6.8 million manufacturing jobs between 1978 and 1982.)[41] Marxist writer Nicole Aschoff explains:

Imports, labor unrest, and the skyrocketing costs of oil and raw materials created a serious profit squeeze in the 1970s. . . . After intense negotiation, Congress passed the Chrysler Loan Guarantee Act in late 1979, creating a federal board to oversee restructuring of the company in exchange for $1.3 billion in loans. Chrysler returned to profitability in 1982, paid back its loans in 1983, and by 1985 all three US automakers were making record profits. But what is most striking about the two crises is that they were both resolved by pushing the costs of the crisis onto working people, allowing the firms to regain profitability and continue on as they always had. As part of the 1979 loan agreement, the Treasury forced the UAW to open its contract, give back $462.5 million in wage and benefit gains, and agree to the permanent elimination of more than a third of Chrysler's hourly workforce. The concessions were an historic blow to autoworkers and signaled to the rest of the country that it was open season on organized labor. GM and Ford quickly secured concessions of their own.[42]

With unions decimated, capital had carte blanche to reorganize labor processes, incorporating new "labor-saving" machinery and robotics. In Detroit, as unemployment skyrocketed between 1980 and 1982, rates of drug overdose doubled and suicides increased 20 percent.[43]

In the early 1970s Huey Newton argued that the coming era of capitalist globalization would mean "the boomeranging of conditions and practices found in the darker nations of the Third World (and ghettos of the US), such as deindustrialisation, structural unemployment, state retrenchment and super-exploitation, back into the general (white) population of the US." If white workers couldn't be organized into a multiracial working-class movement, Newton predicted, they would align with racist demagogues who scapegoated minorities and foreigners for whites' downward mobility.[44]

Unfortunately his analysis proved prescient. Elected president in 1980, Ronald Reagan's plan to "make America great again" by cutting corporate taxes, bolstering military spending, and slashing welfare spending was justified, in part, by a mythology that demonized foreigners as well as black criminals and "welfare queens." As elsewhere, this type of fear-mongering had fatal consequences in Detroit. In 1982 Vincent Chin was murdered in Highland Park by two white Chrysler employees, who blamed the Japanese auto industry for recent layoffs in Detroit and took revenge on the twenty-seven-year-old Chin, a Chinese American draftsman who was celebrating his bachelor party. As unemployment and inequality have continued to rise in the decades since, the nativist mythology that underpinned this hate crime is making an ugly resurgence, as President Trump repeatedly claims that the Chinese are "ripping us off" and that Americans need to be strong enough to take them on.

## The Coleman Young Years Revisited

With this context in mind, we can take a more sober look at the policies of the Young administration. With federal funds lacking and municipal debt accelerating, Young became a fiscal conservative. From 1978 to 1984 he fired

6,000 municipal workers, including at least 1,500 cops. To lure investment he reduced the corporate tax rate; to make up for the subsequent drop in revenue, he raised income taxes. In addition to lowering corporate taxes, Young used public funds to subsidize Downtown investment, in hopes of spurring revitalization. In a deal that eerily resembles the contemporary construction of Little Caesars Arena, the mayor borrowed $40 million against future block grants from the government in order to fund the Red Wings' Joe Louis Arena. As we saw in the introduction, forty years later the Red Wings' owner, Mike Ilitch, wanted a new stadium, and the Detroit public again paid for much of its construction.[45]

In addition to subsidizing Downtown development, Young attempted to lure industrial firms to the city. But this was no easy task. One way that industrial capitalists escaped the economic crisis was by fleeing the United States—with its expensive, rebellious workers—and investing in new low-wage areas throughout the Global South. Between 1970 and 1993 the number of transnational corporations (with headquarters in three or more countries) increased from seven thousand to thirty-seven thousand, accounting for the majority of world trade. Between 1978 and 1992 seventy nation-states underwent structural adjustment programs issued by the International Monetary Fund—largely due to defaulting on their debts after Volcker jacked up interest rates—which opened these countries up to international investors. As a result, foreign direct investment nearly quadrupled in the 1980s.[46]

It was in this context that, in 1980, Coleman Young promised to clear 465 acres of land in Poletown so that General Motors could build a factory there. The government used eminent domain to evict 3,500 people, 114 businesses, a school, a hospital, and sixteen churches. As is shown in the remarkable film *Poletown Lives!*, Young's attempt to displace the racially integrated neighborhood was met with strong resistance. Poletown residents picketed across the city, occupied buildings, and launched a campaign to boycott GM. This struggle drew the attention of Green Party candidate Ralph Nader, who denounced the GM deal as "corporate socialism." One Detroit activist commented, "All I can see is that they're taking from the poor and giving to the rich." Cockrel was the only city council member to vote against the deal. All around the world, he said, governments were "falling over themselves" to attract mobile capital, and companies knew they had municipalities "in a bind."[47] In vain, he insisted his fellow politicians should support the Poletown residents in their struggle against such corporate tyranny.

Lacking support from local politicians, however, the Poletown resistance waned after a suspicious series of arsons drove many longtime residents out of the area. The struggle was brought to a violent climax when a SWAT team descended on an occupied church, removing and arresting twelve people, including four women in their seventies.[48]

Ultimately the site cost Detroit more than $200 million in "procurement and clearing" and was sold to GM for $8 million. Detroit did not have $200 million in spare funds, so it used more than $100 million of grant money, which was meant to support low-income citizens, to fund the project. Detroit also offered GM a twelve-year, 50 percent tax rebate worth $60 million for a factory that created hardly any new jobs, instead replacing jobs from older factories. This was the new logic of global capitalism: Detroit, one of America's poorest cities, was borrowing hundreds of millions of dollars to subsidize the operations of General Motors, at the time the world's second richest company.[49]

The same logic continues to this day, as we saw in the contemporary corporate subsidies detailed in chapter 1. The main difference is that, with a few exceptions, in the 1980s corporate elites still had more profitable places to invest around the world, and so they mostly rejected Detroit's lavish deals. The Renaissance Center stands as the most potent symbol of this rejection. The brainchild of a 1970 public-private partnership spearheaded by Henry Ford II, the RenCen was meant to be the centerpiece of economic revitalization in the wake of the Great Rebellion of 1967. After six years of construction, the Renaissance Center was unveiled in 1977. Part consumption space, part corporate headquarters, and part luxury hotel, the modernist glass towers beckoned commerce to Detroit's waterfront Downtown. But commerce was not forthcoming. The Renaissance Center cost the city $350 million in public money. In 1996 it was sold to Highgate Hotels for $72 million, and then resold to General Motors for what the company's vice chairman described only as "the right price." At the time of its sale, the Renaissance Center had 17 percent vacancy.[50]

Over the next decade unemployment and violent crime rose together, and as Detroit became the country's murder capital, the businesses and residents that could leave generally did: the city's population decreased by 200,000 throughout the 1980s. But for the fleeing workers, there were few places to go in the state; former industrial hubs like Flint and Pontiac were also reeling in the face of deindustrialization. In the 1980s Michigan lost a total of 250,000 jobs.[51]

As levels of poverty grew more dire, Young spent $60 million in public funds to build Millender Center, an upscale apartment building, as part of a broader effort to turn Downtown Detroit into a vibrant commercial center. To stimulate investment, Young also used public housing funds to remove blight, which Mayor Mike Duggan continues to do today. Between 1980 and 1987 the Detroit government demolished 36,000 homes; during that time only 4,500 homes were built.[52] Predictably this aggravated the problem of homelessness, which was already endemic across the United States: between 1981 and 1989 the percentage of Americans who experienced homelessness increased from 5 to 15.[53]

The effort to entice Downtown investment also included the People Mover, a one-track elevated train that circles Downtown Detroit and began operation in 1987. The Mover's original cost was $200 million, with annual running costs of $12 million. Two decades after its opening, the People Mover was running at less than 3 percent of its capacity; almost entirely devoid of passengers, it snaked through Downtown like an apparition of the city's decline. While these projects were being funded, Chrysler threatened to move production away from the Motor City. Young responded by selling $130 million in "limited-tax general obligation bonds, which voters had not approved, to help finance Chrysler's Jefferson North Assembly Plant. At the time, analysts projected the deal would cost the city a total of $235 million in principal and interest over 20 years."[54]

The legacy of the Poletown plant is another stark reminder of capitalism's inherent creative destruction. In late 2018, less than forty years after the city destroyed the neighborhood to make way for GM's factory, the company announced that it was closing the plant as part of a plan to cut $6 billion in costs and lay off 15 percent of its salaried workforce. This was after the federal government spent $51 billion to keep the company afloat during its 2009 Chapter 11 bankruptcy. While GM claims the cuts are necessary to maintain profitability, it has spent over $10 billion buying back its own stock shares since 2015. The city of Hamtramck, which only recently dug itself out from under state emergency management, has been receiving about $850,000 per year in revenue from the plant, over 5 percent of the city's total yearly budget. Hamtramck mayor Karen Majewski summed up capitalism's historical vicissitudes: "They did this in 1980 when they destroyed homes to build the facility. Did GM care? No, they sacrificed little old ladies, their churches and homes for that plant. They did not care, and I don't think there's any reason they do now."[55]

## Crime and Punishment

Michigan, especially Detroit, now looks like a Third World country. . . . People died in Michigan when cuts occurred in the General Assistance. A close friend of mine died for lacking the transportation to get the kidney medicine. —**MARIAN KRAMER**, "Remarks on the National Welfare Rights Union," 1994

In the 1980s crack-cocaine imports into the United States soared (often with CIA complicity).[56] In the Detroit area fifty thousand people became addicted to crack, and its distribution became a $1 billion industry. In urban areas throughout the country, high unemployment and easy access to guns created the conditions for violent struggles to corner this emerging market. Between 1984 and 1989 the homicide rate of black males ages fourteen to twenty-four doubled; in major cities, one-third of *all* homicides were linked to the crack trade in 1988.[57]

This crisis, a result of structural political-economic dynamics that left millions of poor urban residents permanently unemployed, was treated by the government as a problem of crime. This framing served to both legitimate and administer the response to the crisis, offering a simple explanation (crime as moral failing) while also providing a solution (tougher anticrime measures). Throughout the 1980s a series of criminal justice reforms were passed with bipartisan support, resulting in longer prison sentences for drug crimes, the implementation of a 100:1 disparity in sentencing between convictions for arrests related to crack and those related to cocaine, increased funding for police militarization, and further incentives for police departments to participate in the war on drugs. (Departments were allowed to keep 90 percent of any "drug-tainted" property seized in raids.)[58] The number of drug-related arrests in Detroit nearly *tripled* between 1980 and 1988. By 1988 nearly three-quarters of arrestees in Detroit were drug users.[59]

The law-and-order response was justified, in part, by the myth of the "crack baby." In 1986 *Newsweek* declared "crack babies" the largest national news story since the Vietnam War, and *Time* named crack the "issue of the year." The *Detroit Free Press* ran cover stories like "Schools: System's Unprepared to Handle Influx of Crack-Damaged Children."[60] But a recent study led by Dr. Hallam Hurt, the chair of neonatology at the Albert Einstein Medical Center, came to the conclusion that "the crack baby was a myth." As reported by *Al Jazeera*: "'We were really preparing for the worst,' Hurt said. 'We had reports of psychologists saying this was going to be a biologically inferior underclass, might not even be able to dress themselves.' But after 25 years of research she found there were no differences in the health and life outcomes between babies exposed to crack and those who weren't. . . . What did make a difference for those babies, however, was poverty and violence."[61]

The war on drugs went hand in hand with dramatic cuts to welfare. In the early 1990s Republican governor John Engler, who was nearly recalled after hundreds of thousands of Michiganders signed a petition to oust him, eliminated general assistance, removing ninety thousand state residents from the welfare rolls. Meanwhile, between 1985 and 1992 twenty-three new prisons were constructed in Michigan. In 1993 the state spent $1.32 billion to incarcerate forty-four thousand people, each prisoner costing eleven times the average welfare payment.[62]

Throughout the 1980s and 1990s a number of groups in Detroit combated the problems of government neglect and immiseration, questioning the state's law-and-order framework. Marian Kramer helped form the Michigan Welfare Rights Organization (part of the National Welfare Rights Union), which organized welfare recipients against a system that, in her words, "punish[es] people, especially children, for being poor."[63] This organization worked with the Detroit Organization of Tenants in the fight for rent control and affordable housing. At the same time a multitude of groups fought to unify the city's public transport system with the suburbs, though suburbanites consistently blocked this initiative, with devastating effects to Detroit's economy: in the 1980s all jobs created in metro Detroit were in areas where there was no public transport, but nearly one-third of Detroit households had no car.[64]

This era witnessed a flourishing of community groups in the city. Alternatives for Girls formed in 1987 to "serve homeless teenage girls and young women" and participate in AIDS education. The Westside Mothers organized residents in neighborhoods decimated by federal neglect and the crack epidemic. Core City Neighborhoods fought the crack epidemic by organizing for affordable housing and economic uplift.[65] Save Our Sons and Daughters organized against street violence and the crack epidemic. In 1988 the Boggses and Dorothy Garner formed We the People Reclaim Our Streets, an organization that held marches against the ravages of crack-cocaine.[66] And in 1991 the Boggses and other activists held a People's Festival, which celebrated the "new spirit rising in Detroit": "It is found where people are rehabbing abandoned houses, walking against crack and crime, planting gardens, reclaiming our neighborhoods as places of safety and peace for ourselves and our children. It is a spirit born out of the depths of a city crisis. For too long our neighborhoods have been allowed to deteriorate. For too long our scarce tax dollars have gone to subsidize megaprojects with little return to the people. For too long our streets have been places of violence and danger."[67]

But despite the efforts of these and other groups, law-and-order policies were in full effect throughout the poorest and most marginalized parts of the country. On April 30, 1992, this provoked a militant response as impoverished communities of color in Los Angeles took arms in a week-long uprising. The immediate catalyst was the acquittal of the four police officers who pulled over Rodney King, an unarmed black man, on a traffic stop, then proceeded to beat him severely as he lay prone, begging them to stop. In a week of violence, over eleven thousand people were arrested, sixty-three people were killed, and more than $1 billion in property was damaged.[68]

As in the Great Rebellion in Detroit, the national media mythologized this event, describing the protesters as "rioters," "thugs," and "looters." In the *Detroit Free Press*, where the "riot" was front-page news for five straight days, generally unmentioned was the fact that black unemployment was more than 40 percent in Los Angeles. Stripped of most context, the "rioters" were depicted as exploding in "violent rage," and the newspaper concluded that a "gulf of hatred separates races." Protesters in Detroit and Highland Park marched in solidarity with Rodney King and the LA protesters, but the primary coverage they received in the *Free Press* was a story titled "Riot Rumors Make Shop Owners Shaky."[69]

President George H. W. Bush, following long historical precedent, invoked the Insurrection Act of 1807 to send in federal troops to restore order in LA. Military soldiers and Border Patrol agents blasted into poor neighborhoods. Border Patrol agents raided Latino communities and arrested a thousand undocumented immigrants, "despite the fact that most were never formally charged with any riot-related offense."[70]

Later that year Malice Green, an unarmed thirty-five-year-old black man, was pulled over by two white plainclothes police officers in a poor neighborhood on Detroit's West Side, who alleged that he had parked near a drug house. A group of officers, with no justifiable provocation, "beat, kicked and bludgeoned" Green to death. "The attack," the *Press* wrote, "evoked images of Rodney King." In the days that followed, hundreds of Detroiters gathered to mourn Green's death. Wary of the LA uprising, Coleman Young responded by intensifying police patrols in the city's deeply impoverished West Side neighborhoods. No uprising ensued—in large part because the state had successfully repressed and incarcerated the most militant members of Detroit's working class. Only the first two officers on the scene were convicted in Green's killing, and each was released after serving significantly abridged sentences.[71] Malice Green, an unemployed steelworker, was one of many casualties in the war on drugs, a war that treated poor people of color like Green as *enemy combatants*.

In the wake of the Rodney King uprising, the Democratic Party moved all the way to the right on the issue of crime in the 1992 elections. During his presidential campaign, Bill Clinton positioned himself as a law-and-order liberal, and once elected, he signed into law the 1994 Violent Crime Control and Law Enforcement Act and the 1996 Illegal Immigration Reform and Immigrant Responsibility Act. These laws increased mandatory minimum sentences; financed the largest prison construction project in world history; instituted three-strikes legislation (issuing mandatory life sentences for three-time convicts); increased the number of agents controlling the flow of migrants coming across the border following NAFTA (which thrust small farmers into competition with transnational agricultural companies, forcing 1.3 million Mexican farmers off their land in the mid-1990s); and enacted policies that resulted in a 300 percent jump in immigrant detention in the 1990s.[72] "As the violent crime rate plummeted in the 1990s," the political scientist Marie Gottschalk writes, the "number of violent and property offenses prosecuted rose, as did the time served by people convicted of violent offenses."[73]

The 1996 Personal Responsibility and Work Opportunity Reconciliation Act was the second flank of Clinton's assault on the poor. The Act decreased the federal budget for antipoverty programs by more than $500 million; banned parole and probation violators from receiving federal aid and public housing *for a full decade*; placed a lifetime ban on Temporary Assistance for Needy Families and Food Stamp benefits for convicted drug felons; put a five-year lifetime cap on welfare receipt; and issued a mandate to states to decrease those on state doles. Another key part of this Act is what is known as workfare: to keep their benefits, welfare recipients now had to accept *any* job that was offered to them, at *any* wage, or lose their benefits.[74]

In Detroit the Michigan Welfare Rights Organization led the struggle against these draconian policies by organizing impoverished people throughout the city. The Organization denounced the government for creating a "new Great Depression." They called for "adequate income above the poverty level, adequate and affordable housing, employment at prevailing wages, equal and quality healthcare, and quality child care. Although slavery was abolished in this country over 210 years ago, mandatory work legislation has in effect restored slavery in this country, regardless of race."[75]

It was an uphill battle, and it is still being fought. Within seven years of its passage, the number of welfare recipients in the United States decreased from 12.7 million to 5 million. At least 40 percent of those who had been taken off the doles had *not* found jobs, putting them, in their struggle to survive, on a collision course with the country's recently bolstered criminal justice system, whose budget had increased from $22 billion in 1980 to $130 billion in 1997.[76]

## "They'll Be Better Off in Prison"

When he was elected, Young had no program for stopping crime. All he could propose in his inaugural speech was that the criminals should hit 8 Mile road. But he did have a dream, the dream that he could get the corporations to stay in Detroit by bribing them with tax abatements. Today Young's dream has turned into a nightmare. Crime has not hit 8 Mile road, but industry has. —**JAMES BOGGS**, "Rebuilding Detroit: An Alternative to Casino Gambling," 1988

We're going to pay $200,000,000 to $300,000,000 to house a baseball team when we can't house the homeless. —**GENE CUNNINGHAM**, early 1990s, quoted in Mast, *Detroit Lives*

In 1994 Coleman Young left office due to health reasons that soon led to his death. At the time Detroit's population was around one-third of what it had been when Young first took office, and the percentage of Detroiters who were black had increased to around 70. Attempts to transform Downtown into a commercial hub had been an expensive failure: by 1995, 20 percent of the city's 480 Downtown buildings stood "empty, or at best thinly occupied." Camilo Jose Vergara drew national attention for his article in the design and architectural magazine *Metropolis* in which he offered a solution for Downtown Detroit: "I propose that as a tonic for our imagination, as a call for renewal, as a place within our national memory, a dozen city blocks of pre-Depression skyscrapers be stabilized and left standing as ruins: an American Acropolis. We could transform the nearly 100 troubled buildings into a grand national historic park of play and wonder."[77]

Dennis Archer, the city's new mayor, had other plans: not to turn Downtown into a museum but to continue efforts to remake it as a thriving commercial center.[78] The "crown jewel" of Archer's plans to revitalize the city was Comerica Park. In 1997 construction on the new stadium began on twenty-five acres in the heart of Downtown at a cost of $300 million, 38 percent of which was publicly financed.[79] The new stadium, named after Comerica Bank, was leased to Mike Ilitch, owner of the Tigers baseball team. At the time, *Forbes* magazine ranked Ilitch as "one of the nation's wealthiest individuals."[80] Two years later ground broke on a new football stadium that would neighbor Comerica Park. Ford Field, owned by Henry Ford's grandson, cost $430 million to build, 36 percent of which was publicly financed.[81]

The final piece of Archer's vision for a revitalized Downtown was put in place in 1996, when a statewide ballot passed allowing casinos to operate in Michigan. Three casinos were built in Downtown by 2000. In spite of promises that the casino industry would "bring 50,000 to 80,000 jobs," the casinos employed a total of 7,500 people.[82]

Like many of his predecessors, Mayor Archer stated that crime was "the No. 1 problem confronting the city" and that combating it would be integral to the city's attempts to "attract businesses that can provide jobs." By this point the official unemployment rate in Detroit was 25 percent. Throughout the

1990s this reserve army of labor was confronted by an increasingly authoritarian police force. The Malice Green murder was no anomaly: from 1990 to 1998 DPD killed ten citizens per year, making Detroit cops the deadliest in the country.[83]

Police forces across the United States were becoming more militarized: in the late 1990s, $750 million in equipment was sent to police departments, including 181 grenade launchers. The federal government mandated that all subsidized equipment be used within one year, creating a massive local incentive for departments to launch military-style operations.[84] In Detroit these paramilitary units were used mostly on drug raids in the city's poorest neighborhoods.[85]

In 1998 Michigan's legislature passed truth-in-sentencing legislation which drastically reduced prisoners' chances for parole; for prisoners serving the same crime, the average length of sentence increased 50 percent between 1981 and 2005. This increase cannot be linked with crime, only with the mythical perception of increasing crime: between 1986 and 2006 the incarceration rate in Michigan had more than tripled, while violent crime had *dropped* by 30 percent.[86] As the director of the Michigan Department of Corrections put it, "Prisons were a real growth industry for a while."[87]

In 2001 UNICOR, a government-owned corporation, earned $588 million in revenue by selling products made by federal prisoners; two-thirds of UNICOR products were purchased by the U.S. Department of Defense. The minimum wage paid to these inmates was 23 cents per hour.[88] By 1998 in addition to its forty-one correctional institutions, there were fifteen prison camps in Michigan. Heather Ann Thompson notes:

> The Michigan State Industries (MSI)—the division of the Michigan Department of Corrections that oversees prison labor—began making everything from farm equipment to steam engines, boilers, barrels, copper wire, cigars, tombstones, shoes, and laundry products. It was soon operating a textile mill that could compete with operations south of the Mason-Dixon line. By 2000, MSI was running 29 factories in 18 prisons, and, as it reported proudly, its self-sufficiency and employment of more prisoners helped to save "the state the cost of civilian wages, salaries and other costs which were paid out of the Department's budget in the past." Meanwhile of course, factory doors across the City of Detroit were shutting. . . . As one community leader in Detroit noted woefully, "[f]or the first time, I'm seeing guys make a conscious decision they'll be better off in prison than in the community, homeless and hungry."[89]

## Prelude to the Bankruptcy

Since the national attention is on birth control, here's my idea: If we want to fight poverty, reduce violent crime and bring down our embarrassing drop-out rate, we should swap contraceptives for fluoride in Michigan's drinking water. We've got a baby problem in Michigan. Too many babies are born to immature parents who don't have the skills to raise them, too many are delivered by poor women who can't afford them, and too many are fathered by sorry layabouts who spread their seed like dandelions and then wander away from the consequences. —NOAH FINLEY, "Michigan is Breeding Poverty," 2012

Like those who came before him, when Kwame Kilpatrick became mayor in 2002, his options were highly constrained by a harsh reality: hundreds of thousands of people in his city were what James Boggs had called "expendables." The disposability of this population was shown in the U.S. government's response to Hurricane Katrina. Invoking the Insurrection Act of 1807, President George W. Bush ordered federal troops into New Orleans—the U.S. city with the highest per capita prison population and an unemployment rate of 50 percent—on a "shoot to kill" mission against all "looters" attempting to survive a storm that killed more than a thousand people.[90]

Constrained by a political-economic system that had no regard for most of his city's residents, Mayor Kilpatrick's options for governing Detroit—at the time the poorest large city in the country, a city that was more than 80 percent black, a city with a dubious credit rating, declining population, decimated industrial base, and $150 million-plus deficit—were extremely limited. Kilpatrick implemented austerity, reducing the municipal workforce by more than four thousand people, and supported aggressive crime-fighting measures.[91]

In the hysterical political climate following 9/11 the Arab residents in the Detroit suburb of Dearborn were violently targeted by police equipped with the War on Terror's surplus military equipment.[92] As Sally Howell and Andrew Shryock write, in Dearborn the U.S. Border Patrol began "using 'unannounced, rotating checkpoints' to search automobiles for illegal aliens, drugs, and terrorists. . . . a U.S. Justice Department spokesman in Washington, D.C., said of the probe: 'It's the largest investigation in the history of the United States.' . . . The result, so far, has been dozens of arrests—mostly for graft, identity forgery, cigarette smuggling, and other black market crimes—and the purported discovery of an 'operational combat sleeper cell' of four 'al-Qaeda terrorists' (who might just be hapless immigrants who fit the profile . . . )."[93]

In addition to promoting the wars on crime and terror, Kilpatrick would also prove amenable to a brand of neoconservative politics ascendant at this time, embodied most memorably by Bill Cosby. Though his reputation today has been all but destroyed after being convicted of sexual assault and sentenced to ten years in prison (and having been accused by more than sixty women of sexual assault, rape, and many other charges dating back decades), Cosby was in the early 2000s one of the country's most beloved public figures. His political stance is a rehashing of the underclass ideology that has animated debate about the urban poor for over half a century. In Cosby's particular strain of this well-worn doctrine, gangsta rap, baggy jeans, absent male role models, anti-intellectualism in the black community, and other moral failings are the cause of black poverty, problems whose alleviation lies in an amalgam of parental responsibility, mobility through education, and private philanthropy. In a 2004 speech commemorating the fiftieth anniversary of the *Brown v. Board of Education* Supreme Court decision, Cosby blamed poverty on the failings of the poor themselves: "The lower economic people are not holding up their part in this deal."[94] Strange apologetics for police brutality, ridiculous associations between the naming practices of black families and criminality, and the moral contagion of black youth's fashion choices peppered Cosby's tirade. In his formulation, the only barriers keeping the black urban poor from enjoying the prosperity granted to middle- and upper-class blacks by civil rights reforms are their own attitudes.

Cosby's vision was embraced by significant segments of the black political class. After this speech for the NAACP, Cosby was invited to address the National Urban League, Jesse Jackson's Rainbow/PUSH coalition, and the Congressional Black Caucus. Kilpatrick openly endorsed Cosby's remarks, and later that year the mayor invited him "to lead an invitation-only 'town hall' meeting to address Detroit's soaring murder rate."[95] On a speaking tour in 2007, Cosby addressed a packed room at Detroit's St. Paul Church of God in Christ, upbraiding the all-male audience—"Men? Men? Men! Where are you, men?"—to protect their women and children as a remedy for poverty and "black-on-black crime."[96] Rather than falling into the trap of the false consciousness thesis, we should recognize the reasons why this type of thinking "resonates with the black mainstream."[97] Black conservatism does not represent co-optation by white elites, but has rather been a mainstay of African American political life since emancipation, personified by Booker T. Washington and his philosophy of legal segregation and black self-help. The same sentiments animated much of Black Power discourse, with its emphasis on "closing ranks," "community control," and general notions of self-sufficiency, which often scorned integrationism and redress through formal political institutions.

Crucially this type of thinking legitimates the neoliberal order. Another endorsement of Cosby's remarks came from then-senator Barack Obama. "Bill Cosby got into trouble when he said some of these things," Obama explained in an interview with Oprah Winfrey. "But I completely agree with his underlying premise: We have to change attitudes."[98] Understanding crime as a moral problem rather than as a political-economic problem serves to justify both law-and-order policies and the elimination of the social safety net. The social factors that have led to the disintegration of working-class black communities are eliminated, and the market is naturalized as the only legitimate arbiter of human social relations. Regular people, Obama claimed in his celebrated 2004 address to the Democratic National Committee, "don't expect government to solve all their problems" and "don't want their tax money wasted by a welfare agency."[99]

This brand of neoconservatism was also operative in Detroit, as Kilpatrick linked the city's economy to the global financial market in a way that was much more direct than in previous decades. As the city's pension obligations grew and its taxable revenue shrank, Kilpatrick negotiated a deal with Wall Street that he estimated would shave almost $300 million per year in pension obligations. In 2005 the city issued $1.4 billion in securities to Wall Street banks. Kilpatrick then bought swaps from UBS and SBS Financial Products, which locked in Detroit's interest payments on this long-term debt to Wall Street at the *fixed* rate of 6 percent.[100]

At the time, the voices of council members who resisted the deal were drowned out by the mythic belief that Wall Street financial schemes would save the city. The *Free Press* accused the dissenting council members of having their "heads in the sand," calling it a "sound deal . . . akin to refinancing a mortgage." (The irony is that 56 percent of black homeowners who purchased a mortgage in 2006 were foreclosed on within five years by the very same banks that Kilpatrick was negotiating with.) Bond Buyer, Wall Street's premier guide to the municipal investment market, was so enthralled it awarded the deal the 2005 Midwest Regional Deal of the Year.[101]

Three years later, however, after the stock market crashed and interest rates plummeted, Detroit was left in the lurch. By 2012 Detroit's liability on the deal, *in addition to the principal owed*, had increased to $439 million.[102]

After Kilpatrick resigned following an unrelated corruption scandal, David Bing came to office in 2008. He responded to the city's mounting debt by firing nearly one-third of the municipal workforce. These cuts implicated the police department more significantly than previous bouts of downsizing: fewer than two thousand officers were retained, meaning "fewer cops [were] on patrol in the city than at any time since the 1920s." The remaining officers mostly serviced Downtown, and emergency response times in the periphery of the city were soon estimated at an hour.[103]

In 2009 Robert Bobb was appointed emergency manager for Detroit Public Schools, said to be having fiscal problems. As we saw in the introduction, his solution was to close thirty schools and transition DPS to a charter system. When Bobb, who was paid a six-figure salary, stepped down two years later, DPS was in more debt than when he began closing schools, and the school system was well on its way to being the most friendly in the nation to charters.[104]

For all the austerity measures, the city's revenue fell a full 20 percent between 2000 and the end of Bing's first and only term, as the population decreased by another 250,000 people. The city's unemployment rate, meanwhile, was 45 percent (for parolees, this figure was as high as 70 percent). These numbers are only slight exaggerations of the national trend: more than 25 percent of black and Hispanic workers was jobless in 2011. The poverty rate among white workers, meanwhile, increased from 3 to 11 percent in first decade of the millennium; in those same years, the median income for working-age households of all races fell by more than 12 percent.[105]

Following the financial crisis of 2007–8, the U.S. government bailed out the banks and the auto industry with more than $700 billion. For Detroit's working class, no such gifts were forthcoming. Instead the keys to their city were handed to an emergency manager whose job it was to bring Detroit out of its fiscal crisis. As already mentioned in chapter 1, this was to be done by yet more austerity, dispossession, and corporate subsidies. And as Emergency Manager Orr acknowledged in his initial report on the city, in order for the city to become a profitable place to invest in, its "endemic" crime problem had to be addressed. With this in mind, the broken-windows policing advocate James Craig was soon brought in.[106]

As Marx reminds us in *The 18th Brumaire of Louis Bonaparte*, history repeats itself, "the first time as tragedy, the second as farce."[107] We have documented the tragic effects of capitalism's first major attempts in the twentieth century to overhaul Detroit, and now that capitalists are returning to the city en masse, the jubilant support for their profit-seeking efforts can only be seen as a farce—but a farce with fatal consequences. At the same time, with respect to anticrime measures as an ostensible solution to Detroit's social problems, we are well past the realm of the farcical. But for the tens of thousands of Detroiters who will spend some part of their life behind bars, for their friends, families, neighbors, and comrades, it is no laughing matter.

# Competing Visions
### for
# Detroit's New Era

Who remembers all that? History throws its empty bottles out the window. —**CHRIS MARKER**, Sans Soleil, 1983

People always ask us, "Why can't we have another League of Revolutionary Black Workers?" Because those days are over with. When we talk about something now, we're talking about a party for the working class as a whole, the unemployed, or never worked or whatever. It's got to be based on that rising class, and what's happening out here, and the question of technology, and the fact that we need a new society. —**MARIAN KRAMER**, "A Media Project with the League of Revolutionary Black Workers"

The brief history we have told here is an attempt to allow the reader to make sense of the dramatic shifts underway in contemporary Detroit. To conclude, we'd like to offer some thoughts on the challenges faced by those seeking to contest the architects of the so-called New Detroit, and build a city that better serves the needs of all Detroiters.

## Resilience or Resistance?

Post-9/11 politics, according to the Marxist scholar Mark Neocleous, have been defined by the triad anxiety-trauma-resilience, which has become the framework to understand everything from ecology to natural disasters, psychology, urban planning, national security, corporate management, parenting, and all that is in between: "The state now assumes that one of its key tasks is to imagine the worst-case scenario, the coming catastrophe, the crisis to come, the looming war attack, the emergency that could happen, might happen and probably will happen, all in order to be better prepared. . . . Resilience is nothing if not an apprehension of the future, but a future imagined as disaster/attack and then, more importantly, recovery from the disaster/attack."[1]

The concept of resilience also reigns in the economic arena. In financial institutions such as the World Bank and the IMF, the doctrine of resilience has become crucial. The key assumption of this type of thinking is that economies, and economic subjects, must be made more resilient in a situation of global market volatility. Workers must be made more resilient to low wages and underemployment; local and regional economies must be made resilient to the vicissitudes of uneven geographical development, as whole industries move across the globe at the drop of a hat; producers and consumers must become resilient to the wild fluctuations of the commodity market; citizens must be made resilient to withstand retirement without a pension, social security, or public health care; the skyrocketing number of depressed and insomniac individuals must be made resilient to a state of living defined by atomization, hypercompetitiveness, and technological consumption; and ensuring student resilience "is central to improving their academic performance" in underfunded and for-profit schools.[2]

Crucially, all of this resilience works to support capital accumulation. The more resilient the worker, the more docile she will be; the more resilient the consumer, the more he will be able to buy; the more resilient the citizens, the less the state is responsible for their well-being and the more public services can be privatized and turned into avenues for profit; and on and on. Capital "both generates and thrives on the anxiety that lies at the core of bourgeois subjectivity."[3]

Resilience evacuates politics. By always anticipating the traumatic event to come, resilience forecloses the possibility for a political mobilization that would imagine a future in which traumatic disasters would not so readily occur. "We can be individually anxious about the state of the world and about what might happen but our response must be resilience-training, not political struggle."[4]

Resilience is a buzzword in contemporary Detroit. Although this is in some sense nothing new—decades ago, Coleman Young claimed that Detroit was "the most resilient city in America"—the concept seems to have come into fashion especially since the city's supposed revival and can be seen as underpinning the city's ability to have apparently bounced back from years of decline and neglect. Recall that the city's motto is "We hope for better things. It shall rise from the ashes." Resilience appears everywhere that people are talking about the city. The promotional video made by Dan Gilbert's company as part of its bid to host Amazon's second headquarters calls Detroiters "the most resilient people on the planet." A *Huffington Post* article claims, "Together, Detroit's citizens and its leaders are revealing a new playbook for building and rebuilding resilient communities in America." A local artist is quoted in the *New York Times* saying, "People often use the word 'revitalization' in Detroit, but I think of resilience." Dennis Archer Jr., son of the former mayor, says of the city, "We're resilient. We're going to win." An article on the website of the World Bank on the topic is titled "Detroit's Future City Framework Offers Lessons on Resilience." One economist sees in Detroit "resilience in action." The planning director of the City of Detroit gave a presentation in July 2017 called "Putting Design to Work: How Design Is Building a Resilient Detroit." In a 2015 exhibit at the Detroit Institute of Arts on Frida Kahlo and Diego Rivera, NPR sees "A Portrait of a Resilient City."[5] The list could go on.

Where did this resilience come from? Thanks to its history as the manufacturing hub of the world, Detroit is perceived as hard-working, epitomizing the blue-collar, midwestern work ethic. And because of years of neglect and hardship, Detroiters have had to find a way to get by on their own, without the traditional supports of city services and secure jobs. "Detroit hustles harder." Journalists admire the "survivalist spirit of Detroit," the ability of its people, the city's greatest asset, to "adapt."[6] Many, even those with no connection to the city, seem to find themselves rooting for Motown. Detroit, as we noted in the introduction, is a sort of analogy for the fortunes of the country in general, the poster child for processes that have transformed urban life across America. As one writer put it, "If New York is a measure of our financial might and Los Angeles a yardstick for our imagination, Detroit is a gauge of our soul."[7]

Certainly there is truth to these sentiments. Detroit has experienced the worst of the myriad crises plaguing American cities. It ranks near the top on most every metric of urban despair. Despite this, many in the city still thrive, still make do on their own, with the support of their community. However, one is left to wonder, what choice is there other than resilience? *Resilience* seems to indicate nothing other than an attempt to positively frame the creative destruction that has crushed the city. Certainly Detroiters are resilient, but how many have been laid off, imprisoned, beaten by police, had their welfare slashed, been blamed for their own hardship, had their water shut off, their schools closed, their neighborhoods decimated in the name of austerity while Downtown flourishes? Sure, Detroiters are resilient. But what is the alternative? Death? Sheer destruction? One can't help but think that resilience is just another way to romanticize poverty. Given the choice between resilience and prosperity, comfort, and stability, it's obvious which option most Detroiters would choose.

Resilience becomes the ultimate goal of human social relations only within a political-economic system that continually reproduces crises and continually asks the working classes to pay for the cost of those crises. We have seen what resilience has meant in the history of Detroit. The question now is how to avoid the resilience that will become necessary in the future.

## Beyond Mythologies

The demand to give up the illusions about its condition is the demand to give up a condition which needs illusions. . . . Criticism has plucked the imaginary flowers from the chain not so that man will wear the chain without any fantasy or consolation but so that he will shake off the chain and cull the living flower. —**KARL MARX**, quoted in Fromm, *Beyond the Chains of Illusion*, 1962

Fantasy is what people want, but reality is what they need. —**LAURYN HILL**, *MTV Unplugged No. 2.0*, 2002

The interlinked political, moral, ecological, and humanitarian crises facing human civilization are difficult to refute. A report issued by the United Nations in October 2018 warns that humanity has only twelve years to mitigate climate change or face global catastrophe by the end of the century. The changes necessary to prevent this would involve "rapid, far-reaching and unprecedented changes in all aspects of society."[8] We have reached a situation of unprecedented inequality. As the number of billionaires grows—there are more than 600 worldwide—the situation for the working class becomes more desperate and insecure. Wages are stagnant, automation displaces more and more people, and stable jobs are increasingly scarce: in 2011 the number of workers in the world between the ages of twenty-five and fifty-four who were unemployed, vulnerably employed, or economically inactive was 2.4 billion, compared to only 1.4 billion workers that had stable, full-time jobs.[9] At the end of 2018 more than 68 million people had been displaced from their homes due to poverty, dispossession, climate change, or war.[10] Meanwhile, for those privileged groups living in the wealthier parts of the world, mental health is deteriorating. Nearly 16 percent of Americans take antidepressants, 40 percent suffer from insomnia, and nearly 20 percent admit to suffering from an anxiety disorder. Thirty years ago "the average age for the first onset of depression was 30. Today it is 14. . . . At this pace, over 50 per cent of our younger generation, aged 18–29, will succumb to it by middle age." Nor is this mental anguish simply an American problem: the global suicide rate has increased 60 percent in the past forty-five years.[11]

The Marxist psychoanalyst Erich Fromm suggests, "The irrationalities of any given society result in the *necessity* for its members to repress the awareness of many of their own feelings and observations. This necessity is the greater in proportion to the extent to which a society is not representative of all its members. . . . The repression of the awareness of facts is, and must be, supplemented by the acceptance of many fictions. The gaps which exist because we refuse to see many things around us *must be filled so that we may have a coherent picture.*"[12] Since capitalism is a social form that requires obfuscation for its functioning, a politics based on lies and manipulation should be conceived as the fullest expression of capitalist logic. And as the crisis of humanity has deepened, in order to retain their power, political and corporate elites have had to rely on grander mythologies, as well as more robust repressive forces. Authoritarian politicians have gained power in the United States, the Philippines, Brazil, Austria, France, and elsewhere. To seize power, these demagogues have utilized a mythical discourse that acknowledges people's economic and existential insecurities but blames those insecurities on a series of scapegoats: corrupt politicians, socialists, the liberal media, criminals, oppressed minorities, refugees, terrorists, and others—all the while implementing policies that exacerbate the crisis by creating new opportunities for international corporate elites to profit.[13]

The more this dialectic of creative destruction and mythologization develops, the more dangerous and violent things become. But at the same time, the system's legitimacy becomes more precarious, and more space is created for a radical politics based on an awareness of lived personal and political reality, based on a struggle for dignity and well-being rather than immiseration and myth-making. According to Fromm:

> Needs like the striving for happiness, belonging, love, and freedom are inherent in [human] nature. They are also dynamic factors in the historical

process. If a social order neglects or frustrates the basic human needs beyond a certain threshold, the members of such a society will try to change the social order so as to make it more suitable to their human needs. . . . The relation between social change and economic change is not only the one which Marx emphasized, namely, the interests of new classes in changed social and political conditions, but that social changes are at the same time determined by the fundamental human needs which make use, as it were, of favorable circumstances for their realization.[14]

In many ways, Fromm's vision is reflected in the later activism of James and Grace Lee Boggs, the legendary activists who have had a tremendous influence on contemporary Detroit-based activism. Dismayed by the failures of Communist regimes, and by the sexist, racist, and generally closed-off and unimaginative thinking that plagued the U.S. leftist scene, the Boggses increasingly foregrounded their politics on the concept of dialectical humanism, which aims to give a "moral and spiritual dimension" to the materialist struggle for power and resources.[15] Their aim has been to help people to start building, from the ground up, a society that is "more suitable to their human needs." The basic idea is that socialism is not some distant utopia; it is something we must start to build in the here and now.

In the early 1990s the Boggses organized Detroit Summer, which brought young people together with activists to work "in small groups on collaborative projects such as planting gardens, rehabilitating homes, and creating murals."[16] In 2012 Grace Lee Boggs and Scott Kurashige published *The Next American Revolution*, in which they articulated the view that revolutionary politics "should not be mainly a struggle for state power. It should revolve around going to people at the grassroots, helping them to transform their inner and outer lives, and encouraging them to think for themselves in order to create self-reliant local communities."[17] In his recent book, *The Fifty-Year Rebellion*, Kurashige offers a survey of a diverse array of community activists working in this vein, attempting to build a "revolutionary reconstruction of society from the ground up."[18]

Toward the end of her life, Grace Lee Boggs saw Detroit as the ideal place for this revolutionary process to occur:

Detroit, which was once the symbol of miracles of industrialization and then became the symbol of the devastation of deindustrialization, is now the symbol of a new kind of society, of people who grow their own food, of people who try and help each other, to how we begin to think, not so much of getting jobs and advancing our own fortunes, but how we depend on each other. . . . When you look out and all you see is vacant lots, when all you see is devastation, when all you see—do you look at it as a curse, or do you look at it as a possibility, as having potential?[19]

Inspiring though it is, Grace Lee Boggs's vision of contemporary Detroit—as a city full of "possibility," as a place where a "cultural revolution . . . is emerging from the ground up . . . as awesome as the transitions from hunting and gathering to agriculture eleven thousand years ago"—is difficult to reconcile with the continuing devastation of the city and the dominance of global corporations and political elites in Detroit's affairs, elites who have attempted to co-opt and thwart the very initiatives promoted by Kurashige and Boggs.[20]

Consider the James and Grace Lee Boggs School, a radical educational institution founded in 2013 by seasoned Detroit teachers and activists (where one of us briefly worked as a summer intern). Kurashige delineates the structural issues facing the project: "Whereas [other alternative schools] promise (often falsely) to help urban youth move up within the world of education and the global capitalist order, the Boggses maintained that our existing academic and economic systems were set up to promote exploitation and dehumanization." "There's a different way to do education that's not dehumanizing," says Julia Putnam, the school's principal "We get to practice how to be in society with the way we think society should be." The Boggs school recognizes that small pilot schools like itself must be "more than boutique successes or alternatives. Detroiters continue to struggle to build a movement that can apply the best lessons obtainable to revive a public school system that is rooted in the realities and concerns of a majority black and working-class city."[21] But despite this recognition of the need for systemic change, the school has had to make concessions to the powers that be in order to continue operation: "In a sign of stark reality, the Boggs School's founders made the difficult and controversial decision to apply for a charter." Further, the success of the Boggs school has been used by some on the right to justify further privatization of schools, a process which, as we saw in chapter 1, is devastating the city's, and the country's, educational process, as many leaders at the Boggs school acknowledge.[22]

Another sign of activism's co-optation by local elites is the effort to reclaim vacant land. Detroit has experienced an efflorescence of urban farming in recent years, as individuals and organizations take back abandoned lots, sometimes by the hundreds of acres, in an effort to establish neighborhood-level, sustainable food systems. Again, Kurashige recognizes the problems at stake here: "The city's veteran gardeners saw the vast expanse of vacant lots and abandonment as an opening and opportunity, but the issue of what to do with those presumed vacant spaces has become increasingly contentious over the past decade." Despite activists' vision, wherein "members of the community could control and determine the use of land in perpetuity, based on people's needs rather than market value," corporations and powerful individuals have profited from Detroit's land policies, as we saw in chapter 1. One example stands out: the wealthy finance capitalist John Hantz has positioned himself as an advocate of urban farming, piggybacking on the movement's goodwill while promoting large-scale, for-profit urban farming. In 2012 Hantz bought two thousand city-owned parcels on the East Side for *eight cents per acre*, without an appraisal.[23] Despite criticism of the deal, which activists aptly described as a massive "land grab," in early 2019 Hantz was able to manipulate the ideological support for local farming initiatives to secure another 450 parcels of "mostly vacant" properties from the city at the same bargain-basement price, and he intends to put this land to profitable use.[24]

In each case, local movements organizing on the basis of community needs in opposition to market forces met with two interrelated problems: a lack of power over the structural political forces that circumscribe individual action, leading to some necessary capitulation to those forces, and the ability of vested interests to manipulate activist strategies to their own ends, ends which themselves frustrate the goals of community activists and feed into the market mechanisms that dispossess communities. The form of activism championed by Boggs and Kurashige is undoubtedly vital and impactful, as it sees hope in areas of the city long neglected and written off by those in power. There seem to be clear limitations, however, to this vision. When looking at Detroit, people like Grace Lee Boggs may see "possibility" and "potential," but so do people like Dan Gilbert and the Ilitches. The question is: Who is in a strategic position to enact their vision? Political and corporate elites control most of the city's land, resources, and media outlets; they also control the criminal justice system and can bring violence to bear on those who oppose their interests. If it is true, as Fromm and the Boggses suggest, that the next revolution will require the masses to make a "spiritual leap" and affirm their collective humanity, it is also true that there are powerful groups that are fully committed to stopping this spiritual revolution from occurring, insofar as it interferes with the workings of bourgeois society. This is a fundamental issue in capitalism: the power of corporate elites makes genuine democracy very difficult to realize.

Oversimplifying matters a bit, we can highlight a basic contradiction between two types of politics that have animated the city's leftist scene for decades. On the one hand, there is the type of confrontational, class-based politics advocated by the League of Revolutionary Black Workers, many of whose members remain active in the city's political scene; on the other hand, there is the more horizontal, aspirational politics espoused by the Boggses. Over the years, activists from each camp have been critical of the others' approach. Those in the Boggses' camp tend to point out that Marxist organizations have had their day, and that although their ideals sound lofty, in practice they have routinely become dogmatic, non-democratic, non-inclusive, secretive, paranoid, and overly self-righteous. Furthermore, when these groups have become overtly militant, they have regularly been crushed by violent state forces. The Marxist response is basically that although the type of politics espoused by the Boggs is aspirational and inclusive, it is ultimately ineffectual, amorphous, and not up to the monumental task of confronting a very powerful capitalist class.

Both camps have their points. As the history we have provided shows, there is no successful model of leftist politics that can simply be replicated by contemporary activists. If there were, we wouldn't be in this mess. The question is: how will a grassroots politics emerge that can synthesize what is best from both of these camps, and build an organization that stays true to socialist ideals while avoiding political co-optation?

We do not pretend to have an answer to this question, nor do we feel it is our place to put forward some kind of political program. By the time this book is published, neither of us will be living in Detroit, and all we hope is that this book can be of some help to the multitude of Detroiters struggling to forge a more equitable society. We find hope in the diverse cast of activists who came together for the October 28, 2018, "Teach-In on the actual situation facing hundreds of thousands of people who live in the city of Detroit," which was organized around the following premise:

> The city has been underdeveloped by the financial institutions, the service sector and industrial plants. Over the last decade or more some 250,000 people have been forced out of Detroit through job losses, mortgage and property tax foreclosures, utility shut-offs involving water, heating and lighting, school closings and environmental degradation. We have to build fightback movements, which challenge the illegitimate right of the ruling class to govern at our expense by placing the interests of the masses at the forefront of any political and social program. We need to be organized at the grassroots levels to defeat the enemies, which are continuously exploiting and repressing the people of Detroit and other municipalities throughout the state, the country and indeed the world.[25]

Whatever one thinks of the viability of socialism, or of the tactics of various leftist organizations, one thing should be clear from the preceding chapters. So long as Detroit remains organized around the principles of capitalism—private property concentrated in the hands of the few, wage labor for the masses, the endless pursuit of profit—there is no remedy to the problems of poverty, exploitation, inequality, unemployment, dispossession, unsatisfying and degrading working conditions, environmental degradation, etc. These are problems that are *inherent* to capitalism, and they simply cannot be resolved by philanthropy or liberal reforms. All those thinking about Detroit's future should be honest about this. If people decide that capitalism is the only feasible way of organizing society, they are essentially concluding that these issues are acceptable, and that any alternative would probably be worse. It is not our intention to pardon or obscure the atrocities that have been carried out in the name of Socialism or Communism, be they in China, the Soviet Union, Cambodia, or elsewhere. Some of Marx's writings give the impression that, once the capitalist class is overthrown, all of society's problems will magically disappear. This way of thinking has proven to be as dangerous as it is false. So, while any attempt to actualize a communist society would undoubtedly be filled with unforeseeable problems and contradictions, one thing is certain: remaining within the capitalist status quo may be profitable for the elite architects of the New Detroit, but it surely augurs disaster for most people in Detroit.

# Notes

INTRODUCTION: MARX IN DETROIT

1 Matthew Goldstein, "Detroit: From Motor City to Housing Incubator," *New York Times*, November 4, 2017, https://www.nytimes.com/2017/11/04/business/detroit -housing.html; Tresa Baldas, "Detroit Is Once Again the Most Violent City in America, FBI Says Chief Craig Disagrees," *Detroit Free Press*, September 25, 2017, https://www .freep.com/story/news/2017/09/25/detroit-crime-violence/700443001/; Harvey, *Rebel Cities*, 53.

2 LeDuff, *Detroit*, 19.

3 Bedrock Detroit, "Detroit. Move Here. Move the World," directed by Stephen McGee, narration written and performed by Jessica Care Moore, 2017, https://www .youtube.com/watch?v=DO4J_PC1b5M.

4 Kurashige, *The Fifty-Year Rebellion*, 9.

5 The term *hyper-crisis* is from Smith and Kirkpatrick, "Reinventing Detroit," vii.

6 Monica Davey, "Detroit's Mayoral Election Is a Test of Recovery and Legacy," *New York Times*, August 6, 2017, https://www.nytimes.com/2017/08/06/us/detroit-election -mayor-coleman-young-mike-duggan.html.

7 Katherine Rodeghier, "Visitors find Michigan's largest city transformed," *Daily Herald*, December 9, 2016, http://www.dailyherald.com/article/20161209/entlife /161208962/.

8 Reif Larsen, "Detroit: The Most Exciting City in America?," *New York Times*, November 20, 2017, https://www.nytimes.com/2017/11/20/travel/detroit-michigan -downtown.html; Anneke Jong, "Silicon Mitten Is Happening: The Secret Revival of Detroit," *The Muse*, n.d., https://www.themuse.com/advice/silicon-mitten-is -happening-the-secret-revival-of-detroit; Jennifer Bain, "Detroit Is America's Great Comeback Story," *Toronto Star*, September 10, 2016, https://www.thestar.com/life /travel/2016/09/10/detroit-is-americas-great-comeback-story.html.

9 Blair Kamin, "Detroit's downtown revival is real, but road to recovery remains long," *Chicago Tribune*, April 15, 2017, https://www.chicagotribune.com/columns/ct-detroit -revival-kamin-met-0416-20170414-column.html.

10 "Detroit Is American Ingenuity," *Lonely Planet*, n.d., https://www.lonelyplanet.com/usa/great-lakes/detroit.

11 "Detroit, America's most ambitious renovation project," *Lonely Planet*, n.d., https://www.lonelyplanet.com/usa/great-lakes/detroit/travel-tips-and-articles/detroit-americas-most-ambitious-renovation-project/40625c8c-8a11-5710-a052-1479d27680c5.

12 Ben Austen, "The Post-Post-Apocalyptic Detroit," *New York Times*, July 11, 2014, https://www.nytimes.com/2014/07/13/magazine/the-post-post-apocalyptic-detroit.html? mcubz=0&_r=0.

13 "A Phoenix Emerges," *The Economist*, November 7, 2014, http://www.economist.com/blogs/democracyinamerica/2014/11/detroits-bankruptcy-plan.

14 Matt McFarland, "What Will Be the Greatest Turnaround Story in American History? This Author Says Detroit," *Washington Post*, July 8, 2014, https://www.washingtonpost.com/news/innovations/wp/2014/07/08/what-will-be-the-greatest-turnaround-story-in-american-history-this-author-says-detroit/.

15 Tim Alberta, "Is Dan Gilbert Detroit's New Superhero?," *The Atlantic*, February 27, 2014, https://www.theatlantic.com/business/archive/2014/02/is-dan-gilbert-detroits-new-superhero/425742/.

16 Chuck Barney, "TV highlights for the week of July 1-7," *Detroit Free Press*, https://www.freep.com/story/entertainment/television/2018/06/30/tv-highlights-week-july-july/36477709/.

17 Hackworth, "Defiant Neoliberalism and the Danger of Detroit," 547.

18 Frank Witsill, "Detroit Is the No. 2 City in the World to Visit, Lonely Planet Says," *Detroit Free Press*, October 24, 2017, https://www.freep.com/story/travel/michigan/2017/10/24/detroit-global-respect-lonely-planet/791360001/; Larsen, "Detroit: The Most Exciting City in America?"; "Detroit Is American Ingenuity."

19 Samantha Lande, "Meals in Motor City: The Best Restaurants in Detroit," *Food Network*, n.d., https://www.foodnetwork.com/restaurants/photos/restaurant-guide-detroit.

20 Bain, "Detroit Is America's Great Comeback Story."

21 Larsen, "Detroit: The Most Exciting City in America?"

22 Samuel Stebbins and Peter Comen, "50 Worst Cities to Live In," *24/7 Wall St.*, July 19, 2018, https://247wallst.com/special-report/2018/07/19/50-worst-cities-to-live-in-3-ta/11/.

23 Bernadette Atuahene, "Don't Let Detroit's Revival Rest on an Injustice," *New York Times*, July 22, 2017, https://www.nytimes.com/2017/07/22/opinion/sunday/dont-let-detroits-revival-rest-on-an-injustice.html.

24 Diane Bukowski, "We Charge Genocide! Detroit Water Shut-offs, Foreclosures Focus of UN Visit," *Voice of Detroit*, October 26, 2014, http://voiceofdetroit.net/2014/10/26/we-charge-genocide-detroit-water-shut-offs-foreclosures-focus-of-un-visit/.

25 Matthew Heimer, "How JPMorgan Chase Is Fueling Detroit's Revival," *Fortune*, September 7, 2017, http://fortune.com/2017/09/07/jp-morgan-chase-detroit-revival/.

26 Larsen, "Detroit: The Most Exciting City in America?"

27 Davey, "Detroit's Mayoral Election Is a Test of Recovery and Legacy."

28  Joel Kurth and Mike Wilkinson, "Is Detroit Finally Turning the Corner?," *Bridge*, June 19, 2018, https://www.bridgemi.com/detroit-journalism-cooperative/detroit -finally-turning-corner.

29  Joel Kurth, "Poverty Is Detroit's Biggest Problem: Gentrification Doesn't Come Close," *Bridge*, June 19, 2018, https://www.bridgemi.com/detroit-journalism -cooperative/poverty-detroits-biggest-problem-gentrification-doesnt-come-close.

30  George Hunter, "Petraeus Says Detroit's Revival Has Lessons for U.S.," *Detroit News*, April 12, 2018, https://www.detroitnews.com/story/news/local/detroit-city/2018/04 /12/petraeus-speaks-detroit-revival/33773375/.

31  Heimer, "How JPMorgan Chase Is Fueling Detroit's Revival."

32  John Gallagher, "JPMorgan Chase Raises Detroit Investment by $50 Million," *USA Today*, May 10, 2017, https://www.usatoday.com/story/money/2017/05/10/jpmorgan -chase-detroit-investment/101504994/.

33  "Detroit Is American Ingenuity."

34  Witsill, "Detroit Is the No. 2 City in the World to Visit, Lonely Planet Says."

35  Edward Helmore, "Detroit Redefined: City Hires America's First Official 'Chief Storyteller,'" *The Guardian*, September 5, 2017, https://www.theguardian.com/cities /2017/sep/05/detroit-redefined-america-first-official-chief-storyteller.

36  "Taking Back Detroit," directed by Stephen Lighthill (Available Light, 1980), https:// www.youtube.com/watch?v=bzEoyXTf22o.

37  This book draws heavily on past writings about Detroit. We are significantly indebted to the works of James and Grace Lee Boggs, Steve Babson, Martin Glaberman, Daniel J. Clark, Michael Stauch Jr., Stephen Meyer III, Dan Georgakas and Marvin Surkin, Thomas Sugrue, Ahmad Rahman, Heather Ann Thompson, Sidney Fine, Stephen M. Ward, Robert H. Mast, Elizabeth Esch, Nelson Lichtenstein, David Goldberg, Herb Boyd, Wilma Henrickson, A. Muhammad Ahmad, and Scott Martelle. We would also like to acknowledge the great reporting done by Ryan Felton, Abayomi Azikiwe, Allie Gross, Steve Nealing, and Diane Bukowski, among so many others.

38  There have been a tremendous number of films, poems, books, oral histories, and articles that have demonstrated the vibrancy, diversity, and specificity of Detroit's cultural history. Our aim is not to downplay any of these; rather, we hope that our Marxist approach will supplement and give added context to the city's rich cultural history.

39  Christopher McAuley, "On Capitalist Origins," *Solidarity*, November– December 2002, https://solidarity-us.org/atc/101/p724/.

40  Hardt and Negri, *Commonwealth*, 7. Marx spoke often about capital, and the capitalist mode of production, but rarely mentioned capitalism. For Marx, capital is both a process and a thing. It is the private wealth of the capitalist class, but it is also "value in motion," and capital encompasses the range of social relationships that facilitate the ongoing and ever-growing accumulation of private wealth. Throughout this work we follow the common usage among Marxists and refer to *capital* as a shorthand for the capitalist class, or simply as a shorthand for the most powerful corporations.

41 Quoted in Arrighi, *Adam Smith in Beijing*, 18. Tronti's *Operai e capitale* (Workers and Capital), in which this essay appears as a postscript, is not yet, at the time of our writing, available in English translation, so we have relied on Arrighi's interpretation; we have also looked at other works by Tronti that have been published in English.

42 Marx and Engels, *Manifesto of the Communist Party*.

43 Katz-Fishman and Scott, "The League of Revolutionary Black Workers and Race, Class, and Revolution in the Twenty-First Century."

44 Pizzolato, "Transnational Radicals," 25–27. The wildcat strikes launched by the League and other worker groups were of particular interest to Tronti and the Italian *operaismo* movement, which was "not moved by an ethical revolt against factory exploitation, but by political admiration for the practices of insubordination that they invented" (Tronti, "Our Operaismo").

45 Marx and Engels, *Manifesto of the Communist Party*.

46 "Alberto Toscano: Solidarity and Political Work," *Historical Materialism*, n.d., http://www.historicalmaterialism.org/interviews/alberto-toscano-solidarity-and-political-work.

47 Marx and Engels, *The Marx-Engels Reader*, 476. For an incisive analysis of the concept of creative destruction as it relates to the theories of Marx, Schumpeter, and David Harvey, see Arrighi's *Adam Smith in Beijing*.

48 Schumpeter, *Capitalism, Socialism and Democracy*, 83–84.

49 Clark, *Disruption in Detroit*, 97.

50 Harvey, *The New Imperialism*, 101.

51 Bill Shea, "Detroit Rink City: Ilitches' Grand Plan to Supersize the Entertainment District," *Crain's Detroit Business*, July 20, 2014.

52 James Bennet, "A Tribute to Ruin Irks Detroit," *New York Times*, December 10, 1995.

53 Berman, *All That Is Solid Melts into Air*, 99–100. Throughout this book we use the term *creative destruction* as an informal shorthand for the immense destruction that is required for capitalism to reproduce itself on an ever greater scale. Of course, in any process, social or physical, often something must be destroyed so that something else can be created. However, capitalism is set apart from other social systems in that its reproduction "systematically transforms the material conditions to which [it] originally responded" (Perlman, *The Reproduction of Daily Life*, 2). Moreover the level of destruction that capitalism requires is incommensurably large: the environmental degradation inherent in a system that treats nature as a "gigantic gasoline station," city forms and entire ways of life that are built and cultivated only to be demolished, the economic and existential anguish that results when processes of capital flight and automation render workers expendable, brutalizing work conditions and wars fought over access to new markets, violent police tactics and the repression of resistance movements, forced migrations and mass detainments, and on and on. See Heidegger, "Memorial Address."

54 In his analysis of primitive accumulation, Marx wrote that peasants were "first forcibly expropriated from the soil, driven from their homes, turned into vagabonds, then whipped, branded and tortured by grotesquely terroristic laws into accepting

the discipline necessary for the system of wage labor." Only after this spectacular violence occurs, Marx insists, can "the silent compulsion of economic relations [set] the seal on the domination of the capitalist over the worker. Direct extra-economic force is still of course used, but only in exceptional cases. In the ordinary run of things, the worker can be left to the natural laws of production, i.e., it is possible to rely on his dependence on capital, which springs from the conditions of production themselves, and is guaranteed in perpetuity by them" (Marx, *Capital: Vol. 1*, 899). As many scholars and activists have pointed out, however, force is not simply an ir-regular or intermittent requirement for the reproduction of capital; extra-economic force is a constant feature, and primitive accumulation is an ongoing process. See in particular *Caliban and the Witch* by Silvia Federici and *War Power, Police Power* by Mark Neocleous. Our history of Detroit will demonstrate the consistency of extra-economic force in the reproduction of capitalist social relations.

55  Quoted in Georgakas and Surkin, *Detroit, I Do Mind Dying*, 73.

56  Barthes, *Mythologies*, 142–43.

57  The concept of commodity fetishism shows that capitalist social relations are, at their core, centered on the obfuscation of their true nature. Marx begins *Capital* with the primary unit of capitalism: the commodity. At first apparently simple, the commodity is, in reality, "abounding in metaphysical subtleties and theological niceties." To use his classic example, a table is very simple; it is a plane with four legs made of wood. But as soon as a table becomes a commodity, it transforms, becomes imbued with magical capabilities: "It not only stands with its feet on the ground, but . . . it stands on its head, and evolves out of its wooden brain grotesque ideas." On the market, we do not see the producers of the table; all we see is a price tag. It is as if the table, in addition to all its material properties, contains a metaphysical property: its market value. Now tables, and all other commodities, are in reality products of human labor; this is where their value comes from. The money used to buy commodities is, also, an abstract representation of human labor. The exchange of commodities, then, is the exchange of one product of human labor for another. However, the exchange of commodities in the market appears not as an exchange of labor but as an exchange of a table for money. This is the essence of the fetish of the commodity: "It is a definite social relation between men, that assumes, in their eyes, the fantastic form of a relation between things." (Marx, *Capital*, 41, 81–83, emphasis added). So long as I participate in capitalism, I have no choice but to act as if each commodity is necessarily endowed with value. This is what Alfred Sohn-Rethel in *Intellectual and Manual Labor* calls a "real abstraction": although the table does not actually possess any suprasensible quality, our social intercourse is predicated on treating it as if it does. In Marx's philosophy, one finds, "not merely the 'reduction' of ideology to an economic base, and within this base, of exchange to production, but a much more ambiguous and mysterious phenomenon of 'commodity fetishism,' which designates a kind of proto-'ideology' inherent to the economic base itself" (Žižek, *Parallax View*, 170).

58  Lincoln, *Theorizing Myth*.

59  On this point, see Toscano and Kinkle, *Cartographies of the Absolute*.

60 Leonard Michaels, *Time Out of Mind*, 209.

61 Our analysis of myth is inspired by the reading Charles Taylor gives to Hegel's critique of the Enlightenment's dismissal of religion (*Hegel*, 184).

62 As Marx writes, "It is, in reality, much easier to discover by analysis the earthly core of the misty creations of religion, than, conversely, it is to develop from the actual relations of life the corresponding celestialised forms of those relations. The latter method is the only materialistic, and therefore, the only scientific one" (*Capital*, 493–94). In Toscano's words, it is not a matter of referring "representations to a material basis, but of showing the socio-historical necessity and rootedness of the 'phantoms'" that proliferate in capitalist society (*Fanaticism*, 188).

63 Lincoln, *Theorizing Myth*.

## CHAPTER 1: A TALE OF ONE CITY

1 Regina Bell, Jela Ellefson, and Phil Rivera, "7.2 SQ MI: A Report on Greater Downtown Detroit," 2013, http://detroitsevenpointtwo.com./resources/7.2SQ_MI _Section4_LoRes.pdf, p. 82.

2 Bill Bradley, "Detroit Scam City: How the Red Wings Took Hockeytown for All It Had," *Deadspin*, March 3, 2014, http://deadspin.com/detroit-scam-city-how-the-red -wings-took-hockeytown-fo-1534228789.

3 Kathleen Pender, "Quicken Loans Tops Wells Fargo to Become No. 1 in Retail Home Loans," *San Francisco Chronicle*, February 1, 2018, https://www.sfchronicle .com/business/networth/article/Quicken-Loans-bests-Wells-Fargo-in-key-part -of-12544569.php; R. J. King, "Quicken Loans Family of Companies Surpasses 17K Employees in Detroit, More to Come," *dbusiness*, September 5, 2017, http://www .dbusiness.com/daily-news/Annual-2017/Quicken-Loans-Family-of-Companies -Surpasses-17K-Employees-in-Detroit-More-to-Come/.

4 "WXYZ-TV Chooses Detroit Businessman Dan Gilbert as 'Newsmaker of the Year,'" *MLive*, February 23, 2013, https://www.mlive.com/business/detroit/2013/02/wxyz _selects_dan_gilbert_as_it.html; Tim Alberta, "Is Dan Gilbert Detroit's New Super-hero?," *Atlantic*, February 27, 2014, https://www.theatlantic.com/business/archive /2014/02/is-dan-gilbert-detroits-new-superhero/425742/; David Segal, "A Mission-ary's Quest to Remake Motor City," *New York Times*, April 13, 2013, http://www .nytimes.com/2013/04/14/business/dan-gilberts-quest-to-remake-downtown-detroit .html?mcubz=0.

5 Liz Essley Whyte, "Philanthropy Keeps the Lights on in Detroit," *Philanthropy*, Win-ter 2014, https://www.philanthropyroundtable.org/philanthropy-magazine/article /philanthropy-keeps-the-lights-on-in-detroit; Mallach, *The Divided City*, 108.

6 The neighborhoods originally planned for the District have no precedent in actually existing social-cultural formations in the city but, rather, would be built essentially from the ground up, their personality and character predetermined by Olympia Development to attract people to "live, work, and play" in Downtown Detroit. These imitation neighborhoods cannot but remind one of French philosopher Jean Baudrillard's postmodern take on the dialectic of the abstract and the concrete:

"Simulation is no longer that of a territory, a referential being, or a substance. It is the generation by models of a real without origin or reality: a hyperreal" (*Simulacra and Simulation*, 1). However, instead of these neighborhoods, the area around the arena is now filled with new parking lots, and the Neighborhood Advisory Committee assembled by Olympia to advise on the project has complained that the company's promises to invest in housing and other development in the area have gone unfulfilled. See Louis Aguilar, "Cass Corridor Neighbors See Unfulfilled Promises in Little Caesars Arena District," *Detroit News*, November 5, 2018, https://www .detroitnews.com/story/news/local/detroit-city/2018/11/05/ilitch-little-caesars-arena -detroit-development-plans/1850015002/.

7   Bill Shea, "Detroit Rink City: Ilitches' Grand Plan to Supersize the Entertainment District," *Crain's Detroit Business*, July 20 2014, http://www.crainsdetroit.com/article /20140720/news03/140719845/detroit-rink-city-ilitches-grand-plan-to-supersize-the; "Progress in the District Detroit," *District Detroit*, n.d., http://www.districtdetroit .com/progress.

8   Robin Runyan, "Dan Gilbert Talks Transformational Development, Jobs, Amazon Bid," *Curbed Detroit*, September 20, 2017, https://detroit.curbed.com/2017/9 /20/16339982/dan-gilbert-development-jobs-amazon; Leanna Garfield, "Detroit Is Building a $1 Billion 'City within a City' on the Site of a Dead Department Store," *Business Insider*, August 8, 2018, https://www.businessinsider.com/detroit-city-within -a-city-jl-hudson-redevelopment-2018-8; Robin Runyan, "12 Developments Set to Transform Detroit," *Curbed Detroit*, December 17, 2018, https://detroit.curbed.com /maps/development-detroit-transform.

9   Robin Runyan, "Dan Gilbert's Brush Park Development Adds Modern Design to Historic Neighborhood," *Curbed Detroit*, June 14, 2016, https://detroit.curbed.com /2016/6/14/11936040/brush-park-development-dan-gilbert; Robin Runyan, "Details Emerge for Dan Gilbert's Expansive Brewster-Douglass Redevelopment," *Curbed Detroit*, July 26, 2018, https://detroit.curbed.com/2018/7/26/17616932/brewster-douglass -redevelopment-dan-gilbert-plans.

10  Lara Moehlman, "Wayne County Makes Tentative Deal with Dan Gilbert for New Criminal Justice Center," Michigan Radio, March 7, 2018, http://michiganradio.org /post/wayne-county-makes-tentative-deal-gilbert-new-criminal-justice-center; Robin Runyan, "Dan Gilbert, Wayne County Strike Deal for New Jail, Plus Fail Jail Site," *Curbed Detroit*, March 7, 2018, https://detroit.curbed.com/2018/3/7/17090990 /dan-gilbert-wayne-county-tentative-deal-new-jail-gratiot-jail-site.

11  Packard Plant Project, "About Us," n.d., http://packardplantproject.com/about /index.html; Robin Runyan, "The Packard Plant Breaks Ground on First Phase of Massive Redevelopment," *Curbed Detroit*, May 16, 2017, https://detroit.curbed.com /2017/5/16/15647176/packard-plant-groundbreaking-redevelopment; Robin Runyan, "Photos: Visiting the Packard Plant before the Official Groundbreaking," *Curbed Detroit*, May 10, 2017, https://detroit.curbed.com/2017/5/10/15597104/packard-plant -redevelopment-photos.

12  The Platform, "Our Team," n.d., https://www.theplatform.city/our-team-2/; John Gallagher, "Local Developers Join HFZ in Fisher Building Purchase," *Detroit Free*

*Press*, June 25, 2015; Kirk Pinho, "Another Platform Development: 304 Apartments, 28,000 Square Feet of Grocery in New Center," *Crain's Detroit Business*, August 24, 2018, https://www.crainsdetroit.com/article/20180824/news/669186/another -platform-development-304-apartments-28000-square-feet-of; Robin Runyan, "Mapping the Developments in the Works in and around New Center," *Curbed Detroit*, April 26, 2018, https://detroit.curbed.com/maps/new-center-development -construction-map; Robin Runyan, "Cass and York to Bring High-end Condos to New Center," *Curbed Detroit*, January 26, 2018, https://detroit.curbed.com/2018/1 /26/16934714/cass-york-high-end-condos-new-center; Robin Runyan, "First Phase of Baltimore Station to Open This Summer," *Curbed Detroit*, April 11, 2018, https:// detroit.curbed.com/2018/4/11/17225474/first-phase-baltimore-station-open-this -summer; The Platform, "Chroma," n.d., https://www.theplatform.city/chroma/.

13   Robin Runyan, "Henry Ford Breaks Ground on Cancer Center Near New Center," *Curbed Detroit*, June 6, 2017, https://detroit.curbed.com/2017/6/6/15747370/henry -ford-cancer-center-construction.

14   Robin Runyan, "Tech Town Industrial Buildings Sell for $3.1M, Will Be Converted to Mixed-Use Development," *Curbed Detroit*, June 17, 2017, https://detroit.curbed .com/2017/2/17/14650592/tech-town-industrial-buildings-sold-redevelopment.

15   Robin Runyan, "Detroit Snags Brooklyn Bridge Park Designer for West Riverfront," *Curbed Detroit*, April 10, 2018, https://detroit.curbed.com/2018/4/10/17218976/detroit -brooklyn-bridge-park-designer-west-riverfront.

16   Robin Runyan, "Atwater Beach Officially Breaks Ground along Detroit's East Riverfront," *Curbed Detroit*, August 27, 2018, https://detroit.curbed.com/2018/8/27 /17786296/atwater-beach-breaks-ground-detroit-east-riverfront; Robin Runyan, "Detroit RiverFront Conservancy Reveals Plans for East Riverfront Redevelop- ment," *Curbed Detroit*, March 1, 2017, https://detroit.curbed.com/2017/3/1/14785116 /east-riverfront-detroit-development.

17   Visit Detroit, "Marketing Plan," 2018, https://visitdetroit.com/membership /marketing-plan/.

18   Cleve R. Wootson Jr., "Michigan Central Station Is a Towering Symbol of Detroit's Blight: Ford Just Bought It," *Washington Post*, June 11, 2018.

19   Ford, "Michigan Central Station, Centerpiece of Ford's Corktown Campus," accessed February 11, 2019, https://corporate.ford.com/campuses/corktown-campus.html.

20   Robin Runyan, "Here's What We Know about Ford's Move to Detroit," *Curbed De- troit*, June 18, 2018, https://detroit.curbed.com/2018/6/13/17456790/ford-move-detroit -corktown-michigan-central-station.

21   Stephen M. Gillon, "This Train Station Is Poised to Help Detroit Get Back on Track," *History*, June 25, 2018, https://www.history.com/news/detroit-comeback-ford -central-station; Ford Motor Company, "Ford Motor Company: Michigan Central Station Press Conference Recap," June 20, 2018, https://www.youtube.com/watch?v =pGTF104mBOQ.

22   John Gallagher, "Detroit Train Station Is City's Biggest Comeback Moment Yet," *Detroit Free Press*, June 15, 2018, https://www.freep.com/story/money/business/john -gallagher/2018/06/15/ford-detroit-train-station-impact/697756002/.

23  "Central Depot Message: 'A Sentinel of Progress,'" *Detroit News*, June 14, 2018, https://www.detroitnews.com/story/news/local/detroit-city/2018/06/14/central -depot-latin-mottoes-rise-ashes/704129002/.

24  "May 2018 State Occupational Employment and Wage Estimates," *Bureau of Labor Statistics*, https://www.bls.gov/oes/current/oes_mi.htm.

25  Many are attracted by subsidies offered to employees of new businesses who move into Greater Downtown, including up to $20,000 in forgivable loans and $2,500 rent forgiveness. See Bell, Ellefson, and Rivera, "7.2 SQ MI"; Joel Kurth and Mike Wilkinson, "Is Detroit Finally Turning the Corner?," *Bridge*, June 19, 2018, https:// www.bridgemi.com/detroit-journalism-cooperative/detroit-finally-turning-corner.

26  Christina Cannon, "Detroit's Downtown Revival, Led by Dan Gilbert, Gains Momentum," *Rebusiness Online*, May 19, 2016, http://rebusinessonline.com/detroits -downtown-revivalled-by-dan-gilbert-gains-momentum/; "First Look at Models for New Detroit Red Wings Arena Luxury Suites and Entertainment District," WXYZ .com, accessed February 2016. As capital overhauls Detroit, the process serves as a striking illustration of Guy Debord's claim that "Urbanism is the mode of appropriation of the natural and human environment by capitalism, which, true to its logical development toward absolute domination, can (and now must) refashion the totality of space into its own peculiar decor" (*Society of the Spectacle*, 169).

27  Marsha Music, "Just Say Hi! (The Gentrification Blues)," 2015, https://marshamusic .wordpress.com/just-say-hi-the-gentrification-blues/.

28  Nancy Derringer, "In a Gentrifying Detroit, an Uneasy Migration of Urban Millennials," *Bridge*, August 21, 2014, https://www.bridgemi.com/detroit-bankruptcy-and -beyond/gentrifying-detroit-uneasy-migration-urban-millennials.

29  Emma Winowiecki, "Mostly-White 'See Detroit Like We Do' Ad Draws Backlash and Apologies," Michigan Radio, July 24, 2017, http://www.michiganradio.org/post /mostly-white-see-detroit-we-do-ad-draws-backlash-and-apologies.

30  Chris Michael and Ellie Violet Bramley, "Spike Lee's Gentrification Rant— Transcript," *Guardian*, February 14, 2016, https://www.theguardian.com/cities/2014 /feb/26/spike-lee-gentrification-rant-transcript; Roger Wareham, "'Gentrification' Is Ethnic Cleansing," *New York Amsterdam News*, May 10, 2018, http://amsterdamnews .com/news/2018/may/10/gentrification-ethnic-cleansing/.

31  Mallach, *The Divided City*, 111.

32  Lees, Shin, and Lopez-Morales, *Planetary Gentrification*; Harvey, *Social Justice and the City*; Smith, *The New Urban Frontier*.

33  Smith, "New Globalism, New Urbanism," 443.

34  Harvey, "From Managerialism to Entrepreneurialism."

35  Weber, "Extracting Value from the City," 531.

36  Dan Gilbert, "The Elephant in the Room," January 23, 2018, http:// 1md1ifcdgpn3hahxo2l2bzt6.wpengine.netdna-cdn.com/wp-content/uploads/2018/01 /The-Elephant-in-the-Room.pdf.

37  Philip Conklin and Mark Jay, "Opportunity Detroit," *Jacobin*, January 3, 2018, https://www.jacobinmag.com/2018/01/detroit-revival-inequality-dan-gilbert -hudsons.

38  On the fetishization of black grittiness and resilience, see Spence, *Knocking the Hustle*. An "Urban Exploration and Photography Tour" advertised on Trip Advisor for $75 reads, "Explore the city of Detroit and capture images of the crumbling industrial Midwestern metropolis on this guided photography tour. Wander through vacated factories, warehouses, and buildings, while getting photography tips on composition, exposure, and more from your guide who specializes in shooting urban landscapes. There's no fussing with directions as an air-conditioned coach brings you to each location." See: https://www.tripadvisor.com/AttractionProductReview -g42139-d11459396-or5-Detroit_Urban_Exploration_and_Photography_Tour-Detroit _Michigan.html.

39  Samuel Stein, "Capital City: Gentrification and the Real Estate State," *Next City*, March 4, 2019, https://nextcity.org/features/view/capital-city-gentrification-and -the-real-estate-state; Wolf Richter, "Overcapacity Is Destroying Our Economy," *Business Insider*, September 21, 2016, https://www.businessinsider.com/overcapacity-is -destroying-our-economy-2016-9.

40  Stein, "Capital City."

41  Paul Beshouri, "The Griswold Building Becomes 'The Albert,' Releases an Unbearable Promo Video," *Curbed Detroit*, March 13, 2014, https://detroit.curbed.com/2014 /3/13/10132632/the-griswold-building-becomes-the-albert-releases-an-unbearable -promo.

42  Cannon, "Detroit's Downtown Revival."

43  Cannon, "Detroit's Downtown Revival"; Louis Aguilar, "Ilitches Bet Big on Land Near MotorCity Casino," *Detroit News*, 26 August 2015; Abayomi Azikiwe, "Privatizing Detroit: Residents Evicted and Displaced by Corporate Interests," *Global Research*, April 30, 2013, https://www.globalresearch.ca/privatizing-detroit-residents -evicted-and-displaced-by-corporate-interests/5333483.

44  Allie Gross, "Detroit Hotel Residents, Many Low-Income, Given 30 Days to Move," *Detroit Free Press*, October 11, 2018.

45  Aaron Handelsman and LaToya Morgan, "Opinion: As New Development Attracts New People, Detroit Officials Need to Help Keep the City Affordable," *Detroit Metro Times*, June 28, 2017, https://www.metrotimes.com/detroit/opinion-as-new -development-attracts-new-people-detroit-officials-need-to-help-keep-the-city -affordable/Content?oid=4373699.

46  Kurashige, *The Fifty-Year Rebellion*, 48.

47  Mike Wilkinson, "Detroit Jobs Few, Far from Residents," *Detroit News*, August 9, 2015, http://www.detroitnews.com/story/news/local/detroit-city/2015/08/09/detroit -jobs/31392579/.

48  Nina Godlewski, "Amazon Working Conditions," *Newsweek*, September 12, 2018, https://www.newsweek.com/amazon-drivers-warehouse-conditions-workers -complains-jeff-bezos-bernie-1118849; Joe Demanuelle-Hall, "That's Strike One, Amazon," *Jacobin*, March 2019, https://jacobinmag.com/2019/03/minnesota-strike -amazon-somali-awood.

49  "'Still Doin' Time:' Clamoring for Work in the Day Labor Industry," *Working USA* 15 (September 2012): 400–407; Gilmore, "Prisons and Class Warfare."

50 Monica Davey and Mary Williams Walsh, "Billions in Debt, Detroit Tumbles into Insolvency," *New York Times*, July 18, 2013, http://www.nytimes.com/2013/07/19/us /detroit-files-for-bankruptcy.html? mcubz=0; Thomas J. Sugrue, "The Rise and Fall of Detroit's Middle Class," *New Yorker*, July 22, 2013, https://www.newyorker.com /news/news-desk/the-rise-and-fall-of-detroits-middle-class; "Detroit Bankruptcy Plan: A Phoenix Emerges," *The Economist*, November 7, 2014, https://www.economist .com/democracy-in-america/2014/11/07/a-phoenix-emerges; Monica Davey and Mary Williams Walsh, "For Detroit, a Crisis of Bad Decisions and Crossed Fingers," *New York Times*, March 11, 2013, http://www.nytimes.com/2013/03/12/us/for-detroit-a -financial-crisis-was-long-coming.html?mtrref=undefined&gwh=1F3D0777B945EB 2027B94C68C249C3E8&gwt=pay; Aaron Petkov, "Detroit's Grand Bargain," *Jacobin*, June 30, 2014, https://www.jacobinmag.com/2014/06/detroit-s-grand-bargain/; Martha Grevatt, "Victory in Detroit Hotel Strike," *Workers World*, November 6, 2018, https://www.workers.org/2018/11/06/victory-in-detroit-hotel-strike/.

51 Bethany Blankley, "Report: Detroit, Cleveland among 'neediest cities' with highest poverty levels," *The Center Square*, April 17, 2019, https://www.thecentersquare.com /national/report-detroit-cleveland-among-neediest-cities-with-highest-poverty -levels/article_b1725874-5b91-11e9-9155-97b15054e23a.html.

52 "Census: Detroit income rises, poverty rate doesn't improve." *Crain's Detroit Business*, September 13, 2018, https://www.crainsdetroit.com/news/census-detroit-income -rises-poverty-rate-doesnt-improve.

53 Diane Bukowski, "'We the People' Cry Genocide: Detroit Water Shut-offs, Fore-closures Erasing Black Neighborhoods," *Voice of Detroit*, August 25, 2016, http:// voiceofdetroit.net/2016/08/25/we-the-people-cry-genocide-detroit-water-shut-offs -foreclosures-erasing-black-neighborhoods/.

54 Detroit Water Brigade, homepage, http://detroitwaterbrigade.org/; Katrease Staf-ford, "Controversial Water Shutoffs Could Hit 17,461 Detroit Households," *Detroit Free Press*, March 26, 2018, https://www.freep.com/story/news/local/michigan/detroit /2018/03/26/more-than-17–000-detroit-households-risk-water-shutoffs/452801002/.

55 Kurashige, *The Fifty-Year Rebellion*, 69; Bukowski, "'We the People' Cry Genocide"; Drew Philip, "No Water for Poor People," *Guardian*, July 20, 2017, https://www .theguardian.com/us-news/2017/jul/20/detroit-water-shutoffs-marian-kramer-bill -wylie-kellermann; Laura Gottesdiener, "UN Officials 'Shocked' by Detroit's Mass Water Shutoffs," *Al Jazeera America*, October 20, 2014, http://america.aljazeera.com /articles/2014/10/20/detroit-water-un.html. The number of shutoffs through 2017 is based on data from Stafford, "Controversial Water Shutoffs"; Joel Kurth, "Detroit Hits Residents on Water Shut-offs as Businesses Slide," *Detroit News*, April 1, 2016, http://www.detroitnews.com/story/news/local/detroit-city/2016/03/31/detroit-water -shutoffs/82497496/; and Ian Thibodeau, "After 33,607 Water Shut-offs in 2014, De-troit to Focus on Commercial Accounts," *MLive*, March 17, 2015, https://www.mlive .com/news/detroit/index.ssf/2015/03/businesses_next_up_for_detroit.html.

56 Valerie Vande Panne, "Detroiters Fear Losing Their Water May Mean Losing Their Kids," *In These Times*, September 11, 2018, http://inthesetimes.com/article/21412 /detroit-water-shutoffs-child-services-debt; Maria Zamdio and Will Craft, "A Water

Crisis Is Growing in a Place You'd Least Expect It," NPR, February 8, 2019, https://www.npr.org/2019/02/08/691409795/a-water-crisis-is-growing-in-a-place-youd-least-expect-it.

57 Gottesdiener, "UN Officials 'Shocked' by Detroit's Mass Water Shutoffs"; Kurth, "Detroit Hits Residents on Water Shut-offs as Businesses Slide."

58 Bukowski, "'We the People' Cry Genocide."

59 Vande Panne, "Detroiters Fear Losing Their Water May Mean Losing Their Kids."

60 Philip, "No Water for Poor People."

61 Vande Panne, "Detroiters Fear Losing Their Water May Mean Losing Their Kids."

62 Detroit Water Brigade, homepage, http://detroitwaterbrigade.org/.

63 Jerry Goldberg, "Detroit against Foreclosures and for Housing for People, Not Banks," *Workers World*, June 26, 2017, https://www.workers.org/2017/06/26/detroit-against-foreclosures-for-housing-for-people-not-banks/.

64 "People Are Making Big Money Kicking Detroit Residents out of Their Homes," *Vice News*, December 7, 2017, https://www.youtube.com/watch?v=gHLaWw_PnQY; Patrick Sheehan, "Revitalization by Gentrification," *Jacobin*, May 11, 2015, https://www.jacobinmag.com/2015/05/detroit-foreclosure-redlining-evictions/; Ryan Felton, "Redefining Eminent Domain," *Detroit Metro Times*, May 13, 2014.

65 Austen, "The Post-Post-Apocalyptic Detroit," *New York Times*, July 11, 2014, https://www.nytimes.com/2014/07/13/magazine/the-post-post-apocalyptic-detroit.html.

66 Michele Oberholtzer, "Myth-Busting the Detroit Tax Foreclosure Crisis," *Metro Times*, September 13, 2017, https://www.metrotimes.com/detroit/myth-busting-the-detroit-tax-foreclosure-crisis/Content?oid=5552983.

67 Allie Gross, "It Just Got Easier for Poor Detroiters to Get Poverty Tax Exemptions," *Detroit Free Press*, November 20, 2018.

68 "Neighborhood Stabilization Program," City of Detroit Planning and Development Department, 2009, http://www.detroitmi.gov/Portals/0/docs/Planning/PDF/NSP/detroitNSP_R31_29_09_2. pdf; Joel Kurth and Christine MacDonald, "Volume of Abandoned Homes 'Absolutely Terrifying,'" *Detroit News*, May 14, 2015, http://www.detroitnews.com/story/news/special-reports/2015/05/14/detroit-abandoned-homes-volume-terrifying/27237787/; Felton, "Redefining Eminent Domain"; "Demonstration—Stop Foreclosures and Water Shutoffs," Moratorium Now!, June 14, 2016, http://moratorium-mi.org; Allie Gross, "Radical New Program Saves Detroiters on the Brink of Homelessness," *Detroit Free Press*, November 20, 2018, https://www.freep.com/story/news/local/michigan/detroit/2018/11/20/foreclosure-program-detroit-homelessness/1685501002/.

69 Kat Stafford, "Was Contaminated Dirt Used to Fill Detroit Demolition Holes? Feds Ask," *Detroit Free Press*, February 11, 2019, https://www.freep.com/story/news/investigations/2019/02/11/detroit-land-bank-federal-demolition-dirt-probe-sites-across-detroit/2796355002/.

70 Ryan Felton, "What Kind of Track Records Do Quicken Loans and Dan Gilbert Have in Detroit?," *Detroit Metro Times*, November 12, 2014, https://www.metrotimes.com/detroit/what-kind-of-track-record-does-quicken-loans-have-in-detroit-does-anyone-really-care/Content?oid=2266383; Tom Perkins, "On Dan Gilbert's Ever-

Growing Rap Sheet, and Corporate Welfare," *Detroit Metro Times*, August 30, 2017, https://www.metrotimes.com/news-hits/archives/2017/08/30/on-dan-gilberts-ever-growing-rap-sheet-and-corporate-welfare; Chip Jengel, "Billionaire Wants to Drive Out Detroiters," *Workers World*, August 14, 2017, https://www.workers.org/2017/08/04/billionaire-wants-to-drive-out-detroiters/.

71 Austen, "The Post-Post-Apocalyptic Detroit."

72 Joel Kurth, "Foreclosures Lucrative for Wayne County," *Crain's Detroit Business*, 11 June 2017, https://www.crainsdetroit.com/article/20170610/news/631141/foreclosures-lucrative-wayne-county.

73 "Brown v. Ferguson," *Endnotes*, October 2015, https://endnotes.org.uk/issues/4/en/endnotes-brown-v-ferguson; Kelley, "Thug Nation," 30.

74 Gross, "Radical New Program Saves Detroiters on the Brink of Homelessness."

75 Gross, "Radical New Program Saves Detroiters on the Brink of Homelessness"; "Mission," Fitz Forward, accessed January 2019, https://www.fitzforwarddetroit.com/mission/.

76 This has led to the infamous "Count Day." On the day that enrollment numbers are recorded, schools throw pizza parties, raffle Play Stations, and offer myriad other incentives to get the highest possible number of students to show up and be counted, ensuring the highest possible funding from the state. In 2018 students across Detroit boycotted Count Day to protest conditions in the public schools, specifically the recent revelation that the school's water system was tainted by lead.

77 Michael Jackman, "How Boggs School Principal Julia Putnam Is Rethinking Education," *Detroit Metro Times*, July 25, 2018, https://www.metrotimes.com/detroit/how-boggs-school-principal-julia-putnam-is-rethinking-education/Content?oid=14096362.

78 Julie McIntyre, "Superman's Shop Floor: An Inquiry into Charter School Labor in Philadelphia," *Viewpoint Magazine*, September 12, 2013, https://www.viewpointmag.com/2013/09/12/supermans-shop-floor-an-inquiry-into-charter-school-labor-in-philadelphia/.

79 Hella Winston, "How Charter Schools Bust Unions," *Slate*, September 29, 2016, https://slate.com/business/2016/09/the-lengths-that-charter-schools-go-to-when-their-teachers-try-to-form-unions.html.

80 Kurashige, *The Fifty-Year Rebellion*, 84–92; Diane Bukowski, "Genocidal Snyder/Rhodes Plan Harms Detroit," *Voice of Detroit*, May 6, 2016, http://voiceofdetroit.net/2016/05/06/genocidal-snyderrhodes-plan-harms-detroit-public-school-children-workers-residents/; Diane Bukowski, "Detroit Kids in Danger," *Voice of Detroit*, March 29, 2016, http://voiceofdetroit.net/2016/03/29/detroit-kids-in-danger-bills-end-dps-pay-off-banks-with-state-control-tax-levies-closings-charters/; Grover and van der Velde, *A School District in Crisis*; Diane Bukowski, "State War on Public Schools Continues," *Voice of Detroit*, April 24, 2016, http://voiceofdetroit.net/2016/04/24/state-war-on-detroit-public-schools-continues-selling-black-children-to-the-highest-bidder/; Erin Einhorn, "To protect 24 schools from closure, the Detroit school board made a deal with the state. This is what it says, and doesn't say," *Chalkbeat*, April 28, 2017, https://www.chalkbeat.org/posts/detroit/2017/04/28/to-protect

-24-schools-from-closure-the-detroit-school-board-made-a-deal-with-the-state-this
-is-what-it-says-and-doesnt-say/; "Fight Back Unjust School Closures," *482Forward*,
https://www.482forward.org/school-closures.html.

81  League of Revolutionary Black Workers, "Some Lessons Learned," n.d., https://www
.revolutionaryblackworkers.org/video/.

82  Vitale, *The End of Policing*, 58.

83  Annalise Frank, "Former Detroit Police Chief Godbee to Lead City Public Schools'
Force," *Crain's Detroit Business*, August 3, 2018, https://www.crainsdetroit.com/article
/20180803/news/667646/former-detroit-police-chief-godbee-to-lead-city-public
-schools-force.

84  David Arsen and Nicole Geary, "Michigan Schools Face Nation's Worst Decline
in State Education Funding," *MSU Today*, January 23, 2019, https://msutoday.msu
.edu/news/2019/michigan-schools-face-nations-worst-decline-in-state-education
-funding/.

85  Julie McIntyre, "Superman's Shop Floor: An Inquiry into Charter School Labor in
Philadelphia," *Viewpoint Magazine*, September 12, 2013, https://www.viewpointmag
.com/2013/09/12/supermans-shop-floor-an-inquiry-into-charter-school-labor-in
-philadelphia/.

86  As Teju Cole has suggested, when social justice work is divorced from politics, it
becomes little more than "a valve for releasing the unbearable pressures that build
in a system built on pillage." Teju Cole, "The White-Savior-Industrial-Complex,"
*Atlantic*, March 21, 2012, https://www.theatlantic.com/international/archive/2012/03
/the-white-savior-industrial-complex/254843/.

87  Live6 Alliance, "Grow Up in a Diverse Community," *Neighborhood Stories*, http://
www.live6detroit.org/#storiesintro.

88  Marx, *Capital: Vol. 1*, 604.

89  Kurashige, *The Fifty-Year Rebellion*, 104.

90  Petkov, "Detroit's Grand Bargain"; "Detroit Future City 2012," http://
detroitfuturecity.com/wp-content/uploads/2014/12/DFC_ExecutiveSummary_2nd
.pdf.

91  "Detroit Future City 2012"; Bill McGraw, "Redesigning Detroit: Mayor Mike
Duggan's Blueprint Unveiled," *MLive*, August 18, 2015, https://www.mlive.com/news
/detroit/2015/08/redesigning_detroit_the_mayors.html; Jay, "Policing the Poor in
Detroit"; Jonathan Oosting, "Detroit Mayor Dave Bing: Relocation 'Absolutely' Part
of Plan to Downsize City," *MLive*, February 25, 2010, http://www.mlive.com/news
/detroit/index.ssf/2010/02/detroit_mayor_dave_bing_reloca.html; Clement, "The
Spatial Injustice of Crisis-Driven Neoliberal Urban Restructuring in Detroit."

92  Robin Runyan, "The District Detroit: Concept vs. Reality," *Curbed Detroit*,
August 14, 2018, https://detroit.curbed.com/2018/8/14/17680626/district-detroit
-concept-reality-photos-hockey-arena; Joe Guillen, "Ilitches Can Maximize Parking
Money Thanks to Favorable City Ruling on LCA Lot Designs," *Detroit Free Press*,
January 11, 2018.

93  Kirk Pinho, "Dan Gilbert's Newest Development Effort Is a Parking Lot for Employees,
Tenants," *Crain's*, January 11, 2016, http://www.crainsdetroit.com/article/20160111

/BLOG016/160119982/dan-gilberts-newest-development-effort-is-a-parking-lot-for;
Louis Aguilar, "Putting a Price Tag on Properties Linked to Gilbert," *Detroit News*,
April 29, 2016, http://www.detroitnews.com/story/business/2016/04/28/dan-gilbert
-bedrock-downtown-detroit-buildings/83681698/.

94  Ryan Felton. "Off the Rails: How Detroit Ended Up with the Worst Public Transit,"
    *Metro Times*, March 12, 2014, https://www.metrotimes.com/detroit/how-detroit
    -ended-up-with-the-worst-public-transit/Content?oid=2143889; Ryan Felton, "On
    Detroit Transit Woes and James Robertson," *The Periphery*, March 2015, http://www
    .theperipherymag.com/essay-on-detroit-transit-woes-and-james-robertson/.

95  Felton, "What Kind of Track Records Do Quicken Loans and Dan Gilbert Have in
    Detroit?"

96  Bradley, "Detroit Scam City"; Kurashige, *The Fifty-Year Rebellion*, 99.

97  Louis Aguilar, "Gilbert Seals $618M Tax Incentive Package for 4 Detroit Projects,"
    *Detroit News*, May 22, 2018, https://www.detroitnews.com/story/news/local/detroit
    -city/2018/05/22/tax-breaks-dan-gilbert-downtown-detroit-hudson-book-monroe
    -development/629505002/; Tom Perkins, "How Dan Gilbert Just Scored up to
    $1 Billion in Taxpayer Money—and Few Noticed," *Metro Times*, October 4, 2017,
    https://www.metrotimes.com/detroit/how-dan-gilbert-just-scored-up-to-1-billion-in
    -taxpayer-money-and-few-noticed/Content?oid=5981552; Sikha Dalmia, "The Dark
    Side of Detroit's Renaissance," *The Week*, April 27, 2017, https://theweek.com/articles
    /692770/dark-side-detroits-renaissance.

98  Jarett Skorup, "MEGA Failure: Job Projections from Michigan Tax Credit Pro-
    gram Rarely Came True," *Michigan Capitol Confidential*, May 15, 2014, https://www
    .michigancapitolconfidential.com/MEGA-program-a-complete-failure.

99  Conklin and Jay, "Opportunity Detroit."

100 Boyd, *Black Detroit*, 251.

101 Scott Beyer, "Why Has Detroit Continued to Decline?," *Forbes*, July 31, 2018, https://
    www.forbes.com/sites/scottbeyer/2018/07/31/why-has-detroit-continued-to-decline
    /#7b2071f23fbe.

102 Rashida Tlaib, "Transformational Brownfield Bills Are a 'Rebate for the Rich,'"
    *Metro Times*, April 5, 2017, https://www.metrotimes.com/detroit/transformational
    -brownfield-bills-are-a-rebate-for-the-rich/Content?oid=3221084.

103 McNally, *Global Slump*, 5.

104 Kurashige, *The Fifty-Year Rebellion*, 11, 51–52. The original sin of capitalism is what
    Marx termed "primitive accumulation," the foundational process of creation of
    the capital-labor relationship, in which peasants were separated from the means of
    production and forced to become laborers working for a wage. Marxists have rightly
    asserted that despite its name, primitive accumulation is a continuous operation
    of capital. Updating the concept for the contemporary period, David Harvey has
    termed the contemporary process of wealth extraction and redistribution "ac-
    cumulation by dispossession." Under this heading Harvey describes four primary
    processes: commodification and privatization of resources, particularly public assets
    like utilities, pensions, and social services; financialization, in which resources are
    increasingly devoted to and values extracted from the process of circulation of

capital, which has occurred alongside deindustrialization in the United States; the management and manipulation of crises, wherein the implementation of debt turns cities and states into vassals of international financial institutions that administer structural changes to local economies, causing increasing outflow of resources to banks and wealthy countries; and state redistribution, in which taxes and public resources become tools for enrichment of the upper classes at the expense of the poor. Detroit, as we've seen, is a case study of each one of these processes, and the financial coup in the Motor City is part of a long lineage. Harvey, *A Brief History of Neoliberalism*, 159–65.

105 Kurashige, *The Fifty-Year Rebellion*, 63–73, 80; Christine Ferretti and Robert Snell, "Detroit Bankruptcy Fees Top $170M," *Detroit News*, December 31, 2014, http://www .detroitnews.com/story/news/local/wayne-county/2014/12/30/detroit-bankruptcy -fees-top/21074011/.

106 Michael A. Fletcher, "The Man Who Is Trying to Save Detroit," *Washington Post*, July 20, 2013, https://www.washingtonpost.com/business/economy/the-man-who-is -trying-to-save-detroit/2013/07/20/bf3c22c2-f12b-11e2-a1f9-ea873b7e0424_story.html ?noredirect=on&utm_term=.98692518aa92.

107 Kurashige, *The Fifty-Year Rebellion*, 69–70; We the People of Detroit Community Research Collective, *Mapping the Water Crisis*, 15.

108 Hackworth, "Defiant Neoliberalism and the Danger of Detroit," 545.

109 Hackworth, "Defiant Neoliberalism and the Danger of Detroit," 546.

110 Peck, Theodore, and Brenner, "Neoliberalism Resurgent?," 266–67.

111 Thomas J. Sugrue, "The Rise and Fall of Detroit's Middle Class," *New Yorker News Desk*, July 22, 2013; https://www.bridgemi.com/special-report/facts-michigan-safety-net.

112 Moody's, "Announcement: Detroit's Bankruptcy May Change How Other Distressed Cities Approach Their Pension and Debt Obligations," July 26, 2013, https://www.moodys.com/research/Moodys-Detroit-bankruptcy-may-change-how -other-distressed-cities-approach—PR_278692. Soon after leaving Detroit, Orr was branded a man who had the know-how to manage other bankruptcies. He has since returned to his prior firm, Jones Day, where he "provides strategic crisis manage-ment advice" and works with Chrysler and National Century Financial Enterprises to promote "cost-efficient and business-oriented solutions" to their bankruptcies. "Kevyn D. Orr," Jones Day, n.d., https://www.jonesday.com/korr/.

113 Kurashige. *The Fifty-Year Rebellion*, 80.

114 "Not only does this reproduce the hubristic fallacy that policy outcomes are functionally secured through policy designs, but it also indulges a technocratic rep-lication fantasy—that both designs and outcomes are portable from place to place" (Peck, Theodor, and Brenner, "Neoliberalism Resurgent?," 280, 282).

115 Ted Roelofs, "Michiganders Say Emergency Managers Wield Too Much Power," *Bridge*, March 21, 2017, https://www.bridgemi.com/public-sector/michiganders-say -emergency-managers-wield-too-much-power.

116 Kayla Ruble et al., "Flint Water Crisis Deaths Likely Surpass Official Toll," *Frontline*, PBS, July 24, 2018, https://www.pbs.org/wgbh/frontline/article/flint-water-crisis -deaths-likely-surpass-official-toll/.

117 Workers World Detroit Bureau, "United against Capitalism: Detroiters Speak Truth to Power," *Workers World*, October 31, 2017, https://www.workers.org/2017/10/31/united-against-capitalism-detroiters-speak-truth-to-power/.

118 "Demonstration—Defend Detroit Neighborhoods," Moratorium Now!, July 16, 2018, https://moratorium-mi.org/demonstration-defend-detroit-neighborhoods/; Abayomi Azikiwe, "Developing a Program to Defeat Austerity," *Workers World*, March 13, 2018, https://www.workers.org/2018/03/13/developing-a-program-to-defeat-austerity/.

119 Invest Detroit, "Strategic Neighborhood Fund 2.0," https://www.dropbox.com/s/n0r7xjn9p9x6edr/_FINAL%20SNF%202.0%20designed%20book%20-%20single%20page.pdf?dl=0.

120 Mallach, *The Divided City*, 111. One local investment firm pointed out, "These interventions work best in communities that have a key set of assets that can better catalyze investments." Invest Detroit, "Strategic Neighborhood Fund 2.0."

121 Eliza Theiss, "The Rise and Fall of the American Downtown: A Look into the Home Price Evolution of the Nation's Urban Cores in the Decade Since the Downturn," Property Shark, January 14, 2019, https://www.propertyshark.com/Real-Estate-Reports/2019/01/14/the-rise-and-fall-of-the-american-downtown-a-look-into-the-home-price-evolution-of-the-nations-urban-cores-in-the-decade-since-the-downturn/. Home sale prices in University District, Sherwood Forest, and Palmer Woods are taken from Zillow.com, accessed February 2019.

122 "Mission," Fitz Forward.

123 Joe Guillen, "Detroit Land Bank Authority Was Formed Illegally, Activist Says," *Detroit Free Press*, August 26, 2016, https://www.freep.com/story/news/local/michigan/detroit/2016/08/26/detroit-land-bank-authority-formed-illegally-activist-says/89419314/; Erik Trickey, "Detroit's DIY Cure for Urban Blight," *Politico Magazine*, May 18, 2017, https://www.politico.com/magazine/story/2017/05/18/how-detroit-is-beating-its-blight-215160.

124 Trickey, "Detroit's DIY Cure for Urban Blight"; Steve Neavling, "Detroit Is Razing Houses with Money Intended to Save Them," *Metro Times*, July 19, 2017, https://www.metrotimes.com/detroit/detroit-is-razing-houses-with-money-intended-to-save-them/Content?oid=4619015.

125 Sarah Alvarez and Leah Samuel, "Real Estate Is Hot in Detroit but Its Top Owner, the City, Isn't Selling," *Bridge Magazine*, August 21, 2018, https://www.bridgemi.com/detroit-journalism-cooperative/real-estate-hot-detroit-its-top-owner-city-isnt-selling.

126 Trickey, "Detroit's DIY Cure for Urban Blight."

127 "Lessons from Detroit: Cities Find a New Way of Working Together," Reimagining the Civic Commons, September 27, 2018, https://medium.com/reimagining-the-civic-commons/lessons-from-detroit-cities-find-a-new-way-of-working-together-ba29faaad799.

128 Alexa Bush, "Measurement Tools: Early Lessons from Detroit," Reimagining the Civic Commons, January 9, 2019, https://medium.com/reimagining-the-civic-commons/measurement-tools-early-lessons-from-detroit-f12f6b62d4d3.

129 Invest Detroit, "What We Do," n.d., https://investdetroit.com/what-we-do/.

130 Invest Detroit, "An Unprecedented Effort to Strengthen Our Neighborhoods," January 28, 2019, http://investdetroit.com/an-unprecedented-effort-to-strengthen-our -neighborhoods/.

131 LISC, "About," http://www.lisc.org/about-us/; City of Detroit and Local Initiatives Support Corporation, "Affordable Housing Leverage Fund ('AHLF') Notice of Funding Availability ('NOFA') Information and Application Packet," January 15, 2019, https://docs.wixstatic.com/ugd/e14f6d_147059cc497f44df820000292iiab071.pdf; Handelsman and Morgan, "Opinion."

132 Motor City Match, "Frequently Asked Questions and Answers," July 31, 2015, http:// www.motorcitymatch.com/wp-content/files_mf/1438373516MotorCityMatchFAQ _Round2Update.pdf.

133 On these aspects of the history of urban development, see Mollenkopf, *The Contested City*, and Ferguson, *Top Down*.

134 Teresa Ghilarducci, "Amazon's Confusing Breakup with New York," *Forbes*, February 25, 2019, https://www.forbes.com/sites/teresaghilarducci/2019/02/25/amazona -confusing-breakup-with-new-york/#2151f1c87c64.

135 Austen, "The Post-Post-Apocalyptic Detroit."

136 Chad Livengood, "$4.5 billion Fiat Chrysler plan to add 6,500 jobs in Detroit area," *Crain's Detroit Business*, February 26, 2019, https://www.crainsdetroit.com/economic -development/45-billion-fiat-chrysler-plan-add-6500-jobs-detroit-area?CSAuthResp=1% 3A%3A321393%3A1040%3A24%3Asuccess%3AC805749BB5A1BC182AA4F548E5C6A35B.

137 Kimberly Amadeo, "Auto Industry Bailout," *The Balance*, June 25, 2019.

138 JC Reindl, "Fiat Chrysler gets another $92.8M for Mack Avenue plant project," *Detroit Free Press*, July 23, 2019, https://www.freep.com/story/money/business/2019 /07/23/fiat-chrysler-mack-avenue-plant-detroit/1803696001/.

139 Charles Sercombe, "Poletown Plant's future? GM's not saying," *Hamtramck Review*, February 8, 2019, http://www.thehamtramckreview.com/poletown-plants-future-gm -is-not-saying/.

140 Kevyn Orr, "Re: Recommendation Pursuant to Section 18(1) of PA 436," City of Detroit, Emergency Manager's Office, July 16, 2013, https://www.michigan.gov /documents/snyder/Detroit_EM_Kevyn_Orr_Chapter_9_Recommendation_427831 _7.pdf; Stateside Staff, "How Is Crime Hindering the Comeback of Detroit?," Michigan Radio, July 24, 2013, http://michiganradio.org/post/how-crime-hindering -comeback-detroit.

141 "Detroit Police Hire Architects of NYPD's Unconstitutional Stop-and-Frisk Program," ACLU, April 24, 2014, http://www.aclumich.org/article/detroit-police-hire -architects-nypd%E2%80%99s-unconstitutional-stop-and-frisk-program.

142 George Hunter, "Revival of Detroit's Cass Corridor Crowds Out Criminals," *Detroit News*, July 13, 2016, https://apnews.com/bf9e316781534882a9087c685769e38a, emphasis added.

143 Richie Bernardo, "2016's Cities with the Best and Worst ROI on Police Spending," WalletHub, December 17, 2015, https://wallethub.com/edu/cities-with-the-best-and -worst-roi-on-police-spending/9565/; Erika Rawes, "States with the Most People on

Food Stamps," *USA Today*, January 17, 2015, https://www.usatoday.com/story/money
/personalfinance/2015/01/17/cheat-sheet-states-with-most-food-stamps/21877399/;
Jay, "Policing the Poor in Detroit."

144 Bill Laitner, "Count of Homeless Americans Hits Detroit Streets," *Detroit Free Press*,
February 1, 2016; "ACLU Urges Detroit to End Illegal Practice of 'Dumping' Homeless People outside City Limits, Files DOJ Complaint," ACLU, April 18, 2013, https://
www.aclu.org/news/aclu-urges-detroit-end-illegal-practice-dumping-homeless
-people-outside-city-limits-files-doj; "ACLU: Detroit Police Dumping Homeless
outside City," CBS Detroit, April 18, 2013, http://detroit.cbslocal.com/2013/04/18/aclu
-detroit-police-dumping-homeless-outside-city/.

145 Steve Neavling, "Police Wipe Out Homeless Camps in Detroit, Seize Belongings,"
*Metro Times*, February 7, 2019, https://www.metrotimes.com/news-hits/archives
/2019/02/07/police-wipe-out-homeless-camps-in-detroit-seize-belongings; Ameera
David, "Two Homeless Hot Spots Wiped Clean by Detroit, Leaving Dozens Cold
and Empty Handed," WXYZ Detroit, February 6, 2019, https://www.wxyz.com/news
/region/detroit/two-homeless-hot-spots-wiped-clean-by-detroit-leaving-dozens-cold
-and-empty-handed.

146 Allie Gross, "Detroiters in Need of Affordable Housing Are about to Lose a
Lifeline," *Detroit Free Press*, April 9, 2018, https://www.freep.com/story/news/local
/michigan/detroit/2018/04/09/united-community-housing-coalition-hud-funding
/482323002/.

147 "NRRC Facts and Trends," Justice Center, 2017, https://csgjusticecenter.org/nrrc
/facts-and-trends; Camp and Heatherton, *Policing the Planet*, 4.

148 Jon Zemke, "Greater Downtown Detroit Volunteers Work to Improve Public Safety,
Quality of Life," *Huffington Post*, May 22, 2012, http://www.huffingtonpost.com/2012
/05/22/downtown-detroit-volunteers-public-safety-quality-of-life_n_1535998.html.

149 Cedric Johnson, "Coming to Terms with Actually-Existing Black Life," *New Politics*,
April 9, 2019, https://newpol.org/coming-to-terms-with-actually-existing-black-life/.

150 Heather Ann Thompson, "Rescuing America's Inner Cities?," *Huffington Post*,
August 25, 2014, http://www.huffingtonpost.com/heather-ann-thompson/rescuing
-americas-inner-c_b_5526012.html; Doron Levin, "Dan Gilbert Has Another New
Idea for Downtown: Cycling Security Guards," *Deadline Detroit*, November 11, 2012,
http://www.deadlinedetroit.com/articles/2614/dan_gilbert_has_another_new_idea
_for_downtown_cycling_security_guards#.WbV4GrKGOHs; J. C. Reindl, "Detroit's
Rebound Brings Surge in Downtown Security Jobs," *Detroit Free Press*, June 14, 2018.

151 Lauren Ann Davies, "A First Look inside Dan Gilbert's Multimillion-Dollar Security
Hub," *Deadline Detroit*, October 11, 2013, http://www.deadlinedetroit.com/articles
/6760/a_first_look_inside_gilbert_s_downtown_multi-million_dollar_security
_hub; Steve Nealing, "Dan Gilbert's Team Trespasses, Installs Cameras on Down-
town Buildings without Permission," *Motor City Muckraker*, February 23, 2015; Ian
Thibodeau, "Dan Gilbert Loses Cool," *MLive*, April 27, 2015; Steve Nealing, "Dan
Gilbert's Surveillance Team Messes with Wrong Detroit Institution," *Motor City
Muckraker*, April 26, 2015.

152 Thompson, "Rescuing America's Inner Cities?"

153 Paul Beshouri, "The Colony Arms Might Be Detroit's Worst Apartment Building," *Curbed Detroit*, November 15, 2013, http://detroit.curbed.com/2013/11/15/10174776/the-colony-arms-might-be-detroits-worst-apartment-building; Gus Burns, "Detroit Police Chief James Craig after Last Week's Massive Raid," *MLive*, November 19, 2013, http://www.mlive.com/news/detroit/index.ssf/2013/11/detroit_police_chief_james_cra_12.html; Darren Reese-Brown and Mark Jay, "A Resident's Analysis," *The Periphery*, March 2014, http://www.theperipherymag.com/essay-a-residents-analysis/; Jay, "Policing the Poor in Detroit."

154 Mike Wilkinson, "Tracking Progress in Detroit Police Response Times a Fool's Errand," *Bridge*, November 10, 2015, https://www.bridgemi.com/detroit-journalism-cooperative/tracking-progress-detroit-police-response-times-fools-errand.

155 Steve Neavling and Charlie DeDuff, "Part 1: Detroit Dupes Public with False Police Response Times as 911 Calls Spike," *Motor City Muckraker*, January 22, 2019, http://motorcitymuckraker.com/2019/01/22/part-1-detroit-dupes-public-with-false-police-response-times-as-911-calls-spike/.

156 Niraj Warikioo, "Detroit Chief: Comparing City to Ferguson Is 'Appalling,'" *USA Today*, August 19, 2014, https://www.usatoday.com/story/news/nation/2014/08/19/detroit-police-chief-ferguson-comparison-appalling/14277091/.

157 Ryan Felton, "Operation: Restore Public Relations," *Detroit Metro Times*, April 15, 2015, https://www.metrotimes.com/detroit/operation-restore-public-relations/Content?oid=2334953.

158 Hollerman et al., "The Penal State in an Age of Crisis"; Justice Policy Institute, "Rethinking the Blues," 1; "War Comes Home: The Excessive Militarization of American Police," ACLU, June 2014, https://www.aclu.org/sites/default/files/assets/jus14-warcomeshome-report-web-rel1.pdf; "How America's Police Became So Heavily Armed," *Economist*, May 18, 2015, https://www.economist.com/blogs/economist-explains/2015/05/economist-explains-22; Christina Hall, "Michigan Police Also Militarizing with Free Surplus Gear," *Lansing State Journal*, August 17, 2014, https://www.lansingstatejournal.com/story/news/local/michigan/2014/08/17/michigan-police-also-militarizing-with-free-federal-surplus-gear/14173195/.

159 Keith Griffith, "'Don't Run from the State Police, You'll Get F**ked Up,'" *Daily Mail*, April 23, 2018, https://www.dailymail.co.uk/news/article-5613645/Bodycam-reveals-Detroit-cops-harsh-remarks-Damon-Grimes-death.html.

160 Violet Ikonomova, "White Detroit Cops Get Probation for Wrongful Chase That Led to Black Teen's Death," *Metro Times*, October 18, 2018, https://www.metrotimes.com/news-hits/archives/2018/10/18/white-detroit-cops-get-probation-for-wrongful-chase-that-resulted-in-black-teens-death.

161 Quoted in Poulantzas, *State, Power, Socialism*, 46.

162 Jonathan Carlson, "Detroit Police Department's Crackdown on Drug Dens Results in Arrests, Seizures," WXYZ Detroit, March 3, 2015, emphasis added.

163 Jay, "Policing the Poor in Detroit."

164 Reese-Brown and Jay, "A Resident's Analysis"; "Police Make Several Arrests during Raid at Detroit Apartment Complex," WXYZ Detroit, November 15, 2013, https://www.youtube.com/watch?v=iHhJvPZ83ic.

165  "Operation April Showers: Police Raid Homes across Detroit," WXYZ Detroit, April 24, 2014, https://www.youtube.com/watch?v=Rbre9GiR9zw, emphasis added.

166  Sandra Mcneill, "Detroit Police 'April Showers' Raids Bring Multiple Arrests," CBS Detroit, April 24, 2014, http://detroit.cbslocal.com/2014/04/24/detroit-police-april-showers-raids-bring-multiple-arrests/.

167  Bartlett, "Rights, Respectibility, and Responsibility."

168  Forman, *Locking Up Our Own*, 9.

169  Jay, "Cages and Crises."

170  Heather Ann Thompson, interview with Bill McGraw, "The War on Crime, Not Crime Itself, Fueled Detroit's post-1967 Decline," *Bridge*, October 18 2016, http://bridgemi.com/2016/10/ the-war-on-crime-not-crime-itself-fueled-detroits-post-1967-decline/; Kurashige, *The Fifty-Year Rebellion*; John Wisely, "Criminal Tethers Save Money, but What about Lives?," *Detroit Free Press*, November 23, 2015, https://www.freep.com/story/news/local/michigan/2015/11/21/wayne-county-tethers/76184506/.

171  Jay, "Cages and Crises."

172  Lewis, "Mass Incarceration."

173  Forman, "Racial Critiques of Mass Incarceration," 101; Forman, *Locking Up Our Own*, 13.

174  Clegg and Usmani, "The Racial Politics of Mass Incarceration," 26–27.

175  Reed, "Black Exceptionalism and the Militant Capitulation to Economic Inequality."

176  Neocleous, *The Fabrication of Social Order*, xii.

177  "Police activity," write Hall et al., "which is principally directed against this 'workless' stratum of the class, is defined as an attempt to bring the wageless back into wage labour" (*Policing the Crisis*, 363).

178  Marx, *Capital: Vol. 1*, 899; Ylan Q. Mui, "The Shocking Number of Americans Who Can't Cover a $400 Expense," *Washington Post*, May 25, 2016, https://www.washingtonpost.com/news/wonk/wp/2016/05/25/the-shocking-number-of-americans-who-cant-cover-a-400-expense/?noredirect=on&utm_term=.2aeb11249ccb.

179  Tracie McMillan, "The War on Poverty," *Mother Jones*, January/February 2019, 36.

180  Mui, "The Shocking Number of Americans Who Can't Cover a $400 Expense."

181  We analyze STRESS in detail in chapter 4.

182  Schultz, Detroit under STRESS, 10–11, 52.

183  Davies, "A First Look Inside Dan Gilbert's Multimillion-Dollar Security Hub."

184  Bridget Casey, "Apparently Painting 'Free the Water' on a Water Tower Can Land You Jail Time," *ArtReport*, August 1, 2016, http://artreport.com/apparently-painting-free-the-water-on-a-water-tower-can-land-you-jail-time/; Michigan Legislature, The Michigan Penal Code (Excerpt) Act 328 of 1931, http://www.legislature.mi.gov/(S(a05gh2d3a32ay1y2krsuej3a))/mileg.aspx?page=GetMCLDocument&objectname=mcl-750-552c; "Detroit: Artists Fight Felonies for Painting 'Free the Water' on Tower," Democracy Now!, July 14, 2016, https://www.democracynow.org/2016/7/14/headlines/detroit_artists_fight_felonies_for_painting_free_the_water_on_tower. Both artists were eventually acquitted.

185  Steve Neavling, "Researchers alarmed by Detroit's pervasive, expanding facial-recognition surveillance program," *Detroit Metro Times*, May 17, 2019, https://www.metrotimes.com/news-hits/archives/2019/05/17/researchers-alarmed-by-detroits-pervasive-expanding-facial-recognition-surveillance-program; Steve Neavling, "Detroit's facial recognition surveillance technology provokes backlash, proposed bans," *Detroit Metro Times*, July 31, 2019, https://www.metrotimes.com/detroit/detroits-facial-recognition-technology-provokes-backlash-proposed-bans/Content?oid=22272625.

186  Steve Neavling, "Mounting public pressure puts brakes on Detroit's facial-recognition technology," *Detroit Metro Times*, July 3, 2019, https://www.metrotimes.com/detroit/mounting-public-pressure-puts-brakes-on-detroits-facial-recognition-technology/Content?oid=22062719; Steve Neavling, "Detroit police commissioner who was arrested at meeting won't be charged," *Detroit Metro Times*, July 18, 2019, https://www.metrotimes.com/news-hits/archives/2019/07/18/detroit-police-commissioner-who-was-arrested-at-meeting-wont-be-charged; George Hunter, "Detroit chief defends facial recognition technology after Tlaib criticism," *Detroit News*, August 20, 2019, https://www.detroitnews.com/story/news/local/detroit-city/2019/08/20/detroit-chief-defends-facial-recognition-technology-after-tlaib-criticism/2059414001/.

187  Samuel Stein, "Capital City."

188  Tomba, *Marx's Temporalities*, viii. Historical materialism is not a skeleton key for the comprehension of history but "a practical mode of intervention into history. . . . Insofar as it is incomplete, history is produced constructively by a historiography able to trigger off the explosive charge of the past in the present."

### CHAPTER 2: FORDISM AND THE SO-CALLED GOLDEN YEARS

1  Michiko Kakutami, "Review: 'Once in a Great City' Chronicles Detroit's Glory Days," *New York Times*, September 14, 2015, https://www.nytimes.com/2015/09/15/books/review-once-in-a-great-city-chronicles-detroits-glory-days.html; Bomey, *Detroit Resurrected*.

2  Barthes, *Mythologies*, 124.

3  The Henry Ford, Greenfield Village, accessed September 2017, https://www.thehenryford.org/visit/greenfield-village/.

4  The Henry Ford, Ford Rouge Factory Tour, accessed September 2017, https://www.thehenryford.org/visit/ford-rouge-factory-tour/.

5  The Henry Ford, Henry Ford Museum of American Innovation, accessed September 2017, https://www.thehenryford.org/visit/henry-ford-museum/.

6  The Henry Ford, Evolution of Our Collection, accessed September 2017, https://www.thehenryford.org/history-and-mission/evolution-of-our-collection/.

7  The Henry Ford, Creating Our Campus, accessed September 2017, https://www.thehenryford.org/history-and-mission/creating-our-campus/.

8  The Henry Ford, Henry's Assembly Line, accessed September 2017, https://www.thehenryford.org/visit/henry-ford-museum/exhibits/made-in-america-manufacturing/.

9   Marx, *Capital: Vol. 1*, 604.

10  Meyer, *The Five Dollar Day*, 2.

11  Babson et al., *Working Detroit*, 18.

12  Montgomery, *The Fall of the House of Labor*.

13  Marx, *Capital*, 1023.

14  Marx, *Capital*, 1021, 1035.

15  Babson et al., *Working Detroit*, 18–19.

16  Quoted in Zimbalist, "The Limits of Work Humanization," 51.

17  Babson et al., *Working Detroit*, 30. In his classic work, *Labor and Monopoly Capital*, Harry Braverman summarizes the viewpoint of Taylor and his ilk: "Workers who are controlled only by general orders and discipline are not adequately controlled, because they retain their grip on the actual processes of labor. So long as they control the labor process itself, they will thwart efforts to realize the full potential inherent in their labor power. To change this situation, control over the labor process must pass into the hands of management, not only in a formal sense but by the control and dictation of each step of the process" (69). Taylor's precept was that "the cost of production is lowered by separating the work of planning and the brain work as much as possible from the manual labor." This enforced "division between the labour of head and hand" is, for Marxists, a basic definition of alienation. See Sohn-Rethel, *Intellectual and Manual Labor*, 4.

18  Babson et al., *Working Detroit*, 49.

19  This separation between the "head" and the "hands" in Taylorist industrial production is the subject of Fritz Lang's 1927 masterpiece, *Metropolis*. The film depicts faceless masses of exhausted and demoralized workers at the whims of leviathan machines controlled by their capitalist bosses. The plot of the film revolves around the factory owner's son's attempt to lead a revolution among the workers and reconcile the "head" with the "hands."

20  Babson et al., *Working Detroit*, 3, 18.

21  By 1969 the percentage of wage or salaried employees increased to 84 percent, and self-employed workers was down to 9 percent. See Zimbalist, "The Limits of Work Humanization," 52.

22  Meyer, *The Five Dollar Day*, 18.

23  Babson et al., *Working Detroit*, 30, 32. Craft unions, composed of skilled workers, generally took the position that their unique skills gave them a strong bargaining position with the owners, and they resisted "diluting" their ranks by allowing unskilled workers to join. Such a stance is perfectly understandable from the standpoint of these workers and is not so much a product of the prejudice of craft unions as one of myriad internal divisions that have tended to undermine solidarity throughout the labor movement's history.

24  Coopey and McKinlay, "Power without Knowledge?," 111.

25  Lenin, "A 'Scientific' System of Sweating."

26  Shwartz and Fish, "Just-in-Time Inventories in Old Detroit," 53.

27  Murray and Schwartz, "Collateral Damage," 127.

28  Meyer, *The Five Dollar Day*, 111, 120–21.

29 Quoted in Harvey, *The Condition of Postmodernity*, 126.

30 Meyer, *The Five Dollar Day*, 77–78, 115–24; Babson et al., *Working Detroit*, 35.

31 Meyer, *The Five Dollar Day*, 77–78, 115–24, 147–61; Coopey and McKinlay, "Power without Knowledge?," 112; Babson et al., *Working Detroit*, 35.

32 Meyer, *The Five Dollar Day*, 162.

33 Babson et al., *Working Detroit*, 8–21.

34 Babson et al., *Working Detroit*, 32–33.

35 Babson et al., *Working Detroit*, 34.

36 Vargas, *Proletarians of the North*, 59,60, 62; Meyer, *The Five Dollar Day*, 171, 186, 193. Because of this, all the major auto companies kept surplus workers on hand to replace striking or inefficient workers.

37 Wolf, "Spies, Lies and War."

38 Lucia, "The Unemployed Movements of the 1930s"; Meyer, *The Five Dollar Day*, 170–75; Babson et al., *Working Detroit*, 39–40.

39 Babson et al., *Working Detroit*, 56.

40 Baran and Sweezy, *Monopoly Capital*, 251; Marable, *How Capitalism Underdeveloped Black America*, chapter 1; Vargas, *Proletarians of the North*, 59; Boyd, *Black Detroit*, 92.

41 Quoted in Boyd, *Black Detroit*, 92.

42 Robinson, "The Production of Black Violence," 288.

43 Alkalimat, *Introduction to Afro-American Studies*, 124; John Williams, "Interview," League of Revolutionary Black Workers, 2017, https://www .revolutionaryblackworkers.org/video/; Esch, *The Color Line and the Assembly Line*, 96. One anecdote reveals the horrible role that capitalists cast for black workers; it comes from an interview that Lloyd Bailer, one of Detroit's first black economists, conducted with a manager of a Detroit auto factory: "I asked if Negroes were not employed anywhere in the plant. He said 'yes, some jobs white folks will not do; so they have to take niggers in, particularly in duco work, spraying paint on car bodies. This soon kills a white man.' I inquired if it ever killed Negroes. 'Oh, yes,' he replied. 'It shortened their lives, it cuts them down, but they're just niggers.'" Quoted in Norman McRae, "Detroit in Black and White," in Henrickson, *Detroit Perspectives*, 366.

44 McRae, "Detroit in Black and White," 367; Martelle, *Detroit*, 133–34; Karen Dash, "Slum Clearance Farce," *Nation*, April 1, 1936.

45 Babson et al., *Working Detroit*, 44; Vitale, *The End of Policing*, 48.

46 Marable, *Malcolm X*, 26.

47 Schultz, *Detroit under STRESS*, 1.

48 Feeley, "Black Workers, Fordism, and the UAW."

49 Marable, *Malcolm X*, 29; Ward, *In Love and Struggle*, 33; Johnson, "Coming to Terms with Actually-Existing Black Life."

50 Feeley, "Black Workers, Fordism, and the UAW"; Babson et al., *Working Detroit*, 44–45.

51 This was around the same time that Ford established Fordlandia, an industrial town in the Amazon, where Ford expected to create operations that would provide latex for 2 million cars in the United States. There Ford implemented a similar

system of intense labor discipline and moral Puritanism as in Detroit. However, within a couple of years, tired of being treated like "dogs," the workers participated in a massive uprising, destroying much of the newly established company facilities and running their capitalist bosses out of town. See Grandin, *Fordlandia*; George Hunter, "Detroit Police Diversity Issues Predate National Debate," *Detroit News*, March 8, 2015, http://www.detroitnews.com/story/news/local/wayne-county/2015 /03/07/detroit-police-department-diversity/24570427/; Martelle, *Detroit*, 128–32; Forest Davis, "Labor Spies and the Black Legion," in Henrickson, *Detroit Perspectives*, 370–75.

52 Norwood, "'Ford's Brass Knuckles,'" 367.

53 Coopey and McKinlay, "Power without Knowledge?," 115. This aligns with the work of Michel Foucault, who in *Discipline and Punish* argues that one of the major functions of the modern prison is to have a reserve of desperate people who can be used to infiltrate radical movements.

54 Babson et al., *Working Detroit*, 59.

55 Vargas, *Proletarians of the North*, 62.

56 Martelle, *Detroit*, 114; McNally, *Global Slump*, 66; "Automobiles," History Channel, 2010, http://www.history.com/topics/automobiles.

57 Sugrue, *The Origins of the Urban Crisis*, 18; McNally, *Global Slump*, 64.

58 Babson et al., *Working Detroit*, 52.

59 Babson et al., *Working Detroit*, 48.

60 McNally, *Global Slump*, 65–66.

61 Marx, *Capital*, 353.

62 Amin, *Unequal Development*, 101; Robinson, *A Theory of Global Capitalism*, 147.

63 Prabhat Patnaik, "Bubbles, Stocks and Crashes," *MRonline*, March 3, 2018, https://mronline.org/2018/03/03/bubbles-stocks-and-crashes/.

64 McNally, *Global Slump*, 114–15; Harman, *Zombie Capitalism*, 150–53.

65 Murray and Schwartz, "Collateral Damage," 128.

66 Martelle, *Detroit*, 114; Baskin, "The Ford Hunger March," 33.

67 Valocchi, "The Unemployed Workers Movement of the 1930s," 197; Lucia, "The Unemployed Movements of the 1930s"; Martelle, *Detroit*, 114.

68 Government welfare was eventually reduced to just "milk and bread." Lucia, "The Unemployed Movements of the 1930s"; Harvey, *The Condition of Postmodernity*, 127; Martelle, *Detroit*, 121–22; Piven and Cloward, *Poor People's Movements*, 61.

69 Babson et al., *Working Detroit*, 56–57.

70 Burton Folsom, "Michigan Resists the New Deal," Michigan Center for Public Policy, March 2, 1998, https://www.mackinac.org/346.

71 Reed, "Between Obama and Coates," 13. As Reed effectively argues, attempts to portray the New Deal's exclusions primarily in terms of racism or "whiteness" are belied by the overwhelming exclusion of poor white workers.

72 Piven and Cloward, *Poor People's Movements*, 42.

73 Rusche, "Prison Revolts or Social Legislation."

74 On August 14, 1939, the *Detroit Free Press* published an article titled "Preacher Traces Causes of Crime: Negro Duties to Race Are Discussed," in which it was

reported that the "Nation's Negro population [is] 9.6 percent of the whole and the percentage of Negro inmates in penal institutions [is] 27." The preacher insists that whatever the material causes, moral solutions, rather than political-economic ones, would be required: "The church is free enough and has enough man power in it to tackle this problem and solve it to a great extent." We can thus see that the mythological view that crime was not just a political-economic symptom, but also a problem of morality, a view that legitimates processes of dispossession in contemporary Detroit, has a long history in the city; efforts on the part of black elites to moralize and reform the recalcitrant behavior of a black "underclass" are also deeply rooted. See also "African Americans in the United States, Michigan and Metropolitan Detroit," Center for Urban Studies, February 2002, Working Paper Series, No. 8, http://www.cus.wayne.edu/media/1356/aawork8.pdf; Patrick Langan, "Race of Prisoners Admitted to State and Federal Institutions, 1926–1986," U.S. Department of Justice, May 1991, https://www.ncjrs.gov/pdffiles1/nij/125618.pdf, p. 6.

75 Rusche, "Prison Revolts or Social Legislation"; Adrienne Eaton et al., "A History of Jackson Prison, 1920–1975," Research Paper, University of Michigan, Residential College Social Science Research Community, winter 1979.

76 Rusche, "Prison Revolts or Social Legislation."

77 Lorence, *Organizing the Unemployed*, 38–39; Folsom, *Impatient Armies of the Poor*, 305–6; "Murder Charges Asked after Red Mob Fights Police," *Detroit Free Press*, December 8, 1932; John Newsinger, "From Class War to Cold War," *International Socialism*, no. 73 (December 1996), http://pubs.socialistreviewindex.org.uk/isj73/newsing.htm; Babson et al., *Working Detroit*, 54.

78 Black workers were refused housing in Dearborn near the plant; they were forced to live in Inkster. During the Depression, Ford took over Inkster's economically devastated African American neighborhoods. Not trusting black workers to manage their own finances, he withheld more than 80 percent of black workers' wages and spent it as he saw fit to manage the Inkster community—a practice that continued until a minimum wage law was passed in 1933. Esch, *The Color Line and the Assembly Line*, 108–9; Howe and Widick, "The UAW Fights Race Prejudice"; Alan Brinkley, "Last of His Kind," *New York Times*, December 17 1995, http://www.nytimes.com/1995/12/17/books/last-of-his-kind.html?pagewanted=all&src=pm; Babson et al., *Working Detroit*, 44; Esch, *The Color Line and the Assembly Line*, 92.

79 To be sure, "the activities of the Communist Parties in the United States . . . left large sectors of the black population untouched"; however, by 1931—the year that the Communist Party led a campaign to defend the nine young blacks accused of rape in the Scottsboro case—there were over one thousand black members in the CPUSA. Foner and Allen, *American Communism and Black Americans*, 116–17; Sitkoff, *A New Deal for Blacks*, 47; Alkalimat, *Introduction to Afro-American Studies*, 128–33; Jacob Zumoff, "The Party and Black Liberation," *Jacobin*, August 8, 2015, https://www.jacobinmag.com/2015/08/communist-party-scottsboro-cominterm-zumoff-debs-racism/; Kelley, *Hammer and Hoe*; Holger Weiss, "'Negro Workers, Defend the Soviet Union and the Chinese Revolution!' The International Trade Union Committee of Negro Workers and the Political Rhetoric of the Negro Worker,"

*Viewpoint Magazine*, February 1, 2018, https://www.viewpointmag.com/2018/02/01/negro-workers-defend-soviet-union-chinese-revolution-international-trade-union-committee-negro-workers-political-rhetoric-negro-worker/.

80 "A Slap at Moscow," *Detroit Free Press*, October 9, 1935; Martelle, *Detroit*, 129.

81 Sit-down strikes were largely an adaptation of tactics used against workers by capitalists in previous walkouts: Babson et al., *Working Detroit*, 62.

82 Babson et al., *Working Detroit*, 79.

83 Lichtenstein, *State of the Union*, 21–24.

84 Lichtenstein, *State of the Union*, 30–35.

85 McCloud, "Solidarity Forever." McCloud's account is highly critical of Sidney Fine's work, *Sit-Down*, which is the standard account of the strike. She criticizes Fine for his failure to substantially deal with the political attitudes of the workers taking part in the strike and for downplaying the role that militant leftist workers played.

86 McCloud, "Solidarity Forever," 41–43.

87 Murray and Schwartz, "Collateral Damage"; Silver, *Forces of Labor*. While this tactic managed to dissipate and disperse the class struggle, the diffusion of auto plants into a spider-like network caused a significant decline in productivity, allowing more efficient Japanese and German plants to quickly gain much of the Big Three's market share in the postwar years—a process that would have drastic results for the employment prospects of Detroiters in the decades to come.

88 Babson et al., *Working Detroit*, 80–81.

89 Babson et al., *Working Detroit*, 86, 91.

90 Babson et al., *Working Detroit*, 92.

91 Babson et al., *Working Detroit*, 92, 110; Tompkins Bates, *The Making of Black Detroit in the Age of Henry Ford*, 245.

92 Cowie and Salvatore, "The Long Exception," 12; Martelle, *Detroit*, 139; Sugrue, *The Origins of the Urban Crisis*, 19; Boggs, *The American Revolution*, 53; Steve Fraser, "The Good War and the Workers," *American Prospect*, September 20, 2009, http://prospect.org/article/good-war-and-workers-0; Ward, *In Love and Struggle*, 35.

93 Franklin D. Roosevelt, "The Great Arsenal of Democracy," December 29, 1940, American Rhetoric, accessed October 2017, http://www.americanrhetoric.com/speeches/fdrarsenalofdemocracy.html. Note also that Roosevelt's speech opens, "This is not a fireside chat on war. It is a talk on national security." In *Critique of Security*, Mark Neocleous writes that the Roosevelt presidency was a crucial time in the consolidation of the regime of "security" in the United States. The concepts of national security and social security, both originating at this time, were instrumental in securing the order of capital and establishing a mode of citizenship based on wage labor and stratification of the working classes (76–105).

94 Fraser, "The Good War and the Workers"; Woodford, *This Is Detroit*, 155; Sugrue, *The Origins of the Urban Crisis*, 19; Georgakas and Surkin, *Detroit*, 27–28; Babson et al., *Working Detroit*, 120; Jones, "An End to the Neglect of the Problems of the Negro Woman!"

95 Lichtenstein, *The Most Dangerous Man in Detroit*, 75.

96 Lichtenstein, *The Most Dangerous Man in Detroit*, 104–204.

97  Glaberman, *Wartime Strikes*, 3. There is ample evidence that FDR and others in his administration had prior knowledge of the attacks on Pearl Harbor and allowed them to happen anyway. When one considers that defense production, which finally pulled the economy out of the recession, could only be fully mobilized after the attack and the government's subsequent ban on civilian production, one is left with the grim conclusion that the FDR administration saw the attacks as a means to jumpstart the war economy. See *September 11: The New Pearl Harbor*. Directed by Massimo Mazzucco. Italy, Luogo Comune, 2013; Lichtenstein, *The Most Dangerous Man in Detroit*, 154–71.

98  Glaberman, *Wartime Strikes*, 1–5.

99  Lichtenstein, *The Most Dangerous Man in Detroit*, 176–93.

100 Boggs, *The American Revolution*, 20; Brecher, "The World War II and Post-war Strike Wave"; Nelson, "How the UAW Grew," 14.

101 Glaberman, *Wartime Strikes*, 39.

102 Babson et al., *Working Detroit*, 124.

103 Glaberman, *Wartime Strikes*, 37.

104 Roosevelt, "The Great Arsenal of Democracy."

105 Glaberman, *Wartime Strikes*, 42; Babson et al., *Working Detroit*, 123.

106 Glaberman, *Wartime Strikes*, 44.

107 Babson et al., *Working Detroit*, 124.

108 Mollenkopf, *The Contested City*, 25.

109 Glaberman, *Wartime Strikes*, 44, 14, 43.

110 Boggs, *The American Revolution*, 19–20; Brecher, "The World War II and Post-war Strike Wave"; Seidman, *American Labor from Defense to Reconversion*, 78–79; Howe and Widick, "The UAW Fights Race Prejudice"; Glaberman, *Wartime Strikes*, 50; Babson et al., *Working Detroit*, 123.

111 Glaberman, *Wartime Strikes*, 49.

112 Glaberman, *Wartime Strikes*, 98–134.

113 Matthew Goldstein, "Detroit: From Motor City to Housing Incubator," *New York Times*, November 4, 2017, https://www.nytimes.com/2017/11/04/business/detroit-housing.html.

114 Mollenkopf, *The Contested City*, 74.

115 McNally, *Global Slump*, 27.

116 By 1953 the combined U.S. and Canadian share of global steel production was 46 percent; their share of global TV production was 84 percent; their share of cotton woven fabric production was 50 percent; and their share of global auto production was 80 percent. Ikeda, "World Production," 80–83; McNally, *Global Slump*, 27, 89; Magdoff and Sweezy, *The Deepening Crisis of U.S. Capitalism*, 12.

117 Piketty, *Capital in the Twenty-First Century*.

118 Sugrue, *The Origins of the Urban Crisis*, 126; Clark, *Disruption in Detroit*.

119 Clark, *Disruption in Detroit*, 179.

120 As one San Francisco banker explained in 1948, "Labor developments in the last decade may well be the chief contributing factor in speeding regional dispersion of industry. . . . Large aggregations of labor in one [central city] plant are more subject

to outside disrupting influences, and have less happy relations with management, than in smaller [suburban] plants" (quoted in Mollenkopf, *The Contested City*, 143).

121 Neocleous, *Critique of Security*, 95.

122 Neocleous, *Critique of Security*, 98.

123 Neocleous, *Critique of Security*, 102–4.

124 Branko Marcetic, "The FBI's Secret War," *Jacobin*, August 31, 2016, https://www .jacobinmag.com/2016/08/fbi-cointelpro-new-left-panthers-muslim-surveillance. On the Hollywood Blacklist, see *Red Hollywood*. Directed by Thom Andersen and Noël Burch, 1996.

125 Marable, *Race, Reform, and Rebellion*, 19; Taylor, *From #BlackLivesMatter to Black Liberation*, 35; Mast, *Detroit Lives*, 219; Bellamy Foster and McChesney, "Surveillance Capitalism"; Babson et al., *Working Detroit*, 139.

126 Babson et al., *Working Detroit*, 131.

127 Seidman, *American Labor from Defense to Reconversion*, 1; Brecher, "The World War II and Post-war Strike Wave"; Babson et al., *Working Detroit*, 129.

128 Truman, *Memoirs*, 498. The use of the army to repress worker struggles was only one feature of the nascent military-industrial complex. This complex facilitated the pacification of labor movements at the same time as it alleviated the problem of overproduction that plagued the U.S. economy after the war effort ended: real output in the United States rose 65 percent between 1940 and 1944, and the military-industrial complex provided a much-needed outlet for surplus production. Within two decades, for example, more than half of the production in the electronics industry was purchased by the U.S. military. As Jonathan Bellamy Foster and Robert McChesney point out in their important essay, "Surveillance Capitalism," although President Eisenhower is mostly remembered for warning of the specter of the military-industrial complex, it is less often noted that he was instrumental in assembling this complex. In 1946 General Eisenhower, then chief of staff of the army, issued a memo in which he wrote, "The future security of the nation demands that all those civilian resources which by conversion or redirection constitute our main support in time of emergency be associated closely with the activities of the Army in time of peace." In Eisenhower's vision, industrial and technological development would be "organic parts of our military structure. . . . Close integration of military and civilian resources will not only directly benefit the Army, but indirectly contribute to the nation's security."

129 Brecher, "The World War II and Post-war Strike Wave"; Babson et al., *Working Detroit*, 129–30.

130 Babson et al., *Working Detroit*, 130.

131 Brecher, "The World War II and Post-war Strike Wave"; Babson et al., *Working Detroit*, 131.

132 Brecher, "The World War II and Post-war Strike Wave."

133 Brecher, "The World War II and Post-war Strike Wave."

134 Clark, *Disruption in Detroit*, 25, 17, 25, 48, 20, 17.

135 Babson et al., *Working Detroit*, 138–39.

136 Lichtenstein, *State of the Union*, 114–20; Camp, *Incarcerating the Crisis*, 49–50; Boggs, *The American Revolution*, 121–22; Halpern, "'I'm Fighting for Freedom.'"

137 Lichtenstein, "UAW Bargaining Strategy and Shop-Floor Conflict," 363.

138 Appiah and Gates, *Africana*, 181–82; Marable, *Race, Reform, and Rebellion*, 29; West, "The Role of the National Negro Labor Council in the Struggle for Civil Rights"; Marable, *How Capitalism Underdeveloped Black America*.

139 Clark, *Disruption in Detroit*, 37, 41, 46, 43.

140 Lichtenstein, "UAW Bargaining Strategy and Shop-Floor Conflict," 365.

141 Lichtenstein, "UAW Bargaining Strategy and Shop-Floor Conflict," 371.

142 Clark, *Disruption in Detroit*, 53.

143 As Clark writes, "Between 1953 and 1954 independent automakers, such as Hudson and Packard, lost nearly half of their remaining market share. . . . They could not afford much of the newest technology and could no longer compete with the Big Three" (*Disruption in Detroit*, 97, 102).

144 Clark, *Disruption in Detroit*, 107, 95, 144–45.

145 Clark, *Disruption in Detroit*, 120–24; Lichtenstein, "UAW Bargaining Strategy and Shop-Floor Conflict," 370. The corporate media hysterically depicted this deal, which included unemployment insurance, as the coming of communism; in reality, Big Three officials had ensured that unemployment benefits were "low enough to provide [workers] with an incentive to look for another job in the event of a long layoff." See Clark, *Disruption in Detroit*, chapter 7.

146 Cutcher-Gershenfeld et al., "The Decline and Resurgence of the U.S. Auto Industry"; R. E. Houston, "Model T Ford Production," Model T Ford Club of America, February 14, 2007, http://www.mtfca.com/encyclo/fdprod.htm; Baran and Sweezy, *Monopoly Capital*, 108.

147 Clark, *Disruption in Detroit*, 144; Ward, *In Love and Struggle*, 145.

148 Boggs, *The American Revolution*, 22–27.

149 After the massive strikes in 1945–46, the Big Three used automation as a tactic to quell unrest. In 1946 GM introduced the first "successful automated transfer line," and in 1947 Ford introduced his Automation Department.

150 We thank Virginia Leavell for alerting us to this point. Dyer-Witheford, *Cyber-proletariat*, 39.

151 Stein, "Labor History Symposium," 334, 342–43.

152 Boggs, *The American Revolution*, 13.

153 Sugrue, *The Origins of the Urban Crisis*, 141; Georgakas and Surkin, *Detroit*, 25; Clark, *Disruption in Detroit*, 126.

154 Baran and Sweezy, *Monopoly Capital*, 261; Clark, *Disruption in Detroit*, 183. It is important to keep in mind that many unskilled jobs at the time were incorrectly labeled semiskilled. See Braverman, *Labor and Monopoly Capital*, 297.

155 Ward, *In Love and Struggle*, 238.

156 Gonzalez, "Two Reflections on Nelson Peery's Life"; Sugrue, *The Origins of the Urban Crisis*, 151, 147; Luby and Hedegard, "A Study in Civil Disorder in Detroit"; Marable, *Race, Reform, and Rebellion*, 252.

157 Babson et al., *Working Detroit*, 137, 138.

158  Mollenkopf, *The Contested City*.

159  Mollenkopf, *The Contested City*, 104–9.

160  Babson et al., *Working Detroit*, 115.

161  "Scores Hurt in Rioting at Housing Unit," *Detroit Free Press*, March 1, 1942.

162  Glaberman, *Wartime Strikes*, 31; Boyd, *Black Detroit*, 143–44; Denby, *Indignant Heart*; Feeley, "Black Detroit."

163  Jay and Leavell, "The Material Conditions of the Great Rebellion."

164  On the question of arming the black community, see Williams, *Negroes with Guns*; "Martial Law at 10 p.m. US Troops Moved In," *Detroit Free Press*, June 22 1943; Williams, *Our Enemies in Blue*, 141–42; White and Marshall, "June, 1943," 418–28; Sitkoff, "The Detroit Race Riots of 1943"; *Report of the National Advisory Commission on Civil Disorders*, 48; Murakawa, *The First Civil Right*, 31–35.

165  Murakawa, *The First Civil Right*. 31–35.

166  Murakawa, *The First Civil Right*, 31–35; Farley et al., *Detroit Divided*, 36; Conot, *American Odyssey*, 497; Babson et al., *Working Detroit*, 119–20.

167  Chris Wright, "It's Own Peculiar Decor."

168  Mollenkopf, *The Contested City*, 143.

169  Clark, *Disruption in Detroit*, 51, 64.

170  Eisinger, *The Politics of Displacement*, 172; Harold Norris, "Dislocation without Relocation," in Henrickson, *Detroit Perspectives*, 474–76; Woodford, *This Is Detroit*, 155–64; Farley et al., *Detroit Divided*.

171  Wright, "Its Own Peculiar Decor"; Sheehan, "Revitalization by Gentrification."

172  Sugrue, *The Origins of the Urban Crisis*, 205.

173  Reed, "Between Obama and Coates," 16.

174  Sugrue, *The Origins of the Urban Crisis*, 209–58; Ward, *In Love and Struggle*, 54–55. Sugrue notes that the number of these attacks "peaked between 1954 and 1957, when the city's economy was buffeted by plant closings, recession, and unemployment, limiting the housing options of many white, working-class Detroiters" (233). This evidence may give greater credence to Reed's insistence on the economic logic underlying the actions of white homeowners.

175  Marable, *Race, Reform, and Rebellion*, 120; Harvey, "The Right to the City," 34; Harvey, *Rebel Cities*, 50.

176  Babson et al., *Working Detroit*, 160.

177  Babson et al., *Working Detroit*, 135.

178  Wright, "Its Own Peculiar Decor." The state's investment in suburbanization was also deeply influenced by auto industry executives. The Interstate Highway Program, directed by a former GM executive, was, Wright argues, "a thinly disguised way to increase the dominance of the car as the primary means of transport." There is a clear precedent to this sort of collusion: in the 1920s and 1930s a "coalition of companies, including automobile, trucking, steel, rubber, and others, led by the president of General Motors, systematically bought up and destroyed the trolley systems in dozens of cities"—including Detroit.

179  At the same time, during the first negotiations to establish the General Agreement on Tariffs and Trade in the late 1940s, the grounds were being prepared for capital's

flight far beyond U.S. suburbs. Sugrue, *The Origins of the Urban Crisis*, 149; Camp, *Incarcerating the Crisis*, 133; Harvey, *The Enigma of Capital and the Crises of Capitalism*; Gibson and Jung, *Historical Census Statistics on Population Totals*, table 23, "Michigan—Race and Hispanic Origin for Selected Large Cities and Other Places: Earliest Census to 1990"; Woodford, *This Is Detroit*, 155–64; Farley et al., *Detroit Divided*.

180 Goldberg, "From Landless to Landlords," 157.

181 Babson et al., *Working Detroit*, 157.

182 Babson et al., *Working Detroit*, 157–58.

183 Goldberg, "From Landless to Landlords," 158.

184 Mollenkopf, *The Contested City*, 76.

185 Mollenkopf, *The Contested City*, 77–81; Diamond, *Chicago on the Make*, 142.

186 Harvey, "The Right to the City," 34; Berman, *All That Is Solid Melts into Air*.

187 Mollenkopf, *The Contested City*, 80.

188 Diamond, *Chicago on the Make*, 143–47.

189 Mollenkopf, *The Contested City*, 179; Diamond, *Chicago on the Make*, 151.

190 Weber, "Extracting Value from the City," 528, 527.

191 Norris, "Dislocation without Relocation," 474–76; Woodford, *This Is Detroit*, 155–64; Farley et al., *Detroit Divided*; Sheehan, "Revitalization by Gentrification."

192 Ward, *In Love and Struggle*, 147.

193 Da Via, "A Brief History of Detroit's Black Bottom Neighborhood"; Ward, *In Love and Struggle*, 148; George Hunter, "Revival of Detroit's Cass Corridor Crowds Out Criminals."

194 Engels, *The Housing Question*, 74–77.

195 Mollenkopf, *The Contested City*, 173–74.

196 Mollenkopf, *The Contested City*, 176.

197 Quoted in "The 1967 Detroit Rebellion," *Revolutionary Worker*, no. 915 (July 13, 1997), http://revcom.us/a/v19/910-19/915/det67. htm.

198 Murakawa, *The First Civil Right*, 64–65.

199 Warren Stromberg, "What about the Negro Crime Rate?," *Detroit Free Press*, June 23, 1957; emphasis added.

200 Hall et al, *Policing the Crisis*, 102.

201 Reed, *Stirrings in the Jug*, 18.

202 In the words of a former Detroit factory worker, B. J. Widick, "What Detroit needed, Mayor Louis C. Miriani insisted, was more vigorous law enforcement to curb the criminal elements roaming the streets." B. J. Widick, "Mayor Cavanaugh and the Limits of Reform," in Henrickson, *Detroit Perspectives*, 484; Eisinger, *The Politics of Displacement*, 61.

203 Joseph Turrini, "Phooie on Louie," *Michigan History Magazine*, November/December 1999, 10-17; "Who Killed Marilyn? News Offers $5,000 to Solve Crime," *Detroit News*, December 1969; John Mueller, "All Police Ordered on 6-Day Week," *Detroit Free Press*, December 29, 1960; Ron Martin, "Crackdown Draws Fire of NAACP," *Detroit Free Press*, January 1, 1961; John Millhome, "Inner City Is Chief Target in Crime-Reduction Drive," *Detroit Free Press*, July 9, 1962; Taylor-Bonds, *Calling Detroit Home*, 36–37.

204 Hidley Ward, "Crusade on Crime Planned," *Detroit Free Press*, December 31, 1960; Ron Martin, "Crackdown Draws Fire of NAACP," *Detroit Free Press*, January 1, 1961.

### CHAPTER 3: THE CONDITIONS OF THE GREAT REBELLION

1 James Mudge, "Mayor's Secret Riot-Spy Network Flopped," *Detroit Free Press*, July 27 1967.
2 Fine, *Violence in the Model City*, 1.
3 David Simon, "Baltimore," *The Audacity of Despair*, April 27, 2015, http://davidsimon .com/baltimore/.
4 "Brown v. Ferguson."
5 We owe this point to Virginia Hotchkiss.
6 "Difference Engine: Luddite Legacy," *Economist*, November 4, 2011, https://www .economist.com/blogs/babbage/2011/11/artificial-intelligence.
7 Cutcher-Gershenfeld et al., "The Decline and Resurgence of the U.S. Auto Industry"; U.S. Department of Transportation, Bureau of Transportation Statistics, "Table 1-23"; Boggs, *The American Revolution*, 48; Georgakas and Surkin, *Detroit*, 28; Bellamy Foster and McChesney, "Surveillance Capitalism."
8 Marable, *Race, Reform, and Rebellion*, 28; Sugrue, *The Origins of the Urban Crisis*, 126.
9 Boggs, *Living for Change*, 117; B. J. Widick, "Mayor Cavanagh and the Limits of Reform," in Henrickson, *Detroit Perspectives*, 486.
10 Mollenkopf, *The Contested City*, 93.
11 *Report of the National Advisory Commission on Civil Disorders*, 51; Bracey, Meier, and Rudwick, *Black Workers and Organized Labor*, 212–14; Widick, "Mayor Cavanagh and the Limits of Reform," 488–89; Joseph Turrini, "Phooie on Louie," *Michigan History Magazine*, November/December 1999.
12 Georgakas and Surkin, *Detroit*, 28; Luby and Hedegard, "A Study in Civil Disorder in Detroit"; Widick, "Mayor Cavanagh and the Limits of Reform," 489; Marable, *How Capitalism Underdeveloped Black America*, 49.
13 For a summary of the War on Poverty in Detroit, and its Head Start and job-training programs, see Thompson, *Whose Detroit?*, 32–33.
14 Fine, *Violence in the Model City*, 89.
15 Babson et al., *Working Detroit*, 168.
16 Cowie and Salvatore, "The Long Exception," 16.
17 Reed, "Between Obama and Coates," 18.
18 Mast, *Detroit Lives*, 225; Fine, *Violence in the Model City*, 57.
19 Goldberg, "From Landless to Landlords," 161.
20 Goldberg, "From Landless to Landlords," 162–64.
21 *Report of the National Advisory Commission on Civil Disorders*, 51; Peter Eisinger, *The Politics of Displacement*, 63; Georgakas and Surkin, *Detroit*, 156.
22 Fine, *Violence in the Model City*, 97.
23 Widick, "Mayor Cavanagh and the Limits of Reform," 489.
24 Kelley, *Freedom Dreams*, 75.
25 Johnson, *Revolutionaries to Race Leaders*, 14.

26  Babson et al., *Working Detroit*, 107.

27  Ward, *In Love and Struggle*, 50–52; Jones, "An End to the Neglect of the Problems of the Negro Woman!"

28  Johnson, "Coming to Terms with Actually-Existing Black Life."

29  Johnson, *Revolutionaries to Race Leaders*, 20.

30  Ward, *In Love and Struggle*, 118; Johnson, *Revolutionaries to Race Leaders*, 15–16.

31  Ward, *In Love and Struggle*, 158, 166.

32  Denby, *Workers Battle Automation*; Ward, *In Love and Struggle*, 284; Pizzolato, "Transnational Radicals."

33  Johnson, *Revolutionaries to Race Leaders*, 15;

34  Boggs, *The American Revolution*, 84–85.

35  Ward, *In Love and Struggle*, 277, 302, 325.

36  Cleage, *The Black Messiah*, 3.

37  Widick, "Mayor Cavanagh and the Limits of Reform," 488; Herb Boyd, *Black Detroit*, 137, 195.

38  Cleage, "Myths about Malcolm X."

39  Malcolm X, *Malcolm X Speaks*.

40  Johnson, *Revolutionaries to Race Leaders*, 50–51.

41  Marable, *Malcolm X*, 304.

42  Ahmad, "The League of Revolutionary Black Workers"; Kelley, *Freedom Dreams*, 78; Bloom and Martin, *Black against Empire*, 410; Marable, *Malcolm X*, 263.

43  Williams, "The Potential of a Minority Revolution."

44  Mast, *Detroit Lives*, 307.

45  For a comprehensive history of RAM, see Maxwell C. Stanford's thesis, "Revolutionary Action Movement (RAM): A Case Study of an Urban Revolutionary Movement in Capitalist Society"; Kelley, *Freedom Dreams*, 75–84; Rahman, "Marching Blind," 194.

46  When General Baker received his draft notice to serve in the Vietnam War, he responded with a legendary rejection letter: "When the call is made to free the black delta areas of Mississippi, Alabama, South Carolina; when the call is made to FREE 12th STREET HERE IN DETROIT, when these calls are made, send for me, for these shall be Historical Struggles in which it shall be an honor to serve!" ASM began distributing leaflets claiming that if Baker was forced to serve in the armed forces, fifty thousand blacks would show up to the induction to protest. Though this was a bluff—RAM's and ASM's numbers remained relatively small—the government feared an insurrection, and General Baker was subsequently declared unfit for duty. In 1965 RAM published an open statement to the Vietnamese National Liberation Front declaring their solidarity with the Vietnamese people against American imperialism. Azikiwe, "General Gordon Baker, Jr."; Ahmad, "The League of Revolutionary Black Workers"; Bloom and Martin, *Black against Empire*, 32–33.

47  Kelley, *Freedom Dreams*, 71; Bloom and Martin, *Black against Empire*, 28–29.

48  Camp, *Incarcerating the Crisis*, 34.

49  Bloom and Martin, *Black against Empire*, 30.

50  Camp, *Incarcerating the Crisis*, 38.

51 It is important to note that the "nonviolent" civil rights movement was always intricately linked with and received protection from an armed "violent" component. See Williams, *Negroes with Guns*; Marable, *Race, Reform, Rebellion*, 77.

52 Thompson, "Unmaking the Motor City in the Age of Mass Incarceration," 45; Marable, *How Capitalism Underdeveloped Black America*, 124.

53 Widick, "Mayor Cavanagh and the Limits of Reform," 488: Harry Golden, "Mayor Assails 'Irresponsible' Critics of Police," *Detroit Free Press*, October 22, 1965; Marable, *How Capitalism Underdeveloped Black America*, 124; Harry Golden, "New Law Asked to Battle Crime," *Detroit Free Press*, November 19, 1965.

54 Golden, "New Law Asked to Battle Crime."

55 Golden, "New Law Asked to Battle Crime"; John Millhome, "Inner City Is Chief Target in Crime-Reduction Drive," *Detroit Free Press*, July 9, 1962.

56 "Police Kill Woman in Vice Case," *Detroit Free Press*, July 6, 1963; Ward, *In Love and Struggle*, 304.

57 "Lessons Learned from City's Racial Violence," *Detroit Free Press*, August 14, 1966.

58 "Lessons Learned from City's Racial Violence"; "37 Seized in New Outbreaks," *Detroit Free Press*, August 11, 1966; "Lessons Learned from City's Racial Violence"; Ahmad, "The League of Revolutionary Black Workers."

59 *Report of the National Advisory Commission on Civil Disorders* concluded that Kercheval had "the city's most effective police-community relations program" (48). "Lessons Learned from City's Racial Violence."

60 Ahmad, "The League of Revolutionary Black Workers"; "Negro Check on Police Is Criticized," *Detroit Free Press*, October 30, 1966.

61 Don Lenhause, "Three Arraigned in Grocer's Killing," *Detroit Free Press*, December 28, 1966.

62 Eric Morgenthaler, "Blind Queenie Sounds Out a New Home," *Detroit Free Press*, June 26, 1967; Stan Putnam, "Tragedy Stalked His Park of Fun," *Detroit Free Press*, June 26, 1967; *Report of the National Advisory Commission on Civil Disorders*, 48.

63 "5 Freed in Killing in City Park," *Detroit Free Press*, June 27 1967; John Griffith, "Did a Youth in the Gang Actually Fire Fatal Shot?," *Detroit Free Press*, December 31, 1968; Bloom and Martin, *Black against Empire*, 87.

64 "NY Police Seize 16 in Plot to Kill NAACP Chief," *Detroit Free Press*, June 22, 1967; Kelley, *Freedom Dreams*, 90.

65 "Woman Standing in Doorway Is Slain by 2 Men," *Detroit Free Press*, July 2, 1967; Sugrue, *The Origins of the Urban Crisis*, 244; *Report of the National Advisory Commission on Civil Disorders*, 48.

66 Nancy Solomon, "40 Years On, Newark Re-examines Painful Riot Past," NPR, July 14, 2007, http://www.npr.org/templates/story/story.php?storyId=11966375; Bloom and Martin, *Black against Empire*, 85; Mudge, "Mayor's Secret Riot-Spy Network Flopped"; "The 1967 Detroit Rebellion."

67 "The 1967 Detroit Rebellion"; Camp, *Incarcerating the Crisis*, 54; Fine, *Violence in the Model City*, 160.

68 "The 1967 Detroit Rebellion"; "Blind-Pig Raid Was Spark," *Detroit Free Press*, July 24, 1967.

69  Cluster, *They Should Have Served That Cup of Coffee*, 71.

70  Fine, *Violence in the Model City*, 178.

71  *Report of the National Advisory Commission on Civil Disorders*, 40–50; "The 1967 Detroit Rebellion"; "AP Newsman Probe Cause of Race Riots," *Detroit Free Press*, July 31, 1967; Stauch, "Wildcat of the Streets," 61.

72  Dyer, "Rebellion in Detroit."

73  *Report of the National Advisory Commission on Civil Disorders*, 51; Camp, *Incarcerating the Crisis*, 55; "LBJ Approves All-Out Drive to End Strife," *Detroit Free Press*, July 25, 1967.

74  Fine, *Violence in the Model City*, 187, 193; *Report of the National Advisory Commission on Civil Disorders*, 53; Bloom and Martin, *Black against Empire*, 89; "Looter Killed; 724 Held as Riot Spreads," *Detroit Free Press*, July 24, 1967; Dyer, "Rebellion in Detroit."

75  Locke, *The Detroit Riot of 1967*, 41.

76  Fine, *Violence in the Model City*, 200.

77  Rahman, "Marching Blind."

78  Fine, *Violence in the Model City*, 201.

79  "LBJ Approves All-Out Drive to End Strife"; "An Orgy of Pillage Erupts behind Fires and Violence," *Detroit Free Press*, July 25, 1967; "LBJ Vows to Resist Violence," *Detroit Free Press*, July 25, 1967; "Negro Editor Hits Police for Lack of 'Firm Action,'" *Detroit Free Press*, July 26, 1967.

80  Ahmad, "The League of Revolutionary Black Workers"; "LBJ Approves All-Out Drive to End Strife"; "An Orgy of Pillage Erupts behind Fires and Violence"; "LBJ Vows to Resist Violence"; "Negro Editor Hits Police for Lack of 'Firm Action.'"

81  Fine, *Violence in the Model City*, 202–3, 231.

82  Fine, *Violence in the Model City*, 222

83  Fine, *Violence in the Model City*, 231.

84  Ulbrich, "Riot or Rebellion," 112.

85  Saul Friedman, "Expert Fears Long Struggle in Riot Area," *Detroit Free Press*, July 27, 1967; John Griffith, Jerome Hansen, and James C. Dewey, "White Looter Is Killed; Death Toll 36," *Detroit Free Press*, July 27, 1967.

86  Locke, *The Detroit Riot of 1967*, 111.

87  Balbus, *The Dialectics of Legal Repression*, 232–34.

88  Dyer, "Rebellion in Detroit."

89  Griffith, Hansen, and Dewey "White Looter Is Killed; Death Toll 36"; *Report of the National Advisory Commission on Civil Disorders*, 58–60.

90  *Report of the National Advisory Commission on Civil Disorders*, 57; Larue Heard, "A Sniper Was under Fire, but a 4-Year-Old Girl Died," *Detroit Free Press*, July 27, 1967; Ludy Wax, "Legislator Defends Shooting," *Detroit Free Press*, July 26, 1967; Bloom and Martin, *Black against Empire*, 89; John Griffith and James C. Dewey, "2,600 Jailed; New Riots Hit Outstate Area," *Detroit Free Press*, July 26, 1967.

91  Dyer, "Rebellion in Detroit."

92  *Report of the National Advisory Commission on Civil Disorders*, 58–60; Edgar Z. Friedenberg, "Motown Justice," *New York Review of Books*, August 1, 1968, http://www.nybooks.com/articles/1968/08/01/motown-justice/; John Hamilton, "That Was No Racial Incident on Lawton," *Detroit Free Press*, July 27, 1967; Griffith, Hansen, and

Dewey, "White Looter Is Killed; Death Toll 36"; Azikiwe, "Lessons from the Detroit July 1967 Rebellion and Prospects for Social Transformation"; Hershey, *The Algiers Motel Incident*.

93  Fine, *Violence in the Model City*, 233.

94  Thompson, *Whose Detroit?*, 64.

95  *Report of the National Advisory Commission on Civil Disorders*, 59–60; Bloom and Martin, *Black against Empire*, 87; Rahman, "Marching Blind," 184; Fine, *Violence in the Model City*, 259.

96  Author interview with Jerome Scott, March 5, 2019.

97  Vogel, "Capitalism and Incarceration Revisited."

98  Berger, "Social Movements and Mass Incarceration," 62.

99  Camp, *Incarcerating the Crisis*, 53–54.

100  Fine, *Violence in the Model City*, 197.

101  Williams, *Our Enemies in Blue*, 303; Bloom and Martin, *Black against Empire*, 89.

102  Fine, *Violence in the Model City*, 195, 199, 244.

103  Stark, *Police Riots*, 128–29.

104  Bellamy Foster and McChesney, "Surveillance Capitalism."

105  "The 1967 Detroit Rebellion," *Revolutionary Worker*; Babson et al., *Working Detroit*, 171.

106  Bloom and Martin, *Black against Empire*, 86–87. The shift in consciousness that occurred with many rebels evokes the writings of Frantz Fanon. In his seminal work, *The Wretched of the Earth*, Fanon argues that a violent struggle allows "the accumulated libido to dissolve as in a volcanic eruption" and eventually results in the "veritable creation of new men." Fanon, however, also wrote that "'a legitimate desire for revenge' . . . cannot sustain a war of liberation" (52, 37, 139).

107  Georgakas and Surkin, *Detroit*, 14.

108  "Romney Asks Race Reforms," *Detroit Free Press*, July 31, 1967.


CHAPTER 4: REVOLUTIONARIES AND COUNTERREVOLUTIONARIES

1  Brent Lang, "Inside Kathryn Bigelow's Journey to Tell 'Detroit's' Harrowing Story," *Variety*, August 1, 2017, http://variety.com/2017/film/features/detroit-kathryn -bigelow-john-boyega-1202511077/.

2  Boggs and Kurashige, *The Next American Revolution*, 147.

3  John Eligon, "A White Director, the Police and Race in 'Detroit,'" *New York Times*, August 2, 2017, https://www.nytimes.com/2017/08/02/movies/kathryn-bigelow-mark -boal-detroit-police-brutality.html.

4  Reed, "The Kerner Commission and the Irony of Antiracist Politics."

5  Touré Reed writes, "Even as Randolph declared his support for a fair employment practices act at the March on Washington, he stated plainly that antidiscrimination alone would do African Americans little good in the face of 'profit-geared automation' that was destroying 'the jobs of millions of workers black and white.' Randolph and Rustin thus identified public works, full-employment policies, and a minimum-wage hike as essential to closing the racial economic gap" ("Between Obama and Coates," 19).

6  Vitale, *The End of Policing*, 14.

7  Hall et al., *Policing the Crisis*, 240–41, 290–97; Camp, *Incarcerating the Crisis*, 59.
8  Martin Luther King Jr., "Beyond Vietnam," April 4, 1967, Stanford University, Martin Luther King, Jr. Research and Education Institute, http://kingencyclopedia .stanford.edu/encyclopedia/documentsentry/doc_beyond_vietnam/; Bloom and Martin, *Black against Empire*, 3; Bellamy Foster and McChesney, "Surveillance Capitalism."
9  Bloom and Martin, *Black against Empire*, 286; "Streets of Fire: Governor Spiro Agnew and the Baltimore City Riots, April 1968," Maryland State Archives, http://teaching .msa.maryland.gov/000001/000000/000061/html/t61.html.
10 The money used by Americans to purchase foreign goods was no longer recycling back into the United States. Instead, foreigners were increasingly purchasing goods made by non-U.S. firms, and were trading in their U.S. dollars for their gold equivalent, draining the United States of its gold reserves and pushing the U.S. government into debt. "Whereas in 1951, the United States' holdings of gold represented 3.5 times the amount of the country's net short-term indebtedness, in 1971 these holdings covered no more than 22 percent of this external debt." This dynamic was integral to the U.S. government's 1971 decision to terminate the convertibility of the dollar to gold, ending the Bretton Woods system, which had overseen the international monetary system since 1944, paving the way for the rampant currency speculation that continues to this day. Magdoff and Sweezy, *The Deepening Crisis of U.S. Capitalism*, 12; McNally, *Global Slump*, 90; Amin, *Unequal Development*, 120; Arrighi, *Adam Smith in Beijing*.
11 *League of Revolutionary Black Workers: A Media Project with the League of Revolutionary Black Workers*, 2017, https://www.revolutionaryblackworkers.org/video.
12 The working title of the book is "Class, Race and Revolution—Voices from the Point of Production: The Story of the League of Revolutionary Black Workers."
13 John Watson, "Black Editor: An Interview," *Radical America* 2, no. 4 (July–August 1968): 30–38, reprinted in *Viewpoint Magazine*, January 13, 2015, https://www .viewpointmag.com/2015/01/13/black-editor-an-interview-1968/.
14 Watson, "Black Editor."
15 Georgakas and Surkin, *Detroit*, 18–21; Rahman, "Marching Blind," 189.
16 James Dewey, "Chrysler Denies Report of Hamtramck Plant Move," *Detroit Free Press*, October 4, 1968.
17 The League had contacts with black-led organizations such as the United Black Brothers, who had shut down the Ford Mahwah plant in New Jersey for three days in April 1969, and the Black Panther Caucus, which, in addition to their organizational work within GM's plant in Fremont, California, worked hand-in-hand with the United Farmworkers. Camp, *Incarcerating the Crisis*, 61; Fine, *Expanding the Frontier of Civil Rights*, 322–27; "Speech on the League of Revolutionary Black Workers," Second National Conference of the Marxist-Leninist Party, USA, Fall 1984, Communist Voice, http://www.communistvoice.org/WAS8501LRBW.html#WAS; Babson et al., *Working Detroit*, 172.
18 Tripp, "Black Working Class Radicalism."
19 Thompson, *Whose Detroit?*, 124.

20  Babson et al., *Working Detroit*, 181–83.

21  Tripp, "Black Working Class Radicalism in Detroit."

22  "Reuther's Dead: Black Struggle Continues," *Inner City Voice* 2, no. 6 (June 1970): 1, http://freedomarchives.org/Documents/Finder/DOC513_scans/League/513.Leagueof RevolutionaryBlackWokers.InnerCity.June.1970.pdf.

23  Author interview, March 5, 2019.

24  Babson et al., *Working Detroit*, 183–84.

25  Georgakas and Surkin, *Detroit*, 88.

26  *League of Revolutionary Black Workers: A Media Project with the League of Revolutionary Black Workers*; Susan Watson, "Nader Group Says Auto Firms Ignore Health Perils," *Detroit Free Press*, September 8, 1973; Babson et al., *Working Detroit*, 183–84.

27  Tripp, "Black Working Class Radicalism in Detroit."

28  Babson et al., *Working Detroit*, 184.

29  Georgakas and Surkin, *Detroit*, 87.

30  Georgakas and Surkin, *Detroit*, 86.

31  "A Ruling against Reason," *Detroit Free Press*, March 13, 1973; Georgakas and Surkin, *Detroit*, 86; Thompson, *Whose Detroit?*. Management's claims that automation and new machinery were the cause of increased productivity were proved mythical by the failure of the Lordstown plant in Ohio. Designed as a paragon of automation, the computer-controlled plant engineered jobs to a fraction of a second and, claiming a production speed of 103 cars per hour (compared to only 64 at Dodge Main), was the fastest assembly line in the world. "The only problem with Lordstown," write Georgakas and Surkin, "was that it didn't work." The model produced at Lordstown, the Vega, "turned out to be one of the worst-built cars in America." Two years after the factory opened, 97 percent of workers voted to strike over working conditions; this is despite the fact that there were no large minority groups in the factory and the workforce had no known old-time radicals or hardcore unionists. Georgakas and Surkin, *Detroit*, 104–5.

32  Georgakas and Surkin, *Detroit*, 89.

33  "The Role of Black Workers," *League of Revolutionary Black Workers: A Media Project with the League of Revolutionary Black Workers*.

34  Author interview with Jerome Scott, March 5, 2019.

35  "The Role of Political Education," *League of Revolutionary Black Workers: A Media Project with the League of Revolutionary Black Workers*.

36  "The Role of Black Workers," *League of Revolutionary Black Workers: A Media Project with the League of Revolutionary Black Workers*.

37  Azikiwe, "Lessons from the Detroit July 1967 Rebellion."

38  *Finally Got the News*.

39  Mast, *Detroit Lives*, 182.

40  Robé, "Detroit Rising," 131, 147; Lewis-Coleman, *Race against Liberalism*, 105.

41  "The Role of Women," *League of Revolutionary Black Workers: A Media Project with the League of Revolutionary Black Workers*.

42  Robé, "Detroit Rising," 130.

43  Pizzolato, "Transnational Radicals," 28.

44  Ahmad, "The League of Revolutionary Black Workers."

45  Pizzolato, "Transnational Radicals," 20.

46  Georgakas and Surkin, *Detroit*, 86–102.

47  Pizzolato, "Transnational Radicals," 25–27, Tronti, "Our Operaismo."

48  Georgakas, "Finally Got the News," 6.

49  Luke Tripp, "D.R.U.M.—VANGUARD OF THE BLACK REVOLUTION: Dodge Revolutionary Union Movement States History, Purpose and Aims," *South End* 27, no. 62 (1969); 8, http://freedomarchives.org/Documents/Finder/DOC513_scans/League/513 .LeagueofRevolutionaryBlackWorkers.TheSouthEnd.1969.pdf.

50  Mast, *Detroit Lives*, 309.

51  Quoted in Goldberg, "From Landless to Landlords," 162.

52  Goldberg, "From Landless to Landlords," 171–75.

53  Thompson, *Whose Detroit?*, 122; "Speech on the League of Revolutionary Black Workers," Second National Conference of the Marxist-Leninist Party, USA; Dewey, "Chrysler Denies Report of Hamtramck Plant Move."

54  Thompson, *Whose Detroit?*, 102.

55  Stauch, "Wildcat of the Streets," 4, 291.

56  Boyd, *Black Detroit*, 214; Thompson, "Unmaking the Motor City in the Age of Mass Incarceration," 49.

57  Stauch, "Wildcat of the Streets," 289.

58  *Finally Got the News*; "Militant Loses Runoff in Disputed UAW Vote," *Detroit Free Press*, May 29, 1971.

59  Babson et al., *Working Detroit*, 174.

60  Georgakas and Surkin, *Detroit*, 75. As David Goldberg notes, most League activists believe that TULC was behind the failed attempt to assassinate Baker. (The bullet actually hit Fred Lyles, a Black Power activist, who was standing next to Baker.) See Goldberg, "From Landless to Landlords," 183.

61  Mast, *Detroit Lives*.

62  Ernie Allen, "Dying from the Inside: The Decline of the League of Revolutionary Black Workers," in Cluster, *They Should Have Served That Cup of Coffee*, 100.

63  Author interview, March 5, 2019.

64  "On the Split," *League of Revolutionary Black Workers: A Media Project with the League of Revolutionary Black Workers*.

65  "On Political Education," League of Revolutionary Black Workers: A Media Project with the League of Revolutionary Black Workers.

66  These activists also formed the Communist Labor Party in 1974, which ran General Baker as a candidate in the Michigan legislature in 1976.

67  Thompson, *Whose Detroit?*, 203.

68  Sugrue, *The Origins of the Urban Crisis*, 144; Taylor, *From #BlackLivesMatter to Black Liberation*, 59; Stauch, "Wildcat of the Streets," 12; Babson et al., *Working Detroit*, 186; Georgakas and Surkin, *Detroit*, 102.

69  Geschwender, "The League of Revolutionary Black Workers," 9; Georgakas and Surkin, *Detroit*, 166.

70  Marable, *Race, Reform, and Rebellion*, 55–56; Marable, *Malcolm X*, 132–33.

71  Seale, *Seize the Time*, ix–x.

72  Bloom and Martin, *Black against Empire*, 72.

73  Spencer, *The Revolution Has Come*, 131.

74  Bloom and Martin, *Black against Empire*, 292

75  As Robyn C. Spencer points out, while Panthers' work with white radicals caused members like Janice Garrett-Forte to make a "big leap . . . [from,] you know, kill all white people, to understanding that it is a class struggle," many of the rank and file were wary of entering into coalitions with whites. This issue undermined the attempted unification between the Panthers and SNCC, whose leader, Stokely Carmichael, dismissed Marxism as a "white ideology." Spencer observes, however, that the FBI was also complicit here: "The FBI fueled tensions between them with the goal of creating a split" (*The Revolution Has Come*, 81–83, 140).

76  Rahman, "Marching Blind," 191.

77  Rahman, "Marching Blind"; Bloom and Martin, *Black against Empire*, 292.

78  Marcetic, "The FBI's Secret War," *Jacobin*, August 31, 2016, https://www.jacobinmag .com/2016/08/fbi-cointelpro-new-left-panthers-muslim-surveillance.

79  Johnson, *Revolutionaries to Race Leaders*, 98; Bloom and Martin, *Black against Empire*, 210; Marable, *Race, Reform and Rebellion*, 109.

80  Bloom and Martin, *Black against Empire*, 177.

81  Marable, *Race, Reform, and Rebellion*, 124–25; Bloom and Martin, *Black against Empire*, 177, 186; Major, *A Panther Is a Black Cat*, 301; Rahman, "Marching Blind," 210.

82  Rahman, "Marching Blind," 209–10.

83  "Crockett Does Disservice," *Detroit Free Press*, April 24, 1969; Rahman, "Marching Blind," 190.

84  Thompson, *Whose Detroit?*, 128–35.

85  Georgakas and Surkin, *Detroit*, 9–11, 86, 164–67.

86  Jerry M. Flint, "Detroit Lawyer Becomes First Radical Judge in U.S.," *New York Times*, November 12, 1972.

87  Rahman, "Marching Blind," 190–91.

88  Spencer, *The Revolution Has Come*, 76.

89  Spencer, *The Revolution Has Come*, 89.

90  Rahman, "Marching Blind," 192; Marable, *Race, Reform, and Rebellion*, 109.

91  Bloom and Martin, *Black against Empire*; Rahman, "Marching Blind"; Kleffner, "The Black Panthers."

92  Rahman, "Marching Blind," 196–97.

93  Williams, *Our Enemies in Blue*, 218; Rahman, "Marching Blind," 197–99; Andrew Mollison, "Panthers Harassed, Gribbs Told," *Detroit Free Press*, May 23, 1970.

94  Rahman, "Marching Blind," 197–99.

95  Rahman, "Marching Blind," 207.

96  "Policeman Killed, Another Wounded," *Detroit Free Press*, October 25, 1970; "15 Are Arraigned in Slaying of Black Policeman," *Detroit Free Press*, October 26, 1970; Rahman, "Marching Blind," 210–11.

97　Bellamy Foster and McChesney. "Surveillance Capitalism"; Bloom and Martin, *Black against Empire*, 212.

98　"Speech on the League of Revolutionary Black Workers," Second National Conference of the Marxist-Leninist Party, USA.

99　Johnson, *Revolutionaries to Race Leaders*, 74, 88; Dean E. Robinson, "Black Power Nationalism as Ethnic Pluralism: Liberalism's Ethnic Paradigm in Black Radicalism," in Reed and Warren, *Renewing Black Intellectual History*.

100　Johnson, *Revolutionaries to Race Leaders*, 64.

101　Spencer, *The Revolution Has Come*, 143.

102　Thompson, *Whose Detroit?*, 219.

103　Taylor, *From #BlackLivesMatter to Black Liberation*, 59; Johnson, "The Panthers Can't Save Us Now."

104　Reed, "The Black Urban Regime: Structural Origins and Constraints," in *Stirrings in the Jug*, 79–116.

105　Quoted in Johnson, *Revolutionaries to Race Leaders*, 65.

106　Quoted in Johnson, *Revolutionaries to Race Leaders*, 151.

107　Johnson, *Revolutionaries to Race Leaders*, 163, 126, 161.

108　Georgakas and Surkin, *Detroit*, 133.

109　Georgakas and Surkin, *Detroit*, 76.

110　Quoted in Georgakas and Surkin, *Detroit*, 135.

111　"The Role of Political Education," *League of Revolutionary Black Workers: A Media Project with the League of Revolutionary Black Workers.*

112　"The Role of Political Education," *League of Revolutionary Black Workers: A Media Project with the League of Revolutionary Black Workers.*

113　Georgakas and Surkin, *Detroit*, 92.

114　Mast, *Detroit Lives*, 310–13.

115　*Taking Back Detroit*; Mast, *Detroit Lives*, 184–85.

116　Johnson, *Revolutionaries to Race Leaders*, 98–101.

117　Vogel, "Capitalism and Incarceration Revisited."

118　Wacquant, *Punishing the Poor*, 114; Foucault, *Discipline and Punish*, 297, 306; Julia Felsenthal, "Ava Duvernay's *13th* Is a Shocking, Necessary Look at the Link between Slavery and Mass Incarceration," *Vogue*, October 6, 2016, http://www.vogue.com/article/13th-ava-duvernay-review.

119　Jackson, *Soledad Brother*, 14; Camp, *Incarcerating the Crisis*, 71–72.

120　Quoted in Berger, *Captive Nation*, 159, 100.

121　Berger, *Captive Nation*, 129.

122　Marable, *Race, Reform, and Rebellion*, 127.

123　Bloom and Martin, *Black against Empire*, 378.

124　Camp, *Incarcerating the Crisis*, 71.

125　Camp, *Incarcerating the Crisis*, 82.

126　Berger, *Captive Nation*; Pizarro and Stenius, "Supermax Prisons," 251.

127　Camp, *Incarcerating the Crisis*, 88.

128　Pizarro and Stenius, "Supermax Prisons," 251.

129　Berger, "Social Movements and Mass Incarceration," 9.

130 Berger, "Social Movements and Mass Incarceration," 9; Camp, *Incarcerating the Crisis*, 88.

131 Jackson, *Soledad Brother*.

132 Linebaugh, *The London Hanged*, xxii.

133 Marable, *How Capitalism Underdeveloped Black America*, 124.

134 Wenger and Bonomo, "Crime, the Crisis of Capitalism, and Social Revolution," 685.

135 Forman, *Locking Up Our Own*, 76, 20.

136 Mast, *Detroit Lives*, 172.

137 Thompson, *Whose Detroit*, 73; The coalition helped win support for the City of Detroit Fair Housing ordinance, an attempt to ameliorate some of the housing discrimination that had galvanized activists before and after the rebellion. Azikiwe, "Lessons from the Detroit July 1967 Rebellion."

138 Stauch, "Wildcat of the Streets," 179–83.

139 In one striking example of this dynamic, in Chicago there were myriad efforts to "incorporate gangs into the legitimate local power structure" in order to quell dissidence and violence among black youth to leverage more community development funding. In 1967 a $957,000 Office of Economic Opportunity grant "used the Woodlawn area's existing gang structure—the Blackstone Rangers and the Devil's Disciples—as the basis of a program to provide remedial education, recreation, vocational training, and job placement services to youths." Also in 1967 the Vice Lords gang registered as a corporation and the next year received a $15,000 grant for an urban renewal campaign. Diamond, *Chicago on the Make*, 196.

140 Goldberg, "From Landless to Landlords," 170. Azikiwe, "Lessons from the Detroit July 1967 Rebellion."

141 Thompson, *Whose Detroit?*, 85–88, 92, 101.

142 Thompson, *Whose Detroit?*, 80.

143 Thompson, "Unmaking the Motor City in the Age of Mass Incarceration," 46; Usmani, "Did Liberals Give Us Mass Incarceration?"

144 Gibson and Jung, *Historical Census Statistics on Population Totals*, "Table 23. Michigan—Race and Hispanic Origin for Selected Large Cities and Other Places: Earliest Census to 1990."

145 George Hunter, "Dec. Surge Dims Hopes for Dip in Detroit Murders," *Detroit News*, December 28, 2015, http://www.detroitnews.com/story/news/local/detroit-city/2015/12/27/homicides-track-hold-steady-detroit/77959798/; Usmani, "Did Liberals Give Us Mass Incarceration," 174.

146 Stauch, "Wildcat of the Streets," 355.

147 Stauch, "Wildcat of the Streets," 372.

148 Stauch, "Wildcat of the Streets," 355.

149 Georgakas and Surkin. *Detroit*, 167. When considering the scope of the city's crime problem, we have no choice but to disagree with Heather Ann Thompson. In "Unmaking the Motor City in the Age of Mass Incarceration," she argues that rising crime reflected little more than the dubious nature of crime statistics. She also seeks to downplay the scope of the city's homicide problem. "Despite the fact that the national homicide rate had risen from 5.5 per 100,000 people in 1965 to 7.3 in 1968,

the nation's citizenry—be it in the Delta or in Detroit—was not in fact suffering a record-setting crime wave. The murder rate had been far higher in the 1930s—as high as 9.7 per 100,000. Indeed, if one looks at the entire 20th century, it is remarkable how much safer the 1960s were compared to previous decades. Not only was a U.S. citizen less likely to be murdered in the early to mid-1960s than they were at other points in the 20th century, but their risk of meeting a violent death actually went up after the nation began a war on crime" (44). To be sure, the crime problem was exaggerated by political elites, but to deny the reality of a devastating crime problem is highly misleading.

150 Even the dissident group From the Ground Up (which was formed from the Motor City Labor League) wrote in the early 1970s, "One cannot speak of 'high crime areas' in Detroit. The entire city is such an area, though sections of the center city, riddled with poverty, police complicity in drug traffic, and double high rates of unemployment, are, to be sure, the 'highest crime areas'" (Schultz, *Detroit under* STRESS, 9).

151 Forman, "Racial Critiques of Mass Incarceration," 114.

152 Newton, *The Huey Newton Reader*, 156; Spencer, *The Revolution Has Come*; Narayan, "The Wages of Whiteness in the Absence of Wages," 2482–500.

153 Shabazz, "Ahmad A. Rahman's Making of Black 'Solutionaries.'" Shabazz adds, "Long before Michelle Alexander's book about mass incarceration and the 'New Jim Crow,' Rahman saw what was coming and attempted to counter it."

154 Shabazz, "Ahmad A. Rahman's Making of Black 'Solutionaries.'"

155 Jay, "Cages and Crises."

156 Vitale, *The End of Policing*, 14.

157 Parenti, "The Making of the American Police State," *Jacobin*, July 28, 2015, https://www.jacobinmag.com/2015/07/incarceration-capitalism-black-lives-matter/.

158 Vitale, *End of Policing*, 50.

159 Elizabeth Hinton quoted in Kurashige, *The Fifty-Year Rebellion*, 27.

160 Robert Pavich, "The Little Lady May Be a Cop: Disguised Policeman to Fight Detroit Street Crime," *Detroit News*, January 13, 1971. Jerome Scott remembers seeing suspicious things like drunken white guys walking around black neighborhoods with money falling out of their pocket. Author interview. March 5, 2019.

161 Schultz, *Detroit under* STRESS, 15.

162 Darden and Thomas, *Detroit*, 50; Pavich, "The Little Lady May Be a Cop."

163 Schultz, *Detroit under* STRESS, 4.

164 Stephen Cain, "4,000 Join in Orderly Protest against STRESS Killing," *Detroit News*, September 14, 1971.

165 Schultz, *Detroit under* STRESS, 43, 57.

166 Schultz, *Detroit under* STRESS, x.

167 "Black Leaders Support S.T.R.E.S.S.," *Detroit News*, September 24, 1971.

168 "Stress Protest Shows Blacks Short on Foresight: Slayton," *Michigan Chronicle*, November 17, 1971.

169 Georgakas and Surkin, *Detroit*, 168, 171, 169–70. In another remarkable legal victory, Cockrel won a full acquittal for Hayward Brown, the militant accused in the shootout

with police, not by claiming that Brown did not kill the police, but rather that STRESS was an illegitimate institution. Thompson, *Whose Detroit?*, 149–51, 194.

170 Schultz, *Detroit under STRESS*, 51.

171 Thompson, *Whose Detroit?*, 149–51, 194; Georgakas and Surkin, *Detroit*, 220.

172 William K. Stevens, "Mayoral Primary Heed in Detroit," *New York Times*, September 12, 1973, https://www.nytimes.com/1973/09/12/archives/mayoral-primary-held-in -detroit-police-chief-black-liberal-apparent.html.

173 Stauch, "Wildcat of the Streets," 70, 78–79.

174 Stauch, "Wildcat of the Streets," 81; Thompson, *Whose Detroit?*, 198.

175 Robert Pisor, "Young—A Student of the Streets; New Mayor Shares Crime Victims' Concerns," *Detroit News*, November 7, 1973.

176 Inaugural Speech, 1974, in Coleman A. Young Collection, part II, box 106, folders 4–5, Archives of Labor and Urban Affairs, Wayne State University.

177 Stauch, "Wildcat of the Streets," 91–92.

178 Quoted in Stauch, "Wildcat of the Streets," 93–94.


CHAPTER 5: POST-FORDISM AND MASS INCARCERATION

1 "The Curley Effect: The Economics of Shaping the Electorate," *Journal of Law, Economics, and Organization* 21, no. 1 (2000): 2.

2 Mast, *Detroit Lives*, 185.

3 Marable, *Race, Reform, and Rebellion*, 123–24.

4 Goldberg, "From Landless to Landlords," 176.

5 Mast, *Detroit Lives*, 273; Stauch, "Wildcat of the Streets," 21.

6 Reed, *Stirrings in the Jug*, 98–99.

7 Valerie Wilson and William M. Rodgers III, "Black-White Wage Gaps Expand with Rising Wage Inequality," Economic Policy Institute, September 20, 2016, http://www .epi.org/publication/black-white-wage-gaps-expand-with-rising-wage-inequality/; Henry Louis Gates Jr., "Black America and the Class Divide," *New York Times*, February 1, 2016, https://www.nytimes.com/2016/02/07/education/edlife/black -america-and-the-class-divide.html?mcubz=0&_r=0.

8 "Anatomy of Detroit's Decline," *New York Times*, http://www.nytimes.com /interactive/2013/08/17/us/detroit-decline.html.

9 This section is indebted to Michael Stauch Jr.'s meticulously researched dissertation, "Wildcat of the Streets: Race, Class and the Punitive Turn in 1970s Detroit."

10 Stauch, "Wildcat of the Streets," 88–89.

11 Dauenbaugh, "Coleman Young's Detroit," 29–31; Boyd, "Blacks and the Police State," 58–60; Blauner, "Internal Colonialism and Ghetto Revolt"; *Report of the National Advisory Commission on Civil Disorders*; Marable, *How Capitalism Underdeveloped Black America*, 162.

12 Stauch, "Wildcat of the Streets," 120–39.

13 This logic parallels Frantz Fanon's point about the repression of colonial uprisings: "Every time there was a rebellion, the military authorities sent only the colored soldiers to the front line" (*Black Skin, White Masks*, 83).

14  Stauch, "Wildcat of the Streets," 129–30.

15  Stauch, "Wildcat of the Streets," 149.

16  Nadine Brown, "'Hot Summer' of '75: Our Town Keeps Cool," *Michigan Chronicle*, August 9, 1975; Stauch, "Wildcat of the Streets," 120–39.

17  Stauch, "Wildcat of the Streets," 118.

18  "City Recalls 450 Policemen," *Detroit Free Press*, August 17, 1976.

19  Editorial, "Harsh Measures for Harsh Times," *Detroit News*, August 20, 1976.

20  Stauch, "Wildcat of the Streets," 239–44.

21  "Detroit Begins Gang Crackdown," *Chicago Tribune*, August 17 1976; "City Recalls 450 Policemen"; Stauch, "Wildcat of the Streets," 225–37.

22  Stauch, "Wildcat of the Streets," 368–99; Jim Tittsworth and Don Ball, "Busted; Cops Seize 18 in Young Boys Inc. Drug Raid," *Detroit News*, December 8, 1982.

23  Quoted in Dauenbaugh, "Coleman Young's Detroit," 31.

24  Bill McGraw, interview with Heather Ann Thompson, "The War on Crime, Not Crime Itself, Fueled Detroit's Post-1967 Decline," *Bridge*, October 18, 2016, http://bridgemi.com/2016/10/the-war-on-crime-not-crime-itself-fueled-detroits-post-1967-decline/.

25  Vogel, "Capitalism and Incarceration Revisited."

26  Stauch, "Wildcat of the Streets," 156.

27  Stauch, "Wildcat of the Streets," 170, 359, 355.

28  Dauenbaugh, "Coleman Young's Detroit," 37–41.

29  Arrighi, *Adam Smith in Beijing*, 154.

30  McNally, *Global Slump*, 31.

31  McNally, *Global Slump*, 33.

32  Stein, "Labor History Symposium," 343; Prashad, *The Poorer Nations*.

33  Gibson and Jung, *Historical Census Statistics on Population Totals,* "Table 23. Michigan—Race and Hispanic Origin for Selected Large Cities and Other Places: Earliest Census to 1990"; Marable, *How Capitalism Underdeveloped Black America*, 160–62.

34  Sasha Liley and David Harvey, "On Neoliberalism: An Interview with David Harvey," *Monthly Review Online*, June 19, 2006, https://mronline.org/2006/06/19/on-neoliberalism-an-interview-with-david-harvey/.

35  McNally, *Global Slump*, 25.

36  "Neoliberalization has never been about a once-and-for-all liberalization, an evacuation of the state. Instead, it has been about imperfectly repurposing the state and its associated relays of policy intervention, in a manner broadly consistent with the globalizing class project for the regressive social redistribution of incomes and surpluses, and with the ever-shifting currents of transnational financialization and corporate globalization" (Peck, Theodore, and Brenner, "Neoliberalism Resurgent?," 275).

37  Harvey, *A Brief History of Neoliberalism*, 24; McNally, *Global Slump*, 35.

38  The most dramatic effect of this interest rate increase, it should be noted, occurred in the Global South: third world debt had increased from $47.5 billion to $560 billion in 1980. When the interest hike made it impossible for countries to pay back their debts, structural adjustment programs were imposed by the International Monetary Fund, enforcing austerity programs and opening these countries to the

intrusions of foreign capital. The effects were, and continue to be, genocidal: in African countries, per capita healthcare spending halved between 1975 and 1990. See McNally, *Global Slump*, 98–129; Marable, *How Capitalism Underdeveloped Black America*, 242–43.

39 Arrighi, *Adam Smith in Beijing*, 127.

40 During this time, class composition in metro Detroit shifted dramatically: the workers' movement was no longer being led by male workers in private industry. As the manufacturing unions were decimated, public-sector unions grew rapidly, mostly in the suburbs, where the welfare state had expanded dramatically in the postwar era. Meanwhile, as the mostly male manufacturing industries issued mass layoffs, the metro area added 110,000 jobs between 1960 and 1980, and 98 percent of these (mostly low-wage) jobs were taken by women, resulting in a dramatic shift in gender relations throughout the area. More than one-third of metro Detroit workers claimed that they were harassed on the job. Babson et al., *Working Detroit*, 201–4; "Status of Labor Unions," Center of Concern, https://www.coc.org/files/unions .pdf; Adams, "Changing Employment Patterns of Organized Workers"; Aschoff, "Imported from Detroit."

41 Thompson, *Whose Detroit?*, 216; Camp, *Incarcerating the Crisis*, 104. In Detroit the attack on unions only aggravated a long-standing trend: due to union repression, automation, and capital flight, union membership in Detroit's Big Three had already decreased by 50 percent between 1969 and 1980.

42 Aschoff, "Imported from Detroit."

43 Babson et al., *Working Detroit*, 214.

44 Narayan, "Survival Pending Revolution."

45 Boyd, *Black Detroit*, 246; John Gallagher, "How Detroit Went Broke: The Answers May Surprise You—and Don't Blame Coleman Young," *Detroit Free Press*, October 11, 2016, http://www.freep.com/story/news/local/michigan/detroit/2013/09/15/how -detroit-went-broke-the-answers-may-surprise-you-and/77152028/.

46 Robinson, *A Theory of Global Capitalism*, 115, 55, 53, 23, 79, 104.

47 *Poletown Lives!*

48 *Poletown Lives!*

49 Clement, "The Spatial Injustice of Crisis-Driven Neoliberal Urban Restructuring in Detroit," 46–47.

50 Robin Meredith, "G.M. Buys a Landmark of Detroit for Its Home," *New York Times*, May 17, 1996, http://www.nytimes.com/1996/05/17/us/gm-buys-a-landmark-of -detroit-for-its-home.html.

51 "State Incomes Fell in '80s, Census Figures Show," *Detroit Free Press*, July 23, 1992.

52 Maryann Mahaffey, "Hunger in Michigan," in Henrickson, *Detroit Perspectives*, 554.

53 Beckett and Herbert, *Banished*, 25.

54 Clement, "The Spatial Injustice of Crisis-Driven Neoliberal Urban Restructuring in Detroit"; Gallagher, "How Detroit Went Broke."

55 Charles Sercombe, "Future of GM's Poletown Plant Doesn't Look Hopeful," *Hamtramck Review*, April 5, 2019; Lee Devito, "Backlash against General Motors Is Helping Plant the Seeds for a Green Revolution," *Metrotimes*, January 30, 2019.

56 McCoy, *The Politics of Heroin*.

57 Mahaffey, "Hunger in Michigan," 560; Steven D. Levitt and Kevin M. Murphy, "How Bad Was Crack Cocaine?," *Capital Ideas*, April 2006, http://testwww .chicagobooth.edu/capideas/apr06/5.aspx; George Hunter, "Dec. Surge Dims Hopes for Dip in Detroit Murders." *Detroit News*, December 27, 2015, https://www .detroitnews.com/story/news/local/detroit-city/2015/12/27/homicides-track-hold -steady-detroit/77959798/.

58 Murakawa, *The First Civil Right*, 91; Alexander, *The New Jim Crow*, 49; Williams, *Our Enemies in Blue*, 329.

59 Thompson, "Unmaking the Motor City in the Age of Mass Incarceration"; Alexander, *The New Jim Crow*, 49. As the drug war accelerated and law enforcement agencies' budgets skyrocketed, the budget of the rehabilitative projects of the National Institute of Drug Abuse, which the poor relied on for drug relief, was slashed from $274 million in 1981 to $57 million in 1984.

60 Alexander, *The New Jim Crow*, 50–52; "Schools: System's Unprepared to Handle Influx of Crack-Damaged Children," *Detroit Free Press*, March 3, 1991.

61 Todd Reed, "Former Crack Baby: 'It's Another Stigma, Another Box to Put Me In,'" *Al Jazeera America*, May 10, 2015, http://america.aljazeera.com/watch/shows/america -tonight/articles/2015/3/10/crack-baby-myth.html.

62 Wacquant, *Punishing the Poor*, 50–52; Thompson, "Unmaking the Motor City in the Age of Mass Incarceration," 55; Camp, *Incarcerating the Crisis*, 95; Mast, *Detroit Lives*, 107.

63 Kramer, "Remarks on the National Welfare Rights Union," 9.

64 Mast, *Detroit Lives*, 158.

65 Mast, *Detroit Lives*, 109, 247.

66 Ward, *In Love and Struggle*, 330.

67 Ward, *In Love and Struggle*, 330.

68 Camp, *Incarcerating the Crisis*, 99–102.

69 Camp, *Incarcerating the Crisis*, 99–102; Williams, *Our Enemies in Blue*, 166; "L.A.: Hurt, but Healing," *Detroit Free Press*, May 1, 1992; "Anger Boils Over in Los Angeles," *Detroit Free Press*, May 1, 1992; "Riot Rumors Make Shop Owners Shaky," *Detroit Free Press*, May 3, 1992.

70 Dunn, *The Militarization of the US-Mexico Border*, 168.

71 "City Leaders Outraged by Beating," *Detroit Free Press*, November 7, 1992; "300 Mourn Green as Prosecutors Get Case," *Detroit Free Press*, November 11, 1992.

72 Camp, *Incarcerating the Crisis*, 107; Robinson, *Global Capitalism and the Crisis of Humanity*, 88.

73 Marie Gottschalk, "Conservatives against Incarceration?", *Jacobin*, December 23, 2016, https://jacobinmag.com/2016/12/carceral-state-mass-incarceration -conservatives-koch-trump.

74 Wacquant, *Punishing the Poor*, 43, 51, 95; Camp, *Incarcerating the Crisis*, 107; Nathan J. Robinson, "Bill Clinton, Superpredator," *Jacobin*, September 8, 2016, https://www .jacobinmag.com/2016/09/bill-clinton-hillary-superpredators-crime-welfare-african -americans/; Chang, *Disposable Domestics*, 153.

75  Kramer, "Remarks on the National Welfare Rights Union," 10–11.

76  Wacquant, *Punishing the Poor*, 95, 157.

77  James Bennett, "A Tribute to Ruin Irks Detroit," *New York Times*, December 10, 1995, http://www.nytimes.com/1995/12/10/us/a-tribute-to-ruin-irks-detroit.html.

78  Bennett, "A Tribute to Ruin Irks Detroit."

79  Philip Drew, "Sports Teams Score Big Revenues," Walswoth Printing Group, November–December 2013, http://digitaleditions.walsworthprintgroup.com/article /ECONOMY/1572354/186360/article.html; Joseph Lichterman, "In Cash-Strapped Detroit, Few Critics Question New Sports Arena Funding," Reuters, July 29, 2013, http://www.rawstory.com/2013/07/in-cash-strapped-detroit-few-critics-question -new-sports-arena-funding/; Bennett, "A Tribute to Ruin Irks Detroit."

80  Donald W. Nauss, "Detroit Plans to Build Downtown Baseball Stadium," *Los Angeles Times*, October 28, 1995, http://articles.latimes.com/1995-10-28/news/mn-62079_1 _private-projects.

81  Lichterman, "In Cash-Strapped Detroit, Few Critics Question New Sports Arena Funding."

82  Nauss, "Detroit Plans to Build Downtown Baseball Stadium"; Lichterman, "In Cash-Strapped Detroit, Few Critics Question New Sports Arena Funding"; Boggs, "Rebuilding Detroit: An Alternative to Casino Gambling"; Brent Snavely and Matt Helms, "Detroit Leaders Hope Casinos Avert Labor Dispute," *Detroit Free Press*, November 7, 2015, http://www.freep.com/story/money/business/2015/11/07/detroit -leaders-hope-casinos-avert-labor-dispute/75239184/.

83  "In Detroit's Despair, Mayor Sees Hope," *New York Times*, September 28, 1993, http:// www.nytimes.com/1993/11/28/us/in-detroit-s-despair-mayor-sees-hope.html; David Ashenfelter and Joe Swickard, "Detroit Cops Are Deadliest in U.S.," Police Policy Studies Council, May 15, 2000, http://www.theppsc.org/Archives/DF_Articles/Files /Michigan/Detroit/FreePress052000.htm.

84  Spence, *Knocking the Hustle*, 87–88; Balko, *Overkill*, 209–10; "War Comes Home: The Excessive Militarization of American Policing," ACLU, June 2014, 16, https://www .aclu.org/report/war-comes-home-excessive-militarization-american-police.

85  The *Detroit Metro Times* reported in 1999: "'Quite frankly, we get calls that home-less people are frightening folks and that we should move them out, but I tell them I can't arrest them because they are homeless,' said [Police Chief Benny] Napoleon. 'Until the law department says we have the authority to arrest people for panhandling, it does not rise to a level of criminality,' he added. About six weeks ago a police officer had a heavy equipment operator clear a field near Martin Luther King Boulevard and Third Avenue of bags and other items belonging to homeless people who were staying there, according to the heads of several emergency shelters. The possessions were dumped in a truck and not returned, according to emergency service providers." "Harassing the Homeless," *Detroit Metro Times*, November 24, 1999, http://www.metrotimes.com/detroit/harassing-the-homeless/Content?oid =2190657.

86  Thompson, "Unmaking the Motor City in the Age of Mass Incarceration"; Thompson, "The War on Crime, Not Crime Itself, Fueled Detroit's Post-1967 Decline."

87  Jack Lessenberry, "Michigan Has More Than 40,000 Prisoners: She Oversees Them,"
    Michigan Radio, July 21, 2017, https://www.michiganradio.org/post/michigan-has
    -more-40000-prisoners-she-oversees-them.

88  McNally, *Global Slump*, 36; "The Prison Index: Taking the Pulse of the Crime
    Control Industry," Prison Policy Initiative, April 2013, https://www.prisonpolicy.org
    /prisonindex/toc.html.

89  Thompson, "Unmaking the Motor City in the Age of Mass Incarceration." These
    conditions have continued to this day, prompting a massive prison strike in
    2016 on the anniversary of George Jackson's murder. See "Specters of Attica,"
    Rustbelt Abolition Radio, April 25, 2018, https://rustbeltradio.org/2018/04/25
    /makingcontact/.

90  Lily Workneh, "How Black Life In New Orleans Has—And Hasn't—Improved Since
    Katrina," *Huffington Post*, August 27, 2015, http://www.huffingtonpost.com/entry/the
    -state-of-black-new-orleans-is-overwhelmingly-worse-than-it-was-pre-katrina_us
    _55dd57a7e4b04ae49705064c; Camp, *Incarcerating the Crisis*, 116–17.

91  Gallagher, "How Detroit Went Broke";

92  The most definitive and accessible work about the 9/11 conspiracy is Massimo
    Mazzucco's documentary, *September 11—The New Pearl Harbor*. Other serious researchers
    are David Ray Griffin, Christopher Lee Bollyn, and Joseph P. Farrell. It is surprising
    to us how many Marxist theorists have ignored the mountain of evidence suggesting
    a 9/11 inside-job/cover-up, preferring instead to stigmatize the truth community as
    "conspiracy theorists." While many conspiracy theorists are haphazard and sloppy
    thinkers, this should not cause us to make the dire mistake of *a priori* dismissing all
    conspiracies.

93  Howell and Shryock, "Cracking Down on Diaspora," 73–74.

94  Quoted in Johnson, *Revolutionaries to Race Leaders*, 223.

95  Johnson, *Revolutionaries to Race Leaders*, 278n7.

96  Ta-Nehisi Coates, "'This Is How We Lost to the White Man': The Audacity of Bill
    Cosby's Black Conservatism," *The Atlantic*, May 2008.

97  Coates, "'This Is How We Lost to the White Man.'"

98  Quoted in Johnson, *Revolutionaries to Race Leaders*, 279.

99  Quoted in Johnson, *Revolutionaries to Race Leaders*, 279.

100 Gallagher, "How Detroit Went Broke."

101 Gallagher, "How Detroit Went Broke"; McNally, *Global Slump*, 126; Darrell Preston
    and Chris Christoff, "Only Wall Street Wins in Detroit Crisis Reaping $474 Million
    Fee," *Bloomberg*, March 13 2013, https://www.bloomberg.com/news/articles/2013
    -03-14/only-wall-street-wins-in-detroit-crisis-reaping-474-million-fee.

102 Preston and Christoff, "Only Wall Street Wins in Detroit Crisis Reaping $474 Mil-
    lion Fee"; Zac Corrigan, "Hedge Funds Eye Detroit for 'Hostile Takeover,'" WSWS,
    May 20, 2013, https://www.wsws.org/en/articles/2013/05/21/hedg-m20. html.

103 Mike Wilkinson, "Tracking Progress in Detroit Police Response Times a Fool's
    Errand," *Bridge*, November 10, 2015, https://www.bridgemi.com/detroit-journalism
    -cooperative/tracking-progress-detroit-police-response-times-fools-errand; George
    Hunter, "Fewest Cops Are Patrolling Detroit Streets Since 1920s," *Detroit News*,

July 9, 2015, http://www.detroitnews.com/story/news/local/detroit-city/2015/07/08 /detroit-cops/29896105/.

104 Dianne Bukowski, "Genocidal Snyder/Rhodes Plan Harms Detroit Public School Children, Workers, Residents," *Voice of Detroit*, May 6, 2016, http://voiceofdetroit .net/2016/05/06/genocidal-snyderrhodes-plan-harms-detroit-public-school-children -workers-residents/.

105 Gallagher, "How Detroit Went Broke"; Brad Plumer, "We saved the automakers. How come that didn't save Detroit," *Washington Post*, July 19, 2013, https://www .washingtonpost.com/news/wonk/wp/2013/07/19/we-saved-the-automakers -how-come-that-didnt-save-detroit/?noredirect=on&utm_term=.c3bfd417a27c; "Detroit's Unemployment Rate Is Nearly 50%, According to the *Detroit News*," Huffington Post, May 25, 2011, http://www.huffingtonpost.com/2009/12/16/detroits -unemployment-rat_n_394559.html; Heidi Shierholz and Elise Gould, "Already More Than a Lost Decade," Economic Policy Institute, September 12, 2012, http:// www.epi.org/publication/lost-decade-poverty-income-trends-continue-2/; McNally, *Global Slump*, 23; Taylor, *From #BlackLivesMatter to Black Liberation*, 211.

106 Kevyn Orr, "Re: Recommendation Pursuant to Section 18(1) of PA 436," City of Detroit, Emergency Manager's Office, July 16, 2013, https://www.michigan.gov /documents/snyder/Detroit_EM_Kevyn_Orr_Chapter_9_Recommendation _427831_7.pdf.

107 Marx, *The 18th Brumaire of Louis Bonaparte*, 15.


CONCLUSION: COMPETING VISIONS FOR DETROIT'S NEW ERA

1 Neocleous, *War Power, Police Power*, 198. Crucially, Neocleous emphasizes this "train-ing" aspect, for however resilient you are, the future attack could always be worse than anything you have imagined. And so the work of resilience training is never over.

2 Schumaker, "The Demoralized Mind"; Hanson, Austin, and Lee-Bayha, "Ensuring That No Child Is Left Behind," 3.

3 Neocleous, *War Power, Police Power*, 201.

4 Neocleous, *War Power, Police Power*, 203–4. Resilience is widely mobilized in aca-demic and public policy discourse on urban poverty and the educational perfor-mance of minority poor children. In this context, resilience has become a sort of positive version of the "underclass" trope. Instead of blaming the urban poor for their supposed cultural deficiencies, those traits that are presumed to have caused the success of certain individuals in the neoliberal economy are singled out and promoted as the key to success for the group as a whole. We can see the connection of this logic to that of underclass discourse by looking at the obverse: if the success of one individual is the result of her own initiative and inborn traits, then the failure of the rest of the group is likewise the result of inborn traits and personal failings. Singling out those individuals whose resilience allowed them to escape poverty directs attention away from a politics that would attempt to eliminate the structural causes of poverty, while also legitimating the poverty of large segments

of the population by blaming the poor themselves for their condition. One could also connect this to Adolph Reed Jr.'s critique of the prevalence of "self-help" politics in black urban communities. This version of underclass ideology forecloses traditional political avenues for redressing social problems by arguing that initiatives within poor communities themselves are superior to official political responses. "It is," Reed points out, "only with respect to social policy affecting poor minority citizens that such expectations seem reasonable" (Reed, *Stirrings in the Jug*, 127). The ideology of self-help fits easily with that of resilience in legitimating the condition of the urban poor: it separates this population from the rest of the polity, justifying this separation by arguing that their poverty is best addressed through their own initiative. Our thanks to an anonymous reviewer for pointing out this aspect of resilience.

5  "Coleman A. Young, 79, Mayor of Detroit and Political Symbol for Blacks, Is Dead," *New York Times*, December 1, 1997, http://www.nytimes.com/1997/12/01/us/coleman -a-young-79-mayor-of-detroit-and-political-symbol-for-blacks-is-dead.html; "Move Here. Move the World," n.d., www.detroitmovestheworld.com; Tracy Hoover, "Detroit: A Resilient Community We All Got to See," *Huffington Post*, August 9, 2016, https://www.huffingtonpost.com/tracy-hoover/detroit—a-resilient-com_b_11392476 .html; Melena Ryzik, "For Detroit Artists, Almost Anything Goes," New York Times, July 15, 2015, https://www.nytimes.com/2015/07/16/arts/design/for-detroit -artists-almost-anything-goes.html?_r=0; Frank Bruni, "The Spirit and Promise of Detroit," *New York Times*, Septeber 9, 2015, https://www.nytimes.com/2015/09/09 /opinion/frank-bruni-the-spirit-and-promise-of-detroit.html; Chisako Fukuda, "Detroit's Future City Framework Offers Lessons on Resilience," World Bank, March 22, 2014, http://blogs.worldbank.org/sustainablecities/detroit-s-future-city -framework-offers-lessons-resilience; Noah Enelow, "Beyond Bankruptcy: The Resilience of Detroit," Ecotrust, August 19, 2013, https://ecotrust.org/beyond-bankruptcy -the-resilience-of-detroit/; Maurice Cox, "Putting Design to Work: How Design Is Building a Resilient Detroit," July 10, 2017, https://melkinginstitute.org/events /putting-design-work-how-design-building-resilient-detroit; "In Detroit's Rivera and Kahlo Exhibit, a Portrait of a Resilient City," NPR, March 16, 2015, https://www .npr.org/2015/03/16/393393697/in-detroits-rivera-and-kahlo-exhibit-a-portrait-of-a -resilient-city.

6  Reif Larsen, "Detroit: The Most Exciting City in America?," *New York Times*, November 20, 2017, https://www.nytimes.com/2017/11/20/travel/detroit-michigan -downtown.html?_r=0.

7  Bruni, "The Spirit and Promise of Detroit."

8  "U.N. Climate Panel: Only 12 Years Left to Mitigate Climate Catastrophe," Democracy Now!, October 8, 2018, https://www.democracynow.org/2018/10 /8/headlines/un_climate_panel_only_12_years_left_to_mitigate_climate _catastrophe; Sinéad Baker, "Trump Suggests the Climate May Actually Be 'Fabulous' after an Ominous UN Report on Looming Disaster," *Business Insider*, October 10, 2018, https://www.businessinsider.com/trump-doubt-un-climate -change-report-2018–10.

9   Bellamy Foster and McChesney, *The Endless Crisis*, 145.

10  Vijay Prashad, "There Is No Refugee Crisis: There Is Only a Crisis of Humanity," *Monthly Review Online*, September 15, 2018, https://mronline.org/2018/09/15/there-is -no-refugee-crisis-there-is-only-a-crisis-of-humanity/.

11  Bellamy Foster, "This Is Not Populism"; "Brazil: Far-Right Bolsonaro Wins First Round of Presidential Election," Democracy Now!, October 8, 2018, https://www .democracynow.org/2018/10/8/headlines/brazil_far_right_bolsonaro_wins_first _round_of_presidential_election; "How Far-Right Parties Are Faring across Europe," *The Local*, October 14, 2017, https://www.thelocal.fr/20171014/how-far-right -parties-are-faring-across-europe; "Facts and Statistics," Anxiety and Depression Association of America, n.d., https://adaa.org/about-adaa/press-room/facts-statistics; Amy P. Cohen, Deborah Azrael, and Mathew Miller, "Rate of Mass Shootings Has Tripled Since 2011, Harvard Research Shows," *Mother Jones*, October 25, 2014, http://www.motherjones.com/politics/2014/10/mass-shootings-increasing-harvard -research; Sabrina Tavernise, "U.S. Suicide Rate Surges to a 30-Year High," *New York Times*, April 22, 2016, www.nytimes.com/2016/04/22/health/us-suicide-rate-surges -to-a-30-year-high.html?hp&action=click&pgtype=Homepage&clickSource=story -heading&module=first-column-region&region=top-news&WT.nav=top-news&_r =0; Schumaker, "The Demoralized Mind"; Tricontinental Research Institute, "In the Ruins of the Present," *Monthly Review*, March 26, 2018, https://mronline.org/2018 /03/26/in-the-ruins-of-the-present/.

12  Fromm, *Beyond the Chains of Illusion*, 123–24, emphasis added.

13  Tricontinental Research Institute, "In the Ruins of the Present."

14  Fromm, *Beyond the Chains of Illusion*, 81–82.

15  Ward, *In Love and Struggle*, 326.

16  Ward, *In Love and Struggle*, 331.

17  Boggs and Kurashige, *The Next American Revolution*, 89.

18  Kurashige, *The Fifty-Year Rebellion*, 115.

19  Boggs and Kurashige, *The Next American Revolution*, 89, 148–49; "'The Answers Are Coming from the Bottom': Legendary Detroit Activist Grace Lee Boggs on the US Social Forum and Her 95th Birthday," Democracy Now!, June 22, 2010, https://www .democracynow.org/2010/6/22/legendary_detroit_activist_grace_lee_boggs.

20  Boggs and Kurashige, *The Next American Revolution*, xxii.

21  Kurashige, *The Fifty-Year Rebellion*, 123–25; Michael Jackman, "How Boggs School Principal Julia Putnam Is Rethinking Education," *Detroit Metro Times*, July 25, 2018, https://www.metrotimes.com/detroit/how-boggs-school-principal-julia-putnam-is -rethinking-education/Content?oid=14096362.

22  Kurashige, *The Fifty-Year Rebellion*, 123–25.

23  Kurashige, *The Fifty-Year Rebellion*, 126–31.

24  Chad Livengood, "Detroit strikes land deal with Hantz Farms as part of FCA plant project," *Crain's Detroit Business*, April 15, 2019, https://www.crainsdetroit.com/real -estate/detroit-strikes-land-deal-hantz-farms-part-fca-plant-project.

25  "Teach-In on City Lab: Real Detroiters Speak Out," Moratorium Now!, October 19, 2018, https://moratorium-mi.org/. The political ambitions of this book consciously

mirror the authors of *Policing the Crisis*: "We cannot presume to offer quick solutions to these problems of strategy and struggle. We have deliberately refrained from entering directly into this question, because it is a matter which we believe must be resolved in struggle, rather than on paper. We hope, nevertheless, that our argument has served to highlight certain aspects and to clarify the terrain on which answers can be sought" (Hall et al., *Policing the Crisis*, 393–94).

# Bibliography

Adams, Larry T. "Changing Employment Patterns of Organized Workers." *Monthly Labor Review*, February 1985. http://www.bls.gov/opub/mlr/1985/02/art3full.pdf.

Ahmad, Muhammad. "The League of Revolutionary Black Workers." *History Is a Weapon*. http://www.historyisaweapon.com/defcon1/rbwstudy.html.

Alexander, Michelle. *The New Jim Crow*. New York: New Press, 2010.

Alkalimat, Abdul. *Introduction to Afro-American Studies*. Urbana: University of Illinois Press, 1984.

Amin, Samir. *Unequal Development*. New York: Monthly Review Press, 1976.

Appiah, Kwame Anthony, and Henry Louis Gates Jr. *Africana: The Encyclopedia of the African and African American Experience*. Oxford: Oxford University Press, 2005.

Arrighi, Giovanni. *Adam Smith in Beijing: Lineages of the Twenty-First Century*. New York: Verso, 2007.

Austen, Ben. "The Post-Post-Apocalyptic Detroit," *New York Times*, July 11, 2014, https://www.nytimes.com/2014/07/13/magazine/the-post-post-apocalyptic-detroit.html.

Azikiwe, Aboyomi. "General Gordon Baker, Jr.: Pioneer in African American Working Class Resistance." *Pambazuka News*, June 19, 2014, http://www.pambazuka.org/resources/general-gordon-baker-jr-pioneer-african-american-working-class-resistance.

Azikiwe, Abayomi. "Lessons from the Detroit July 1967 Rebellion and Prospects for Social Transformation: Part 1 and 2." *21st Century*, July 28, 2017. https://www.21cir.com/2017/07/lessons-from-the-detroit-july-1967-rebellion-and-prospects-for-social-transformation-part-i-ii/.

Babson, Steve, with Ron Alpern, Dave Elsila, and John Revitte. *Working Detroit: The Making of a Union Town*. New York: Adama Books, 1984.

Baker, General Gordon. "General Baker Speaks!" Talk delivered at the 2010 United States Social Forum, 2010, https://www.youtube.com/watch?v=wCkMz70QP8Q.

Balbus, Isaac D. *The Dialectics of Legal Repression*. New York: Russell Sage Foundation, 1973.

Balko, Radley. *Overkill: The Rise of Paramilitary Police Raids in America*. Washington, DC: Cato Institute, 2006.

Baran, Paul, and Paul Sweezy. *Monopoly Capital*. New York: Monthly Review Press, 1966.

Barthes, Roland. *Mythologies*. Translated by Annette Lavers. New York: Noonday Press, 1991.

Bartlett, Jackson Christopher. "Rights, Respectability, Responsibility: Black Middle-Class Frameworks for Understanding Neighborhood Decline." *Race and Society* 5 (fall 2017).

Baskin, Alex. "The Ford Hunger March 1932." *Labor History* 13 (1972): 331–60.

Baudrillard, Jean. *Simulacra and Simulation*. Ann Arbor: University of Michigan Press, 1992.

Beckett, Katherine, and Steve Herbert. *Banished: The New Social Control in Urban America*. Oxford: Oxford University Press, 2010.

Bellamy Foster, John. "This Is Not Populism." *Monthly Review* 69, no. 2 (2017): 1–24. https://monthlyreview.org/2017/06/01/this-is-not-populism/.

Bellamy Foster, John, and Robert W. McChesney, *The Endless Crisis: How Monopoly-Finance Capital Produces Stagnation and Upheaval from the USA to China*. New York: Monthly Review Press, 2012.

Bellamy Foster, Jonathan, and Robert W. McChesney. "Surveillance Capitalism: Monopoly-Finance Capital, the Military-Industrial Complex, and the Digital Age." *Monthly Review* 66, no. 3 (2014). http://monthlyreview.org/2014/07/01/surveillance -capitalism/.

Benjamin, Walter. *The Arcades Project*. Translated by Howard Eiland and Kevin McLaughlin. Cambridge, MA: Belknap Press, 1999.

Berger, Dan. *Captive Nation: Black Prison Organizing in the Civil Rights Era*. Chapel Hill: University of North Carolina Press, 2014.

Berger, Dan. "Social Movements and Mass Incarceration: What Is to Be Done?" *Souls* 15, nos. 1–2 (2015).

Berman, Marshall. *All That Is Solid Melts into Air*. New York: Penguin, 1988.

Blauner, Robert. "Internal Colonialism and Ghetto Revolt," *Social Problems* 16, no. 4 (1969): 393–408.

Bloom, Joshua, and Waldo E. Martin Jr. *Black against Empire: The History and Politics of the Black Panther Party*. Berkeley: University of California Press, 2012.

Boggs, Grace Lee. *Living for Change: An Autobiography*. Minneapolis: University of Minnesota Press, 1998.

Boggs, Grace Lee, with Scott Kurashige. *The Next American Revolution: Sustainable Activism for the Twenty-First Century*. Berkeley: University of California Press, 2012.

Boggs, James. *The American Revolution: Pages from a Negro Worker's Notebook*. New York: Monthly Review Press, 1963.

Boggs, James. "Rebuilding Detroit: An Alternative to Casino Gambling." June 24, 1988. {R}evolution: James and Grace Lee Boggs Center to Nurture Community Leadership, August 29, 2015, http://boggscenter.org/rebuilding-detroit-an-alternative-to-casino -gambling-by-james-boggs/.

Bomey, Nathan. *Detroit Resurrected: To Bankruptcy and Back*. New York: W. W. Norton, 2016.

Boyd, Herb. *Black Detroit: A People's History of Self-Determination*. New York: HarperCollins, 2017.

Boyd, Herb. "Blacks and the Police State: A Case Study of Detroit." *Black Scholar* 12, no. 1 (January/February1981): 58–61.

Bracey, John, Jr., August Meier, and Elliott Rudwick, eds. *Black Workers and Organized Labor*. Belmont, CA: Wadsworth, 1971.

Braverman, Harry. *Labor and Monopoly Capital*. New York: Monthly Review Press, 1998.

Brecher, Jeremy. "The World War II and Post-war Strike Wave." *Libcom*, December 17, 2009. https://libcom.org/history/world-war-ii-post-war-strike-wave.

"Brown v. Ferguson." *Endnotes* 4 (October 2015). https://endnotes.org.uk/issues/4/en/endnotes-brown-v-ferguson.

Camp, Jordan. *Incarcerating the Crisis*. Berkeley: University of California Press, 2016.

Camp, Jordan T., and Christina Heatherton, eds. *Policing the Planet*. London: Verso, 2016.

Chang, *Disposable Domestics: Immigrant Women Workers in the Global Economy*. Boston: South End Press, 2000.

Clark, Daniel. *Disruption in Detroit*. Champaign: University of Illinois Press, 2018.

Cleage, Albert B., Jr. *The Black Messiah*. New York: Sheed and Ward, 1968.

Cleage, Albert. "Myths about Malcolm X: A Speech." *International Socialist Review* 28 (1967). https://www.marxists.org/history/etol/newspape/isr/vol28/n005/cleage.htm.

Cleaver, Eldridge. *Soul on Ice*. New York: Delta Books, 1968.

Clegg, John, and Adaner Usmani. "The Racial Politics of Mass Incarceration." *SSRN*, February 15, 2017. https://papers.ssrn.com/sol3/papers.cfm?abstract_id=3025670.

Clement, Daniel. "The Spatial Injustice of Crisis-Driven Neoliberal Urban Restructuring in Detroit." Paper 406. *Open Access Theses*, 2013. http://scholarlyrepository.miami.edu/cgi/viewcontent.cgi?article=1415&context=oa_theses.

Cluster, Dick, ed. *They Should Have Served That Cup of Coffee: Seven Radicals Remember the '60s*. Boston: South End Press, 1979.

Conot, Robert. *American Odyssey*. New York: Bantam Books, 1973.

Coopey, Richard, and Alan McKinlay. "Power without Knowledge? Foucault and Fordism, c. 1900–1950." *Labor History* 51, no. 1 (2010): 107–25.

Cowie, Jefferson, and Nick Salvatore. "The Long Exception: Rethinking the Place of the New Deal in American History." *International Labor and Working-Class History*, no. 74 (2008).

Cutcher-Gershenfeld, Joel, et al. "The Decline and Resurgence of the U.S. Auto Industry." Economic Policy Institute, May 6, 2015. http://www.epi.org/publication/the-decline-and-resurgence-of-the-u-s-auto-industry/.

Darden, Joe T., and Richard W. Thomas. *Detroit: Race Riots, Racial Conflicts and Efforts to Bridge the Racial Divide*. East Lansing: Michigan State University Press, 2013.

Dauenbaugh, Rachel S. "Coleman Young's Detroit: A Vision for a City 1974–1994." *Student Research* 9 (2014).

Da Via, Carrie. "A Brief History of Detroit's Black Bottom Neighborhood." Rogue Haa, May 18, 2012. http://www.roguehaa.com/a-brief-history-of-detroits-black-bottom-neighborhood/.

Debord, Guy. *Society of the Spectacle*. Translated by Donald Nicholson-Smith. New York: Zone, 1994.

Denby, Charles [Simon Owens]. *Indignant Heart: A Black Worker's Journal*. Detroit: Wayne State University Press, 1979.

Denby, Charles [Simon Owens]. *Workers Battle Automation*. Detroit: News and Letters, 1960.

Diamond, Andrew J. *Chicago on the Make: Power and Inequality in a Modern City*. Berkeley: University of California Press, 2017.

Dunn, Timothy. *The Militarization of the US-Mexico Border 1978–1992*. Austin, TX: CMAS Books, 1996.

Dyer, Patrick. "Rebellion in Detroit." *Socialist Worker* (2007). https://socialistworker.org /2007-2/639/639_10_Detroit.php.

Dyer-Witheford, Nick. *Cyber-proletariat: Global Labour in the Digital Vortex*. Toronto: Pluto Press, 2015.

Eisinger, Peter. *The Politics of Displacement*. New York: Academic Press, 1980.

Engels, Friedrich. *The Housing Question*. New York: Pathfinder Press, 1935.

Esch, Elizabeth D. *The Color Line and the Assembly Line: Managing Race in the Ford Empire*. Berkeley: University of California Press, 2018.

Fanon, Frantz. *Black Skin, White Masks*. New York: Grove Press, 2008.

Fanon, Frantz. *The Wretched of the Earth*. Translated by Constance Farrington. New York: Grove Weidenfeld, 1963.

Farley, Reynolds, et al. *Detroit Divided*. New York: Russell Sage, 2000.

Federici, Silvia. *Caliban and the Witch: Women, the Body, and Primitive Accumulation*. New York: Autonomedia, 2004.

Feeley, Diane. "Black Workers, Fordism, and the UAW." *Solidarity*, January– February 2014. https://solidarity-us.org/atc/168/p4071/.

Felton, Ryan. "Not just Detroit: Residents of Nearby Michigan city Face $11,000 Water Bills." *Guardian*, July 6, 2015. https://www.theguardian.com/us-news/2015/jul/06 /detroit-water-bills-michigan-highland-park.

Ferguson, Karen. *Top Down: The Ford Foundation, Black Power, and the Reinvention of Racial Liberalism*. Philadelphia: University of Pennsylvania Press, 2013.

*Finally Got the News*. Directed by Stewart Bird, Rene Lichtman, and Peter Gessner. Produced in association with the League of Revolutionary Black Workers. Detroit: Black Star Productions, 1970.

Fine, Sidney. *Expanding the Frontier of Civil Rights: Michigan, 1948–1968*. Detroit: Wayne State University Press, 2000.

Fine, Sidney. *Sit-Down: The General Motors Strike of 1936–1937*. Ann Arbor: University of Michigan Press, 1960.

Fine, Sidney. *Violence in the Model City: The Cavanagh Administration, Race Relations, and the Detroit Riot of 1967*. Ann Arbor: University of Michigan Press, 1989.

Folsom, Franklin. *Impatient Armies of the Poor: The Story of Collective Action of the Unemployed, 1808–1942*. Niwot: University Press of Colorado, 1991.

Foner, Philip, and James Allen. *American Communism and Black Americans: A Documentary History, 1919–1929*. Philadelphia: Temple University Press, 1977.

Forman, James, Jr. *Locking Up Our Own*. New York: Farrar, Straus and Giroux.

Forman, James, Jr. "Racial Critiques of Mass Incarceration: Beyond the New Jim Crow." *New York University Law Review* 87 (2012): 101–46.

Foucault, Michel. *Discipline and Punish*. Translated by Alan Sheridan. New York: Vintage Books, 1995.

Fromm, Erich. *Beyond the Chains of Illusion: My Encounter with Marx and Freud*. New York: Simon and Schuster, 1962.

Georgakas, Dan. "Finally Got the News: The Making of a Radical Film." *Cineast* 5 (1973). https://fadingtheacsthetic.files.wordpress.com/2013/08/finally-got-the-news.pdf.

Georgakas, Dan, and Marvin Surkin. *Detroit: I Do Mind Dying*. Cambridge, MA: South End Press, 1998.

Geschwender, James A. "The League of Revolutionary Black Workers." *Journal of Ethnic Studies* 2, no. 3 (1974).

Gibson, Campbell, and Kay Jung. *Historical Census Statistics on Population Totals by Race, 1790 to 1990, and by Hispanic Origin, 1970 to 1990, for the United States, Regions, Divisions, and States*. Working Paper 56. Washington, DC: U.S. Census Bureau, Population Division, September 2002. https://census.gov/content/dam/Census/library/working -papers/2002/demo/POP-twps0056.pdf.

Gilmore, Ruth Wilson. "Prisons and Class Warfare: Interview with Ruth Wilson Gilmore." *Historical Materialism*, 2018. http://www.historicalmaterialism.org/interviews /prisons-and-class-warfare.

Glaberman, Martin. *Wartime Strikes: The Struggle against the No-Strike Pledge in the UAW during World War II*. Detroit: Bewick Editions, 1980.

Goldberg, David. "From Landless to Landlords: Black Power, Black Capitalism, and the Co-optation of Detroit's Tenants' Rights Movement, 1964–1969." In *The Business of Black Power: Community Development, Capitalism and Corporate Responsibility in Postwar America*, ed. Laura Warren Hill and Julia Rabig. Rochester, NY: University of Rochester Press, 2012.

Gonzalez, Nacho. "Two Reflections on Nelson Peery's Life." *League of Revolutionary Black Workers: A Media Project with the League of Revolutionary Black Workers*. September 8, 2015. https://www.revolutionaryblackworkers.org/reflections-on-nelson-peerys-life/.

Grandin, Greg. *Fordlandia: The Rise and Fall of Henry Ford's Forgotten Jungle City*. New York: Metropolitan Books, 2009.

Grover, John, and Yvette van der Velde. *A School District in Crisis*. Detroit: Loveland Technologies, 2016.

Hackworth, Jason. "Defiant Neoliberalism and the Danger of Detroit," *Tijdschrift voor Economische en Sociale Geografie* 107, no. 5 (2016). https://onlinelibrary.wiley.com/doi/abs /10.1111/tesg.12184.

Hall, Stuart, et al. *Policing the Crisis: Mugging, the State, and Law and Order*. Basingstoke, UK: Palgrave Macmillan, 1978.

Halpern, Martin. "'I'm Fighting for Freedom': Coleman Young, HUAC and the Detroit African American Community." *Journal of American Ethnic History* 17, no. 1 (1997).

Hanson, Thomas L., Gregory Austin, and June Lee-Bayha. "Ensuring That No Child Is Left Behind: How Are Student Health Risks and Resilience Related to the Academic Progress of Schools?" WestEd, 2004. https://data.calschls.org/resources /EnsuringNCLB.pdf.

Hardt, Michael, and Antonio Negri. *Commonwealth*. Cambridge, MA: Harvard University Press, 2011.

Harman, Chris. *Zombie Capitalism: Global Crisis and the Relevance of Marx*. Chicago: Haymarket Books, 2009.

Harvey, David. *A Brief History of Neoliberalism*. Oxford: Oxford University Press, 2007.

Harvey, David. *The Condition of Postmodernity*. Oxford: Blackwell, 1990.

Harvey, David. *The Enigma of Capital and the Crises of Capitalism*. Oxford: Oxford University Press, 2010.

Harvey, David. "The Enigma of Capital and the Crisis This Time," DavidHarvey.org, August 30, 2010. http://davidharvey.org/2010/08/the-enigma-of-capital-and-the-crisis-this-time/.

Harvey, David. "From Managerialism to Entrepreneurialism: The Transformation in Urban Governance in Late Capitalism." *Geografiska Annaler: Series B, Human Geography* 71, no. 1 (1989).

Harvey, David. *The New Imperialism*. Oxford: Oxford University Press, 2003.

Harvey, David. *Rebel Cities: From the Right to the City to the Urban Revolution*. London: Verso, 2013.

Harvey, David. "The Right to the City." *New Left Review*, no. 53 (2008).

Harvey, David. *Social Justice and the City*. Athens: University of Georgia Press, 2009.

Heidegger, Martin. "Memorial Address." In *Discourse on Thinking*, translated by John M. Anderson and E. Hans Freund. New York. Harper and Row, 1966.

Henrickson, Wilma, editor. *Detroit Perspectives: Crossroads and Turning Points*. Detroit: Wayne State University Press, 1991.

Hershey, John. *The Algiers Motel Incident*. Baltimore: Johns Hopkins University Press, 1997.

Hollerman, Hannah, et al. "The Penal State in an Age of Crisis." *Monthly Review* 61, no. 2 (June 2009).

Howe, Irving, and B. J. Widick. "The UAW Fights Race Prejudice." *Commentary* 8, no. 3 (1949).

Howell, Sally, and Andrew Shryock. "Cracking Down on Diaspora: Arab Detroit and America's 'War on Terror.'" In *Arab Detroit 9/11*, ed. Nabeel Abraham, Sally Howell, and Andrew Shryock. Detroit: Wayne State University Press, 2011.

Howell, Shea. "Asking Questions," *The Boggs Blog*, October 27, 2013.

Ikeda, Satoshi. "World Production." In *The Age of Transition: Trajectory of the World-System 1945–2025*, ed. Terence Hopkins and Immanuel Wallerstein. London: Zed Books, 1998.

Jackson, George. *Soledad Brother: The Prison Letters of George Jackson*. Chicago: Lawrence Hill Books, 1994.

Jay, Mark. "Cages and Crises." *Historical Materialism* 29, no. 1 (2019): 182–223.

Jay, Mark. "Policing the Poor in Detroit." *Monthly Review* 68, no. 8 (January 2017).

Jay, Mark, and Virginia Leavell. "The Material Conditions of the Great Rebellion." *Social Justice* 4 (fall 2018): 27–54.

Johnson, Cedric. "Coming to Terms with Actually-Existing Black Life." *New Politics*, April 9, 2019. https://newpol.org/coming-to-terms-with-actually-existing-black-life/.

Johnson, Cedric. "The Panthers Can't Save Us Now." *Catalyst* 1, no. 1 (2017).

Johnson, Cedric. *Revolutionaries to Race Leaders: Black Power and the Making of African American Politics*. Minneapolis: University of Minnesota Press, 2007.

Jones, Claudia. "An End to the Neglect of the Problems of the Negro Woman!" *Political Affairs*, June 1949, 3–19.

Justice Policy Institute. "Rethinking the Blues: How We Police in the U.S. and at What Cost." May 2012. http://www.justicepolicy.org/uploads/justicepolicy/documents /rethinkingtheblues_final.pdf.

Katz-Fishman, Walda, and Jerome Scott. "The League of Revolutionary Black Workers and Race, Class, and Revolution in the Twenty-First Century." In *The Oxford Handbook of Karl Marx*, ed. Matt Vidal et al. November 2018. http://www.oxfordhandbooks.com /view/10.1093/oxfordhb/9780190695545.001.0001/oxfordhb-9780190695545-e-21.

Kelley, Robin D. G. *Freedom Dreams*. Boston: Beacon Press, 2002.

Kelley, Robin D. G. *Hammer and Hoe: Alabama Communists During the Great Depression*. Chapel Hill: University of North Carolina Press, 1990.

Kelley, Robin D. G. "Thug Nation: On State Violence and Disposability." In *Policing the Planet: Why the Policing Crisis Led to Black Lives Matter*, edited by Jordan Camp and Christina Heatherton. New York: Verso, 2016.

Kenyon, Amy. "Detroit's Road to Ruin: How the Suburbs Accelerated Detroit's Downfall," *Financial Times*, December 11, 2013. https://www.ft.com/content/c9add7c4-48aa-11e3-8237-00144feabdc0.

Kleffner, Heike. "The Black Panthers: Interviews with Geronimo ji-jaga Pratt and Mumia Abu-Jamal," *Race and Class* 35, no. 1 (1993): 3–26.

Kramer, Marian. "Marian Kramer." *League of Revolutionary Black Workers: A Media Project with the League of Revolutionary Black Workers*. n.d. https://www .revolutionaryblackworkers.org/video/.

Kramer, Marian. "Remarks on the National Welfare Rights Union." *Social Justice* 21, no. 1 (1994): 9–11.

Kurashige, Scott. *The Fifty-Year Rebellion: How the U.S. Political Crisis Began in Detroit*. Berkeley: University of California Press, 2017.

LeDuff, Charlie. *Detroit: An American Autopsy*. New York: Penguin, 2013.

Lees, Loretta, Hyun Bang Shin, and Ernesto Lopez-Morales. *Planetary Gentrification*. Cambridge: Polity Press, 2016.

Lenin, V. I. "A 'Scientific' System of Sweating." *Pravda*, March 13, 1913. https://www .marxists.org/archive/lenin/works/1913/mar/13.htm.

Lewis, Nathaniel. "Mass Incarceration: New Jim Crow, Class War, or Both?" *People's Policy Project*, January 30, 2018.

Lewis-Colman, David M. *Race against Liberalism: Black Workers and the UAW in Detroit*. Champagne: University of Illinois Press, 2008.

Lichtenstein, Nelson. *The Most Dangerous Man in Detroit: Walter Reuther and the Fate of American Labor*. New York: Basic Books, 1995.

Lichtenstein, Nelson. *State of the Union: A Century of American Labor*. Princeton, NJ: Princeton University Press, 2002.

Lichtenstein, Nelson. "UAW Bargaining Strategy and Shop-Floor Conflict: 1946–1970." *Industrial Relations* 24 (1985).

Lincoln, Bruce. *Theorizing Myth*. Chicago: University of Chicago Press, 1999.

Linebaugh, Peter. *The London Hanged*. London: Verso, 2003.

Linkner, Josh. "Wish You Bought Gold in '06? You'll Wish You Bought Detroit in '12." *Forbes*, August 30, 2012. https://www.forbes.com/sites/joshlinkner/2012/08/30/wish -you-bought-gold-in-06-youll-wish-you-bought-detroit-in-12/#4ca88b1346fd.

Locke, Hubert. *The Detroit Riot of 1967*. Detroit: Wayne State University Press, 1969.

Lorence, James. *Organizing the Unemployed: Community and Union Activists in the Industrial Heartland*. Albany: State University of New York Press, 1996.

Luby, Elliot D., and James Hedegard. "A Study of Civil Disorder in Detroit." *William and Mary Law Review* 10, no. 3 (1969). http://scholarship.law.wm.edu/cgi/viewcontent.cgi ?article=2892&context=wmlr.

Lucia, Danny. "The Unemployed Movements of the 1930s." *International Socialist Review* 71 (2010). http://isreview.org/issue/71/unemployed-movements-1930s.

Magdoff, Harry, and Paul M. Sweezy. *The Deepening Crisis of U.S. Capitalism*. New York: Monthly Review Press, 1981.

Major, Reginald. *A Panther Is a Black Cat*. Baltimore: Black Classic Press, 1971.

Malcolm X. *Malcolm X Speaks*. Edited by George Breitman. New York: Grove Press, 1994.

Mallach, Allan. *The Divided City: Poverty and Prosperity in Urban America*. Washington, DC: Island Press, 2018.

Marable, Manning. *How Capitalism Underdeveloped Black America*. Boston: South End Press, 1983.

Marable, Manning. *Malcolm X: A Life of Reinvention*. New York: Penguin, 2012.

Marable, Manning. *Race, Reform, and Rebellion*. Jackson: University Press of Mississippi, 2007.

Martelle, Scott. *Detroit (A Biography)*. Chicago: Chicago Review Press, 2012.

Marx, Karl. *Capital: A Critique of Political Economy*. Vol. 3. Translated by David Fernbach. London: Penguin, 1993.

Marx, Karl. *Capital: Vol. 1*. Translated by David Fernbach. London: Penguin, 1992.

Marx, Karl. *Economic and Philosophical Manuscripts*. Translated by Martin Milligan. Marxists Internet Archive. https://www.marxists.org/archive/marx/works/1844 /manuscripts/preface.htm

Marx, Karl. *The 18th Brumaire of Louis Bonaparte*. New York: International Publishers, 2008.

Marx, Karl, and Friedrich Engels. *Manifesto of the Communist Party*. Translated by Samuel Moore. Marxists Internet Archive. https://www.marxists.org/archive/marx/works /1848/communist-manifesto/.

Marx, Karl, and Friedrich Engels. *The Marx-Engels Reader*. Edited by Robert C. Tucker. New York: W. W. Norton, 1972.

Mast, Robert H. *Detroit Lives*. Philadelphia: Temple University Press, 1994.

McCloud, Brandi Nicole. "Solidarity Forever: The Story of the Flint Sit-Down Strike and the Communist Party from the Perspective of the Rank and File Auto Workers." Paper 1416. *Electronic Theses and Dissertations*. May 2012. http://dc.etsu.edu/etd/1416.

McCoy, Alfred W. *The Politics of Heroin: CIA Complicity in the Global Drug Trade*. Chicago: Lawrence Hill Books, 2003.

McNally, David. *Global Slump*. Oakland, CA: PM Press, 2011.

Meyer, Stephen, III. *The Five Dollar Day: Labor Management and Social Control in the Ford Motor Company 1908–1921*. Albany: State University of New York Press, 1981.

Michaels, Leonard. *Time Out of Mind: The Diaries of Leonard Michaels*. New York: River-head Books, 1999.

Mollenkopf, John H. *The Contested City*. Princeton, NJ: Princeton University Press, 1983.

Montgomery, David. *The Fall of the House of Labor: The Workplace, the State, and American Labor Activism, 1865–1925*. Cambridge: Cambridge University Press, 1987.

Murakawa, Naomi. *The First Civil Right*. New York: Oxford University Press, 2014.

Murray, Joshua, and Michael Schwartz. "Collateral Damage: How Capital's War on Labor Killed Detroit." *Catalyst* 1, no. 1 (2017).

Narayan, John. "Survival Pending Revolution: Self-Determination in the Age of Proto-neo-liberal Globalization." Unpublished manuscript, 2018.

Narayan, John. "The Wages of Whiteness in the Absence of Wages: Racial Capitalism, Reactionary Intercommunalism and the Rise of Trumpism." *Third World Quarterly* 38, no. 11 (2017): 2482–500.

Nelson, Daniel. "How the UAW Grew," *Labor History* 35, no. 1: 5-24.

Neocleous, Mark. *Critique of Security*. Edinburgh: Edinburgh University Press, 2008.

Neocleous, Mark. *The Fabrication of Social Order: A Critical Theory of Police Power*. London: Pluto Press, 2000.

Neocleous, Mark. *War Power, Police Power*. Edinburg: Edinburgh University Press, 2014.

Newton, Huey P. *The Huey Newton Reader*. Edited by David Hillard and Donald Weise. New York: Seven Stories Press.

"The 1967 Detroit Rebellion." *Revolutionary Worker*, no. 915 (1997).

Norwood, Stephen. "'Ford's Brass Knuckles: Harry Bennett, the Cult of Muscularity, and Anti-Labor Terror. 1920-1945." *Labor History* 37 (1996).

Peck, Jamie, Nik Theodore, and Neil Brenner. "Neoliberalism Resurgent? Market Rule after the Great Recession." *South Atlantic Quarterly* 111, no. 2 (spring 2012): 265–88.

Perlman, Fredy. *The Reproduction of Daily Life*. Detroit: Black and Red, 2002.

Piketty, Thomas. *Capital in the Twenty-First Century*. Translated by Arthur Goldhammer. Cambridge, MA: Belknap Press, 2014.

Piven, Francis Fox, and Richard Cloward. *Poor People's Movements: Why They Succeed, How They Fail*. New York: Vintage Books, 1979.

Pizarro, Jesenia, and Vanja M. K. Stenius. "Supermax Prisons: Their Rise, Current Practices, and Effect on Inmates." *Prison Journal* 84, no. 2 (2004). https://journals.sagepub.com/doi/10.1177/0032885504265080.

Pizzolato, Nicola. "Transnational Radicals: Dissent and Political Activism in Detroit and Turin (1950–1970)."*ISRH* 56 (2011).

*Poletown Lives!* Directed by George Corsetti. Detroit: Information Factory, 1983.

Poulantzas, Nicos. *State, Power, Socialism*. London: Verso, 2014.

Prashad, Vijay. *The Poorer Nations: A Possible History of the Global South*. London: Verso, 2014.

Rahman, Ahmad A. "Marching Blind: The Rise and Fall of the Black Panther Party in Detroit." In *Liberated Territory: Untold Perspectives on the Black Panther Party*, ed. Yohuru Williams and Jama Lazerow. Durham, NC: Duke University Press, 2009.

Reed, Adolph, Jr. "The Kerner Commission and the Irony of Antiracist Politics." *Labor: Studies in Working-Class History* 14, no. 4 (2017).

Reed, Adolph, Jr. *Stirrings in the Jug: Black Politics in the Post-Segregation Era*. Minneapolis: University of Minnesota Press, 1999.

Reed, Adolph, Jr., and Kenneth W. Warren, eds. *Renewing Black Intellectual History: The Ideological and Material Foundations of African American Thought*. New York: Routledge, 2016.

Reed, Touré. "Between Obama and Coates." *Catalyst* 4, no. 1 (2018).

Reed, Touré F. "Black Exceptionalism and the Militant Capitulation to Economic Inequality." *New Politics* (winter 2019). https://newpol.org/issue_post/black -exceptionalism-and-the-militant-capitulation-to-economic-inequality/.

Reese-Brown, Darren, and Mark Jay. "A Resident's Analysis." *The Periphery*, May 2014. http://www.theperiphery mag.com/essay-a-residents-analysis.

*Report of the National Advisory Commission on Civil Disorders*. New York: Bantam Books, 1968.

Robé, Chris. "Detroit Rising: The League of Revolutionary Black Workers, Newsreel, and the Making of *Finally Got the News*." *Film History* 28, no. 4 (2016).

Robinson, Cyril. "The Production of Black Violence." In *Crime and Capitalism: Readings in Marxist Criminology*, ed. David F. Greenberg. Philadelphia: Temple University Press, 1993.

Robinson, William I. *Global Capitalism and the Crisis of Humanity*. New York: Cambridge University Press, 2014.

Robinson, William I. *A Theory of Global Capitalism*. Baltimore: Johns Hopkins University Press, 2004.

Rudin, A. James. "The Dark Legacy of Henry Ford's Anti-Semitism (Commentary)," *Washington Post*, October 10, 2014, https://www.washingtonpost.com/national/religion /the-dark-legacy-of-henry-fords-anti-semitism-commentary/2014/10/10/c95b7df2 -509d-11e4-877c-335b53ffe736_story.html?noredirect=on&utm_term=.2d36c7cee8ed.

Rusche, Georg. "Prison Revolts or Social Legislation: On the Events in America." Translated by Heinz D. Osterle and Kevin Anderson. *Frankfurter Zeitung*, June 1, 1930.

Schultz, Kathleen. *Detroit under STRESS*. Detroit: From the Ground Up, 1973.

Schumaker, John F. "The Demoralized Mind." *New Internationalist*, April 1, 2016. https:// newint.org/columns/essays/2016/04/01/psycho-spiritual-crisis.

Schumpeter, Joseph. *Capitalism, Socialism and Democracy*. London: Routledge, [1942] 1994.

Seale, Bobby. *Seize the Time: The Story of the Black Panther Party and Huey P. Newton*. Baltimore: Black Classic Press, 1968.

Seidman, Joel. *American Labor from Defense to Reconversion*. Chicago: University of Chicago Press, 1953.

Shabazz, Amilcar. "Ahmad A. Rahman's Making of Black 'Solutionaries.'" *Journal of Pan African Studies* 8, no. 9 (2015). https://pdfs.semanticscholar.org/60b8/964c204d46b979 ac9678e79eff51d201c9bc.pdf.

Shwartz, Michael, and Drew Fish. "Just-in-Time Inventories in Old Detroit." *Business History* 40, no. 3 (1998).

Silver, Beverly J. *Forces of Labor: Workers' Movements and Globalization since 1870*. New York: Cambridge University Press, 2003.

Sitkoff, Harvard. *A New Deal for Blacks: The Emergence of Civil Rights as a National Issue. The Depression Decade*. New York: Oxford University Press, 1981.

Sitkoff, Harvard. "The Detroit Race Riots of 1943," *Michigan History* 53 (fall 1969): 183–206.

Smith, Michael Peter, and L. Owen Kirkpatrick. "Reinventing Detroit: Urban Decline and the Politics of Possibility." In *Reinventing Detroit: The Politics of Possibility*, ed. Michael Peter Smith and L. Owen Kirkpatrick. London: Routledge, 2015.

Smith, Neil. "New Globalism, New Urbanism: Gentrification as Global Urban Strategy." *Antipode* 2002. https://onlinelibrary.wiley.com/doi/abs/10.1111/1467-8330.00249.

Smith, Neil. *The New Urban Frontier: Gentrification and the Revanchist City*. New York: Routledge, 1996.

Snyder, Rick. "Michigan Gov. Rick Snyder's 2013 State of the State Speech," *Governing*, January 6, 2013. https://www.governing.com/news/state/michigan-snyder-2013-speech.html.

Sohn-Rethel, Alfred. *Intellectual and Manual Labor*. Atlantic Highlands, NJ: Humanities Press, 1978.

Spence, Lester K. *Knocking the Hustle: Against the Neoliberal Turn in Black Politics*. New York: Punctum Books, 2015.

Spencer, Robyn C. *The Revolution Has Come: Black Power, Gender, and the Black Panther Party in Oakland*. Durham, NC: Duke University Press, 2016.

Stanford, Maxwell C. "Revolutionary Action Movement (RAM): A Case Study of an Urban Revolutionary Movement in Capitalist Society." ETD Collection for AUC Robert W. Woodruff Library. MA Thesis 2051. 1986. http://digitalcommons.auctr.edu/dissertations/2051/.

Stark, Rodney. *Police Riots: Collective Violence and Law Enforcement*. Belmont, CA: Focus Books, 1972.

Stauch, Michael, Jr. "Wildcat of the Streets: Race, Class and the Punitive Turn in 1970s Detroit," Unpublished dissertation, 2015. Cite Seer X. http://citeseerx.ist.psu.edu/viewdoc/download?doi=10.1.1.845.3092&rep=rep1&type=pdf.

Stein, Judith. "Labor History Symposium: Judith Stein, Pivotal Decade." *Labor History* 52, no. 3 (2011).

Stein, Samuel. "Capital City: Gentrification and the Real Estate State." *Next City*, March 4, 2019.

Sugrue, Thomas J. *The Origins of the Urban Crisis: Race and Inequality in Postwar Detroit*. Princeton, NJ: Princeton University Press, 1996.

*Taking Back Detroit*. Directed by Stephen Lighthill. Detroit: Available Light, 1980.

Taylor, Charles. *Hegel*. Cambridge: Cambridge University Press, 1977.

Taylor, Keeanga-Yamahtta. *From #BlackLivesMatter to Black Liberation*. Chicago: Haymarket Books, 2016.

Taylor-Bonds, Darlena. *Calling Detroit Home: Life within the Motor City*. Detroit: Taylor-Bonds Books, 2007.

Thompson, Heather Ann. "Unmaking the Motor City in the Age of Mass Incarceration." *Law and Society* 15 (December 2014).

Thompson, Heather Ann. *Whose Detroit? Politics, Labor, and Race in a Modern American City*. Ithaca, NY: Cornell University Press, 2001.

Tomba, Massimiliano. *Marx's Temporalities*. Translated by Peter D. Thomas and Sarah R. Farris. Leiden: Brill, 2013.

Tompkins Bates, Beth. *The Making of Black Detroit in the Age of Henry Ford.* Chapel Hill: University of North Carolina Press, 2012.

Toscano, Alberto. *Fanaticism: On the Uses of an Idea.* London: Verso, 2010.

Toscano, Alberto, and Jeff Kinkle. *Cartographies of the Absolute.* London: Zero Books, 2015.

Trilling, Daniel. "A Nightmare Experience? The Tories Economic Adviser on the Thatcher Years." *New Statesman*, March 8, 2010. https://www.newstatesman.com/blogs /the-staggers/2010/03/thatcher-economic-budd-dispatches.

Tripp, Luke S. "Black Working Class Radicalism in Detroit, 1960–1970." Ethnic and Women's Studies Working Papers 7. 1994. https://repository.stcloudstate.edu/ews_wps/7/.

Tronti, "Our Operaismo." *New Left Review* 73 (January–February 2012). http://www .newleftreview.org/II/73/mario-tronti-our-operaismo.

Truman, Harry. *Memoirs.* Vol. 1. Garden City, NY: Doubleday, 1955.

Ulbrich, Casandra E. "Riot or Rebellion: Media Framing and the 1967 Uprising." PhD dissertation. Wayne State University, 2011. https://digitalcommons.wayne .edu/cgi/viewcontent.cgi?referer=https://www.google.com/&httpsredir=1&article =1337&context=oa_dissertations.

U.S. Department of Transportation, Bureau of Transportation Statistics. "Table 1–23: World Motor Vehicle Production, Selected Countries (Thousands of Vehicles)." May 23, 2017. https://www.bts.gov/archive/publications/national_transportation _statistics/table_01_23.

Usmani, Adaner. "Did Liberals Give Us Mass Incarceration?" *Catalyst* 1, no. 3, 2017. https://catalyst-journal.com/vol1/no3/did-liberals-give-us-mass-incarceration

Valocchi, Steve. "The Unemployed Workers Movement of the 1930s: A Reexamination of the Piven and Cloward Thesis." *Social Problems* 37 (May 1990).

Vargas, Zaragosa. *Proletarians of the North.* Berkeley: University of California Press, 1999.

Vitale, Alex S. *The End of Policing.* New York: Verso, 2017.

Vogel, Richard. "Capitalism and Incarceration Revisited." *Monthly Review*, September 1, 2003. https://monthlyreview.org/2003/09/01/capitalism-and-incarceration-revisited/.

Wacquant, Loïc. *Punishing the Poor.* Durham, NC: Duke University Press, 2009.

Ward, Stephen M. *In Love and Struggle.* Chapel Hill: University of North Carolina Press, 2016.

Weber, Rachel. "Extracting Value from the City: Neoliberalism and Urban Development." *Antipode* 34, no. 3 (2002): 519–40.

Wenger, Morton, and Thomas Bonomo. "Crime, the Crisis of Capitalism, and Social Revolution." In *Crime and Capitalism: Readings in Marxist Criminology*, ed. David F. Greenberg. Philadelphia: Temple University Press, 1993.

West, Clara. "The Role of the National Negro Labor Council in the Struggle for Civil Rights." *Political Affairs*, February 16, 2007. http://www.politicalaffairs.net/the-role-of -the-national-negro-labor-council-in-the-struggle-for-civil-rights/.

We the People of Detroit Community Research Collective. *Mapping the Water Crisis.* Detroit: We the People of Detroit Community Research Collective, 2016.

White (unkown first name) and Thurgood Marshall, "June 1943." In *Detroit Perspectives: Crossroads and Turning Points.*, ed. Wilma Henrickson, 418–28. Detroit: Wayne State University Press, 1991.

Williams, Kristian. *Our Enemies in Blue: Police and Power in America*. Chico, CA: AK Press, 2015.

Williams, Robert. "The Potential of a Minority Revolution." *The Crusader* 4 (1964). https://archive.org/stream/ThePotentialOfAMinorityRevolution/The%20Potential%20of%20a%20Minority%20Revolution_djvu.txt.

Williams, Robert F. *Negroes with Guns*. Detroit: Wayne State University Press, 1998.

Wolf, Sherry. "Spies, Lies and War: The Lessons of COINTELPRO." *International Socialist Review* 49 (2006). http://www.isreview.org/issues/49/cointelpro.shtm.

Woodford, Arthur. *This Is Detroit, 1701–2001*. Detroit: Wayne State University Press, 2001.

Wright, Chris. "Its Own Peculiar Décor." *Endnotes* 4 (October 2015). https://endnotes.org/issues/4/en/chris-wright-its-own-peculiar-decor.

Zimbalist, Andrew. "The Limits of Work Humanization." *Review of Radical Political Economics* 7, no. 2 (1975).

Žižek, Slavoj. *Parallax View*. Cambridge, MA: MIT Press, 2006.

# Index

investment in, 17–20, 41, 236n6; policing of, 28, 56–60, 58f, 59f, 200, 219; rent hikes in, 2; revitalization efforts of mayors and, 197, 202, 208–9, 214; unemployment, 29–31, 88–89, 89f

Duggan, Mike, 2, 39, 51; on anticrime measures, 68; on homelessness, 57; revitalization efforts of, 34, 41, 49–51, 54, 208

Dunayevskaya, Raya, 136

East Side of Detroit, 29, 31, 54, 64, 65, 146, 228; Kercheval Street, 141, 265n59

emergency management: of black Michiganders, 47; of debt, 44–45; of Hamtramck, 209; of school system, 35. See also Orr, Kevyn

Engels, Friedrich, 8–9, 10, 124, 172

Engler, John, 47, 188, 210

FBI, 33–34, 170, 176, 189; Counterintelligence Program (COINTELPRO) of the, 173–74, 182–83, 188

fetishization: commodity, 12, 235n57; of Detroit's grittiness and resilience, 26, 240n38; ruin porn as, 2, 11, 23, 240n38

Fiat Chrysler Automobiles (FCA), 54–55. See also Chrysler

Finally Got the News (film), 165–67, 168, 187. See also League of Revolutionary Black Workers (LRBW)

Fitzgerald Neighborhood Revitalization project, 48–51, 54

Five Dollar Day, 80–81, 86. See also Ford Motor Company

Flint, 47, 93, 187, 208

Ford, Henry, 150; Great Depression and, 88; labor management and, 78, 80–81, 86, 254n51; mythology of, 76–77; racism of, 81–82, 90–91, 114, 256n78. See also Ford Motor Company

Ford, Henry, II, 10, 131, 193, 208

Fordism: as labor management, 77–81; worker dissent against, 83–86. See also Ford Motor Company

Ford Motor Company, 23–24, 109, 114, 161, 166, 168, 170, 268n17; at the Battle of the Overpass, 95; Crystal Palace of, 78, 80, 115; Great Depression and, 86–96; labor management and, 77–81; Piquette Avenue Plant of, 78, 115; production of military equipment by, 96; production of the Model T by, 80; River

Rouge factory complex, 76, 80, 86, 91, 95, 111; Service Department of, 86, 90–91, 95; suburbanization and, 115; Treaty of Detroit and, 111–13; worker turnover at, 82. See also Ford, Henry; Fordism

Forman, James, 165, 181

Freedom Now Party, 138

From the Ground Up, 69, 190, 274n150

gangs, 86, 95, 169, 200, 201

General Motors (GM), 44, 100, 131, 161, 166, 261n178, 268n17, 269n31; Great Depression and, 86–88; Poletown Plant of, 55, 207, 209; post-WWII struggles with workers at, 107–12; production of military equipment by, 96; sitdown strike of 1936–37 at, 92–93, 97

gentrification, 3, 24–28, 39–48, 52, 208; crime and, 56–57; fallacy of investment as philanthropy and, 39–40, 43, 49–50, 72–73; in Poletown, 207–9; policing and, 68–70, 71; public subsidies and, 40–44; uneven development and, 72–73. See also New Detroit

Georgakas, Dan, 133, 167, 180, 191 92

Gilbert, Dan, 3, 25, 42; Amazon bid by, 26, 223; Downtown real estate investment and, 18–20, 27, 41, 53; Downtown security and, 58–59, 70; role in home foreclosures, 34; as "savior" of Detroit, 18, 43, 44

Glaberman, Martin, 98, 136

Goldberg, David, 122, 134, 168, 196, 270n60

Grand Bargain. See bankruptcy of Detroit

Great Boom, 181, 203

Great Depression, the, 14, 86–96, 115–16, 171, 256n78

Great Rebellion (1967), 2, 5, 6, 127, 146f, 147f, 148f, 149f; auto industry and, 153; civil rights movement's contribution to, 131–40; day-by-day account of, 143–51; in Detroit (film), 155–56; as justification for militarization of police, 151–52; mythologies of, 129–31, 212; political consciousness after, 153, 160, 164, 267n106; revitalization as response to, 5, 15, 69, 185, 208; stop-and-frisk's role in catalyzing, 140–43

Great Society, 132, 134

Green, Malice, 212

Gribbs, Roman, 186–87, 189

Group on Advanced Leadership, 138

Wayne County tax foreclosure auction, 20, 21, 33–35
Wayne State University, 19, 21, 56, 60, 133, 138, 164, 165, 169, 186
West Central Organization, 165, 168
West Side of Detroit, 29, 31, 65–66, 143, 147, 212
We the People of Detroit, 32, 73
white flight, 40–41, 133, 156, 195, 277n41
Widick, B. J., 135, 262n202
Williams, John, 164. *See also* League of Revolutionary Black Workers
Williams, Robert F., 139
women: in the League of Revolutionary Black Workers, 165, 167; sit-down strikes and, 92; as workers, 96–97, 109, 112, 136, 277n40

Woodward Avenue, 18, 21, 42, 133
Wooten, Chuck, 170
World Production Board (WPB), 115–16
World War I, 83–84
World War II, 96–100, 115, 116, 136; aftermath of, 6, 7, 40, 102, 136, 157, 195

Young, Coleman, 44, 55, 67, 110, 192–94, 195–97, 202–3, 214; on Detroit's resiliency, 223; as a fiscal conservative, 206; urban renewal and, 208–9; war on crime of, 198–202, 212
Young, Coleman A., Jr., 3, 39

Zedong, Mao, 139

# FOREWORD

The feeling one has when entering the ministry can be described as both a burden and a blessing. It's a blessing because we have a "desire" (1 Timothy 3:1) to serve God, and there is no greater joy; it's a burden because there are "cares" and responsibilities in the ministry (2 Corinthians 11:28). The thought that God would use sinners like us to proclaim His word is humbling indeed, and sometimes overwhelming. Add to that a lack of experience, and a few church-related problems, and you have the potential for a shipwreck of your ministry. Many sincere God-called preachers leave or destroy their ministries simply because they lack the wherewithal to handle a problem, or perhaps because they have adopted an unbiblical approach from the outset.

The Bible admonishes us to "[h]ear instruction, and be wise, and refuse it not" (Proverbs 8:33). Preachers need preaching too, and pastors need pastoring from time to time. This book does both. It addresses questions and situations that pastors face, and it provides biblical answers. It is written by a man admired and respected by many pastors, including myself. Dr. David Peacock is both a "preacher's preacher" and a "pastor's pastor." I know I would not be where I am today without Dr. Peacock's influence and help through the years.

Dr. Peacock is a perceptive pupil of the scriptures as well as a powerful preacher of the gospel. If you've ever heard him preach, you know this to be true. He is also a compassionate pastor whom the Lord has used to grow his congregation at Bible Believers Baptist Church, both spiritually and in numbers, over the past twenty years.

To the veteran preacher who has heard it all, I challenge you. This book may hold some ideas you've never thought of or heard expressed quite this way. To the young preacher just starting out, take notes! In the following pages lies a wealth of information that is both biblical and practical for the man, the message, and the ministry.

Dr. David E. Walker, Pastor
Calvary Baptist Church, Monticello, Florida

# PREFACE

Let me say, by way of introduction, that the material presented in this book is by no means the absolute authority regarding preaching or the pastoral ministry. The things that I would like to share with you are simply suggestions for you to consider, as they come from my years of personal experience in the ministry. Many things I have learned the hard way through failure instead of success, but I trust they may be a blessing to you.

This book is designed not only for those currently in the ministry, but for those who feel God's call to begin or start a work. It is my prayer that you may avoid some of the pitfalls to which I have fallen prey, and have a fruitful ministry for the Lord.

Let me also affirm that the ideas presented in this work are not given as commands but rather suggestions. Please take what you want and throw out what doesn't work for you.

Many of the storms that I experienced in the early years of my ministry were caused by the fact that I didn't know better. I didn't have any instruction. People normally learn three ways: God teaches them, they learn from their own mistakes, or they learn from the mistakes of others.

It is my prayer that you may learn from my experience.

Dr. David Peacock, Pastor
Bible Believers Baptist Church, Jacksonville, Florida

# $The$ M A N

## THE GOD-CALLED PREACHER

I have been around the ministry and in the ministry long enough to see people who have genuinely been called and those who have not. A God-called preacher is not a preacher because that is something that he does; he does it because it is something that he is.

Real God-called preachers seem to be an extinct species. There are not many men who stand behind pulpits anymore. Instead we have these effeminate "men" or women attempting to fill an office they were never called to in the first place.

Biblical preaching is supposed to be "male oriented," in the sense that it is to have a thrust and present a charge to the people in such a way that it is authoritative on behalf of God. Women can minister better in some areas, but God ordained that men are to be the leaders and preachers of the word of God.

## THE PREPARATION OF THE MINISTER

The first thing that you must do before any other preparation is to be willing to admit that you have been wrong in the past.

Acts 26:9-11

9 I verily thought with myself, that I ought to do many things contrary to the name of Jesus of Nazareth.

10 Which thing I also did in Jerusalem: and many of the saints did I shut up in prison, having received authority from the chief priests; and when they were put to death, I gave my voice against them.

11 And I punished them oft in every synagogue, and compelled them to blaspheme; and being exceedingly mad against them, I persecuted them even unto strange cities.

In the above passage we know that Paul was a very religious man, doing those things that he thought he should be doing. He was even doing those things in the name of God.

When the Lord spoke to him on the road to Damascus, Paul thought of himself as the Lord's right-hand man. He thought he was honestly serving God by persecuting the church. He thought he was doing God a service, but the first thing God revealed to Paul was that everything he was doing was wrong.

After that revelation Paul had a choice to make. He could choose to justify himself and make excuses or he could repent and admit before God that he was wrong.

This is the first step in surrendering to the ministry and the first step in future growth. As God reveals more and more of Himself, you must be willing to say, "I have been wrong, and I acknowledge that what I have been doing is wrong. I was going the wrong way, doing the wrong things." That is step one. If there is no recognition of past failures there can be no promise of future success. Until the foundation is cleared of everything corrupt, nothing pure and right can be built on it.

# TRUE SURRENDER

Second, there has to be a true surrender for the purpose of God in your life. This is where you say, "I count all things but loss for the excellency of the knowledge of Christ Jesus my Lord: for whom I have suffered the loss of all things, and do count them but dung, that I may win Christ" (Phil. 3:8). This is the total and complete sacrifice of everything that we plan, everything that we are, and everything that we hope for. At this point there is no "fence-straddling." If you desire to be "God's man" instead of "the man of God" you will have to take this step. Being "God's man" is being a man that God can control. It means God can say, "Do you love me? Are you willing to lay down your life for me?"

There is a message I preach called "What is your Isaac?" As preachers, our "Isaacs" can be our jobs, our reputations, our families, our friends, or our finances. You must understand that before your preaching can have any power or take effect you must make this choice to surrender fully. You must be willing to do what the Lord would have you to do in his time frame. This step concerns willingness, plain and simple.

You can know a lot of things about preaching and how to preach, but unless your heart, mind, body, and soul are surrendered to preach, you are only a "sounding brass, or a tinkling cymbal" (1 Cor. 13:1). If your service is just something you do because there is a need, or there is nothing else to do, then it will never be the right kind of service. You must give yourself to the Lord wholly; completely.

If God can save your soul and preserve you for all eternity, you shouldn't have a problem surrendering your life to Him. God can run our lives better than we can. And He will never do anything to hurt you or harm you in any way.

Anything that stands between you and full surrender to Jesus Christ should be "counted as dung" (Phil. 3:8). Those things are actually idols because you worship them instead of God. They can be careers, sports, family, or money.

Complete surrender is taking Isaac to the top of the mountain and saying, "Here it is, Lord; you do with it what you want." Paul says, "I count all things but dung." The reason was so Paul could "win Christ." He wanted to get closer to the Lord and the only way to do that was to get rid of what was standing between him and the Lord. Paul was willing to suffer the loss of all things that he might know the Lord in a personal way and be closer to him—full surrender.

Any ministry or message without Jesus is of no point anyway. Therefore, surrender is one of the most important elements when it comes to preaching. We sing a hymn called "I Surrender All." But I fear, if we were honest, we would sing, "I surrender some." The fact is, when the Lord comes to take what we supposedly surrendered (for example, child, house, car, job, family, reputation, career, or health), we often find that we never gave it to Him in the first place. If you never surrender totally, when the Lord does take some things, you may harbor bitterness and anger at the Lord instead of love and worship. The key to a successful, joyous Christian life is not stopping this or that and doing this or that; it is the surrender to Jesus Christ. It is putting Jesus Christ first above everything and everyone else.

People say that Dr. Jim Lince was a great preacher, and he was. What people don't realize is that he didn't become a great preacher overnight. Neither did he become a great preacher because of his brilliant mind, Bible studies, and doctoral thesis. He became a great preacher because he suffered. He was willing to keep preaching despite everything he had been through, and God blessed him and used him mightily. Power comes from pressure, which comes from suffering.

## A PREACHER'S PURPOSE

Your purpose as a preacher of the gospel is to turn people from the power of Satan to God, not to yourself:

Acts 26:17-18

17 Delivering thee from the people, and from the Gentiles, unto whom now I send thee,

18 To open their eyes, and to turn them from darkness to light, and from the power of Satan unto God, that they may receive forgiveness of sins, and inheritance among them which are sanctified by faith that is in me.

Our object in preaching is to make sure the sinner is converted to Jesus Christ, not to us or our way of thinking. We are not converting them to a religion, but to Jesus Christ. The sinner should see Christ, not our formalistic religion. Salvation is in Christ; there is no other way. The main purpose of our calling is to convert lost people to Jesus Christ, to show them the way to heaven. The second purpose is to give instruction to them for their Christian life.

You are not called to put people in bondage to religion—that is Catholicism. You are called to set people free (John 8:32–36) from the bondage of Satan to the liberty that is found in Jesus Christ. You must be careful and not take people from the bondage of Satan and replace their rusted iron handcuffs and barbed wired fences with platinum handcuffs and padded cells and straitjackets. We have been given a great responsibility to set people free, to give them the liberty that can only be enjoyed in Christ. Don't turn your beliefs into a padded prison cell.

In Jesus Christ there is liberty. When people are saved, they do not lose their right to make their own decisions. You as a pastor must let God be the one who changes them. You are to persuade and point them in the right direction. They have the choice to pursue that path in their own way and own time. The pathway to God, once you are saved, is like a stream. No two streams are identical. They all vary to some degree. Because the way of salvation is the same for everyone in this age, by grace through faith through the blood of Jesus Christ,

many think that the Christian life and growth should all be the same. This is not at all true.

Our growth varies based on who we are and the circumstances we find ourselves in. We must not attempt to clone our experience with God. All Christians must experience their own growth with God. If their relationship with God is a clone of ours then they might know us better but they will fail to know God. It is better to be acquainted with God than with us.

# SETTING PEOPLE FREE

We as preachers are to follow the same calling of our Lord with regard to preaching liberty to the captives:

> Isa 61:1 The Spirit of the Lord GOD is upon me; because the LORD hath anointed me to preach good tidings unto the meek; he hath sent me to bind up the brokenhearted, to proclaim liberty to the captives, and the opening of the prison to them that are bound;

We must remember that our calling has in its very root the responsibility to set people free. When I was a policeman we would take people out of a caged car up to a jail cell. Then we would take off the handcuffs, giving them some liberty, but they were still in an eight by ten cell with bars and a locked door. They were still in prison.

After they went to their first court appearance, they were then put in "general population." They had a little more freedom (a bigger cell) but they were still in jail. They still could not leave when they wanted, or go when they wanted to go, or do what they wanted to do.

Then, after their trial, if they were found guilty they were sent to what we called "The Big House," meaning a big prison facility. This meant that they then had the opportunity to get out of their cell

into a yard for recreation, but they were still in prison! They still had a desire to be set free. They had a little more freedom than being in the back seat of a police car, but they were still in prison, still bound, still in bondage.

We have to understand that it is not our job to imprison people and become their "god." We are not called to preach in order to determine what God's people should and shouldn't do. We are to proclaim what the Bible says, letting the Lord say what He needs to say to His people. They are His, not ours. We are merely "under shepherds" for the "chief Shepherd" (1 Peter 5:4).

If you have kids, how do you feel when someone else gets on to them? You know your own kids, you spend time with them, you invest in their lives, and you are the one who knows best. You are the one who knows how much discipline they need. If someone came into your house and pulled out a belt and spanked your kids, how would you react? How do you think God feels when we as preachers belittle and berate His children? Preacher, we are dealing with God's children and must be careful how we treat them.

Now I say all of that, realizing that there is a proper time to preach rebuking or reproving types of messages. I understand this. But we must be careful.

## LEGISLATING INSTEAD OF PREACHING

Unfortunately, some Bible believers have decided to legislate spirituality. I've seen some base their thoughts of spirituality on just about anything you can imagine. They determine whether or not you are spiritual based on whether or not you have children and how many children you have. They stay hung up on Gen. 1:28; 9:1.

Some people can have children and some people can't. Paul never had children; are you going to say that he wasn't as spiritual as Lot? To preach that having children is God's way of increasing the church puts pressure on people to have more children when

they may not be able to handle everything that comes with having those children.

While I believe in homeschooling where and when possible, and understand that public schools (and many private and Christian schools) often harm the development of a child, it is not the "fix- all" for every family. All women are not natural-born teachers and some do not have the flexibility to stay at home. If you set up homeschooling as a spiritual standard, what impression is that going to give the single mom who has to work in order to support her children? You say, "She shouldn't be divorced." Yes, in a perfect world, but churches are made up of broken people from broken homes and relationships.

I have seen churches that started out on the right foundation, but then split right down the middle. One group said, "You must homeschool." And the other said, "We can't." The group that didn't homeschool felt looked down upon. They didn't think they measured up to the spirituality of the "homeschool" group, so they left. They are gone. Now you can't help them at all. They left over a nonbiblical issue that was caused by the preacher or people in the church superimposing and legislating spirituality.

Our object is to help people. And when as a preacher you move outside of the realm of the heart, you begin treading dangerous ground. Instead of preaching biblical convictions, you begin to place nonbiblical burdens on people that they might not be able to bear.

# CONFRONTATION

Anytime you try to do something for the Lord, there will be spiritual forces at work that you cannot see, which will oppose you. Things may be naturally peaceful, but then all of a sudden the volcano erupts, the kids get upset, the phone rings off the hook, the tires on the car go flat, and so on.

The pathway to God is most often lined with minefields. There is opposition to doing God's will. There will be things that block your

pathway in order to prevent you from doing what God wants you to do. These things may also arise in your life in order to test your motive for why you are doing what you are doing. If you are committed to the cause of Jesus Christ, you will step around those obstacles and move on. Sometimes sickness, age, other Christians, or your own flesh will hinder you in the ministry.

Those who follow the prosperity gospel think that all God wants to do for you after you get saved is give you a better job, a newer car, a bigger house, and more monetary possessions. These false teachers do not emphasize the gospel of Jesus Christ, or the suffering that comes along with the call to the ministry. They use God, and take out of context the blessings given to Israel, and falsely apply them to the church. If and when the period of prosperity comes to a close in America, many Christians will see that they have been worshipping and serving the wrong concept of "god."

# THE NUMBERS EQUATION

You cannot determine what a substance is by how many gather around it. Flies gather around a coconut cake but they also gather around the outhouse. Just because a ministry has numerical growth doesn't necessarily mean it is successful in God's eyes. Often as preachers we judge success by how many attend instead of by how biblically based the ministry is.

Eph 4:11-12
11 And he gave some, apostles; and some, prophets; and some, evangelists; and some, pastors and teachers;
12 For the perfecting of the saints, for the work of the ministry, for the edifying of the body of Christ:

The above passage teaches us that preachers are simply a gift that has been given by God to the church to become their servants. Notice

the following verses which teach that the primary job of the pastor is to feed the church. Preachers are not to fleece or skin the sheep: You can only skin a sheep one time and he is dead. The object is to feed the sheep.

> Acts 20:28 Take heed therefore unto yourselves, and to all the flock, over which the Holy Ghost hath made you overseers, to feed the church of God, which he hath purchased with his own blood.

> John 21:15 So when they had dined, Jesus saith to Simon Peter, Simon, son of Jonas, lovest thou me more than these? He saith unto him, Yea, Lord; thou knowest that I love thee. He saith unto him, Feed my lambs.

The pastor is a gift from God to the saints of God for the expressed purpose of edifying and strengthening the body of Christ. The healthiest sheep are the ones that are fed the best. If they are fed properly, they will not be as prone to sickness and disease. If you feed them the right food they will be able to detect the wrong food.

## PERSONALITY AND PREACHING

As preachers, we must be careful of not mimicking or copying someone else. Study preachers. Study what works and what doesn't work and learn from that. But you must be the preacher God wants you to be. If you copy someone else, you lose the advantage of how God made you and will not be as effective ministering to the people God called you to minister to.

Some preachers are more animated and excited, while others are more serious and somber. No one preacher has discovered the one right way. You must be aware of how God made you and the type of people you are called to preach to. Someone preaching in the

Southern United States will most likely preach with a different style from someone in the Northern U.S.

However, as it concerns the emotions, your congregation should understand from your delivery that you believe what you are preaching about. This emotional side of preaching is more than just volume and excitement. It has to do with your attitude and your actions. You can say something and not follow through with what you say, which will make your words of no value.

So, while we can learn from other preachers by taking a little here and there, we should be careful not to be clones. We should let God use us where He has us and learn to let the word of God be the authority over us and our ministries. The Bible should draw the people, not us or our delivery. If you lift up the Book, it will act as a natural magnet. If you place yourself above the Bible, your ministry will not be biblically based, no matter how successful it may be in the eyes of men.

## LEADING SHEEP

The ministry of being a pastor is different from the ministry of a missionary, jail minister, or street preacher. Each call of God is different and we have to be careful not to judge another brother because he doesn't feel led of the Lord to serve the Lord the same way we do.

Often preachers make the mistake of coercing their people into some type of Christian service (jail ministry, nursing home, visitation, street preaching, and so on). Because their people are interested in pleasing the Lord and their preacher, they are persuaded against their will to do something that is spiritual, when it is in fact mimicking what their preacher is doing. If God has called you to do it, you should do it whether anyone else does it or not. You are not a success in the ministry because you duplicate yourself in someone else. Some preachers think their spirituality is based on how busy they can make their congregation.

Everyone has a place. Some men are called to preach, some are not. Neither is any better than the other. We must be careful not to manipulate people, but rather, to allow God to work in their lives.

When I was getting ready to leave the sheriff's office, I sought out some counsel from a man who has been in the ministry for many years. Over dinner, I told him that I thought the Lord was leading me to quit my current job and enter the ministry full time. The church we had started was still rather small and this would be a huge step for me to make. His response when I asked him what he thought I should do was, "Pass the salt." With tears in my eyes, in a serious tone, I asked him if he had heard what I said. He looked squarely at me and said, "Did you hear what I said? Pass the salt." Years later, he told me that he was careful not to give me an opinion because he didn't want me relying on what he thought instead of how the Lord had dealt with me. If I had based my decision on what he thought, I probably would have quit The Ministry when things grew difficult. But, because I knew it was God's voice and His will, I could fall back on His promises when things got rough. It was my relationship with God, not with my mentor, that sustained me.

When it comes to God dealing with others, our job is to point them to God and simply get out of the way. Everyone has his or her place and part in the body of Christ. When men reproduce themselves in others, they will always reproduce a flaw. But when God does something in a man, it will last.

# PAUL'S PATTERN

1 Thess 2:1-2

1 For yourselves, brethren, know our entrance in unto you, that it was not in vain:

2 But even after that we had suffered before, and were shamefully entreated, as ye know, at Philippi, we were bold

in our God to speak unto you the gospel of God with much contention.

Oftentimes we as preachers say things that are better left unsaid. Paul said that he was "bold in our God," not his preferences, prejudices, or personal convictions. When the contention came it was because of the gospel, not his pet peeves. All too often we use the pulpit as a platform to promote ourselves and our way of thinking instead of God and His purpose. We are not to be "busybody[ies] in other men's matters" (1 Peter 4:15). Just because you are a preacher doesn't mean you have the right to meddle in other people's personal lives. If a visitor to your church feels that his or her personal life is going to be put under a microscope or on public display for all to see, he or she will draw back and probably not come back. Preaching against sin is one thing, but embarrassing people is not biblical preaching. If God was to put everything He knows about you on display, you probably wouldn't have anyone to preach to next Sunday.

If contention arises because of the gospel, fine. But if it arises because we are overstepping our bounds, then we are going to lose more people than we gain. Sometimes before we get an opportunity to reach people, we try to correct them and we move so quickly we lose them. They do not stay long enough to see Christ in us and the benefits of being a Christian or growing as a Christian.

1 Thess 2:3 For our exhortation was not of deceit, nor of uncleanness, nor in guile:

The pulpit must be respected. While you may have much literary license, there are some things that just shouldn't be said. One time I used a very common word from the pulpit that was slang and kind of questionable. I didn't think anything of it until a little boy came to church and said that word. After his mother scolded him, he retorted,

"The preacher says it." Right then and there the Lord smote my heart and told me to clean up my language (Titus 2:8).

Things we say from the pulpit shouldn't represent anything unclean or paint a picture that is unclean. People traffic in trash, and if you are not careful you will fall into that trap.

> 1 Thess 2:4 But as we were allowed of God to be put in trust with the gospel, even so we speak; not as pleasing men, but God, which trieth our hearts.

We are not to preach in order to please men, and this goes for ourselves as well. Sometimes we want to preach a message because we feel we can preach it well, and maybe even the Lord has blessed it in the past. But we are to preach to please God first in our preaching. It doesn't matter if the people are pleased or if it is a message we want to preach. God first, men second.

> 1 Thess 2:5-9
> 5 For neither at any time used we flattering words, as ye know, nor a cloak of covetousness; God is witness:
> 6 Nor of men sought we glory, neither of you, nor yet of others, when we might have been burdensome, as the apostles of Christ.
> 7 But we were gentle among you, even as a nurse cherisheth her children:
> 8 So being affectionately desirous of you, we were willing to have imparted unto you, not the gospel of God only, but also our own souls, because ye were dear unto us.
> 9 For ye remember, brethren, our labour and travail: for labouring night and day, because we would not be chargeable unto any of you, we preached unto you the gospel of God.

If our churches are going to be built on preaching, we need to become better preachers. We should never get to the point where we

think we have arrived and know everything there is to know about preaching. When that happens we become our own standard and instead of improving, we settle in rut and can eventually rot.

Many times in my early ministry I preached on things that did no one any eternal good. I might have made a lot of thunder and lightning, but there was not much rain. The thunder and lightning may be loud, but the growth comes from the rain. We must deliver what God wants us to deliver minus all of our personal agendas and carnality. We have to move aside so the Lord can get in the message.

Notice again in 1 Thess 2 that Paul compares his ministry to that of being a nurse (verse 7). Many of us are good at being a father (verse 11) because we can straighten people out and demand and demean. But many are not good at comforting those who are downcast. We are all too quick to use our swords to cut off heads rather than ward off foes. You can't give out judgment all the time or you will create a false balance (Prov. 11:1). Just because the world creates a false balance about God (accenting the "love of God" all the time), this should not affect us. We are not here to balance out the world; we are to feed the sheep. You might consider not giving out correction at every service. Compassion, care, and concern must be a component of the biblical message. Not everyone is a soldier on the march. Not everyone is going to keep up with you if all you preach is judgment and condemnation. Until they are fed, nurtured, and grown, they will need more "nursing" than judging. It is difficult, but it is necessary.

When David went after the Amalekites (1 Samuel 30), there are some men who could not continue any further than the brook Besor. David left those two hundred behind and continues chasing the Amalekites and recovers everything they had lost and then some. After the battle, David commands the men to divide everything equally among all the men, including the two hundred. There were some men of Belial that didn't think the two hundred deserved

anything, but David made it clear that "as his part is that goeth down to the battle, so shall his part be that tarrieth by the stuff: they shall part alike" (1 Sam. 30:24). The men of Belial were among the warriors, not the waiters or the watchers (those men of Judah who had invested much in David).

All the people in our churches are not warriors, but that doesn't mean they are not important. Everyone can't go out on the street; everyone can't go on visitation, but that doesn't mean they are not spiritual. If your church is nothing but warriors they will eventually kill one another or they will kill you.

> 2 Sam 2:26 Then Abner called to Joab, and said, Shall the sword devour forever? Knowest thou not that it will be bitterness in the latter end? How long shall it be then, ere thou bid the people return from following their brethren?

I am not saying that you should never preach judgment. You just need to be careful to maintain a balance between being a "father" and a "nurse." It is much better to have someone that serves the Lord Jesus because they love the Lord instead of someone who serves because they are compelled to out of fear and judgment.

> 1 Thess 2:11 As ye know how we exhorted and comforted and charged every one of you, as a father doth his children,

Now notice that the father's job is not just correction and judgment. It is also exhortation and comfort. All too often preachers raise the standard so high that the people begin to resent the Lord and get frustrated to the point that they quit. The underlying message is that they are never good enough, never do enough, never give enough, and so on. We must be careful how we present the Lord and that we comfort as well as condemn when necessary.

1 Thess 2:13 For this cause also thank we God without ceasing, because, when ye received the word of God which ye heard of us, ye received it not as the word of men, but as it is in truth, the word of God, which effectually worketh also in you that believe.

As pastors, we have a responsibility to make sure biblical preaching is properly applied. The word of God can impart life or it can impart death. In the name of God you can do a lot of damage with the Bible. It is a two-edged sword (Heb. 4:12). We must be careful to use this sword for the purpose of killing the wolves, and protecting—not killing—the sheep.

## SACRIFICING THE SHEEP

Don't use your sheep as a stepping-stone to make yourself a legend in your own mind. Years ago the Lord gave me some little lambs. These were folks who wanted to learn the Bible and were interested in the scriptures. They were saved but were babes in the Lord. A few years passed and the Lord came by to check on His little lambs. When He asked how they were doing, all I could do was point to the wall and show Him their hides. Instead of growing them, teaching them, and helping them to become full grown sheep I skinned them and hung their hides on the wall.

Those sheep were sacrificed for me to learn some lessons that I could never have learned otherwise. It was a costly lesson. There was damage done based on how I perceived what they should be and should be doing. Even though my heart was pure, it was all zeal, not knowledge. I was trying to force compliance in an outward way, and using the Bible to do so, instead of allowing them time to grow.

If you are called to preach, be very careful how you treat and take care of God's sheep. They are not there for our use and abuse. They are there to be fed and protected by us. Don't get caught in

the trap that says, "If I am not preaching hard judgment sermons all the time, then I'm not preaching." Preach what God tells you to preach, but keep in mind that people need rest, they need comfort, and they need assurance. A soft touch, a tender smile, and reassuring words will go a long way with people, especially those who are worn and weary in the battle or those who are about to cross over to the other side.

Preaching in the nursing homes will help to teach you many lessons. Those saints are just as much God's people as those who are out on the front lines. Preaching in a place like a nursing home is much like adjusting a thermostat. You are not compromising in that you are not always telling people about judgment. Yes, you should preach judgment, but never without telling people how they can escape judgment and find mercy with a gracious God. Remember, most of them are close to the end.

It is much the same way you deal with children. You warn them of judgment if they fail to do what you tell them. But you also give them a way out if they obey you. Over time you want the child to obey you because he loves and respects you, not because he is always afraid of the judgment you might impose on him. This is called growth.

## THE PASTOR AND DISCOURAGEMENT

The fact of the matter is that we all go through depression and discouragement because we want to see results. We are often let down when people reject the truth of the gospel or when Christians refuse fellowship with the Lord. Our excitement for what the Lord has done for us is often not shared by those we are trying to minster to, and when it is not, it causes us to get discouraged.

Some preachers have a hard time admitting that they are disappointed with the lack of results in their ministries. It is for this reason that I want to emphasize again the importance of sticking to the Book.

The first thing that happens when discouragement sets in is that you begin to look to other sources. Then you think about change and finally you start to doubt your calling, and question whether or not God really called you into the ministry.

When I was first called to pastor we met in a living room. After a while we outgrew that and because of zoning restrictions had to rent a small building to meet in. This small building had no comfort amenities (no heat, no air conditioning, no bathroom). This building was located in a section of town where you had to make sure you took everything home with you or it might be stolen before you met again. We stayed in that building for a long time with only twelve to fifteen people. After a while I wondered whether or not God really called me and what I could do differently to make things better. Fortunately, I had been taught to stick with the Bible; the book that had brought me to where I was. Some are not taught that and they quickly attempt to change things in order to manufacture results.

## PREACHING FOR RESULTS

There is a grave danger in not preaching the Bible or forsaking the right paths just for the sake of results. When we do this, we produce Ishmaels instead of Isaacs. Ishmael was born out of haste. Abraham and Sarah didn't think God was responding as quickly as He should, so they decided to "help God out." After all, they did have God's promise; what would be wrong if they went about fulfilling that promise in a quick way?

The problem was that they were producing a child after the flesh instead of after the promise of God. And eventually that child would become an outcast and the perpetual enemy of God's chosen people.

Later God gave them Isaac who was produced supernaturally according to the promise of God when circumstances (Abraham and Sarah were both past childbearing and producing age) were not in their favor. It was Isaac that God blessed, not Ishmael.

The lesson is clear. Whenever we stray from what God promises, we may have results, but we could potentially produce Ishmaels that are devised of our own thoughts, ideas, and perception. It will ultimately lead to the spiritual demise of our work and not the blessings of God.

Let me encourage you to stick with the promises of God, realizing that He very seldom does things according to our timing. He often moves slowly, but you can rest assured that His movements are sure. When we get to the judgment seat of Christ, the Lord will not grade you according to the perceived success of other ministries, but based on your faithfulness and willingness. The most important thing to God is that you be willing.

> 2 Cor 8:12 For if there be first a willing mind, it is accepted according to that a man hath, and not according to that he hath not.

If all you have is five barley loaves and two fish, God is satisfied with that seemingly meager supply. Oftentimes early in my ministry I was frustrated as I watched some preachers flourish with exceptional growth, while at the same time they compromised in areas I never would (like music and the King James Bible). I even saw some of the people in our church get discouraged as they watched these same trends transpire. They felt like an outcast because the ministry was not growing even though we were faithful to the truth and trying to do things according to the scriptures. It seemed like everything was a fight and a struggle.

The Lord taught me a few things during that period in my ministry. The first thing He reaffirmed was that He didn't settle His accounts now, and my faithfulness would eventually be rewarded, if not here in Eternity. Second, I learned that the things that are most valuable come at the greatest price.

So if you think you are not successful, but you are doing your best according to what God has called you to do, be encouraged!

Your willingness to suffer and sacrifice for the benefit of other people without immediate results will be rewarded; if not in this life, then at the Judgment Seat of Christ.

# THE PREACHER'S ADVERSARY

You don't have to read the Bible very long (three chapters) before the devil shows up ready to deceive and destroy. Likewise, it will not be very long in the ministry after you are walking with God and preaching for God that Satan will try to trip you up and get you off track. He begins by making you question God ("Yea, hath God said").

When we get away from the Bible, we begin to do what Eve did (Gen. 3:1): start listening to other voices. Those other voices will lead you in a different direction. God gives you a promise when you are called and you start out standing bold and strong for the Lord. But after a while when you see few or no results, you begin to doubt and wonder if maybe you misunderstood God or He said something different: "Yea hath God said?" If God has called you, there will be times in your life (because you do not see results) that you will doubt your calling. But that is not the time to doubt the source of your calling or the Bible.

Also we notice from Gen. 3:4 that when a person begins listening to other voices they can be easily deceived. The moment that you begin to question God and His calling for your life, you open yourself up for deception. We all question God. Don't feel bad about questioning from time to time. But, when you question, do not base your answer on your feelings. Your feelings change with the times; God's word never changes. We are emotional beings and are tempted to judge things based on feelings alone. But when it comes to questioning God, you must go by the facts instead of the feelings. When you get away from the facts, you open yourself up to easy deception, which leads to compromise.

# YOUR PAST

There will always be people who will try to hold your past against you. But don't let that keep you from doing what God would have you do now. There will always be those "snotty, uppity" people who think that they are God's gift to the ministry. When someone brings up your past, first accept the fact that you might have to reap some things from your past. Second, don't dwell on your past. Admit your faults and then move on. Don't let someone use your past as a boat anchor to keep you down.

# REAL SUCCESS

Success in the ministry, whether it be preaching, pastoring, or missionary work, is not dependent on a pedigree. It doesn't matter who your family was, how much college training you have, how smart you are, or how talented you are. Success in God's eyes is determined by your willingness to surrender and sacrifice what you want to do for what God wants you to do. We should pray as our Lord, "not my will, but thine, be done" (Luke 22:42).

No man can measure the potential a certain individual has for success in the ministry. God chooses who He wants to bless. Often He uses the "base things of the world" (1 Cor. 1:28) to carry out His will. The naturally talented have more of a tendency to fail because they might trust in their own abilities instead of God. These types of ministers often work at pleasing the people for the sake of their reputation, instead of trying to please God.

# THE PREACHER'S WIFE

Next to the Bible and the Holy Spirit, the most important thing a preacher has is a wife who will stand beside him and help him. He needs the kind of wife who will love him even though she

knows everything about him. He needs a wife who will stick with him through the difficult times as well as the good times. This is absolutely crucial.

In order to be this kind of wife, she must understand the pressure that is on her husband in the ministry.

Over the years of my ministry, I can truly say that my wife has been a help to me, not a hindrance. Back a few years ago when I was sick, she put her own personal needs aside in order to minister to me. She knew that taking care of me would help me to be able to continue the work of the ministry and help others. I don't know if I would have recovered had not my wife cared for me twenty-four hours a day. And, consequently, the ministry God has given us continues.

## PREACHING FOR REPUTATION

There is a common thread that ties all Bible believers together — the Book. While pastors in different areas may do things a bit differently, the common thread can still be seen. All too often preachers get into running gun battles. Just because a preacher doesn't do everything exactly like you doesn't mean you can't be in fellowship with him. No one does everything exactly the same, because God has called each person to a specific place and wants him to carry out His will in a particular manner.

We as preachers must be careful not to misuse and abuse our office in order to try to build a work that is appealing to our preacher friends. You must divorce yourself from the opinions of the brethren and do what God has called you to do, not what everyone else is called to do. You can't do the same thing that a church of forty years and five hundred people is doing. You must do what you can for the size you are and the strength you are until you grow and expand.

Often preachers feel so much pressure to please the brethren that they force their people to do things before they are ready. Their people (trying to please their pastor) step up and obey but make a mess

because they were not prepared or ready. The devil is good at getting behind us and pushing us, making us go faster than we are ready to go. If you go into the battle unprepared, you will get into trouble. When David prepared to face Goliath, he took some time at the brook and gathered five stones. He knew that after he killed Goliath that he might have to face Goliath's four brothers. David planned before he went into the battle. He had been preparing for years as he tended and cared for the sheep. He had defeated a bear and a lion, all according to God's plan and timing. So when Goliath showed up, David had had enough experience to know that he needed to prepare for what he might face.

Frequently we try to prove our spirituality by going to the pinnacle of the temple, jumping off and expecting God to catch us. There is a fine line between faith and stupidity. I believe a man must be willing to surrender and sacrifice everything, but I also know that the Devil is very good at counterfeiting the Lord (2 Cor. 11:14) by getting you to do something before you are ready (see the Temptation of our Lord). You don't need to prove your spirituality to the Devil; you simply need to prove your willingness to the Lord. It does not matter who thinks you are spiritual or who thinks you are not spiritual. What matters is that we please God by doing what He wants us to do, how He wants us to do it, in the manner in which He wants it, and at the right time.

I'm just suggesting that you never preach as much to the hands and feet as you preach to the heart. The apostle Paul saw himself as the Lord's right-hand man. He thought he was honestly serving God by persecuting the church. He thought he was doing God a service, but the first thing God revealed to Paul was that everything he was doing was wrong.

After that revelation, Paul had a choice to make. He could choose to justify himself and make excuses or he could repent and admit before God that he was wrong.

I'm suggesting that as you move forward in the ministry, you may find that you were wrong about some things, no matter how pure

your motive. You must be willing to admit the wrong, correct it, and move on. The Lord knows I've made plenty of mistakes, and I pray that you'll learn from what I've done wrong and not have to repeat those mistakes yourself.

# *The* MESSAGE

## A MESSAGE FROM GOD

I believe that when the preacher stands in the pulpit to preach on Sunday, God has a message He wants imparted to the congregation. If we, as preachers, are not careful, we can get in the way of that message. So often preachers look at their congregations and think, "Well, they need this," or "They need that." But the truth is that none of us really knows what the people are going through and what they need from God. I've been preaching over twenty-five years and I was a policeman for over twenty years. I know a little bit about people because I was trained to watch people and pick out their behavior. But I only know people based on what I see on the outside, and then it will be interpreted by my own experience or by the deceitfulness of my heart (Jer. 17:9). If, then, I access them and give an opinion based on my point of view, we are headed for trouble. Approaching the ministry and preaching that way is a dangerous position to take. God knows what the people need; we don't. None of us are as good as the Holy Spirit in determining what people need.

## A SERMON'S FOUNDATION

Preaching must be rooted and grounded in the Bible. If the Bible is not the authority and foundation, the preacher becomes the

foundation. Any man can run off into a ditch. No man is perfect. The pressures of life, personal problems, and difficulties can come along and sway a preacher off in one direction or another if he is not biblically anchored.

# DON'T COMPROMISE ON THE BIBLE

The only place where there is no room for compromise or differing opinion is the Book. I will not move or change my position on the authority of the Authorized Version. No matter how good a ministry may look on the outside, no matter how pure and righteous it may seem, if it is not founded on the Book of God, it is not the right work. I don't care how nice the people are, how godly they appear to be or how well the pastor preaches. If it is not based on the right source it is not the right work. I am very dogmatic about this. I believe that God has His pure fountain and Satan has his corrupt fountain. If God has the ability to preserve your soul He has the ability to preserve a Book without error and fallibility. My soul rests in the fact that He did preserve the Book, the King James Bible. If I am planting tomato seeds I will not expect an orange tree when the crop comes up. If I plant the right seed (from the right Book), I know that it will produce the right fruit. Any other fruit, even if it resembles the right fruit, is corrupt fruit.

Preachers today are abandoning the King James Bible and that is like pulling a thread from a jacket. When you pull one thread the whole thing begins to come apart. The only thing that will keep your church together doctrinally is the King James Bible rightly divided (2 Tim. 2:15). Therefore, you can't waver from the Book. If someone tries to talk you out of believing the Book, you must see it as a direct attack on God Almighty.

There will always be people that appear to be godly and intellectual who will attempt to discredit and malign the Authorized Version. They appear to be peaceful little sheep and shepherds, but they are

really ravening wolves that are used by Satan to destroy you and your ministry.

Do not falter in your faith concerning the inspiration of the King James Bible (2 Tim. 3:16). I don't care if Grandma, Grandpa, Dad, and your dearest mentor in the ministry change their belief about the Bible, don't you change!

The most important tool you have as a preacher is the King James Bible. Some may think that you are mean or obnoxious because of your strong stance on the Bible. Don't let that bother you. This doesn't mean that you must purposefully act rude or uncouth. But when you stand for the King James Bible, people and preachers will attack you for it. Your faith in the Bible will transfer to your people. If you are strong and confident in it, your folks will be. If you are timid and unsure, your sheep will be shallow and the first time a storm comes they will be blown away.

# FINDING THE RIGHT MESSAGE

I do not claim to be the "preacher of all preachers" or claim to know all there is to know about preaching. But I do know that preaching must be the center point or focus of a Bible-believing work. If we want God to be pleased with what we are doing, preaching must be the focus. If preaching is the main thing, then we as preachers must strive to do it right. There is a right and a wrong way to preach a message.

As elementary as it sounds, the source of the message should be the Bible. When you begin preparing your message, you should not first consult commentaries, another preacher's outline, or Internet sermons. The Bible itself should be the starting point.

We have all experienced Saturday night rush hour with time running out and no Sunday message. The temptation during those times is to grab an outline from somewhere and preach it just for the sake of having something to say. It might have been a great outline, but there was no message from God. An old preacher used to say, "I

have a great outline, If God gets in it and breathes on it, I'll have a great message."

It is our job to deliver a great message. And this message must come from the right source; otherwise it will be corrupt from its beginning. Preachers are often tempted to look to outside sources in order to "spruce up" a message. Outside sources are good for support, but not for the backbone and foundation of the sermon. The sermon might be "fluffy" but will lack the meat and nutrition to feed the people properly.

When it comes to preparing a message, you should approach God with the Bible and ask Him to show you what He wants you to preach to your people. If you can't feel it, it is likely the people will not either. You must have a message that first speaks to your heart if you want it to speak to the hearts of others.

It is a must, a necessity, that the preacher of the word of God be familiar with the Bible. As a carpenter is familiar with the tools of his trade (saw, hammer, and so on), so the preacher must be with his tools. The Bible will keep you clean. Its effect on other people through your messages is no greater than its its effect on you personally. If people see the Bible having a personal effect on your life, then it will have a greater impact when they hear you preach. They will know that you "practice what you preach." You, as a preacher, are to be a living example. You should never have the mentality that you have "arrived," that there is no reason for you to repent and get right with God. You are not "above" the people as a "Baptist pope." You should constantly keep yourself under subjection to the word of God and be ready to repent and change just as you expect your flock to repent and change.

# OUTWARD CONFORMITY

We all talk about hating popery, yet sometimes, especially as young preachers, we have a tendency to force the people to outward conformity before we get them in subjection to the word of God.

People can look right on the outside but be headed toward Egypt in their hearts (Acts 7:39).

When people go to prison, they get their hair cut the right length, wear clothes that are not offensive, are told when to go to bed, when to get up, when to have recreation and so on. But when they get out, there is an eighty percent chance that they will land back in prison. This happens because for most prisoners they have simply conformed on the outside and had no change take place inside.

The same is true with congregations. You may get outward conformity during a Sunday morning service, but if you want something that lasts, they must be changed from the inside. A person can look right on the outside but be as wicked as the Devil on the inside.

Sometimes pastors can become very manipulative by putting pressure on a congregation. Let's say a pastor believes a woman should always wear a dress. If he is not careful he can put pressure on all the women to conform to his conviction and thus give the idea that how a person dresses makes her spiritual or unspiritual. It would be better for a woman to understand the biblical teaching regarding modest apparel (1 Tim. 3:9; 1 Peter 3:3), and make the change on her own, than to copy another person blindly, for the sake of pleasing the pastor. There are many women who wear dresses but still can't control their mouths. Spirituality is not in a dress or an outward appearance.

Outward conformity is often short lived. A pastor can frustrate himself and stunt the growth of his church by being in too big of a hurry for reputation's sake. Just because you force your people to look a certain way, act a certain way, and do certain things means very little.

For example, Mormons dress right, look right, knock on doors, and visit, but their beliefs are not right and their doctrine is not in line with the word of God. There are some Roman Catholics who are good, solid, moral people, but they are on their way to Hell. So, outward conformity is not a good foundation to build a church on.

When people go to a hospital they come with broken legs, diseases, and things for which they need medical attention. No one stands at the door of a hospital and demands that they be healed and cleaned up before entering. A church is much like a hospital for the soul. We offer the "balm of Gilead" (Jer. 8:22), but if we never let them get in we can't help them with their diseases. Some people might consider what I'm saying as compromise because all they get out of the Bible is a list of do's and don'ts. Some pastors are only interested in making people be like them. We should be interested in making people the way Jesus Christ wants them to be, not our impression of who they should be.

I believe in the autonomy and independence of the local church, but I also believe in the independence and freedom of the people who compose the church. I do not believe that any pastor or any parishioner has the right to dictate to anyone else how to act or be. That job is reserved for the Bible and the Holy Spirit.

Many people become Bible-believers because they are rebels at heart and cannot take orders. Unfortunately, many pastors have this mentality and are not happy unless they are bearing rule over everyone else. This is a dangerous way to operate a ministry because it undermines the authority of God and His word. If a man rises even a half-inch above the Bible, he is a half-inch too tall.

If the Bible is not the authority and preaching is not biblical, the foundation of the ministry will be cracked, thus leading to disunity, carnality, and division.

## BIBLICAL PREACHING

Preaching today is watered down. Preaching is supposed to stir the emotions and the heart. Any preacher who is preaching should intend to strike deep into the heart. The intent in preaching should be to help the listener from the scriptures. God did not raise up preachers in the Bible who never offended anyone. Real preaching will put God

in His proper place and man in his. God will be exalted and man will be brought down, and man does not like to be put down.

If you want a successful church in the eyes of God, it must be built on God's idea of success, not man's. This type of success may not bring man's praises. Success is not determined by the size of your congregation. The measuring stick for success is the Lord Jesus Christ, not some ministerial association or preachers' fellowship. The Judgment Seat of Christ will reveal which ministries were truly successful in His eyes.

Notice from 1 Corinthians 1 what biblical preaching should be and accomplish:

1. Biblical preaching is supposed to be plain.

1 Cor 1:17 For Christ sent me not to baptize, but to preach the gospel: not with wisdom of words, lest the cross of Christ should be made of none effect.

This does not mean that preaching must be loud, or necessarily hard. But preaching should be hard enough to drive the point home. The preacher must be able to distinguish between when to use the hammer and when to use the sledgehammer. You wouldn't use a sledgehammer for a finishing nail. Finish work must be done with the tack hammer. By the same token, you can't tear something down with the tack hammer. Discretion is the key.

When I first started preaching, I used the sledgehammer effect all the time (i.e., "don't touch, don't go here, don't go there, and the like). My preaching was harsh and similar to telling people to put themselves in a straitjacket in order to keep themselves from sin. When I preached like this, my heart was right, my intentions were good, but the Lord had to show me that I couldn't beat the sheep down all the time. That type of preaching will frustrate people. The sentiment will be that they are never good enough, never right

enough, never clean enough, and never serve enough. They will be torn down all the time and never able to enjoy the blessings of the freedom that is offered in Christ.

When I trained police officers, I learned that I had to train them how to think like policemen, not civilians. If all I did was focus on everything they did wrong, I could never instruct them on how to start doing things the right way. It is all a matter of balance (Prov. 11:1).

Your preaching must be plain. Preachers often make the Bible too complicated. Sometimes preachers will use an obscure passage and they think that it is very deep, but in reality it is not deep, only muddy. It might make them look intelligent, but it hasn't helped the people at all. In my opinion, the best preaching is simple, plain preaching, so that the people know where you are coming from. You do not have to prove to your sheep that you know more than they do. You are to aim at the target you are trying to hit. It is more important to get the message across than to show everything you know.

Preaching should convict people of their sins and let them know where they are going without Jesus Christ. But the plainness of it means that it should be on common ground with those who are listening. You do not have to know Greek or Hebrew in order to make your message have power. God is the One who gives power to the sermon, not the wisdom of elaborate words that no one understands.

2.   Biblical preaching should create division.

1 Cor 1:18 For the preaching of the cross is to them that perish foolishness; but unto us which are saved it is the power of God.

As I said earlier, God has a message that He wants us to preach, but many times we get in the way of that message. In the book of Jonah, we see that Jonah created a storm because he did something

God didn't want him to do. Often times storms in our churches are created because we go against God's will. Preachers can cause storms.

Sometimes the storms are caused by the preacher when he decides what he thinks needs to be preached instead of following the scriptures. Storms can also arise when a preacher puts a scope on his Bible in order to preach against one individual in the church. When he does that, the rest of the flock starves and God can't be glorified because God is nowhere in the message.

If our purpose in preaching is to lift up Jesus Christ, it follows reason that wrong motives in preaching will not glorify God, and it will not be long before the sheep starve to death. We can't feed them spiritually; only the Holy Spirit through the preaching of the word of God can feed the sheep. The preacher is to subject himself to the word of God, study, and pray, so that we can be the "mouthpiece" for God and say what He has given us to say.

> Heb 4:12 For the word of God is quick, and powerful, and sharper than any two edged sword, piercing even to the dividing asunder of soul and spirit, and of the joints and marrow, and is a discerner of the thoughts and intents of the heart.

Preaching will naturally create divisions; we do not have to attempt to make these divisions ourselves. If you preach the word, there will be people who love it and praise the Lord for it. There will also be people that will claim that it is foolish and they will get angry.

If you are ridiculed for preaching the word of God, so be it. But if you are ridiculed for being stupid, arrogant, or obnoxious, you are the one out of line. Some preachers think they are "suffering for Jesus" when people get mad when the fact is their brash rude comments had nothing to do with the scriptures! Instead of drawing people to Jesus

Christ, they turn people away and make it harder for those of us who are simply trying to preach the cross of Christ.

The gospel will create its own division. Those who accept the gospel will love it, and those who reject it will hate it. We have to remember that it is not our job to make divisions. The Bible and the preaching of the Bible will do that by itself. You don't have to draw a line in the sand and say, "If you don't believe this, then you're out!" If you will just preach the Bible, it will clearly call into question which side people are on without your having to make the choice for them.

3.    Biblical preaching should delight God instead of man.

1 Cor 1:21-22
21 For after that in the wisdom of God the world by wisdom knew not God, it pleased God by the foolishness of preaching to save them that believe.
22 For the Jews require a sign, and the Greeks seek after wisdom:

If preaching the gospel is what pleases God, why then would we want to preach anything else? Why then, would we want to put our own spin on it? Some preachers spin it in order to get people to conform to their image, instead of allowing God through the Holy Spirit to reveal to them how they should live.

Preaching that deviates from the Bible creates a false sense of conviction. In other words, the hearers will conform to the preacher's convictions instead of having their own from the word of God. They will mimic the preacher instead of following the Lord.

In order to delight the heart of God with biblical preaching, you must be willing to preach against things that are not doctrinally correct. Compromise for the sake of numbers is not acceptable to the God-called preacher. The idea that a preacher should never say

anything to his congregation about any other religion or Christian denomination comes from Hell itself. Jesus Christ spoke against the Pharisees. It is biblical to draw attention to doctrinal imperfections and heresies that might affect and harm His sheep. It is perfectly acceptable for a Bible preacher to condemn the so-called tongues movement, or any other heretical deviation. The Bible preacher must divorce himself from friends, family, fans, foes, and finances. The preacher is to preach the truth, even if it means preaching against popular movements and trends like contemporary music. God never built a church on singing. I like singing and music, but the music is the salad before the steak. The music can set the tone, but it should never be the main course. Music might prepare the emotions and the soil, but preaching sets the seed in the heart.

The God-called preacher must be willing to go against the modern effeminate shift in Christianity. God's order has been established in the scriptures (1 Cor. 11) and whenever a church begins to put women in charge of leadership, trouble will inevitably come. I am not against women, and I am not saying that they are "second-hand" creations, but if you are going to draw families and men, you are not going to do it with women leaders. Many churches are predominantly women and as such are emotionally driven. Some preachers draw large feminine crowds because they use psychology, and smiles exhort all the time, but refuse to preach on sin and judgement. This "preaching" is pleasing to the people and makes them happy. But does it follow biblical preaching to reprove, rebuke and exhort?

If you preach the Bible, people's flesh will crawl but their spirits will rejoice. Don't be afraid to preach the Book and in doing so you will expose the doctrinal inconsistencies and heresies of other groups. This does not have to be done in an arrogant, mean, or hateful manner. But at the same time you must caution and warn the people about movements such as the Charismatic movement.

Rom 16:17 Now I beseech you, brethren, mark them which cause divisions and offences contrary to the doctrine which ye have learned; and avoid them.

Let me also qualify this by stating that the place to address these heresies is not on the street corner when you are trying to preach the gospel to the lost. Neither should you go to these churches and try to straighten out their followers by protesting. People have a right to choose where they want to go to church. It is not your job to demean people, make fun of them, mock them, or belittle them. They are going to give account to God themselves (Rom. 14:12).

Notice also from 1 Cor. 1:22 that preaching rebukes worldly wisdom. When it comes to preaching, among others, the world says that preaching should be about how to have a happy marriage or how to be prosperous and financially secure.

Some preachers fall prey to the carnal demands of carnal Christians and try to teach through the Bible only on the topics that tickle people's ears. Along this road they then claim that God is obligated to bless them because they have followed some "formula" found in the scriptures.

Biblical preaching encourages the saint to focus on Heaven and eternity, not on the things in the world (Col. 3:1-3). God teaches spiritual things and they exceed the value of worldly things.

The Bible-believing preacher must be careful to avoid the modern attitude that says a church should address social issues. Getting involved in the community and politics has no place in the church. God's house was set apart for the worship of God, not to be a political vehicle. Many Christians and preachers honestly think, "If we can just get a Christian elected then things will be better for us." In all honesty the motive behind the concern of most Christians boils down to an attempt to protect their own prosperity. They simply use the "God factor" as an axis by which to sway things in their direction.

Never do we find the Lord Jesus Christ, the apostle Paul, or any of the twelve preaching on politics. Paul himself subjected himself to the powers that be (Rom. 13; Acts 25:11). Be careful. Examine your messages. Ask yourself, 'Am I preaching the Bible or making the Bible fit my political view, preference, prejudice, or for prosperity?'

4.   Biblical preaching should define the believer.

1 Cor 1:26-28

26 For ye see your calling, brethren, how that not many wise men after the flesh, not many mighty, not many noble, are called:

27 But God hath chosen the foolish things of the world to confound the wise; and God hath chosen the weak things of the world to confound the things which are mighty;

28 And base things of the world, and things which are despised, hath God chosen, yea, and things which are not, to bring to nought things that are:

Preaching will define what an individual is. It will define your family, it will define your friends, it will even define your enemies. This is taken for granted that you are in obedience to the preaching and you are doing what the Bible says.

5.   Biblical preaching should display God's glory.

1 Cor 1:29-31

29 That no flesh should glory in his presence.

30 But of him are ye in Christ Jesus, who of God is made unto us wisdom, and righteousness, and sanctification, and redemption:

31 That, according as it is written, He that glorieth, let him glory in the Lord.

The flesh is crucified in verse 29 and Christ is magnified in verse 31. A pulpit must have a preacher who is willing to preach but understands that he is to preach Jesus Christ. He should magnify the person of Christ, not the people or the preacher.

I know that this all sounds elementary. But think about how many sermons you hear that talk about everything under the sun without magnifying Christ.

6.  Preaching debases the preacher's knowledge.

1 Cor 2:1-2
1 And I, brethren, when I came to you, came not with excellency of speech or of wisdom, declaring unto you the testimony of God.
2 For I determined not to know any thing among you, save Jesus Christ, and him crucified.

True Bible preaching debases the preacher's knowledge. The Lord is not interested in how much you know about everything else. He is interested in how you know Him! Biblical preaching will manifest the wisdom of God over the preacher's wisdom.

7.  Preaching debases the preacher's personal strength.

1 Cor 2:3 And I was with you in weakness, and in fear, and in much trembling.

When we are in the pulpit as preachers, we are preaching under the power of His might, His strength, and we are not relying on our ability, but on Him. If we are not preaching by His power we are missing the mark.

8.   Preaching debases the preacher's boldness.

1 Cor 2:4 And my speech and my preaching was not with enticing words of man's wisdom, but in demonstration of the Spirit and of power:

Sometimes biblical preaching can be mimicked by someone who has a gift or ability as an orator. Some preachers are simply good actors. This can sometimes be faked by those who have the ability to carry on conversation and tell stories, but it is not God's power. You know this because, even though the people might like it, it does nothing for them spiritually.

9.   Preaching will debase the hearer.

1 Cor 2:5 That your faith should not stand in the wisdom of men, but in the power of God.

The only way I know for the foregoing to take place, is for us as preachers to be anchored in the Book. As a preacher you are basically asking your flock to subject themselves to you spiritually. And it will be much easier for them to subject themselves to you if they know that you are subjected to the Bible and that it is the final authority in all matters of faith and practice. The Book comes before the preacher. If it is not the authority, then there really is no point in preaching and anyone's opinion is just as valid as yours.

The Bible is not subjective authority, but rather, it is the authority even when it shows where and when we are wrong. God established the church this way so we wouldn't fall prey to what the Israelites did in the book of Judges—"every man did that which was right in his own eyes" (Judges 21:25).

# THINGS TO ASK YOURSELF ABOUT YOUR PREACHING

1. Does it enlighten the intellect?

In other words, does it teach something? Do they learn something about the Lord that they didn't know before?

2. Does it stir the emotion?

Is there enough fire in the pulpit, enough excitement in the pulpit for people to sense that you believe what you are saying? We get excited about everything under the sun except when it comes to spiritual matters. People get loud at ball games; they get emotional at funerals, when they are in arguments, and even when they are passionate about their political opinions. Preaching should not be "starchy." If you believe what you are saying, preach like it! If you were in a public building and there was a fire, you wouldn't whisper in a monotone—"Fire." You would yell it at the top of your lungs— "F-I-R-E!!!" As a preacher you can't be afraid to get outside of yourself for Him and His glory!

3. Does it move the will to a decision?

A preacher is trying to get the people to see things God's way. The preacher is trying to get across a message that is important, that invokes a decision. Preaching should make the people think about the point of the message and what they are going to do about that point.

2 Cor 5:11 Knowing therefore the terror of the Lord, we persuade men...

4. Does it have a direction?

Preaching must have a point. The message must not be random thoughts that are not woven together without a purpose. The thoughts or points within the message should be integrated along the same general theme of the message.

5. Does it nourish and strengthen the sheep?

Does your message puff up the sheep and make them feel good about themselves because they don't commit some of the sins you preach about? Or does it edify them and encourage them? Does it feed them the word of God by which they are corrected and instructed (2 Tim. 3:16)?

6. Does it pull or draw them closer to Christ?

Does your preaching draw people closer to Jesus or push them further away from Him? The preaching is not to draw people to the preacher or the preacher's convictions, but to Jesus Christ.

# HARSH PREACHING

Too often preachers stomp on other people in order to maintain their own position. Maybe they were never leaders in any other profession before becoming a pastor, so they have some insecurities, and they relieve those insecurities by belittling others in order to make themselves look big.

As pastors, we must be strong enough to avoid stepping on others, but in turn allowing others to step on us in order that they may get to the top of the hill. This is illustrated by the story of two goats that were coming and going down a mountain trail. The narrow trail left absolutely no room for both goats to pass each other, and seeing

there was a large ravine below, the larger, older goat coming down the mountain laid down allowing the younger goat to walk over him and continue up to the top.

The Lord Jesus Christ laid down His life, thus making it possible for us to get to where He came from. As preachers we must remember that our primary job is to be servants! We must allow them if necessary to use us and abuse us if it will result in them getting closer to Jesus Christ. It is not about us winning the battle in the here and now, but where they will wind up in the hereafter.

## ALL JUDGMENT; NO LOVE

If you had visited our church in the early years and heard me preach, you probably would have said, "There is no way I am coming back to hear that man again!" I preached and taught the Bible like a policeman training recruits. It was good for some because it kept them from the horrors of sin, but it was bad for others. Over time the Lord has helped me become more balanced and, I hope, become a better pastor. My problem was that I preached nothing more than judgment and condemnation. Nearly every sermon was about God's wrath and judgment and the wickedness of sin. I preached hard and harshly, to the point that people might have gotten the idea from my preaching that God hated them. When I began to preach people probably thought, "I wonder what God is mad at me about today." My police background didn't help matters. I saw firsthand the results of sin and so I constantly pounded sin so hard and I never showed the other side of God—His love, mercy, and grace.

As a policeman, I was paid to find bad behavior in people. They never paid me to write tickets to people who were doing good. This transferred itself into the pulpit and in a matter of time I could spot the Christians who were not "up to par." After I identified my "target," I would get out the sniper scope and put it on my Bible, using the pulpit as a rifle rest and then I could pick off individuals during

the preaching. The ones who were getting shot didn't particularly like it, while the ones who were not in the crosshairs enjoyed it. Some would "A-men" and others would "O-me." I can only pray that those who were hurt while I was learning can forgive my inexperience and stupidity.

The Lord finally dealt with me about how I was portraying Him and convinced me to start preaching the other attributes of God as well—His mercy, longsuffering, and love. I was pretty hard. I had no tears. I thought it was somewhat effeminate to cry because of the things I had seen and done. I was molded into a soldier's mentality and it was transferring itself over to the congregation.

This was a difficult change for me to make. I had a reputation of being known as a judgment preacher that would gut everyone as he preached. My type of preaching used intimidation to get results. This is often a bad mistake many preachers and pastors make. Putting people through a "guilt trip" might get a large altar call at the end of the service but if it is not Holy Ghost conviction, it will not last. Using God's Bible to strong-arm people into a decision is not biblical and gives the wrong impression of God and preaching.

The Lord used the story of the prodigal son to show me how I was misrepresenting the image of God. When the son finally came home, did the father kick him in the teeth? Did the father reject him? Did he cast him away from his presence? Did he alienate him? Did he restore him to a lower position? No. He restored him to the place he was before, as his son. He had mercy and compassion!

So, when I began to turn this corner with the Lord, many of my messages were now focused on the love of God and the grace of God. I would preach on God's goodness and His longsuffering. Many of my "soldier" preacher friends now called me a compromiser. They claimed that I had "gone soft."

I learned that my reputation in the eyes of other preachers was not what was important. What was important was what God thought about me and that I was preaching His word as He would have me

preach it. I began to realize that I could reach people more with a towel in my hand (John 13) than with a sword, trying to force them into subjection.

I believe in hard judgment preaching at the right time and in its right format. I don't believe in presenting God as a God of love to the extent that the balanced side of God is not understood. However, if we force people into submission, we are doing no more than putting them in prison and making them conform outwardly. Inwardly they are screaming, "I want out!" Their service is not willing, but forced. If service is forced, eventually it will lead to bitterness (Ex. 1:14) and the person will not be able to stand when things get tough. They will quit because their heart is not in it.

# GLOOM-AND-DOOM PREACHING

Many pastors have developed this dig in, foxhole, hang on until the rapture mentality. People who are not Bible believers do not understand Murphy's Law: "Cheer up, things are going to get worse." They really don't want to hear, "Now that you are saved things are really going to get bad," especially every single Sunday. And although preaching about political espionage, nuclear holocaust, and financial crashes might be true, it wears on the ears when you hear it week in and week out.

Preaching and teaching with this attitude is like sitting kids down and telling them horror stories of how bad things are going to be when they get older instead of letting them enjoy the sunshine and growing up.

It's not good to preach all gloom and doom. The world is going to come to an end; there is a fire in the basement. I believe that one hundred percent. I believe the judgment of God is coming. I believe the rapture could take place very soon. But, now that I know all those things, what should I do? Go in the foxholes, get my helmet on, gather all my foodstuffs, close the door and sit in the bomb shelter until the

Lord comes back? No! I am to serve the Lord and enjoy my salvation and the life that God has given me.

You don't have to preach "the sky is falling" every sermon. If you do, then your people will tend to watch current events just as much as they read their Bibles and walk with Jesus Christ. They will have a tendency to be glued to the newspapers and the T.V. more than to the scriptures. I'm not looking for the Antichrist. I'm not trying to find out who the Antichrist is so I can determine when the Lord is going to come back. I'm looking for Jesus Christ:

> Titus 2:13 Looking for that blessed hope, and the glorious appearing of the great God and our Saviour Jesus Christ;

This gloom-and-doom preaching can cause people to get distracted and in turn it stagnates the growth of the people.

If your church has grown stagnant, the best thing to do is to give them a good meal. You will be surprised how well fresh water and fresh bread will solve many problems.

## BALANCED PREACHING

There is a big difference between forcing people into subjection and drawing them (John 6:44) into willing submission. Unbalanced false preaching gives a lopsided view of God. Bible-believing groups tend to lean toward the hard, judgmental side of things without emphasizing God's love, mercy, and understanding.

A good way to keep balance is to ask yourself how God has treated you. Has He been merciful to you? Has He been gracious and longsuffering with you? None of us has fully experienced God's judgment for what we have done. To the contrary, we have been over-showered with His love, mercy, and grace! He has been merciful to all of us!

It is not a sign of weakness to show the other side of God. For example, my wife and I have been married for over thirty years. If my wife stayed married to me only because she was concerned what people might think about her if she was divorced, or just because she was afraid she might lose the house, or because of how people might treat her as a divorcee, I would rather not be married to her. If the only reason my wife comes home at night is because she is worried about getting caught doing something else, if she is not coming home because she loves me, I would rather not be married to her. I want her to come home because she loves me, not because she is forced into being there. If she is forced into being there, the moment that threat is taken away she will be gone.

When it comes to our relationship to Jesus Christ, it is right to fear Him. But your relationship must grow beyond fear into love. I'm not preaching because I'm afraid He is going to backhand me if I don't. I preach because I love Jesus Christ and I am grateful that He gave me an opportunity to serve Him. I do fear Him, but I do not serve Him out of fear. I serve Him because I love Him. I stay married to my wife because I love her. It is not a duty or an obligation.

If preaching becomes a duty or an obligation it will transfer into your preaching. Your congregation will sense the bitterness in your heart if you view yourself as a slave, not a servant. A slave is someone who has no other choice but to obey. A servant receives the same command, but he obeys because he wants to and because he loves his master.

When you are preaching, what is the people's perception of God? We must remember that every time we preach, we paint a picture of the Lord.

## THE PREACHER'S TARGET

When you preach, it is important to know what your target is. All too often preachers appeal to the intellect. Preaching to

the head is okay, but it must always be tempered with the heart. Preaching on current events, politics, or social ills that are going on in the world generally aims at the head instead of the heart. Too much preaching to the head leads to an enlarging of the head, a bigger hat for the head, and a bigger door in order to get the head out! Intellectual preaching pleases the people because it makes them feel educated, wise, and smart. The heart is the governor of the head, not the other way around. Affections are seated in the heart, not the head.

## PREACHING ON MOVEMENTS

Currently, there is a movement called the Constitutional Movement where preachers preach all about "the people" and the people's rights in the U.S.A. This humanistic type of preaching exalts the people and inadvertently demotes Jesus Christ. This type of political preaching is very appealing because no one likes to be ruled over. However, the scriptures teach that we are to be in subjection to the government and authorities, whether we agree with their policies or not (Rom. 13:1-7; 1 Peter 2:7). I know that the Bible trumps the government, but not until they tell us we can't preach Jesus Christ and Him crucified. A good rule of thumb to govern yourself by is to ask yourself if you could preach that sermon anywhere else in the world.

## PREACHING TO THE INTELLECT

When we preach to the head, often we invent a list of "do's and don'ts." I know that God is a God of order, but frequently we expect compliance immediately after one sermon. Think about it. You didn't get things right with the Lord immediately, so why do you expect others to do so? People must have time to think and there must be time for the Lord to work in their hearts.

We must not teach people that the way to God is through outward conformity. I do believe in standards, but often they are our preferences more than God's standard. When people do conform to a set of standards, they are no closer to God, and then they become disappointed and disillusioned. They think, "Well, I did this and this and this, but where is God?" The fact is, God is not found in the performing of a duty. He is found in a relationship, not in a religion.

Preaching to the head is something that can create outward conformity. And because people want God, they will have a tendency to do whatever you tell them to do in order to "obtain" God. If we allow the Lord Jesus Christ to have His way in their hearts, it will result in outward conformity according to the time frame to which the Lord would have them conform. Let the Lord work on them from the inside out. Be glad that they are still interested in church and are coming to hear the word of God. Let Him change them in His time.

# PREACHING TO THE STOMACH

Much preaching done from the pulpit today is what I call "diet gospels." Preaching how to lose weight or how to be healthy, in my opinion, has no place in the pulpit. Preachers are simply following the way of the world by promoting and marketing health ideas because it is the big craze today. Since there is a "market" for these things, preachers go into the Bible and preach their particular "snake oil" or cure-all. And the sheep flock to them by the thousands. The best way to preach diet is by example and lose the "preacher's profile."

This modern-day preaching according to "fads" appeals to the flesh. Preachers think they are doing "God's will" because they are "helping people." I mean, after all, wouldn't God want them to know how to lose weight, or look ten years younger?

While these things may work and may be true, God has called us to preach the gospel of Jesus Christ. He hasn't called us to be dieticians.

We are not called to placate the needs of the people. We are called to preach the Bible. Unless you are a doctor, please remember there is a responsibility, and even liability and repercussions, to giving people dietary or medical advice.

# PREACHING ON THE GOSPEL OF 'DO'

Many Churches can be likened to a football game where you have seventy to eighty thousand people cheering for a few dozen players on the field. The folks cheering are enjoying the game but they are only watching; they are not participating.

If you are a pastor or missionary you must realize that when you accepted the call to the ministry you accepted the responsibility of bearing the majority of the load and burden of the church. God knew you had in your character the ability to bear the load that would accompany the ministry – namely, doing things that others refuse or don't see the need to do.

As pastors we must be careful not to get bitter with some of the menial tasks (especially if you have a smaller church) and therefore manifesting that bitterness in our preaching and pastoring. It is easy to preach the gospel of "do's and don'ts," particularly when it takes some of the pressure off of us. Getting people to do things that they may not be comfortable with or ready to do, may give them a false sense of spirituality. If they are pressured to go on visitation or teach a Sunday school class, then they may think that they are a better Christian than those who don't do those things.

People can be right with God and not be called to do certain things. The hand cannot do the same thing that the head can do. If we force the hand to become the head, we are asking it to do something that will only frustrate it. It does not have the ability to be the head. It can remain a hand and only do that which the hand does, and in doing so remain confident and comfortable. If, however, we say, "We need a foot" so we ask the hand to support the weight of

the body, the hand will be misused, bruised, battered, and eventually worn out.

What pastor truly knows which position his church members possess? It is a dangerous thing for a pastor to identify those positions because of personal opinion and perception. Our senses are as sinful and corrupt as anyone's. The object is for the church members to find the place God has for them in the body. If they happen to be an ear, where all they do is sit and listen, that's what they need to do. If someday the Lord tells them to be more of a "mouth" or a "hand", then they will be getting their orders from the Lord.

# PREACHING TO THE HEART

Heb 4:12 For the word of God is quick, and powerful, and sharper than any two edged sword, piercing even to the dividing asunder of soul and spirit, and of the joints and marrow, and is a discerner of the thoughts and intents of the heart.

Preaching that is aimed at the heart will fix the head. The relationship with the Lord is developed in the heart. Getting the word in the heart is how a person discovers what God likes and doesn't like. God is more interested in the vertical sins against Him than the horizontal sins against man.

It is the sins against God that send a person to Hell, not sins against his fellow man. If all we preach are sermons on how to treat your fellow man or how to have a happy marriage, or how to be financially successful, we may get people to conform on the outside, but have we helped their relationship with Jesus Christ?

Too often man is venerated and worshiped more than Jesus Christ. When we preach sermons that are focused on the outward sins to our fellow man, we are saying in effect that how we treat man is more important than how we treat God. We must put Jesus

first above all things. The acronym "JOY" stands for "Jesus, Others, You." Your relationship with Jesus Christ is not dependent on how you treat others. It may sound like a very good philosophy. Some think that if they can just get people into church, they can change the community, the city, the county, the country, and eventually the world. But the purpose of biblical preaching is not to change the community; it is to change the heart of man toward God. If as a result the community changes, that is great, but today too many are focused on changing the outside in order to make a better society.

The focus of a preacher's preaching is not to clean up a drunkard. It is to get the man's heart in line with God and hope that God will give him the victory over the sin that he struggles with. If we are honest, we look down on some that have not gained the victory over some of the outward sins (like drinking) while at the same time concealing our easy-to-hide sins like covetousness and murmuring, bitterness and gossip.

Preach to the heart first. If God gets their heart, He will take care of the rest. Just leave it up to Him.

# KEEPING IT SIMPLE

Sometimes as preachers we make messages too complicated for those who are listening. We forget that we have been studying the passage all week long, and then we expect the congregation to understand what has taken us a week to understand. Don't be intimidated by the simplicity of the gospel and by preaching sermons that are easy and simple for your people to understand and apply. A practical, easy to understand, usable message will stick with folks longer than an intellectual discussion.

# STICK TO THE POINT

Preaching should be for the purpose of turning people from darkness to light; from Satan to God. It should not be centered on the things of this world. It should persuade them to repent of their sins and turn to God.

Acts 26:18-20

18 To open their eyes, and to turn them from darkness to light, and from the power of Satan unto God, that they may receive forgiveness of sins, and inheritance among them which are sanctified by faith that is in me.

19 Whereupon, O king Agrippa, I was not disobedient unto the heavenly vision:

20 But shewed first unto them of Damascus, and at Jerusalem, and throughout all the coasts of Judaea, and then to the Gentiles, that they should repent and turn to God, and do works meet for repentance.

Preaching must be devoid of our own ideas or our own thoughts, otherwise we seek to control people by what we think they should be instead of what God says they should be. We then become, for all practical purposes, God to them, instead of letting God be God to them. They, in turn, develop a relationship with us, instead of developing a relationship with Him. The last time I checked, we can't save anyone from Hell.

Biblical preaching is not propagating your personal pet peeves, politics, preferences, or prejudices. If you focus on the simplicity of the gospel and salvation, and then attempt to help them in their Christian walk after they are saved, you will be surprised how it will take care of a multitude of sins and problems.

# TOO NEGATIVE

Don't spend so much time magnifying the sin that it seems greater and larger than the Lord. If you magnify the Lord, it will contrast properly with the sin.

If you were diagnosed with cancer and sat down with the doctor and all he said was "You have cancer, and cancer is bad; cancer eats away at you like Pac-Man. Cancer can lead to a horrible death; cancer is terrible," you will leave feeling like you had no hope and not even any options. Sometimes our preaching is like that. We hammer into people's heads how bad and rotten sin is but we don't offer any cure; we don't offer any hope or remedy for the sin. I am not saying that we are not to point out the disease (which is sin). But what I am saying is that we magnify the solution (Christ) more than the sin. After you expose sin, you must give the solution. The blood of Jesus Christ is the answer for both lost and saved!

If you spend all your time on the negatives (blasting this and condemning that), the sheep will not grow right. All condemnation and no praise is not a proper balance.

Yes, you should preach against sin; yes, you should condemn the things that are wrong. Sometimes you have to preach hard truths, but you must do it in love, not anger or hate. You must remember that if it wasn't for God's grace you might have fallen into the same sins that some of your people have fallen in to.

Jesus preached on Hell, but He spoke about it with a broken heart and in love. He was not glad that people were going to hell. He was concerned and compassionate and preaches it because he didn't want people to go there.

# MAD OR GLAD?

I heard a preacher say once that sometimes preachers preach like a gorilla whose last banana has been stolen. They preach like

they are mad at the world and even mad at the sheep God has called them to pastor. I heard a man preach on Hell one time and it seemed from the way that he preached that he didn't care if people went to Hell and he was even somewhat glad that they were going. He might have been preaching the truth, but he wasn't preaching it in love.

The object of preaching is to preach Jesus Christ and Him crucified. Jesus Christ is the answer, not our churches, sermons, or programs. The Bible is the answer, not us. The Bible and the Lord Jesus Christ must be magnified, not us or our solutions.

When you preach, stick to the simplicity of the gospel.

# PERSONAL PREACHING AND CONFRONTATION

You will notice in Acts 26 when Paul preached to Agrippa and the leaders present that he said nothing at all about their personal sins, their families, their marriages or their finances. He preached Jesus Christ. So you wouldn't think that he would receive a negative reaction. But because the gospel is the living word, it causes confrontation.

If you preach the gospel, there will be confrontation, and if confrontation comes, it should come because of the power of the gospel, not because of our foolishness. A good sermon should present the Lord Jesus Christ, and those listening will have to face Him, not you.

# HANDLING CONFRONTATION

Do not take it personally when someone becomes confrontational when you are preaching the gospel. It is not you who offend but the Holy Spirit inside of you and the word of God. Don't feel persecuted to the point that you are so offended you quit or give up. They are not rejecting you but the Lord.

# FALSE GUILT

Preaching that purposely attempts to embarrass or cause guilt is not Holy Ghost preaching. If someone comes into your church improperly attired, and you change your message and aim it at them, you have ceased preaching. When we preach so pointedly that a person knows we are talking about him, we offend him to the point that he will probably never come back. You say, "Yeah, but it was the truth." There are several ways to present the truth to a person and the best way is to present Jesus Christ.

It is one thing to be called in by your boss at the office and get reprimanded for poor work performance, and quite another thing for him to call you out in front of all your co-workers. He might get a response from you, but he will have lost your respect for him.

If people feel alienated or picked on when we preach, it will cause them to put up a wall and be confrontational. If people feel ostracized, they will not feel comfortable and will not listen to the message.

# THE USE OF ILLUSTRATIONS

Acts 26:25 But he said, I am not mad, most noble Festus; but speak forth the words of truth and soberness.

It is fine and good to use some humor when you are preaching, but not the entire time. It is great to use illustrations, but not for the entire sermon. The sermon gets the power of God from the words of God, not from humorous illustrations. Humor and illustrations help the congregation remember the words of God and sometimes help relax the listener, but they shouldn't overpower the Bible. Power doesn't come from volume or delivery, it comes from speaking the words of God. Paul didn't tell animal stories, fables, or fairy tales; he gave them the word of God.

## STAYING FOCUSED

Paul preached publicly (Acts 26:26). He did this because the gospel was not given to be hidden but to be shared. We are not here as a conspiracy to hide from the government or city officials. We are not here to change laws or sign petitions; we exist to publicly declare the gospel. Our doors are open in our churches for visitors to come freely. We have nothing up our sleeves, nothing to hide; our testimony is open as a witness for God.

## THE CONCLUSION AND INVITATION

Acts 26:27 King Agrippa, believest thou the prophets? I know that thou believest.

Paul didn't just preach and quit. He preached and brought his sermon to a conclusion and invitation. There is a reason Paul said all that he said. Now he put the pressure on Agrippa to respond to what was said.

After all the preaching, after all that sweat and persuading, Paul asked Agrippa, and Agrippa said, "Almost thou persuadest me..." He was not convinced. Paul did his job and the ball was in Agrippa's court.

Preaching should cause those that listen either to accept or to reject the message. If people reject the gospel you shouldn't take it personally or become angry. They are rejecting the Lord, not you.

## SUGGESTIONS ON WHAT TO KEEP OUT OF THE PULPIT

As a preacher and a pastor, you need to be very careful not to vent your aggravations, frustrations, and disappointments from the pulpit. If you need to vent, call a friend in the ministry (someone not in your church) or another pastor friend. You will get depressed and

discouraged and you will sometimes need an ear to talk to. Sometimes you will get "fighting mad" because you are pouring your life into people and will find that they will pull your heart out, throw it on the ground, stomp on it, and leave. That is the ministry. But be careful not to take your frustrations out during your preaching because, chances are, many listening have nothing to do with the problem anyway, especially visitors. And they don't understand the pressures that are associated with the ministry anyway. If visitors come in, or others that are trying to serve the Lord, and you say, "Well, nobody is here today. I guess nobody wants the truth. What's the point of my preparing a message when no one shows up at church?" they probably will not stay long because no one wants to board a sinking ship. I'm not saying that every time you preach you should be like someone who sugarcoats everything to the point of lying. But I'm saying that you need to be balanced, and part of that means being careful in bringing your personal frustrations into the pulpit.

## UNDERNOURISHING THE SHEEP

Sometimes I think problems in the church are not caused because the sheep are out of line and wicked. I think sometimes they are simply malnourished and that causes them to pick on one another and cause problems.

I have found that those who are successful in the ministry for a number of years (say, forty to fifty) have a common thread: they consistently and continually feed the sheep. And by feeding them the sheep naturally grow. When natural growth takes place, they will not become stale. Sheep are happiest when they are fed.

# *The* MINISTRY

A church must have the proper foundation. Modern ministries build their churches not how God would have them to be built but like businesses. God's church was originally built on the foundation of Jesus Christ, through biblical preaching.

> 1 Cor 3:11 For other foundation can no man lay than that is laid, which is Jesus Christ.

> Rom 16:25 Now to him that is of power to establish you according to my gospel, and the preaching of Jesus Christ...

This is sometimes easier said than done, especially when you, the pastor, are hit with the pressures of trying to be what the world or other ministries consider a success. Some ministries judge success by the attendance at your church, the offering amount, the number of missionaries your church supports, how many "ministries" (jail ministries, visitation, and so on) you have. In other words, they consider the success of your church to be something they can see with their eyes.

When the Lord led us to start a new work, we didn't have the finances to do all the things people would think necessary to be called a church. We began with family and friends, and that was it. It

was later on, as the Lord grew our congregation both spiritually and numerically that we could add particular ministries as He led.

It is important to understand that churches should be developed by preaching.

> 1 Cor 1:21 For after that in the wisdom of God the world by wisdom knew not God, it pleased God by the foolishness of preaching to save them that believe.

The modern church has been built on everything but preaching. And what little preaching does take place has been perverted to the point that philosophical ideas, humanism, and psychology dominate the majority of the messages.

You must understand that what you use to draw people to your church must continue to be used in order to keep them. If your ministry is built on carnal programs or "self-help" type of ministries, the type of people that will gravitate toward your church will not stay around if you begin to preach the Bible. On the other hand, if you begin with the foundation of biblical preaching, and keep the emphasis on the preaching of the word of God, the people that come will come for the right reasons.

## THE PASTOR'S AUTHORITY

The last thing our churches need are pastoral popes vaunting themselves above the Bible. I believe the Bible is the authority and the "go-to" book for every answer. I don't believe the preacher is the answer. Some pastors think that because they have been called to preach they have been imparted with some special wisdom that gives them the right to determine direction in people's personal lives. The pastor's authority ends with spiritual matters. Just because he is a preacher does not give him the wisdom or the right to choose whom you marry, what kind of car you buy, or whether or not you

should take a job promotion. Unless you want the responsibility and repercussions that come with these discussions, you might want to stay out of them and let God direct them.

# BUILT ON THE BOOK

When a new Bible-believing work is started, it normally has its inception in one of three ways. It will be founded on one man, around some people who have gathered, or on the Bible itself. If its foundation is anything other than the Bible, then you open yourself up to strife and contention. Eventually something will happen to cause authority to be questioned. If the foundation is a man or personal opinion, you will have no recourse when you are brought into question.

If the ministry is founded on the Bible, and the party chooses to reject what the Book says, then that is their choice, but your foundation remains the same. One of the most detrimental things that can happen to a pastor is a split in the church. It can ruin him and make him bitter. It can hurt the man and his family to the point that he quits the ministry for good. Even if the church is founded on the Book, it is certainly no guarantee against a split, but I do believe it will lessen the fall out.

# COMPROMISE

Compromise justifies itself by the adage—"If it brings more people in, it must be okay." But keep in mind that whatever you use to get people to come to church, you must continue to implement in order to keep them coming. Bob Jones, Sr. often stated that "It is never right to do wrong in order to get a chance to do right."

So, when the pressure to produce results is bearing down on you and you begin to doubt the promise of God, you need to ask yourself if you want an Isaac or an Ishmael. Do you want an Isaac after God's blessing or an Ishmael after your own making?

Notice in Genesis 3:5 that this mentality leads one to become independent of God. After a pastor compromises, he falls into the trap of no longer asking God for direction. Instead he simply asks other preachers, reads a book by a successful pastor, or gets ideas from the Internet. His preaching then strays from straight, hard, biblical preaching to "feel-good" sermons in order to keep people attending. He doesn't ask God what the people need anymore; instead he gives them what they want. He reasons that he knows "his people" and can give them what they need. All the while he is rejecting God's will and God's method for biblical pastoring and preaching.

The decisions of this pastor who thinks independently of God are based on fleshly choices and things that are important to him, not God (Genesis 3:6). He bases things on his own heart, which is deceitful and wicked ( Jer. 17:9).

The next stage in this deceitful paradigm concerns seeking confirmation with other people. Eve gave the fruit to Adam. She didn't want to be deceived alone. Pastors who compromise and leave the old paths will seek fellowship with other compromisers, not true Bible believers. Their mentality changes from staying with the old paths to following the new and modern way.

The ridicule and pressure from the world might be removed, but they instantly begin making excuses (Genesis 3:8-13) for their compromising ministry. If you see these steps as found in Genesis 3 taking place in your own life and ministry, you simply must return to your roots and reestablish the foundation that has been laid.

# RECOGNITION

If you do what God tells you to do, it matters little if the world recognizes you. You should not look to the world for approval, anyway, because the world doesn't understand what you are trying to do. Your measuring stick is God Almighty. As long as He is pleased with your preaching and your ministry, that is all that matters.

Whether or not anyone else is pleased or recognizes you means nothing.

I have some friends in the ministry who have very small churches. Sometimes they get discouraged because they are doing everything they know to do, they are preaching the gospel, they are trying to get people saved and in church, but the church just simply doesn't grow. If that is the case for you, I simply want to encourage you not to be "weary in well doing" (Gal. 6:9). Sometimes it takes years of people watching you to see if your actions line up with your words, especially in small rural communities. It might take a while for people to warm up to you to the point that they will have confidence in what you are saying.

## BEING PATIENT

There is a danger of getting into such a hurry that you push people because of your zeal when they are not ready. If you are patient and will allow people to watch you year after year, you may find that your words may have more gravity and weight when they come to realize you are no longer an outsider, but one of them. Consistency is the best testimony.

A good example of this is found in 1 Peter 3, in which the wife of an unsaved husband is told to lead by a meek and quiet life in submission to him and God. The passage teaches that she is more likely to win him that way than if she tries to "cram it down his throat," so to speak. People are going to have to see how we live first before they will listen to what we say.

## WHEN TO START A CHURCH

It is very important not only that you are called into the ministry, but that you follow the Lord's timing in that ministry. If you have been called to begin a new work, not only should you begin at the

right location, you should know when to begin it. Most of us have learned from experience if we get ahead of the Lord things will not work out.

I would like to use my own example to help you in this matter.

My wife and I had been attending church faithfully, but that church had drifted away from the authority of the word of God (KJV). The more we grew in our faith and understood the importance of the Bible, the more we saw that this church was not established on the Bible, but on men and tradition. We soon thought it best to leave the church and try to find one that believed in the authority of the King James Bible. We left quietly without stirring up trouble.

On Sunday mornings I began teaching my family and a few others, and on Sunday night or Wednesday night we would visit churches that professed to be Bible-believing churches. Since I was still a policeman working shift work, my wife would call the pastors and ask them specific questions about what they believed. After narrowing down the list, we would visit the church and listen to see if it was a place where we could be fed the word of God.

During this time the Lord began to deal with me about pastoring. I had already surrendered to preach years before but I did not want to be a pastor. I had no desire to start a church. I enjoyed being a policeman and being able to preach on the side, but I didn't want the ridicule and responsibility of being a pastor. We would visit some of these churches and sometimes stay for a while but would soon discover that they really didn't believe what they professed to believe. We were having conflict in our life because we couldn't justify attending a church that didn't believe what we believed. We rode this roller coaster for a while until we faced the fact that there was no place for us to go and feel comfortable and confident that we were following the Lord.

So, we continued meeting on Sunday morning (all eight of us) and I would basically teach the Bible. I did this under the presumption that we would not start a church until the Lord brought us a pastor. I still didn't want to pastor. I was a preacher and a teacher but not a pastor.

Some time passed and it wasn't long before the Lord said, "I think I have found a pastor for you." 'I said "Wonderful, who is it?"' The Lord said, "Look in the mirror." There was a need and a necessity but the need did not dictate my decision. God had called me and through a process of time showed me clearly that He wanted me to be a pastor.

I knew how to be a policeman, but I didn't know how to be pastor. I knew how to be a teacher, but I didn't know how to pastor a church. The need was so great and the burden so heavy on my heart to the point that I couldn't condone or send anyone to a church where I knew the church didn't believe right. The Lord tapped me on the shoulder and said, "You're it."

Now over the past twenty years the Lord has developed the pastor part of me, but I wasn't a pastor in the beginning.

If you are convinced that you need a church and there is no place for you to attend without compromising, and that God has called you to preach His word, maybe it is incumbent on you to accept the responsibilities of starting a ministry.

## THE TIMING IN STARTING A CHURCH

If you ask, "When do I begin a new work?", the answer is, when God shows you the need for the work where you are. We had a saying in police work: "You are guilty by association," which simply meant that if you were present with someone engaged in a crime, you would be punished along with the culprit. So if you align yourself with someone who is not a Bible believer, then you are guilty by being joined to that church.

You need to exercise wisdom in these matters. Don't leave a Bible believing church over nitpicking things. We don't need more King James churches that are divided over minute differences. If you are not called to preach and you are attending a Bible believing work, then the best thing for you to do is to submit to your pastor and stay in the church.

Starting a church is much like raising a child. There will be a natural progression and the Lord will teach you how to do things as you grow. Just as most of us are better grandparents than we were parents, so it will be in the ministry. The more experience you get, the more you will look back and say, "I can't believe I did such and such!" Never be afraid to ask those who have been in the ministry for a long time for their counsel and advice. It may save you some heartache along the way.

## THE APPEARANCE OF THE CHURCH BUILDING

The appearance of your church, on the outside as well as the inside, is an important truth that is often overlooked. It does make a difference how people perceive your church when they come in the door. They will come to what they see first, before they will come for what they think they will hear.

Let me illustrate it this way. When you travel and decide to stop for the night, the first thing you do is look at the exterior of the motel where you are considering staying. If the outside looks dirty and not well kept you will probably never go inside. This applies to a doctor's office or other professional offices and even restaurants. Before you ever taste the food you look at the place where it is served. You make a natural connection between the appearance and cleanliness of the place where the food is served and the quality of the food served.

Please do not misunderstand what I am saying. I'm not saying that our churches have to look like ornate temples. I'm saying that your church should be clean, neat, and well kept so that when people visit for the first time they will not be turned off by the appearance. You don't want your visitors uneasy before they even sit down or walk into the church.

Remember, we are asking these people to trust us with their souls. But if we cannot maintain the place where we are meeting, they are

not going to have confidence in us. Choosing a pastor and a church is the most important decision a person will make outside of salvation and marriage.

Some churches have the mentality that their houses should be well kept with new updates, but the church should always look for a deal and just be bland. This mentality takes the emphasis and importance off of God and places it on ourselves.

When we first began, we rented a room in a building that was only about fifteen by fifteen. We met in this room for several months. Every time we finished we cleaned it so that the next time we met it would be ready and no one would feel uncomfortable. It wasn't big, and it wasn't pretty, but at least it was clean.

If the shrubbery outside needs pruning, prune it. If the carpet needs vacuuming, vacuum it. If the doors need painting, paint them. If people see that the church is taken care of aesthetically, they won't be as suspicious about whether or not you can watch for their souls. People do make preconceived judgments based on outer appearance. This is seen in the courtroom. I used to be a detective in sex crimes – a horrible job, by the way. These perverts that we would catch would not come to the courtroom unshaven with shabby clothes on. They would appear in suits as respectable, fine looking business people. They did this so the jury's first impression would be a good one. You don't want to rise above the culture of the area God has called you. Then you would be like a Pharisee. But you don't want to go below it, either. There is a balance to all of this.

## THE ATTITUDE OF THE CONGREGATION

How you as a pastor and your people appear and act toward visitors is very important. I know of some churches and pastors where their attitude is a "take it or leave it" one. They don't care what they look like, how friendly they are or what kind of first impression they give to newcomers. When their churches remain small, they

think it is because "people just don't want the truth" when it is in fact because they never felt like you were the ones to give them the truth.

You don't want to turn someone off to what you say based on your appearance and attitude. There is nothing wrong with being friendly and kind. This approach of "if they want the truth it doesn't matter what our church looks like" will not take you far. That mentality prevents people who might receive the truth from ever having the opportunity. They are immediately turned off by this ogre who says, "I don't care what you think about me."

# A LEVEL OF CONFIDENCE

If you need surgery, you don't go to a butcher; you go to a professional in the field who deals with the type of surgery you need. You have never seen them do surgery but you are willing to be put to sleep and cut on. Why? You are confident in what they have told you. They have a reputation of competence.

When people come to church, you are asking them to let down their guard and open up so you can do spiritual surgery on them. And this kind of surgery is more invasive than physical surgery. If you fail to show competence, you will not gain the trust and respect of those under your care.

Competence can be shown through compassion and concern. You must realize that you are asking these people to trust you with their eternal souls, so you must be willing to gain their trust, and that takes time.

When they evaluate you, will they think you are a butcher or a surgeon who can operate with exacting precision? Are you the type of preacher and pastor who amputates or heals?

# A LEVEL OF COMPETENCE

If you are not competent, people are not going to trust you. For example, if I was sitting in an airplane getting ready for departure and the pilot came on the intercom saying that he had never flown a plane before but it wouldn't be a problem because it is much like a flight simulator, I would be nervous, to say the least, and most likely leave the plane.

I daresay if you spoke to a surgeon just prior to surgery and he told you that he used to be a veterinarian and has never operated on a person before, you would get up and walk out of the hospital.

It is the same way when people come into our churches. People want to feel that they can trust us enough to let down their guard and listen without worrying that you are lying to them. We should be familiar enough with the Bible and sound Bible doctrine that we can discuss and explain it thoroughly. I am not saying that you should be cocky or arrogant, but simply confident and competent. You should know what the Lord would have you preach and teach, and you should be authoritative enough that people know you believe what you are saying.

We should also be transparent to a degree, and honest. If you make a mistake you should be able to publicly own up to it to your people. Some pastors are afraid and ashamed to admit that they have made mistakes. I can't tell you how many mistakes I've made. I've made enough that I've had to stand in front of the congregation and correct where I have erred. (I'm not talking about confessing your sins and getting so personal that you destroy the respect and confidence the people may have in you.)

# HOW TO TREAT VISITORS

When people attend your church, do they feel welcomed, or do they feel like a piece of meat? By that I mean, do they feel like you want

them to stay so bad that you are too invasive? Asking a first time visitor questions like, "What do you do for a living? Are you married? Do you have kids? Are you saved? Are you a member of another church?" are too persistent and can be harmful instead of helpful. Often we attempt to extract too much information from them, and in so doing destroy any type of lasting relationship built on trust.

When a church acts this way toward a visitor, they make the church look desperate, and the pressure is so great that the visitor will probably never return.

You want to make the visitor feel welcome but not pushed. You want people to come because they have a desire to be there. You don't want them to come because they feel forced or threatened.

It might be a good idea for your ushers to hand out welcome packets to the visitors. This welcome packet can contain some information about the church and a visitor's card for them to fill out. The card should ask if they would like a phone call or a visit. If they do not want a visit, you are not obligated to visit them. You are not compromising if you do not go to their house on the following Tuesday and knock on their door trying to beg them to come back. The person more than likely will feel that you are chasing him down with the same fervor as other solicitors and salesmen. Americans are bombarded with commercials, telemarketing calls, junk mail, and so on. Visiting without being asked may be more of a hindrance than a help.

When someone visits, let them have some breathing room. Most of the time when someone visits a church, especially if it is a small one, they stand out as if they had Christmas tree lights on. They already know they are the stranger. They already feel different coming into a church they have never been before. They already feel a bit isolated. Let them get to know you and your members. Give them some time to develop some trust before you invade their space by getting too personal. After they have visited

for a while you could take them out to lunch or something, but don't be too pushy.

Let people know that you are glad they are there. Don't be rude or ignore them. But at the same time don't get in the way of what the Holy Spirit may want to do for them during the preaching. Don't turn them off before the Lord has a chance to help them.

In our zeal to get people in church, let's be careful and let Jesus Christ draw them instead of being like sheepdogs nipping at their heels until they come. If we do that, eventually the sheep will stray when you are not constantly on them, driving them. Sheep are to be led, not driven.

## GREETING VISITORS

It is a good idea to have someone to stand at the door or foyer of the church to welcome visitors when they come in. If you have parking issues, it would be a good idea to have someone in the parking lot, as well.

The greeter is one who welcomes guests by introducing them to the church grounds. He tells them where the bathrooms and water fountain are. If they have children he can direct them to the nursery and even introduce them to the pastor or another church family. Asking them, "Is there anything we can do for you?" is a good way to be non-intrusive yet welcoming.

There is nothing wrong in saying "Thank you for visiting. We are glad you are here." I am glad people attend church. I would much rather preach to people than a church full of empty pews.

If you sit down in a restaurant, I don't care how good the food is, if the waitress acts like you are a burden instead of a blessing, you are most likely not going to go back. If the people are not appreciated and made to feel welcome, they will not come back.

# BEING A SHEPHERD INSTEAD OF A HOUND DOG

It is not your responsibility as a pastor to chase people down. If you spend all your time calling everyone who misses church, the people will develop the mentality that they are indispensable. They will think if they don't get a card or phone call they don't matter. You want people to come of their own volition, because they love the Lord, not because you guilt trip them into coming. Use some discernment here. An occasional call or card can be helpful.

# DECENTLY AND IN ORDER

1 Cor 14:40 Let all things be done decently and in order.

Having an order to your service is very important because it demonstrates that there is some level of competence. If you want to effectually reach people and build a church, you can't just go through the service unprepared. Letting the Holy Spirit have liberty is one thing, but not being organized and ready is downright sin. God created everything in order and expects us to have some order in our churches.

People gravitate toward order. They are comfortable when things are orderly. They are peaceable when things are orderly. When there is chaos, people get nervous and out of sorts.

I'm not saying that you should make things ritualistic and so formalistic that the Lord can't get through. I'm simply suggesting that you have some sort of order as to when you are going to do things. For example, when are you going to have congregational singing, special singing, taking up of the offering, announcements, preaching, and so on. People will be more relaxed knowing there is some order and it will help them be focused on what the Lord is saying through the message.

The Lord is not the author of confusion. If you have a song leader, he should be prepared with the songs ahead of time. Your ushers should know when it is time to take up the offering. Those singing specials should know and be prepared when it is time for them to sing. People's lives are disheveled enough without coming to church and seeing chaos. If your services are always confused and disorderly, it will turn people away. They will not think you could possibly be competent with spiritual things if you can't run an orderly service.

Again, I'm not saying that you are to run things so rigidly that you can never change things, but that you should have enough organization that things run smoothly and peaceably.

## GROWING AS A PASTOR

You must learn to maintain your independence while at the same time learning from others. You have to minister to the people the Lord has called you to minister to, in that particular area and culture. Every church should take on its uniqueness based on its location and the pastor.

You must remember that you as a pastor will grow as well as your sheep. Often pastors are in a hurry to build large works quickly, and if that happens, the pastor may not be ready to handle such a task and the pressure that comes with it. Since a good pastor is willing to "be spent" (2 Cor. 12:15) for his people, it will take a huge toll on his life and his family. It will literally drain him because he is imparting his life to the sheep by way of sacrifice.

So sometimes the Lord prevents the church from growing too fast so that the shepherd can get stronger and more sturdy. The Lord doesn't want the weight of the ministry to be too heavy and crush the pastor at an early time in his ministry.

You must trust the Lord that He will grow your church at a pace that you are equally able to withstand.

# SPIRITUAL GROWTH

Often we think of growth in terms of numbers. But spiritual growth is the foundation for what the Lord may be building for later on down the road. The deeper the foundation, the studier the building. When you develop people it is the same way. Don't get discouraged or be in a hurry. Let the Lord build the foundation as He sees fit and then He will build it numerically.

However, if something does not appear to have little green shoots in the springtime and buds that eventually turn into blossoms, it appears dead. So we must look for growth, spiritual growth.

For something to grow, it must have the right amount of food, water, and sunshine. It also has to be weeded on a regular basis.

Many times when we see a small sapling, we immediately cover it with fertilizer, trying to get it to grow as quickly as possible. But too much fertilizer can burn a plant up. It can also make the plant shoot up quickly, but the fruit that comes out is either very bitter or the branches are not strong enough to support the fruit.

It is better to allow the tree to get its roots solidly into the ground. A fruit tree may grow as much as five to seven years before it produces fruit, because it is establishing a root system that will be able to support the fruit in the coming years.

I have seen young Christians who have grown very fast only to last about three to five years before they fizzle out. They don't lose their salvation, but they lose their fellowship.

# LOOKING FOR GROWTH

Ex 15:23 And when they came to Marah, they could not drink of the waters of Marah, for they were bitter: therefore the name of it was called Marah.

Here in Ex. 15:23 Moses and the Israelites come to a place where water is still and stagnant. Only the Bread of Life and the Water of Life impart spiritual life.

When you start a church, your goal must be to feed the flock the Lord has given you and nothing else (at least not yet). The Lord will bless the reading, preaching, and studying of His word, and when He is ready for it to show fruit on the outside, it will. But in the meantime we are to nourish and grow people with strong spiritual roots. It is more important to grow people spiritually than it is to grow them in an outward sense.

Notice this passage and how it is a great illustration of a church:

> Gen 33:13 And he said unto him, My lord knoweth that the children are tender, and the flocks and herds with young are with me: and if men should overdrive them one day, all the flock will die.

Sometimes in our eagerness to appear that we are not stagnant or dead, we drive people to produce fruit that they are not ready to produce. You are called to pastor the sheep, and that is more important than your reputation or your opinion of where you think they should be and what they should be doing.

## LOCAL CHURCH FIRST

You can't build a ministry outside the local church. The foundation must be built first and then other ministries can grow out from there. The local church is the strong point. It comes first.

When you start any kind of a ministry you are taking from the strong point and dividing it out. So you want to make sure that you move into those ministries in the Lord's time so that you will not weaken that nucleus.

# TAKING CARE OF THE PASTOR

I do not believe in pastoral popery. I do not believe in fleecing the sheep. I believe that the pastor is on the same level as others in the body of Christ but that he holds a different office or position. I don't believe he should be exalted like some kind of pope where he can "lord" over the people.

Having said that, let's look at what the Bible says concerning taking care of a pastor as far as monetary things are concerned:

> 1 Cor 9:7-14
>
> 7 Who goeth a warfare any time at his own charges? who planteth a vineyard, and eateth not of the fruit thereof? Or who feedeth a flock, and eateth not of the milk of the flock?
>
> 8 Say I these things as a man? Or saith not the law the same also?
>
> 9 For it is written in the law of Moses, Thou shalt not muzzle the mouth of the ox that treadeth out the corn. Doth God take care for oxen?
>
> 10 Or saith he it altogether for our sakes? For our sakes, no doubt, this is written: that he that ploweth should plow in hope; and that he that thresheth in hope should be partaker of his hope.
>
> 11 If we have sown unto you spiritual things, is it a great thing if we shall reap your carnal things?
>
> 12 If others be partakers of this power over you, are not we rather? Nevertheless we have not used this power; but suffer all things, lest we should hinder the gospel of Christ.
>
> 13 Do ye not know that they which minister about holy things live of the things of the temple? And they which wait at the altar are partakers with the altar?
>
> 14 Even so hath the Lord ordained that they which preach the gospel should live of the gospel.

Gal 6:6-10

6 Let him that is taught in the word communicate unto him that teacheth in all good things.

7 Be not deceived; God is not mocked: for whatsoever a man soweth, that shall he also reap.

8 For he that soweth to his flesh shall of the flesh reap corruption; but he that soweth to the Spirit shall of the Spirit reap life everlasting.

9 And let us not be weary in well doing: for in due season we shall reap, if we faint not.

10 As we have therefore opportunity, let us do good unto all men, especially unto them who are of the household of faith.

The verses are clear. If a man is taking care of the church spiritually, the church is to take care of his carnal needs. It works like a circle. Church members work secular jobs so they can support the ministry, and the preacher devotes his time to spiritual matters so he can take care of the church. When the church takes care of the pastor, he is free to give his time to the ministry.

Galatians 6 is used many times to convict people about fleshly sins, when in the context it is also dealing with being liberal in taking care of spiritual leaders in our lives. If a church is not trying to take care of their pastor, then God says, "I will not be mocked. If that is the value you place on spiritual things, then you are going to reap what you sow." Many churches come apart because they do not take care of the man the Lord has given to them to feed them.

At some point the church must be able to take care of itself and its pastor. When I first started preaching I had a very good job and my wife worked as well and was very successful in what she did. So when we started the church I didn't take a salary from the church; we had all our needs met, so we just supported ourselves.

Then I went to preach a meeting in the mountains and was sitting at the table with an elderly preacher. He said, "Young man, I

understand that you are a policeman and you are a pastor." I said, "Yes, sir." He said, "Do your people take care of you?" I said, "Yes, they are very good to me." He said, "That's not what I mean. I mean do they pay you anything?" I said, "Oh, no! I don't need a salary. I can take care of things. I make good money and don't want to be in debt or in bondage to anyone, anyway." He said, "You are a very proud man." I was thinking, "What?" And I started to puff up and get a little red. He said, "You have your people in bondage." I said, "Pardon me?" He asked, "Have your folks ever tried to do anything for you, give you anything?" I said, "Yes, sir, they've tried before, but I have never let them. I don't need it." He said, "Yeah, you don't need it, but they need it." He said, "What they are trying to do is to pay you for giving them God's word. They are trying to show you that you are appreciated. When you don't allow them to give, you are holding them in bondage because they feel that they owe you something." That hit me like a ton of bricks. He went on to say, "I have one word of advice to you. When the people want to take care of you, let them do it. If you don't keep it, or want to give it away to missions or something, fine. But let them give."

I never forgot that conversation. You see, up until that time my attitude was, "If you don't like my preaching, there is the door, you can leave." But the Lord wanted me to trust Him instead of myself. When I left the sheriff's office, what the church gave me wasn't even enough to take care of my mortgage payment. I had to become dependent on people taking care of me. That is hard to do for a proud man. The Lord wanted me to trust Him to use the sheep to take care of me. It might be a hard thing to do, but it is a biblical principal. You do your part, they do their part, and trust the Lord. If you or they break that circle you can lose God's blessings.

To what extent a pastor should be taken care of is to be left up to your congregation, the size of your church, and so on. The idea is that you are to "live of the gospel."

# SPECIAL MEETINGS

Some churches that have been around thirty to fifty years are more capable financially than a small church to handle special meetings, multiple ministries, and large missions programs.

Sometimes pastors feel undue pressure to have a meeting just for the sake of having a meeting. But the fact remains: If you can't afford it, you shouldn't buy it. When people come to meetings, there will be expenses involved, and you want to avoid a situation where people might get bitter because you didn't consider the cost of the meeting. It is great to have a revival meeting, but not to the detriment of the church. If you are not properly prepared, you will not be able to handle the pressures that come with having a meeting. You should never sit down and say, "Well, we don't have the money for this meeting, but we are going to pray and God will provide." You have to plan for things. Take out a piece of paper and write out how much it will cost the church. You must remember that it is proper for you to take care of all the expenses of your guests (such as rooms, food, travel) and give them a decent offering.

For a small church, meetings can be a backbreaker and very expensive. So you might want to consider the following:

1. Can we afford it?
2. Are we spiritually mature enough to handle the attacks that are going to come?
3. Can the people withstand the pressure of meeting however many days the meeting lasts?

Let me call the baby ugly. Meetings can overburden the people with guilt, especially if you are constantly passing the offering plate and putting pressure on them to bear the load. A good rule of thumb to follow is to allow for meetings in your church budget. If you can't

afford to pay for the meeting, don't have it. By that I mean do not depend on offerings to pay the expenses of special meetings.

If God wants you to have a meeting, He will provide the means and give you enough sense to plan ahead. If you are not prepared, you might get in over your head, causing your budget to go in the red, affecting other things (like paying rent, light bills, and so on).

Also, don't fall into the trap of attempting to finance everything on your own. If you do, then it might lead to bitterness and anger where you will browbeat the people because they are not giving enough, and it may even lead to your checking the tithing records to see who is and who is not contributing. That is a very dangerous place to go. A pastor should never look at any of the tithing records. A pastor also needs to guard against jealousy and bitterness that might set in after a meeting. You might hear your people comment on how well the guest preacher preached, or they might give him a bigger offering than they pay you. People have a tendency to take "Old Faithful" for granted. Once people know that there will be a guest preacher, the crowds may get a little larger and the people may seem a bit more excited. If you're not careful, you can get bitter that your folks stepped up for the visiting preacher and haven't done anything for you.

## MISSIONS

Supporting missions is a good thing. It is a noble thing and something every church should eventually be a part of. But a church should only support missions when the timing is right and they are financially able to do so. The priorities must be right. The pastor of a church must be taken care of first; then you might be ready to take on some missionaries and branch out into some other ministries.

It is your responsibility to take care of your missionaries by providing their expenses and giving them a decent offering. Missionaries are people, too. Yes, they want to be a blessing and

present their burden, but they have to eat like the rest of us and they have travel expenses to take care of.

When a missionary calls me in order to get a chance to present his work, if our church is not financially able to take care of his expenses and give him a reasonable offering, I tell him we can't have him in. Missionaries are not to be taken advantage of. It would be better to let them go somewhere where they might be taken on for support than to let them come to your church just so you can use them to fill the pulpit or get your folks burdened about missions.

Let me also say that I think it is better to support one missionary well than ten at five dollars a month. Some churches put up a mission board full of missionaries with the appearance of super spirituality, when in actuality they are not giving the missionaries enough money to pay for their postage to send their prayer letters.

God does bless sacrificial giving. God does bless you when you give to missions. But you must keep everything in proper perspective. A small church can have so many pressures to support things outside the church that people quit giving as much to the general needs of the church. They may feel pressure to support missions to the point that they give some of the money that they would have normally given in the offering to missions or some project.

## THE MISSIONARY

To our discredit, many pastors and church members think missionaries are to be accountable to us as to how they spend every dime of the money that we give them. Some think they shouldn't have nice clothes, a decent car, or any luxuries of life. We think we have the authority to dictate to how missionaries are to spend their money. Does your church dictate to you how you spend your money? Do your church members buy new clothes every now and then?

When you give a missionary money, it is between him and the Lord what he does with it. We gave a pretty decent offering to a

missionary one time and he didn't have any furniture. I told him to spend some of it on some furniture. He said, "I can't use God's money to buy furniture." I said, "Look, you had better buy your wife a bed to lay her head on. She's leaving everything over here to go on the field. You better make her nest as comfortable as you can when you get there, or she might be ready to bail out when the going gets tough." He said, "You mean I can use God's money to buy furniture?" I said, "You need to take care of your family, and yes, you can use God's money to do that."

## ACCOUNTABILITY AND MISSIONS

When you support other missions, you need to be accountable for those works. At some point you need to check with those missions and make sure they are still on the field and doing the work they told you they would do. I'm not saying that you demand to know what they are doing with "your money" but just that you should know that they are still actively in the ministry and not just sitting at home collecting checks.

Some missionaries have figured out that Americans are stupid and lazy. They will send out a prayer letter and the pastor and church just take it for granted that they are doing what they said they were doing. Don't feel intimated in calling the mission board and checking on the missionary, or emailing and calling the missionary himself. You don't have to be rude to him, just ask him what's going on and how he is doing. Keep your missionaries somewhat accountable because we are also accountable for how we direct the Lord's money.

## OTHER MINISTRIES

Sometimes as a church we feel a responsibility to branch into ministries before we can handle the pressure of that ministry. When

you begin jail and prison ministries, you will draw the attention of "your adversary the Devil" (1 Peter 5:8). When it comes to a nursing home ministry, you must be very consistent. Those people will look for you each and every week, and you shouldn't start something that you are not able to finish. You can't just go when you feel like going; you must be consistent.

The need to start a ministry doesn't dictate a calling. When we first thought about establishing a nursing home ministry, we saw the need all around us, but we waited until the Lord raised up some people who were willing to go on a regular basis.

If you let the Lord develop a ministry, you will find it will help with attitudes within that ministry. Instead of people serving because they have to or feel pressured to or to prove their spirituality, they will serve out of a desire to please the Lord.

Pastors sometimes feel pressure from other pastors because they do not have all these outside ministries. They think the only way to be spiritual is to be covered up in "doing, doing, doing." The Devil will spread you so thin that you will be weak.

If you want to start a ministry, start slow and let the Lord open the door instead of kicking it down yourself.

## STREET PREACHING

Most street preaching done by Bible believers is done with the wrong spirit and attitude. They stand on the corner using the "shock and awe effect" with hard and harsh words, all the while supposedly concerned and compassionate. When a person turns down a gospel tract, they quip back with some rude comment like, "Well, you are going to burn in Hell like a hot dog." That's not the way to do it.

A public street ministry brings pressure from the community, the authorities, and the Devil himself. It is easier to get in the flesh preaching on the street than almost anywhere else. But if you go in the spirit of meekness and check with the authorities, things may go a

lot easier than you think. You must realize that much land is privately owned (like shopping malls, and so on). You say, "Well, I'm willing to go to jail for Jesus." If you trespass on private property and preach there, you won't be going to jail for Jesus, you will be going to jail for your own stupidity.

If someone came to your house and got on your front steps and began preaching about Allah and Islam, what would you say? You would throw him off your land. The shopping malls have spent their money for advertising, for the land itself, and have drawn the crowds there. When you go to preach on private property, you are acting like a leach. They have spent their money to draw people to come to their businesses to buy products from them and you show up, blocking or hindering them from making money.

So when it comes to doing street ministry you must check things out first. You might do more harm than good. You might ruin the reputation of your church. You must have the right spirit and do it with compassion. Are you called to build a church or a street ministry? You had better count the cost and make sure your church is ready for this type of ministry.

## MOTIVES OF STREET PREACHING

Often street preaching is done to prove something either to the world or to the brethren. Not everybody is called to be a street preacher. I appreciate the courage that it takes to publicly preach on the street, but the preacher should not portray himself like he is angry at the world. Some of these guys get up with their sword drawn, ready to take someone's head off. No wonder many people have a skewed view of Christianity and the gospel. They think that Christians are glad people are going to Hell instead of burdened with compassion.

There is nothing wrong with lifting up your voice, but you must do it in a nonconfrontational, noncontending manner. You can give

the gospel clear and plain and some people will mock, laugh, and make fun, but they shouldn't get upset because you have an arrogant, argumentative attitude. If they get offended because of the gospel, tough apples. But if they get offended because of our attitude, we have failed to propagate the gospel properly.

## COUNSELING—THE DANGER ZONE

There a few avenues that the Devil might enter into in order to destroy the work that you have started. If you have been called in the ministry, there will be times that you will have to counsel people and give advice. Some pastors get the idea that since they are called they have been given a green light to say anything. All across our country, pastors are being sued not only for what they are saying in the pulpit, but privately.

Pastors' wives will have to tread carefully here as well because many times other women come to a pastor's wife for counsel. The tears and emotionalism sometimes can sway people one way or the other, oftentimes without the other side of the story.

I just want to suggest that if the Bible doesn't give a concrete answer regarding a particular situation that you simply say, "I don't know." There are many pastors that are giving medical advice and other types of counsel where they have no expertise. Our field is to be an expert in the scriptures, not people's personal lives.

The goal in counseling is to help people based on the Bible, but not in a manner whereby we get too close to them personally. We are not to become a priest to our congregation. We have a high priest— Jesus Christ. There is "one mediator between God and men, the man Christ Jesus" (2 Tim. 2:5). Sometimes people feel the need to confess and tell a pastor their sins, but sins against God need to be confessed to God. Keep in mind that once a person divulges his past to you it does two things:

1. It makes you remember his past every time you see him.
2. It makes you feel indebted to him to tell him something private about your life in order to help him.

You can see the danger in trying to "understand" the person you are counseling. She might say, "My boyfriend did such and such," and you say, "Well, I know how that feels because at times my wife/ husband has done such and such." Trying to relate personally with the person you are counseling opens up too many doors and can lead to being too transparent, so much so that respect and admiration are lost.

I'm not saying that you shouldn't be compassionate and try to help people. But you must understand that the Devil is real good at slipping in places that seem good (Gen. 3:1, where his first word is positive— "Yea"). The best counseling you can do is from the pulpit with the Bible. There you have a pulpit between you and the individual. It also prevents things from getting too personal.

There are times when people will need to sit down with you and get some advice and counsel, but we as pastors must make sure we protect ourselves and also that we don't become the person they repent to. We should point them to the Lord.

We can gain some insight from the story of the prodigal son (Luke 15), where the father never asks for details of every place the prodigal had been and every sin he had done. Nowhere in the passage do we read that! The father forgives him without drilling him and takes care of his son while preparing to move on instead of digging up the past.

In today's society, and unfortunately in the church, we have a propensity to traffic in trash. We become like these trash magazines you see at the checkout counters. In some churches they demand people to openly confess their sins in front of the church. This is ridiculous. Why would someone want to come home when they knew they were going to have to stand up in front of people and relive their

sin? The Bible tells us to be "simple concerning evil" (Rom. 16:19) and to "abstain from all appearance of evil" (1 Thess. 5:22).

Sins against God should be confessed to God and God alone. Sins against a brother should be confessed to that brother and him alone. It should not be made public. If it is a sin that has a public effect on the church (like embezzlement) and affects a multitude of people, then it can be brought before the church. But moral sins of the flesh are better confessed to Jesus Christ and left alone.

You have to realize that but for the grace of God we would all be in horrible sin today. Anyone is capable of doing anything. I do not believe in condoning sin, but I do not believe in embarrassing people and trafficking in other people's sin. All it does is glorify sin, make them look bad, and give people who haven't committed those sins a self-righteous attitude.

Once people tell you their sins there is a link formed between you and them. This chain can put them in bondage because they know that you know something about their private lives. It can also put you in bondage. It is better not to know everything about everybody. It is just not that important. In twenty-five years of ministry I have never seen it beneficial for anybody under any circumstances for everybody to know everything about everybody. Ignorance is bliss, except for the fact that people sin and mess up and knowing every detail is not beneficial.

## LEGAL ACCOUNTABILITY

If something of a dangerous nature is revealed, you had better act. I happened to be in a church where a man I had arrested for pedophilia wanted to become a Sunday school teacher. The pastor didn't know his history. In that situation I felt a responsibility to tell the pastor. I didn't tell him to kick him out of the church; I just cautioned him about making this guy a Sunday school teacher.

The pastor didn't bring him up in front of the church, but he pulled the man aside and warned him that he was being watched and that he wouldn't be allowed to be around children in the church. He told him that if he saw or heard anything suspicious he would assume that it was true and he would no longer be welcome.

Many years ago I was in a church where the pastor was confronted by a man who wanted to teach Sunday school in the church but was denied because the pastor knew his wicked past. The man insisted that he had been forgiven by God and should be allowed to teach. He further insisted that this matter be brought before the church. He thought the pastor was being unfair.

The man stood in front of the church and revealed his past and asked the church to consider allowing him to teach the class. The pastor responded by saying that he would not be responsible for anything bad happening and if the church chose to override his decision he would resign on the spot. Of course the church supported the pastor and the man ran out claiming he was "shamed" in the church. But he brought it on himself. The pastor was just being responsible and cautious.

## LEGAL ENTANGLEMENTS

Sometimes when people come to you for counseling they will tell you something they have done that is not only morally wrong, but legally wrong as well. If a person tells you about a person-to-person crime, you have a legal obligation to report it. You can't view yourself as a lawyer and claim attorney/client privilege.

Don't risk your ministry or reputation of the church covering up a crime. It is important that the person trusts you and has a level of confidence in you, but don't let someone put you in a box. If a legal matter is brought to your attention, be upfront and turn it over to the proper officials. If you choose not to report these matters and

someone gets hurt, you can be charged with guilt by association. Be very careful.

# HOW TO HELP OTHERS

In Acts 27 we have a great example of a pastor attempting to help others who are in storms. You will notice in the passage, they were told to stay in the port but they chose to reject the pastor's counsel and do what they wanted to do.

You need to understand from the start that some people will reject biblical counsel no matter how many warnings you give them or how compassionate and concerned you are toward them. Human nature has not changed.

So what are we to do as pastors when we see people in storms? Let's learn from Acts 27:

1. Don't steer their ship.

Acts 27:15 And when the ship was caught, and could not bear up into the wind, we let her drive.

You have to be careful not to steer the person's ship you are counseling. Sometimes you have to let the storm take the ship where it is supposed to go, instead of jumping in there and becoming their hero. Remember, many times people get themselves into a storm and bailing them out too quickly might cause them not to learn the lesson of the storm.

You don't have to have an immediate solution to everyone's problems. There are many times people come to me and ask, "What do you think about so-and-so?" A lot of times I think, "I know exactly what will straighten this out." But then the Lord will say, "Be quiet." So I'll instruct them to pray and seek the Lord's direction. You see,

there is a danger in bailing them out too quickly because they might have a tendency to depend on you instead of the Lord.

2. Encourage them.

Next, notice they used "helps, undergirding the ship" (Acts 27:17). There is nothing wrong with encouraging and strengthening the person going through the storm. You are not condoning their sin, but let's be honest. There have been times you made a mess of things and found yourself in the middle of a storm. What you needed was some help and encouragement, not someone to berate and belittle you. You don't want the person to think he is going to get the "I told you so" attitude.

If you visited someone dying of cancer and you saw him lying there gasping for breath because the cancer had eaten up his lungs, the last thing you should say is, "Hey there, I told you that you would reap what you sow That's what you get for smoking. God's judgment is real and true."

Those words may be true, but have you helped the person by those words? I mean, he is in the storm about to die and the last thing he will remember is someone had a foot on his chest, saying "I told you so."

When people are seeking counsel and wanting help they have already learned the lesson. They know that they messed up. They don't need to be reminded again.

When I was a policeman on the road, I had a predisposition to be more lenient to those citizens who admitted their guilt (running a red light, not wearing a seat belt, and so on) than I was to those who wanted to argue and attempt to justify themselves. You see, those who admitted their guilt were already humbled enough to see their fault. They didn't need more antagonizing from me to convince them to change their ways.

It is the same in counseling. The repercussions of sin will do enough damage; we don't have to add to it and become "God's punisher." We are to help "lighten the ship" (verse 18), not add to it.

3.   Rebuke them with grace.

This rebuking should be done gently (Acts 27:21). Be gracious and gentle with them. It is okay to remind them what the scripture says and that they are reaping some things, but do it in the right spirit. You will have to correct improper behavior, but you can do it in a way that will help them, not hurt them or turn them away.

The most important advice I can give you concerning counseling is a familiar saying: "Unsolicited advice is rarely heeded." If people come to you for help, they are likely to listen to what you have to say. But if you chase someone down, making it your business to "help" him, normally he will not listen.

4.   Point them to Jesus.

Another thing Paul does on the ship is to "exhort" them (Acts 27:22). When you counsel, tell them it is going to get better; exhort them; encourage them. Don't paint a false picture. You are not giving them a magic pill that will fix everything overnight. Salvation is instantaneous, but getting out of problems sometimes takes a long time. People don't change quickly. None of us ever changed fast. Gradual changes are much better than fast changes, anyway, because if you change too quickly you might adopt the wrong things.

Paul mentions in Acts 27:23 "the angel of God," which we know is Jesus Christ. Make sure you point people in the direction of our Lord when you counsel. Go back to the Book, back to the Saviour.

5.   Feed them the Bible.

Paul also gives them something to eat (Acts 27:33–35). You want to feed them the word of God, but don't feed them too much too quick. They are in a storm. They will get seasick. Feed them a little.

Keep it simple. Give them small bites. I've had couples come to me in marital distress. They haven't had any biblical training, but they realize they need to find the right direction. You will discover how serious they are about getting help when you give them an assignment (like writing out some things, reading together, praying together, and so on) and see if they have completed it the next week. If they don't complete the first assignment, I simply say, I have nothing today until you complete your assignment from last week.

That might sound harsh, but why should we spend our precious time and effort pouring our lives into them when they refuse to make any effort? Their marriage is in trouble because they are not making an effort.

I'm not saying that you give them huge assignments and unattainable goals. Just give them little bites, little things to accomplish at first. After they make a little headway, give them more.

If I have a husband-and-wife situation I usually get them to look up four or five verses about being a husband/wife and get them to write comments on what they learned in each verse. The result is their learning from the Bible, not me, the right and wrong ways to act. Eventually the couple learns to depend on God and the scriptures instead of just asking the pastor. The goal of counseling is to counsel yourself out of a job.

What you want is for them to develop a relationship with the Lord through the Bible, and that in turn will draw them together.

6.   Cut them loose.

Next, notice in Acts 27:40 they took up the "anchors." You must turn people loose from what is holding them back. People do feel guilt and it is a real emotion. You have to let them know about the cleansing and forgiveness found in the blood of Jesus Christ.

I worked a case where a young man had killed someone. I talked to him in the interview room and he professed to be a Christian and

wanted to ask for God's forgiveness. I prayed with him and he said, "Do you think God forgave me?" I assured him that God had, and then he said to me the strangest thing: "You think I can go home now?" He didn't understand that there are some mistakes in this life that you can be forgiven for but must still bear the repercussions. But you can help to relieve their guilt.

7.   Be honest.

Never paint an untrue picture of the situation when you are counseling. Sometimes their problem will be with them for the rest of their lives and they are going to have to learn to deal with it.

But by the same token, don't be afraid to cut the anchor that holds a person in a boat of guilt. You need to let him know he can go forward and there is forgiveness and restoration with the Lord. When you are plowing you must keep your eyes on where you are going, not where you have been.

You must maintain a balance. You don't want people to get a sense of "Can I go home now?" but you want to be free to move forward. Let the anchors go.

We must also keep in mind that some people are going to try to "jump ship" anyway (Acts 27:43). We must be faithful and try to help them regardless of that fact. Also, there will be times that you must be willing to lead them out of a situation. You will have to befriend them and help them even though it may be hard to do. You must go first.

8.   Give hope.

Finally, you must give them something to float on (Acts 27:44). You must give them some hope. Don't give them false hope. I mean, if you are sitting with someone on their death bed, it is not the time to say, "Something wonderful is going to happen to you today!"

I visited an old police buddy of mine who was dying of colon cancer. I listened to that man (down from over two hundred pounds to a little over one hundred) talk about so many regrets he had and mistakes he had made in life. I asked him if he was saved. When he assured me that he was, I just gave him a little "piece" of the ship to float on. I comforted him as best I could from the scriptures that everything would be all right once he made it to the other side. I couldn't say he was going to get well, nor was I there to magnify all of his regrets or say, "I told you so." I simply gave him some hope about the future, some comfort. That was what I was there for.

## TIME AND COUNSELING

Another thing to watch out for is letting people become dependent on you. If you are not careful, people will eat all of your time. Every psychologist, doctor, dentist, and other professional understands the time principle. Pastors just don't seem to get it. When you schedule to meet with someone, give him a block of time and realize that you are not going to fix everything in one session.

You must guard your time carefully. Anything that takes away from your preparation and prayer is out of balance.

## COUNSELING AND PERSONAL ADVICE

Some pastors have the idea that they can help their congregations make every decision, from which car and house to buy to which person to marry. I don't want to have those responsibilities and the scriptures do not regulate that kind of authority to a pastor. I don't want to deal with the repercussions of giving out counsel and watching it go bad. If I tell someone whom to marry, what if it turns out wrong?

If God gives you some wisdom about some things, that is great. But be careful how you give out the counsel. You might just say with a warning, "You do what God tells you to do. Don't do this because this is what the preacher says. I am not God."

# THE CHURCH AND MONEY

The number one cause of church splits is not over doctrinal issues or spiritual issues. The number one cause for church splits has to do with how churches handle their money.

People are funny when it comes to money. I will not go into great detail about what the scripture says concerning giving and the ministry of the church. Most of you know that we are to give spiritually, willingly, gratefully, and so on, but we give:

1. So the pastor can be taken care of.
2. So the work of the ministry can continue (all the business expenses, operation costs, and so on).
3. To enable mission work to proceed.
4. For benevolent ministries.

Unfortunately, churches and pastors are too flippant and haphazard when it concerns the handling of money. Some surmise that they can do whatever they want because it has been given by the people. But if we are not somewhat accountable and wise with money, it will show that we are not competent or appreciative with their giving. I'm not saying we have to give recognition to people when they give, but I am saying that church members should know when they give a dollar or a dime it is overseen and properly handled. They should know that God's money is handled honestly and will be properly dispensed according to the decisions of the church.

# HELPFUL GUIDELINES

All it takes is an accusation concerning the mishandling of money to destroy your church. If someone argues that you have used money that was given to God for other purposes, it will bring reproach on your church.

Everyone knows of a preacher, deacon, or treasurer who took money from the church, ran off with money, or embezzled money. There is nothing more reproachful than a church that is known for misappropriating funds.

The scriptures do not teach the idea that one person should "float the boat" for the entire church. Everyone collectively should have an opportunity to give to the work of the ministry. So, when you take up a collection, do it publicly. We, as many churches do, use offering plates and pass them around the church in plain sight.

Next, you should never leave one person alone with the money. Until it is properly counted, sealed in the bag, and deposited, two people should be with the money at all times, or the money should be placed in a safe until it is counted or taken to the bank.

In our church, after the offering is taken, the treasurer and one of our trustees take the money and put it into the safe until after the evening service. There are only two people in our church who know the combination to the safe, and I am not one of them. We do this for precautionary measures. I want to live above reproach. I do not want to be accused of taking money or even writing checks to myself. My name is not on the checking account. This is all done for the protection of the ministry.

I do have a credit card with a limit that I can use for expenses. But there again, every receipt must be turned in and accounted for. I do not want anyone to question whether or not the preacher is dipping his hand into the collection plate.

Always have a minimum of two people counting the money. After it is counted, there is a count sheet that is signed by both individuals

and then the deposit slip is filled out and everything is placed in the deposit bag. At the end of the month, every deposit slip is checked with the corresponding bank statement. So we have a three-way check: the count sheet signed by both counters, the deposit slip, and the bank statement.

We also have a system with every purchase that is made for the church. Each receipt must be accounted for.

At the end of every year we have an open audit where a CPA comes in and oversees all of our books. They check to make sure we are in accordance with our personal practices (outlined in our constitution and bylaws) and that we are in accordance with the federal and state laws. If anyone ever questions anything we can show him to the penny where the money came from and where it went.

Honesty and common sense will save you a lot of headache in dealing with church finances. I don't get up in front of the church and say, "Last week we spent thirty-five dollars on toilet paper," but we do have everything listed and categorized so every penny can be accounted for.

It is important to stay above reproach. If someone thinks you are a thief, your reputation is done. There is a rather large church in Jacksonville where the pastor said they were sending money to a certain missionary. They gave the pastor a check every month and he was putting it in an account, but it was his account! When someone questioned him, he tried to claim pastoral authority saying, "I'm the pastor, and you shouldn't be questioning me." Well, later they did a public investigation and arrested him in front of everyone. You can imagine the embarrassment for the entire church.

You need to put some things in place in the beginning, when you first start a church. Open a checking account and practice proper accounting measures. As a pastor, you need to divorce yourself from handling the money. People need to know you don't have your hands on the money.

I know in small churches it may take a while before you are able to trust someone to handle the books, but as soon as you can, break away from the finances.

## BUILDING PROJECTS

Finally, at some point you will have to consider building a building or expanding grounds and buildings of your ministry. You need to communicate what the cost is going to be so your congregation can know what to expect and how to pray and give accordingly.

Before you make a huge move and expense, it is a good idea to work from a budget. Counting the cost (Luke 9) is not compromise; it is good sense! "Let's just trust God" is not going to pay the bills. Be wise enough to tell the people what is going on and what the cost will be.

Never assume anything when it comes to money. If someone hands you some money, don't be afraid to say, "Where do you want this to go?" I treat money like a snake. If someone gives me some money and says, "Put this in the plate," I don't take it; I tell him to give it to someone else. I am not going to open myself up to accusations like, "I gave that preacher some money. He took it. I wonder if he really put it in the plate."

Be careful how you handle money. Be upfront in the money business of the church. Always have a witness so that there is never any question. If you do this, you will avoid the number one reason for church splits in this country.

## STAY WITH IT!

Sometimes a Bible-believing work exists in a place as a testimony for the Lord. Your work may not be large and successful in the eyes of man, but it may be that the Lord has you at that particular place as a

witness for the truth. When the Judgment comes, no one will be able to say, "I didn't have a church I could go to and get the truth."

Your church may be located in a hard area. Maybe you don't see people getting saved as much as you want to. It is in areas like this where it becomes hard to keep going. I just want to encourage you to keep your eyes on eternity. Your reward is not always seen on the earth. If God has called you to that area and church, just be faithful to Him and let Him deal with the results or lack of results. Just because you don't see it here does not mean God doesn't see it up there.

# CONTENTS

Scripture quotations are from the Authorized King James Version.

WestBow Press books may be ordered through booksellers or by contacting:

WestBow Press
A Division of Thomas Nelson & Zondervan
1663 Liberty Drive
Bloomington, IN 47403
www.westbowpress.com
1 (866) 928-1240

Published by Bible Believers Baptist Church
3857 Hartley Road. Jacksonville, FL 3225/

ISBN: 978-1-4908-1988-4 (sc)
ISBN: 978-1-4908-1990-7 (hc)
ISBN: 978-1-4908-1989-1 (e)

Library of Congress Control Number: 2013923609

Printed in the United States of America.

WestBow Press rev. date: 02/04/2014

*The*
# MAN
*The*
# MESSAGE
*The*
# MINISTRY

David Peacock

Bible Believers Baptist Church
3857 Hartley Road, Jacksonville, Florida 32257

WESTBOW®
PRESS
A DIVISION OF THOMAS NELSON
& ZONDERVAN

# CONTENTS

## III LIBERALISM, PLURALISM, AND COMMUNITY

# PUBLIC PHILOSOPHY

The re-election of President George W. Bush prompted a new wave of soul-searching among Democrats. Exit polls found that more voters based their presidential vote on "moral values" than on any other issue—more than terrorism, the war in Iraq, or the state of the economy. And those who cited moral values voted overwhelmingly (80 to 18 percent) for Bush over his opponent, John Kerry. Commentators were perplexed. "Somewhere along the line," a CNN reporter confessed, "all of us missed this moral values thing."

Skeptics warned against over-interpreting the "moral values" issue. They pointed out that the majority of voters did not share Bush's opposition to abortion and same-sex marriage, the most morally charged issues in the campaign. Other factors helped explain the Bush victory: Kerry's campaign had lacked a compelling theme; it is not easy to defeat an incumbent president during wartime; and Americans were still reeling from the terrorist attacks of September 11. Still, in the wake of the 2004 election, Democrats found themselves casting about for ways to speak more convincingly to Americans' moral and spiritual yearnings.

It was not the first time that Democrats had missed the "moral values thing." In the four decades following Lyndon Johnson's landslide victory in 1964, only two Democrats won the presidency. One was Jimmy Carter, a born-again Christian from Georgia who, in the wake of Watergate, promised to restore honesty and morality to government; the other was Bill Clinton who, despite his personal foibles, displayed a keen instinctive grasp of the religious and spiritual dimensions of politics. Other Democratic standard-bearers—Walter Mondale, Michael Dukakis, Al Gore, and John Kerry—eschewed soul talk, cleaving instead to the language of policies and programs.

When Democrats in recent times have reached for moral and religious resonance, their efforts have taken two forms, neither wholly convincing. Some, following the example of George W. Bush, have sprinkled their speeches with religious rhetoric and biblical references. (Bush has employed this strategy more brazenly than any modern president; his inaugural addresses and State of the Union speeches mention God more frequently than even Ronald Reagan did.) So intense was the competition for divine favor in the 2000 and 2004 campaigns that a Web site, *beliefnet.com,* established a "God-o-meter" to track the candidates' references to God.

The second approach Democrats have taken is to argue that moral values in politics are not only about cultural issues, such as abortion, school prayer, same-sex marriage, and the display of the Ten Commandments in courthouses, but also about economic issues, such as health care, child care, education funding, and Social Security. John Kerry offered a version of this approach in his acceptance speech at the 2004 Democratic convention, using the V-words ("value" and "values") no less than 32 times.

Though the impulse is right, the hortatory fix for the values deficit comes across as stilted and unconvincing, for two reasons: First, Democrats have had trouble articulating, with clarity and conviction, the vision of economic justice that underlies their social and economic policies. Second, even a strong argument for economic justice does not by itself constitute a governing vision. Providing everyone a fair opportunity to reap the rewards of an affluent society is one aspect of the good society. But fairness isn't everything. It does not answer the hunger for a public life of larger meaning, because it ___

—

does not connect the project of self-government with people's desire to participate in a common good greater than themselves.

Notwithstanding the outpouring of patriotism in the immediate aftermath of September 11, and the sacrifices being made by the soldiers in Iraq, American politics lacks an animating vision of the good society, and of the shared obligations of citizenship. A few weeks after the terrorist attacks of 2001, President Bush, who insisted on his tax cuts even as he led the nation into war, was asked why he had not called for any sacrifices from the American people as a whole. He replied that the American people were sacrificing by enduring longer lines at airports. In a 2004 interview in Normandy, France, on the anniversary of D-Day, NBC's Tom Brokaw asked the President why he was not asking the American people to sacrifice more so that they would feel connected with their fellow citizens fighting and dying in Iraq. Bush seemed mystified, replying, "What does that mean, 'sacrifice more'?" Brokaw offered the example of World War II rationing and restated his question: "There's a great sense, I think, that there's a disconnect between what American military people are doing overseas and what Americans are doing at home." Bush replied: "America has been sacrificing. Our economy hasn't [been] as strong as it should be, and there's—people haven't been working. Fortunately, our economy's now strong, and it's getting stronger."

That Democrats did not seize the theme of sacrifice, and that Bush scarcely understood the question, testifies to the dulled civic sensibilities of American politics in the early years of the twenty-first century. Without a compelling account of the public purpose, the electorate settled, in a time of terror, for the security and moral certitude they associated with the incumbent President.

The essays in this volume explore the moral and civic dilemmas that animate American public life. Part I, "American Civic Life," offers an overview of the American political tradition. It shows that the "moral values" predicament in which liberals find themselves today represents something of a reversal; conservatives have not always held a monopoly on the faith-based aspects of political argument. Some of the great movements of moral and political reform in American history—from the abolitionist movement to the Progressive era to the civil rights movement of the 1960s—drew powerfully on moral, religious, and spiritual sources. By recalling American political debates from Thomas Jefferson to the present, these essays show how liberalism lost its moral and civic voice, and ask whether the project of self-government can be rejuvenated in our time.

Part II, "Moral and Political Arguments," takes up some of the hotly contested moral and political issues of the last two decades, including affirmative action, assisted suicide, abortion, gay rights, stem cell research, pollution permits, presidential lying, criminal punishment, the moral limits of markets, the meaning of toleration and civility, individual rights and the claims of community, and the role of religion in public life. Running through the discussion of these controversies are several recurring questions: Individual rights and freedom of choice are the most prominent ideals in our moral and political life. But are they an adequate basis for a democratic society? Can we reason our way through the hard moral questions that arise in public life without recourse to controversial ideas about the good life? If (as I maintain) our political arguments cannot avoid questions of the good life, how can we contend with the fact that modern societies are teeming with disagreement about such questions?

Part III, "Liberalism, Pluralism, and Community," steps back from the particular moral and political controversies discussed in Part II to examine the varieties of liberal political theory prominent today, and to assess their strengths and weaknesses. It offers some examples of political theories that draw openly and explicitly on moral and religious ideals, and yet retain a commitment to pluralism. Connecting the themes running through the volume as a whole, the essays in this section argue for a politics that gives greater emphasis to citizenship, community, and civic virtue, and that grapples more directly with questions of the good life. Liberals often worry that inviting moral and religious argument into the public square runs the risk of intolerance and coercion. The essays in this volume respond to that worry by showing that substantive moral discourse is not at odds with progressive public purposes, and that a pluralist society need not shrink from engaging the moral and religious convictions its citizens bring to public life.

Many of these essays blur the line between political commentary and political philosophy. They constitute a venture in public philosophy, in two senses: they find in the political and legal controversies of our day an occasion for philosophy, and they represent an attempt to do philosophy in public—to bring moral and political philosophy to bear on contemporary public discourse. Most of the essays in this volume originally appeared in publications aimed at an audience beyond the academy, such as the *Atlantic Monthly*, the *New Republic*, the *New York Times*, and the *New York Review of Books*. Others appeared in law reviews or scholarly publications. But all are addressed to citizens as well as scholars, and seek to shed light on contemporary public life.

# Part I

# AMERICAN CIVIC LIFE

The essays in this section seek in the American political tradition sources of civic renewal for our time. Chapter 1, "America's Search for a Public Philosophy," is an essay in retrieval though not, I hope, in nostalgia. It shows that our political debates have not always focused on the size and distribution of the national product; nor is the consumerist, individualist understanding of freedom so familiar in our time the only way of conceiving liberty. From Thomas Jefferson to the New Deal, a more demanding, civic conception of freedom has also informed American political argument. The scale of political life in a global age complicates the civic project; we cannot invigorate self-government simply by reviving civic virtue as traditionally conceived. But recalling the civic strand of our tradition can help us reimagine present possibilities. At the very least, it can remind us of questions we have forgotten how to ask: How can powerful economic forces be brought to democratic account? Is self-government possible under conditions of a global economy? In a pluralist age marked by multiple identities and complex selves, what forms of commonality can democratic societies hope to inspire?

Chapters 2–7 are shorter essays that explore the changing terms of American political discourse in recent decades. "Beyond Individualism: Democrats and Community" was first published as Michael Dukakis and Gary Hart competed for the 1988 Democratic nomination. I argued that the Democratic Party had ceded to Ronald Reagan the language of community, and had lost its moral and civic voice. Not long after the article appeared, I received an appreciative letter from a reader in Little Rock. Bill Clinton, then the Governor of Arkansas, wrote that he had been making speeches around the country sounding similar themes, and was struck by two points in particular: "one, that we have something to learn from Reagan's conservative vision and his success in 'speaking the language of self-government and community,'" and second, "that we must focus less on macroeconomic issues and more on 'questions of economic structure' and 'building communities capable of self-government on a manageable scale.'"

Chapters 3–5 are essays written eight years later, in the midst of Clinton's presidency. They reflect on his partially successful attempt to wrest from Republicans the language of community and moral values and on his somewhat less successful attempt to articulate large governing themes for progressive politics at the end of the twentieth century. Both efforts were disrupted by the impeachment proceedings of 1998–99, touched off by a Clinton sex scandal involving a White House intern. Chapter 6 contrasts the largely partisan attempt by House Republicans to impeach Clinton with the more sober impeachment hearings that led to the resignation of Richard Nixon, hearings I had witnessed as a young journalist.

The section concludes with an essay recalling the civic voice of Robert F. Kennedy, drawn from a talk I gave at a gathering at the John F. Kennedy Library in 2000, celebrating the seventy-fifth anniversary of Robert Kennedy's birth.

# one

# AMERICA'S SEARCH FOR A PUBLIC PHILOSOPHY

## LIBERAL VERSUS REPUBLICAN FREEDOM

The central idea of the public philosophy by which we live is that freedom consists in our capacity to choose our ends for ourselves. Politics should not try to form the character or cultivate the virtue of its citizens, for to do so would be to "legislate morality." Government should not affirm, through its policies or laws, any particular conception of the good life; instead it should provide a neutral framework of rights within which people can choose their own values and ends.

The aspiration to neutrality finds prominent expression in our politics and law. Although it derives from the liberal tradition of political thought, its province is not limited to those known as liberals, rather than conservatives, in American politics; it can be found across the political spectrum. Liberals invoke the ideal of neutrality when opposing school prayer or restrictions on abortion or attempts by Christian fundamentalists to bring their morality into the public square. Conservatives appeal to neutrality when opposing attempts by government to impose certain moral restraints—for the sake of workers' safety or environmental protection or distributive justice—on the operation of the market economy.

The ideal of free choice also figures on both sides of the debate over the welfare state. Republicans have long complained that taxing the rich to pay for welfare programs for the poor is a form of coerced charity that violates people's freedom to choose what to do with their own money. Democrats have long replied that government must assure all citizens a decent level of income, housing, education, and health care, on the grounds that those who are crushed by economic necessity are not truly free to exercise choice in other domains. Despite their disagreement about how government should act to respect individual choice, both sides assume that freedom consists in the capacity of people to choose their own ends.

So familiar is this vision of freedom that it might seem a permanent feature of the American political tradition. But as a reigning public philosophy, it is a recent arrival, a development of the past half century. Its distinctive character can best be seen by comparison with a rival public philosophy that it gradually displaced: a version of republican political theory.

Central to republican theory is the idea that liberty depends on sharing in self-government. This idea is not by itself inconsistent with liberal freedom. Participating in politics can be one among the ways in which people choose to pursue their individual ends. According to republican political theory, however, sharing in self-rule involves something more. It involves deliberating with fellow citizens about the common good and helping to shape the destiny of the political community. But to deliberate well about the common good requires more than the capacity to choose one's ends and to respect others' rights to do the same. It requires a knowledge of public affairs and also a sense of belonging, a concern for the whole, a moral bond with the community whose fate is at stake. To share in self-rule therefore requires that citizens possess, or come to acquire, certain civic virtues. But this means that republican politics cannot be neutral toward the values and ends its citizens espouse. The republican conception of freedom, unlike the liberal conception, requires a formative politics, a politics that cultivates in citizens the qualities of character that self-government requires.

Both the liberal and the republican understandings of freedom have been present throughout our political experience, but in shifting measure and relative importance. In recent decades the civic, or formative, aspect of our politics has given way to a procedural republic, concerned less with cultivating virtue than with enabling persons to choose their own values. This shift sheds light on our present discontent. For despite its appeal, the liberal vision of freedom lacks the civic resources to sustain self-government. The public philosophy by which we live cannot secure the liberty it promises, because it cannot inspire the sense of community and civic engagement that liberty requires.

### THE POLITICAL ECONOMY OF CITIZENSHIP

If American politics is to recover its civic voice, it must find a way to debate questions we have forgotten how to ask. Consider the way we think and argue about economics today, in contrast to the way Americans debated economic policy through much of our history. These days most of our economic arguments revolve around two considerations: prosperity and fairness. Whatever tax policies or budget proposals or regulatory schemes people may favor, they usually defend them on the grounds that they will increase the size of the economic pie or distribute the pieces of the pie more fairly or both.

So familiar are these ways of justifying economic policy that they might seem to exhaust the possibilities. But our debates about economic policy have not always focused solely on the size and the distribution of the national product. Throughout much of American history they have also addressed a different question: What economic arrangements are most hospitable to self-government?

Thomas Jefferson gave classic expression to the civic strand of economic argument. In his *Notes on the State of Virginia* (1787) he argued against developing large-scale domestic manufactures on the grounds that the agrarian way of life made for virtuous citizens, well suited to self-government. "Those who labour in the earth are the chosen people of God," he wrote—the embodiments of "genuine virtue." The political economists of Europe claimed that every nation should manufacture for itself, but Jefferson worried that large-scale manufacturing would create a propertyless class, lacking the independence that republican citizenship requires: "Dependance begets subservience and venality, suffocates the germ of virtue, and prepares fit tools for the designs of ambition." Jefferson thought it better to "let our work-shops remain in Europe" and avoid the moral corruption they brought; better to import manufactured goods than the manners and habits that attended their production. "The mobs of great cities add just so much to the support of pure government, as sores do to the strength of the human body," he wrote. "It is the manners and spirit of a people which preserve a republic in vigour. A degeneracy in these is a canker which soon eats to the heart of its laws and constitution."

Whether to encourage domestic manufacturing or to retain the nation's agrarian character was the subject of intense debate in the early decades of the republic. In the end, Jefferson's agrarian vision did not prevail. But the republican assumption underlying his economics—that public policy should cultivate the qualities of character that self-government requires—found broader support and a longer career. From the Revolution to the Civil War the political economy of citizenship played a prominent role in American national debate. In fact, the civic strand of economic argument extended even into the twentieth century, when Progressives grappled with big business and its consequences for self-government.

## THE CURSE OF BIGNESS

The political predicament of the Progressive Era bears a striking similarity to our own. Then as now, Americans sensed the unraveling of community and feared for the prospects of self-government. Then as now, there was a gap, or a lack of fit, between the scale of economic life and the terms in which people conceived their identities—a gap that many experienced as disorienting and disempowering. The threat to self-government at the turn of the century took two forms: the concentration of power amassed by giant corporations, and the erosion of those traditional forms of authority and community that had governed the lives of most Americans through the first century of the republic. A national economy dominated by vast corporations diminished the autonomy of local communities, traditionally the site of self-government. Meanwhile, the growth of large, impersonal cities, teeming with immigrants, poverty, and disorder, led many to fear that Americans lacked sufficient moral and civic cohesiveness to govern according to a shared vision of the good life.

Despite the dislocation they wrought, the new forms of industry, transportation, and communication seemed to offer a new, broader basis for political community. In many ways Americans of the early twentieth century were more closely connected than ever before. Railroads spanned the continent. The telephone, the telegraph, and the daily newspaper brought people into contact with events in distant places. And a complex industrial system connected people in a vast scheme of interdependence that coordinated their labors. Some saw in the new industrial and technological interdependence a more expansive form of community. "Steam has given us electricity and has made the nation a neighborhood," wrote William Allen White. "The electric wire, the iron pipe, the street railroad, the daily newspaper, the telephone, the lines of transcontinental traffic by rail and water . . . have made us all of one body—socially, industrially, politically. . . . It is possible for all men to understand one another."

More sober observers were not so sure. That Americans found themselves implicated in a complex scheme of interdependence did not guarantee that they would identify with that scheme or come to share a life with the unknown others who were similarly implicated. As the social reformer Jane Addams observed, "Theoretically, 'the division of labor' makes men more interdependent and human by drawing them together into a unity of purpose." But whether this unity of purpose is achieved depends on whether the participants take pride in their common project and regard it as their own; "the mere mechanical fact of interdependence amounts to nothing."

Political debate in the Progressive Era focused on two different responses to the power of big business. Some sought to preserve self-government by decentralizing economic power and thus bringing it under democratic control. Others considered economic concentration irreversible and sought to control it by enlarging the capacity of national democratic institutions. The decentralizing strand of progressivism found its ablest advocate in Louis D. Brandeis, who before his appointment to the Supreme Court was an activist attorney and an outspoken critic of industrial concentration. Brandeis's primary concern was with the civic consequences of economic arrangements. He opposed monopolies and trusts not because their market power led to higher consumer prices but because their political power undermined democratic government.

In Brandeis's view, big business threatened self-government in two ways—directly, by overwhelming democratic institutions and defying their control, and indirectly, by eroding the moral and civic capacities that equip workers to think and act as citizens. Brandeis brought long-standing republican themes into the twentieth-century debate: like Jefferson, he viewed concentrated power, whether economic or political, as inimical to liberty. His solution was not to confront big business with big government—that would only compound "the curse of bigness"—but to break up the trusts and restore competition. Only in this way would it be possible to preserve a decentralized economy of locally based enterprises amenable to democratic control.

Brandeis favored industrial democracy not for the sake of improving workers' incomes, desirable though that was, but for the sake of improving their civic capacities. For him, the formation of citizens capable of self-government was an end even higher than distributive justice. "We Americans are committed not only to social justice in the sense of avoiding . . . [an] unjust distribution of wealth; but we are committed primarily to democracy." The "striving for democracy" was inseparable from a "striving for the development of men," he said. "It is absolutely essential in order that men may develop that they be properly fed and properly housed, and that they have proper opportunities of education and recreation. We cannot reach our goal without those things. But we may have all those things and have a nation of slaves."

## THE NEW NATIONALISM

The other branch of the Progressive movement offered a different response to the threat posed by corporate power. Rather than decentralize the economy, Theodore Roosevelt proposed a "New Nationalism" to regulate big business by increasing the capacity of the national government.

Like Brandeis, Roosevelt feared the political consequences of concentrated economic power. Where Roosevelt disagreed with the decentralizers was over how to reassert democratic authority. He considered big business an inevitable product of industrial development and saw little point in trying to recover the decentralized political economy of the nineteenth century. Since most big corporations operated in interstate or foreign commerce, beyond the reach of individual states, only the federal government was suited to the task of controlling them. The power of the national government had to grow to match the scale of corporate power.

Like republicans since Jefferson's time, Roosevelt worried about the civic consequences of economic arrangements. His aim was not only to reduce the domination of government by big business but also to enlarge the self-understanding of American citizens, to instill what he called "a genuine and permanent moral awakening," "a spirit of broad and far-reaching nationalism." More than a program of institutional reform, the New Nationalism was a formative project that sought to cultivate a new sense of national citizenship.

Roosevelt was the leading spokesman for the New Nationalism; Herbert Croly was its leading philosopher. In *The Promise of American Life* (1909), Croly laid out the political theory underlying the nationalist strand of progressivism: given "the increasing concentration of American industrial, political, and social life," American government "demands more rather than less centralization." But, according to Croly, the success of democracy also required the nationalization of politics. The primary form of political community had to be recast on a national scale. This was the way to ease the gap, felt so acutely in the Progressive Era, between the scale of American life and the terms of American identity. Given the national scale of the modern economy, democracy required "an increasing nationalization of the American people in ideas, in institutions, and in spirit."

Although Croly renounced Jefferson's notion that democracy depends on dispersed power, he shared Jefferson's conviction that economic and political arrangements should be judged by the qualities of character they promote. For him, the project of nationalizing the American character was "an essentially formative and enlightening political transformation." American democracy could advance only as the nation became more of a nation, which required in turn a civic education that inspired in Americans a deeper sense of national identity.

The decentralizing and nationalizing versions of Progressive reform found memorable expression in the 1912 contest between Woodrow Wilson and Theodore Roosevelt. In retrospect, however, the greater significance of that campaign lies in the assumptions the protagonists shared. Brandeis and Wilson on one side, and Croly and Roosevelt on the other, agreed despite their differences that economic and political institutions should be assessed for their tendency to promote or erode the moral qualities that self-government requires. Like Jefferson before them, they worried about the sort of citizens that the economic arrangements of their day were likely to produce. They argued, in different ways, for a political economy of citizenship.

The economic arguments of our day bear little resemblance to the issues that divided the Progressive reformers. They were concerned with the structure of the economy and debated how to preserve democratic government in the face of concentrated economic power. We are concerned with the overall level of economic output and debate how to promote economic growth while assuring broad access to the fruits of prosperity. In retrospect it is possible to identify the moment when our economic questions displaced theirs. Beginning in the late New Deal and culminating in the early 1960s, the political economy of growth and distributive justice displaced the political economy of citizenship.

## THE NEW DEAL AND THE KEYNESIAN REVOLUTION

As the New Deal began, political debate continued to reflect the alternatives defined in the Progressive Era. When Franklin D. Roosevelt took office, in the midst of the Depression, two traditions of reform offered competing approaches to economic recovery. One group of reformers, heirs to the philosophy of Louis Brandeis, sought to decentralize the economy through antitrust laws and other measures aimed at restoring competition. Another group, indebted to the New Nationalism of Teddy Roosevelt, sought to rationalize the economy through national economic planning. Despite their differences, both the antitrusters and the planners assumed that overcoming the Depression required a change in the structure of industrial capitalism. They also agreed that the concentration of power in the economy, left to its own devices, posed a threat to democratic government.

The competition between these approaches persisted, unresolved, through much of the New Deal. In different policies and different moods, Roosevelt experimented with both, never fully embracing or rejecting either. In the end neither the antitrusters nor the planners prevailed. Recovery, when it came, was due not to structural reform but to heavy government spending. The Second World War supplied the occasion for the spending, and Keynesian economics supplied the rationale. But Keynesian fiscal policy had political appeal even before the war demonstrated its economic success. For unlike the various proposals for structural reform, such as vigorous antitrust action or national economic planning, Keynesian economics offered a way for the government to control the economy without having to choose among controversial views of the good society. Where earlier reformers had sought economic arrangements that would cultivate citizens of a certain kind, Keynesians undertook no formative mission; they proposed simply to accept existing consumer preferences and to regulate the economy by manipulating aggregate demand.

By the end of the Second World War, the central issues of economic policy had little to do with the debates that had preoccupied Americans earlier in the century. The old debates about how to reform industrial capitalism faded from the scene, and the macroeconomic issues familiar in our day came to the fore. By 1960 most economists and policymakers agreed, as Herbert Stein has written, that "the chief economic problem of the country was to achieve and maintain high and rapidly rising total output." Steps to distribute income more equally were deemed desirable but secondary to the aim of full employment and economic growth.

Debate would continue, of course, about the relative claims of economic growth and distributive justice, about tradeoffs between inflation and unemployment, about tax policies and spending priorities. But these debates reflected the assumption that economic policy is concerned above all with the amount and the distribution of national wealth. With the triumph of fiscal policy, the political economy of citizenship gave way to the political economy of growth and distributive justice.

## KEYNESIANISM AND LIBERALISM

The advent of the new political economy marked a decisive moment in the demise of the republican strand of American politics and the rise of contemporary liberalism. According to this liberalism, government should be neutral as to conceptions of the good life, in order to respect persons as free and independent selves, capable of choosing their own ends. Keynesian fiscal policy both reflected this liberalism and deepened its hold on American public life. Although those who practiced Keynesian economics did not defend it in precisely these terms, the new political economy displayed two features of the liberalism that defines the procedural republic. First, it offered policymakers and elected officials a way to "bracket," or set aside, controversial views of the good society, and so promised a consensus that programs for structural reform could not offer. Second, by abandoning the formative project, it denied government a stake in the moral character of its citizens and affirmed the notion of persons as free and independent selves.

The clearest expression of faith in the new economics as a neutral instrument of national governance was offered by President John F. Kennedy. In a commencement address at Yale University in 1962, he argued that modern economic problems could best be resolved if people set aside their ideological convictions. "The central domestic issues of our time," he observed, "are more subtle and less simple" than the large moral and political issues that commanded the nation's attention in earlier days. "They relate not to basic clashes of philosophy or ideology but to ways and means of reaching common goals. . . . What is at stake in our economic decisions today is not some grand warfare of rival ideologies which will sweep the country with passion but the practical management of a modern economy." Kennedy urged the country "to face technical problems without ideological preconceptions" and to focus on "the sophisticated and technical questions involved in keeping a great economic machinery moving ahead."

As Keynesian fiscal policy took hold in the 1960s, the civic strand of economic argument faded from American political discourse. Confronted with an economy too vast to admit republican hopes of mastery, and tempted by the prospect of prosperity, Americans of the postwar decades found their way to a new understanding of freedom. According to this understanding, our liberty depends not on our capacity as citizens to share in shaping the forces that govern our collective destiny but rather on our capacity as persons to choose our values and ends for ourselves.

From the standpoint of republican political theory, this shift represents a fateful concession; to abandon the formative ambition is to abandon the project of liberty as the republican tradition conceives it. But Americans did not experience the new public philosophy as disempowering—at least not at first. To the contrary, the procedural republic appeared to be a triumph of mastery and self-command. This was owing partly to the historical moment and partly to the promise of the liberal conception of freedom.

### THE MOMENT OF MASTERY

The procedural republic was born at a rare moment of American mastery. At the end of the Second World War, the United States stood astride the world, an unrivaled global power. This power, combined with the buoyant economy of the postwar decades, accustomed a generation of Americans to seeing themselves as masters of their circumstances. John Kennedy's inaugural address gave stirring expression to a generation's conviction that it possessed powers of Promethean proportions. "The world is very different now," Kennedy proclaimed. "For man holds in his mortal hands the power to abolish all forms of human poverty and all forms of human life." We would "pay any price, bear any burden," to assure the success of liberty.

Beyond the bounty of American power, the promise of mastery in the postwar decades had another source in the public philosophy of contemporary liberalism itself. The image of persons as free and independent selves, unbound by moral or communal ties they have not chosen, is a liberating, even exhilarating, ideal. Freed from the dictates of custom or tradition, the liberal self is installed as sovereign, cast as the author of the only obligations that constrain. This image of freedom found expression across the political spectrum. Lyndon Johnson argued the case for the welfare state not in terms of communal obligation but instead in terms of enabling people to choose their own ends: "For more than thirty years, from Social Security to the war against poverty, we have diligently worked to enlarge the freedom of man," he said upon accepting the 1964 Democratic presidential nomination. "And as a result Americans tonight are freer to live as they want to live, to pursue their ambitions, to meet their desires . . . than at any time in all of our glorious history." Welfare-rights advocates opposed work requirements, mandatory job training, and family-planning programs for welfare recipients on the grounds that all people, including the poor, "should have the freedom to choose how they may express the meaning of their lives." For their part, conservative critics of Johnson's Great Society also made their arguments in the name of the liberal conception of freedom. The only legitimate functions of government, Barry Goldwater insisted, were those that made it "possible for men to follow their chosen pursuits with maximum freedom." The libertarian economist Milton Friedman opposed Social Security and other mandatory government programs on the grounds that they violated people's rights "to live their lives by their own values."

And so for a time the special circumstances of American life obscured the passing of the civic conception of freedom. But when the moment of mastery expired—when, in 1968, Vietnam, riots in the ghettos, campus unrest, and the assassinations of Martin Luther King Jr. and Robert Kennedy brought a shattering of faith—Americans were left ill equipped to contend with the dislocation that swirled about them. The liberating promise of the freely choosing self could not compensate for the loss of self-government more broadly conceived. Events spun out of control at home and abroad, and government seemed helpless to respond.

## REAGAN'S CIVIC CONSERVATISM

There followed a season of protest that is with us still. As disillusionment with government grew, politicians groped to articulate the frustrations that the reigning political agenda did not address. The most successful, at least in electoral terms, was Ronald Reagan. Although he ultimately failed to allay the discontent he tapped, it is instructive nonetheless to consider the source of his appeal and the way it departed from the prevailing terms of political discourse.

Reagan drew, in different moods and moments, on both the libertarian and the civic strands of American conservatism. The most resonant part of his political appeal derived from the second of these, from his skillful evocation of communal values such as family and neighborhood, religion and patriotism. What set Reagan apart from laissez-faire conservatives also set him apart from the public philosophy of his day: his ability to identify with Americans' yearnings for a common life of larger meanings on a smaller, less impersonal scale than that the procedural republic provides.

Reagan blamed big government for disempowering citizens and proposed a "New Federalism" that would shift power to states and localities, recalling the long-standing republican worry about concentrated power. But Reagan revived this tradition with a difference. Previous advocates of republican political economy had worried about big government and big business alike. For Reagan, the curse of bigness attached to government alone. Even as he evoked the ideal of community, he had little to say about the corrosive effects of capital flight or the disempowering consequences of economic power organized on a vast scale.

Reagan-era Democrats did not challenge Reagan on this score, nor did they otherwise join the debate about community and self-government. Tied to the terms of rights-oriented liberalism, they missed the mood of discontent. The anxieties of the age concerned the erosion of those communities intermediate between the individual and the nation—families and neighborhoods, cities and towns, schools and congregations. But Democrats, once the party of dispersed power, had learned in recent decades to view intermediate communities with suspicion. Too often such communities had been pockets of prejudice, outposts of intolerance, places where the tyranny of the majority held sway. And so, from the New Deal to the civil-rights movement to the Great Society, the liberal project was to use federal power to vindicate individual rights that local communities had failed to protect. This unease with the middle terms of civic life, however honorably acquired, left Democrats ill equipped to attend to the erosion of self-government.

The civic strand of Reagan's rhetoric enabled him to succeed, where Democrats failed, in tapping the mood of discontent. In the end, however, Reagan's presidency did little to alter the conditions underlying the discontent. He governed more as a market conservative than as a civic conservative. The unfettered capitalism he favored did nothing to repair the moral fabric of families, neighborhoods, and communities and much to undermine them.

## THE RISKS OF REPUBLICAN POLITICS

Any attempt to revitalize the civic strand of freedom must confront two sobering objections. The first doubts that it is possible to revive republican ideals; the second doubts that it is desirable. The first objection holds that given the scale and complexity of the modern world, it is unrealistic to aspire to self-government as the republican tradition conceives it. From Aristotle's polis to Jefferson's agrarian ideal, the civic conception of freedom found its home in small and bounded places, largely self-sufficient, inhabited by people whose conditions of life afforded the leisure, learning, and commonality to deliberate well about public concerns. But we do not live that way today. To the contrary, we live in a highly mobile continental society, teeming with diversity. Moreover, even this vast society is not self-sufficient but is situated in a global economy whose frenzied flow of money and goods, information and images, pays little heed to nations, much less neighborhoods. How, under conditions such as these, could the civic strand of freedom possibly take hold?

In fact, this objection continues, the republican strand of American politics, for all its persistence, has often spoken in a voice tinged with nostalgia. Even as Jefferson exalted the yeoman farmer, America was becoming a manufacturing nation. And so it was with the artisan republicans of Andrew Jackson's day, the apostles of free labor in Abraham Lincoln's time, and the shopkeepers and pharmacists Brandeis defended against the curse of bigness. In each of these cases—or so it is argued—republican ideals found their expression at the last moment, too late to offer feasible alternatives, just in time to offer an elegy for a lost cause. If the republican tradition is irredeemably nostalgic, then whatever its capacity to illuminate the defects of liberal politics, it offers little that could lead us to a richer civic life.

The second objection holds that even were it possible to recover republican ideals, to do so would not be desirable; given the difficulty of instilling civic virtue, republican politics always runs the risk of coercion. This peril can be glimpsed in Jean-Jacques Rousseau's account of the formative undertaking necessary to a democratic republic. The task of the republic's founder or great legislator, he writes, is no less than "to change human nature, to transform each individual . . . into a part of a larger whole from which this individual receives, in a sense, his life and his being." The legislator "must deny man his own forces" in order to make him reliant on the community as a whole. The more nearly each person's individual will is "dead and obliterated," the more likely that person is to embrace the general will. "Thus if each citizen is nothing and can do nothing except in concert with all the others . . . one can say that the legislation has achieved the highest possible point of perfection."

The coercive face of soulcraft is by no means unknown among American republicans. For example, Benjamin Rush, a signer of the Declaration of Independence, wanted "to convert men into republican machines" and to teach each citizen "that he does not belong to himself, but that he is public property." But civic education need not take so harsh a form. In practice, successful republican soulcraft involves a gentler kind of tutelage. For example, the political economy of citizenship that informed nineteenth-century American life sought to cultivate not only commonality but also the independence and judgment to deliberate well about the common good. It worked not by coercion but by a complex mixture of persuasion and habituation—what Alexis de Tocqueville called "the slow and quiet action of society upon itself."

The dispersed, differentiated character of American public life in Tocqueville's day and the indirect modes of character formation this differentiation allowed are what separate Rousseau's republican exertions from the civic practices Tocqueville described. Unable to abide disharmony, Rousseau's republican ideal seeks to collapse the distance between persons so that citizens stand in a kind of speechless transparence, or immediate presence to one another. Where the general will prevails, the citizens "consider themselves to be a single body" and there is no need for political argument. "The first to propose [a new law] merely says what everybody has already felt; and there is no question of intrigues or eloquence" to secure its passage.

It is this assumption, that the common good is unitary and uncontestable, not the formative ambition as such, that inclines Rousseau's politics to coercion. It is, moreover, an assumption that republican politics can do without. As America's experience with the political economy of citizenship suggests, the civic conception of freedom does not render disagreement unnecessary. It offers a way of conducting political argument, not transcending it.

Unlike Rousseau's unitary vision, the republican politics Tocqueville described is more clamorous than consensual. It does not despise differentiation. Instead of collapsing the space between persons, it fills this space with public institutions that gather people together in various capacities, that both separate and relate them. These institutions include the townships, schools, religions, and virtue-sustaining occupations that form the "character of mind" and "habits of the heart" a democratic republic requires. Whatever their more particular purposes, these agencies of civic education inculcate the habit of attending to public things. And yet given their multiplicity, they prevent public life from dissolving into an undifferentiated whole.

So the civic strand of freedom is not necessarily coercive. It can sometimes find pluralistic expression. To this extent the liberal objection to republican political theory is misplaced. But the liberal worry does contain an insight that cannot be dismissed: republican politics is risky politics, a politics without guarantees, and the risks it entails inhere in the formative project. To accord the political community a stake in the character of its citizens is to concede the possibility that bad communities may form bad characters. Dispersed power and multiple sites of civic formation may reduce these dangers but cannot remove them.

## WHERE LIBERALS FEAR TO TREAD

What to make of this complaint depends on the alternatives. If there were a way to secure freedom without attending to the character of citizens, or to define rights without affirming a conception of the good life, then the liberal objection to the formative project might be decisive. But is there such a way? Liberal political theory claims that there is. The voluntarist conception of freedom promises to lay to rest, once and for all, the risks of republican politics. If liberty can be detached from the exercise of self-government and conceived instead as the capacity of persons to choose their own ends, then the difficult task of forming civic virtue can finally be dispensed with. Or at least it can be narrowed to the seemingly simpler task of cultivating toleration and respect for others.

In the voluntarist conception of freedom, statecraft no longer needs soulcraft, except in a limited domain. Tying freedom to respect for the rights of freely choosing selves dampens old disputes about how to form the habits of self-rule. It spares politics the ancient quarrels about the nature of the good life. Once freedom is detached from the formative project, "the problem of setting up a state can be solved even by a nation of devils," in Kant's memorable words. "For such a task does not involve the moral improvement of man."

But the liberal attempt to detach freedom from the formative project confronts problems of its own, problems that can be seen in both the theory and the practice of the procedural republic. The philosophical difficulty lies in the liberal conception of citizens as freely choosing, independent selves, unencumbered by moral or civic ties antecedent to choice. This vision cannot account for a wide range of moral and political obligations that we commonly recognize, such as obligations of loyalty or solidarity. By insisting that we are bound only by ends and roles we choose for ourselves, it denies that we can ever be claimed by ends we have not chosen—ends given by nature or God, for example, or by our identities as members of families, peoples, cultures, or traditions.

Some liberals concede that we may be bound by obligations such as these but insist that they apply to private life alone and have no bearing on politics. But this raises a further difficulty. Why insist on separating our identity as citizens from our identity as persons more broadly conceived? Why should political deliberation not reflect our best understanding of the highest human ends? Don't arguments about justice and rights unavoidably draw on particular conceptions of the good life, whether we admit it or not?

The problems in the theory of procedural liberalism show up in the practice it inspires. A politics that brackets morality and religion too completely soon generates its own disenchantment. Where political discourse lacks moral resonance, the yearning for a public life of larger meaning finds undesirable expression. The Christian Coalition and similar groups seek to clothe the naked public square with narrow, intolerant moralisms. Fundamentalists rush in where liberals fear to tread. The disenchantment also assumes more secular forms. Absent a political agenda that addresses the moral dimension of public questions, attention becomes riveted on the private vices of public officials. Political discourse becomes increasingly preoccupied with the scandalous, the sensational, and the confessional as purveyed by tabloids, talk shows, and eventually the mainstream media as well. It cannot be said that the public philosophy of contemporary liberalism is wholly responsible for these tendencies. But liberalism's vision of political discourse is too spare to contain the moral energies of democratic life. It creates a moral void that opens the way for intolerance and other misguided moralisms.

A political agenda lacking substantive moral discourse is one symptom of the public philosophy of the procedural republic. Another is a loss of mastery. The triumph of the voluntarist conception of freedom has coincided with a growing sense of disempowerment. Despite the expansion of rights in recent decades, Americans find to their frustration that they are losing control of the forces that govern their lives. This has partly to do with the insecurity of jobs in the global economy, but it also reflects the self-image by which we live. The liberal self-image and the actual organization of modern social and economic life are sharply at odds. Even as we think and act as freely choosing, independent selves, we confront a world governed by impersonal structures of power that defy our understanding and control. The voluntarist conception of freedom leaves us ill equipped to contend with this condition. Liberated though we may be from the burden of identities we have not chosen, entitled though we may be to the range of rights assured by the welfare state, we find ourselves overwhelmed as we turn to face the world on our own resources.

## GLOBAL POLITICS AND PARTICULAR IDENTITIES

If the public philosophy of contemporary liberalism fails to address democracy's discontent, the question remains how a renewed attention to republican themes might better equip us to contend with our condition. Is self-government in the republican sense even possible under modern conditions, and if so, what qualities of character would be necessary to sustain it?

A partial, inchoate answer can be glimpsed in the shifting terms of contemporary political argument. Some conservatives, and recently some liberals, have gestured toward a revival of civic virtue, character formation, and moral judgment as considerations in public policy and political discourse. From the 1930s to the 1980s conservatives criticized the welfare state on libertarian grounds. Since the mid-1980s, however, the conservative argument has focused on the moral and civic consequences of federal social policy. Welfare is at odds with freedom, many conservatives now argue, not because it coerces taxpayers but because it breeds dependence and irresponsibility among recipients and so deprives them of the independence that full citizenship requires.

Liberals came more reluctantly to the revolt against the procedural republic, but they too have begun to articulate civic themes. In November of 1993, speaking in the Memphis church where Martin Luther King Jr. preached the night before his assassination, Bill Clinton ventured onto moral and spiritual terrain that liberals of recent times had sought to avoid. Restoring work to the life of the inner city was essential, he explained, not only for the income it would bring but also for its character-forming effects, for the discipline, structure, and pride that work confers on family life.

But suppose that the civic intimations present in our politics did find fuller voice and succeeded in reorienting the terms of political discourse. What is the prospect that a revitalized politics could actually alleviate the loss of mastery and the erosion of community that lie at the heart of democracy's discontent? Even a politics that engaged rather than avoided substantive moral discourse and managed to revive the formative project would confront a daunting obstacle. This obstacle consists in the formidable scale on which modern economic life is organized and the difficulty of achieving the democratic political authority necessary to govern it.

The difficulty actually involves two related challenges. One is to devise political institutions capable of governing the global economy. The other is to cultivate the civic identities necessary to sustain those institutions, to supply them with the moral authority they require. It is not obvious that both these challenges can be met.

In a world where capital and goods, information and images, pollution and people, flow across national boundaries with unprecedented ease, politics must assume transnational, even global, forms, if only to keep up. Otherwise, economic power will go unchecked by democratically sanctioned political power. Nation-states, traditionally the vehicles of self-government, will find themselves increasingly unable to bring their citizens' judgments to bear on the economic forces that govern their destinies. If the global character of the economy suggests the need for transnational forms of governance, however, it remains to be seen whether such political units can inspire the identification and allegiance—the moral and civic culture—on which democratic authority ultimately depends.

In striking ways, the challenge to self-government in the global economy resembles the predicament American politics faced in the early decades of the twentieth century. Then as now, new forms of commerce and communication spilled across familiar political boundaries and created networks of interdependence among people in distant places. But the new interdependence did not carry with it a new sense of community. Jane Addams's insight, that "the mere mechanical fact of interdependence amounts to nothing," is no less apt today. What railroads, telegraph wires, and national markets were to her time, satellite hookups, CNN, cyberspace, and global markets are to ours—instruments that link people without necessarily making them neighbors or fellow citizens or participants in a common venture.

Given the similarity between their predicament and ours, it is tempting to think that the logic of the Progressives' solution can be extended to our time. If the way to respond to a national economy was to strengthen the national government and cultivate a sense of national citizenship, perhaps the way to respond to a global economy is to strengthen global governance and cultivate a corresponding sense of global or cosmopolitan citizenship. Internationally minded reformers have already begun to articulate this impulse. The Commission on Global Governance, a group of twenty-eight public officials from around the world, recently published a report calling for greater authority for international institutions. The commission also called for efforts to inspire "broad acceptance of a global civic ethic," to transform "a global neighborhood based on economic exchange and improved communications into a universal moral community."

The analogy between the globalizing impulse of our time and the nationalizing project of the Progressives' time does hold to this extent: We cannot hope to govern the global economy without transnational political institutions, and we cannot expect to sustain such institutions without cultivating more-expansive civic identities. Human-rights conventions, global environmental accords, and world bodies governing trade, finance, and economic development are among the undertakings that will depend for public support on inspiring a greater sense of engagement in a shared global destiny.

But the cosmopolitan vision is wrong to suggest that we can re-store self-government simply by pushing sovereignty and citizenship upward. The hope for self-government today lies not in relocating sovereignty but in dispersing it. The most promising alternative to the sovereign state is not a cosmopolitan community based on the solidarity of humankind but a multiplicity of communities and po-litical bodies—some more extensive than nations and some less—among which sovereignty is diffused. Only a politics that disperses sovereignty both upward and downward can combine the power re-quired to rival global market forces with the differentiation required of a public life that hopes to inspire the allegiance of its citizens.

In some places dispersing sovereignty may entail according greater cultural and political autonomy to subnational communi-ties—such as Catalans and Kurds, Scots and Quebecois—even while strengthening and democratizing the European Union and other transnational structures. Arrangements like these may avoid the strife that arises when state sovereignty is an all-or-nothing affair. In the United States, which never was a nation-state in the European sense, proliferating sites of political engagement may take a different form. America was born of the conviction that sovereignty need not reside in a single place. From the start the Constitution divided power among branches and levels of government. Over time, how-ever, we too have pushed sovereignty and citizenship upward, in the direction of the nation.

The nationalizing of American political life occurred largely in response to industrial capitalism. The consolidation of economic power called forth the consolidation of political power. Present-day conservatives who rail against big government often ignore this fact. They wrongly assume that rolling back the power of the national government would liberate individuals to pursue their own ends, in-stead of leaving them at the mercy of economic forces beyond their control.

Conservative complaints about big government find popular resonance, but not for the reasons conservatives articulate. The American welfare state is politically vulnerable because it does not rest on a sense of national community adequate to its purpose. The nationalizing project that unfolded from the Progressive Era to the New Deal to the Great Society succeeded only in part. It managed to create a strong national government but failed to cultivate a shared national identity. As the welfare state developed, it drew less on an ethic of social solidarity and mutual obligation and more on an ethic of fair procedures and individual rights. But the liberalism of the procedural republic proved an inadequate substitute for the strong sense of citizenship that the welfare state requires.

If the nation cannot summon more than a minimal commonality, it is unlikely that the global community can do better, at least on its own. A more promising basis for a democratic politics that reaches beyond nations is a revitalized civic life nourished in the more particular communities we inhabit. In the age of NAFTA the politics of neighborhood matters more, not less. People will not pledge allegiance to vast and distant entities, whatever their importance, unless those institutions are somehow connected to political arrangements that reflect the identity of the participants.

### BEYOND SOVEREIGN STATES AND SOVEREIGN SELVES

The growing aspiration for the public expression of communal identities reflects a yearning for political arrangements that can situate people in a world increasingly governed by vast and distant forces. For a time the nation-state promised to answer this yearning, to provide the link between identity and self-rule. In theory at least, each state was a more or less self-sufficient political and economic unit that gave expression to the collective identity of a people defined by a common history, language, or tradition. The nation-state laid claim to the allegiance of its citizens on the ground that its exercise of sovereignty expressed their collective identity.

In the contemporary world, however, this claim is losing its force. National sovereignty is eroded from above by the mobility of capital, goods, and information across national boundaries, the integration of world financial markets, and the transnational character of industrial production. And national sovereignty is challenged from below by the resurgent aspirations of subnational groups for autonomy and self-rule. As their effective sovereignty fades, nations gradually lose their hold on the allegiance of their citizens. Beset by the integrating tendencies of the global economy and the fragmenting tendencies of group identities, nation-states are increasingly unable to link identity and self-rule. Even the most powerful states cannot escape the imperatives of the global economy; even the smallest are too heterogeneous to give full expression to the communal identity of any one ethnic or national or religious group without oppressing others who live in their midst.

Since the days of Aristotle's polis, the republican tradition has viewed self-government as an activity rooted in a particular place, carried out by citizens loyal to that place and the way of life it embodies. Self-government today, however, requires a politics that plays itself out in a multiplicity of settings, from neighborhoods to nations to the world as a whole. Such a politics requires citizens who can abide the ambiguity associated with divided sovereignty, who can think and act as multiply situated selves. The civic virtue distinctive to our time is the capacity to negotiate our way among the sometimes overlapping and sometimes conflicting obligations that claim us, and to live with the tension to which multiple loyalties give rise.

The global media and markets that shape our lives beckon us to a world beyond boundaries and belonging. But the civic resources we need to master these forces, or at least to contend with them, are still to be found in the places and stories, memories and meanings, incidents and identities, that situate us in the world and give our lives their moral particularity. The task for politics now is to cultivate these resources, to repair the civic life on which democracy depends.

# two

# BEYOND INDIVIDUALISM
## DEMOCRATS AND COMMUNITY

This essay appeared as the 1988 presidential primary season began. Michael Dukakis won the Democratic nomination that year, and was defeated by George H. W. Bush in the general election.

For half a century, the Democratic Party was sustained by the public philosophy of New Deal liberalism. Democrats and Republicans debated the role of government in the market economy, and the responsibility of the nation for the collective provision of basic needs. The Democrats won that debate, and elected every president but Eisenhower from 1932 to 1964.

In time the Republicans stopped attacking the welfare state and argued instead that they could manage it better. But the New Deal agenda continued to define the terms of debate, and the meaning of liberalism and conservatism. Liberals favored a greater federal role in the social and economic life of the nation, conservative less.

Between these alternatives flowed the rhythms of American politics. Arthur Schlesinger Jr. has written that American politics moves in cycles, from activism to quietude and back again. Since progress demands passions that cannot last for long, liberalism advances by seasons, punctuated by conservative interludes that set the stage for further reforms.

Thus the complacent Republican '20s gave way to the activism of

FDR and Truman, which receded in turn to the languid years of Eisenhower. A time of consolidation prepared the way for renewed political exertions, for Kennedy's call to "get the country moving again," and Lyndon Johnson's Great Society. By the end of the '60s, exhausted and divided, the country collapsed into Richard Nixon's awkward embrace.

This account of the political pendulum explains the predominance of the Democratic Party in recent times. Although it assigns to each party a distinctive vocation—the Democrats reform, the Republicans repose—it casts the Democratic Party as the primary agent of moral and political improvement. And so, for half a century, the Democrats have been. The welfare state took shape under Democratic auspices, and the great issues of the 1960s—civil rights and the Vietnam War—were fought out not between the parties but within the Democratic Party.

If the cycles of American politics hold up, 1988 should be a Democratic year. If the world turns as the conventional wisdom suggests, eight years of Ronald Reagan will have left a country ripe for reform.

But there is reason to think that the cycle has stalled, the pattern dissolved. By the 1970s the New Deal agenda had become obsolete. The alternatives it posed lost their capacity to inspire the electorate or animate meaningful debate. Voter turnout steadily declined from the '60s to the '80s, party loyalties eroded, and disillusion with government grew. Meanwhile, politicians groped to articulate frustrations and discontents that the reigning political agenda did not capture. From the left and the right came a politics of protest. In the 1972 primaries, pollsters found to their surprise that many supporters of George Wallace favored George McGovern as their second choice. Despite their ideological differences, both appealed to a tradition of populist protest.

In 1976 Jimmy Carter brought the Southern and progressive strands of populist protest together in a single candidacy. Like Wallace and McGovern, he campaigned as a political outsider, a critic of the federal bureaucracy and the Washington establishment. But Carter's presidency only deepened the discontent he had tapped as a candidate. Four years later another self-described political outsider, Ronald Reagan, ran for president by running against government, and won.

In different ways, both Carter and Reagan spoke to anxieties that the New Deal agenda failed to address. Both sensed a growing fear that, individually and collectively, we are less and less in control of the forces that govern our lives. Despite the extension of rights and entitlements in recent decades, and despite the expansion of the franchise, Americans increasingly find themselves in the grip of impersonal structures of power that defy their understanding and control.

By the 1970s a generation weaned on ever-rising standards of living and unrivaled American power suddenly confronted a world it could not summon or command. A decade of inflation and declining real wages undercut Americans' confidence that we could shape our personal destinies. Meanwhile, events in the world at large symbolized the loss of collective mastery—in Vietnam, a war we could not win, in Iran, a hostage-taking we could not avenge, and in 1987, a stock market crash that even the experts could not explain.

To make matters worse, the flow of power to large-scale institutions coincided with the decline of traditional communities. Families and neighborhoods, cities and towns, religious and ethnic and regional communities were eroded or homogenized, leaving the individual to confront the impersonal forces of the economy and the state without the moral or political resources that intermediate communities provide.

It is clear by now that Ronald Reagan's presidency has not addressed the worries and longings his candidacy so effectively evoked. For all the talk of "America standing tall," it neither restored our sense of self-mastery nor reversed the erosion of community. The

Marines killed in Lebanon, the failed attempt to trade arms for hostages, the Wall Street plunge, and a gaping trade deficit are Reagan-era reminders of a world spinning out of control.

Still, Democrats will not reap the fruits of Reagan's failures until they learn from his success at speaking the language of self-government and community. Oddly enough, a new public philosophy for American liberalism has something to learn from Ronald Reagan's conservative vision.

Political genius is more instinctive than deliberate, especially so in the case of Reagan. His genius was to bring together in a single voice two contending strands in American conservatism. The first is individualistic, libertarian, and laissez-faire, the second communal, traditionalist, and Moral Majoritarian. The first seeks a greater role for markets in public life, the second a greater role for morals.

Individualist conservatives believe people should be free to do as they please so long as they do not harm others. They are the conservatives who talk about "getting government off people's backs." Communal conservatives, by contrast, believe government should affirm moral and religious values. They want to ban abortion, restrict pornography, and restore prayer to public schools. While the first favor a volunteer army in the name of individual liberty, the second favor conscription in hopes of cultivating civic virtue. The first oppose the welfare state as a form of coerced charity; the second favor a welfare state that promotes conservative values.

Reagan managed to affirm both ethics without ever choosing between them. In his capacious conservatism, Milton Friedman met Jerry Falwell, and the two coexisted for a time. But Reagan's political achievement was not simply to make bedfellows of libertarian economists and fundamentalist preachers. It was to draw from conservative ideals a set of themes that spoke to the troubles of the time.

And here lies the lesson that American liberalism has still to learn: the themes that resonated most deeply came from the second strand, the communal strand of conservative thought. For all Reagan's talk of individual liberty and market solutions, the most potent part of his appeal was his evocation of communal values—of family and neighborhood, religion and patriotism. What Reagan stirred was a yearning for a way of life that seems to be receding in recent times—a common life of larger meanings, on a smaller, less impersonal scale than the nation-state provides.

To their political misfortune, Democrats in recent years have not spoken convincingly about self-government and community. More than a matter of rhetoric, the reasons run deep in liberal political theory. For, unlike conservatism, contemporary liberalism lacks a second voice, or communal strand. Its predominant impulse is individualistic.

Like laissez-faire conservatives, liberals believe that government should be neutral on moral and religious questions. Rather than affirm in law a particular vision of the good life, liberals would leave individuals free to choose their values for themselves. They believe government should protect people's rights, not promote civic virtue. It should offer a framework of rights, neutral among ends, within which its citizens may pursue whatever values they happen to have.

Though they share the ideal of a neutral state that protects individual rights, individualist conservatives and liberals disagree about what rights are fundamental, and about *what* political arrangements the ideal of neutrality requires. Conservatives emphasize private property rights, and claim that freedom of choice is most fully realized in an unfettered market economy. Liberals reply that genuine freedom requires certain social and economic prerequisites, and so argue for rights to welfare, education, employment, housing, health care, and the like.

And so, for half a century, the argument has gone. Locked in battle with laissez-faire conservatives, liberals defended the welfare state in the individualistic language of rights and entitlements. For example, the Social Security system was set up from the start to resemble a private insurance scheme rather than a social welfare program, funded by payroll "contributions," not general tax revenues. FDR rightly thought this would assure its political survival.

Compared with the social democracies of Europe, the American welfare state draws less on notions of communal obligation and social solidarity and more on notions of individual rights. Given the individualism of American political culture, this may have been the only way to win broad support for the public provision of basic human goods.

But political considerations aside, liberals are troubled in principle by strong notions of self-government and community. If government is not neutral, they ask, then what is to prevent an intolerant majority from imposing its values on those who disagree? Didn't the struggle for civil rights show that "local control" can be a code word for racism, that "community" is the first refuge of prejudice and intolerance? And hasn't the rise of the religious right taught the danger of mixing morality and politics?

When Democrats do speak of community, they usually mean the national community. FDR argued for "extending to our national life, the old principle of the local community," and encouraged Americans to think of themselves as "neighbors" bound in national community. More recently, Democrats have used the family as a metaphor for the ties of national citizenship. Urging the Great Society, Lyndon Johnson saw "America as a family, its people bound together by common ties of confidence and affection." In 1984 Walter Mondale and Mario Cuomo also compared the nation to a family. As Mondale proclaimed, "Let us be a community, a family where we care for each other, knit together by a band of love."

But the yearning for community can no longer be satisfied by depicting the nation as a family or a neighborhood. The metaphor is by now too strained to carry conviction. The nation is too vast to sustain more than a minimal commonality, too distant to permit more than occasional moments of participation.

Local attachments can serve self-government by engaging citizens in a common life beyond their private pursuits, and by cultivating the habit of attending to public things. They can enable citizens, in Tocqueville's phrase, to "practice the art of government in the small sphere within their reach."

Ideally at least, the reach extends as the sphere expands. Civic capacities first awakened in neighborhoods and town halls, churches and synagogues, trade unions and social movements, find national expression. For example, the civic education and social solidarity cultivated in the black Baptist churches of the South were a crucial prerequisite for the civil rights movement that ultimately unfolded on a national scale. What began as a bus boycott in Montgomery later became a general challenge to segregation in the South, which led in turn to a national campaign for equal citizenship and the right to vote. But more than a means of winning the vote, the movement itself was a moment of self-government, an instance of empowerment. It offered an example of the kind of civic engagement that can flow from local attachments and communal ties.

From the New Deal to the Great Society, the individualistic ethic of rights and entitlements offered an energizing, progressive force. But by the 1970s it had lost its capacity to inspire. Lacking a communal sensibility, liberals missed the mood of the discontent. They did not understand how people could be more entitled but less empowered at the same time.

The anxieties of the age concern the erosion of those communities intermediate between the individual and the nation, from families and neighborhoods to cities and towns to communities defined by religious or ethnic or cultural traditions. American democracy has long relied on communities like these to cultivate a public spirit that the nation alone cannot command. Self-government requires community, for people aspire to control their destiny not only as individuals, but as participants in a common life with which they can identify.

But the public philosophy of rights and entitlements left Democrats suspicious of intermediate communities. From the New Deal to the civil rights movement to the Great Society, the liberal project was to use the federal government to vindicate individual rights that local communities had failed to protect. Unable to fulfill the longing for self-government and community, Democrats allowed Ronald Reagan and the religious right to capture these aspirations and bend them to conservative purposes.

This abdication was politically costly, for as Reagan has shown, the communal dimension of politics is too potent to ignore. But it was also philosophically unnecessary, for there is nothing intrinsically conservative about family or neighborhood or community or religion. To the contrary, under modern conditions, traditional values cannot be vindicated by conservative policies. This can be seen in Reagan's failure to govern by the vision he evoked.

Reagan's proposed solution to the erosion of self-government was to shift power from the federal government to states and localities—to cut federal domestic spending, to decentralize and deregulate. A revitalized federal system would restore people's control over their lives by locating power closer to home. Meanwhile, a less activist federal judiciary would strengthen traditional values by allowing communities to legislate morality in the areas of abortion, pornography, homosexuality, and school prayer.

But this approach was bound to fail, because it ignored the conditions that led to the growth of federal power in the first place, including the growth of corporate power on a national, and now international, scale.

In its origins, federalism was designed to promote self-government by dispersing political power. But this arrangement presupposed the decentralized economy prevailing at the time. As national markets and large-scale enterprise grew, the political forms of the early republic became inadequate to self-government. Since the turn of the century, the concentration of political power has been a response to the concentration of economic power, an attempt to preserve democratic control.

Decentralizing government without decentralizing the economy, as Reagan proposed, is only half a federalism. And from the standpoint of self-government, half a federalism is worse than none. Leaving local communities to the mercy of corporate decisions made in distant places does not empower them; if anything it diminishes their ability to shape their destiny.

For similar reasons, conservative policies cannot answer the aspiration for community. The greatest corrosive of traditional values are not liberal judges but features of the modern economy that conservatives ignore. These include the unrestrained mobility of capital, with its disruptive effects on neighborhoods, cities, and towns; the concentration of power in large corporations unaccountable to the communities they serve; and an inflexible workplace that forces working men and women to choose between advancing their careers and caring for their children.

In the end, Reagan's presidency was an evocative success and a practical failure. In both respects, it offers insights that can inform a public philosophy for American liberalism.

First, liberalism must learn the language of self-government and community. It needs a vision of self-government that goes beyond voting rights, important though they are. And it needs a vision of community that embraces the rich array of civic resources intermediate between the individual and the nation.

Second, no amount of exhortation can rejuvenate communities unless people identify with them and have reason to participate in them. So Democrats need a revitalized federalism of their own, and should begin to debate the political responsibilities best suited to local control. A Democratic theory of federalism might begin by defining the basic rights of national citizenship, and seek ways, consistent with those rights, of giving local communities a greater role in the decisions that govern their lives. It might ask, for example, how to enhance local control of schools consistent with nationally assured rights to racial equality and a decent education for all citizens.

Third, Democrats must acknowledge, as Republicans do not, that any meaningful devolution of political power requires reform in the structure of the modern economy. They need policies to deal with the unprecedented mobility of capital, the unaccountable power of large corporations, and the adversarial relations of labor and management. A public philosophy that put self-government first would focus less on macroeconomic issues such as budget deficits and tax rates and more on questions of economic structure. And it would address these questions not only from the standpoint of maximizing GNP, but also from that of building communities capable of self-government on a manageable scale.

In this respect, it would recall an older debate in the progressive tradition, a debate about the economic arrangements most amenable to democratic government. Some New Dealers favored national economic planning as a way of preserving democracy in the face of economic power, others anti-trust policy and economic decentralization. Earlier in the century, the New Nationalism of Theodore Roosevelt opposed the New Freedom of Woodrow Wilson. Despite their differences, the participants in those debates understood that economic policy was not only about consumption but also about self-government. Democrats today would do well to recover that insight of their progressive forebears.

Finally, Democrats should overcome the impulse to banish moral and religious discourse from public life. They should reject the idea that government can be neutral. A public life empty of moral meanings and shared ideals does not secure freedom but offers an open invitation to intolerance. As the Moral Majority has shown, a politics whose moral resources are diminished with disuse lies vulnerable to those who would impose narrow moralisms. Fundamentalists rush in where liberals fear to tread. The answer for liberals is not to flee moral arguments but to engage them. In any case, liberals have long been making moral arguments, often explicitly so. The civil rights movement "legislated morality," and drew without apology on religious themes.

In recent years liberalism has faltered because of its failure to argue for a vision of the common good. This has conceded to conservatives the most potent resources of American politics. A public philosophy of self-government and community would reclaim those resources for liberal purposes, and enable Democrats to resume their career as the party of moral and political progress.

# three

# THE POLITICS
# OF EASY VIRTUE

This essay and the next appeared during the presidential campaign of 1996, between Bill Clinton and his Republican challenger, Bob Dole. Clinton was re-elected by a comfortable margin.

Ever since Richard Nixon won the presidency by standing for law and order and against the counterculture, Democrats have been on the defensive about values. Until now. In one of the great reversals of contemporary American politics, Bill Clinton has seized the upper hand in the politics of virtue. Over the past year, Clinton has promoted the V-chip, curfews, and school uniforms, and condemned teenage pregnancy, smoking, and truancy. Some mock this agenda as a litany of small favors, and wonder when the president will come out against cussing. But, as Republicans have known for some time, easy virtue goes a long way in American politics, longer perhaps than more strenuous versions.

No one understood this better than Ronald Reagan. He skillfully evoked family and neighborhood, religion and patriotism, even while promoting an unfettered capitalism that undermined the traditions and communities he praised. Other Republicans followed. George H. W. Bush, who invoked values more out of strategy than conviction, posed in a flag factory and introduced us to Willie Horton. Dan Quayle criticized the television character Murphy Brown for bearing a child out of wedlock. William Bennett led a campaign against the violent lyrics of rap music. Patrick Buchanan demanded that we "take back our culture and take back our country." Democrats, meanwhile, resisted the politics of virtue, not by disputing conservatives' particular moral judgments but by rejecting the idea that moral judgments have a place in the public realm. When Republicans tried to ban abortion, oppose gay rights, or promote school prayer, liberals replied that government should not legislate morality or concern itself with the moral character of citizens. Turning statecraft into soulcraft, they argued, runs the risk of coercion. Politics should not be about telling people how to live but about giving people the freedom to choose for themselves.

The liberals' insistence that politics be neutral on moral and religious matters was misguided in principle and costly in practice. As a philosophical matter, it is by no means clear that government can or should be neutral on the pressing moral questions of the day. The civil rights laws legislated morality, and rightly so. Not only did they ban odious practices, like the segregation of lunch counters; they also aimed at changing moral sentiments.

Philosophy aside, the Democrats' rejection of the politics of virtue carried a high price, for it left conservatives with a monopoly on moral discourse in politics. This helped Republicans win five of the six presidential elections between 1968 and 1988. Bill Clinton finally broke the pattern, winning as a "New Democrat" who stressed responsibility as well as rights. But Clinton's success at wresting the values issue from Republicans became clear only in the summer of 1996.

Two things made it possible. The first was the Republican takeover of Congress in the mid-term elections. Once Clinton could no longer hope to legislate, he fell back on the presidency's rhetorical dimension. And with the bully pulpit comes an invitation to soulcraft.

The second was the nomination of Bob Dole, a man who lacks both the gift and the taste for talk of virtue. In his one valiant attempt to bring morals to bear on markets, he delivered a speech in Hollywood a year ago denouncing movie-makers for pandering to the public's taste for violence, sex, and depravity. But his heart was not in it. He recently returned to Hollywood to declare that there was no conflict between markets and morals after all. Movie-makers could make plenty of money by catering to our nobler instincts, as in the box office hit Independence Day, a high-tech shoot-up about alien space invaders. No longer the scolding prophet, Dole now spoke as an earnest public relations consultant. "In Hollywood today, the big story is that responsibility is good business. You can watch your ratings rise and your box-office receipts go up and still look yourself in the mirror." The ticket window, Dole argued, was a "cultural ballot box" that proved Americans' preference for "the good over the grotesque, excellence over exploitation, quiet virtue over gratuitous violence."

Faced with the need to energize his candidacy, Dole had to choose between the two great enthusiasms of modern Republican politics: the moral fervor of the religious right or the tax-cutting fervor of the supply-side true-believers. Weary of the abortion struggle that has divided his party, Dole opted for the second, leaving Clinton an opening on the values front. In an interview on values with *USA Today*, Dole could not conceal his impatience with the whole subject. His acceptance speech, he said, would be "pretty heavy on values." He would make the point that "it doesn't take a village, it takes a family. And whatever." But even this grudging concession to the politics of virtue seemed to offend his laconic sensibility. "What, do you run around saying, 'I'm the Values Candidate, c'mon in. I'll give you some values'?"

Clinton, hampered by no such reticence, had still to find some content for his soulcraft. How to do so was far from obvious. Previous presidents had mounted the bully pulpit to ask great sacrifices of their fellow citizens—to risk their lives in war, or to share their bounty with the less fortunate, or to forgo material consumption for the sake of civic virtue. And true to liberal worries, the most ambitious episodes of soulcraft often involved a measure of coercion, as in nineteenth-century efforts to Americanize immigrants and Progressive era attempts to combat poverty through settlement houses and other means of moral uplift.

But what kind of soulcraft is suited to a nation hungry for community but unwilling to abide restraint, yearning for moral purpose but in no mood for sacrifice? By design or intuition, Clinton has discovered a solution: don't impose moral restraints on adults; impose them on children. What V-chips, curfews, school uniforms, and campaigns against truancy, teenage pregnancy, and underage smoking have in common is that they all address people's anxieties about the erosion of moral authority by attending to the moral character of their children. Clinton's politics of virtue avoids the objection of paternalism by becoming, strictly speaking, paternal.

Some may complain that, compared to historic projects of moral and civic improvement, Clinton's sermonizing amounts to soulcraft lite, an exercise in easy virtue that does little to challenge the civic habits and dispositions of grown-ups. But perhaps that is all we can expect these days. Clinton's politics of virtue is at least an improvement over flag factories and Willie Horton. And it just might help make him become the first Democratic president since FDR to win re-election.

# four

# BIG IDEAS

This presidential campaign offers a choice between one big, unworthy idea and many worthy little ones. The big but unworthy idea is at the heart of Bob Dole's proposed tax cut: people should keep more of what they earn. It is not clear why they should. First, given the budget deficit and unmet public needs, the government needs the money. Second, Americans already pay a smaller share of national income in taxes than do citizens of any other industrial democracy. Finally, by offering no higher purpose than lower taxes, Dole contradicts the admirable declaration in his acceptance speech that presidents should place moral considerations above material ones. Dole tries, on occasion, to elevate the moral status of tax cuts, arguing that too much taxation encroaches on liberty. But it is difficult to see how shifting a few hundred dollars per person to private consumption will make Americans more free.

Bill Clinton's campaign, bereft of big ideas, is littered with small ones—a volunteer literacy program, vouchers for job training, a ban on bullets that pierce bulletproof vests, new curbs on cigarettes, a law against forcing women out of maternity wards less than forty-eight hours after giving birth, a plan to reduce busy signals when people dial 911. These are good ideas, but they don't add up to a governing vision. Clinton has decided, probably rightly, that he does not need one to win.

This is the Dole campaign's most important failure: it has made life too easy for Clinton. It has absolved him of the challenge to rethink progressive politics or to grapple with the forces that, sooner or later, will transform American political debate. Had Pat Buchanan been the Republican nominee, Clinton would have been forced to confront the anxieties produced by the changing nature of work, the erosion of traditional communities, the rise of global markets, and the declining sovereignty of nations. Faced with a Republican whose political imagination runs in the well-worn grooves of tired party politics, however, Clinton can cleave to the conventional center without addressing the larger questions looming on the horizon. For all the president's talk of a bridge to the twenty-first century, this election will be remembered, if it is remembered at all, not as the beginning of a new era in American politics, but as the fading expression of an old one.

The defining election of the twenty-first century may not come for a decade or more. The questions that animate an age only become clear when, under pressure of events, people find ways of explaining the new circumstances in which they live. The election that "built the bridge" to the twentieth century did not occur until 1912. It was then that Woodrow Wilson, the Democrat, and Theodore Roosevelt, running on the Bull Moose ticket, articulated the big ideas that gave shape to the politics of the twentieth century.

Their predicament was similar to ours. Then, as now, there was an uneasy fit between the scale of economic life and the terms of political community. Railroads, telephones, telegraph wires, and daily newspapers spilled across local boundaries, bringing people into contact with events in distant places. National markets and a complex industrial system made workers and consumers interdependent. But Americans, accustomed to finding their bearings in small communities, felt powerless in the face of forces beyond their control. A decentralized political system, invented for a nation of farmers and shopkeepers, was dwarfed by the power of giant corporations.

How could a locally based democracy govern an economy national in scope? That question divided Wilson and Roosevelt. Wilson argued for breaking up the trusts and decentralizing economic power so it could be held accountable by local political units. Big business had become "vastly more centralized than the political organization of the country itself," Wilson declared. Corporations had bigger budgets than states "and loomed bigger than whole commonwealths in their influence over the lives and fortunes of entire communities of men." Simply to accept and regulate monopoly power was, according to Wilson, a kind of capitulation. "Have we come to a time," he asked, "when the President of the United States must doff his cap in the presence of this high finance, and say, 'You are our inevitable master, but we will see how we can make the best of it?'"

Teddy Roosevelt considered big business an inevitable product of industrial development and saw little point in trying to restore the decentralized economy of the nineteenth century. The only way to contend with national economic power, he argued, was to enlarge the capacity of national democratic institutions. The solution to big business was big government. Roosevelt sought to meet national economic power with national political power. But he insisted that a national democracy required more than the centralization of government; it also required the nationalization of politics. The political community had to be recast on a national scale. Roosevelt's "New Nationalism" sought to inspire in Americans "a genuine and permanent moral awakening," a new sense of national citizenship.

Wilson won the election, but Roosevelt's "New Nationalism" won the future. From the New Deal through the Great Society, and even to the age of Reagan and Gingrich, the nationalizing project gave energy and purpose to American political debate—to liberals who sought to expand the responsibilities of the federal government and to conservatives who sought to constrain them.

But today we face a new predicament similar to the one Americans confronted early in this century. Now, as then, new forms of commerce and communication spill across political boundaries, creating networks of interdependence while disrupting familiar forms of community. What railroads, telegraph wires, and national markets were to their time, cyberspace, CNN, and global markets are to ours—instruments that link people in distant places without making them neighbors, or fellow citizens, or participants in a common venture. Once again, the scale of economic life has outgrown the reach of existing democratic institutions. This explains the sense of disempowerment that hovers over our politics, the gnawing doubt that either party can do much to allay the anxieties of the age.

That we are not debating questions analogous to those that preoccupied Wilson and Roosevelt reveals the poverty of our politics. Is democracy possible within a global economy? How can emerging transnational arrangements from NAFTA to GATT to the International Court of Justice possibly inspire the loyalty of neighborhoods and nations? If civic virtues must be nourished closer to home—in schools, congregations, and workplaces—how can such communities equip us to exercise citizenship on a global scale? The bridge to the twenty-first century will not be built with a lot of small answers but by a few big questions.

# five

# THE PROBLEM
# WITH CIVILITY

Worries about incivility and partisanship are a recurring motif of American politics. Such worries received renewed attention in the aftermath of the 1996 election, in which President
Clinton won re-election but Republicans retained control of
both houses of Congress.

Meanness is out of season in American life, and calls for civility echo
across the land. Fed up with attack ads, negative campaigns and partisan rancor, Americans are also distressed at the coarsening of everyday life—rudeness on the highways, violence and vulgarity in
Hollywood movies and popular music, the brazenly confessional fare
of daytime television, the baseball star who spits at an umpire.

Sensing the backlash against incivility, President Clinton and
Republican leaders promise to rise above partisanship and to seek
common ground. Members of Congress plan a bipartisan weekend
retreat to get to know one another better and to discuss ways of conducting their disagreements with greater civility. Meanwhile, a growing number of national commissions ponder ways of renewing citizenship and community.

Americans are right to worry about the erosion of civility in everyday life. But it is a mistake to think that better manners and decorum can solve the fundamental problems of American democracy. In
politics, civility is an overrated virtue.

The problem with civility is the very thing that tempts politicians to extol it: it is uncontroversial. But democratic politics, properly conducted, is filled with controversy. We elect politicians to debate hotly contested public questions—for example, how much to spend on education and defense and care for the poor, how to punish crime, whether to permit abortion. We should not recoil at the clamor and contention that result; it is the sound and the spectacle of democracy.

It is desirable, of course, that political debate be conducted in a spirit of mutual respect rather than enmity. But too often these days, the plea for more civility in politics is a high-minded way of pleading for less critical scrutiny of illicit campaign contributions or other misdeeds. Likewise, the call to rise above partisanship can blur legitimate policy differences or justify a politics that lacks principle or conviction.

From the New Deal to the civil rights movement, principled politics has always been partisan politics, at least in the sense of requiring the mobilization of like-minded citizens to fight for a cause that others oppose.

The incivility now rampant in American life will not be cured by exhortation or by a muting of political differences. It is a symptom of a problem with our public life more fundamental than can be solved by a softening of partisan voices. Americans' worries about incivility express a deeper fear that the moral fabric of community is unraveling around us. From families and neighborhoods to cities and towns to schools, congregations and trade unions, the institutions that traditionally provided people with moral anchors and a sense of belonging are under siege.

Taken together, these forms of community are sometimes described as the institutions of "civil society." A healthy civil society is important not only because it promotes civility (though this may be a welcome byproduct) but because it calls forth the habits, skills and qualities of character that make effective democratic citizens.

Of course, every institution of civil society has its own distinctive purposes. Schools are for educating the young, churches and synagogues for worship, and so on. But when we participate in schools or congregations, we also develop civic virtues, qualities that equip us to be good citizens. We learn, for example, how to think about the good of the whole, how to exercise responsibility for others, how to deal with conflicting interests, how to stand up for our views while respecting the views of others. Above all, the institutions of civil society draw us out of our private, self-interested concerns and get us in the habit of attending to the common good.

A century and a half ago, Alexis de Tocqueville praised America's vibrant civil society for producing the "habits of the heart" on which democracy depends. If Tocqueville was right, there is reason to worry about the health of civil society, even beyond its effect on the manners people display in stores and on the streets.

For if families, neighborhoods and schools are in ill repair, they may be failing to produce the active, public-spirited citizens a successful democracy requires. (The dismal turnout in the recent election may be one indication of this effect.)

This at least is the hunch underlying a profusion of national commissions sprouting up to explore ways to renew citizenship and community. They include the Penn National Commission on Society, Culture and Community, which convened this month in Philadelphia; the National Commission on Civic Renewal, led by William Bennett and retiring Senator Sam Nunn of Georgia; the National Commission on Philanthropy and Civic Renewal, whose chairman is former Education Secretary Lamar Alexander, and the Boston-based Institute for Civil Society, which recently announced a project on civic renewal to be led by retiring Representative Patricia Schroeder of Colorado.

Whether these efforts can help rejuvenate American civic life will depend on their willingness to grapple with hard, controversial questions about the factors that have undermined virtue-sustaining communities in the first place. They must resist the temptation, endemic to such commissions, to steer clear of politically charged questions.

On the surface, the project of renewing civil society has the same kind of nonpartisan appeal as the call for civility in public life. Who could oppose efforts to strengthen families, neighborhoods and schools? But the attempt to repair civil society will be uncontroversial only as long as it remains hortatory—the stuff of Fourth of July speeches and State of the Union addresses.

Any serious effort to shore up value-laden communities must face up to the forces that have undermined them. Conservatives like Mr. Bennett locate the threat to virtue-sustaining institutions in two sources: popular culture and big government.

Rap music and vulgar movies corrupt the youth, they argue, while big government and the welfare state sap individual initiative, enervate the impulse for local self-help, and pre-empt the role of mediating institutions. Prune the shade tree of big government, they insist, and families, neighborhoods and church-based charities will flourish in the sun and space now crowded out by the overgrown tree.

The cultural conservatives are right to worry about the coarsening effects of popular entertainment, which, taken together with the advertising that drives it, induces a passion for consumption and a passivity toward politics at odds with civic virtue. But they are wrong to ignore the most potent force of all—the corrosive power of an unfettered market economy.

When corporations use their power to extract tax reductions, zoning changes and environmental concessions from cities and states desperate for jobs, they disempower communities more profoundly than any federal mandate ever did. When the growing gap between rich and poor leads the affluent to flee public schools, public parks and public transportation for privileged enclaves, civic virtue becomes difficult to sustain, and the common good fades from view.

Any attempt to revitalize community must contend with the economic as well as the cultural forces eating away at the social fabric. We need a political philosophy that asks what economic arrangements are hospitable to self-government and the civic virtues that sustain it. The project of civic renewal is important, not because it offers a way of muting political differences but because the health of American democracy requires it. So, too, does the prospect of civility.

# six

# IMPEACHMENT—
# THEN AND NOW

This commentary appeared as the House began impeachment proceedings against Bill Clinton in 1998. The House, voting mainly along party lines, eventually approved two counts of impeachment. But Clinton retained popular support, and the Senate voted to acquit him.

I, too, was once a 21-year-old Washington intern. Between my junior and senior years of college, I worked as a reporter in the Washington bureau of the *Houston Chronicle*. It was the summer of 1974, and the House Judiciary Committee was considering the impeachment of Richard Nixon.

"Let others wallow in Watergate," Nixon once said. I was a happy wallower. On July 8, I sat in the Supreme Court chamber, listening to Leon Jaworski, the special prosecutor, and James St. Clair, the president's lawyer, debate whether Nixon should be compelled to turn over his tapes. (I actually heard only half of the oral argument. So intense was the crush of press coverage that most newspaper reporters had to share a seat in the Court chamber, rotating in and out every half-hour.) A few days later, the House Judiciary Committee released volumes of evidence prepared by its staff. Unlike the "document dumps" of today, which appear instantly on the Web, the volumes were often given out at the Capitol in the evening, embargoed for release the following morning. I volunteered to pick up the copies designated for our paper, lugged them to my apartment behind Capitol

Hill, and read late into the night, culling the massive tomes for new revelations. When the summer ended, I was allowed to keep one of our bureau's sets as a bulky souvenir.

The recent impeachment stirrings prompted me to pull the beige-covered volumes down from the shelf. Read in the light of the Starr report, the 1974 committee's "Statement of Information" is striking for its restraint. It consists solely of facts and supporting documents, without argument or conclusions. It also includes a parallel set of volumes, prepared by Nixon's lawyers and published by the committee, emphasizing evidence more favorable to the president.

Despite some surface similarities, the impeachment hearings I witnessed that summer differed in several ways from those now unfolding in Washington. Then, as now, the majority party in Congress was investigating a president of the opposing party serving his second term. The party balance on the committees was roughly the same—a 21–17 Democratic majority in Committee Chair Peter Rodino's day, a 21–16 Republican majority in Henry Hyde's. Rodino's inquiry, like the one House Republicans now propose, was not limited by time or subject matter. Almost six months passed from the authorization of the inquiry to the final vote. In the end, Rodino was able to secure a bipartisan majority for impeachment—and, with it, a national consensus.

Hyde's committee will not likely achieve either, for three reasons. The first has to do with changes in the Congress. Many have observed that the House today, and especially the Judiciary Committee, are more bitterly partisan than they were a quarter-century ago. To some extent, the comparison is clouded by nostalgia. The Nixon impeachment hearings were not devoid of partisan passions. Twelve of the Democrats on the committee, including Robert Drinan of Massachusetts, Charles Rangel and Elizabeth Holtzman of New York, and John Conyers Jr. of Michigan (who is now the committee's senior minority member), voted to impeach Nixon for his secret bombing of Cambodia. (The article failed.) On the GOP side, Charles Wiggins, who represented Nixon's former district in California, and Charles Sandman Jr., a combative New Jersey Republican, vigorously defended their president to the bitter end. Then, as now, the minority complained about leaks and unfair treatment.

Still, the climate was less contentious. Party and ideology were less clearly aligned than they are today. Of the 21 Democrats on Rodino's committee, three were conservative Southern Democrats. Walter Flowers (Alabama), James Mann (South Carolina), and Ray Thornton (Arkansas) all came from districts that had voted heavily for Nixon in 1972, and their votes were in doubt until late in the proceedings. The Republican ranks included Northern moderates such as William Cohen of Maine (now secretary of defense), Hamilton Fish Jr. of New York, and Tom Railsback of Illinois. The Southern Democrats and moderate Republicans met frequently, softening the partisan edge of the proceedings. In the end, all Democrats and seven Republicans voted to recommend impeachment.

The second big difference is in the nature of the presidential misdeeds. Nixon's offenses—the cover-up of the Watergate burglary (Article of Impeachment I) and the use of the FBI, CIA, and IRS against political enemies (Article of Impeachment II)—were classic examples of the "serious offenses against the system of government" that, as the committee rightly argued, impeachment is designed to remedy. When Nixon released the "smoking gun" tape shortly after the committee's votes, proving his involvement in the Watergate cover-up conspiracy, even his ten die-hard Republican supporters on the committee announced that they favored impeachment. A president should be removed, they wrote in a minority addendum, "only for serious misconduct dangerous to the system of government established by the Constitution." Among the Nixon loyalists who endorsed that statement was Trent Lott, then a freshman representative. Hyde,

Lott, and their fellow Republicans will have a hard time persuading Democrats—and the country—that Clinton's misdeeds, deplorable though they are, pose a serious threat to our constitutional system.

A third factor that makes it difficult to imagine a national consensus for impeaching Bill Clinton has to do with the changing role of the presidency in American life. Vietnam, Watergate, and now the Clinton sex scandal have deflated the majesty and aura of the presidency. So has a style of media coverage that encourages presidential candidates to bare their souls and confess their foibles on national television. Bill Clinton is more liked but less revered than Richard Nixon. Paradoxically, this lack of reverence protects Clinton from the sense of outrage and injured idealism that made the impeachment of Nixon possible.

On the evening of July 27, I sat in Room 2141 of the Rayburn House Office Building as Chairman Rodino asked the clerk to call the roll. The room fell silent as, one by one, the members of the committee answered "aye" or "no." The "ayes" were softly spoken, barely audible. It was a moment of almost religious solemnity. When the first article of impeachment was voted, Rodino's gavel came down, and the press surged forward, as it always did, to the front of the room where the members sat. My task was to get a quote from the formidable Barbara Jordan, the Democratic congresswoman from Houston who had distinguished herself throughout the hearings with her forceful eloquence. "I don't want to talk to anyone about anything right now," she exploded. With tears in her eyes, she escaped to a back room. I retreated, shaken by the encounter. Even Democrats hostile to Nixon felt the awesome burden of impeaching him. It is difficult to imagine a similar moment of civic trembling today.

# seven

# ROBERT F. KENNEDY'S PROMISE

Robert F. Kennedy was assassinated in 1968, on the night of his victory in the California primary. To recall his death is to wonder what might have been. For as he campaigned for the presidency, he was finding his way to a political vision that challenged the complacencies of postwar American liberalism. Had he lived, he might have set progressive politics on a new, more successful course. In the decades since his death, the Democratic Party has failed to recover the moral energy and bold public purpose to which RFK gave voice.

Despite his commitment to the poor and his opposition to the war in Vietnam, Kennedy was not, by temperament or ideology, a liberal. His political outlook was in some ways more conservative and in other ways more radical than the mainstream of his party. Unlike most liberals, he worried about the remoteness of big government, favored decentralized power, criticized welfare as "our greatest domestic failure," challenged the faith in economic growth as a panacea for social ills, and took a hard line on crime.

Some viewed RFK's departure from liberal orthodoxy as a shrewd attempt to win support from white working-class ethnic voters while retaining the support of minorities and the poor. It certainly had that effect. In the 1968 Indiana primary, Kennedy managed, remarkably, to win 86 percent of the black vote while also sweeping the counties that had given George Wallace his greatest support in 1964. The journalist Jack Newfield aptly described RFK as the only candidate of protest who "was able to talk to the two polarities of powerlessness at the same time."

But Kennedy's unease with the conventional wisdom of 1960s liberalism was more than a matter of political calculation. What gave his message its resonance was that it drew on a vision of citizenship and community that the managerial politics of the modern age had crowded from view. As he groped to articulate a public philosophy adequate to the turmoil of his times, RFK revived an older, more demanding vision of civic life. According to this ideal, freedom does not simply consist in fair access to the bounty of a consumer society; it also requires that citizens share in self-rule, that they participate in shaping the forces that govern their collective destiny.

The civic strand of Kennedy's politics enabled him to address anxieties of the late sixties that have persisted to our time—mistrust of government, a sense of disempowerment, and the fear that the moral fabric of community was unraveling. Liberals often cast their arguments in individualistic terms, or appeal to the ideal of national community. By contrast, Kennedy emphasized the importance for self-government of communities intermediate between the individual and the nation, and lamented the loss of such communities in the modern world: "Nations or great cities are too huge to provide the values of community . . . The world beyond the neighborhood has become more impersonal and abstract," beyond the reach of individual control. "Cities, in their tumbling spread, are obliterating neighborhoods and precincts. Housing units go up, but there is no place for people to walk, for women and their children to meet, for common activities. The place of work is far away through blackened tunnels or over impersonal highways. The doctor and lawyer and government official is often somewhere else and hardly known. In far too many places—in pleasant suburbs as well as city streets—the home is a place to sleep and eat and watch television; but the community is not where we live. We live in many places and so we live nowhere."

In addressing the nation's urban ills, Democrats of the sixties emphasized unemployment, while Republicans spoke of crime. Kennedy spoke convincingly about joblessness and crime, and linked both to civic themes. The tragedy of crime, he argued, was not only the danger it posed to life and limb but also its destructive effect on public spaces, such as neighborhoods and communities: "No nation hiding behind locked doors is free, for it is imprisoned by its own fear. No nation whose citizens fear to walk their own streets is healthy, for in isolation lies the poisoning of public participation." Similarly, unemployment posed a civic challenge, not just an economic one. The problem was not simply that the jobless lacked an income but that they could not share in the common life of citizenship: "Unemployment means having nothing to do—which means having nothing to do with the rest of us. To be without work, to be without use to one's fellow citizens, is to be in truth the Invisible Man of whom Ralph Ellison wrote."

Kennedy's clearest difference with mainstream liberal opinion was on the issue of welfare. Unlike conservatives, who opposed federal spending for the poor, Kennedy criticized welfare on the grounds that it corrupted the civic capacity of recipients. It rendered "millions of our people slaves to dependency and poverty, waiting on the favor of their fellow citizens to write them checks. Fellowship, community, shared patriotism—these essential values of our civilization do not come from just buying and consuming goods together. They come from a shared sense of individual independence and personal effort." The solution to poverty was not a guaranteed income paid by the government, but "dignified employment at decent pay, the kind of employment that lets a man say to his community, to his family, to his country, and most important, to himself, 'I helped to build this country. I am a participant in its great public ventures.'" A guaranteed income, whatever good it might do, "simply cannot provide the sense of self-sufficiency, of participation in the life of the community, that is essential for citizens of a democracy."

Had Democrats taken up RFK's toughness on crime, they would have deprived a generation of Republicans of one of its most effective issues. Had Democrats heeded Kennedy's worries about welfare, they could have reformed it without abandoning the poor, and avoided decades of public resentment toward welfare that fed a broader hostility toward government. Had Democrats learned from RFK the importance of community, self-government, and civic virtue, they would not have ceded these powerful ideals to conservatives like Ronald Reagan. Three decades later, the progressive impulse has yet to recover a compelling voice. We still need a strenuous idealism that recalls us to a citizenship that consists of something more than basic training for a consumer society.

# Part II

# MORAL AND POLITICAL ARGUMENTS

The essays in this section take up moral arguments prompted by recent legal and political controversies, ranging from affirmative action to pollution permits to stem cell research. A number of the essays deal with the moral limits of markets, a subject I plan to examine more systematically in a future book. In Chapters 8–13 I argue that market practices and commercial pressures can corrupt civic institutions and degrade the public realm. The growing tendency to fund education and other public purposes through state lotteries and commercial advertising in schools are two conspicuous examples. Less obvious but also insidious is the extension of branding, commercialism, and market imperatives into spheres of life (including government, sports, and universities) traditionally governed, at least to some extent, by non-market norms.

Chapter 14, "Should We Buy the Right to Pollute?", takes issue with the U.S. insistence that global environmental agreements include a tradable emissions scheme that would allow countries to buy and sell the right to pollute. This article brought a torrent of criticism from economists, for whom tradable pollution permits represent a cherished example of the way market mechanisms promote the public good. Soon after the article appeared, I received a note from my college economics professor. He was surprisingly sympathetic to my argument, but asked that I not publicly divulge that I had learned my economics from him.

More often than we realize, the question of moral desert lurks just below the surface of disputes about the just distribution of opportunities, honors, and rewards. Chapters 15–17 try to make sense of the competing notions of desert at stake in contemporary debates about the rights of the disabled, affirmative action, and criminal punishment. Chapter 18, "Clinton and Kant on Lying," uses President Clinton's alleged perjury about his sexual misconduct as an occasion to examine Immanuel Kant's moral distinction between lying and misleading.

When politicians, activists, and political commentators speak of morality in politics, they usually have in mind the morally and religiously charged issues that have figured in the culture wars—abortion, gay rights, assisted suicide, and, more recently, stem cell research. Chapters 19–21 deal with these issues. Running through these essays is the argument that liberal toleration is flawed insofar as it tries to adjudicate rights without attending to the substantive moral and religious claims in contention.

Some people claim it is not possible to conduct reasoned argument about deeply held moral and religious convictions, especially those involving the origins and sanctity of human life. These essays challenge that claim. Chapter 20, on the ethics of stem cell research, grew out of debates I encountered as a member of the President's Council on Bioethics, a body appointed by President George W. Bush to examine the ethical implications of new biomedical technologies. The debates I found myself engaged in with colleagues on the Council confirmed my sense that even questions as fraught as those concerning the moral status of the human embryo are susceptible to reasoned argument. (This is not to suggest that reasoned argument necessarily leads to agreement; the views expressed in this essay are mine alone, and do not represent those of the Council.) Chapter 21 takes up the hotly contested issues of abortion and gay rights. I assess the U.S. Supreme Court's reasoning on these subjects, from the privacy rights cases of the 1960s to a 2003 case that struck down a law banning gay and lesbian sexual practices.

# eight

# AGAINST STATE
# LOTTERIES

Political corruption comes in two forms. Most familiar is the hand-in-the-till variety: bribes, payoffs, influence-peddling, lobbyists lining the pockets of public officials in exchange for access and favors. This corruption thrives in secrecy, and is usually condemned when exposed.

But another kind of corruption arises, by degree, in full public view. It involves no theft or fraud, but rather a change in the habits of citizens, a turning away from public responsibilities. This second, civic corruption, is more insidious than the first. It violates no law, but enervates the spirit on which good laws depend. And by the time it becomes apparent, the new habits may be too pervasive to reverse.

Consider the most fateful change in public finance since the income tax: the rampant proliferation of state lotteries. Illegal in every state for most of the century, lotteries have suddenly become the fastest-growing source of state revenue. In 1970, two states ran lotteries; today, forty states and the District of Columbia run them. Nationwide, lottery sales exceeded $48 billion a year by 2004, up from $9 billion in 1985.

The traditional objection to lotteries is that gambling is a vice. This objection has lost force in recent decades, partly because notions of sin have changed but also because Americans are more reluctant than they once were to legislate morality. Even people who find gambling morally objectionable shy away from banning it on that ground alone, absent some harmful effect on society as a whole.

Freed from the traditional, paternalistic objections to gambling, proponents of state lotteries advance three seemingly attractive arguments: first, lotteries are a painless way of raising revenue for important public services without raising taxes; unlike taxes, lotteries are a matter of choice, not coercion. Second, they are a popular form of entertainment. Third, they generate business for the retail outlets that sell lottery tickets (such as convenience stores, gas stations and supermarkets) and for the advertising firms and media outlets that promote them.

What, then, is wrong with state-run lotteries? For one thing, they rely, hypocritically, on a residual moral disapproval of gambling that their defenders officially reject. State lotteries generate enormous profits because they are monopolies, and they are monopolies because privately operated numbers games are prohibited, on traditional moral grounds. (In Las Vegas, where casinos compete with one another, the slot machines and blackjack tables pay out around 90 percent of their take in winnings. State lotteries, being monopolies, only pay out about 50 percent.) Libertarian defenders of state lotteries can't have it both ways. If a lottery is, like dry cleaning, a morally legitimate business, then why should it not be open to private enterprise? If a lottery is, like prostitution, a morally objectionable business, then why should the state be engaged in it?

Lottery defenders usually reply that people should be free to decide the moral status of gambling for themselves. No one is forced to play, they point out, and those who object can simply abstain. To those troubled by the thought that the state derives revenue from sin, advocates reply that government often imposes "sin taxes" on products (like liquor and tobacco) that many regard as undesirable. Lotteries are better than taxes, the argument goes, because they are wholly voluntary, a matter of choice.

But the actual conduct of lotteries departs sharply from this laissez-faire ideal. States do not simply provide their citizens the opportunity to gamble; they actively promote and encourage them to do so. The nearly $400 million spent on lottery advertising each year puts lotteries among the largest advertisers in the country. If lotteries are a form of "sin tax," they are the only kind in which the state spends huge sums to encourage its citizens to commit the sin.

Not surprisingly, lotteries direct their most aggressive advertising at their best customers—the working class, minorities and the poor. A billboard touting the Illinois lottery in a Chicago ghetto declared, "This could be your ticket out." Ads often evoke the fantasy of winning the big jackpot and never having to work again. Lottery advertising floods the airwaves around the first of each month, when Social Security and welfare payments swell the checking accounts of recipients. In sharp contrast to most other government amenities (say, police protection), lottery ticket outlets saturate poor and blue-collar neighborhoods and offer less service to affluent ones.

Massachusetts, with the highest grossing per capita lottery sales in the country, offers stark evidence of the blue collar bias. A 1997 series in the *Boston Globe* found that Chelsea, one of the poorest towns in the state, has one lottery agent for every 363 residents; upscale Wellesley, by contrast, has one agent for every 3,063 residents. In Massachusetts, as elsewhere, this "painless" alternative to taxation is a sharply regressive way of raising revenue. Residents of Chelsea spent a staggering $915 per capita on lottery tickets last year, almost 8 percent of their income. Residents of Lincoln, an affluent suburb, spent only $30 per person, one-tenth of 1 percent of their income.

For growing numbers of people, playing the lottery is not the free, voluntary choice its promoters claim. Instant games such as scratch tickets and Keno (a video numbers game with drawings every five minutes), now the biggest money-makers for the lottery, are a leading cause of compulsive gambling, rivaling casinos and racetracks. Swelling the ranks of Gamblers Anonymous are lottery addicts, like the man who scratched $1,500 worth of tickets per day, exhausted his retirement savings and ran up debt on eleven credit cards.

Meanwhile, the state has grown as addicted to the lottery as its problem gamblers. Lottery proceeds now account for 13 percent of state revenues in Massachusetts, making radical change all but unthinkable. No politician, however troubled by the lottery's harmful effects, would dare raise taxes or cut spending sufficiently to offset the revenue the lottery brings in.

With states hooked on the money, they have no choice but to continue to bombard their citizens, especially the most vulnerable ones, with a message at odds with the ethic of work, sacrifice and moral responsibility that sustains democratic life. This civic corruption is the gravest harm that lotteries bring. It degrades the public realm by casting the government as the purveyor of a perverse civic education. To keep the money flowing, state governments across America must now use their authority and influence not to cultivate civic virtue but to peddle false hope. They must persuade their citizens that with a little luck they can escape the world of work to which only misfortune consigns them.

# nine

# COMMERCIALS
# IN THE CLASSROOM

When the Boston Red Sox first installed a display of giant Coke bottles above the left field wall, local sportswriters protested that such tacky commercialism tainted the sanctity of Fenway Park. But ballparks have long been littered with billboards and ads. Today, teams routinely sell corporations the right to name the stadium: the Colorado Rockies, for example, play in Coors Field. However distasteful, such commercialism does not seem to corrupt the game or diminish the play.

The same cannot be said of the newest commercial frontier—the public schools. The corporate invasion of the classroom threatens to turn schools into havens for hucksterism. Eager to cash in on a captive audience of consumers-in-training, companies have flooded teachers with free videos, posters and "learning kits" designed to sanitize corporate images and emblazon brand names in the minds of children. Students can now learn about nutrition from curricular materials supplied by Hershey's Chocolate or McDonald's, or study the effects of the Alaska oil spill in a video made by Exxon. According to *Giving Kids the Business,* by Alex Molnar, a Monsanto video teaches the merits of bovine growth hormone in milk production, while Procter & Gamble's environmental curriculum teaches that disposable diapers are good for the earth.

Not all corporate-sponsored educational freebies promote ideological agendas; some simply plug the brand name. A few years ago, the Campbell Soup Company offered a science kit that showed students how to prove that Campbell's Prego spaghetti sauce is thicker than Ragu. General Mills distributed science kits containing free samples of its Gusher fruit snacks, with soft centers that "gush" when bitten. The teacher's guide suggested that students bite into the Gushers and compare the effect to geothermal eruptions. A Tootsie Roll kit on counting and writing recommends that, for homework, children interview family members about their memories of Tootsie Rolls.

While some marketers seek to insinuate brand names into the curriculum, others take a more direct approach: buying advertisements in schools. When the Seattle School Board faced a budget crisis a few years ago, it voted to solicit corporate advertising. School officials hoped to raise $1 million a year with sponsorships like "the cheerleaders, brought to you by Reebok" and "the McDonald's gym." Protests from parents and teachers forced the Seattle schools to suspend the policy, but such marketing is a growing presence in schools across the country.

Corporate logos now clamor for student attention from school buses to book covers. In Colorado Springs, advertisements for Mountain Dew adorn school hallways, and ads for Burger King decorate the sides of school buses. A Massachusetts firm distributes free book covers hawking Nike, Gatorade and Calvin Klein to almost 25 million students nationwide. A Minnesota broadcasting company pipes music into school corridors and cafeterias in fifteen states, with twelve minutes of commercials every hour. Forty percent of the ad revenue goes to the schools.

The most egregious example of the commercialization in schools is Channel One, a twelve-minute television news program seen by 8 million students in 12,000 schools. Introduced in 1990 by Whittle Communications, Channel One offers schools a television set for each classroom, two VCRs and a satellite link in exchange for an agreement to show the program every day, including the two minutes of commercials it contains. Since Channel One reaches over 40 percent of the nation's teenagers, it is able to charge advertisers a hefty $200,000 per thirty-second spot. In its pitch to advertisers, the company promises access to the largest teen audience in history in a setting free of "the usual distractions of telephones, stereos, remote controls, etc." The Whittle program shattered the taboo against outright advertising in the classroom. Despite controversy in many states, only New York has banned Channel One from its schools.

The rampant commercialization of schools is corrupting in two ways. First, most corporate-sponsored learning supplements are ridden with bias, distortion and superficial fare. A recent study by Consumers Union found that nearly 80 percent of classroom freebies are slanted toward the sponsor's product. An independent study of Channel One released earlier this year found that its news programs contributed little to students' grasp of public affairs. Only 20 percent of its airtime covers current political, economic or cultural events. The rest is devoted to advertising, sports, weather and natural disasters.

But, even if corporate sponsors supplied objective teaching tools of impeccable quality, commercial advertising would still be a pernicious presence in the classroom because it undermines the purposes for which schools exist. Advertising encourages people to want things and to satisfy their desires: education encourages people to reflect on their desires, to restrain or to elevate them. The purpose of advertising is to recruit consumers; the purpose of public schools is to cultivate citizens.

It is not easy to teach students to be citizens, capable of thinking critically about the world around them, when so much of childhood consists of basic training for a commercial society. At a time when children come to school as walking billboards of logos and labels and licensed apparel, it is all the more difficult—and all the more important—for schools to create some distance from a popular culture drenched in the ethos of consumerism.

But advertising abhors distance. It blurs the boundaries between places, and makes every setting a site for selling. "Discover your own river of revenue at the schoolhouse gates!" proclaims the brochure for the 4th Annual Kid Power Marketing Conference, held last May in New Orleans. "Whether it's first-graders learning to read or teen-agers shopping for their first car, we can guarantee an introduction of your product and your company to these students in the tradi-tional setting of the classroom!" Marketers are storming the school-house gates for the same reason that Willie Sutton robbed banks—because that's where the money is. Counting the amount they spend and the amount they influence their parents to spend, 6- to 19-year-old consumers now account for $485 billion in spending per year.

The growing financial clout of kids is itself a lamentable symp-tom of parents abdicating their role as mediators between children and the market. Meanwhile, faced with property tax caps, budget cuts and rising enrollments, cash-strapped schools are more vulnera-ble to the siren song of corporate sponsors. Rather than raise the public funds we need to pay the full cost of educating our schoolchil-dren, we choose instead to sell their time and rent their minds to Burger King and Mountain Dew.

# ten

# BRANDING
# THE PUBLIC REALM

The branding of public spaces has proliferated since 1998, when this article was written. "Municipal marketing" companies have sprung up to help cities sell naming rights. In 2003, the mayor of New York hired the city's first chief marketing officer. One of his first deals was a $166 million contract with Snapple to be the official drink of New York City.

It is getting hard to tell the difference between companies and countries. Earthwatch Inc. of Longmont, Colorado, recently launched the world's first commercial spy satellite into space. Now, anyone with a few hundred dollars can buy surveillance photos of missile sites in the Middle East or the swimming pool in a celebrity's backyard. Once the prerogative of governments, spying from space has become a commercial enterprise.

Even where countries retain their functions, governance and marketing are increasingly entangled. For decades, candidates for office have sold themselves like breakfast cereal. Today, entire countries do. Consider the "rebranding" of Britain. A few months ago, Prime Minister Tony Blair's advisers recommended that he update the country's image. It was time to "rebrand" Britain as "one of the world's pioneers rather than one of its museums." Red telephone booths are being replaced by transparent glass ones. The box-like London taxicab is getting a sleeker, aerodynamic design. "Rule Britannia!" is giving way to "Cool Britannia," the new slogan of the British Transit Authority, whose logo is now a jaunty Union Jack tinged with yellow and green for vibrancy. "The image of Britain," Blair explained, "which used to be bowler hats and pinstripe trousers and very old-fashioned and very stuffy, has been replaced by something far more dynamic and open and forward-looking. . . . I'm proud of my country's past, but I don't want to live in it." The "rebranding" of Britain is not an isolated episode but a sign of the times. It reflects a new image-savvy, commercialized approach to government that threatens to turn national identities into brand names, anthems into advertising jingles, flags into corporate logos.

Last year, the U.S. Postal Service issued a stamp of Bugs Bunny. Critics complained that stamps should honor historic figures, not commercial products. But the post office, facing stiff competition from email, fax machines, and Federal Express, sees licensing rights as key to its future. Every Bugs Bunny stamp that is saved rather than mailed contributes 32 cents to post office profits. And stamp collecting is the least of it. The licensing deal with Warner Bros. enables the Postal Service to market Looney Tunes ties, hats, videos, and other products at more than 500 postal stores nationwide.

Also for sale is a new product line called Postmark America that seeks to capitalize on the brand name of the Postal Service itself. Products include a $2.95 Pony Express youth cap, infantwear emblazoned with the logo "Just Delivered," and an airmail pilot's leather jacket—which sells for $345. A Postal Service executive explained that the retailing effort is modeled after companies like Warner Bros. and Walt Disney: "They've turned their icons into product lines. That's what we're trying to do. We're trying to key off our stamps and our stamp image."

Sometimes, however, the attempt to turn national symbols into brand names meets with resistance. In 1995, the Royal Canadian Mounted Police sold Disney the right to market the Mountie image worldwide. Disney paid Canada's federal police $2.5 million per year in marketing rights plus a share of the licensing fees for Mountie t-shirts, coffee mugs, teddy bears, maple syrup, diaper bags, and other merchandise. Many Canadians protested that the Mounties were selling out a sacred national symbol to a U.S. corporate giant. "It's not the price that rankles. It's the sale," complained an editorial in the Toronto-based *Globe and Mail.* "The Mounted Police have miscalculated on a crucial point. Pride."

Canada has learned to live with the marketing of the Mounties, but the critics had a point: there is reason to worry about an excessive commingling of governance and commerce. At a time when politics and government are widely disliked, public officials will inevitably seek to tap the appeal of popular culture, advertising, and entertainment. The problem is not that this borrowed authority fails, but that it succeeds too completely. According to polls, the two most popular agencies of the U.S. government are the post office and the military. Not coincidentally, perhaps, both advertise heavily on television. In a media-saturated world, citizens' judgments about government increasingly depend on the image it projects.

Not only is this unfair to government programs that lack advertising budgets (who ever saw a commercial for welfare?); it distorts the priorities of agencies that lavish money on their public image. After a time, their mission becomes indistinguishable from their marketing. Once the post office sold stamps and delivered the mail; today it sells stamp-related images and licensed apparel. Postmaster General Marvin Runyon articulated well the theory behind the new commercialized style of governance: "We have to be market-driven and customer-friendly, and make products that people want."

But citizens are not customers, and democracy is not simply a matter of giving people what they want. Self-government, properly practiced, leads people to reflect on their wants and to revise them in the light of competing considerations. Unlike customers, citizens sometimes sacrifice their wants for the sake of the common good. This is the difference between politics and commerce, between patriotism and brand loyalty.

When government leans too heavily on the borrowed appeal of cartoon characters and cutting-edge ads, it may boost its approval ratings but squander the dignity and authority of the public realm. And without a public realm in good repair, democratic citizens have little hope of directing the market forces and commercial pressures that quicken by the day and shape our lives in untold ways.

Margaret Thatcher, no friend of the rebranding of Britain, inadvertently contributed to this phenomenon when, as prime minister, she privatized the national airline. At a recent Conservative Party conference, she came upon a British Airways booth and was dismayed to find that the tail fin of the model plane on display no longer bore the Union Jack, but a multicultural motif designed to represent British Airways' new global identity. Drawing a tissue from her handbag, she covered the tail fin in protest. As Lady Thatcher should have known, markets, for all their glories, exact a price in honor and pride.

When capitalism and community collide, as they increasingly do these days, community needs all the help it can get. Consider the case of sports. Like few institutions in American life, professional baseball, football, basketball, and hockey provide a source of social glue and civic pride. From Yankee Stadium to Candlestick Park, sports stadiums are the cathedrals of our civil religion, public spaces that gather people from different walks of life in rituals of loss and hope, profanity and prayer. The common sentiments reach beyond the ballpark or arena. When the Boston Celtics and the Los Angeles Lakers faced off in the NBA playoffs some years ago, one could walk the streets of Boston and from every open window hear the echoes of the game.

But professional sports is not only a source of civic identity. It is also a business. And these days the money in sports is driving out the community. Of course, when fans go to the ballpark, they don't go for the sake of a civic experience. They go to see Ken Griffey Jr. hit the ball a long way or make a sparkling catch in center field. But what they experience at the game are two important features of democratic public life: One is a broad equality of condition; another is a sense of belonging to a particular place. While box seats have always cost more than the bleachers, the ballpark is one of the few public places where CEOs sit side by side with mailroom clerks, where all eat the same soggy hot dogs, where rich and poor alike get wet when it rains, where all hearts sink and soar with the fate of the home team.

Or so it was until recently. Today, the allure of greater profit is leading team owners to transform their games in ways that destroy the class-mixing habits and sense of place on which sports and democracy thrive. The proliferation of luxury skyboxes segregates the upper crust from the common folk in the stands below. At the same time, owners are constantly relocating teams, or threatening to do so, if the home town is unwilling or unable to shell out huge public subsidies for stadiums.

The skybox trend began when the Dallas Cowboys installed luxury suites at Texas Stadium, where corporations pay up to 1.5 million dollars for the right to entertain executives and clients in posh settings above the crowd. Through the 1980s, more than a dozen teams followed the Cowboys' lead, cosseting privileged fans behind Plexiglas perches in the sky. In the late 1980s, Congress cut back on the tax deduction corporations could claim for skybox expenses, but this did not stem the demand for the climate-controlled retreats. Although skybox revenues represent a windfall for the teams, they change the fans' relation to the game and to one another. The sweaty, egalitarian intensity of the Boston Garden in Larry Bird's day has given way to Boston's commodious but class-stratified FleetCenter, where executive-suite patrons dine on pistachio-encrusted salmon in a restaurant so elevated that they cannot see the court below.

If skyboxes separate fans by class, relocation deprives a community of its home team, as the notorious case of the Cleveland Browns illustrates. Arthur Modell, for 35 years the owner of the Browns, could not complain about the Cleveland fans, who filled the 70,000 seats in Municipal Stadium game after game. But, in 1995, he announced he was moving his team to Baltimore, where local officials were offering him $65 million, a new stadium free of rent, and revenues from luxury boxes.

Cleveland is not the only community whose home-team loyalty

went unrequited by a profit-maximizing owner. In fact, Baltimore's extravagant bid for the Browns was prompted by a desire to replace its own beloved Baltimore Colts, who bolted for Indianapolis in 1984. ("This is my team," the Colt's owner bluntly declared at the time. "I own it, and I'll do whatever I want with it.") In the last six years, eight major-league teams have abandoned their host cities for sweeter deals elsewhere, and another 20 cities paid the blackmail teams demanded in the form of new or renovated stadiums. Many other teams are currently demanding subsidies as a condition of staying put. The Super Bowl champion Denver Broncos, for example, are threatening to leave unless taxpayers fork over $266 million for a new stadium.

From the standpoint of market principles, there is nothing wrong with selling teams to the highest bidder. Cities and states often compete with one another to attract new businesses to their communities. If it is all right to offer tax breaks and subsidies to persuade an auto plant to relocate, why not bid for a sports franchise as well? The answer is that all bidding wars among states are objectionable because they allow corporations to extract revenue that should go to education and other pressing public needs. In the case of sports, the bidding is doubly damaging because it mocks the loyalty and civic pride that communities invest in their teams.

What, if anything, can be done to render communities less vulnerable to extortion by the teams they love? David Morris, cofounder of a Minneapolis-based group called the Institute for Local Self-Reliance, suggests a promising solution: Since teams are now demanding subsidies that exceed the value of the teams, why not allow communities to take ownership themselves? The sole example of community ownership in big-league sports is the Green Bay Packers, incorporated in 1923 as a nonprofit organization. Despite their small market, the Packers have won three Super Bowls and sold out their games for more than 30 consecutive seasons. The waiting list for season tickets is 36,000 names long. Their 108,000 shareholder-fans know that they will not make a profit. But they do not need to worry that their Packers will leave town.

As Morris points out, the NFL now prohibits community ownership (with an exception for the Packers), and Major League Baseball has an informal policy against it. He therefore endorses legislation proposed by Representative Earl Blumenauer of Oregon that would require leagues to permit public ownership of teams. Leagues that refused would lose the valuable antitrust exemption that allows teams to collaborate in selling broadcast rights. The bill, dubbed the Give Fans a Chance Act, would also require teams to give 180 days notice before moving and afford local groups the opportunity to make ownership bids or other proposals to retain the team.

Whether or not Congress acts, the movement for community ownership may hold growing appeal for voters reluctant to subsidize millionaire owners and players as the price of keeping the home team at home. Activists in Denver plan a statewide initiative that would tie any stadium subsidy to a public share in the Broncos. In Minnesota, the danger of losing the Twins baseball franchise to Charlotte, North Carolina, has led some Minnesota legislators to propose a bill that would enable the state to buy the team and sell it to the fans. The drive for community ownership has won support both from conservatives who oppose stadium subsidies and from progressives who prize community and want government to level the playing field between private wealth and the public good.

# twelve

# HISTORY FOR SALE

The recent auction of John F. Kennedy memorabilia displayed two distasteful features of American culture in the 1990s: one is the obsession with celebrity; the other is the willingness to turn everything into a commodity. Among the items sold: a JFK rocking chair ($300,000), a sheet of presidential doodles ($12,250), the black alligator briefcase Kennedy carried with him to Dallas ($700,000), his Harvard sweater ($27,500), long underwear ($3,000), and a plastic comb ($1,100). The auction consisted largely of items that Robert L. White, an avid collector of JFK memorabilia, had inherited from Kennedy's longtime secretary, Evelyn Lincoln.

Kennedy's children, Caroline Kennedy and John F. Kennedy Jr., opposed the auction, disputing the ownership of some items and seeking to claim them for the John F. Kennedy Library in Boston. "Mrs. Lincoln never owned the vast majority of items that Mr. White received from her," they stated. "They once belonged to our father. They now belong to our family, to history, and to the American people." Defenders of the auction charged the Kennedy children with hypocrisy, citing their own $34.4 million auction of Jacqueline Kennedy Onassis's belongings two years ago. White's lawyer accused them of trying to "pick things out of the collection like it's an L.L. Bean catalog." The wrangle ended when White agreed to hand over two Kennedy diaries and other personal items in exchange for an agreement by the Kennedy children not to challenge the auction in court. Legal rights and wrongs aside, the auction reflects a tawdry trend that is gaining momentum by the day: the commodification of memory, the peddling of national pride and pain, the consignment of our past to mail-order catalogs and home shopping channels. In the case of Kennedy-related artifacts, the memorabilia market is fueled not only by sentiment but also by a lurid desire to possess the trappings of tragedy. Items related to the assassination are especially prized by collectors. Last year, an auction house sold a teletype printout of the Associated Press's report of the Kennedy assassination. Several years ago, the gun Jack Ruby used to kill Lee Harvey Oswald fetched $200,000.

Many feel a sense of moral queasiness at the spectacle of history on the auction block, but what exactly is wrong with selling presidential diaries, documents, and underwear to the highest bidder? At least two things, depending on the artifact: the first is that it privatizes what should be public; the second is that it publicizes what should be private.

When significant historical documents are at stake, selling them off to private collectors deprives the public of access (through libraries, museums, and archives) to sources of collective identity and memory. To commodify the past is to diminish the public realm. This is why many in the art world oppose the "deaccessioning," or selling off, of masterpieces from museum collections to raise funds for expenses. It is also reason to regret the sale to a private collector several years ago of a newly discovered first printing of the Declaration of Independence (for $2.4 million). Some scholars and civil rights figures have raised similar objections to efforts by the family of Martin Luther King Jr. to cash in on his legacy. Last year, the King family entered into a multimedia deal with Time Warner to market the words and image of Dr. King; the deal is projected to bring the estate $30 million to $50 million. Since the deal with Time Warner is to sell books, recordings, and cd-roms, it might be argued that commercialism in this case promotes, rather than restricts, public access.

But the aggressive marketing of King's legacy has coincided with severe limits on scholarly access to the King Center's archive. The estate has also been unusually stringent about enforcing its licensing rights. It sued CBS for selling a videotape containing footage of King's "I Have a Dream" speech and *USA Today* for publishing the speech without paying a licensing fee.

Of course, many of the things that collectors crave have less to do with history than celebrity. The public domain is not diminished by the fact that someone paid a fortune for a presidential comb. Still, there is something distasteful about buying and selling the personal effects of public figures. Perhaps it is the prying, prurient interest that lies behind the desire to possess such things. A few months ago, in another hotly disputed auction, Mickey Mantle's former agent and companion, Greer Johnson, sought to sell a bounty of Mantle memorabilia, including a lock of the Yankee slugger's hair, his American Express card, bathrobe, jockstrap, worn socks, golf shoes, and four vials of prescription decongestant. Under threat of a lawsuit from Mantle's family, Johnson agreed to withdraw some personal items from the sale, including the prescription bottles. In another celebrity auction last year, collectors from around the world bid via satellite and telephone in a Tokyo-based auction of Beatles memorabilia. Paul McCartney won a court order blocking the sale of a handwritten draft of his song "Penny Lane," but his birth certificate (once sold by his stepmother for $14,613) went for $73,064.

The worship of celebrities—sports heroes, rock stars, and movie idols—is nothing new. But the frenzied drive to commodify celebrity, to buy it and possess it, has reached unprecedented intensity. For generations, children came early to the ballpark in hopes of meeting a player and getting his autograph. Today, the autograph market is a $500 million industry, with dealers paying players to sign thousands of items, which are sold through catalog companies, cable television channels, mail-order houses, and sports-memorabilia stores in shopping malls across the country. In 1992, Mantle earned a reported $2.75 million for autographs and appearances, more than he made during his entire playing career with the Yankees.

Ironically, the cultural icons whose images and belongings are in greatest demand today—JFK, Mickey Mantle, the Beatles, Martin Luther King Jr.—are figures from the 1960s, a more innocent, idealistic time. It was a time before the personal foibles of public figures were relentlessly exposed, a time before presidents spoke of their boxer shorts on television. Perhaps, in our market-crazed way, we are struggling vainly to buy our way back to a world where not everything was for sale or open to public view.

# thirteen

# THE MARKET
# FOR MERIT

As high school seniors across America ponder their choice of colleges, their parents wonder how they will pay the bill. The price of tuition, room, and board at some private colleges and universities now tops $40,000 per year. For many families, however, the actual cost is not as staggering as it seems. As with airline tickets, not everyone pays full fare. For several decades, colleges have offered financial aid to students whose families cannot afford the full price. And, in recent years, a growing number of colleges have offered merit scholarships to desirable students regardless of financial need.

The trend toward merit scholarships has been a boon for families who don't qualify for need-based financial aid, and a valuable recruiting tool for colleges eager to compete for the best students. But, from the standpoint of higher education, merit scholarships are a mixed blessing. More money for students who can afford to pay their way may mean less money for the needy. Merit-based aid increased at an annual rate of 13 percent during the 1980s (adjusting for inflation), faster than the increase in need-based aid. The effect is most dramatic among second-tier schools trying to compete with those in the top tier for the most qualified students. Private colleges and universities ranked in the top fifth of selectivity offer little merit-based aid. In contrast, at liberal arts colleges ranked in the second tier, almost half of all scholarship funds are awarded according to merit.

The strongest argument against merit scholarships is that "merit" is a euphemism for "market." According to this argument, merit scholarships represent the intrusion of market values into education. Colleges that offer top students a discount on tuition are not simply honoring high academic achievement; they are buying better students than would attend their institution if financial aid were tied to need alone.

Unlike ordinary businesses, colleges and universities do not seek to maximize profits. But they do seek to maximize qualities such as academic selectivity, excellence, and prestige, all of which cost money. The drive to compete has led many colleges to adopt market-like policies in admissions and financial aid. From the standpoint of the market, a merit scholarship, like a supersaver airfare, is a discount on a product designed to help the bottom line. Like the airlines, many colleges now employ computer-driven "enrollment management" policies that predict the "willingness to pay" of student applicants in various categories. These days the price of a seat in the freshman class may vary not only according to the financial circumstances and academic standing of the applicant, but also according to race, gender, geography, or proposed field of study. Some schools have found that those who come for a campus interview are more eager to attend and therefore more willing to accept a leaner financial package.

Whether market-like practices rationalize or corrupt college financial aid policy depends on the purpose of higher education. Insofar as education is a commodity—an investment in human capital that yields a stream of future earnings—there is a case for allocating it according to market principles. To the extent that education advances non-market ideals—the pursuit of truth, the cultivation of moral and civic sensibilities—there is reason to worry that market principles may be corrupting.

These two visions of college education clashed a few years ago in a remarkable antitrust case brought by the Justice Department against a group of elite Northeast colleges and universities. Since the late 1950s, the eight Ivy League schools and MIT had agreed to offer financial aid solely on the basis of need, as defined by a common formula. To implement their agreement, representatives of the schools met each year to compare financial aid offers and adjust for discrepancies. A student admitted to Harvard, Princeton, and Columbia, for example, would receive a comparable financial aid offer from all three.

The Justice Department brought an antitrust action against the schools, claiming the practice amounted to price-fixing. The schools replied that they were not profit-making firms but educational institutions advancing two worthy social purposes: assuring equal access for those unable to afford an elite college education, and enabling all admitted students to make their college choice untainted by financial considerations. Financial aid was not a discount on a product, they argued, but a charitable gift that schools bestowed in order to advance their educational mission.

The federal courts ultimately rejected this view. "Discounting the price of educational services for needy students is not charity when a university receives tangible benefits in exchange," stated the U.S. Court of Appeals. Those tangible benefits were not profits, but the exceptional students Ivy League schools were able to attract who would otherwise be unable to enroll. The ability to avoid competition with peer institutions in awarding financial aid also enabled Ivy League schools to set higher tuition rates than might otherwise be possible. While the Ivies can continue to share common principles for awarding aid, they can no longer compare individual cases.

Not surprisingly, the case against merit scholarships is advanced most strongly by the schools that need them least. In virtue of their prestige, the nation's most selective colleges do best in the competition for students when the financial playing field is level. One educational benefit of the merit scholarships offered by second-tier schools may be to disperse top students among a wider range of colleges rather than concentrate them among a handful of elite ones.

Still, the principled objections to merit scholarships cannot easily be waved aside. At a time when government support for education is waning, the principle of access for needy students has become difficult to sustain for all but the richest institutions. And even schools that reap a competitive benefit from the use of merit scholarships should not be lulled into ignoring the dangers of creeping commodification. The most ardent advocates of markets would still, to some degree, insulate higher education from market pressures. For example, if it is all right to offer full scholarships to attract top students, what about offering salaries? Why should the NCAA not allow open bidding for the services of star athletes? Or, if colleges find that certain courses or majors are oversubscribed, why not charge a premium for them? If an unpopular professor draws persistently low enrollments, why not offer his courses at a discount?

At a certain point, market solutions sully the character of the good they allocate, at least where higher education is concerned. The growing use of merit scholarships may be approaching that point.

# fourteen

# SHOULD WE BUY THE
# RIGHT TO POLLUTE?

At the 1997 conference on global warming in Kyoto, Japan, the United States found itself at loggerheads with developing nations on two important issues: The United States wanted those countries to commit themselves to restraints on emissions, and it wanted any agreement to include a trading scheme that would let countries buy and sell the right to pollute.

The Clinton administration was right on the first point, but wrong on the second. Creating an international market in emission credits would make it easier for us to meet our obligations under the treaty but undermine the ethic we should be trying to foster on the environment.

Indeed, China and India threatened to torpedo the talks over the issue. They were afraid that such trading would enable rich countries to buy their way out of commitments to reduce greenhouse gases. In the end, the developing nations agreed to allow some emissions trading among developed countries, with details to be negotiated the following year.

The Clinton administration made emission trading a centerpiece of its environmental policy. Creating an international market for emissions, it argues, is a more efficient way to reduce pollution than imposing fixed levels for each country.

Trading in greenhouse gases could also make compliance cheaper and less painful for the United States, which could pay to reduce some other country's carbon dioxide emissions rather than reduce its own. For example, the United States might find it cheaper (and more politically palatable) to pay to update an old coal-burning factory in a developing country than to tax gas-guzzling sports utility vehicles at home.

Since the aim is to limit the global level of these gases, one might ask, what difference does it make which places on the planet send less carbon to the sky?

It may make no difference from the standpoint of the heavens, but it does make a political difference. Despite the efficiency of international emissions trading, such a system is objectionable for three reasons.

First, it creates loopholes that could enable wealthy countries to evade their obligations. Under the Kyoto formula, for example, the United States could take advantage of the fact that Russia has already reduced its emissions 30 percent since 1990, not through energy efficiencies but through economic decline. The United States could buy excess credits from Russia, and count them toward meeting our obligations under the treaty.

Second, turning pollution into a commodity to be bought and sold removes the moral stigma that is properly associated with it. If a company or a country is fined for spewing excessive pollutants into the air, the community conveys its judgment that the polluter has done something wrong. A fee, on the other hand, makes pollution just another cost of doing business, like wages, benefits and rent.

The distinction between a fine and a fee for despoiling the environment is not one we should give up too easily. Suppose there were a $100 fine for throwing a beer can into the Grand Canyon, and a wealthy hiker decided to pay $100 for the convenience. Would there be nothing wrong in his treating the fine as if it were simply an expensive dumping charge?

Or consider the fine for parking in a place reserved for the disabled. If a busy contractor needs to park near his building site and is willing to pay the fine, is there nothing wrong with his treating that space as an expensive parking lot?

In effacing the distinction between a fine and a fee, emission trading is like a recent proposal to open carpool lanes on Los Angeles freeways to drivers without passengers who are willing to pay a fee. Such drivers are now fined for slipping into carpool lanes; under the market proposal, they would enjoy a quicker commute without opprobrium.

A third objection to emission trading among countries is that it may undermine the sense of shared responsibility that increased global cooperation requires.

Consider an illustration drawn from an autumn ritual: raking fallen leaves into great piles and lighting bonfires. Imagine a neighborhood where each family agrees to have only one small bonfire a year. But they also agree that families can buy and sell their bonfire permits as they choose.

The family in the mansion on the hill buys permits from its neighbors—paying them, in effect, to lug their leaves to the town compost heap. The market works, and pollution is reduced, but without the spirit of shared sacrifice that might have been produced had no market intervened.

Those who have sold their permits, and those who have bought them, come to regard the bonfires less as an offense against clean air than as a luxury, a status symbol that can be bought and sold. And the resentment against the family in the mansion makes future, more demanding forms of cooperation more difficult to achieve.

Of course, many countries that attended the Kyoto conference have already made cooperation elusive. They have not yet agreed to restrict their emissions at all. Their refusal undermines the prospect of a global environmental ethic as surely as does our pollution trading scheme.

But the United States would have more suasion if these developing countries could not rightly complain that trading in emissions allows wealthy nations to buy their way out of global obligations.

# fifteen

# HONOR AND RESENTMENT

The politics of the ancients was about virtue and honor, but we moderns are concerned with fairness and rights. There is some truth in this familiar adage, but only to a point. On the surface, our political debates make little mention of honor, a seemingly quaint concern best suited to a status-ridden world of chivalry and duels. Not far beneath the surface, however, some of our fiercest debates about fairness and rights reflect deep disagreement about the proper basis of social esteem.

Consider the fuss over Callie Smartt, a 15-year-old cheerleader at a high school in West Texas. For a year she was a popular freshman cheerleader, despite the fact that she has cerebral palsy and moves about in a wheelchair. As Sue Anne Pressley reported in the *Washington Post,* "She had plenty of school spirit to go around. . . . The fans seemed to delight in her. The football players said they loved to see her dazzling smile." But at the end of the season, Callie was kicked off the squad. Earlier this fall, she was relegated to the status of honorary cheerleader; now, even that position is being abolished. At the urging of some other cheerleaders and their parents, school officials have told Callie that, to make the squad next year, she will have to try out like anyone else, in a rigorous routine involving splits and tumbles.

The head cheerleader's father opposes Callie's participation. He claims he is only concerned for Callie's safety. If a player comes flying off the field, he worries, "the cheerleader girls who aren't handi-capped could move out of the way a little faster." But Callie has never been hurt cheerleading. Her mother suspects the opposition may be motivated by resentment of the acclaim Callie has received.

But what kind of resentment might motivate the head cheer-leader's father? It cannot be fear that Callie's inclusion deprives his daughter of a place; she is already on the team. Nor is it the simple envy he might feel toward a girl who outshines his daughter at tum-bles and splits, which Callie, of course, does not. The resentment more likely reflects the conviction that Callie is being accorded an honor she does not deserve, in a way that mocks the pride he takes in his daughter's cheerleading prowess. If great cheerleading is some-thing that can be done from a wheelchair, then what becomes of the honor accorded those who excel at tumbles and splits? Indignation at misplaced honor is a moral sentiment that figures prominently in our politics, complicating and sometimes inflaming arguments about fairness and rights.

Should Callie be allowed to continue on the team? Some would answer by invoking the right of nondiscrimination: provided she can perform well in the role, Callie should not be excluded from cheer-leading simply because, through no fault of her own, she lacks the physical ability to perform gymnastic routines. But the nondiscrimi-nation argument begs the question at the heart of the controversy: What does it mean to perform well in the role of cheerleader? This question, in turn, is about the virtues and excellences that the prac-tice of cheerleading honors and rewards. The case for Callie is that, by roaring up and down the sidelines in her wheelchair, waving her pom-poms and motivating the team, she does well what cheerleaders are supposed to do: inspire school spirit.

But if Callie should be a cheerleader because she displays, despite her disability, the virtues appropriate to her role, her claim does pose a certain threat to the honor accorded the other cheerleaders. The gymnastic skills they display no longer appear essential to excellence in cheerleading, only one way among others of rousing the crowd. Ungenerous though he was, the father of the head cheerleader correctly grasped what was at stake. A social practice once taken as fixed in its purpose and in the honors it bestowed was now, thanks to Callie, redefined.

Disputes about the allocation of honor underlie other controversies about fairness and rights. Consider, for example, the debate over affirmative action in university admissions. Here too, some try to resolve the question by invoking a general argument against discrimination. Advocates of affirmative action argue it is necessary to remedy the effects of discrimination, while opponents maintain that taking race into account amounts to reverse discrimination. Again the nondiscrimination argument begs a crucial question. All admissions policies discriminate on some ground or other. The real issue is, what kind of discrimination is appropriate to the purposes universities serve? This question is contested, not only because it decides how educational opportunities are distributed but also because it determines what virtues universities define as worthy of honor.

If the sole purpose of a university were to promote scholarly excellence and intellectual virtues, then it should admit the students most likely to contribute to these ends. But if another mission of a university is to cultivate leadership for a pluralistic society, then it should seek students likely to advance civic purposes as well as intellectual ones. In a recent court case challenging its affirmative action program, the University of Texas Law School invoked its civic purpose, arguing that its minority admissions program had helped equip black and Mexican-American graduates to serve in the Texas legislature, on the federal bench and even in the president's Cabinet.

Some critics of affirmative action resent the idea that universities should honor qualities other than intellectual ones, for to do so implies that standard meritocratic virtues lack a privileged moral place. If race and ethnicity can be relevant to university admissions, then what becomes of the proud parent's conviction that his daughter is worthy of admission by virtue of her grades and test scores alone? Like the father's pride in his cheerleader daughter's tumbles and splits, it would have to be qualified by the recognition that honor is relative to social institutions, whose purposes are open to argument and revision.

Perhaps the most potent instance of the politics of honor plays itself out in debates about work. One reason many working-class voters despise welfare is not that they begrudge the money it costs but that they resent the message it conveys about what is worthy of honor and reward. Liberals who defend welfare in terms of fairness and rights often miss this point. More than an incentive to elicit effort and skills in socially useful ways, income is a measure of the things we prize. For many who "work hard and play by the rules," rewarding those who stay at home mocks the effort they expend and the pride they take in the work they do. Their resentment against welfare is not a reason to abandon the needy. But it does suggest that liberals need to articulate more convincingly the notions of virtue and honor that underlie their arguments for fairness and rights.

# sixteen

# ARGUING AFFIRMATIVE ACTION

Affirmative action has been the subject of recurring political and constitutional controversy since the 1970s. In 1996, California voters enacted Proposition 209, a state constitutional amendment banning preferential treatment in public education and employment. In 2003, the U.S. Supreme Court struck down an undergraduate admissions policy at the University of Michigan that used a point system to give minority applicants an advantage. But it upheld a more flexible affirmative action policy used in Michigan's law school, and ruled that race could be considered as a factor in admissions.

Some say it is all in the wording. When a 1997 referendum in Houston asked voters to end affirmative action, they refused to do so. When Proposition 209 asked California voters to end preferential treatment based on race, they obliged.

Controlling the language of a political debate is the first step toward winning it. Yet, in the case of affirmative action, the different answers reflect more than just political manipulation; they reflect a conflicted public mind. Critics of affirmative action say this is because Americans are reluctant to remedy past wrongs with new discrimination, whereas supporters say it is because of the public's lingering racism. Both are mistaken. Affirmative action is difficult to defend for a reason that has nothing to do with race. The real problem is that the best case for affirmative action challenges the sacred American myth that landing a job, or a seat in the freshman class, is a prize one deserves thanks solely to one's own efforts. Consider the two main arguments for counting race as a factor in university admissions: one argues for compensation, the other for diversity. The compensatory argument views affirmative action as a remedy for past wrongs. Minority students should be given preference now to make up for a history of discrimination that has placed them at an unfair disadvantage. This argument treats admission primarily as a benefit to the recipient and seeks to distribute the benefit in a way that compensates for past discrimination.

But the compensatory argument is the weaker of the two. As opponents of affirmative action note, those who benefit are not necessarily those who have suffered, and those who pay the compensation are seldom those responsible for the wrongs being rectified. Many beneficiaries of affirmative action are middle-class minority students who did not suffer the hardships that afflict young blacks and Hispanics from the inner city. And those who lose out under affirmative-action programs may have suffered obstacles of their own.

Those who defend affirmative action on compensatory grounds must be able to explain why otherwise qualified applicants should bear the burden of redressing the historic wrongs that minorities have suffered. Even if it can be argued that compensation should not be understood as a specific remedy for particular acts of discrimination, the compensatory rationale is too narrow to justify the range of programs advanced in the name of affirmative action.

The diversity argument is more compelling. It does not depend upon showing that the minority student given preference today actually suffered discrimination in the past. This is because it treats admission less as a reward to the recipient than as a means of advancing a socially worthy aim. The diversity argument holds that a racially mixed student body is desirable because it enables students to learn more from one another than they would if they all came from similar backgrounds. Just as a student body drawn from one part of the country would limit the range of intellectual perspectives, so would one reflecting a homogeneity of race, class, or ethnicity. Moreover, equipping disadvantaged minorities to assume positions of leadership in key public and professional roles advances the university's civic purpose and contributes to the common good.

Critics of affirmative action might concede the goal but question the means. Even if a diverse student body is desirable, isn't it unfair to exclude those who may have high enough test scores but lack, through no fault of their own, the racial or ethnic background that admissions officers need to advance their worthy purposes? Don't the students with the highest academic achievement and promise deserve to be admitted?

The honest answer to this question is: no, they don't. Here lies the far-reaching assumption underlying the diversity argument for affirmative action: admission is not an honor bestowed to reward superior virtue. Neither the student with high test scores nor the student who comes from a disadvantaged minority group morally deserves to be admitted. Provided the criteria of admission are reasonably related to a worthy social purpose, and provided applicants are admitted accordingly, no one has a right to complain.

The moral force of the diversity argument is that it detaches admissions from individual claims and connects them to considerations of the common good. But this is also the source of its political vulnerability. The belief that jobs and opportunities are rewards for those who deserve them runs deep in the American soul. Politicians constantly remind us that those who "work hard and play by the rules" deserve to get ahead, and insist that those who realize the American dream should view their success as the measure of their virtue.

The case for affirmative action and for other acts of social solidarity would be easier if the myth were weaker, if one day Americans grew skeptical of the faith that worldly success reflects moral desert. But what politician is up to the task of explaining that, even at their best, the rules of the game do not reward virtue after all, but simply call forth the qualities required, at any given moment to advance the common good?

# seventeen

# SHOULD VICTIMS HAVE A SAY IN SENTENCING?

Before sentencing Timothy McVeigh to death, the jury in the Oklahoma City bombing case heard heart-wrenching testimony from survivors and from victims' families. Some say that such testimony, no matter how moving, has no place in the courtroom. Whether a criminal defendant should be put to death should be decided by reasoned reflection on the facts and the law, they argue, and not by the anger and rage that the victims' families rightly feel. Others maintain that victims should have a voice in the punishment a perpetrator receives. If the punishment should fit the crime, they contend, juries must know the full measure of the victims' suffering and loss.

Judge Richard Matsch, who presided over the McVeigh trial, seemed torn between these two positions. While he allowed some victims to testify during the sentencing phase, he ruled out the use of emotionally loaded evidence like poems, wedding photographs and the testimony of a 9-year-old boy whose mother died in the bombing. He took pains to prevent testimony that might "inflame or incite the passions of the jury with respect to vengeance or . . . empathy for grief." Such emotions, he said, were "inappropriate in making a measured and deliberate moral judgment as to whether the defendant should be put to death." The judge's ambivalence reflects competing notions of the purpose of criminal punishment. Those who favor giving victims a voice in criminal sentencing rely, sometimes unwittingly, on two different arguments—one therapeutic, the other retributive. The first treats punishment as a source of solace for the victim, a cathartic expression, a moment of closure. If punishment is for the benefit of the victim, then the victim should have a say in what the punishment is. The therapeutic theory of punishment finds its clearest expression in state laws that invite victims not only to describe their pain and suffering but also to express their opinions of the defendant, making for raucous courtroom scenes resembling daytime talk shows. Texas law even allows victims or their relatives to berate the defendant in open court after sentencing.

But the therapeutic case for victim testimony is flawed. It confuses an effect of criminal punishment (that victims and their families take satisfaction in the outcome) with its primary justification—to give the perpetrator what he deserves. The most compelling reason to allow victim impact statements is a retributive one: to provide the jury with a full account of the moral gravity of the crime. Though we may be aware that 168 people died in the Oklahoma bombing, only those agonizing stories of bewildered toddlers asking plaintively for their mothers convey the full moral measure of the crime.

In the retributive view, victim impact statements are not for the sake of allowing victims to vent their emotions but rather for the sake of doing justice, of getting at the moral truth of the matter. To the extent that emotions distort rather than clarify the nature of the crime, the judge should restrain their role in sentencing.

Though the retributive argument offers the best case for victim testimony, it is open to two apparent objections. First, the use of evidence about the character of particular victims and their importance to family or community implies that some lives are worthier than others. Otherwise, what moral difference does it make whether a murderer kills a beloved parent of four children or an unmarried drifter whose death goes unmourned, a Martin Luther King Jr. or the town drunk? Unless there is some basis for judgments of this kind, it is difficult to explain the moral relevance of testimony about the life or character of particular victims.

Second, even if certain murders are morally more grievous than others, isn't it unfair to give extra punishment for aspects of a crime about which the perpetrator was unaware? If an assailant kills a stranger, should his penalty depend on whether the victim turns out to have been a sinner or a saint? The Supreme Court emphasized this objection in *Booth v. Maryland,* a 1987 case that held victim impact statements in capital cases to be unconstitutional. Allowing the jury to consider the victim's character or family circumstances "could result in imposing the death sentence because of factors about which the defendant was not aware, and that were irrelevant to the decision to kill."

The second objection is less weighty than the first. We do not punish murderers only for their "decision to kill," but also for the harm they cause. A would-be assassin whose gun fails to fire receives a lesser punishment than a successful assassin, even though both made a "decision to kill." A drunk driver who kills a pedestrian is subject to a heavier penalty than an equally drunk driver who is lucky enough to kill no one, even though neither made a "decision to kill."

The first objection, on the other hand, is not as easy to dismiss. That the retributive case for victim testimony implies a moral hierarchy among murders (and perhaps also victims) is difficult to deny. The notion of moral discrimination is at odds with the nonjudgmental instinct of our time. But that is not an argument against it. We cannot make sense of our judgments about crime and punishment without some notion of moral discrimination.

Judge Matsch is not the only one wrestling with these competing theories of punishment. The use of impact statements has burgeoned in recent years, prompted by a victims' rights movement and a 1991 Supreme Court decision, *Payne v. Tennessee,* that overruled Booth and allowed victim testimony in death penalty cases. Most states now accord victims the right to be heard, and Congress included provisions for victim testimony in the 1994 federal crime bill. In March, President Clinton signed legislation that would let victims of the Oklahoma bombing witness the trial even if they were being called to testify. "When someone is a victim, he or she should be at the center of the criminal justice process," Clinton said, "not on the outside looking in."

The increasing concern for victims' rights is a morally ambiguous tiding. It reflects the rising therapeutic impulse in American public life—a defense attorney called victim testimony "the Oprahization of sentencing"—and also the growing appeal of traditional notions of retributive justice. As the therapeutic ethic represents the flight from moral responsibility, the retributive ethic represents the yearning to recover it. The challenge is to disentangle the second impulse from the first. Victim testimony, properly controlled, can serve justice by shedding light on the moral gravity of the crime. But there is a danger in placing the victim "at the center of the criminal justice process." It is the danger, as old as the practice of private vengeance, that the psychological needs of the victim will swamp the moral imperative that the punishment fit the crime.

# eighteen

# CLINTON AND KANT
# ON LYING

Suppose, for the sake of argument, that the president was sexually involved with Monica Lewinsky. Would it be wrong for him to deny it? The obvious answer is yes—an extramarital dalliance with a White House intern is bad enough, and lying only compounds the sin. But while a public lie about private misconduct may not be a morally admirable thing, such a lie does not necessarily add to the wrong of the conduct it conceals. It might even be justified.

Consider a different case of presidential deceit—a denial of plans to lead the country into war. During the 1964 presidential campaign, Lyndon Johnson concealed his intention to escalate the war in Vietnam, much as Franklin Roosevelt had denied plans to enter World War II. "I have said this before, but I shall say it again and again and again," FDR declared during the 1940 campaign. "Your boys are not going to be sent into any foreign wars." Both presidents deceived the public—Roosevelt for the sake of a just cause, Johnson for the sake of an unjust one. The moral status of their respective deceits differs accordingly. Johnson's lie was less justified than Roosevelt's, not because it was any less truthful, but because it served an unworthy end. The Clinton case differs in that the conduct in question is not a public undertaking but an alleged private misdeed. It certainly lacks the high moral purpose of Roosevelt's cause. But there may be a case, in the name of privacy and decorum, for the president to deny a scurrilous charge even if true, provided it has no bearing on public responsibilities. The Talmud allows three exceptions to the requirement of truthfulness—involving knowledge, hospitality, and sex. A scholar who is asked whether he knows a certain passage of Talmud may say, falsely, that he does not, to avoid an immodest display of knowledge. He may also lie if asked about the quality of hospitality he has received in order to spare his host a parade of unwelcome guests. Finally, he is entitled to lie if asked about such intimate matters as the performance of his conjugal duties. (This last exemption applies only loosely to the case of Clinton. On the one hand, it suggests that the right to lie can arise from the impropriety of the question. On the other, it covers inquiries about marital relations, not alleged infidelity.)

The morality of deceit is complicated by the fact that it is possible to mislead without actually lying. Much has been made of Clinton's tendency to give carefully worded, loophole-ridden denials to embarrassing allegations. When asked, during his first presidential campaign, whether he had ever used recreational drugs, Clinton replied that he had never broken the anti-drug laws of his country or state. He later conceded that he had tried marijuana while a student in England. A close reading of his famous 1992 interview on "60 Minutes" reveals that he never actually denied an extramarital affair with Gennifer Flowers. Asked about Flowers's tabloid account of a twelve-year affair, Clinton replied, "That allegation is false." This answer is technically consistent with Clinton's reported admission in his sealed deposition in the Paula Jones case that he did have a sexual involvement with Flowers.

Is there a moral difference between an artful dodge and a bald-faced lie? No, say Clinton critics, and many ethicists as well. They argue that a misleading truth has the same purpose and, if successful, the same effect as an outright lie: to deceive the listener. One of the greatest moralists of all time, however, disagreed. Immanuel Kant, an eighteenth-century German philosopher, insisted there is all the difference in the world between a lie and a technically truthful dodge.

Kant yielded to no one in his opposition to lying. Even if a murderer came to your door looking for a person hiding in your house, Kant held, it is not morally permissible to lie. The duty to tell the truth holds irrespective of the consequences. At one point, Benjamin Constant, a French contemporary of Kant's, took issue with this uncompromising stance. The duty to tell the truth only applies, Constant argued, to those who deserve the truth, as surely the murderer does not. Kant replied that lying to a murderer is wrong, not because it harms him, but because it violates the very principle of right and offends the human dignity of the person who lies. "To be truthful (honest) in all declarations is, therefore, a sacred and unconditionally commanding law of reason that admits of no expediency whatsoever," Kant said.

Despite his categorical prohibition on lying, or perhaps because of it, Kant drew a sharp distinction between lies and statements that are misleading but not, in the formal sense, untrue. A few years before his exchange with Constant, Kant found himself in trouble with King Friedrich Wilhelm II. The King and his censors demanded that Kant refrain from any lectures or writings they deemed a distortion or depreciation of Christianity. Kant, who planned to speak and publish further on religion, responded with a carefully worded statement, promising that "as your Majesty's faithful subject, I shall in the future completely desist from all public lectures or papers concerning religion."

When the King died a few years later, Kant considered himself absolved of the promise, which bound him only as "His Majesty's faithful subject." Kant later explained that he had chosen his words "most carefully, so that I should not be deprived of my freedom . . . forever, but only so long as His Majesty was alive." By this clever evasion, the paragon of Prussian probity succeeded in misleading the censors without lying to them.

Many thought Clinton was employing a similar maneuver when, early in the scandal, he repeatedly employed the present tense to deny allegations of past impropriety, stating, "There is no sexual relationship." When journalists seized on the possible evasion, he finally issued a less equivocal denial.

If the president has shifted from a misleading truth (like Kant's) to an actual lie, there might still be a mitigating factor. Even the most righteous among us would not welcome the prying, prurient scrutiny to which public figures are exposed. Consider, again, the Talmud. It tells of a rabbinic sage so exemplary that his disciple once hid under his bed to learn the proper way to make love to one's wife. When the rabbi discovered his student's presence and asked him to leave, the disciple replied, "It is Torah and deserves to be studied." The president's popularity is unimpaired, not because the American people believe he is telling the truth, but because they have decided that his sex life is not Torah and does not deserve to be studied.

# nineteen

# IS THERE A RIGHT TO ASSISTED SUICIDE?

This essay was written as the Supreme Court contemplated two cases involving state laws that banned physician-assisted suicide. The Court unanimously upheld the laws and rejected the notion of a constitutional right to physician-assisted suicide.

The Supreme Court will soon decide whether terminally ill patients have a constitutional right to physician-assisted suicide. Most likely, the Court will say no. Almost every state prohibits assisted suicide, and in oral arguments earlier this year the justices voiced doubts about striking down so many state laws on so wrenching a moral issue.

If the Court rules as expected, it will not simply be overruling the two federal courts that declared suicide a constitutional right. It will also be rejecting the advice of six distinguished moral philosophers who filed a friend of the court brief. The authors of the brief comprise the Dream Team of liberal political philosophy—Ronald Dworkin (Oxford and NYU), Thomas Nagel (NYU), Robert Nozick (Harvard), John Rawls (Harvard), Thomas Scanlon (Harvard), and Judith Jarvis Thomson (MIT).[1]

At the heart of the philosophers' argument is the attractive but mistaken principle that government should be neutral on controversial moral and religious questions. Since people disagree about what gives meaning and value to life, the philosophers argue, government should not impose through law any particular answer to such questions. Instead, it should respect a person's right to live (and die) according to his own convictions about what makes life worth living. Mindful that judges are reluctant to venture onto morally contested terrain, the philosophers insist that the Court can affirm a right to assisted suicide without passing judgment on the moral status of suicide itself. "These cases do not invite or require the Court to make moral, ethical, or religious judgments about how people should approach or confront their death or about when it is ethically appropriate to hasten one's own death or to ask others for help in doing so," they write. Instead, say the philosophers, the Court should accord individuals the right to make these "grave judgments for themselves, free from the imposition of any religious or philosophical orthodoxy by court or legislature."

Despite their claim to neutrality, the philosophers' argument betrays a certain view of what makes life worth living. According to this view, the best way to live and die is to do so deliberately, autonomously, in a way that enables us to view our lives as our own creations. The best lives are led by those who see themselves not as participants in a drama larger than themselves but as authors of the drama itself "Most of us see death . . . as the final act of life's drama," the brief states, "and we want that last act to reflect our own convictions." The philosophers speak for those who would end their lives upon concluding that living on "would disfigure rather than enhance the lives they had created." Citing the Court's language in a recent abortion case, *Planned Parenthood v. Casey* (1992), the philosophers stress the individual's right to make "choices central to personal dignity and autonomy." Such freedom includes nothing less than "the right to define one's own concept of existence, of meaning, of the universe, and of the mystery of human life."

The philosophers' emphasis on autonomy and choice implies that life is the possession of the person who lives it. This ethic is at odds with a wide range of moral outlooks that view life as a gift, of which we are custodians with certain duties. Such outlooks reject the idea that a person's life is open to unlimited use, even by the person whose life it is. Far from being neutral, the ethic of autonomy invoked in the brief departs from many religious traditions and also from the views of the founders of liberal political philosophy, John Locke and Immanuel Kant. Both Locke and Kant opposed a right to suicide, and both rejected the notion that our lives are possessions to dispose of as we please.

Locke, the philosopher of consent argued for limited government on the grounds that certain rights are so profoundly ours that we cannot give them up, even by an act of consent. Since the right to life and liberty is unalienable, he maintained, we cannot sell ourselves into slavery or commit suicide: "No body can give more Power than he has himself, and he that cannot take away his own Life, cannot give another power over it."

For Kant, respect for autonomy entails duties to oneself as well as others, most notably the duty to treat humanity as an end in itself. This duty constrains the way a person can treat himself. According to Kant, murder is wrong because it uses the victim as a means rather than respects him as an end. But the same can be true of suicide. If a person "does away with himself in order to escape from a painful situation," Kant writes, "he is making use of a person merely as a means to maintain a tolerable state of affairs till the end of his life. But man is not a thing—not something to be used as a means: he must always in his actions be regarded as an end in himself." Kant concludes that a person has no more right to kill himself than to kill someone else.

The philosophers' brief assumes, contrary to Kant, that the value of a person's life is the value he or she attributes to it, provided the person is competent and fully informed. "When a competent person does want to die," the philosophers write, "it makes no sense to appeal to the patient's right not to be killed as a reason why an act designed to cause his death is impermissible." Kant would have disagreed. The fact that a person wants to die does not make it morally permissible to kill him, even if his desire is uncoerced and well-informed.

The philosophers might reply that permitting assisted suicide does no harm to those who find it morally objectionable; those who prefer to view their lives as episodes in a larger drama rather than as autonomous creations would remain free to do so.

But this reply overlooks the way that changes in law can bring changes in the way we understand ourselves. The philosophers rightly observe that existing laws against assisted suicide reflect and entrench certain views about what gives life meaning. But the same would be true were the Court to declare, in the name of autonomy, a right to assisted suicide. The new regime would not simply expand the range of options, but would encourage the tendency to view life less as a gift and more as a possession. It might heighten the prestige we accord autonomous, independent lives and depreciate the claims of those seen to be dependent. How this shift would affect policy toward the elderly, the disabled, the poor and the infirm, or reshape the attitudes of doctors toward their ailing patients or children toward their aging parents, remains to be seen.

To reject the autonomy argument is not necessarily to oppose assisted suicide in all cases. Even those who regard life as a sacred trust can admit that the claims of compassion may sometimes override the duty to preserve life. The challenge is to find a way to honor these claims that preserves the moral burden of hastening death, and that retains the reverence for life as something we cherish, not something we choose.

# twenty

# EMBRYO ETHICS

## THE MORAL LOGIC OF
## STEM CELL RESEARCH

At first glance, the case for federal funding of embryonic stem cell research seems too obvious to need defending. Why should the government refuse to support research that holds promise for the treatment and cure of devastating conditions such as Parkinson's disease, diabetes, and spinal cord injury? Critics of stem cell research offer two main objections: some hold that despite its worthy ends, stem cell research is wrong because it involves the destruction of human embryos; others worry that even if research on embryos is not wrong in itself, it will open the way to a slippery slope of dehumanizing practices, such as embryo farms, cloned babies, the use of fetuses for spare parts, and the commodification of human life.

Neither objection is ultimately persuasive, though each raises questions that proponents of stem cell research should take seriously. Consider the first objection. Those who make it begin by arguing, rightly, that biomedical ethics is not only about ends but also about means; even research that achieves great good is unjustified if it comes at the price of violating fundamental human rights. For example, the ghoulish experiments of Nazi doctors would not be morally justified even if they resulted in discoveries that alleviated human suffering.

Few would dispute the idea that respect for human dignity imposes certain moral constraints on medical research. The question is whether the destruction of human embryos in stem cell research amounts to the killing of human beings. The "embryo objection" insists that it does. For those who adhere to this view, extracting stem cells from a blastocyst is morally equivalent to yanking organs from a baby to save other people's lives.

Some base this conclusion on the religious belief that ensoulment occurs at conception. Others try to defend it without recourse to religion, by the following line of reasoning: Each of us began life as an embryo. If our lives are worthy of respect, and hence inviolable, simply by virtue of our humanity, one would be mistaken to think that at some younger age or earlier stage of development we were not worthy of respect. Unless we can point to a definitive moment in the passage from conception to birth that marks the emergence of the human person, this argument claims, we must regard embryos as possessing the same inviolability as fully developed human beings.

But this argument is flawed. The fact that every person began life as an embryo does not prove that embryos are persons. Consider an analogy: although every oak tree was once an acorn, it does not follow that acorns are oak trees, or that I should treat the loss of an acorn eaten by a squirrel in my front yard as the same kind of loss as the death of an oak tree felled by a storm. Despite their developmental continuity, acorns and oak trees are different kinds of things. So are human embryos and human beings. Sentient creatures make claims on us that nonsentient ones do not; beings capable of experience and consciousness make higher claims still. Human life develops by degrees.

Those who view embryos as persons often assume that the only alternative is to treat them with moral indifference. But one need not regard the embryo as a full human being in order to accord it a certain respect. To regard an embryo as a mere thing, open to any use we desire or devise, does, it seems to me, miss its significance as potential human life. Few would favor the wanton destruction of embryos or the use of embryos for the purpose of developing a new line of cosmetics. Personhood is not the only warrant for respect. For example, we consider it an act of disrespect when a hiker carves his initials in an ancient sequoia—not because we regard the sequoia as a person, but because we regard it as a natural wonder worthy of appreciation and awe. To respect the old-growth forest does not mean that no tree may ever be felled or harvested for human purposes. Respecting the forest may be consistent with using it. But the purposes should be weighty and appropriate to the wondrous nature of the thing.

The notion that an embryo in a petri dish has the same moral status as a person can be challenged on further grounds. Perhaps the best way to see its implausibility is to play out its full implications. First, if harvesting stem cells from a blastocyst were truly on a par with harvesting organs from a baby, then the morally responsible policy would be to ban it, not merely deny it federal funding. If some doctors made a practice of killing children to get organs for transplantation, no one would take the position that the infanticide should be ineligible for federal funding but allowed to continue in the private sector. If we were persuaded that embryonic stem cell research were tantamount to infanticide, we would not only ban it but treat it as a grisly form of murder and subject scientists who performed it to criminal punishment.

Second, viewing the embryo as a person rules out not only stem cell research, but all fertility treatments that involve the creation and discarding of excess embryos. In order to increase pregnancy rates and spare women the ordeal of repeated attempts, most in vitro fertilization clinics create more fertilized eggs than are ultimately implanted. Excess embryos are typically frozen indefinitely or discarded. (A small number are donated for stem cell research.) But if it is immoral to sacrifice embryos for the sake of curing or treating devastating diseases, it is also immoral to sacrifice them for the sake of treating infertility.

Third, defenders of in vitro fertilization point out that embryo loss in assisted reproduction is less frequent than in natural pregnancy, in which more than half of all fertilized eggs either fail to implant or are otherwise lost. This fact highlights a further difficulty with the view that equates embryos and persons. If natural procreation entails the loss of some embryos for every successful birth, perhaps we should worry less about the loss of embryos that occurs in in vitro fertilization and stem cell research. Those who view embryos as persons might reply that high infant mortality would not justify infanticide. But the way we respond to the natural loss of embryos suggests that we do not regard this event as the moral or religious equivalent of the death of infants. Even those religious traditions that are the most solicitous of nascent human life do not mandate the same burial rituals and mourning rites for the loss of an embryo as for the death of a child. Moreover, if the embryo loss that accompanies natural procreation were the moral equivalent of infant death, then pregnancy would have to be regarded as a public health crisis of epidemic proportions; alleviating natural embryo loss would be a more urgent moral cause than abortion, in vitro fertilization, and stem cell research combined.

Even critics of stem cell research hesitate to embrace the full implications of the embryo objection. President George W. Bush has prohibited federal funding for research on embryonic stem cell lines derived after August 9, 2001, but has not sought to ban such research, nor has he called on scientists to desist from it. And as the stem cell debate heats up in Congress, even outspoken opponents of embryo research have not mounted a national campaign to ban in vitro fertilization or to prohibit fertility clinics from creating and discarding excess embryos. This does not mean that their positions are unprincipled—only that their positions cannot rest on the principle that embryos are inviolable.

What else could justify restricting federal funding for stem cell research? It might be the worry that embryo research will lead down a slippery slope of exploitation and abuse. This objection raises legitimate concerns, but curtailing stem cell research is the wrong way to address them. Congress can stave off the slippery slope by enacting sensible regulations, beginning with a simple ban on human reproductive cloning. Following the approach adopted by the United Kingdom, Congress might also require that research embryos not be allowed to develop beyond 14 days, restrict the commodification of embryos and gametes, and establish a stem cell bank to prevent proprietary interests from monopolizing access to stem cell lines. Regulations such as these could save us from slouching toward a brave new world as we seek to redeem the great biomedical promise of our time.

# twenty-one

# MORAL ARGUMENT AND LIBERAL TOLERATION
## ABORTION AND HOMOSEXUALITY

People defend laws against abortion and homosexual conduct in two different ways: Some argue that abortion and homosexuality are morally reprehensible and therefore worthy of prohibition; others try to avoid passing judgment on the morality of these practices, and argue instead that, in a democracy, political majorities have the right to embody in law their moral convictions.

In a similar way, arguments against antiabortion and antisodomy laws take two different forms: Some say the laws are unjust because the practices they prohibit are morally permissible, indeed sometimes desirable; others oppose these laws without reference to the moral status of the practices at issue, and argue instead that individuals have a right to choose for themselves whether to engage in them.

These two styles of argument might be called, respectively, the "naive" and the "sophisticated." The naive view holds that the justice of laws depends on the moral worth of the conduct they prohibit or protect. The sophisticated view holds that the justice of such laws depends not on a substantive moral judgment about the conduct at stake, but instead on a more general theory about the respective claims of majority rule and individual rights, of democracy on the one hand, and liberty on the other.

I shall try in this essay to bring out the truth in the naive view, which I take to be this: The justice (or injustice) of laws against abortion and homosexual conduct depends, at least in part, on the morality (or immorality) of those practices.[1] This is the claim the sophisticated view rejects. In both its majoritarian and its liberal versions, the sophisticated view tries to set aside or "bracket" controversial moral and religious conceptions for purposes of justice. It insists that the justification of laws be neutral among competing visions of the good life.

In practice, of course, these two kinds of argument can be difficult to distinguish. In the debate over cases like *Roe v. Wade*[2] and *Bowers v. Hardwick*,[3] both camps tend to advance the naive view under cover of the sophisticated. (Such is the prestige of the sophisticated way of arguing.) For example, those who would ban abortion and gay and lesbian sex out of abhorrence often argue in the name of deference to democracy and judicial restraint. Similarly, those who want permissive laws because they approve of abortion and homosexuality often argue in the name of liberal toleration.

This is not to suggest that all instances of the sophisticated argument are disingenuous attempts to promote a substantive moral conviction. Those who argue that law should be neutral among competing conceptions of the good life offer various grounds for their claim, including most prominently the following:

(1) the *voluntarist* view holds that government should be neutral among conceptions of the good life in order to respect the capacity of persons as free citizens or autonomous agents to choose their conceptions for themselves; (2) the *minimalist* or pragmatic view says that, because people inevitably disagree about morality and religion, government should bracket these controversies for the sake of political agreement and social cooperation.

In order to bring out the truth in the naive way of arguing, I look to the actual arguments judges and commentators have made in recent cases dealing with abortion and homosexuality. Their arguments, unfailingly sophisticated, illustrate the difficulty of bracketing moral judgments for purposes of law. Although much of my argument criticizes leading theories of liberal toleration, I do not think it offers any comfort to majoritarianism. The cure for liberalism is not majoritarianism, but a keener appreciation of the role of substantive moral discourse in political and constitutional argument.

## PRIVACY RIGHTS: INTIMACY AND AUTONOMY

In the constitutional right of privacy, the neutral state and the voluntarist conception of the person are often joined. In the case of abortion, for example, no state may, "by adopting one theory of life,"[4] override a woman's right to decide "whether or not to terminate her pregnancy."[5] Government may not enforce a particular moral view, however widely held, for "no individual should be compelled to surrender the freedom to make that decision for herself simply because her 'value preferences' are not shared by the majority."[6]

As with religious liberty and freedom of speech, so with privacy, the ideal of neutrality often reflects a voluntarist conception of human agency. Government must be neutral among conceptions of the good life in order to respect the capacity of persons to choose their values and relationships for themselves. So close is the connection between privacy rights and the voluntarist conception of the self that commentators frequently assimilate the values of privacy and autonomy: Privacy rights are said to be "grounded in notions of individual autonomy," because "the human dignity protected by constitutional guarantees would be seriously diminished if people were not free to choose and adopt a lifestyle which allows expression of their uniqueness and individuality."[7] In "recognizing a constitutional right to privacy," the Court has given effect to the view "that persons have the capacity to live autonomously and the right to exercise that capacity."[8] Supreme Court decisions voiding laws against contraceptives "not only protect the individual who chooses not to procreate, but also the autonomy of a couple's association."[9] They protect men and women "against an unchosen commitment" to unwanted children, and "against a compelled identification with the social role of parent."[10]

In Supreme Court decisions and dissents alike, the justices have often tied privacy rights to voluntarist assumptions. The Court has thus characterized laws banning the use of contraceptives as violating "the constitutional protection of individual autonomy in matters of childbearing."[11] It has defended the right to an abortion on the grounds that few decisions are "more properly private, or more basic to individual dignity and autonomy, than a woman's decision . . . whether to end her pregnancy."[12] Justice Douglas, concurring in an abortion case, emphasized that the right of privacy protects such liberties as "the autonomous control over the development and expression of one's intellect, interests, tastes, and personality," as well as "freedom of choice in the basic decisions of one's life respecting marriage, divorce, procreation, contraception, and the education and upbringing of children."[13] And four justices would have extended privacy protection to consensual homosexual activity on the grounds that "much of the richness of a relationship will come from the freedom an individual has to *choose* the form and nature of these intensely personal bonds."[14]

Although the link between privacy and autonomy is now so familiar as to seem natural, even necessary, the right of privacy need not presuppose a voluntarist conception of the person. In fact, through most of its history in American law, the right of privacy has implied neither the ideal of the neutral state nor the ideal of a self freely choosing its aims and attachments.

Where the contemporary right of privacy is the right to engage in certain conduct without government restraint, the traditional version is the right to keep certain personal facts from public view. The new privacy protects a person's "independence in making certain kinds of important decisions," whereas the old privacy protects a person's interest "in avoiding disclosure of personal matters."[15]

The tendency to identify privacy with autonomy not only obscures these shifting understandings of privacy; it also restricts the range of reasons for protecting it. Although the new privacy typically relies on voluntarist justifications, it can also be justified in other ways. A right to be free of governmental interference in matters of marriage, for example, can be defended not only in the name of individual choice, but also in the name of the intrinsic value or social importance of the practice it protects.

## FROM THE OLD PRIVACY TO THE NEW

The right to privacy first gained legal recognition in the United States as a doctrine of tort law, not constitutional law. In an influential article in 1890, Louis Brandeis, then a Boston lawyer, and his one-time law partner Samuel Warren argued that the civil law should protect "the right to privacy."[16] Far from later-day concerns with sexual freedoms, Brandeis and Warren's privacy was quaint by comparison, concerned with the publication of high society gossip by the sensationalist press, or the unauthorized use of people's portraits in advertising.[17] Gradually at first, then more frequently in the 1930s, this right to privacy gained recognition in the civil law of most states.[18] Prior to the 1960s, however, privacy received scant attention in constitutional law.

The Supreme Court first addressed the right of privacy as such in 1961 when a Connecticut pharmacist challenged the state's ban on contraceptives in *Poe v. Ullman*.[19] Although the majority dismissed the case on technical grounds,[20] Justices Douglas and Harlan dissented, arguing that the law violated the right of privacy. The privacy they defended was privacy in the traditional sense. The right at stake was not the right to use contraceptives but the right to be free of the surveillance that enforcement would require. "If we imagine a regime of full enforcement of the law," wrote Douglas, "we would reach the point where search warrants issued and officers appeared in bedrooms to find out what went on. . . . If [the State] can make this law, it can enforce it. And proof of its violation necessarily involves an inquiry into the relations between man and wife."[21] Banning the sale of contraceptives would be different from banning their use, Douglas observed. Banning the sale would restrict access to contraceptives but would not expose intimate relations to public inspection. Enforcement would take police to the drugstore, not the bedroom, and so would not offend privacy in the traditional sense.[22]

Justice Harlan also objected to the law on grounds that distinguish the old privacy from the new. He did not object that the law against contraceptives failed to be neutral among competing moral conceptions. Although Harlan acknowledged that the law was based on the belief that contraception is immoral in itself, and encourages such "dissolute action" as fornication and adultery by minimizing their "disastrous consequence,"[23] he did not find this failure of neutrality contrary to the Constitution. In a statement clearly opposed to the strictures of neutrality, Harlan argued that morality is a legitimate concern of government.

> Society is not limited in its objects only to the physical well-being of the community, but has traditionally concerned itself with the moral soundness of its people as well. Indeed to attempt a line between public behavior and that which is purely consensual or solitary would be to withdraw from community concern a range of subjects with which every society in civilized times has found it necessary to deal.[24]

Though he rejected the ideal of the neutral state, Harlan did not conclude that Connecticut could prohibit married couples from using contraceptives. Like Douglas, he reasoned that enforcing the law would intrude on the privacy essential to the prized institution of marriage. He objected to the violation of privacy in the traditional sense, to "the intrusion of the whole machinery of the criminal law into the very heart of marital privacy, requiring husband and wife to render account before a criminal tribunal of their uses of that intimacy."[25] According to Harlan, the state was entitled to embody in law the belief that contraception is immoral, but not to implement "the obnoxiously intrusive means it ha[d] chosen to effectuate that policy."[26]

Four years later, in *Griswold v. Connecticut*,[27] the dissenters prevailed. The Supreme Court invalidated Connecticut's law against contraceptives and for the first time explicitly recognized a constitutional right of privacy. Although the right was located in the Constitution rather than tort law, it remained tied to the traditional notion of privacy as the interest in keeping intimate affairs from public view. The violation of privacy consisted in the intrusion required to enforce the law, not the restriction on the freedom to use contraceptives. "Would we allow the police to search the sacred precincts of marital bedrooms for telltale signs of the use of contraceptives?" wrote Justice Douglas for the Court. "The very idea is repulsive to the notions of privacy surrounding the marriage relationship."[28]

The justification for the right was not voluntarist but based on a substantive moral judgment; the privacy the Court vindicated was not for the sake of letting people lead their sexual lives as they choose, but rather for the sake of affirming and protecting the social institution of marriage.

> Marriage is a coming together for better or for worse, hopefully enduring, and intimate to the degree of being sacred. It is an association that promotes a way of life, . . . a harmony in living, . . . a bilateral loyalty. . . . [I]t is an association for as noble a purpose as any involved in our prior decisions.[29]

Although commentators and judges often view *Griswold* as a dramatic constitutional departure, the privacy right it proclaimed was consistent with traditional notions of privacy going back to the turn of the century. From the standpoint of shifting privacy conceptions, the more decisive turn came seven years later in *Eisenstadt v. Baird*,[30] a seemingly similar case. Like *Griswold,* it involved a state law restricting contraceptives. In *Eisenstadt,* however, the challenged law restricted the distribution of contraceptives, not their use. While it therefore limited access to contraceptives, its enforcement could not be said to require governmental surveillance of intimate activities. It did not violate privacy in the traditional sense.[31] Furthermore, the law prohibited distributing contraceptives only to unmarried persons, and so did not burden the institution of marriage as the Connecticut law did.

Despite these differences, the Supreme Court struck down the law with only a single dissent. Its decision involved two innovations, one explicit, the other unacknowledged. The explicit innovation redescribed the bearers of privacy rights from persons *qua* participants in the social institution of marriage to persons *qua* individuals, independent of their roles or attachments. As the Court explained, "It is true that in *Griswold* the right of privacy in question inhered in the marital relationship. Yet the marital couple is not an independent entity with a mind and heart of its own, but an association of two individuals each with a separate intellectual and emotional makeup."[32]

The subtler, though no less fateful change in *Eisenstadt* was in the shift from the old privacy to the new. Rather than conceiving privacy as freedom from surveillance or disclosure of intimate affairs, the Court found that the right to privacy now protected the freedom to engage in certain activities without governmental restriction. Although privacy in *Griswold* prevented intrusion into "the sacred precincts of marital bedrooms,"[33] privacy in *Eisenstadt* prevented intrusion into *decisions* of certain kinds. Moreover, as the meaning of privacy changed, so did its justification. The Court protected privacy in *Eisenstadt* not for the social practices it promoted but for the individual choice it secured. "If the right of privacy means anything, it is the right of the *individual,* married or single, to be free from unwarranted governmental intrusion into matters so fundamentally affecting a person as the decision whether to bear or beget a child."[34]

One year later, in *Roe v. Wade*,[35] the Supreme Court gave the new privacy its most controversial application by striking down a Texas law against abortion and extending privacy to "encompass a woman's decision whether or not to terminate her pregnancy."[36] First with contraception, then with abortion, the right of privacy had become the right to make certain sorts of choices, free of interference by the state.

The voluntarist grounds of the new privacy found explicit statement in a 1977 case invalidating a New York law prohibiting the sale of contraceptives to minors under age sixteen.[37] For the first time, the Court used the language of autonomy to describe the interest privacy protects, and argued openly for the shift from the old privacy to the new. Writing for the Court in *Carey v. Population Services International*, Justice Brennan admitted that *Griswold* focused on the fact that a law forbidding the *use* of contraceptives can bring the police into marital bedrooms.[38] "But subsequent decisions have made clear that the constitutional protection of individual autonomy in matters of childbearing is not dependent on that element."[39] Surveying the previous cases, he emphasized that *Eisenstadt* protected the "*decision* whether to bear or beget a child,"[40] and *Roe* protected "a woman's *decision* whether or not to terminate her pregnancy."[41] He concluded that "the teaching of *Griswold* is that the Constitution protects individual decisions in matters of childbearing from unjustified intrusion by the State."[42]

Given the voluntarist interpretation of privacy, restricting the *sale* of contraceptives violates privacy as harshly as banning their *use;* the one limits choice as surely as the other. "Indeed, in practice," Brennan observed, "a prohibition against all sales, since more easily and less offensively enforced, might have an even more devastating effect upon the freedom to choose contraception."[43] Ironically, the very fact that a ban on sales does *not* threaten the old privacy makes it a greater threat to the new.

Later decisions upholding abortion rights also used the language of autonomy to describe the privacy interest at stake. "Few decisions are . . . more properly private, or more basic to individual dignity and autonomy," held the Court in one such case, "than a woman's decision . . . whether to end her pregnancy. A woman's right to make that choice freely is surely fundamental."[44] The notion of privacy as autonomy found perhaps its fullest expression in a 1992 abortion rights opinion authored by Justices Sandra Day O'Connor, Anthony Kennedy, and David Souter. Privacy rights protect "the most intimate and personal choices a person may make in a lifetime, choices central to personal dignity and autonomy." The justices went on to draw an explicit connection between privacy as autonomy and the voluntarist conception of the person: "At the heart of liberty is the right to define one's own concept of existence, of meaning, of the universe, and of the mystery of human life. Beliefs about these matters could not define the attributes of personhood were they formed under compulsion of the State."[45]

Despite its increasing tendency to identify privacy with autonomy, the Court refused, in a 5–4 decision, to extend privacy protection to consensual homosexual activity. Writing for the majority, Justice White emphasized that the Court's previous privacy cases protected choice only with respect to child rearing and education, family relationships, procreation, marriage, contraception, and abortion. "We think it evident," he held, "that none of the rights announced in those cases bears any resemblance to the claimed constitutional right of homosexuals to engage in acts of sodomy."[46] He also rejected the claim that Georgia's citizens could not embody in law their belief "that homosexual sodomy is immoral and unacceptable."[47] Neutrality to the contrary, "the law . . . is constantly based on notions of morality, and if all laws representing essentially moral choices are to be invalidated under the Due Process Clause, the courts will be very busy indeed."[48]

Writing for the four dissenters, Justice Blackmun argued that the Court's previous privacy decisions did not depend on the virtue of the practices they protected but on the principle of free individual choice in intimate matters. "We protect those rights not because they contribute . . . to the general public welfare, but because they form so central a part of an individual's life. 'The concept of privacy embodies the "moral fact that a person belongs to himself and not others nor to society as a whole."'"[49]

Blackmun argued for the application of earlier privacy rulings in the considerations of homosexual practices by casting the Court's concern for conventional family ties in individualist terms: "We protect the decision whether to have a child because parenthood alters so dramatically an individual's self-definition . . . And we protect the family because it contributes so powerfully to the happiness of individuals, not because of a preference for stereotypical households."[50] Because the right of privacy in sexual relationships protects "the freedom an individual has to *choose* the form and nature of these intensely personal bonds,"[51] it protects homosexual activity no less than other intimate choices.

Defending the ideal of the neutral state, Blackmun added that traditional religious condemnations of homosexuality "give the State no license to impose their judgments on the entire citizenry."[52] To the contrary, the State's appeal to religious teachings against homosexuality undermines its claim that the law "represents a legitimate use of secular coercive power."[53]

Despite the Court's reluctance to extend privacy rights to homosexuals, the privacy cases of the last twenty-five years offer ample evidence of assumptions drawn from the liberal conception of the person. They also raise two questions about the liberalism they reflect: First, whether bracketing controversial moral issues is even possible;

and second, whether the voluntarist conception of privacy limits the range of reasons for protecting privacy.

## THE MINIMALIST CASE FOR TOLERATION: ABORTION

Unlike the voluntarist grounds for the neutral state, minimalist liberalism seeks a conception of justice that is political not philosophical, that does not presuppose any particular conception of the person, autonomous or otherwise. It proposes bracketing controversial moral and religious issues for the sake of securing social cooperation in the face of disagreement about ends, not for the sake of such "comprehensive" liberal ideals as autonomy or individuality.[54] One objection to minimalist liberalism is that the case for bracketing a particular moral or religious controversy may partly depend on an implicit answer to the controversy it purports to bracket. In the case of abortion, for example, the more confident we are that fetuses are, in the relevant moral sense, different from babies, the more confident we can be in bracketing the question about the moral status of fetuses for political purposes.

The Court's argument in *Roe v. Wade*[55] illustrates the difficulty of deciding constitutional cases by bracketing controversial moral and religious issues. Although the Court claimed to be neutral on the question of when life begins, its decision presupposes a particular answer to that question. The Court began by observing that Texas's law against abortion rests upon a particular theory of when life begins. "Texas urges that . . . life begins at conception and is present throughout pregnancy, and that, therefore, the State has a compelling interest in protecting that life from and after conception."[56]

The Court then claimed to be neutral on that question: "We need not resolve the difficult question of when life begins. When those trained in the respective disciplines of medicine, philosophy, and theology are unable to arrive at any consensus, the judiciary . . . is not in a position to speculate as to the answer."[57] It then noted "the wide divergence of thinking on this most sensitive and difficult question," throughout the western tradition and in the law of various American states.[58]

From this survey, the Court concluded that "the unborn have never been recognized in the law as persons in the whole sense."[59] Accordingly, it argued that Texas was wrong to embody in law a particular theory of life. Since no theory was conclusive, it held that Texas erred in "adopting one theory of life . . . [which would] override the rights of the pregnant woman that are at stake."[60]

However, contrary to its professions of neutrality, the Court's decision presupposed a particular answer to the question it claimed to bracket.

> With respect to the State's important and legitimate interest in potential life, the "compelling" point is at viability. This is so because the fetus then presumably has the capability of meaningful life outside the mother's womb. State regulation protective of fetal life after viability thus has both logical and biological justifications.[61]

That the Court's decision in *Roe* presupposes a particular answer to the question it purports to bracket is no argument against its decision, only an argument against its claim to have bracketed the controversial question of when life begins. It does not replace Texas's theory of life with a neutral stance, but with a different theory of its own.

The minimalist case for neutrality is subject to a further difficulty: Even given an agreement to bracket controversial moral and religious issues for the sake of social cooperation, it may be controversial what counts as bracketing; and this controversy may require for its solution either a substantive evaluation of the interests at stake, or the autonomous conception of agency that minimalist liberalism resolves to avoid. *Thornburgh v. American College of Obstetri-*

*cians & Gynecologists,*[62] a 1986 abortion case upholding *Roe,* offers an example of this difficulty.

Writing in dissent, Justice White urged the Court in *Thornburgh* to overrule *Roe v. Wade* and "return the issue to the people."[63] He agreed that abortion was a controversial moral issue, but argued that the best way for the Court to bracket this controversy was to let each state decide the question for itself. He proposed, in effect, to bracket the intractable controversy over abortion as Stephen Douglas proposed to bracket the intractable controversy over slavery—by refusing to impose a single answer on the country as a whole. "Abortion is a hotly contested moral and political issue," White wrote. "Such issues, in our society, are to be resolved by the will of the people, either as expressed through legislation or through the general principles they have already incorporated into the Constitution they have adopted."[64] For the Court to do otherwise is not to be neutral but to "impose its own controversial choices of value upon the people."[65]

Justice Stevens responded to White by arguing for a different way of bracketing. Given the controversial moral issues at stake, he urged that individual women, not legislatures, should decide the question for themselves. For the Court to insist that women be free to choose for themselves is not to impose the *Court's* values, but simply to prevent local majorities from imposing *their* values on individuals. "No individual should be compelled to surrender the freedom to make that decision for herself simply because her 'value preferences' are not shared by the majority."[66] For Stevens, the basic question is not which theory of life is true, but "whether the 'abortion decision' should be made by the individual or by the majority 'in the unrestrained imposition of its own, extraconstitutional value preferences.'"[67]

What is striking is that both ways of bracketing are in principle consistent with minimalist liberalism: The practical interest in social cooperation under conditions of disagreement about the good offers no grounds for choosing one over the other. Even given agreement to bracket an intractable moral or religious controversy for the sake of social cooperation, it may still be unclear what counts as bracketing. Moreover, resolving that question—deciding between White's position and Stevens'—requires either a substantive view about the moral and religious interests at stake or an autonomous conception of the person such as the voluntarist view affirms. Both solutions, however, would deny minimalist liberalism its minimalism; each would implicate its putatively political conception of justice in precisely the moral and philosophical commitments that it seeks to avoid.

## THE VOLUNTARIST CASE FOR TOLERATION: HOMOSEXUALITY

The dissenters' argument for toleration in *Bowers v. Hardwick*[68] illustrates the difficulties with the version of liberalism that ties toleration to autonomy rights alone. In refusing to extend the right of privacy to homosexuals, the majority in *Bowers* declared that none of the rights announced in earlier privacy cases resembled the rights homosexuals were seeking: "No connection between family, marriage, or procreation on the one hand and homosexual activity on the other has been demonstrated."[69] Any reply to the Court's position would have to show some connection between the practices already subject to privacy protection and the homosexual practices not yet protected. What then is the resemblance between heterosexual intimacies on the one hand, and homosexual intimacies on the other, such that both are entitled to a constitutional right of privacy?

This question might be answered in at least two different ways—one voluntarist, the other substantive. The first argues from the autonomy the practices reflect, whereas the second appeals to the human goods the practices realize. The voluntarist answer holds that people should be free to choose their intimate associations for themselves, regardless of the virtue or popularity of the practices they choose so long as they do not harm others. In this view, homosexual relationships resemble the heterosexual relationships the Court has already protected in that all reflect the choices of autonomous selves.

By contrast, the substantive answer claims that much that is valuable in conventional marriage is also present in homosexual unions. In this view, the connection between heterosexual and homosexual relations is not that both result from individual choice but that both realize important human goods. Rather than rely on autonomy alone, this second line of reply articulates the virtues homosexual intimacy may share with heterosexual intimacy, along with any distinctive virtues of its own. It defends homosexual privacy the way *Griswold* defended marital privacy, by arguing that, like marriage, homosexual union may also be "intimate to the degree of being sacred . . . a harmony in living . . . a bilateral loyalty," an association for a "noble . . . purpose."[70]

Of these two possible replies, the dissenters in *Bowers* relied wholly on the first. Rather than protect homosexual intimacies for the human goods they share with intimacies the Court already protects, Justice Blackmun cast the Court's earlier cases in individualist terms, and found their reading applied equally to homosexuality because "much of the richness of a relationship will come from the freedom an individual has to *choose* the form and nature of these intensely personal bonds."[71] At issue was not homosexuality as such but respect for the fact that "different individuals will make different choices" in deciding how to conduct their lives.[72]

Justice Stevens, in a separate dissent, also avoided referring to the values homosexual intimacy may share with heterosexual love. Instead, he wrote broadly of "'the individual's right to make certain unusually important decisions'" and "'respect for the dignity of individual choice,'"[73] rejecting the notion that such liberty belongs to heterosexuals alone. "From the standpoint of the individual, the homosexual and the heterosexual have the same interest in deciding how he will live his own life, and, more narrowly, how he will conduct himself in his personal and voluntary associations with his companions."[74]

The voluntarist argument so dominates the *Bowers* dissents that it seems difficult to imagine a judicial rendering of the substantive view. But a glimmer of this view can be found in the appeals court opinion in the same case.[75] The United States Court of Appeals had ruled in Hardwick's favor and had struck down the law under which he was convicted. Like Blackmun and Stevens, the appeals court constructed an analogy between privacy in marriage and privacy in homosexual relations. But unlike the Supreme Court dissenters, it did not rest the analogy on voluntarist grounds alone. It argued instead that both practices may realize important human goods.

The marital relationship is significant, wrote the court of appeals, not only because of its procreative purpose but also "because of the unsurpassed opportunity for mutual support and self-expression that it provides."[76] It recalled the Supreme Court's observation in *Griswold* that "marriage is a coming together for better or for worse, hopefully enduring, and intimate to the degree of being sacred."[77] And it went on to suggest that the qualities the Court so prized in *Griswold* could be present in homosexual unions as well: "For some, the sexual activity in question here serves the same purpose as the intimacy of marriage."[78]

Ironically, this way of extending privacy rights to homosexuals depends on an "old-fashioned" reading of *Griswold* as protecting the human goods realized in marriage, a reading the Court has long since renounced in favor of an individualist reading.[79] By drawing on the aspect of *Griswold* that affirms certain values and ends, the substantive case for homosexual privacy offends the liberalism that insists on neutrality. It grounds the right of privacy on the good of the practice it would protect, and so fails to be neutral among conceptions of the good.

The more frequently employed precedent for homosexual rights is not *Griswold* but *Stanley v. Georgia*,[80] which upheld the right to possess obscene materials in the privacy of one's home. *Stanley* did not hold that the obscene films found in the defendant's bedroom served a "noble purpose," only that he had a right to view them in private. The toleration *Stanley* defended was wholly independent of the value or importance of the thing being tolerated.[81]

In the 1980 case of *People v. Onofre*,[82] the New York Court of Appeals vindicated privacy rights for homosexuals on precisely these grounds. The court reasoned that if, following *Stanley,* there is a right to the "satisfaction of sexual desires by resort to material condemned as obscene," there should also be a right "to seek sexual gratification from what at least once was commonly regarded as 'deviant' conduct," so long as it is private and consensual.[83] The court emphasized its neutrality toward the conduct it protected: "We express no view as to any theological, moral or psychological evaluation of consensual sodomy. These are aspects of the issue on which informed, competent authorities and individuals may and do differ."[84] The court's role was simply to ensure that the State bracketed these competing moral views, rather than embodying any one of them in law.[85]

The case for toleration that brackets the morality of homosexuality has a powerful appeal. In the face of deep disagreement about values, it seems to ask the least of the contending parties. It offers social peace and respect for rights without the need for moral conversion. Those who view sodomy as sin need not be persuaded to change their minds, only to tolerate those who practice it in private. By insisting only that each respect the freedom of others to live the lives they choose, this toleration promises a basis for political agreement that does not await shared conceptions of morality.

Despite its promise, however, the neutral case for toleration is subject to two related difficulties. First, as a practical matter, it is by no means clear that social cooperation can be secured on the strength of autonomy rights alone, absent some measure of agreement on the moral permissibility of the practices at issue. It may not be accidental that the first practices subject to the right of privacy were accorded constitutional protection in cases that spoke of the sanctity of marriage and procreation. Only later did the Court abstract privacy rights from these practices and protect them without reference to the human goods they were once thought to make possible. This suggests that the voluntarist justification of privacy rights is dependent—politically as well as philosophically—on some measure of agreement that the practices protected are morally permissible.

A second difficulty with the voluntarist case for toleration concerns the quality of respect it secures. As the New York case suggests, the analogy with *Stanley* tolerates homosexuality at the price of demeaning it; it puts homosexual intimacy on a par with obscenity—a base thing that should nonetheless be tolerated so long as it takes place in private. If *Stanley* rather than *Griswold* is the relevant analogy, the interest at stake is bound to be reduced, as the New York court reduced it, to "sexual gratification." (The only intimate relationship at stake in *Stanley* was between a man and his pornography.)

The majority in *Bowers* exploited this assumption by ridiculing the notion of a "fundamental right to engage in homosexual sodomy."[86] The obvious reply is that *Bowers* is no more about a right to homosexual sodomy than *Griswold* was about a right to heterosexual intercourse. But by refusing to articulate the human goods that homosexual intimacy may share with heterosexual unions, the voluntarist case for toleration forfeits the analogy with *Griswold* and makes the ridicule difficult to refute.

The problem with the neutral case for toleration is the opposite side of its appeal; it leaves wholly unchallenged the adverse views of homosexuality itself. Unless those views can be plausibly addressed, even a Court ruling in their favor is unlikely to win for homosexuals more than a thin and fragile toleration. A fuller respect would require, if not admiration, at least some appreciation of the lives homosexuals live. Such appreciation, however, is unlikely to be cultivated by a legal and political discourse conducted in terms of autonomy rights alone.

The liberal may reply that autonomy arguments in court need not foreclose more substantive, affirmative arguments elsewhere; bracketing moral argument for constitutional purposes does not mean bracketing moral argument altogether. Once their freedom of choice in sexual practice is secured, homosexuals can seek, by argument and example, to win from their fellow citizens a deeper respect than autonomy can supply.

The liberal reply, however, underestimates the extent to which constitutional discourse has come to constitute the terms of political discourse in American public life. While most at home in constitutional law, the main motifs of contemporary liberalism—rights as trumps, the neutral state, and the unencumbered self—figure with increasing prominence in our moral and political culture. Assumptions drawn from constitutional discourse increasingly set the terms of political debate in general.

Admittedly, the tendency to bracket substantive moral questions makes it difficult to argue for toleration in the language of the good. Defining privacy rights by defending the practices privacy protects seems either reckless or quaint; reckless because it rests so much on moral argument, quaint because it recalls the traditional view that ties the case for privacy to the merits of the conduct privacy protects. But as the abortion and sodomy cases illustrate, the attempt to bracket moral questions faces difficulties of its own. They suggest the truth in the "naive" view, that the justice or injustice of laws against abortion and homosexual conduct may have something to do with the morality or immorality of these practices after all.

### EPILOGUE

Since this essay was written, the U.S. Supreme Court, in the case of *Lawrence v. Texas* (2003),[87] reversed *Bowers v. Hardwick*, and struck down a law that criminalized so-called "deviate sexual intercourse" between persons of the same sex. The Court's opinion, written by Justice Anthony Kennedy, drew to some extent on the autonomy-based, nonjudgmental line of reasoning I have criticized: "Liberty presumes an autonomy of self that includes freedom of thought, belief, expression, and certain intimate conduct."[88] And it cited with approval the extravagant statement of the voluntarist conception of the person announced in *Casey:* "At the heart of liberty is the right to define one's own concept of existence, of meaning, of the universe, and of the mystery of human life. Beliefs about these matters could not define the attributes of personhood were they formed under compulsion of the State."[89]

But despite its rhetoric of autonomy and choice, Justice Kennedy's opinion also gestured toward a different, more substantive reason for striking down the Texas law—that it wrongly demeaned a morally legitimate mode of life. First, the opinion pointed out that *Bowers* was no more about a right to homosexual sodomy than *Griswold* was about a right to heterosexual intercourse: "To say that the issue in *Bowers* was simply the right to engage in certain sexual conduct demeans the claim the individual put forward, just as it would demean a married couple were it to be said marriage is simply about the right to have sexual intercourse." Privacy rights should protect the sexual intimacy of gays and straights alike, not because sex reflects autonomy and choice, but because it expresses an important human good. "When sexuality finds overt expression in intimate conduct with another person, the conduct can be but one element in a personal bond that is more enduring."[90]

Second, the Court insisted on reversing *Bowers,* even though it could have ruled more narrowly and invalidated the Texas law on equal protection grounds. (Unlike the law in *Bowers,* the law in *Lawrence* banned sodomy by same-sex but not opposite-sex couples.) "If protected conduct is made criminal and the law which does so remains unexamined for its substantive validity, its stigma might remain even if it were not enforceable as drawn for equal protection reasons." In seeking to remove the stigma that antisodomy laws attach to gay sexual intimacy, the Court went beyond liberal toleration to affirm the moral legitimacy of homosexuality. To allow *Bowers* to stand as precedent would "demean[] the lives of homosexual persons."[91]

Justice Antonin Scalia saw the moral stakes clearly. In a biting dissent, he castigated the Court for signing on to "the agenda promoted by some homosexual activists directed at eliminating the moral opprobrium that has traditionally attached to homosexual conduct," and for "tak[ing] sides in the culture war."[92] Grasping the moral logic of *Lawrence*, he worried that once the Court rejected "moral disapprobation of homosexual conduct" as a legitimate state interest for purposes of criminal law, it would be difficult to justify prohibitions on same-sex marriage.[93]

Scalia did not argue openly for preserving the moral disapproval of homosexuality. He claimed, for his part, to take no side in the culture war. Rather than defend the antisodomy law on its merits, he supported it in the name of majoritarianism. The "promotion of majoritarian sexual morality" was a legitimate state interest, and the Court's role was simply to assure, "as neutral observer, that the democratic rules of engagement" were observed.[94] But Scalia's confidence that stigmatizing homosexual conduct is a legitimate state interest seems to depend on more than a value-neutral commitment to majoritarianism. (His own moral view can be glimpsed in the analogy he draws between Texas's antisodomy law and laws banning bestiality and incest.) At the very least, the case for letting majorities ban homosexual intimacy is far stronger if homosexuality is immoral than if it is morally permissible.

Ironically, just as the liberals in *Lawrence* were freeing themselves from the assumption that privacy rights can be adjudicated without reference to the moral status of the practices that rights protect, the conservatives were embracing it. But neither liberal toleration nor deference to majoritarianism can avoid the need for substantive moral argument. Scalia's dissent in *Lawrence* and Justice Blackmun's opinion in *Roe v. Wade* have this in common: Both illustrate the difficulty of bracketing moral judgment, whether in the name of respecting individual choice or deferring to majoritarian sentiment.

# Part III

# LIBERALISM, PLURALISM, AND COMMUNITY

The essays in this section explore the varieties of liberalism prominent in contemporary political philosophy, and the encounter between liberalism and its critics. They develop two lines of criticism: First, given liberalism's emphasis on individual choice, it does not offer an adequate account of community, solidarity, and membership. Second, given its emphasis on the fact that people in pluralist societies often hold conflicting visions of the good life, liberalism wrongly insists that citizens relegate their moral and religious convictions to the private realm, or at least set them aside for political purposes.

In Chapters 22 ("Morality and the Liberal Ideal") and 23 ("The Procedural Republic and the Unencumbered Self") I argue that the liberalism of Immanuel Kant and John Rawls is more persuasive than the utilitarianism they reject. Their conception of the person as a freely choosing, independent self offers a powerful corrective to the utilitarian idea that we are simply the sum of our preferences and desires. But the Kantian and Rawlsian self raises problems of its own; we cannot conceive ourselves as "unencumbered selves" without cost to those loyalties and traditions that situate us in the world and give our lives their moral particularity.

Chapters 24–26 take up several non-Kantian varieties of liberalism. Chapter 24, "Justice as Membership," discusses Michael Walzer's *Spheres of Justice*, an important contribution to what came to be known as the communitarian critique of liberalism. Chapter 25, "The Peril of Extinction," responds to the ardent individualism of George Kateb, who argued that the moral peril of nuclear war consists in its threat to individual rights. Chapter 26, "Dewey's Liberalism and Ours," recalls the liberalism of America's leading public philosopher of the early twentieth century, John Dewey. Richard Rorty has tried to appropriate Dewey for the liberalism that asserts the priority of the right over the good. But Dewey was not a Kantian or a rights-based liberal. To the contrary, his concern with cultivating a public realm that draws on the moral and spiritual energies of citizens actually makes him a more natural ally of today's communitarians.

Liberals often worry about religion in politics because they associate religion with intolerance. The resolve to avoid wars of religion has shaped much liberal political thought. In recent years, Christian, Jewish, and Islamic theologians have wrestled with sources of intolerance to be found in the teachings and traditions of their faiths. Chapter 27, "Mastery and Hubris in Judaism," examines the quest of Rabbi David Hartman, one of the foremost Jewish thinkers of our time, to articulate a pluralist ethic from within the Jewish tradition. I include the essay here in hopes of showing how religious and theological reflections can illuminate contemporary moral and political questions, even for those who may not share the faith from which those reflections derive.

By the 1990s, the debate between utilitarians and Kantian liberals had largely given way to the "liberal-communitarian" debate. In 1993 John Rawls published *Political Liberalism,* a book that recast the version of liberalism he presented in his classic work, *A Theory of Justice* (1971). Chapter 28, "Political Liberalism," examines Rawls's revised view. Chapter 29, "Remembering Rawls," is a memorial to Rawls on the occasion of his death in 2002. Chapter 30, "The Limits of Communitarianism," looks back on the liberal-communitarian debate and explains why some of those labeled "communitarians" (including me) are reluctant to embrace the term.

# twenty-two

# MORALITY AND THE LIBERAL IDEAL

Liberals often take pride in defending what they oppose—pornography, for example, or unpopular views. They say the state should not impose on its citizens a preferred way of life, but should leave them as free as possible to choose their own values and ends, consistent with a similar liberty for others. This commitment to freedom of choice requires liberals constantly to distinguish between permission and praise, between allowing a practice and endorsing it. It is one thing to allow pornography, they argue, something else to affirm it.

Conservatives sometimes exploit this distinction by ignoring it. They charge that those who would allow abortions favor abortion, that opponents of school prayer oppose prayer, that those who defend the rights of Communists sympathize with their cause. And in a pattern of argument familiar in our politics, liberals reply by invoking higher principles; it is not that they dislike pornography less, but rather that they value toleration, or freedom of choice, or fair procedures more.

But in contemporary debate, the liberal rejoinder seems increasingly fragile, its moral basis increasingly unclear. Why should toleration and freedom of choice prevail when other important values are also at stake? Too often the answer implies some version of moral relativism, the idea that it is wrong to "legislate morality" because all morality is merely subjective. "Who is to say what is literature and what is filth? That is a value judgment, and whose values should decide?"

Relativism usually appears less as a claim than as a question. "Who is to judge?" But it is a question that can also be asked of the values that liberals defend. Toleration and freedom and fairness are values too, and they can hardly be defended by the claim that no values can be defended. So it is a mistake to affirm liberal values by arguing that all values are merely subjective. The relativist defense of liberalism is no defense at all.

What, then, can be the moral basis of the higher principles the liberal invokes? Recent political philosophy has offered two main alternatives—one utilitarian, the other Kantian. The utilitarian view, following John Stuart Mill, defends liberal principles in the name of maximizing the general welfare. The state should not impose on its citizens a preferred way of life, even for their own good, because doing so will reduce the sum of human happiness, at least in the long run; better that people choose for themselves, even if, on occasion, they get it wrong. "The only freedom which deserves the name," writes Mill in *On Liberty*, "is that of pursuing our own good in our own way, so long as we do not attempt to deprive others of theirs, or impede their efforts to obtain it." He adds that his argument does not depend on any notion of abstract right, only on the principle of the greatest good for the greatest number. "I regard utility as the ultimate appeal on all ethical questions; but it must be utility in the largest sense, grounded on the permanent interests of man as a progressive being."

Many objections have been raised against utilitarianism as a general doctrine of moral philosophy. Some have questioned the concept of utility, and the assumption that all human goods are in principle commensurable. Others have objected that by reducing all values to preferences and desires, utilitarians are unable to admit qualitative distinctions of worth, unable to distinguish noble desires from base ones. But most recent debate has focused on whether utilitarianism offers a convincing basis for liberal principles, including respect for individual rights.

In one respect, utilitarianism would seem well suited to liberal purposes. Seeking to maximize overall happiness does not require judging people's values, only aggregating them. And the willingness to aggregate preferences without judging them suggests a tolerant spirit, even a democratic one. When people go to the polls we count their votes, whatever they are.

But the utilitarian calculus is not always as liberal as it first appears. If enough cheering Romans pack the Colosseum to watch the lion devour the Christian, the collective pleasure of the Romans will surely outweigh the pain of the Christian, intense though it be. Or if a big majority abhors a small religion and wants it banned, the balance of preferences will favor suppression, not toleration. Utilitarians sometimes defend individual rights on the grounds that respecting them now will serve utility in the long run. But this calculation is precarious and contingent. It hardly secures the liberal promise not to impose on some the values of others. As the majority will is an inadequate instrument of liberal politics—by itself it fails to secure individual rights—so the utilitarian philosophy is an inadequate foundation for liberal principles.

The case against utilitarianism was made most powerfully by Immanuel Kant. He argued that empirical principles, such as utility, were unfit to serve as basis for the moral law. A wholly instrumental defense of freedom and rights not only leaves rights vulnerable, but fails to respect the inherent dignity of persons. The utilitarian calculus treats people as means to the happiness of others, not as ends in themselves, worthy of respect.

Contemporary liberals extend Kant's argument with the claim that utilitarianism fails to take seriously the distinction between persons. In seeking above all to maximize the general welfare, the utilitarian treats society as a whole as if it were a single person; it conflates our many, diverse desires into a single system of desires. It is indifferent to the distribution of satisfactions among persons, except insofar as this may affect the overall sum. But this fails to respect our plurality and distinctness. It uses some as means to the happiness of all, and so fails to respect each as an end in himself.

In the view of modern-day Kantians, certain rights are so fundamental that even the general welfare cannot override them. As John Rawls writes in his important work, *A Theory of Justice*, "Each person possesses an inviolability founded on justice that even the welfare of society as a whole cannot override. . . . The rights secured by justice are not subject to political bargaining or to the calculus of social interests."

So Kantian liberals need an account of rights that does not depend on utilitarian considerations. More than this, they need an account that does not depend on any particular conception of the good, that does not presuppose the superiority of one way of life over others. Only a justification neutral about ends could preserve the liberal resolve not to favor any particular ends, or to impose on its citizens a preferred way of life. But what sort of justification could this be? How is it possible to affirm certain liberties and rights as fundamental without embracing some vision of the good life, without endorsing some ends over others? It would seem we are back to the relativist predicament—to affirm liberal principles without embracing any particular ends.

The solution proposed by Kantian liberals is to draw a distinction between the "right" and the "good"—between a framework of basic rights and liberties, and the conceptions of the good that people may choose to pursue within the framework. It is one thing for the state to support a fair framework, they argue, something else to affirm some particular ends. For example, it is one thing to defend the right to free speech so that people may be free to form their own opinions and choose their own ends, but something else to support it on the grounds that a life of political discussion is inherently worthier than a life unconcerned with public affairs, or on the grounds that free speech will increase the general welfare. Only the first defense is available in the Kantian view, resting as it does on the ideal of a neutral framework.

Now, the commitment to a framework neutral with respect to ends can be seen as a kind of value—in this sense the Kantian liberal is no relativist—but its value consists precisely in its refusal to affirm a preferred way of life or conception of the good. For Kantian liberals, then, the right is prior to the good, and in two senses. First, individual rights cannot be sacrificed for the sake of the general good; and second, the principles of justice that specify these rights cannot be premised on any particular vision of the good life. What justifies the rights is not that they maximize the general welfare or otherwise promote the good, but rather that they comprise a fair framework within which individuals and groups can choose their own values and ends, consistent with a similar liberty for others.

Of course, proponents of the rights-based ethic notoriously disagree about what rights are fundamental, and about what political arrangements the ideal of the neutral framework requires. Egalitarian liberals support the welfare state, and favor a scheme of civil liberties together with certain social and economic rights—rights to welfare, education, health care, and so on. Libertarian liberals defend the market economy, and claim that redistributive policies violate peoples' rights; they favor a scheme of civil liberties combined with a strict regime of private property rights. But whether egalitarian or libertarian, rights-based liberalism begins with the claim that we are separate, individual persons, each with our own aims, interests, and conceptions of the good; it seeks a framework of rights that will enable us to realize our capacity as free moral agents, consistent with a similar liberty for others.

Within academic philosophy, the last decade or so has seen the ascendance of the rights-based ethic over the utilitarian one, due in large part to the influence of Rawls's *A Theory of Justice*. The legal philosopher H. L. A. Hart recently described the shift from "the old faith that some form of utilitarianism must capture the essence of political morality" to the new faith that "the truth must lie with a doctrine of basic human rights, protecting specific basic liberties and interests of individuals. . . . Whereas not so long ago great energy and much ingenuity of many philosophers were devoted to making some form of utilitarianism work, latterly such energies and ingenuity have been devoted to the articulation of theories of basic rights."

But in philosophy as in life, the new faith becomes the old orthodoxy before long. Even as it has come to prevail over its utilitarian rival, the rights-based ethic has recently faced a growing challenge from a different direction, from a view that gives fuller expression to the claims of citizenship and community than the liberal vision allows. The communitarian critics, unlike modern liberals, make the case for a politics of the common good. Recalling the arguments of Hegel against Kant, they question the liberal claim for the priority of the right over the good, and the picture of the freely choosing individual it embodies. Following Aristotle, they argue that we cannot justify political arrangements without reference to common purposes and ends, and that we cannot conceive of ourselves without reference to our role as citizens, as participants in a common life.

This debate reflects two contrasting pictures of the self. The rights-based ethic, and the conception of the person it embodies, were shaped in large part in the encounter with utilitarianism. Where utilitarians conflate our many desires into a single system of desire, Kantians insist on the separateness of persons. Where the utilitarian self is simply defined as the sum of its desires, the Kantian self is a choosing self, independent of the desires and ends it may have at any moment. As Rawls writes, "The self is prior to the ends which are affirmed by it; even a dominant end must be chosen from among numerous possibilities."

The priority of the self over its ends means I am never defined by my aims and attachments, but always capable of standing back to survey and assess and possibly to revise them. This is what it means to be a free and independent self, capable of choice. And this is the vision of the self that finds expression in the ideal of the state as a neutral framework. On the rights-based ethic, it is precisely because we are essentially separate, independent selves that we need a neutral framework, a framework of rights that refuses to choose among competing purposes and ends. If the self is prior to its ends, then the right must be prior to the good.

Communitarian critics of rights-based liberalism say we cannot conceive ourselves as independent in this way, as bearers of selves wholly detached from our aims and attachments. They say that certain of our roles are partly constitutive of the persons we are—as citizens of a country, or members of a movement, or partisans of a cause. But if we are partly defined by the communities we inhabit, then we must also be implicated in the purposes and ends characteristic of those communities. As Alasdair MacIntyre writes in his book, *After Virtue,* "What is good for me has to be the good for one who inhabits these roles." Open-ended though it be, the story of my life is always embedded in the story of those communities from which I derive my identity—whether family or city, tribe or nation, party or cause. In the communitarian view, these stories make a moral difference, not only a psychological one. They situate us in the world and give our lives their moral particularity.

What is at stake for politics in the debate between unencumbered selves and situated ones? What are the practical differences between a politics of rights and a politics of the common good? On some issues, the two theories may produce different arguments for similar policies. For example, the civil rights movement of the 1960s might be justified by liberals in the name of human dignity and respect for persons, and by communitarians in the name of recognizing the full membership of fellow citizens wrongly excluded from the common life of the nation. And where liberals might support public education in hopes of equipping students to become autonomous individuals, capable of choosing their own ends and pursuing them effectively, communitarians might support public education in hopes of equipping students to become good citizens, capable of contributing meaningfully to public deliberations and pursuits.

On other issues, the two ethics might lead to different policies. Communitarians would be more likely than liberals to allow a town to ban pornographic bookstores, on the grounds that pornography offends its way of life and the values that sustain it. But a politics of civic virtue does not always part company with liberalism in favor of conservative policies. For example, communitarians would be more willing than some rights-oriented liberals to see states enact laws regulating plant closings, to protect their communities from the disruptive effects of capital mobility and sudden industrial change. More generally, where the liberal regards the expansion of individual rights and entitlements as unqualified moral and political progress, the communitarian is troubled by the tendency of liberal programs to displace politics from smaller forms of association to more comprehensive ones. Where libertarian liberals defend the private economy and egalitarian liberals defend the welfare state, communitarians worry about the concentration of power in both the corporate economy and the bureaucratic state, and the erosion of those intermediate forms of community that have at times sustained a more vital public life.

Liberals often argue that a politics of the common good, drawing as it must on particular loyalties, obligations, and traditions, opens the way to prejudice and intolerance. The modern nation-state is not the Athenian polis, they point out; the scale and diversity of modern life have rendered the Aristotelian political ethic nostalgic at best and dangerous at worst. Any attempt to govern by a vision of the good is likely to lead to a slippery slope of totalitarian temptations.

\*      \*      \*

Communitarians reply, rightly in my view, that intolerance flourishes most where forms of life are dislocated, roots unsettled, traditions undone. In our day, the totalitarian impulse has sprung less from the convictions of confidently situated selves than from the confusions of atomized, dislocated, frustrated selves, at sea in a world where common meanings have lost their force. As Hannah Arendt has written, "What makes mass society so difficult to bear is not the number of people involved, or at least not primarily, but the fact that the world between them has lost its power to gather them together, to relate and to separate them." Insofar as our public life has withered, our sense of common involvement diminished, we lie vulnerable to the mass politics of totalitarian solutions. So responds the party of the common good to the party of rights. If the party of the common good is right, our most pressing moral and political project is to revitalize those civic republican possibilities implicit in our tradition but fading in our time.

# twenty-three

# THE PROCEDURAL REPUBLIC AND THE UNENCUMBERED SELF

Political philosophy seems often to reside at a distance from the world. Principles are one thing, politics another, and even our best efforts to "live up" to our ideals typically founder on the gap between theory and practice.[1]

But if political philosophy is unrealizable in one sense, it is unavoidable in another. This is the sense in which philosophy inhabits the world from the start; our practices and institutions are embodiments of theory. To engage in a political practice is already to stand in relation to theory.[2] For all our uncertainties about ultimate questions of political philosophy—of justice and value and the nature of the good life—the one thing we know is that we live *some* answer all the time.

In this essay I will try to explore the answer we live now, in contemporary America. What is the political philosophy implicit in our practices and institutions? How does it stand, as philosophy? And how do tensions in the philosophy find expression in our present political condition?

It may be objected that it is a mistake to look for a single philosophy, that we live no "answer," only answers. But a plurality of answers is itself a kind of answer. And the political theory that affirms this plurality is the theory I propose to explore.

## THE RIGHT AND THE GOOD

We might begin by considering a certain moral and political vision. It is a liberal vision, and like most liberal visions gives pride of place to justice, fairness, and individual rights. Its core thesis is this: a just society seeks not to promote any particular ends, but enables its citizens to pursue their own ends, consistent with a similar liberty for all; it therefore must govern by principles that do not presuppose any particular conception of the good. What justifies these regulative principles above all is not that they maximize the general welfare, or cultivate virtue, or otherwise promote the good, but rather that they conform to the concept of *right*, a moral category given prior to the good, and independent of it.

This liberalism says, in other words, that what makes the just society just is not the *telos* or purpose or end at which it aims, but precisely its refusal to choose in advance among competing purposes and ends. In its constitution and its laws, the just society seeks to provide a framework within which its citizens can pursue their own values and ends, consistent with a similar liberty for others.

The ideal I've described might be summed up in the claim that the right is prior to the good, and in two senses: the priority of the right means first, that individual rights cannot be sacrificed for the sake of the general good (in this it opposes utilitarianism), and second, that the principles of justice that specify these rights cannot be premised on any particular vision of the good life. (In this it opposes teleological conceptions in general.)

This is the liberalism of much contemporary moral and political philosophy, most fully elaborated by Rawls, and indebted to Kant for its philosophical foundations.[3] But I am concerned here less with the lineage of this vision than with what seem to me three striking facts about it.

First, it has a deep and powerful philosophical appeal. Second, despite its philosophical force, the claim for the priority of the right over the good ultimately fails. And third, despite its philosophical failure, this liberal vision is the one by which we live. For us in late twentieth-century America, it is our vision, the theory most thoroughly embodied in the practices and institutions most central to our public life. And seeing how it goes wrong as philosophy may help us to diagnose our present political condition. So first, its philosophical power; second, its philosophical failure; and third, however briefly, its uneasy embodiment in the world.

But before taking up these three claims, it is worth pointing out a central theme that connects them. And that is a certain conception of the person, of what it is to be a moral agent. Like all political theories, the liberal theory I have described is something more than a set of regulative principles. It is also a view about the way the world is, and the way we move within it. At the heart of this ethic lies a vision of the person that both inspires and undoes it. As I will try to argue now, what make this ethic so compelling, but also, finally, vulnerable, are the promise and the failure of the unencumbered self.

### KANTIAN FOUNDATIONS

The liberal ethic asserts the priority of right, and seeks principles of justice that do not presuppose any particular conception of the good.[4] This is what Kant means by the supremacy of the moral law, and what Rawls means when he writes that "justice is the first virtue of social institutions."[5] Justice is more than just another value. It provides the framework that *regulates* the play of competing values and ends; it must therefore have a sanction independent of those ends. But it is not obvious where such a sanction could be found.

Theories of justice, and for that matter, ethics, have typically founded their claims on one or another conception of human purposes and ends. Thus Aristotle said the measure of a polis is the good at which it aims, and even J. S. Mill, who in the nineteenth century called "justice the chief part, and incomparably the most binding part of all morality," made justice an instrument of utilitarian ends.[6]

This is the solution Kant's ethic rejects. Different persons typically have different desires and ends, and so any principle derived from them can only be contingent. But the moral law needs a *categorical* foundation, not a contingent one. Even so universal a desire as happiness will not do. People still differ in what happiness consists of, and to install any particular conception as regulative would impose on some the conceptions of others, and so deny at least to some the freedom to choose their *own* conceptions. In any case, to govern ourselves in conformity with desires and inclinations, given as they are by nature or circumstance, is not really to be *self*-governing at all. It is rather a refusal of freedom, a capitulation to determinations given outside us.

According to Kant, the right is "derived entirely from the concept of freedom in the external relationships of human beings, and has nothing to do with the end which all men have by nature [i.e., the aim of achieving happiness] or with the recognized means of attaining this end."[7] As such, it must have a basis prior to all empirical ends. Only when I am governed by principles that do not presuppose any particular ends am I free to pursue my own ends consistent with a similar freedom for all.

But this still leaves the question of what the basis of the right could possibly be. If it must be a basis prior to all purposes and ends, unconditioned even by what Kant calls "the special circumstances of human nature,"[8] where could such a basis conceivably be found? Given the stringent demands of the Kantian ethic, the moral law would seem almost to require a foundation in nothing, for any empirical precondition would undermine its priority. "Duty!" asks Kant at his most lyrical, "What origin is there worthy of thee, and where is to be found the root of thy noble descent which proudly rejects all kinship with the inclinations?"[9]

His answer is that the basis of the moral law is to be found in the *subject*, not the object of practical reason, a subject capable of an autonomous will. No empirical end, but rather "a subject of ends, namely a rational being himself, must be made the ground for all maxims of action."[10] Nothing other than what Kant calls "the subject of all possible ends himself" can give rise to the right, for only this subject is also the subject of an autonomous will. Only this subject could be that "something which elevates man above himself as part of the world of sense" and enables him to participate in an ideal, unconditioned realm wholly independent of our social and psychological inclinations. And only this thoroughgoing independence can afford us the detachment we need if we are ever freely to choose for ourselves, unconditioned by the vagaries of circumstance.[11]

Who or what exactly *is* this subject? It is, in a certain sense, *us.* The moral law, after all, is a law we give *ourselves;* we don't *find* it, we *will* it. That is how it (and we) escape the reign of nature and circumstance and merely empirical ends. But what is important to see is that the "we" who do the willing are not "we" *qua* particular persons, you and me, each for ourselves—the moral law is not up to us as individuals—but "we" *qua* participants in what Kant calls "pure practical reason," "we" *qua* participants in a transcendental subject.

Now what is to guarantee that I *am* a subject of this kind, capable of exercising pure practical reason? Well, strictly speaking, there *is* no guarantee; the transcendental subject is only a possibility. But it is a possibility I must *presuppose* if I am to think of myself as a free moral agent. Were I wholly an empirical being, I would not be capable of freedom, for every exercise of will would be conditioned by the desire for some object. All choice would be heteronomous choice, governed by the pursuit of some end. My will could never be a first cause, only the effect of some prior cause, the instrument of one or another impulse or inclination. "When we think of ourselves as free," writes Kant, "we transfer ourselves into the intelligible world as members and recognize the autonomy of the will."[12] And so the notion of a subject prior to and independent of experience, such as the Kantian ethic requires, appears not only possible but indispensible, a necessary presupposition of the possibility of freedom.

How does all of this come back to politics? As the subject is prior to its ends, so the right is prior to the good. Society is best arranged when it is governed by principles that do not presuppose any particular conception of the good, for any other arrangement would fail to respect persons as being capable of choice; it would treat them as objects rather than subjects, as means rather than ends in themselves.

We can see in this way how Kant's notion of the subject is bound up with the claim for the priority of right. But for those in the Anglo-American tradition, the transcendental subject will seem a strange foundation for a familiar ethic. Surely, one may think, we can take rights seriously and affirm the primacy of justice without embracing the *Critique of Pure Reason*. This, in any case, is the project of Rawls.

He wants to save the priority of right from the obscurity of the transcendental subject. Kant's idealist metaphysic, for all its moral and political advantage, cedes too much to the transcendent, and wins for justice its primacy only by denying it its human situation. "To develop a viable Kantian conception of justice," Rawls writes, "the force and content of Kant's doctrine must be detached from its background in transcendental idealism" and recast within the "canons of a reasonable empiricism."[13] And so Rawls's project is to preserve Kant's moral and political teaching by replacing Germanic obscurities with a domesticated metaphysic more congenial to the Anglo-American temper. This is the role of the original position.

## FROM TRANSCENDENTAL SUBJECT TO UNENCUMBERED SELF

The original position tries to provide what Kant's transcendental argument cannot—a foundation for the right that is prior to the good, but still situated in the world. Sparing all but essentials, the original position works like this: it invites us to imagine the principles we would choose to govern our society if we were to choose them in advance, before we knew the particular persons we would be—whether rich or poor, strong or weak, lucky or unlucky—before we knew even our interests or aims or conceptions of the good. These principles— the ones we would choose in that imaginary situation—are the principles of justice. What is more, if it works, they are principles that do not presuppose any particular ends.

What they *do* presuppose is a certain picture of the person, of the way we must be if we are beings for whom justice is the first virtue. This is the picture of the unencumbered self, a self understood as prior to and independent of its purposes and ends.

Now the unencumbered self describes first of all the way we stand toward the things we have, or want, or seek. It means there is always a distinction between the values I *have* and the person I *am*. To identify any characteristics as *my* aims, ambitions, desires, and so on, is always to imply some subject "me" standing behind them, at a certain distance, and the shape of this "me" must be given prior to any of the aims or attributes I bear. One consequence of this distance is to put the self *itself* beyond the reach of its experience, to secure its identity once and for all. Or to put the point another way, it rules out the possibility of what we might call *constitutive* ends. No role or commitment could define me so completely that I could not understand myself without it. No project could be so essential that turning away from it would call into question the person I am.

For the unencumbered self, what matters above all, what is most essential to our personhood, are not the ends we choose but our capacity to choose them. The original position sums up this central claim about us. "It is not our aims that primarily reveal our nature," writes Rawls, "but rather the principles that we would acknowledge to govern the background conditions under which these aims are to be formed . . . We should therefore reverse the relation between the right and the good proposed by teleological doctrines and view the right as prior."[14]

Only if the self is prior to its ends can the right be prior to the good. Only if my identity is never tied to the aims and interests I may have at any moment can I think of myself as a free and independent agent, capable of choice.

This notion of independence carries consequences for the kind of community of which we are capable. Understood as unencumbered selves, we are of course free to join in voluntary association with others, and so are capable of community in the cooperative sense. What is denied to the unencumbered self is the possibility of membership in any community bound by moral ties antecedent to choice; he cannot belong to any community where the self *itself* could be at stake. Such a community—call it constitutive as against merely cooperative—would engage the identity as well as the interests of the participants, and so implicate its members in a citizenship more thoroughgoing than the unencumbered self can know.

For justice to be primary, then, we must be creatures of a certain kind, related to human circumstance in a certain way. We must stand to our circumstance always at a certain distance, whether as transcendental subject in the case of Kant, or as unencumbered selves in the case of Rawls. Only in this way can we view ourselves as subjects as well as objects of experience, as agents and not just instruments of the purposes we pursue.

The unencumbered self and the ethic it inspires, taken together, hold out a liberating vision. Freed from the dictates of nature and the sanction of social roles, the human subject is installed as sovereign, cast as the author of the only moral meanings there are. As participants in pure practical reason, or as parties to the original position, we are free to construct principles of justice unconstrained by an order of value antecedently given. And as actual, individual selves, we are free to choose our purposes and ends unbound by such an order, or by custom or tradition or inherited status. So long as they are not unjust, our conceptions of the good carry weight, whatever they are, simply in virtue of our having chosen them. We are, in Rawls's words, "self-originating sources of valid claims."[15]

This is an exhilarating promise, and the liberalism it animates is perhaps the fullest expression of the Enlightenment's quest for the self-defining subject. But is it true? Can we make sense of our moral and political life by the light of the self-image it requires? I do not think we can, and I will try to show why not by arguing first within the liberal project, then beyond it.

## JUSTICE AND COMMUNITY

We have focused so far on the foundations of the liberal vision, on the way it derives the principles it defends. Let us turn briefly now to the substance of those principles, using Rawls as our example. Sparing all but essentials once again, Rawls's two principles of justice are these: first, equal basic liberties for all, and second, only those social and economic inequalities that benefit the least-advantaged members of society (the difference principle).

In arguing for these principles, Rawls argues against two familiar alternatives—utilitarianism and libertarianism. He argues against utilitarianism that it fails to take seriously the distinction between persons. In seeking to maximize the general welfare, the utilitarian treats society as whole as if it were a single person; it conflates our many, diverse desires into a single system of desires, and tries to maximize. It is indifferent to the distribution of satisfactions among persons, except insofar as this may affect the overall sum. But this fails to respect our plurality and distinctness. It uses some as means to the happiness of all, and so fails to respect each as an end in himself. While utilitarians may sometimes defend individual rights, their defense must rest on the calculation that respecting those rights will serve utility in the long run. But this calculation is contingent and uncertain. So long as utility is what Mill said it is, "the ultimate appeal on all ethical questions,"[16] individual rights can never be secure. To avoid the danger that their life prospects might one day be sacrificed for the greater good of others, the parties to the original position therefore insist on certain basic liberties for all, and make those liberties prior.

If utilitarians fail to take seriously the distinctness of persons, libertarians go wrong by failing to acknowledge the arbitrariness of fortune. They define as just whatever distribution results from an efficient market economy, and oppose all redistribution on the grounds that people are entitled to whatever they get, so long as they do not cheat or steal or otherwise violate someone's rights in getting it. Rawls opposes this principle on the ground that the distribution of talents and assets and even efforts by which some get more and others get less is arbitrary from a moral point of view, a matter of good luck. To distribute the good things in life on the basis of these differences is not to do justice, but simply to carry over into human arrangements the arbitrariness of social and natural contingency. We deserve, as individuals, neither the talents our good fortune may have brought, nor the benefits that flow from them. We should therefore regard these talents as common assets, and regard one another as common beneficiaries of the rewards they bring. "Those who have been favored by nature, whoever they are, may gain from their good fortune only on terms that improve the situation of those who have lost out . . . In justice as fairness, men agree to share one another's fate."[17]

This is the reasoning that leads to the difference principle. Notice how it reveals, in yet another guise, the logic of the unencumbered self. I cannot be said to deserve the benefits that flow from, say, my fine physique and good looks, because they are only accidental, not essential facts about me. They describe attributes I *have*, not the person I *am*, and so cannot give rise to a claim of desert. Being an unencumbered self, this is true of *everything* about me. And so I cannot, as an individual, deserve anything at all.

However jarring to our ordinary understandings this argument may be, the picture so far remains intact; the priority of right, the denial of desert, and the unencumbered self all hang impressively together.

But the difference principle requires more, and it is here that the argument comes undone. The difference principle begins with the thought, congenial to the unencumbered self, that the assets I have are only accidentally mine. But it ends by assuming that these assets are therefore *common* assets and that society has a prior claim on the fruits of their exercise. But this assumption is without warrant. Simply because I, as an individual, do not have a privileged claim on the assets accidentally residing "here," it does not follow that everyone in the world collectively does. For there is no reason to think that their location in society's province or, for that matter, within the province of humankind, is any *less* arbitrary from a moral point of view. And if their arbitrariness within *me* makes them ineligible to serve *my* ends, there seems no obvious reason why their arbitrariness within any particular society should not make them ineligible to serve that society's ends as well.

To put the point another way, the difference principle, like utilitarianism, is a principle of sharing. As such, it must presuppose some prior moral tie among those whose assets it would deploy and whose efforts it would enlist in a common endeavor. Otherwise, it is simply a formula for using some as means to others' ends, a formula this liberalism is committed to reject.

But on the cooperative vision of community alone, it is unclear what the moral basis for this sharing could be. Short of the constitutive conception, deploying an individual's assets for the sake of the common good would seem an offense against the "plurality and distinctness" of individuals this liberalism seeks above all to secure.

If those whose fate I am required to share really are, morally speaking, *others*, rather than fellow participants in a way of life with which my identity is bound, the difference principle falls prey to the same objections as utilitarianism. Its claim on me is not the claim of a constitutive community whose attachments I acknowledge, but rather the claim of a concatenated collectivity whose entanglements I confront.

What the difference principle requires, but cannot provide, is some way of identifying those *among* whom the assets I bear are properly regarded as common, some way of seeing ourselves as mutually indebted and morally engaged to begin with. But as we have seen, the constitutive aims and attachments that would save and situate the difference principle are precisely the ones denied to the liberal self; the moral encumbrances and antecedent obligations they imply would undercut the priority of right.

What, then, of those encumbrances? The point so far is that we cannot be persons for whom justice is primary, and also be persons for whom the difference principle is a principle of justice. But which must give way? Can we view ourselves as independent selves, independent in the sense that our identity is never tied to our aims and attachments?

I do not think we can, at least not without cost to those loyalties and convictions whose moral force consists partly in the fact that living by them is inseparable from understanding ourselves as the particular persons we are—as members of this family or community or nation or people, as bearers of that history, as citizens of this republic. Allegiances such as these are more than values I happen to have, and to hold, at a certain distance. They go beyond the obligations I voluntarily incur and the "natural duties" I owe to human beings as such. They allow that to some I owe more than justice requires or even permits, not by reason of agreements I have made but instead in virtue of those more or less enduring attachments and commitments that, taken together, partly define the person I am.

To imagine a person incapable of constitutive attachments such as these is not to conceive an ideally free and rational agent, but to imagine a person wholly without character, without moral depth.

For to have character is to know that I move in a history I neither summon nor command, which carries consequences nonetheless for my choices and conduct. It draws me closer to some and more distant from others; it makes some aims more appropriate, others less so. As a self-interpreting being, I am able to reflect on my history and in this sense to distance myself from it, but the distance is always precarious and provisional, the point of reflection never finally secured outside the history itself. But the liberal ethic puts the self beyond the reach of its experience, beyond deliberation and reflection. Denied the expansive self-understandings that could shape a common life, the liberal self is left to lurch between detachment on the one hand, and entanglement on the other. Such is the fate of the unencumbered self, and its liberating promise.

### THE PROCEDURAL REPUBLIC

But before my case can be complete, I need to consider one powerful reply. While it comes from a liberal direction, its spirit is more practical than philosophical. It says, in short, that I am asking too much. It is one thing to seek constitutive attachments in our private lives; among families and friends, and certain tightly knit groups, there may be found a common good that makes justice and rights less pressing. But with public life—at least today, and probably always— it is different. So long as the nation-state is the primary form of political association, talk of constitutive community too easily suggests a darker politics rather than a brighter one; amid echoes of the Moral Majority, the priority of right, for all its philosophical faults, still seems the safer hope.

This is a challenging rejoinder, and no account of political community in the twentieth century can fail to take it seriously. It is challenging not least because it calls into question the status of political philosophy and its relation to the world. For if my argument is correct, if the liberal vision we have considered is not morally self-sufficient but parasitic on a notion of community it officially rejects, then we should expect to find that the political practice that embodies this vision is not *practically* self-sufficient either—that it must draw on a sense of community it cannot supply and may even undermine. But is that so far from the circumstance we face today? Could it be that through the original position darkly, on the far side of the veil of ignorance, we may glimpse an intimation of our predicament, a refracted vision of ourselves?

How does the liberal vision—and its failure—help us make sense of our public life and its predicament? Consider, to begin, the following paradox in the citizen's relation to the modern welfare state. In many ways, we stand near the completion of a liberal project that has run its course from the New Deal through the Great Society and into the present. But notwithstanding the extension of the franchise and the expansion on individual rights and entitlements in recent decades, there is a widespread sense that, individually and collectively, our control over the forces that govern our lives is receding rather than increasing. This sense is deepened by what appear simultaneously as the power and the powerlessness of the nation-state. On the one hand, increasing numbers of citizens view the state as an overly intrusive presence, more likely to frustrate their purposes than advance them. And yet, despite its unprecedented role in the economy and society, the modern state seems itself disempowered, unable effectively to control the domestic economy, to respond to persisting social ills, or to work America's will in the world.

This is a paradox that has fed the appeals of recent politicians (including Carter and Reagan), even as it has frustrated their attempts to govern. To sort it out, we need to identify the public philosophy implicit in our political practice, and to reconstruct its arrival. We need to trace the advent of the procedural republic, by which I mean a public life animated by the liberal vision and self-image we've considered.

The story of the procedural republic goes back in some ways to the founding of the republic, but its central drama begins to unfold around the turn of the century. As national markets and large-scale enterprise displaced a decentralized economy, the decentralized political forms of the early republic became outmoded as well. If democracy was to survive, the concentration of economic power would have to be met by a similar concentration of political power. But the Progressives understood, or some of them did, that the success of democracy required more than the centralization of government; it also required the nationalization of politics. The primary form of political community had to be recast on a national scale. For Herbert Croly, writing in 1909, the "nationalizing of American political, economic, and social life" was "an essentially formative and enlightening political transformation." We would become more of a democracy only as we became "more of a nation . . . in ideas, in institutions, and in spirit."[18]

This nationalizing project would be consummated in the New Deal, but for the democratic tradition in America, the embrace of the nation was a decisive departure. From Jefferson to the populists, the party of democracy in American political debate had been, roughly speaking, the party of the provinces, of decentralized power, of small-town and small-scale America. And against them had stood the party of the nation—first Federalists, then Whigs, then the Republicans of Lincoln—a party that spoke for the consolidation of the union. It was thus the historic achievement of the New Deal to unite, in a single party and political program, what Samuel Beer has called "liberalism and the national idea."[19]

What matters for our purpose is that, in the twentieth century, liberalism made its peace with concentrated power. But it was understood at the start that the terms of this peace required a strong sense of national community, morally and politically to underwrite the extended involvements of a modern industrial order. If a virtuous republic of small-scale, democratic communities was no longer a possibility, a national republic seemed democracy's next best hope. This was still, in principle at least, a politics of the common good. It looked to the nation, not as a neutral framework for the play of competing interests, but rather as a formative community, concerned to shape a common life suited to the scale of modern social and economic forms.

But this project failed. By the mid- or late twentieth century, the national republic had run its course. Except for extraordinary moments, such as war, the nation proved too vast a scale across which to cultivate the shared self-understandings necessary to community in the formative, or constitutive sense. And so the gradual shift, in our practices and institutions, from a public philosophy of common purposes to one of fair procedures, from a politics of good to a politics of right, from the national republic to the procedural republic.

## OUR PRESENT PREDICAMENT

A full account of this transition would take a detailed look at the changing shape of political institutions, constitutional interpretation, and the terms of political discourse in the broadest sense. But I suspect we would find in the *practice* of the procedural republic two broad tendencies foreshadowed by its philosophy: first, a tendency to crowd out democratic possibilities; second, a tendency to undercut the kind of community on which it nonetheless depends.

Where liberty in the early republic was understood as a function of democratic institutions and dispersed power,[20] liberty in the procedural republic is defined in opposition to democracy, as an individual's guarantee against what the majority might will. I am free insofar as I am the bearer of rights, where rights are trumps.[21] Unlike the liberty of the early republic, the modern version permits—in fact even requires—concentrated power. This has to do with the universalizing logic of rights. Insofar as I have a right, whether to free speech or a minimum income, its provision cannot be left to the vagaries of local preferences but must be assured at the most comprehensive level of political association. It cannot be one thing in New York and another in Alabama. As rights and entitlements expand, politics is therefore displaced from smaller forms of association and relocated at the most universal form—in our case, the nation. And even as politics flows to the nation, power shifts away from democratic institutions (such as legislatures and political parties) and toward institutions designed to be insulated from democratic pressures, and hence better equipped to dispense and defend individual rights (notably the judiciary and bureaucracy).

These institutional developments may begin to account for the sense of powerlessness that the welfare state fails to address and in some ways doubtless deepens. But it seems to me a further clue to our condition recalls even more directly the predicament of the unencumbered self—lurching, as we left it, between detachment on the one hand, entanglement on the other. For it is a striking feature of the welfare state that it offers a powerful promise of individual rights, and also demands of its citizens a high measure of mutual engagement. But the self-image that attends the rights cannot sustain the engagement.

As bearers of rights, where rights are trumps, we think of ourselves as freely choosing, individual selves, unbound by obligations antecedent to rights, or to the agreements we make. And yet, as citizens of the procedural republic that secures these rights, we find ourselves implicated willy-nilly in a formidable array of dependencies and expectations we did not choose and increasingly reject.

In our public life, we are more entangled, but less attached, than ever before. It is as though the unencumbered self presupposed by the liberal ethic had begun to come true—less liberated than disempowered, entangled in a network of obligations and involvements unassociated with any act of will, and yet unmediated by those common identifications or expansive self-definitions that would make them tolerable. As the scale of social and political organization has become more comprehensive, the terms of our collective identity have become more fragmented, and the forms of political life have outrun the common purpose needed to sustain them.

Something like this, it seems to me, has been unfolding in America for the past half-century or so. I hope I have said at least enough to suggest the shape a fuller story might take. And I hope in any case to have conveyed a certain view about politics and philosophy and the relation between them—that our practices and institutions are themselves embodiments of theory, and to unravel their predicament is, at least in part, to seek after the self-image of the age.

# twenty-four

# JUSTICE AS MEMBERSHIP

There are some things money can't buy and other things it tries to buy but shouldn't—elections, for example, or in an earlier day, salvation. But the sale of elections, like the sale of indulgences, usually brings a demand for reform. What is wrong with buying these things? And where else should money's writ not rule? How the good things in life should be distributed is the subject of Michael Walzer's book *Spheres of Justice,* which offers an imaginative alternative to the ongoing debate over distributive justice.

The debate is typically carried on between libertarians on the one hand and egalitarians on the other. Libertarians argue that money, the medium of free exchange, should buy whatever those who possess it want; people should be free to use their money as they choose. Egalitarians reply that money could be a fair instrument of distribution only if everyone had the same amount. So long as some have more and others less, some will deal from strength, others from weakness, and the so-called free market can hardly be fair. But critics of the egalitarian approach respond that even if all wealth were equally distributed, the equality would end when the dealing began. Those favorably endowed by fortune or circumstance would do well; those less favorably endowed less well. So long as people have different abilities and desires the reign of perfect equality can never last for long.

Walzer rescues the case for equality from its critics and defenders alike, by shifting the ground of the libertarian-egalitarian debate. The key to his solution is to worry less about the distribution of money and more about limiting the things that money can buy. This is the point of talking about spheres of justice. He maintains that different goods occupy different spheres, which are properly governed by different principles—welfare to the needy, honors to the deserving, political power to the persuasive, offices to the qualified, luxuries to those able and willing to pay for them, divine grace to the pious, and so on.

For Walzer, the injustice of unequal wealth lies not in the yachts and gourmet dinners that money commands but in money's power to dominate in spheres where it does not belong, as when it buys political influence. And while money may be the worst offender, it is not the only currency that wrongly rules beyond its own sphere. For example, when an office is obtained by kinship instead of ability, that is nepotism. Nepotism and bribery are easy to condemn because they result in goods being distributed by principles alien to their spheres.

But as Walzer acknowledges, the idea of spheres, taken alone, does not tell us how to distribute this or that good. Most of our political arguments arise over precisely what goods belong to what spheres. What sort of goods, for example, are health care and housing and education? Should we regard them as basic needs to be publicly provided as required or as goods and services to be sold in the market? Or, to take a different sort of example, in what sphere does sex belong? Should sexual pleasure be "distributed" only on the basis of love and commitment or also in exchange for cash or other goods?

Whether we are debating the welfare state or sexual mores, we need some way of deciding which goods fit which distributive principles. One way of deciding, perhaps the most familiar way, is to try to identify certain universal natural or human rights and to deduce from these whatever particular rights may follow—the right to housing or health care or the right to engage in prostitution, as the case may be.

Walzer rejects the appeal to rights and adopts in its place a conception of membership in a community, a conception that poses a powerful challenge to political theories that put rights first. For him, distributive justice must begin with such membership because we are all members of political communities before we are bearers of rights. Whether we have a right to a particular good depends on the role that good plays in our communal life and on its importance to us as members.

Walzer illustrates this point with an argument for greater public provision of medical care, an argument that appeals not to a universal "right to treatment," but instead to the character of contemporary American life and the shared understandings that define it. What the care of souls meant to the medieval Christians, he argues, the cure of bodies means to us. For them, eternity was a socially recognized need—"hence, a church in every parish, regular services, catechism for the young, compulsory communion, and so on." For us, a long and healthy life is a socially recognized need—"hence, doctors and hospitals in every district, regular checkups, health education for the young, compulsory vaccination, and so on." Medical care becomes a matter of membership in the society. To be cut off from it is "not only dangerous but degrading," a kind of excommunication.

In Walzer's conception, then, the case for equality is tied to the case for membership. Different communities invest different goods with different meanings and values, which give rise, in turn, to different understandings of membership. For example, Walzer reminds us that in different times and places, bread has been "the staff of life, the body of Christ, the symbol of the Sabbath, the means of hospitality and so on." What matters is that each community be faithful to its shared understandings and open to political debate about what those understandings require.

This is a humane and hopeful vision, and Walzer conveys it with a wry and gentle grace. His book is laced with specific illustrations and historical examples, designed to bring out our own understanding of social goods—of offices and honors, security and welfare, work and leisure, schooling and dating, property and power—often by contrast with other cultures and traditions. If his approach is at times more evocative than systematic, this is in keeping with his purpose—to resist the universalizing impulse of philosophy, to affirm the rich particularity of our moral lives.

Some may take issue with this purpose on the grounds that it is essentially conservative and uncritical. Societies faithful to the shared understandings of their members do not make for just societies, it may be said, only consistent ones. If the notion of justice is to have any critical force, one can further argue, it must be based on standards independent of any particular society; otherwise justice is left hostage to the very values it must judge. Walzer sometimes seems vulnerable to this challenge, as when he doubts that we can ever judge the meanings of communities other than our own.

But I don't think his pluralism requires that kind of moral relativism. Walzer's relativist voice is in tension with a more affirmative voice that gives his case its moral force. Implicit in his argument is a particular vision of community, the kind that cultivates the common life we share as members.

One expression of the kind of community Walzer has in mind is the public holiday, an institution that he contrasts with the modern vacation. Whereas vacations are private occasions, free of obligations, a time to "go away" from our usual place, holidays are public occasions (sometimes religious, sometimes civic), that we celebrate together. In our own time, those holidays that survive are increasingly attached to long weekends, to our private vacations.

He uses the history of the word "vacation" to show how far we have come from the communal life: "In Ancient Rome, the days on which there were no religious festivals or public games were called dies vacantes, 'empty days.' The holidays, by contrast, were full—full of obligation but also of celebration, full of things to do, feasting and dancing, rituals and plays. This was when time ripened to produce the social goods of shared solemnity and revelry. Who would give up days like that? But we have lost that sense of fullness; and the days we crave are the empty ones, which we can fill by ourselves as we please."

Though Walzer leaves little doubt which form of rest makes for the richer common life, he concludes nonetheless (in his relativist voice) that justice doesn't choose between holidays and vacations but simply requires public support for whichever form happens to prevail. But this is at odds with the deeper suggestion implicit in his account that a community that values vacations over holidays not only lacks a certain fullness but is unlikely to sustain the sense of belonging necessary if the community is to provide for such holidays.

It is one thing to expect a community to share the expenses of public celebrations and another to demand that it subsidize private vacations. The eclipse of holidays by vacations suggests the weakening of those moral ties that any case for public provision must presuppose. This seems to me the larger force of Walzer's claim. Where justice begins with membership, it cannot be concerned with distribution alone; it must also attend to the moral conditions that cultivate membership.

# twenty-five

# THE PERIL OF EXTINCTION

There are many things wrong with destroying humankind—the lives lost, the suffering and pain, the futures denied. But these terrible things are also wrong with wars that spare the species. What makes the nuclear nightmare different is not simply the scale of suffering or the number of deaths, but the possibility that human history could come to an end. Unlike other instruments of destruction, nuclear war introduces the possibility of extinction, and this possibility makes a moral difference. But what does this difference consist in? What is the moral difference between the loss of human lives and the end of human life?

Such speculation may seem as idle as it is grim. But as George Kateb rightly insists, policy must answer to philosophy, even a policy so powerfully governed by military and technological imperatives as nuclear deterrence. What is puzzling is not his enterprise but his answer. According to Kateb, the moral crux of the nuclear peril consists in the fact that nuclear war violates individual rights. If this seems a small complaint for so fateful an event, Kateb claims nonetheless that the doctrine of individualism is "the most adequate idealism" for the nuclear age, the moral philosophy best suited "to see the nuclear predicament truly and to protest and resist its perpetuation."[1]

Kateb believes that individualist principles rule out the use of "any nuclear weapon, of any size, for any purpose, by any country." This he calls "the no-use doctrine." Since the only end of legitimate government is to protect individual rights, and since nuclear war violates those rights, no use of nuclear weapons is morally permissible. Those who use nuclear weapons forfeit their right to govern, and can justifiably be overthrown, by violence if need be, by their fellow citizens or others. Indeed, even the threat to use nuclear weapons, implicit in the doctrine of deterrence, is at odds with legitimate government, and gives rise to the right to resist.

Kateb's hard line against nuclear war seems to offer a firmness appropriate to the peril. And as Kateb reminds us, it is the peril of extinction that makes the nuclear world "utterly distinct." But why, from the standpoint of individualism, *is* the destruction of humankind a loss beyond the loss of lives? Why should we worry about the survival of the world, apart from the reasons we have to worry about the survival of the millions who comprise it? By tying his case to an individualistic ethic, Kateb obscures the distinctness of the peril he would confront; he makes it difficult to see how extinction could be, so to speak, a fate worse than death.

There are at least two ways of accounting for the special loss of extinction; neither fits well with the individualism Kateb defends. The first appeals to the common world we share as human beings. As Hannah Arendt writes,

> The common world is what we enter when we are born and what we leave behind when we die. It is what we have in common not only with those who live with us, but also with those who were here before and with those who will come after us.

According to Arendt, the permanence of the common world is essential to the possibility of human meaning. Only by engaging in significant action can mere mortals aspire to an "earthly immortality." But to escape the ruin of time, such acts must be remembered; meaning depends on memory. As the common world is the carrier of memory, no less than the possibility of human meaning depends on its survival. It is from this point of view that Jonathan Schell describes the nuclear predicament as "a crisis of life in the common world."

A second case against extinction appeals to those particular common worlds defined by peoples and nations, cultures and communities. The memories they bear draw their resonance from local references and traditions. The events they recall have meaning for their members even when they lack universal significance. To care for the fate of a community is to care for a way of life more enduring than an individual life, but less expansive than humanity in general.

This explains why genocide is a crime more heinous than the many murders it entails. To destroy not only persons but also a people is to extinguish a language and culture, a distinctive way of being. By destroying a world, even one more bounded than the world of humankind, genocide intimates the ultimate extinction. It diminishes our humanity by effacing one of its distinctive expressions.

The idea that we should cherish the common worlds we inhabit draws Kateb's emphatic rebuke. "Such a way of conceiving a people does not answer to the American experience." It is alien, "Old World," "folk-mystique," a piece of superstition. Far from an argument against annihilation, the conviction that cultures and peoples are worth preserving "constitutes a fertile source of the possibility of extinction." Once we believe that a people outlives the individuals who at any moment comprise it, we are more likely to prefer our own kind, to fight for abstractions, to travel down the road of massive ruin. "The idea of a people is a pernicious atavism," the very thing modern individualism is meant to cure.

Those who prize communal ties need to guard against the decay of pride into chauvinism, especially where the community commands, as it sometimes does, the power of a state. The suggestion that solidarity as such is a slippery slope to statism, however, is a caricature of vast proportions. Nor does Kateb say enough about his individualistic alternative to show whether it can overcome such familiar difficulties as sustaining a scheme of rights without appealing to a sense of community beyond the social contract. But leaving aside these broader questions of political theory, the question remains how Kateb can cast extinction as a special kind of peril, while at the same time denying any notion of a common world worth preserving. If individualism teaches us to outgrow all solidarities, what reason does it leave to love the world? And if we have no reason, why worry so about extinction?

The nuclear peril is different because it threatens us whole; it threatens the continuities that situate us in the world. In the individualist view, the extinction of the species can only be another case, a bigger case, of murder. Kateb seems to concede as much when he writes, "The emphasis is on the death of millions of individuals." But this denies our sense that the loss of the world is a loss beyond the loss of lives. The language of individual rights does not help us say what is wrong with nuclear war. Without some kind of communal language, the distinctness of the nuclear age is likely to defy description.

# twenty-six

# DEWEY'S LIBERALISM AND OURS

## 1.

In the first half of the twentieth century, John Dewey was America's most celebrated philosopher. More than a philosopher, he was a public intellectual who wrote about politics and education, science and faith, for an audience beyond the academy. When Dewey died in 1952, at age ninety-three, Henry Commager described him as "the guide, the mentor, and the conscience of the American people; it is scarcely an exaggeration to say that for a generation no issue was clarified until Dewey had spoken."

In the decades following his death, however, Dewey's work was largely ignored. Academic philosophy became increasingly technical and regarded Dewey's broad speculations as fuzzy and old-fashioned. Even moral and political philosophers, embroiled in debates about utilitarian versus Kantian ethics, found little reason to turn to Dewey. Except in schools of education, where his influence persisted, few students read his books. Meanwhile, the central political debates of the day—about the scope of rights and entitlements, about the relation between government and the economy—had little to do, or so it seemed, with Dewey's political teaching.

In recent years, Dewey has made a comeback. Why this is so, and whether the Dewey revival holds promise for contemporary philosophy and politics, are among the questions that Alan Ryan poses in

*John Dewey and the High Tide of American Liberalism* (1995). Ryan's book is itself an expression of the Dewey revival it describes. It follows the publication a few years ago of Robert Westbrook's excellent biography, *John Dewey and American Democracy,* and coincides with the appearance of other books and articles on aspects of Dewey's thought.[1] Ryan, a political theorist who teaches at Oxford, is a spirited and sympathetic guide to Dewey's life and thought. He describes his book less as a full-fledged biography than as "a friendly but critical tour of the ideas that established Dewey's astonishing hold over the educated American public of his day." In this aim, Ryan admirably succeeds.

If the narrative occasionally flags, the fault lies less with the author than with his subject. Rarely has so eventful a life been led by so colorless a figure. Like few philosophers of his day or ours, Dewey lived a life of public engagement. A leading voice of Progressive reform, he founded an experimental school in Chicago, worked with the social reformer Jane Addams at Hull House, and supported women's suffrage and Margaret Sanger's birth control movement. He became the nation's foremost apostle of what came to be called progressive education and a hero to school teachers. He helped to establish the American Association of University Professors, the New School for Social Research, and the American Civil Liberties Union. He traveled to Japan, China, Turkey, Mexico, and the Soviet Union to lecture and advise on educational reform, and chaired an unsuccessful attempt to form a new political party based on social democratic principles. At the age of seventy-eight, Dewey led a commission of inquiry that cleared Leon Trotsky of Stalin's charge, made at the Moscow trials of 1936, that Trotsky had committed sabotage and treason against the Soviet regime. Notwithstanding this remarkable variety of activities, Dewey found time to write more than a thousand essays and books, many for a general audience, which have recently been gathered in thirty-seven volumes of collected works.[2]

*   *   *

But Dewey himself was scarcely as imposing a person as his activism and influence might suggest. He was a shy, impassive man, an awkward writer, and a poor public speaker. Even when writing for a general audience, he was not particularly adept at making complex ideas accessible. Sidney Hook, one of Dewey's greatest admirers, acknowledged that America's greatest philosopher of education was not impressive as a classroom teacher:

> He made no attempt to motivate or arouse the interest of his auditors, to relate problems to their own experiences, to use graphic, concrete illustrations in order to give point to abstract and abstruse positions. He rarely provoked a lively participation and response from students . . . Dewey spoke in a husky monotone . . . His discourse was far from fluent. There were pauses and sometimes long lapses as he gazed out of the window or above the heads of his audience.

Dewey's lack of presence as a writer, speaker, or personality makes his popular appeal something of a mystery. The mystery is compounded by the fact that the political positions he espoused were often at odds with conventional opinion. A non-Marxist critic of capitalism, he voted for Eugene Debs over Woodrow Wilson in 1912, opposed the New Deal as too tepid a response to the crisis of industrial capitalism, and always voted for Norman Thomas over Franklin Roosevelt. What was it then, that won Dewey so broad an audience for half a century?

The answer, Ryan persuasively suggests, is that Dewey's philosophy helped Americans make their peace with the modern world. It did so by easing the seemingly stark alternatives that confronted Americans in the early twentieth century—between science and faith, individualism and community, democracy and expertise. Dewey's philosophy blurred these familiar distinctions. Science, he wrote, was not necessarily opposed to faith, but another way of making sense of the world as we experience it. Individualism, properly understood, was not the rampant pursuit of self-interest but the unfolding of a person's distinctive capacities in a "common life" that calls them forth. Democracy was not simply a matter of counting up people's preferences, however irrational, but a way of life that educates citizens to be capable of "intelligent action."

Dewey argued, in short, that Americans could embrace the modern world without forsaking some of their most cherished allegiances. Raised in Vermont as a Congregationalist, a member of the first generation of university teachers of philosophy who were not clergymen, Dewey was not aggressively secular. He retained the vocabulary of faith, of moral and religious uplift, and applied it to democracy and education. This position, as Ryan argues, appealed to people who were seeking moral and religious ideals and ways to express them that were compatible with the assumptions of secular society. During a century of wars, vast social and economic changes, and widespread anxiety about them, Dewey offered a reassuring message, even a consoling one.

Dewey's tendency to blur distinctions, the subject of much annoyance among his critics, did not spring simply from a desire to soothe the anxieties of his readers. It reflected the two central tenets of his philosophy; pragmatism and liberalism. Recent debates about Dewey's work have concentrated on these two doctrines and on the relation between them. Since pragmatism and liberalism are often used in ways at odds with Dewey's meaning, it is important to see how he understood them.

In common usage, pragmatism describes a merely expedient approach to things, ungoverned by moral principle. But this is not what Dewey meant by it. For him, pragmatism described a challenge to the way philosophers understood the search for truth. Since the time of the Greeks, philosophers had assumed that the quest for truth was a quest for knowledge of an ultimate reality, or metaphysical order, independent of our perceptions and beliefs. Philosophers disagreed among themselves about whether the meaning of this ultimate reality was something we supply or something we discover; they disagreed as well about the nature of relations between mind and body, subject and object, and between the ideal and the real. But they shared the assumption that the test of truth is the correspondence between our thoughts about the world and the world as it really is. Dewey rejected this assumption. At the heart of his pragmatism was the notion that the truth of a statement or belief depends on its usefulness in making sense of experience and guiding action, not on its correspondence to an ultimate reality that exists outside or beyond our experience. According to Dewey, philosophy should "surrender all pretension to be peculiarly concerned with ultimate reality" and accept the pragmatic notion that "no theory of Reality in general, *Uberhaupt*, is possible or needed."[3]

If Dewey is right, important consequences follow for philosophers. If philosophy lacks a distinctive subject matter, if the validity of a belief can only be determined by testing it in experience, then conventional distinctions between thought and action, knowing and doing, must be reconsidered. The process of knowing does not consist in grasping something accurately from the outside; it involves taking part in events in a purposive, intelligent way. Philosophers should give up their search for conditions of knowledge in general and attend to the particular problems for thought and action that arise in everyday life. "Philosophy," Dewey writes, "recovers itself when it ceases to be a device for dealing with the problems of philosophers and becomes a method, cultivated by philosophers, for dealing with the problems of men."[4]

The idea of philosophy as unavoidably practical and experimental suggests that the philosopher must respond to the events of his or her time not only as a concerned citizen but also as a philosopher. It therefore suggests a closer connection between philosophy and democracy than most philosophers would accept. As Ryan observes,

"Dewey came to think that every aspect of philosophy was an aspect of understanding a modern democratic society." So close a link between philosophy and democracy runs counter to the familiar contrast between philosophy, understood as the pursuit of truth, and democracy, understood as a way of representing opinions and interests. But Dewey viewed philosophy as less detached and democracy as more elevated than the familiar contrast assumes. More than a system of majority rule, democracy was, for Dewey, a way of life that fosters communication and deliberation among citizens, deliberation that issues in intelligent collective action.

Ardent democrat though he was, Dewey did not defend democracy as founded in consent or the general will. Instead, he viewed democracy as the political expression of an experimental, pragmatic attitude to the world. Dewey's pragmatism led him to celebrate democracy for much the same reasons that he celebrated science. Ryan explains the parallel between democracy and science in Dewey's thought as follows:

> There is no truth legitimating the observations and experiments of scientists and no will legitimating democratic decision making . . . [Dewey] eschewed any suggestion that "democracy" was uniquely legitimate either because it was government by the general will or because it was uniquely apt to uncover the truth. The nearest he got to a single account of democracy's virtues was that they were like those of science: It excluded the fewest alternatives, allowed all ideas a fair shot at being tried out, encouraged progress, and did not rely on authority.

Dewey's pragmatism gave his liberalism a distinctive, and in some ways unfamiliar, cast. Most versions of liberal political theory rest on moral and metaphysical assumptions at odds with Dewey's pragmatism. John Locke held that legitimate government is limited by natural, inalienable rights; Immanuel Kant argued that no policy, however popular or conducive to utility, may violate principles of justice and right that are not derived from experience but are prior to it; even John Stuart Mill, who based justice and rights on "utility," broadly conceived, relied on a strong distinction between public and private spheres of action.

Dewey rejected all of these versions of liberalism, for they rested on moral or metaphysical foundations that were held to be prior to politics and prior to experience. Unlike these classical liberals and many contemporary ones, Dewey did not base his political theory on the existence of fundamental rights or a social contract. Although he favored civil liberties, he was not primarily concerned with defining the rights that limit majority rule; nor did he try to derive principles of justice that would govern the basic structure of society, or to identify a realm of privacy free from government intrusion.

Central to Dewey's liberalism was the idea that freedom consists in participating in a common life that enables individuals to realize their distinctive capacities. The problem of freedom is not how to balance individual rights against the claims of community, but how, as he put it to establish "an entire social order, possessed of a spiritual authority that would nurture and direct the inner as well as the outer life of individuals."[5] Civil liberties are vital for such a society, not because they enable individuals to pursue their own ends but because they make possible the social communication, the free inquiry and debate, that democratic life requires.

The overriding importance of democracy for Dewey is not that it provides a mechanism for weighing everyone's preferences equally, but that it provides a "form of social organization, extending to all the areas and ways of living," in which the full powers of individuals can be "fed, sustained and directed."[6] For Dewey, the "first object of a renascent liberalism" was not justice or rights but education, the task of "producing the habits of mind and character, the intellectual and moral patterns," that suited citizens to the mutual responsibilities of a shared public life.[7] Democratic education of this kind, he stressed,

was not only a matter of schooling but the essential task of liberal social and political institutions as well. Schools would be small communities that would prepare children to engage in a democratic public life, which would in turn educate citizens to advance the common
good.

## 2.

Ryan's observation that Dewey's life and thought represent the "high
tide of American liberalism" raises the question of Dewey's relevance
today. Does the marked difference, in argument and emphasis, between Dewey's liberalism and ours reflect the obsolescence of his liberalism or the inadequacy of our own? Ryan himself seems divided
about this question. On the one hand, he is wary of Dewey's view
that freedom is bound up with membership in a community, a view
that reflects Dewey's debt to Hegel. Dewey's "urge to close the gap
between what we desire for ourselves and what we want for other
people," Ryan writes, "contains more wishful thinking than is decent in a philosophical theory." On the other hand, Ryan describes
Dewey's liberalism as a desirable corrective to the preoccupation
with rights that characterizes much liberal political theory and practice today. "Rights-obsessed liberalism is only one liberalism," Ryan
writes, "and not the most persuasive."

In the end, Ryan suggests, a liberalism grounded in rights and
Dewey's more communitarian version of liberalism may not differ as
sharply in practice as they do in theory. Despite Dewey's rejection of
natural rights, for example, he endorsed traditional liberal rights on
other grounds—as a necessary condition for a democratic community hospitable to communication, intelligent action, and the full realization of human capacities. "The traditional political liberties remain firmly in place" in Dewey's liberalism, Ryan observes,

> not because they are "natural rights"—there are no natural rights—
> or because there is a chronic problem of defending each individual

in a democracy from the potential ill will of a majority. They remain in place as part of the machinery that allows a truly democratic public to form . . . The diehard rights-obsessed liberal will not be persuaded by this, but Dewey would not be persuaded by him. Nor does this matter as much as it may seem. Dewey was quite ready to agree that the full battery of *legal* rights that the liberal traditionally demands are the indispensable way to institutionalize the ground rules of a democratic community.

While it is true that Dewey's liberalism and the contemporary version of liberalism associated with such theorists as John Rawls and Ronald Dworkin both affirm a familiar range of rights, the differences between the two are not without consequence for politics. This can be seen by considering the attempt by Richard Rorty to enlist Dewey's pragmatism in the service of his own version of contemporary liberalism, which holds that political argument should be detached from moral and religious argument. In a number of influential works, Rorty has praised Dewey's attempt to set epistemology aside and abandon the idea that philosophy can provide a foundation for knowledge.[8]

More recently, in an article entitled "The Priority of Democracy to Philosophy," Rorty has sought to show that Dewey's pragmatism can provide support for the kind of liberalism he favors. Just as philosophy should set aside the search for knowledge of an ultimate reality beyond experience, Rorty argues, so politics should set aside competing visions of morality and religion. Politics should not aim at any particular conception of the good life, but should settle for a society in which people tolerate one another in public and pursue their moral and religious ideals in private. A liberal democracy should not only avoid legislating morality, Rorty maintains; it should also banish moral and religious argument from political discourse. "Such a society will become accustomed to the thought that social policy needs no more authority than successful accommodation among individuals."

Rorty acknowledges that encouraging citizens to set aside their moral convictions for political purposes is likely to make them philosophically "light-minded" and lead to a spiritual "disenchantment" of public life. People will gradually give up the tendency to view politics as the appropriate vehicle for the expression of moral and spiritual ideals. But Rorty argues that such a result is precisely the wisdom of the pragmatic liberalism that he and, allegedly, Dewey endorse. "For Dewey, communal and public disenchantment is the price we pay for individual and private spiritual liberation."[9]

It is a measure of Rorty's philosophical ingenuity that he derives from Dewey's pragmatism a political theory sharply at odds with the one that Dewey himself affirmed. Dewey rejected the notion that government should be neutral among conceptions of the good life. He lamented rather than celebrated the moral and spiritual disenchantment of public life. He rejected a sharp distinction between public and private life and defended the view, derived from Hegel and the British idealist philosopher T. H. Green, that individual freedom can only be realized as part of a social life that cultivates the moral and civic character of citizens and inspires a commitment to the common good.

Rorty sets aside the communal aspect of Dewey's thought. Drawing instead on Dewey's pragmatism, he constructs a liberalism that renounces moral or philosophical foundations. Rorty argues that pragmatism teaches us to abandon the idea that philosophy supplies the foundations of knowledge; similarly, liberalism teaches us to abandon the idea that moral and religious ideals supply the justifications for political arrangements. Rorty's liberalism asserts that democracy takes precedence over philosophy in the sense that the case for democracy need not presuppose any particular vision of the good life. Rorty's creative rewriting (some would say hijacking) of Dewey's liberalism helps to clarify what is at stake in the contrast between

Dewey's communitarian liberalism and the rights-based liberalism more familiar in our time.

For Dewey, the primary problem with American democracy in his day was not an insufficient emphasis on justice and rights, but the impoverished character of public life. The source of this impoverishment was the discrepancy between the impersonal and organized character of modern economic life and the ways Americans conceived of themselves. Americans of the early twentieth century increasingly thought of themselves as freely choosing individuals, even as the huge scale of economic life dominated by large corporations undermined their capacity to direct their own lives. Paradoxically, Dewey observed, people clung to an individualistic philosophy "at just the time when the individual was counting for less in the direction of social affairs, at a time when mechanical forces and vast impersonal organizations were determining the frame of things."[10]

Central among the mechanical forces were steam, electricity, and railroads. Their effect was to dissolve the local forms of community that had prevailed in American life through much of the nineteenth century without substituting a new form of political community. As Dewey wrote, "The machine age in developing the Great Society has invaded and partially disintegrated the small communities of former times without generating a Great Community."[11] The erosion of traditional forms of community and authority at the hands of commerce and industry seemed at first a source of individual liberation. But Americans soon discovered that the loss of community had very different effects. Although the new forms of communication and technology brought a new, more extensive interdependence, they did not bring a sense of engagement in common purposes and pursuits. "Vast currents are running which bring men together," Dewey wrote, but these currents did nothing to build a new kind of political community. As Dewey stressed, "No amount of aggregated collective action of itself constitutes a community." In spite of the increasing use of railroads, telegraph wires, and the increasingly complex division of labor, or perhaps because of them, "the Public seems to be lost."[12] The new national economy had "no political agencies worthy of it," leaving the democratic public atomized, inchoate, and unorganized.[13] According to Dewey, the revival of democracy awaited the recovery of a shared public life, which depended in turn on creating new communitarian institutions, especially schools, that could equip citizens to act effectively within the modern economy. "Till the Great Society is converted into a Great Community, the Public will remain in eclipse."[14]

Like many liberals of his day and since, Dewey assumed that the Great Community would take the form of a national community; American democracy would flourish insofar as it managed to inspire a sense of mutual responsibility and allegiance to the nation as a whole. Since the economy was now national in scale, political institutions had to become national as well, if only to keep up. National markets called forth big government, which required in turn a strong sense of national community to sustain it.

From the Progressive era to the New Deal to the Great Society, American liberalism sought to cultivate a deeper sense of national community and civic engagement, but with only mixed success. Except in extraordinary moments, such as war, the nation proved too vast for anything resembling a Great Community to be formed, too disparate to serve as a forum for the public deliberation Dewey rightly prized. Partly as a result, American liberals in the postwar years gradually turned their attention from the character of public life to the expansion of both rights against the government and entitlements backed by the government. By the 1980s and 1990s, however, the liberalism of rights and entitlements was in retreat, having lost much of its moral energy and political appeal.

As in Dewey's day, there is today a widespread fear that citizens are losing control of the forces that govern their lives, that people are turning away from public responsibilities, and that the politicians and parties lack the moral or civic imagination to respond. Once again there is reason to worry that the "Public," as Dewey conceived it, is in eclipse, while the play of powerful interests and the din of strident voices leave little room for reasoned public discourse. Now as then it could be said, with Dewey, that "the political elements in the constitution of the human being, those having to do with citizenship, are crowded to one side."[15] Now, however, it is conservatives, rather than liberals, who speak most explicitly of citizenship, community, and the moral prerequisites of a shared public life. Although the conservatives' conception of community is often narrow and ungenerous, liberals often lack the moral resources to mount a convincing reply. What Ryan calls the "rights-obsessed liberalism" familiar in our time insists that government must be neutral on questions of the good life, that it must avoid taking sides on moral and religious controversies. The great service of Ryan's book is to remind us that liberalism was not always reluctant to speak the language of morality, community, and religion. "Deweyan liberalism," he writes,

> is different. It is a genuine liberalism, unequivocally committed to progress and the expansion of human tastes, needs, and interests . . . Nonetheless, it comes complete with a contentious world view and a contentious view of what constitutes a good life; it takes sides on questions of religion, and it is not obsessed with the defense of rights . . . The individual it celebrates is someone who is thoroughly engaged with his or her work, family, local community and its politics, who has not been coerced, bullied, or dragged into these interests but sees them as fields for a self-expression quite consistent with losing himself or herself in the task at hand.

At a time when the liberalism of rights and entitlements finds itself at low ebb, we might do well to recall the more robust civic liberalism for which Dewey spoke.

# twenty-seven

# MASTERY AND HUBRIS IN JUDAISM

## WHAT'S WRONG WITH PLAYING GOD?

David Hartman, one of the leading religious thinkers of our time, is also our most important Jewish public philosopher. In his teachings and writings, he has fostered a rich encounter between the Jewish tradition and modern moral and political philosophy. As Maimonides drew Aristotle into conversation with Moses and Rabbi Akiva, so Hartman has renovated Jewish thought by bringing the liberal sensibilities of Immanuel Kant and John Stuart Mill to bear on Talmudic argument.

Much of Hartman's work is devoted to showing that it is possible to reconcile halakhic Judaism with modern pluralism.[1] The pluralism he defends is not simply a pragmatic response to the moral and religious disagreements that abound in modern societies, a compromise for the sake of peace. To the contrary, Hartman's pluralism has its source in his theology, in his distinctive vision of covenantal Judaism.

### PLURALISM: ETHICAL AND INTERPRETIVE

At the heart of Hartman's theology is the notion of God as a self-limiting being who restrains himself in order to make room for human freedom and responsibility. The notion of divine self-limitation is first intimated in the biblical account of creation. God creates human beings in his own image, but as distinct from himself, as free and independent creatures, capable of violating his commands (as Adam shows when he eats from the tree of knowledge), and also of arguing with him (as Abraham does before the destruction of Sodom). But for Hartman, the fullest expression of God's self-limitation is the Sinai covenant. In giving the Torah to the Jewish people at Sinai, God enlists human beings as partners in his project for history. Rather than achieve his purposes directly, through miraculous intervention or prophetic revelation, God ties his hopes to a community that undertakes to live by his commandments. But the Torah he hands down at Sinai is not transparent or self-interpreting. God leaves it to human beings—the scholars and rabbis—to determine the meaning of his law. Here is a further sense in which God limits himself and makes room for human initiative. "God's self-limiting love for human beings is expressed in His entrusting the elaboration and expansion of the Torah to rabbinic scholars."[2] The successive elaborations, embodied in Talmud and Midrash, become constitutive of the Torah revealed at Sinai. "With the development of the oral tradition, Israel became a partner in the development of revelation; revelation ceased being the divine Word completely given at Sinai and became an open-ended Word creatively elaborated by countless generations of students."[3]

Hartman argues for two forms of pluralism—one interpretive, the other ethical. His interpretive pluralism emerges directly from his covenantal theology and reflects the open-ended character of Talmudic argument. Different rabbis, however learned, can come to different conclusions. Even God cannot intervene to resolve a Talmudic dispute, as a well-known *midrash* attests. ("It is not in heaven.") Minority opinions are not condemned as heretical but are legitimized and preserved. The open-ended character of interpretation makes room for pluralism within halakhic Judaism.

But Hartman also defends a more far-reaching, ethical pluralism that takes seriously the ethical systems of other faiths, and of secular morality. According to Hartman, God's covenant with the Jewish people does not mean that Judaism is the only authentic way to worship God. Nor must a system of ethics be founded on divine revelation.[4] Hartman rejects the notion that, without revelation, there can be no rational grounding of ethical norms. "Human history has shown that individuals are capable of developing viable ethical systems not rooted in divine authority. God's revelation of the ethical is not meant to compensate for a presumed inability of human reason to formulate an ethical system."[5] Unlike many religious thinkers, Hartman maintains that "secular humanism is a viable and morally coherent position."[6]

Hartman does not claim that ethical pluralism is mandated by biblical and Talmudic Judaism, only that it is a possible interpretation. He acknowledges that some aspects of the tradition are at odds with pluralism. Hartman's claim might prompt one to ask which interpretation is truest to the Jewish tradition taken as a whole—the pluralist reading or the exclusivist one? But Hartman does not focus on this question, and I will not pursue it here. Instead, I would like to explore a different issue raised by Hartman's ethical pluralism: If people can reason their way to morality without divine revelation, then what is religion for? Or, to put the question another way: Why does the possibility of a valid secular morality pose no threat to halakhic Judaism as Hartman understands it? In support of his own willingness to accept secular ethics as legitimate, Hartman cites Maimonides, who drew freely on Aristotle's ethics: "Maimonides demonstrated that covenantal halakhic spirituality is in no way threatened or undermined by admitting the validity of ethical norms whose source is independent of the notion of revelation."[7]

Many people with strong religious convictions believe they have a stake in denying the adequacy of secular morality. That Hartman, as a halakhic Jew, has no such stake reflects more than a tolerant stance toward the beliefs of others. It also reflects a deep conviction that religion is about more than grounding moral principles. Notwithstanding the importance of the ethical *mitzvot,* Hartman is critical of those who identify Judaism with certain ethical precepts said to be unique or distinctive to Jews. "In order to appreciate the seriousness with which Judaism takes the ethical mitzvoth, it is not necessary to claim some special Jewish ethical sensibility or to adduce the moral genius of the Hebrew prophets."[8] To identify Judaism with the ethical not only fails to notice similar ethical norms in many other traditions; it also reflects an impoverished understanding of Jewish religious and spiritual life.

## RELIGIOUS ANTHROPOLOGY

For Hartman, religion is about more than ethical precepts, more than ritual and celebration. It is also a way of making sense of our relation to God, nature, and the cosmos, and of determining the mode of being appropriate to that relation. At the heart of Hartman's covenantal theology lie fundamental questions of religious anthropology: What does it mean for a human being to live in the presence of God? What dispositions, sensibilities, and stance toward the world does a religious person have? Is he humble and submissive, or assertive and bold? What sort of religious personality does halakhic Judaism, properly understood, cultivate and affirm? What limits on human powers, if any, should we recognize and observe?

As these questions suggest, religious anthropology is at once metaphysical and normative. It is metaphysical in that it seeks an account of the universe, and of the place of human beings within it. It is normative in that any account of our relation to God and nature carries implications for the way we should be and the lives we should live. Those who insist on a purely formal or positivist view of law might deny that any such account carries normative weight; whatever the law prohibits may not be done, and whatever the law does not prohibit is permissible. But if Hartman is right that halakhah is open to competing interpretations, the best interpretation may be the one that fits with the larger theological picture. In this way, Hartman's religious anthropology informs his understanding of ethics and law.

In order to illustrate the importance of Hartman's religious anthropology, I would like to consider a set of moral and political questions, increasingly prominent in contemporary public discourse, that cannot be resolved by invoking familiar moral principles or ethical precepts alone. Although Hartman has not addressed these questions directly, his religious anthropology provides a fruitful way of thinking about them, and a language in which to do so.

## BIOTECHNOLOGY: PLAYING GOD?

Many of the most difficult issues we face in the modern world concern the proper use of our growing technological power to remake nature, including human nature. Arguments about the limits, if any, of human dominion over nature have figured in debates about environmental policy for some time. Recent advances in biotechnology have sharpened the question, as illustrated by debates over genetically modified food, the bioengineering of animals, human cloning, new reproductive technologies, and other techniques that give human beings the power to choose or change their children's (or their own) genetic characteristics. While few object to the cloning of Dolly the sheep, many are troubled by the prospect of cloning human beings or using genetic technologies that would enable parents to create "designer babies" by specifying in advance the sex, height, eye color, athletic prowess, musical ability, or IQ of their children.

Troubling though these scenarios are, it is not easy to say exactly what is wrong with them. There is, of course, the safety objection: attempting such practices prematurely poses grave risk of genetic abnormalities and other medical harms. But even assuming the medical risks can eventually be overcome, there remains a lingering unease. The standard lexicon of ethical principles—utility, rights, and informed consent—does not capture the features of genetic engineering that trouble us most deeply. And so those who worry about these practices—including those who otherwise argue within secular moral frameworks—find themselves invoking the idea that human beings shouldn't "play God." By this they suggest that certain human interventions in nature represent a kind of "hubris," a drive to mastery and dominion that exceeds the bounds of properly human endeavor. Whether or not the "playing God" objection to genetic engineering is decisive, it prompts us to consider the proper relation of human beings to God and nature. It forces us onto the terrain of religious anthropology.

Judaism is more permissive than many traditions with respect to human dominion over nature. As Hartman points out, the God of creation is not one with nature, as in pantheistic conceptions, nor embodied in nature, as in pagan cosmologies, but a transcendent being whose existence is prior to nature. So if human intervention in nature is subject to certain limits, these limits do not arise from the idea that nature is enchanted or sacred as such, as some "deep green" ecologists believe. The limits on the exercise of human powers over nature arise not from nature itself but from a proper understanding of the relation between human beings and God. If it is wrong to clone ourselves in a quest for immortality, or to genetically alter our children so that they will better fulfill our ambitions and desires, the sin is not the desecration of nature but the deification of ourselves.

But at what point does the exercise of scientific or technological power amount to deification, or a hubristic quest to usurp God's role? In rabbinic times, some saw the physician's practice of medicine as a failure of faith, as an illegitimate intrusion on God's role as healer of the sick. But the Talmud rejects this view, and teaches that "permission has been given to the physician to heal" (*Berakhot* 60a).

A midrashic story explains the permission to heal by comparing it to the permission given the farmer to rework nature in planting and cultivating crops:

> R. Ishmael and R. Akiva were strolling in the streets of Jerusalem accompanied by another person. They were met by a sick person. He said to them, "My masters, tell me by what means I may be Healed." They told him, "Do thus and so and be healed." He asked them, "And who afflicted me?" They replied, "The Holy One, blessed be He." [The sick person] responded, "You intrude in a realm which is not yours; He has afflicted and you heal! Are you not transgressing His will?"
>   They asked him, "What is your occupation?" He answered, "I am a tiller of the soil and here is the sickle in my hand." They asked him, "Who created the orchard?" He answered, "The Holy One, blessed be He." Said they, "You too intrude in a realm which is not yours. [God] created it and you cut away its fruit!" He said to them, "Do you not see the sickle in my hand? If I did not plow, sow, fertilize and weed it, nothing would grow." They said to him, "Oh you fool! Does your occupation not teach you this, as Scripture says 'as for man, his days are as grass: as grass of the field, so he flourishes' (Psalms 103:15). Just as a tree, without weeding, fertilizing, and plowing will not grow; and even if it grows, then without irrigation and fertilizing it will not live but will surely die—so it is with regard to the body. Drugs and medical procedures are the fertilizer, and the physician is the tiller of the soil."[9]

The permission of the physician to heal the sick does not resolve the question of whether certain forms of genetic engineering wrongly intrude in God's realm. Many uses of the new biotechnology, such as choosing to have a boy rather than a girl, or gaining a competitive edge in sports through the use of performance-enhancing drugs or genetic alteration, have nothing to do with healing the sick or curing disease. My inability to run a three-minute mile or hit seventy home runs, however disappointing, is not a disease; my doctor has no obligation to provide me with a cure. But it is a further question whether there is anything wrong with using science and technology to acquire these powers.

## THE PROMETHEAN SPIRIT

Hartman's teacher, Rabbi Joseph Soloveitchik, accords human beings almost boundless scope for the exercise of their powers. For Soloveitchik, man's creation in the image of God implies that human beings have a divine mandate to participate in the act of creation itself. He argues that God deliberately created an imperfect universe so that human beings would be empowered to improve it. "The most fervent desire of halakhic man is to behold the replenishment in the deficiency in creation," Soloveitchik writes. "The dream of creation is the central idea in the halakhic consciousness—the idea of the importance of man as a partner of the Almighty in the act of creation, man as creator of worlds."[10]

According to Soloveitchik, the incompleteness of creation was an expression of God's love for humankind. "The Creator of the world diminished the image and stature of creation in order to leave something for man, the work of his hands, to do, in order to adorn man with the crown of creator and maker." Soloveitchik includes in the mandate of creativity the project of self-creation. "Herein is embodied the entire task of creation and the obligation to participate in the renewal of the cosmos. The most fundamental principle of all is that man must create himself. It is this idea that Judaism introduced into the world."[11]

The Promethean spirit of Soloveitchik's religious anthropology would seem to sanction a boundless human dominion over nature. It is hard to imagine a scientific pursuit he would condemn as hubristic. He might even sympathize with James Watson's famous reply to those who criticized modern scientists for playing God. "If we don't play God," Watson is reported to have said, "who will?" As

Hartman observes, Soloveitchik's vision of Jewish spirituality supports "the whole modern technological spirit, which has often been viewed as a threat to the religious quest."[12]

What then becomes of religious humility? What prevents so empowered and autonomous a human being from mistaking himself for God? Soloveitchik answers this question by attributing to halakhic man a second mandate—to imitate not only the creativity of God but also His withdrawal from the world, and His acceptance of defeat. "Jewish ethics, then, requires man, in certain situations, to withdraw. Man must not always be a victor."[13] The majesty of human mastery and dominion is reined in by an obligation of sacrifice and submission to the ultimately inscrutable will of God, as exemplified by Abraham's willingness to sacrifice his son. For Soloveitchik, the religious personality, riven by contrasting orientations to life, is bound to oscillate between two radically different spiritual sensibilities: Facing nature, he displays a heady sense of mastery and dominion; facing God, his sense of agency gives way to the unquestioning sacrifice and utter submission of the *Akedah*.

Hartman rejects Soloveitchik's religious anthropology on two grounds. First, Hartman does not believe that a wrenching oscillation between radical polarities of assertiveness and submissiveness is true to human experience, either spiritually or psychologically. Second, his covenantal theology moderates the polarities from the start. Without the Promethean vision of human mastery and dominion, the temptation to hubris can be contained without recourse to what Hartman calls "the ultimate principle of authoritarian religion," the claim that God's will is inscrutable.[14]

> The enormous elation that [Soloveitchik's] halakhic man feels in exercising his creative powers in the majestic gesture of subduing nature must be counteracted by the move of sacrificial surrender based on the *Akedah*. I would argue, however, that this drastic cure

is unnecessary because the disease need not arise in the first place. Judaism contains its own internal corrective mechanisms, which can protect against any inclination to hubris.[15]

## RESTRAINING HUBRIS: AFFIRMING FINITUDE

I would like to bring out the features of Hartman's religious anthropology that stave off the temptation to hubris even while affirming human adequacy and dignity. Hartman acknowledges the tension, running throughout the rabbinic tradition, between self-assertion and submission. Since his primary aim, at least in *A Living Covenant*, is to reconcile halakhic Judaism with modernity, he begins by emphasizing the openness of the tradition to human initiative, creativity, and freedom. His primary target is the image of the halakhic Jew as passive and submissive, bound by the yoke of the law to the authoritative teachings of the past. Against this image, Hartman offers a covenantal anthropology that makes room for human adequacy and dignity. Given his target, he emphasizes the creative, autonomous spirit of rabbinic Judaism. But his appeal to the Sinai covenant as the warrant for human initiative also implies certain restraints on the human drive for mastery and dominion. If applied to contemporary debates about genetic engineering, these restraints might help articulate the "hubris objection," and offer a corrective to the drift to deification.

The sources of restraint can be glimpsed in three themes of Hartman's religious anthropology: (1) human finitude, (2) Shabbat, and (3) idolatry. For Hartman, the celebration of human finitude means that a religious life can affirm and embrace the limits and imperfections of the world. Notwithstanding the messianic yearning that runs through the Jewish tradition, "the vitality of the covenant does not presuppose belief in messianic redemption, the immortality of the soul, or the resurrection of the dead."[16] Hartman acknowledges the perspective within Judaism that views death and suffering as a punishment for sin. From such a perspective, observing the *mitzvot* and living according to halakhah will prepare the way for divine deliverance from suffering and affliction. "Even the body's vulnerability to disease will ultimately be eliminated."[17]

Hartman does not rule out the possibility of messianic redemption, but he argues that covenantal Judaism does not require it. Moreover, he suggests that human finitude can be affirmed as an expression of the irreducible difference between God and the world. "Finite human beings who accept their creatureliness know that they remain separate from their Creator," Hartman writes. Although the human intellect may be tempted to believe that it can "be freed from finitude, and think the thoughts of God," this is an illusion that has led to dogmatism and wars in the name of truth. Our embodiment restrains this impulse and recalls us to our human situation. "Rooted in our bodies, we are always reminded of the limited, fragile, but dignified quality of human finitude."[18] A "religious sensibility that celebrates finitude and creatureliness as permanent features of covenantal life"[19] is one of the restraints internal to Hartman's vision that reins in the tendency to hubris.

### SHABBAT AND SLEEP

A second theme of restraint in Hartman's religious anthropology is the Sabbath. Like the celebration of human finitude, the obligation to keep the Sabbath serves to check our drive to dominion. "On the Sabbath, Jews celebrate God as the Creator . . . Awe, wonder, and humility are expressed by giving up mastery and control over the world for a day. Nature is not our absolute possession."[20] Sabbath observance restrains the human tendency to self-deification by releasing us from the activities of mastery and control that prevail during the rest of the week. "On the Sabbath, a person may not stand over and against the universe as a Promethean figure . . . The halakhic notion of the holiness of the Sabbath aims at controlling the human impulse to mastery by setting limits to human dominance of nature."[21] When the sun sets and the Sabbath arrives, nature ceases to be a mere instrument to human purposes:

> Halakhah prohibits my plucking a flower from my garden or doing with it as I please. At sunset the flower becomes a "thou" with a right to existence irrespective of its instrumental value for me. I stand silently before nature as before a fellow creature and not as before an object of my control. By forcing us to experience the meaning of being creatures of God, the Sabbath aims at healing the human grandiosity of technological arrogance.[22]

What are the implications of Shabbat for genetic engineering and other feats of biotechnology? Hartman's account can be interpreted in two ways—one permissive, the other restrictive: The permissive interpretation holds that nature becomes a "thou" only one day in seven, and remains a mere instrument of human desires the rest of the week. The restrictive interpretation, by contrast, would carry something of Shabbat into our everyday stance toward the natural world, and impose some limits on the project of mastery.

Of the two interpretations, the second seems more plausible, and truer to Hartman's concern with the way halakhah shapes religious character. Since the point of Shabbat is to cultivate a certain humility toward God's creation, shouldn't that humility inform our orientation to the world when our work resumes? Although Hartman does not elaborate an ethic of nature and human dominion, he clearly implies that the experience of Shabbat should shape our behavior and check our hubris throughout the week: "The Sabbath develops the characteristic of gratitude, the sense that life is a gift, and the need to give up the longing for absolute power."[23]

Even if I am right that Hartman's Shabbat teaching implies an ethic of restraint in our everyday dealings with nature, it is difficult to know which transformations of the world and of ourselves carry the risk of self-deification. One way of thinking about this question is to ask what projects of bioengineering, if successfully carried out and practiced on a wide scale, would erode our appreciation of life as a gift.

Consider a small but suggestive example: the case of sleep. Sleep is a biological necessity, not a disease in need of a cure. But suppose we devised a way of banishing sleep, or radically reducing our need for it. The possibility is not entirely hypothetical. A new drug, invented to treat narcolepsy (excessive sleepiness), is increasingly popular among people who want to stay awake for extended periods of time. Without the side effects of caffeine or other stimulants, it enables people to think and work effectively without sleep. In military use, it has enabled soldiers to function well for 40 hours, and then, after 8 hours of sleep, to fight for another 40 hours without rest.[24] Suppose such a drug were safe, and imagine that an improved version of it enabled people to forgo sleep for a week, or a month, or even a year. At what point, if any, would the use of this drug become ethically troubling? And on what grounds? From the standpoint of utility, it would surely lead to greater productivity and wealth. Worries about unfairness could be met, in principle at least, by making the drug accessible to all. And assuming its use were voluntary, no one could claim that it violated people's rights. If we would still find it troubling, it must be for reasons connected to the "hubris objection," which takes us back to Hartman's themes of Shabbat and the affirmation of human finitude.

In explaining the meaning of Shabbat, Hartman cites a *midrash* about the danger of human self-deification: When God created Adam, the angels mistook him for a divine being. "What did the Holy One, blessed be He, do? He caused sleep to fall upon him and thus all knew he was a human being."[25] Hartman reads this *midrash* as responding to the tendency of human power to blur the gap between God and human beings, a theological problem for which sleep provides the solution. "Sleep . . . destroys the illusion of omnipotence, forcing us to recognize our humanity. Sleep symbolizes a state of consciousness in which human beings give up mastery and control." He compares Adam's sleep in the *midrash* to "the restful joy of 'Sabbath sleep.'"[26] Sleep, like Shabbat, recalls us to human limits by regulating our lives according to a rhythm of rest beyond our control. To rid ourselves, by technological means, of the need for sleep would deprive us of a feature of human life that checks our impulse to mastery and dominion.

## IDOLATRY

A third source of restraint in Hartman's religious anthropology is the rejection of idolatry. He cites Maimonides' view that rejecting idolatry is central to halakhic Judaism. "Whoever denies idolatry," Maimonides writes in the *Mishneh Torah*, "confesses his faith in the whole Torah, in all the prophets and all that the prophets were commanded, from Adam to the end of time. And this is the fundamental principle of all commandments."[27]

Hartman points out that the prohibition of idolatry does not only apply to the ancient idols of pagan worship. If idolatry had no broader meaning, it would pose no threat in the modern world, and the struggle against it would be of merely antiquarian interest. The rejection of idolatry depends for its normative significance on the enduring presence of false gods, objects or pursuits that exert an appeal sufficiently seductive to inspire misplaced worship and allegiance.

What form does idolatry take in the modern world? In Talmudic times, the rabbis worried most about the worship of emperors and kings, whose sovereignty and power posed the most potent rival to religious commitment. Hartman observes that the idolatry of absolute power persists in our time in "the demand for total and uncritical allegiance to a political state."[28] This was certainly true of the great tyrannies of the twentieth century, as in the notorious cases of

Hitler's Germany and Stalin's Soviet Union. But with the fall of Communism, the locus of idolatry may have shifted. Although local tyrants and charismatic rulers still hold sway in various places, political rule today does not rivet the attention or absorb the energies or inspire the allegiance that render it a rival good to God. This is not to claim that liberal democracy has triumphed throughout the world; it is only to suggest that, in liberal and illiberal societies alike, the pull of the political is less compelling, less seductive, and therefore less capable of stirring idolatrous passions.

In the contemporary world, the idolatrous temptation has migrated from politics to other domains—consumerism, entertainment, and technology. The obsession with consumption in affluent market societies erodes the sacred by turning everything into a commodity. The entertainment industry, now global in its reach, makes idols of celebrities and promotes their worship on a scale that Roman emperors would have envied. Finally, biotechnology in the age of the genome promises not only to remedy devastating diseases but also to empower us to choose our genetic characteristics and those of our progeny. It is difficult to imagine a more exhilarating prospect, or a more demanding test of human humility and restraint. If idolatry is the ultimate sin, if arrogance and hubris are the dispositions most at odds with religious character, then the ancient struggle against self-deification is likely to find renewed occasion in our time.

# twenty-eight

# POLITICAL LIBERALISM

Rare is the work of political philosophy that provokes sustained debate. It is a measure of its greatness that John Rawls's *A Theory of Justice*[1] inspired not one debate, but three.

The first, by now a starting point for students of moral and political philosophy, is the argument between utilitarians and rights-oriented liberals. Should justice be founded on utility, as Jeremy Bentham and John Stuart Mill argue, or does respect for individual rights require a basis for justice independent of utilitarian considerations, as Kant and Rawls maintain? Before Rawls wrote, utilitarianism was the dominant view within Anglo-American moral and political philosophy. Since *A Theory of Justice*, rights-oriented liberalism has come to predominate.[2]

The second debate inspired by Rawls's work is an argument within rights-oriented liberalism. If certain individual rights are so important that even considerations of the general welfare cannot override them, it remains to ask which rights these are. Libertarian liberals, like Robert Nozick and Friedrich Hayek, argue that government should respect basic civil and political liberties, and also the right to the fruits of our labor as conferred by the market economy; redistributive policies that tax the rich to help the poor thus violate our rights.[3] Egalitarian liberals like Rawls disagree. They argue that we cannot meaningfully exercise our civil and political liberties without the provision of basic social and economic needs; government should therefore assure each person, as a matter of right, a decent level of such goods as education, income, housing, health care, and the like. The debate between the libertarian and egalitarian versions of rights-oriented liberalism, which flourished in the academy in the 1970s, corresponds roughly to the debate in American politics, familiar since the New Deal, between defenders of the market economy and advocates of the welfare state.

The third debate prompted by Rawls's work centers on an assumption shared by libertarian and egalitarian liberals alike. This is the idea that government should be neutral among competing conceptions of the good life. Despite their various accounts of what rights we have, rights-oriented liberals agree that the principles of justice that specify our rights should not depend for their justification on any particular conception of the good life.[4] This idea, central to the liberalism of Kant, Rawls, and many contemporary liberals, is summed up in the claim that the right is prior to the good.[5]

## CONTESTING THE PRIORITY OF THE RIGHT OVER THE GOOD

For Rawls, as for Kant, the right is prior to the good in two respects, and it is important to distinguish them. First, the right is prior to the good in the sense that certain individual rights "trump," or outweigh, considerations of the common good. Second, the right is prior to the good in that the principles of justice that specify our rights do not depend for their justification on any particular conception of the good life. It is this second claim for the priority of the right that prompted the most recent wave of debate about Rawlsian liberalism, an argument that has flourished in the last decade under the somewhat misleading label of the "liberal-communitarian debate."

A number of political philosophers writing in the 1980s took issue with the notion that justice can be detached from considerations of the good. Challenges to contemporary rights-oriented liberalism found in the writings of Alasdair MacIntyre,[6] Charles Taylor,[7] Michael Walzer,[8] and also in my own work,[9] are sometimes described as the "communitarian" critique of liberalism. The term "communitarian" is misleading, however, insofar as it implies that rights should rest on the values or preferences that prevail in any given community at any given time. Few, if any, of those who have challenged the priority of the right are communitarians in this sense.[10] The question is not whether rights should be respected, but whether rights can be identified and justified in a way that does not presuppose any particular conception of the good. At issue in the third wave of debate about Rawls's liberalism is not the relative weight of individual and communal claims, but the terms of relation between the right and the good.[11] Those who dispute the priority of the right argue that justice is relative to the good, not independent of it. As a philosophical matter, our reflections about justice cannot reasonably be detached from our reflections about the nature of the good life and the highest human ends. As a political matter, our deliberations about justice and rights cannot proceed without reference to the conceptions of the good that find expression in the many cultures and traditions within which those deliberations take place.

Much of the debate about the priority of the right has focused on competing conceptions of the person and of how we should understand our relation to our ends. Are we, as moral agents, bound only by the ends and roles we choose for ourselves, or can we sometimes be obligated to fulfill certain ends we have not chosen—ends given by nature or God, for example, or by our identities as members of families, peoples, cultures, or traditions? In various ways, those who have criticized the priority of right have resisted the notion that we can make sense of our moral and political obligations in wholly voluntarist or contractual terms.

In *A Theory of Justice*, Rawls linked the priority of the right to a voluntarist, or broadly Kantian, conception of the person. According to this conception, we are not simply defined as the sum of our desires, as utilitarians assume, nor are we beings whose perfection consists in realizing certain purposes or ends given by nature, as Aristotle held. Rather, we are free and independent selves, unbound by antecedent moral ties, capable of choosing our ends for ourselves. This is the conception of the person that finds expression in the ideal of the state as a neutral framework. It is precisely because we are free and independent selves, capable of choosing our own ends, that we need a framework of rights that is neutral among ends. To base rights on some conception of the good would impose on some the values of others and so fail to respect each person's capacity to choose his or her own ends.

This conception of the person, and its link to the case for the priority of the right, are expressed throughout *A Theory of Justice*. Its most explicit statement comes toward the end of the book, in Rawls's account of "the good of justice." There Rawls argues, following Kant, that teleological doctrines are "radically misconceived" because they relate the right and the good in the wrong way:

> We should not attempt to give form to our life by first looking to the good independently defined. It is not our aims that primarily reveal our nature but rather the principles that we would acknowledge to govern the background conditions under which these aims are to be formed and the manner in which they are to be pursued. For the self is prior to the ends which are affirmed by it; even a dominant end must be chosen from among numerous possibilities . . . We should therefore reverse the relation between the right and the good proposed by teleological doctrines and view the right as prior.[12]

In *A Theory of Justice*, the priority of the self to its ends supports the priority of the right to the good. "A moral person is a subject with ends he has chosen, and his fundamental preference is for conditions that enable him to frame a mode of life that expresses his nature as a free and equal rational being as fully as circumstances permit."[13] The notion that we are free and independent selves, unclaimed by prior moral ties, assures that considerations of justice will always outweigh other, more particular aims. In an eloquent expression of Kantian liberalism, Rawls explains the moral importance of the priority of the right in the following terms:

The desire to express our nature as a free and equal rational being can be fulfilled only by acting on the principles of right and justice as having first priority . . . It is acting from this precedence that expresses our freedom from contingency and happenstance. Therefore in order to realize our nature we have no alternative but to plan to preserve our sense of justice as governing our other aims. This sentiment cannot be fulfilled if it is compromised and balanced against other ends as but one desire among the rest . . . How far we succeed in expressing our nature depends upon how consistently we act from our sense of justice as finally regulative. What we cannot do is express our nature by following a plan that views the sense of justice as but one desire to be weighed against others. For this sentiment reveals what the person is, and to compromise it is not to achieve for the self free reign but to give way to the contingencies and accidents of the world.[14]

In different ways, those who disputed the priority of the right took issue with Rawls's conception of the person as a free and independent self, unencumbered by prior moral ties.[15] They argued that a conception of the self given prior to its aims and attachments could not make sense of certain important aspects of our moral and political experience. Certain moral and political obligations that we commonly recognize—such as obligations of solidarity, for example, or religious duties—may claim us for reasons unrelated to a choice. Such obligations are difficult to dismiss as merely confused, and yet difficult to account for if we understand ourselves as free and independent selves, unbound by moral ties we have not chosen.[16]

## DEFENDING THE PRIORITY OF THE RIGHT OVER THE GOOD

In *Political Liberalism,* Rawls defends the priority of the right over the good. He sets aside, for the most part, issues raised in the first two waves of debate, about utility versus rights and libertarian versus egalitarian notions of distributive justice. *Political Liberalism* focuses instead on issues posed by the third wave of debate, about the priority of the right.

Given the controversy over the Kantian conception of the person that supports the priority of the right, at least two lines of reply are possible. One is to defend liberalism by defending the Kantian conception of the person; the other is to defend liberalism by detaching it from the Kantian conception. In *Political Liberalism,* Rawls adopts the second course. Rather than defend the Kantian conception of the person as a moral ideal, he argues that liberalism as he conceives it does not depend on that conception of the person after all. The priority of the right over the good does not presuppose any particular conception of the person, not even the one advanced in Part III of *A Theory of Justice.*

### Political Versus Comprehensive Liberalism

The case for liberalism, Rawls now argues, is political, not philosophical or metaphysical, and so does not depend on controversial claims about the nature of the self (pp. 29–35). The priority of the right over the good is not the application to politics of Kantian moral philosophy, but a practical response to the familiar fact that people in modern democratic societies typically disagree about the good. Because people's moral and religious convictions are unlikely to converge, it is more reasonable to seek agreement on principles of justice that are neutral with respect to those controversies (pp. xvi–xvii).

Central to Rawls's revised view is the distinction between political liberalism and liberalism as part of a comprehensive moral doctrine (pp. 154–158). Comprehensive liberalism affirms liberal political arrangements in the name of certain moral ideals, such as autonomy or individuality or self-reliance. Examples of liberalism as a comprehensive moral doctrine include the liberal visions of Kant and John Stuart Mill.[17] As Rawls acknowledges, the version of liberalism presented in *A Theory of Justice* is also an instance of comprehensive liberalism. "An essential feature of a well-ordered society associated with justice as fairness is that all its citizens endorse this conception on the basis of what I now call a comprehensive philosophical doctrine" (p. xvi). It is this feature that Rawls now revises, by recasting his theory as a "political conception of justice" (p. xvi).

Unlike comprehensive liberalism, political liberalism refuses to take sides in the moral and religious controversies that arise from comprehensive doctrines, including controversies about conceptions of the self. "Which moral judgments are true, all things considered, is not a matter for political liberalism" (p. xx). "To maintain impartiality between comprehensive doctrines, it does not specifically address the moral topics on which those doctrines divide" (p. xxviii). Given the difficulty of securing agreement on any comprehensive conception, it is unreasonable to expect that, even in a well-ordered society, all people will support liberal institutions for the same reason—as expressing the priority of the self to its ends, for example. Political liberalism abandons this hope as unrealistic and contrary to the aim of basing justice on principles that adherents of various moral and religious conceptions can accept. Rather than seek a philosophical foundation for principles of justice, political liberalism seeks the support of an "overlapping consensus" (p. 134). This means that different people can be persuaded to endorse liberal political arrangements, such as equal basic liberties, for different reasons, reflecting the various comprehensive moral and religious conceptions they espouse. Because political liberalism does not depend for its justification on any one of those moral or religious conceptions, it is presented as a "freestanding" view; it "applies the principle of toleration to philosophy itself" (p. 10).

Although political liberalism renounces reliance on the Kantian conception of the person, it does not do without a conception of the person altogether. As Rawls acknowledges, some such conception is necessary to the idea of the original position, the hypothetical social contract that gives rise to the principles of justice. The way to think about justice, Rawls argued in *A Theory of Justice,* is to ask which principles would be agreed to by persons who found themselves gathered in an initial situation of equality, each in temporary ignorance of his or her race and class, religion and gender, aims and attachments.[18] But in order for this way of thinking about justice to carry weight, the design of the original position must reflect something about the sort of persons we actually are, or would be in a just society.

One way of justifying the design of the original position would be to appeal to the Kantian conception of the person that Rawls advanced in Part III of *A Theory of Justice.* If our capacity to choose our ends is more fundamental to our nature as moral persons than are the particular ends we choose, if "it is not our aims that primarily reveal our nature but rather the principles that we would acknowledge to govern the background conditions under which these aims are to be formed,"[19] if "the self is prior to the ends which are affirmed by it,"[20] then it makes sense to think about justice from the standpoint of persons deliberating prior to any knowledge of the ends they will pursue. If "a moral person is a subject with ends he has chosen, and his fundamental preference is for conditions that enable him to frame a mode of life that expresses his nature as a free and equal rational being as fully as circumstances permit,"[21] then the original position can be justified as an expression of our moral personality and the "fundamental preference" that flows from it.

Once Rawls disavows reliance on the Kantian conception of the person, however, this way of justifying the original position is no longer available. But this raises a difficult question: what reason remains for insisting that our reflections about justice should proceed without reference to our purposes and ends? Why must we "bracket," or set aside, our moral and religious convictions, our conceptions of the good life? Why should we not base the principles of justice that govern the basic structure of society on our best understanding of the highest human ends?

## The Political Conception of the Person

Political liberalism replies as follows: the reason we should think about justice from the standpoint of persons who abstract from their ends is not that this procedure expresses our nature as free and independent selves given prior to our ends. Rather, this way of thinking about justice is warranted by the fact that, for *political* purposes, though not necessarily for all moral purposes, we should think of ourselves as free and independent citizens, unclaimed by prior duties or obligations (pp. 29–35). For political liberalism, what justifies the design of the original position is a "political conception of the person" (p. 29). The political conception of the person embodied in the original position closely parallels the Kantian conception of the person, with the important difference that its scope is limited to our public identity, our identity as citizens. Thus, for example, our freedom as citizens means that our public identity is not claimed or defined by the ends we espouse at any given time. As free persons, citizens view themselves "as independent from and not identified with any particular such conception with its scheme of final ends" (p. 30). Our public identity is not affected by changes over time in our conceptions of the good.

In our personal or nonpublic identity, Rawls allows, we may regard our "ends and attachments very differently from the way the political conception supposes" (p. 31). There, persons may find themselves claimed by loyalties and commitments "they believe they would not, indeed could and should not, stand apart from and evaluate objectively. They may regard it as simply unthinkable to view themselves apart from certain religious, philosophical, and moral convictions, or from certain enduring attachments and loyalties" (p. 31). But however encumbered we may be in our personal identities, however claimed by moral or religious convictions, we must bracket our encumbrances in public, and regard ourselves, *qua* public selves, as independent of any particular loyalties or attachments or conceptions of the good (p. 31).

A related feature of the political conception of the person is that we are "self-authenticating sources of valid claims" (p. 32). The claims we make as citizens carry weight, whatever they are, simply by virtue of our making them (provided they are not unjust). That some claims may reflect high moral or religious ideals, or notions of patriotism and the common good, while others express mere interests or preferences, is not relevant from the standpoint of political liberalism. From a political point of view, claims founded on duties and obligations of citizenship or solidarity or religious faith are just things people want—nothing more, nothing less. Their validity as political claims has nothing to do with the moral importance of the goods they affirm, but consists solely in the fact that someone asserts them. Even divine commandments and imperatives of conscience count as "self-authenticating" claims, politically speaking.[22] This ensures that even those who regard themselves as claimed by moral or religious or communal obligations are nonetheless, for political purposes, unencumbered selves.

This political conception of the person explains why, according to political liberalism, we should reflect about justice as the original position invites us to do, in abstraction from our ends. But this raises a further question: why should we adopt the standpoint of the political conception of the person in the first place? Why should our political identities not express the moral and religious and communal convictions we affirm in our personal lives? Why insist on the separation between our identity as citizens and our identity as moral persons more broadly conceived? Why, in deliberating about justice, should we set aside the moral judgments that inform the rest of our lives?

Rawls's answer is that this separation or "dualism" between our identity as citizens and our identity as persons "originates in the special nature of democratic political culture" (p. xxi). In traditional societies, people sought to shape political life in the image of their comprehensive moral and religious ideals. But in a modern democratic society like our own, marked as it is by a plurality of moral and religious views, we typically distinguish between our public and personal identities. Confident though I may be of the truth of the moral and religious ideals I espouse, I do not insist that these ideals be reflected in the basic structure of society. Like other aspects of political liberalism, the political conception of the person as a free and independent self is "implicit in the public political culture of a democratic society" (p. 13).

But suppose Rawls is right, and the liberal self-image he attributes to us is implicit in our political culture. Would this provide sufficient grounds for affirming it, and for adopting the conception of justice it supports? Some have read Rawls's recent writings as suggesting that justice as fairness, being a political conception of justice, requires no moral or philosophical justification apart from an appeal to the shared understandings implicit in our political culture. Rawls seemed to invite this interpretation when he wrote, in an article published after *A Theory of Justice* but before *Political Liberalism*, as follows:

> What justifies a conception of justice is not its being true to an order antecedent to and given to us, but its congruence with our deeper understanding of ourselves and our aspirations, and our realization that, given our history and the traditions embedded in our public life, it is the most reasonable doctrine for us.[23]

Richard Rorty, in an insightful article, interprets (and welcomes) Rawls's revised view as "thoroughly historicist and antiuniversalist."[24] Although *A Theory of Justice* seemed to base justice on a Kantian conception of the person, Rorty writes, Rawls's liberalism "no longer seems committed to a philosophical account of the human self, but only to a historico-sociological description of the way we live now."[25] On this view, Rawls is not "supplying philosophical foundations for democratic institutions, but simply trying to systematize the principles and intuitions typical of American liberals."[26] Rorty endorses what he takes to be Rawls's pragmatic turn, a turn away from the notion that liberal political arrangements require a philosophical justification, or "extrapolitical grounding" in a theory of the human subject. "Insofar as justice becomes the first virtue of a society," Rorty writes, "the need for such legitimation may gradually cease to be felt. Such a society will become accustomed to the thought that social policy needs no more authority than successful accommodation among individuals, individuals who find themselves heir to the same historical traditions and faced with the same problems."[27]

In *Political Liberalism*, Rawls pulls back from this purely pragmatic account. Although justice as fairness begins "by looking to the public culture itself as the shared fund of implicitly recognized basic ideas and principles" (p. 8), it does not affirm these principles simply on the grounds that they are widely shared. Though Rawls argues that his principles of justice could gain the support of an overlapping consensus, the overlapping consensus he seeks "is not a mere modus vivendi" (p. 147), or compromise among conflicting views. Adherents of different moral and religious conceptions begin by endorsing the principles of justice for reasons drawn from within their own conceptions. But, if all goes well, they come to support those principles as expressing important political values. As people learn to live in a pluralist society governed by liberal institutions, they acquire virtues that strengthen their commitment to liberal principles.

> The virtues of political cooperation that make a constitutional regime possible are . . . very great virtues. I mean, for example, the virtues of tolerance and being ready to meet others halfway, and the virtue of reasonableness and the sense of fairness. When these vir-

tues are widespread in society and sustain its political conception of justice, they constitute a very great public good. (p. 157)

Rawls emphasizes that affirming liberal virtues as a great public good and encouraging their cultivation is not the same as endorsing a perfectionist state based on a comprehensive moral conception. It does not contradict the priority of the right over the good. The reason is that political liberalism affirms liberal virtues for political purposes only—for their role in supporting a constitutional regime that protects people's rights. Whether and to what extent these virtues should figure in people's moral lives generally is a question that political liberalism does not claim to answer (pp. 194–195).

### ASSESSING POLITICAL LIBERALISM

If *Political Liberalism* defends the priority of right by detaching it from the Kantian conception of the person, how convincing is its defense? As I shall try to argue, *Political Liberalism* rescues the priority of the right from controversies about the nature of the self only at the cost of rendering it vulnerable on other grounds. Specifically, I shall try to show that liberalism conceived as a political conception of justice is open to three objections.

First, notwithstanding the importance of the "political values" to which Rawls appeals, it is not always reasonable to bracket, or set aside for political purposes, claims arising from within comprehensive moral and religious doctrines. Where grave moral questions are concerned, whether it is reasonable to bracket moral and religious controversies for the sake of political agreement partly depends on which of the contending moral or religious doctrines is true.

Second, for political liberalism, the case for the priority of the right over the good depends on the claim that modern democratic societies are characterized by a "fact of reasonable pluralism" about the good (p. xvii). Though it is certainly true that people in modern democratic societies hold a variety of conflicting moral and religious views, it cannot be said that there is a "fact of reasonable pluralism" about morality and religion that does not also apply to questions of justice.

Third, according to the ideal of public reason advanced by political liberalism, citizens may not legitimately discuss fundamental political and constitutional questions with reference to their moral and religious ideals. But this is an unduly severe restriction that would impoverish political discourse and rule out important dimensions of public deliberation.

## Bracketing Grave Moral Questions

Political liberalism insists on bracketing our comprehensive moral and religious ideals for political purposes, and on separating our political from our personal identities. The reason is this: in modern democratic societies like ours, where people typically disagree about the good life, bracketing our moral and religious convictions is necessary if we are to secure social cooperation on the basis of mutual respect. But this raises a question that political liberalism cannot answer within its own terms. Even granting the importance of securing social cooperation on the basis of mutual respect, what is to guarantee that this interest is always so important as to outweigh any competing interest that could arise from within a comprehensive moral or religious view?

One way of assuring the priority of the political conception of justice (and hence the priority of the right) is to deny that any of the moral or religious conceptions it brackets could be true.[28] But this would implicate political liberalism in precisely the sort of philosophical claim it seeks to avoid. Time and again Rawls emphasizes that political liberalism does not depend on skepticism about the claims of comprehensive moral and religious doctrines. If political liberalism therefore allows that some such doctrines might be true, then what is to assure that none can generate values sufficiently compelling to burst the brackets, so to speak, and morally outweigh the political values of toleration, fairness, and social cooperation based on mutual respect?

One might reply that political values and values arising from within comprehensive moral and religious doctrines address different subjects. Political values, one might say, apply to the basic structure of society and to constitutional essentials, whereas moral and religious values apply to the conduct of personal life and voluntary associations. But if it were simply a difference of subject matter, no conflict between political values and moral and religious values could ever arise, and there would be no need to assert, as Rawls repeatedly does, that in a constitutional democracy governed by political liberalism, "political values normally outweigh whatever nonpolitical values conflict with them" (p. 146).

The difficulty of asserting the priority of "political values" without reference to the claims of morality and religion can be seen by considering two political controversies that bear on grave moral and religious questions. One is the contemporary debate about abortion rights. The other is the famous debate between Abraham Lincoln and Stephen Douglas over popular sovereignty and slavery.

Given the intense disagreement over the moral permissibility of abortion, the case for seeking a political solution that brackets the contending moral and religious issues—that is neutral with respect to them—would seem especially strong. But whether it is reasonable to bracket, for political purposes, the comprehensive moral and religious doctrines at stake largely depends on which of those doctrines is true. If the doctrine of the Catholic Church is true, if human life in the relevant moral sense does begin at conception, then bracketing the moral-theological question when human life begins is far less reasonable than it would be on rival moral and religious assumptions. The more confident we are that fetuses are, in the relevant moral sense, different from babies, the more confident we can be in affirming a political conception of justice that sets aside the controversy about the moral status of fetuses.

The political liberal might reply that the political values of toleration and equal citizenship for women are sufficient grounds for concluding that women should be free to choose for themselves whether to have an abortion; government should not take sides on the moral and religious controversy over when human life begins.[29] But if the Catholic Church is right about the moral status of the fetus, if abortion is morally tantamount to murder, then it is not clear why the political values of toleration and women's equality, important though they are, should prevail. If the Catholic doctrine is true, the political liberal's case for the priority of political values must become an instance of just-war theory; he or she would have to show why these values should prevail even at the cost of some 1.5 million civilian deaths each year.

Of course, to suggest the impossibility of bracketing the moral-theological question of when human life begins is not to argue against a right to abortion. It is simply to show that the case for abortion rights cannot be neutral with respect to that moral and religious controversy. It must engage rather than avoid the comprehensive moral and religious doctrines at stake. Liberals often resist this engagement because it violates the priority of the right over the good. But the abortion debate shows that this priority cannot be sustained. The case for respecting a woman's right to decide for herself whether to have an abortion depends on showing—as I believe can be shown—that there is a relevant moral difference between aborting a fetus at a relatively early stage of development and killing a child.

A second illustration of the difficulty with a political conception of justice that tries to bracket controversial moral questions is offered by the 1858 debates between Abraham Lincoln and Stephen Douglas. Douglas's argument for the doctrine of popular sovereignty is perhaps the most famous case in American history for bracketing a controversial moral question for the sake of political agreement. Because people were bound to disagree about the morality of slavery, Douglas argued, national policy should be neutral on that question. The doctrine of popular sovereignty he defended did not judge slavery right or wrong, but left the people of each territory free to make their own judgments. "To throw the weight of federal power into the scale, either in favor of the free or the slave states," would violate the fundamental principles of the Constitution and run the risk of civil war. The only hope of holding the country together, he argued, was to agree to disagree, to bracket the moral controversy over slavery and respect "the right of each state and each territory to decide these questions for themselves."[30]

Lincoln argued against Douglas's case for a political conception of justice. Policy should express rather than avoid a substantive moral judgment about slavery. Though Lincoln was not an abolitionist, he believed government should treat slavery as the moral wrong that it was, and prohibit its extension to the territories. "The real issue in this controversy—the one pressing upon every mind—is the sentiment on the part of one class that looks upon the institution of slavery *as a wrong,* and of another class that *does not* look upon it as a wrong."[31] Lincoln and the Republican party viewed slavery as a wrong and insisted that it "*be treated* as a wrong, and one of the methods of treating it as a wrong is to *make provision that it shall grow no larger.*"[32]

Whatever his personal moral views, Douglas claimed that, for political purposes at least, he was agnostic on the question of slavery; he did not care whether slavery was "voted up or voted down."[33] Lincoln replied that it was reasonable to bracket the question of the morality of slavery only on the assumption that it was not the moral evil he regarded it to be. Any man can advocate political neutrality

> who does not see anything wrong in slavery, but no man can logically say it who does see a wrong in it; because no man can logically

say he don't care whether a wrong is voted up or voted down. He may say he don't care whether an indifferent thing is voted up or down, but he must logically have a choice between a right thing and a wrong thing. He contends that whatever community wants slaves has a right to have them. So they have if it is not a wrong. But if it is a wrong, he cannot say people have a right to do wrong.[34]

The debate between Lincoln and Douglas was not primarily about the morality of slavery, but about whether to bracket a moral controversy for the sake of political agreement. In this respect, their debate over popular sovereignty is analogous to the contemporary debate over abortion rights. As some contemporary liberals argue that government should not take a stand one way or the other on the morality of abortion, but let each woman decide the question for herself, so Douglas argued that national policy should not take a stand one way or the other on the morality of slavery, but let each territory decide the question for itself. There is of course the difference that in the case of abortion rights, those who would bracket the substantive moral question typically leave the choice to the individual, while in the case of slavery, Douglas's way of bracketing was to leave the choice to the territories.

But Lincoln's argument against Douglas was an argument against bracketing as such, at least where grave moral questions are at stake. Lincoln's point was that the political conception of justice defended by Douglas depended for its plausibility on a particular answer to the substantive moral question it claimed to bracket. This point applies with equal force to those arguments for abortion rights that claim to take no side in the controversy over the moral status of the fetus. Even in the face of so dire a threat to social cooperation as the prospect of civil war, Lincoln argued that it made neither moral nor political sense to bracket the most divisive moral controversy of the day.

I say, where is the philosophy or the statesmanship based on the assumption that we are to quit talking about it . . . and that the public mind is all at once to cease being agitated by it? Yet this is the policy . . . that Douglas is advocating—that we are to care nothing about it! I ask you if it is not a false philosophy? Is it not a false statesmanship that undertakes to build up a system of policy upon the basis of caring nothing about *the very thing that every body does care the most about?*[35]

Present-day liberals will surely resist the company of Douglas and want national policy to oppose slavery, presumably on the grounds that slavery violates people's rights. The question is whether liberalism conceived as a political conception of justice can make this claim consistent with its own strictures against appeals to comprehensive moral ideals. For example, a Kantian liberal can oppose slavery as a failure to treat persons as ends in themselves, worthy of respect. But this argument, resting as it does on a Kantian conception of the person, is unavailable to political liberalism. Other historically important arguments against slavery are unavailable to political liberalism for similar reasons. American abolitionists of the 1830s and 1840s, for example, typically cast their arguments in religious terms, arguments that political liberalism cannot invoke.

How, then, can political liberalism escape the company of Douglas and oppose slavery without presupposing some comprehensive moral view? It might be replied that Douglas was wrong to seek social peace at any price; not just any political agreement will do. Even conceived as a political conception, justice as fairness is not merely a modus vivendi. Given the principles and self-understandings implicit in our political culture, only an agreement on terms that treat persons fairly, as free and equal citizens, can provide a reasonable basis for social cooperation. For us twentieth-century Americans, at least, the rejection of slavery is a settled matter. The historical demise of Douglas's position is by now a fact of our political tradition that any political agreement must take as given.

This appeal to the conception of citizenship implicit in our political culture might explain how political liberalism can oppose slavery today; our present political culture was importantly shaped, after all, by the Civil War, Reconstruction, the adoption of the Thirteenth, Fourteenth, and Fifteenth Amendments, *Brown v. Board of Education*,[36] the civil rights movement, the Voting Rights Act,[37] and so on. These experiences, and the shared understanding of racial equality and equal citizenship they formed, provide ample grounds for holding that slavery is at odds with American political and constitutional practice as it has developed over the past century.

But this does not explain how political liberalism could oppose slavery in 1858. The notions of equal citizenship implicit in American political culture of the mid-nineteenth century were arguably hospitable to the institution of slavery. The Declaration of Independence proclaimed that all men are created equal, endowed by their Creator with certain unalienable rights, but Douglas argued, not implausibly, that the signers of the Declaration were asserting the right of the colonists to be free of British rule, not the right of their Negro slaves to equal citizenship.[38] The Constitution itself did not prohibit slavery, but to the contrary accommodated it by allowing states to count three-fifths of their slave population for apportionment purposes,[39] providing that Congress could not prohibit the slave trade until 1808,[40] and requiring the return of fugitive slaves.[41] And in the notorious *Dred Scott* case,[42] the Supreme Court upheld the property rights of slaveholders in their slaves and ruled that African-Americans were not citizens of the United States.[43] To the extent that political liberalism refuses to invoke comprehensive moral ideals and relies instead on notions of citizenship implicit in the political culture, it would have a hard time explaining, in 1858, why Lincoln was right and Douglas was wrong.

## The Fact of Reasonable Pluralism

The abortion debate today and the Lincoln-Douglas debate of 1858 illustrate the way a political conception of justice must presuppose some answer to the moral questions it purports to bracket, at least where grave moral questions are concerned. In cases such as these, the priority of the right over the good cannot be sustained. A further difficulty with political liberalism concerns the reason it gives for asserting the priority of the right over the good in the first place. For Kantian liberalism, the asymmetry between the right and the good arises from a certain conception of the person. Because we must think of ourselves as moral subjects given prior to our aims and attachments, we must regard the right as regulative with respect to the particular ends we affirm; the right is prior to the good because the self is prior to its ends.

For political liberalism, the asymmetry between the right and the good is not based on a Kantian conception of the person but instead on a certain feature of modern democratic societies. Rawls describes this feature as "the fact of reasonable pluralism" (p. xvii). "A modern democratic society is characterized not simply by a pluralism of comprehensive religious, philosophical, and moral doctrines but by a pluralism of incompatible yet reasonable comprehensive doctrines. No one of these doctrines is affirmed by citizens generally" (p. xvi). Nor is it likely that sometime in the foreseeable future this pluralism will cease to hold. Disagreement about moral and religious questions is not a temporary condition but "the normal result of the exercise of human reason" under free institutions (p. xvi).

Given the "fact of reasonable pluralism," the problem is to find principles of justice that free and equal citizens can affirm despite their moral, philosophical, and religious differences. "This is a problem of political justice, not a problem about the highest good" (p. xxv). Whatever principles it generates, the solution to this problem must be one that upholds the priority of the right over the good. Otherwise, it will fail to provide a basis for social cooperation among adherents of incompatible but reasonable moral and religious convictions.

But here there arises a difficulty. For even if the fact of reasonable pluralism is true, the asymmetry between the right and the good depends on a further assumption. This is the assumption that, despite our disagreements about morality and religion, we do not have, or on due reflection would not have, similar disagreements about justice. Political liberalism must assume not only that the exercise of human reason under conditions of freedom will produce disagreements about the good life, but also that the exercise of human reason under conditions of freedom will *not* produce disagreements about justice. The "fact of reasonable pluralism" about morality and religion only creates an asymmetry between the right and the good when coupled with the further assumption that there is no comparable "fact of reasonable pluralism" about justice.

It is not clear, however, that this further assumption is justified. We need only look around us to see that modern democratic societies are teeming with disagreements about justice. Consider, for example, contemporary debates about affirmative action, income distribution and tax fairness, health care, immigration, gay rights, free speech versus hate speech, and capital punishment, to name just a few. Or consider the divided votes and conflicting opinions of Supreme Court justices in cases involving religious liberty, freedom of speech, privacy rights, voting rights, the rights of the accused, and so on. Do not these debates display a "fact of reasonable pluralism" about justice? If so, how does the pluralism about justice that prevails in modern democratic societies differ from the pluralism about morality and religion? Is there reason to think that, sometime in the foreseeable future, our disagreements about justice will dissolve even as our disagreements about morality and religion persist?

The political liberal might reply by distinguishing two different kinds of disagreement about justice. There are disagreements about what the principles of justice should be and disagreements about how these principles should be applied. Many of our disagreements about justice, it might be argued, are of the second kind. Although we generally agree, for example, that freedom of speech is among the basic rights and liberties, we disagree about whether the right to free speech should protect racial epithets, or violent pornographic depictions, or commercial advertising, or unlimited contributions to political campaigns. These disagreements, vigorous and even intractable though they may be, are consistent with our agreeing at the level of principle that a just society includes a basic right to free speech. Our disagreements about morality and religion, by contrast, might be seen as more fundamental. They reflect incompatible conceptions of the good life, it might be argued, not disagreements about how to put into practice a conception of the good life that commands, or on reflection would command, widespread agreement. If our controversies about justice concern the application of principles we share or would share on due reflection, while our controversies about morality and religion run deeper, then the asymmetry between the right and the good advanced by political liberalism would be vindicated.

But with what confidence can this contrast be asserted? Do all of our disagreements about justice concern the application of principles we share or would share on due reflection, rather than the principles themselves? What of our debates about distributive justice? Here it would seem that our disagreements are at the level of principle, not application. Some maintain, consistent with Rawls's difference principle, that only those social and economic inequalities that improve the condition of the least-advantaged members of society are just. They argue, for example, that government must ensure the provision of certain basic needs, such as income, education, health care, housing, and the like, so that all citizens will be able meaningfully to exercise their basic liberties. Others reject the difference principle. Libertarians argue, for example, that it may be a good thing for people to help those less fortunate than themselves, but that this should be a matter of charity, not entitlement. Government should not use its coercive power to redistribute income and wealth, but should respect people's rights to exercise their talents as they choose, and to reap their rewards as defined by the market economy.[44]

The debate between liberal egalitarians like Rawls and libertarians like Robert Nozick and Milton Friedman is a prominent feature of political argument in modern democratic societies. This debate reflects disagreement about what the correct principle of distributive justice is, not disagreement about how to apply the difference principle. But this would suggest that there exists in democratic societies a "fact of reasonable pluralism" about justice as well as about morality and religion. And if this is the case, the asymmetry between the right and the good does not hold.

Political liberalism is not without a reply to this objection, but the reply it must make departs from the spirit of toleration it otherwise evokes. Rawls's reply must be that, although there is a fact of pluralism about distributive justice, there is no fact of *reasonable* pluralism.[45] Unlike disagreements about morality and religion, disagreements about the validity of the difference principle are not reasonable; libertarian theories of distributive justice would not be sustained on due reflection. Our differences about distributive justice, unlike our differences of morality and religion, are not the natural outcome of the exercise of human reason under conditions of freedom.

At first glance, the claim that disagreements about distributive justice are not reasonable may seem arbitrary, even harsh, at odds with political liberalism's promise to apply "the principle of toleration to philosophy itself" (p. 10). It contrasts sharply with Rawls's apparent generosity toward differences of morality and religion. These differences, Rawls repeatedly writes, are a normal, indeed desirable feature of modern life, an expression of human diversity that only the oppressive use of state power can overcome (pp. 303–304). Where comprehensive moralities are concerned, "it is not to be expected that conscientious persons with full powers of reason, even after free discussion, will all arrive at the same conclusion" (p. 58). Since the exercise of human reason produces a plurality of reasonable moral and religious doctrines, "it is unreasonable or worse to want to use the sanctions of state power to correct, or to punish, those who disagree with us" (p. 138). But this spirit of toleration does not extend to our disagreements about justice. Because disagreements between, say, libertarians and advocates of the difference principle do not reflect a reasonable pluralism, there is no objection to using state power to implement the difference principle.

Intolerant though it may seem at first glance, the notion that theories of distributive justice at odds with the difference principle are not reasonable, or that libertarian theories of justice would not survive due reflection, is no arbitrary claim. To the contrary, in *A Theory of Justice* Rawls offers a rich array of compelling arguments on behalf of the difference principle and against libertarian conceptions: the distribution of talents and assets that enables some to earn more and others less in the market economy is arbitrary from a moral point of view; so is the fact that the market happens to prize and reward, at any given moment, the talents you or I may have in abundance; libertarians would agree that distributive shares should not be based on social status or accident of birth (as in aristocratic or caste societies), but the distribution of talents given by nature is no less arbitrary; the notion of freedom that libertarians invoke can be meaningfully exercised only if persons' basic social and economic needs are met; if people deliberated about distributive justice without reference to their own interests, or without prior knowledge of their talents and the value of those talents in the market economy, they would agree that the natural distribution of talents should not be the basis of distributive shares; and so on.[46]

My point is not to rehearse Rawls's argument for the difference principle, but only to recall the kind of reasons he offers. Viewing justification as a process of mutual adjustment between principles and considered judgments that aims at a "reflective equilibrium,"[47] Rawls tries to show that the difference principle is more reasonable than the alternative offered by libertarians. To the extent that his arguments are convincing—as I believe they are—and to the extent they can be convincing to citizens of a democratic society, the principles they support are properly embodied in public policy and law. Disagreement will doubtless remain. Libertarians will not fall silent or disappear. But their disagreement need not be regarded as a "fact of reasonable pluralism" in the face of which government must be neutral.

But this leads to a question that goes to the heart of political liberalism's claim for the priority of the right over the good: if moral argument or reflection of the kind Rawls deploys enables us to conclude, despite the persistence of conflicting views, that some principles of justice are more reasonable than others, what guarantees that reflection of a similar kind is not possible in the case of moral and religious controversy? If we can reason about controversial principles of distributive justice by seeking a reflective equilibrium, why can we not reason in the same way about conceptions of the good? If it can be shown that some conceptions of the good are more reasonable than others, then the persistence of disagreement would not necessarily amount to a "fact of reasonable pluralism" that requires government to be neutral.

Consider, for example, the controversy in our public culture about the moral status of homosexuality, a controversy based in comprehensive moral and religious doctrines. Some maintain that homosexuality is sinful, or at least morally impermissible; others argue that homosexuality is morally permissible, and in some cases gives expression to important human goods. Political liberalism insists that neither of these views about the morality of homosexuality should play a role in public debates about justice or rights. Government must be neutral with respect to them. This means that those who abhor homosexuality may not seek to embody their view in law; it also means that proponents of gay rights may not base their arguments on the notion that homosexuality is morally defensible. From the standpoint of political liberalism, each of these approaches would wrongly base the right on some conception of the good; each would fail to respect the "fact of reasonable pluralism" about comprehensive moralities.

But does the disagreement in our society about the moral status of homosexuality constitute a "fact of reasonable pluralism" any more than does the disagreement about distributive justice? According to political liberalism, the libertarian's objection to the difference principle does not constitute a "fact of reasonable pluralism" that requires government neutrality, because there are good reasons to conclude, on due reflection, that the arguments for the difference principle are more convincing than the ones that support libertarianism. But isn't it possible to conclude, with equal or greater confidence, that on due reflection, the arguments for the moral permissibility of homosexuality are more convincing than the arguments against it? Consistent with the search for a reflective equilibrium among principles and considered judgments, such reflection might proceed by assessing the reasons advanced by those who assert the moral inferiority of homosexual to heterosexual relations.

Those who consider homosexuality immoral often argue, for example, that homosexuality cannot fulfill the highest end of human sexuality, the good of procreation.[48] To this it might be replied that many heterosexual relations also do not fulfill this end, such as contracepted sex, or sex among sterile couples, or sex among partners beyond the age of reproduction. This might suggest that the good of procreation, important though it is, is not necessary to the moral worth of human sexual relations; the moral worth of sexuality might also consist in the love and responsibility it expresses, and these goods are possible in homosexual as well as heterosexual relations. Opponents might reply that homosexuals are often promiscuous, and hence less likely to realize the goods of love and responsibility. The reply to this claim might consist in an empirical showing to the contrary, or in the observation that the existence of promiscuity does not argue against the moral worth of homosexuality as such, only against certain instances of it.[49] Heterosexuals also engage in promiscuity and other practices at odds with the goods that confer on sexuality its moral worth, but this fact does not lead us to abhor heterosexuality as such. And so on.

My point is not to offer a full argument for the moral permissibility of homosexuality, only to suggest the way such an argument might proceed. Like Rawls's argument for the difference principle, it would proceed by seeking a reflective equilibrium between our principles and considered judgments, adjusting each in the light of the other. That the argument for the morality of homosexuality, unlike the argument for the difference principle, explicitly addresses claims about human ends and conceptions of the good does not mean that the same method of moral reasoning cannot proceed. It is unlikely, of course, that such moral reasoning would produce conclusive or irrefutable answers to moral and religious controversies. But as Rawls acknowledges, such reasoning does not produce irrefutable answers to questions of justice either; a more modest notion of justification is appropriate. "In philosophy questions at the most fundamental level are not usually settled by conclusive argument," writes Rawls, referring to arguments about justice. "What is obvious to some persons and accepted as a basic idea is unintelligible to others. The way to resolve the matter is to consider after due reflection which view, when fully worked out, offers the most coherent and convincing account" (p. 53). The same could be said of arguments about comprehensive moralities.

If it is possible to reason about the good as well as the right, then political liberalism's claim for the asymmetry between the right and good is undermined. For political liberalism, this asymmetry rests on the assumption that our moral and religious disagreements reflect a "fact of reasonable pluralism" that our disagreements about justice do not. What enables Rawls to maintain that our disagreements about distributive justice do not amount to a "fact of reasonable pluralism" is the strength of the arguments he advances on behalf of the difference principle and against libertarianism. But the same could be said of other controversies, including, conceivably, some moral and religious controversies. The public culture of democratic societies includes controversies about justice and comprehensive moralities alike. If government can affirm the justice of redistributive policies even in the face of disagreement by libertarians, why cannot government affirm in law, say, the moral legitimacy of homosexuality, even in the face of disagreement by those who regard homosexuality as sin?[50] Is Milton Friedman's objection to redistributive policies a less "reasonable pluralism" than Pat Robertson's objection to gay rights?

With morality as with justice, the mere fact of disagreement is no evidence of the "reasonable pluralism" that gives rise to the demand that government must be neutral. There is no reason in principle why in any given case, we might not conclude that, on due reflection, some moral or religious doctrines are more plausible than others. In such cases, we would not expect all disagreement to disappear, nor would we rule out the possibility that further deliberation might one day lead us to revise our view. But neither would we have grounds to insist that our deliberations about justice and rights may make no reference to moral or religious ideals.

## The Limits of Liberal Public Reason

Whether it is possible to reason our way to agreement on any given moral or political controversy is not something we can know until we try. This is why it cannot be said in advance that controversies about comprehensive moralities reflect a "fact of reasonable pluralism" that controversies about justice do not. Whether a moral or political controversy reflects reasonable but incompatible conceptions of the good, or whether it can be resolved by due reflection and deliberation, can only be determined by reflecting and deliberating. But this raises a further difficulty with political liberalism. For the political life it describes leaves little room for the kind of public deliberation necessary to test the plausibility of contending comprehensive moralities—to persuade others of the merits of our moral ideals, to be persuaded by others of the merits of theirs.

Although political liberalism upholds the right to freedom of speech, it severely limits the kinds of arguments that are legitimate contributions to political debate, especially debate about constitutional essentials and basic justice.[51] This limitation reflects the priority of the right over the good. Not only may government not endorse one or another conception of the good, but citizens may not even introduce into political discourse their comprehensive moral or religious convictions, at least when debating matters of justice and rights (pp. 15–16).[52] Rawls maintains that this limitation is required by the "ideal of public reason" (p. 218). According to this ideal, political discourse should be conducted solely in terms of "political values" that all citizens can reasonably be expected to accept. Because citizens of democratic societies do not share comprehensive moral and religious conceptions, public reason should not refer to such conceptions (pp. 216–220).

The limits of public reason do not apply, Rawls allows, to our personal deliberations about political questions, or to the discussions we may have as members of associations such as churches and universities, where "religious, philosophical, and moral considerations" (p. 215) may properly play a role.

> But the ideal of public reason does hold for citizens when they engage in political advocacy in the public forum, and thus for members of political parties and for candidates in their campaigns and for other groups who support them. It holds equally for how citizens are to vote in elections when constitutional essentials and matters of basic justice are at stake. Thus, the ideal of public reason not only governs the public discourse of elections insofar as the issues involve those fundamental questions, but also how citizens are to cast their vote on these questions. (p. 215)

How can we know whether our political arguments meet the requirements of public reason, suitably shorn of any reliance on moral or religious convictions? Rawls offers a novel test. "To check whether we are following public reason we might ask: how would our argument strike us presented in the form of a supreme court opinion?" (p. 254). For citizens of a democracy to allow their political discourse about fundamental questions to be informed by moral and religious ideals is no more legitimate, Rawls suggests, than for a judge to read his or her moral and religious beliefs into the Constitution.

The restrictive character of this notion of public reason can be seen by considering the sorts of political arguments it would rule out. In the debate about abortion rights, those who believe that the fetus is a person from the moment of conception and that abortion is therefore murder could not seek to persuade their fellow citizens of this view in open political debate. Nor could they vote for a law that would restrict abortion on the basis of this moral or religious conviction. Although adherents of the Catholic teaching on abortion could discuss the issue of abortion rights in religious terms within their church, they could not do so in a political campaign, or on the floor of the state legislature, or in the halls of Congress. Nor for that matter could opponents of the Catholic teaching on abortion argue their case in the political arena. Relevant though it clearly is to the question of abortion rights, Catholic moral doctrine cannot be debated in the political arena that political liberalism defines.

The restrictive character of liberal public reason can also be seen in the debate about gay rights. At first glance, these restrictions might seem a service to toleration. Those who consider homosexuality immoral and therefore unworthy of the privacy rights accorded heterosexual intimacy could not legitimately voice their views in public debate. Nor could they act on their belief by voting against laws that would protect gay men and lesbians from discrimination. These beliefs reflect comprehensive moral and religious convictions and so may not play a part in political discourse about matters of justice.

But the demands of public reason also limit the arguments that can be advanced in support of gay rights, and so restrict the range of reasons that can be invoked on behalf of toleration. Those who oppose antisodomy laws of the kind at issue in *Bowers v. Hardwick*[53] cannot argue that the moral judgments embodied in those laws are wrong, only that the law is wrong to embody any moral judgments at all.[54] Advocates of gay rights cannot contest the substantive moral judgment lying behind antisodomy laws or seek, through open political debate, to persuade their fellow citizens that homosexuality is morally permissible, for any such argument would violate the canons of liberal public reason.

The restrictive character of liberal public reason is also illustrated by the arguments offered by American abolitionists of the 1830s and 1840s. Rooted in evangelical Protestantism, the abolitionist movement argued for the immediate emancipation of the slaves on the grounds that slavery is a heinous sin.[55] Like the argument of some present-day Catholics against abortion rights, the abolitionist case against slavery was explicitly based on a comprehensive moral and religious doctrine.

In a puzzling passage, Rawls tries to argue that the abolitionist case against slavery, religious though it was, did not violate the ideal of liberal public reason. If a society is not well-ordered, he explains, it may be necessary to resort to comprehensive moralities in order to bring about a society in which public discussion is conducted solely in terms of "political values" (p. 251 n.41). The religious arguments of the abolitionists can be justified as hastening the day when religious arguments would no longer play a legitimate role in public discourse. The abolitionists "did not go against the ideal of public reason," Rawls concludes, "provided they thought, or on reflection would have thought (as they certainly could have thought), that the comprehensive reasons they appealed to were required to give sufficient strength to the political conception to be subsequently realized" (p. 251).

It is difficult to know what to make of this argument. There is little reason to suppose, and I do not think Rawls means to suggest, that the abolitionists opposed slavery on secular political grounds and simply used religious arguments to win popular support. Nor is there reason to think that the abolitionists sought by their agitation to make a world safe for secular political discourse. Nor can it be assumed that, even in retrospect, the abolitionists would take pride in having contributed, by their religious arguments against slavery, to the emergence of a society inhospitable to religious argument in political debate. If anything the opposite is more likely the case, that by advancing religious arguments against so conspicuous an injustice as slavery, the evangelicals who inspired the abolitionist movement were hoping to encourage Americans to view other political questions in moral and religious terms as well. In any case, it is reasonable to suppose that the abolitionists meant what they said, that slavery is wrong because it is contrary to God's law, a heinous sin, and that this is the reason it should be ended. Absent some extraordinary assumptions, it is difficult to interpret their argument as consistent with the priority of the right over the good, or with the ideal of public reason advanced by political liberalism.

The cases of abortion, gay rights, and abolitionism illustrate the severe restrictions liberal public reason would impose on political debate. Rawls argues that these restrictions are justified as essential to the maintenance of a just society, in which citizens are governed by principles they may reasonably be expected to endorse, even in the light of their conflicting comprehensive moralities. Although public reason requires that citizens decide fundamental political questions without reference "to the whole truth as they see it" (p. 216), this restriction is justified by the political values, such as civility and mutual respect, that it makes possible. "The political values realized by a well-ordered constitutional regime are very great values and not easily overridden and the ideals they express are not to be lightly abandoned" (p. 218). Rawls compares his case for restrictive public reason with the case for restrictive rules of evidence in criminal trials. There too we agree to decide without reference to the whole truth as we know it—through illegally obtained evidence, for example—in order to advance other goods (pp. 218–219).

The analogy between liberal public reason and restrictive rules of evidence is instructive. Setting aside the whole truth as we know it carries moral and political costs, for criminal trials and for public reason alike. Whether those costs are worth incurring depends on how significant they are compared to the goods they make possible, and whether those goods can be secured in some other way. To assess restrictive rules of evidence, for example, we need to know how many criminals go free as a result and whether less restrictive rules would unduly burden innocent persons suspected of a crime, lead to undesirable law enforcement practices, violate important ideals such as respect for privacy (exclusionary rule) and spousal intimacy (spousal privilege), and so on. We arrive at rules of evidence by weighing the importance of deciding in the light of the whole truth against the importance of the ideals that would be sacrificed if all evidence were admissible.

Similarly, to assess restrictive rules of public reason, we need to weigh their moral and political costs against the political values they are said to make possible; we must also ask whether these political values—of toleration, civility, and mutual respect—could be achieved under less-restrictive rules of public reason. Although political liberalism refuses to weigh the political values it affirms against competing values that may arise from within comprehensive moralities, the case for restrictive rules of public reason must presuppose some such comparison.

The costs of liberal public reason are of two kinds. The strictly moral costs depend on the validity and importance of the moral and religious doctrines liberal public reason requires us to set aside when deciding questions of justice. These costs will necessarily vary from case to case. They will be at their highest when a political conception of justice sanctions toleration of a grave moral wrong, such as slavery in the case of Douglas's argument for popular sovereignty. In the case of abortion, the moral cost of bracketing is high if the Catholic doctrine is correct, otherwise much lower. This suggests that, even given the moral and political importance of toleration, the argument for tolerating a given practice must take some account of the moral status of the practice, as well as the good of avoiding social conflict, letting people decide for themselves, and so on.

This way of thinking about the moral cost of liberal public reason is admittedly at odds with political liberalism itself. Although Rawls repeatedly states that a political conception of justice expresses values that normally outweigh whatever other values conflict with them (pp. 138, 146, 156, 218), he also insists that this involves no substantive comparison of the political values to the moral and religious values they override.

> We need not consider the claims of political justice against the claims of this or that comprehensive view; nor need we say that political values are intrinsically more important than other values and that is why the latter are overridden. Having to say that is just what we hope to avoid. (p. 157)

But because political liberalism allows that comprehensive moral and religious doctrines can be true, such comparisons cannot reasonably be avoided.

Beyond the moral costs of liberal public reason are certain political costs. These costs are becoming increasingly apparent in the politics of those countries, notably the United States, whose public discourse most closely approximates the ideal of public reason advanced by political liberalism. With a few notable exceptions, such as the civil rights movement, American political discourse in recent decades has come to reflect the liberal resolve that government be neutral on moral and religious questions, that fundamental questions of public policy be debated and decided without reference to any particular conception of the good.[56] But democratic politics cannot long abide a public life as abstract and decorous, as detached from moral purposes, as Supreme Court opinions are supposed to be. A politics that brackets morality and religion too completely soon generates its own disenchantment. Where political discourse lacks moral resonance, the yearning for a public life of larger meanings finds undesirable expressions. Groups like the Moral Majority seek to clothe the naked public square with narrow, intolerant moralisms. Fundamentalists rush in where liberals fear to tread. The disenchantment also assumes more secular forms. Absent a political agenda that addresses the moral dimension of public questions, public attention becomes riveted on the private vices of public officials. Public discourse becomes increasingly preoccupied with the scandalous, the sensational, and the confessional as purveyed by tabloids, talk shows, and eventually the mainstream media as well.

It cannot be said that the public philosophy of political liberalism is wholly responsible for these tendencies. But its vision of public reason is too spare to contain the moral energies of a vital democratic life. It thus creates a moral void that opens the way for the intolerant and the trivial and other misguided moralisms.

If liberal public reason is too restrictive, it remains to ask whether a more spacious public reason would sacrifice the ideals that political liberalism seeks to promote, notably mutual respect among citizens who hold conflicting moral and religious views. Here it is necessary to distinguish two conceptions of mutual respect. On the liberal conception, we respect our fellow citizens' moral and religious convictions by ignoring them (for political purposes), by leaving them undisturbed, or by carrying on political debate without reference to them. To admit moral and religious ideals into political debate about justice would undermine mutual respect in this sense.

But this is not the only, or perhaps even the most plausible way of understanding the mutual respect on which democratic citizenship depends. On a different conception of respect—call it the deliberative conception—we respect our fellow citizen's moral and religious convictions by engaging, or attending to them—sometimes by challenging and contesting them, sometimes by listening and learning from them—especially if those convictions bear on important political questions. There is no guarantee that a deliberative mode of respect will lead in any given case to agreement or even to appreciation for the moral and religious convictions of others. It is always possible that learning more about a moral or religious doctrine will lead us to like it less. But the respect of deliberation and engagement affords a more spacious public reason than liberalism allows. It is also a more suitable ideal for a pluralist society. To the extent that our moral and religious disagreements reflect the ultimate plurality of human goods, a deliberative mode of respect will better enable us to appreciate the distinctive goods our diffcrent lives express.

# twenty-nine

# REMEMBERING RAWLS

John Rawls, America's greatest political philosopher, died last week at the age of 81. Rawls taught philosophy at Harvard from 1962 to 1994. He is best known for his book *A Theory of Justice* (1971), which offers the most compelling account of liberal political principles since John Stuart Mill. In the 1950s and 1960s, Anglo-American political theory was virtually moribund, consigned to irrelevance by linguistic analysis and moral relativism. Rawls revived political theory by showing that it was possible to argue rationally about justice, rights, and political obligation. He inspired a new generation to take up classic questions of morality and politics.

*A Theory of Justice* is not an easy read. But its distinctive contribution can be seen in the way it develops three key ideas: individual rights, the social contract, and equality. Before Rawls wrote, the dominant conception of justice in the English-speaking world was utilitarian: Laws and public policies should seek the greatest good for the greatest number. Rawls rejected this view as failing to respect individual rights. Suppose, for example, that a large majority despises a minority religion and wants it banned. Utilitarian principles might support the ban. But Rawls argued that certain rights are so important that the desires of the majority should not override them.

If rights cannot be based on utilitarian principles, how can they be justified? Rawls answered this question with a version of social-contract theory based on a novel thought experiment: Imagine making a social contract without knowing whether we are rich or poor; strong or weak; healthy or unhealthy; without knowing our race, religion, gender, or class. The principles we would choose behind this "veil of ignorance" would be just, Rawls argued, because they would not be tainted by unfair bargaining conditions. If we imagined ourselves behind the veil of ignorance, Rawls maintained, we would choose two principles to govern society. The first would require equal basic liberties for all citizens (speech, association, religion). The second would permit only those inequalities of income and wealth that work to the advantage of the least well-off members of society. So it might be just for doctors to make more money than janitors, for example, but only if such pay differentials were necessary to attract talented people to medicine, and only if doing so helped the least advantaged members of society. This is Rawls's famous "difference principle."

Some critics of Rawls's egalitarianism reply that people behind the veil of ignorance might gamble on inequality and choose a principle that gives people the right to keep whatever wealth they can accumulate. Rawls's best answer to this challenge steps outside the contract argument and draws on the moral impulse behind his theory: The reason we do not deserve, as a matter of right, the benefits that flow from the exercise of our talents is that we cannot take credit for those talents in the first place. That a market society values the skills some people happen to have is their good fortune, not a measure of their moral merit. So we should not regard the bounty and prestige the market bestows on athletes and anchormen, entrepreneurs and stockbrokers, academics and professionals, as a reward for superior virtue. Instead, we should design our tax and educational system so the accidents of nature and social circumstance work for the benefit of everyone. This challenges a meritocratic assumption that runs deep in American life: that success and virtue go hand in hand, that the United States is wealthy because it is good. If Rawls is right, the meritocratic assumption should give way to a more generous stance toward those less favored by fortune and circumstance.

Shortly after his retirement, Rawls joined me for a discussion with students in an undergraduate course I teach on justice. I asked him about Immanuel Kant, his philosophical hero. Despite the similarities in their philosophies, did Kant go wrong in concluding that the equality of human beings is "perfectly consistent with the utmost inequality" of material possessions? Rawls answered with a wry evasion: "I want to say that Kant is really, truly a very great man. One doesn't even think of criticizing him without being aware of that. No, I wouldn't say that Kant goes wrong . . . He was ahead of his time. That you get anything at all out of East Prussia in the eighteenth century is wonderful. And that you get Immanuel Kant is a miracle."

It is something of a miracle, or at least a surprise, to find an American philosopher mentioned in the company of Thomas Hobbes, John Locke, Jean-Jacques Rousseau, Karl Marx, and John Stuart Mill. Political philosophy is one of the few intellectual fields to which America's contribution has been meager. Some attribute this dearth to the success of American democracy. Wars of religion, decaying empires, failed states, and class struggles offer richer fare for philosophy than do stable institutions. This may be why the most notable expressions of American political thought have come not from philosophers but from participants in American public life: Thomas Jefferson, James Madison, Alexander Hamilton, John C. Calhoun, Abraham Lincoln, Frederick Douglass, Jane Addams, Oliver Wendell Holmes, Louis D. Brandeis. Rawls is one of the few nonpractitioners of politics to loom large in American political thought.

When Alexis de Tocqueville visited the United States in the 1830s, he observed that "no country in the civilized world pays less attention to philosophy than the United States." Tocqueville's observation was borne out 170 years later by the public notice of Rawls's death.

The major newspapers of Europe—*Le Monde* in France, *The Times,* *The Guardian, The Independent,* and *The Daily Telegraph* in England—all marked the passing of America's political philosopher with more extensive obituaries than appeared in *The New York Times* or *The Washington Post.* This may suggest that Rawls's egalitarianism has more resonance for European welfare states than for America's market-driven society. But it also reflects the fact that philosophy continues to play a more prominent role in the public discourse of the Old World than the New.

Rawls's modesty was legendary, as was his kindness to students and junior colleagues. I first read *A Theory of Justice* as a graduate student at Oxford in 1975 and made it the subject of my dissertation. When I came to Harvard as a young assistant professor in the government department, I had never met the figure whose great work on liberalism I had studied. Shortly after I arrived, my phone rang. A hesitant voice on the other end said, "This is John Rawls, R-A-W-L-S." It was as if God himself had called to invite me to lunch and spelled his name just in case I didn't know who he was.

# thirty

# THE LIMITS OF COMMUNITARIANISM

## WHERE COMMUNITARIANISM GOES WRONG

Along with the works of other contemporary critics of liberal political theory, notably Alasdair MacIntyre,[1] Charles Taylor,[2] and Michael Walzer,[3] my book *Liberalism and the Limits of Justice (LLJ)* has come to be identified with the "communitarian" critique of rights-oriented liberalism. Since part of my argument is that contemporary liberalism offers an inadequate account of community, the term fits to some extent. In many respects, however, the label is misleading. The "liberal-communitarian" debate that has raged among political philosophers in recent years describes a range of issues, and I do not always find myself on the communitarian side.

The debate is sometimes cast as an argument between those who prize individual liberty and those who think the values of the community or the will of the majority should always prevail, or between those who believe in universal human rights and those who insist there is no way to criticize or judge the values that inform different cultures and traditions. Insofar as "communitarianism" is another name for majoritarianism, or for the idea that rights should rest on the values that predominate in any given community at any given time, it is not a view I would defend.

What is at stake in the debate between Rawlsian liberalism and the view I advance in *LLJ* is not whether rights are important but whether rights can be identified and justified in a way that does not presuppose any particular conception of the good life. At issue is not whether individual or communal claims should carry greater weight but whether the principles of justice that govern the basic structure of society can be neutral with respect to the competing moral and religious convictions its citizens espouse. The fundamental question, in other words, is whether the right is prior to the good.

For Rawls, as for Kant, the priority of the right over the good stands for two claims, and it is important to distinguish them. The first is the claim that certain individual rights are so important that even the general welfare cannot override them. The second is the claim that the principles of justice that specify our rights do not depend for their justification on any particular conception of the good life, or, as Rawls has put it more recently, on any "comprehensive" moral or religious conception. It is the second claim for the priority of right, not the first, that *LLJ* seeks to challenge.

The notion that justice is relative to the good, not independent of it, connects *LLJ* to writings by others commonly identified as the "communitarian critics" of liberalism. But there are two versions of the claim that justice is relative to the good, and only one of them is "communitarian" in the usual sense. Much of the confusion that has beset the liberal-communitarian debate arises from failing to distinguish the two versions.

One way of linking justice with conceptions of the good holds that principles of justice derive their moral force from values commonly espoused or widely shared in a particular community or tradition. This way of linking justice and the good is communitarian in the sense that the values of the community define what counts as just or unjust. On this view, the case for recognizing a right depends on showing that such a right is implicit in the shared understandings that inform the tradition or community in question. There can be disagreement, of course, about what rights the shared understandings of a particular tradition actually support; social critics and political reformers can interpret traditions in ways that challenge prevailing practices. But these arguments always take the form of recalling a community to itself, of appealing to ideals implicit but unrealized in a common project or tradition.

A second way of linking justice with conceptions of the good holds that principles of justice depend for their justification on the moral worth or intrinsic good of the ends they serve. On this view, the case for recognizing a right depends on showing that it honors or advances some important human good. Whether this good happens to be widely prized or implicit in the traditions of the community would not be decisive. The second way of tying justice to conceptions of the good is therefore not, strictly speaking, communitarian. Since it rests the case for rights on the moral importance of the purposes or ends rights promote, it is better described as teleological, or (in the jargon of contemporary philosophy) perfectionist. Aristotle's political theory is an example: Before we can define people's rights or investigate "the nature of the ideal constitution," he writes, "it is necessary for us first to determine the nature of the most desirable way of life. As long as that remains obscure, the nature of the ideal constitution must also remain obscure."[4]

Of the two ways of linking justice to conceptions of the good, the first is insufficient. The mere fact that certain practices are sanctioned by the traditions of a particular community is not enough to make them just. To make justice the creature of convention is to deprive it of its critical character, even if allowance is made for competing interpretations of what the relevant tradition requires. Arguments about justice and rights have an unavoidably judgmental aspect. Liberals who think the case for rights should be neutral toward substantive moral and religious doctrines and communitarians who think rights should rest on prevailing social values make a similar mistake; both try to avoid passing judgment on the content of the ends that rights promote. But these are not the only alternatives. A third possibility, more plausible in my view, is that rights depend for their justification on the moral importance of the ends they serve.

## THE RIGHT TO RELIGIOUS LIBERTY

Consider the case of religious liberty. Why should the free exercise of religion enjoy special constitutional protection? The liberal might reply that religious liberty is important for the same reason individual liberty in general is important—so that people may be free to live autonomously, to choose and pursue their values for themselves. According to this view, government should uphold religious liberty in order to respect persons as free and independent selves, capable of choosing their own religious convictions. The respect the liberal invokes is not, strictly speaking, respect for religion, but respect for the self whose religion it is, or respect for the dignity that consists in the capacity to choose one's religion freely. On the liberal view, religious beliefs are worthy of respect, not in virtue of their content but instead in virtue of being "the product of free and voluntary choice."[5]

This way of defending religious liberty puts the right before the good; it tries to secure the right to religious freedom without passing judgment on the content of people's beliefs or on the moral importance of religion as such. But the right to religious liberty is not best understood as a particular case of a more general right to individual autonomy. Assimilating religious liberty to a general right to choose one's own values misdescribes the nature of religious conviction and obscures the reasons for according the free exercise of religion special constitutional protection. Construing all religious convictions as products of choice may miss the role that religion plays in the lives of those for whom the observance of religious duties is a constitutive end, essential to their good and indispensable to their identity. Some may view their religious beliefs as matters of choice, others not. What makes a religious belief worthy of respect is not its mode of acquisition—be it choice, revelation, persuasion, or habituation—but its place in a good life, or the qualities of character it promotes, or (from a political point of view) its tendency to cultivate the habits and dispositions that make good citizens.

To place religious convictions on a par with the various interests and ends an independent self may choose makes it difficult to distinguish between claims of conscience, on the one hand, and mere preferences, on the other. Once this distinction is lost, the right to demand of the state a special justification for laws that burden the free exercise of religion is bound to appear as nothing more weighty than "a private right to ignore generally applicable laws."[6] If an orthodox Jew is granted the right to wear a yarmulke while on duty in an air force health clinic, then what about servicemen who want to wear other head coverings prohibited by military dress codes?[7] If Native Americans have a right to the sacramental use of peyote, then what can be said to those who would violate state drug laws for recreational purposes?[8] If Sabbath observers are granted the right to schedule their day off from work on the day corresponding to their Sabbath, does not the same right have to be accorded those who want a certain day off to watch football?[9]

Assimilating religious liberty to liberty in general reflects the liberal aspiration to neutrality. But this generalizing tendency does not always serve religious liberty well. It confuses the pursuit of preferences with the performance of duties. It therefore ignores the special concern of religious liberty with the predicament of conscientiously encumbered selves—claimed by duties they cannot choose to renounce, even in the face of civil obligations that may conflict.

But why, it might be asked, should the state accord special respect to conscientiously encumbered selves? Part of the reason is that for government to burden practices central to the self-definition of its citizens is to frustrate them more profoundly than to deprive them of interests less central to the projects that give meaning to their lives. But encumbrance as such is not a sufficient basis for special respect.

Defining projects and commitments can range from the admirable and heroic to the obsessive and demonic. Situated selves can display solidarity and depth of character or prejudice and narrow-mindedness.

The case for according special protection to the free exercise of religion presupposes that religious belief, as characteristically practiced in a particular society, produces ways of being and acting that are worthy of honor and appreciation—either because they are admirable in themselves or because they foster qualities of character that make good citizens. Unless there were reason to think religious beliefs and practices contribute to morally admirable ways of life, the case for a right to religious liberty would be weakened. Pragmatic considerations would, of course, remain; upholding religious liberty could still be justified as a way of avoiding the civil strife that can result when church and state are too closely intertwined. But the moral justification for a right to religious liberty is unavoidably judgmental; the case for the right cannot wholly be detached from a substantive judgment about the moral worth of the practice it protects.

## THE RIGHT TO FREE SPEECH

The link between rights and the goods rights protect is also illustrated by recent debates about free speech and hate speech. Should neo-Nazis have the right to march in Skokie, Illinois, a community with large numbers of Holocaust survivors?[10] Should white-supremacist groups be allowed to promulgate their racist views?[11] Liberals argue that government must be neutral toward the opinions its citizens espouse. Government can regulate the time, place, and manner of speech—it can ban a noisy rally in the middle of the night—but it cannot regulate the content of speech. To ban offensive or unpopular speech imposes on some the values of others and so fails to respect each citizen's capacity to choose and express his or her own opinions.

Liberals can, consistent with their view, restrict speech likely to cause significant harm—violence, for example. But in the case of hate speech, what counts as harm is constrained by the liberal conception of the person. According to this conception, my dignity consists not in any social roles I inhabit but instead in my capacity to choose my roles and identities for myself. But this means that my dignity could never be damaged by an insult directed against a group with which I identify. No hate speech could constitute harm in itself, for on the liberal view, the highest respect is the self-respect of a self independent of its aims and attachments. For the unencumbered self, the grounds of self-respect are antecedent to any particular ties and attachments, and so beyond the reach of an insult to "my people." The liberal would therefore oppose restrictions on hate speech, except where it is likely to provoke some actual physical harm—some harm independent of the speech itself.

The communitarian might reply that the liberal conception of harm is too narrow. For people who understand themselves as defined by the ethnic or religious group to which they belong, an insult to the group can inflict a harm as real and as damaging as some physical harms. For Holocaust survivors, the neo-Nazi march was aimed at provoking fears and memories of unspeakable horrors that reached to the core of their identities and life stories.

But to acknowledge the harm that hate speech can inflict does not establish that the speech should be restricted. The harm such speech inflicts has to be weighed against the good of upholding free speech. With speech as with religion, it is not enough simply to invoke the claims of thickly constituted selves. What matters is the moral importance of the speech in relation to the moral status of the settled identities the speech would disrupt or offend. If Skokie could keep out the Nazis, why could not the segregationist communities of the South keep out civil-rights marchers of the 1950s and 1960s? The Southern segregationists did not want Martin Luther King, Jr., to march in their communities any more than the residents of Skokie wanted the neo-Nazis to march in theirs. Like the Holocaust survivors, the segregationists could claim to be thickly constituted selves, bound by common memories that would be deeply offended by the marchers and their message.

Is there a principled way of distinguishing the two cases? For liberals who insist on being neutral with respect to the content of speech, and for communitarians who define rights according to the prevailing values of the communities in question, the answer must be no. The liberal would uphold free speech in both cases, and the communitarian would override it. But the need to decide both cases in the same way displays the folly of the nonjudgmental impulse liberals and communitarians share.

The obvious ground for distinguishing the cases is that the neo-Nazis promote genocide and hate, whereas Martin Luther King, Jr., sought civil rights for blacks. The difference consists in the content of the speech, in the nature of the cause. There is also a difference in the moral worth of the communities whose integrity was at stake. The shared memories of the Holocaust survivors deserve a moral deference that the solidarity of the segregationists does not. Moral discriminations such as these are consistent with common sense but at odds with the version of liberalism that asserts the priority of the right over the good and the version of communitarianism that rests the case for rights on communal values alone.

If the right to free speech depends for its justification on a substantive moral judgment about the importance of speech in relation to the risks it entails, it does not follow that judges should try, in each particular case, to assess the merits of the speech for themselves. Nor, in every case involving religious liberty, should judges undertake to assess the moral importance of the religious practice at issue. On any theory of rights, certain general rules and doctrines are desirable to spare judges the need to recur to first principles in every case that comes before them. But sometimes, in hard cases, judges cannot apply such rules without appealing directly to the moral purposes that justify rights in the first place.

One striking example is the opinion of Judge Frank Johnson in the 1965 case that permitted Martin Luther King's historic march from Selma to Montgomery. Alabama Governor George Wallace tried to prevent the march. Judge Johnson acknowledged that the states had the right to regulate the use of their highways, and that a mass march along a public highway reached "to the outer limits of what is constitutionally allowed." Nevertheless, he ordered the state to permit the march, on grounds of the justice of its cause: "The extent of the right to assemble, demonstrate and march peaceably along the highways," he wrote, "should be commensurate with the enormity of the wrongs that are being protested and petitioned against. In this case, the wrongs are enormous. The extent of the right to demonstrate against these wrongs should be determined accordingly."[12]

Judge Johnson's decision was not content-neutral; it would not have helped the Nazis in Skokie. But it aptly illustrates the difference between the liberal approach to rights and the approach that would rest rights on a substantive moral judgment of the ends rights advance.

**NOTES**
**CREDITS**
**INDEX**

### 19. Is There a Right to Assisted Suicide?

1. See "Assisted Suicide: The Philosophers' Brief," *New York Review of Books*, vol. 44, March 27, 1997.

### 21. Moral Argument and Liberal Toleration

1. I do not defend the stronger claim that the morality (or immorality) of a practice is the only relevant reason in deciding whether there should be a law against it.
2. 410 U.S. 113 (1973).
3. 478 U.S. 186 (1986).
4. Roe v. Wade, 410 U.S. 113, 162 (1973).
5. Ibid., 153.
6. Thornburgh v. American College of Obstetricians & Gynecologists, 476 U.S. 747, 777 (1986) (Stevens, J., concurring).
7. Eichbaum, "Towards an Autonomy-Based Theory of Constitutional Privacy: Beyond the Ideology of Familial Privacy," 14 *Harv. C.R.-C.L. L. Rev.* 361, 362, 365 (1979).
8. Richards, "The Individual, the Family, and the Constitution: A Jurisprudential Perspective," 55 *N.Y.U. L. Rev.* 1, 31 (1980).
9. Karst, "The Freedom of Intimate Association," 89 *Yale L.J.* 624, 641 (1980). For articles discussing the connection between privacy and autonomy rights, see also Henkin, "Privacy and Autonomy," 74 *Colum. L. Rev.* 1410 (1974); Smith, "The Constitution and Autonomy," 60 *Tex. L. Rev.* 175 (1982); Wilkinson III and White, "Constitutional Protection for Personal Lifestyles," 62 *Cornell L. Rev.* 563 (1977).
10. Karst, "The Freedom of Intimate Association," 641.
11. Carey v. Population Services Int'l, 431 U.S. 678, 687 (1977).

12. Thornburgh v. American College of Obstetricians & Gynecologists, 476 U.S. 747, 772 (1986).
13. Doe v. Bolton, 410 U.S. 179, 211 (1973) (Douglas, J., concurring) (emphasis omitted).
14. Bowers v. Hardwick, 478 U.S. 186, 205 (1986) (Blackmun, J., dissenting).
15. Whalen v. Roe, 429 U.S. 589, 599–600 (1977).
16. Warren and Brandeis, "The Right to Privacy," 4 *Harv. L. Rev.* 193 (1890).
17. Ibid., 195–196.
18. Prosser, "Privacy," 48 *Calif. L. Rev.* 383 (1960) (discussing the ensuing recognition and development of a right to privacy).
19. 367 U.S. 497 (1961).
20. Ibid., 509.
21. Ibid., 519–521 (Douglas, J., dissenting).
22. Ibid., 519.
23. Ibid., 545 (Harlan, J., dissenting).
24. Ibid., 545–546.
25. Ibid., 553.
26. Ibid., 554.
27. 381 U.S. 479 (1965).
28. Ibid., 485–486.
29. Ibid., 486.
30. 405 U.S. 438 (1972).
31. In fact, the case arose when a man was convicted for giving away a contraceptive device at a public lecture. Ibid., 440.
32. Ibid., 453.
33. *Griswold,* 381 U.S. at 485.
34. *Eisenstadt,* 405 U.S. at 453. The Court's opinion in *Eisenstadt* camouflages the shift from the old privacy to the new with a false hypothetical premise: "If under *Griswold* the distribution of contraceptives to married persons cannot be prohibited, a ban on distribution to unmarried persons would be equally impermissible." Ibid. But *Griswold* did not hold that distribution to married persons cannot be prohibited.
35. 410 U.S. 113 (1973).
36. Ibid., 153.
37. Carey v. Population Services Int'l, 431 U.S. 678 (1977).
38. Ibid., 687.
39. Ibid.

40. Ibid. (quoting *Eisenstadt,* 405 U.S. at 453) (emphasis added in *Carey*).
41. Ibid. (quoting *Roe,* 410 U.S. at 153) (emphasis added in *Carey*).
42. Ibid.
43. Ibid., 688.
44. Thornburgh v. American College of Obstetricians, 476 U.S. 747, 772 (1986).
45. Planned Parenthood v. Casey, 505 U.S. 833, 851 (1992).
46. Bowers v. Hardwick, 478 U.S. 186, 190–191 (1986).
47. Ibid., 196.
48. Ibid.
49. Ibid., 204 (Blackmun, J., dissenting) (quoting Thornburgh v. American College of Obstetricians & Gynecologists, 476 U.S. at 777 n.5 (Stevens, J., concurring) (quoting Fried, "Correspondence," 6 *Phil. and Pub. Aff.* 288–289 [1977])).
50. Ibid., 205.
51. Ibid.
52. Ibid., 211.
53. Ibid. In striking down a similar sodomy law, the New York Court of Appeals clearly expressed the idea that government must be neutral among competing conceptions of the good. "It is not the function of the Penal Law in our governmental policy to provide either a medium for the articulation or the apparatus for the intended enforcement of moral or theological values." People v. Onofre, 51 N.Y.2d 476, 488 n.3, 415 N.E.2d 936, 940 n.3, 434 N.Y.S.2d 947, 951 n.3 (1980), *cert. denied,* 451 U.S. 987 (1981).
54. Rawls, "Justice as Fairness: Political Not Metaphysical," 14 *Phil. and Pub. Aff.* 223, 245 (1985); Rorty, "The Priority of Democracy to Philosophy," in *The Virginia Statute for Religious Freedom,* 257 (M. Peterson and R. Vaughan, eds., 1988).
55. 410 U.S. 113 (1973).
56. Ibid., 159.
57. Ibid.
58. Ibid., 160–162.
59. Ibid., 162.
60. Ibid.
61. Ibid., 163.
62. 476 U.S. 747 (1986).

63. Ibid., 797 (White, J., dissenting).

64. Ibid., 796.

65. Ibid., 790. Justice Harlan suggested a similar way of bracketing the moral controversy over contraception in Poe v. Ullman, 367 U.S. 497, 547 (1961) (Harlan, J., dissenting): "The very controversial nature of these questions would, I think, require us to hesitate long before concluding that the Constitution precluded Connecticut from choosing as it has among these various views."

66. Ibid., 777 (Stevens, J., concurring).

67. Ibid., 777–778 (quoting ibid. at 794 (White, J. dissenting)).

68. 478 U.S. 186 (1986).

69. Ibid., 191.

70. The phrases are from Griswold v. Connecticut, 381 U.S. 479, 486 (1965).

71. 478 U.S. at 205 (Blackmun, J., dissenting) (emphasis added).

72. Ibid., 206.

73. Ibid., 217 (Stevens, J., dissenting) (quoting Fitzgerald v. Porter Memorial Hospital, 523 F.2d 716, 719–720 (7th Cir. 1975), *cert. denied*, 425 U.S. 916 (1976)).

74. Ibid., 218–219.

75. Hardwick v. Bowers, 760 F.2d 1202 (11th Cir. 1985), *rev'd*, 476 U.S. 747 (1986).

76. Ibid., 1211–1212.

77. Ibid., 1212 (quoting Griswold v. Connecticut, 381 U.S. 479, 486 (1965)).

78. Ibid., 1212.

79. For individualist readings of *Griswold*, see Eisenstadt v. Baird, 405 U.S. 438, 453 (1972) and Carey v. Population Services Int'l, 431 U.S. 678, 687 (1977).

80. 394 U.S. 557 (1969).

81. Ibid., 564–566, 568 ("This right to receive information and ideas, *regardless of their social worth*, is fundamental to our free society . . . The States retain broad power to regulate obscenity; that power simply does not extend to mere possession by the individual in the privacy of his own home.") (emphasis added) (citation omitted).

82. 51 N.Y.2d 476, 415 N.E.2d 936, 434 N.Y.S.2d 947 (1980), *cert. denied*, 451 U.S. 987 (1981).

83. Ibid., 487–488, 415 N.E.2d at 939–41, 434 N.Y.S.2d at 950–951.

84. Ibid., 488 n.3, 415 N.E.2d at 940 n.3, 434 N.Y.S.2d at 951 n.3.

85. Ibid.
86. Bowers v. Hardwick, 478 U.S. 186, 191 (1986).
87. Lawrence v. Texas, 539 U.S. 558 (2003).
88. Ibid., 562.
89. Ibid., 574, quoting *Casey,* 505 U.S. 833, 851 (1992).
90. Lawrence v. Texas, 567.
91. Ibid., 575.
92. Ibid., 602.
93. Ibid., 604.
94. Ibid., 602.

### 23. The Procedural Republic and the Unencumbered Self

1. An excellent example of this view can be found in Samuel Huntington, *American Politics: The Promise of Disharmony* (Cambridge, Mass.: Harvard University Press, 1981). See especially his discussion of the "ideals versus institutions" gap, pp. 10–12, 39–41, 61–84, 221–262.
2. See, for example, the conceptions of a "practice" advanced by Alasdair MacIntyre and Charles Taylor. MacIntyre, *After Virtue* (Notre Dame: University of Notre Dame Press, 1981), pp. 175–209; Taylor, "Interpretation and the Sciences of Man," *Review of Metaphysics* 25 (1971), pp. 3–51.
3. John Rawls, *A Theory of Justice* (Oxford: Oxford University Press, 1971); Immanuel Kant, *Groundwork of the Metaphysics of Morals,* trans. H. J. Paton (1785; New York: Harper and Row, 1956); Kant, *Critique of Pure Reason,* trans. Norman Kemp Smith (1781, 1787; London: Macmillan, 1929); Kant, *Critique of Practical Reason,* trans. L. W. Beck (1788; Indianapolis: Bobbs-Merrill, 1956); Kant, "On the Common Saying: 'This May Be True in Theory, But It Does Not Apply in Practice,'" in Hans Reiss, ed., *Kant's Political Writings* (1793; Cambridge: Cambridge University Press, 1970). Other recent versions of the claim for the priority of the right over good can be found in Robert Nozick, *Anarchy, State, and Utopia* (New York: Basic Books, 1974); Ronald Dworkin, *Taking Rights Seriously* (London: Duckworth, 1977); Bruce Ackerman, *Social Justice in the Liberal State* (New Haven: Yale University Press, 1980).
4. This section, and the two that follow, summarize arguments developed more fully in Michael Sandel, *Liberalism and the Limits of Justice* (Cambridge: Cambridge University Press, 1982).

5. Rawls, *A Theory of Justice*, p. 3.
6. John Stuart Mill, *Utilitarianism*, in *The Utilitarians* (1893; Garden City: Doubleday, 1973), p. 465; Mill, *On Liberty*, in *The Utilitarians*, p. 485 (originally published 1849).
7. Kant, "On the Common Saying," p. 73.
8. Kant, *Groundwork*, p. 92.
9. Kant, *Critique of Practical Reason*, p. 89.
10. Kant *Groundwork*, p. 105.
11. Kant, *Critique of Practical Reason*, p. 89.
12. Kant, *Groundwork*, p. 121.
13. Rawls, "The Basic Structure as Subject," *American Philosophical Quarterly* (1977), p. 165.
14. Rawls, *A Theory of Justice*, p. 560.
15. Rawls, "Kantian Constructivism in Moral Theory," *Journal of Philosophy* 77 (1980), p. 543.
16. Mill, *On Liberty*, p. 485.
17. Rawls, *A Theory of Justice*, pp. 101–102.
18. Croly, *The Promise of American Life* (Indianapolis: Bobbs-Merrill, 1965), pp. 270–273.
19. Beer, "Liberalism and the National Idea," *The Public Interest* (Fall 1966), pp. 70–82.
20. See, for example, Laurence Tribe, *American Constitutional Law* (Mineola: The Foundation Press, 1978), pp. 2–3.
21. See Ronald Dworkin, "Liberalism," in Stuart Hampshire, ed., *Public and Private Morality* (Cambridge: Cambridge University Press, 1978), p. 136.

### 25. The Peril of Extinction

1. George Kateb, "Nuclear Weapons and Individual Rights," *Dissent*, Spring 1986.

### 26. Dewey's Liberalism and Ours

1. Robert B. Westbrook, *John Dewey and American Democracy* (Cornell University Press, 1991); Stephen Rockefeller, *John Dewey: Religious Faith*

and *Democratic Humanism* (Columbia University Press, 1991); Jennifer Welchman, *Dewey's Ethical Thought* (Cornell University Press, 1995); Debra Morris and Ian Shapiro, eds., *John Dewey: The Political Writings* (Hackett, 1993); Richard Rorty, *Consequences of Pragmatism* (University of Minnesota Press, 1982); Richard J. Bernstein, "John Dewey on Democracy," in *Philosophical Profiles: Essays in a Pragmatic Mode* (University of Pennsylvania Press, 1986), pp. 260–272.

2. *John Dewey: The Early Works, 1882–1898,* Volumes 1–5; *John Dewey: The Middle Works, 1899–1924,* Volumes 1–15; *John Dewey: The Later Works, 1925–1953,* Volumes 1–17, edited by Jo Ann Boydston (Southern Illinois University Press, 1969–1991).

3. Dewey, "The Need for a Recovery of Philosophy" (1917), in *The Middle Works,* Volume 10.

4. Ibid.

5. Dewey, *Liberalism and Social Action* (1935), in *The Later Works,* Volume 11, p. 24.

6. Ibid., p. 25.

7. Ibid., p. 44.

8. See Rorty, *Philosophy and the Mirror of Nature* (Princeton University Press, 1979), and Rorty, *Consequences of Pragmatism* (University of Minnesota Press, 1982).

9. Richard Rorty, "The Priority of Democracy to Philosophy," in Merrill D. Peterson and Robert C. Vaughan, eds., *The Virginia Statute for Religious Freedom* (Cambridge University Press, 1988), pp. 257–282.

10. Dewey, *The Public and Its Problems* (1927), in *The Later Works,* Volume 2, p. 295.

11. Ibid., p. 314.

12. Ibid., pp. 301, 330, 308.

13. Ibid., p. 303.

14. Ibid., p. 324.

15. Ibid., p. 321.

### 27. Mastery and Hubris in Judaism

1. Halakhic Judaism is the Judaism of those who live in accordance with the precepts of Jewish law.

2. David Hartman, *A Living Covenant: The Innovative Spirit in Traditional Judaism* (New York: The Free Press, 1985), 32.

3. Ibid., 36.

4. Ibid., 3.

5. Ibid., 98.

6. Ibid., 183.

7. Ibid., 99.

8. Ibid., 96.

9. *Midrash Terumah,* chapter 2, quoted in Noam J. Zohar, *Alternatives in Jewish Bioethics* (Albany: State University of New York Press, 1997), 20–21. On religious naturalism, see Zohar, ibid., 19–36.

10. Rabbi Joseph B. Soloveitchik, *Halakhic Man,* trans. Lawrence Kaplan (Philadelphia: Jewish Publication Society of America, 1983; originally published in Hebrew, 1944), 99.

11. Ibid., 107, 109.

12. Hartman, *Living Covenant,* 79.

13. Soloveitchik, "The Lonely Man of Faith," *Tradition* 7:2 (Summer 1965), 35–36, quoted in Hartman, *Living Covenant,* 82.

14. Hartman, *Living Covenant,* 84.

15. Ibid., 88.

16. Ibid., 257.

17. Ibid., 256.

18. Ibid., 260.

19. Ibid., 18.

20. Ibid., 260.

21. David Hartman, *A Heart of Many Rooms: Celebrating the Many Voices within Judaism* (Woodstock, Vt.: Jewish Lights Publishing, 1999), 77–78.

22. Ibid., 78.

23. Ibid., 201–202.

24. Carey Goldberg, "Who Needs Sleep? New Pill Hits Scene," *Boston Globe,* Sept. 22, 2002, A1, A20.

25. Midrash Rabbah, Genesis VIII, 4,5; quoted in Hartman, *Heart of Many Rooms,* 77.

26. Ibid., 77–78.

27. *Mishneh Torah, Avodah Zarah* II, 4; quoted in Hartman, *Heart of Many Rooms,* 106.

28. Ibid., 107.

## 28. Political Liberalism

1. John Rawls, *A Theory of Justice* (1971).
2. See, e.g., H. L. A. Hart, "Between Utility and Rights," in *The Idea of Freedom*, 77 (Alan Ryan, ed., 1979).
3. See Friedrich A. Hayek, *The Constitution of Liberty* (1960); Robert Nozick, *Anarchy, State, and Utopia* (1974).
4. See Bruce A. Ackerman, *Social Justice in the Liberal State*, pp. 349–378 (1980); Ronald Dworkin, *Taking Rights Seriously*, pp. 90–100, 168–177 (1977); Charles Fried, *Right and Wrong*, pp. 114–119 (1978); Charles E. Larmore, *Patterns of Moral Complexity*, pp. 42–68 (1987); Nozick, *Anarchy, State, and Utopia*, p. 33; Rawls, *A Theory of Justice*, pp. 30–32, 446–451, 560; Ronald Dworkin, "Liberalism," in *Public and Private Morality*, pp. 113, 127–136 (Stuart Hampshire, ed., 1978); Thomas Nagel, "Moral Conflict and Political Legitimacy," *Phil. and Pub. Aff.*, 16, pp. 215, 227–237 (1987).
5. See Immanuel Kant, *Critique of Pure Reason* (Norman K. Smith, trans., St. Martin's Press, 1965) (1788); Immanuel Kant, *Groundwork of the Metaphysic of Morals* (H. J. Paton, trans., Harper & Row, 3d ed., 1964) (1785); Immanuel Kant, "On the Common Saying: 'This May Be True in Theory, but It Does Not Apply in Practice,'" in *Kant's Political Writings*, pp. 61, 73–74 (Hans Reiss, ed., and H. B. Nisbet, trans., 1970); Rawls, *A Theory of Justice*, pp. 30–32, 446–451, 560.
6. See Alasdair MacIntyre, *After Virtue* (2d ed., 1984) [hereafter cited as MacIntyre, *After Virtue*]; Alasdair MacIntyre, *Is Patriotism a Virtue?: The Lindley Lecture* (1984) [hereafter cited as MacIntyre, *Is Patriotism a Virtue?*]; Alasdair MacIntyre, *Whose Justice? Which Rationality?* (1988).
7. See Charles Taylor, "The Nature and Scope of Distributive Justice," in *Philosophy and the Human Sciences, Philosophical Papers*, 2, p. 289 (1985); Charles Taylor, *Sources of the Self: The Making of the Modern Identity* (1989) [hereafter cited as Taylor, *Sources of the Self*].
8. See Michael Walzer, *Spheres of Justice: A Defense of Pluralism and Equality* (1983).
9. See Michael J. Sandel, *Liberalism and the Limits of Justice* (1982); Michael J. Sandel, "The Procedural Republic and the Unencumbered Self," *Pol. Theory*, p. 81 (1984).
10. Michael Walzer comes close to this view when he writes: "Justice is rela-

tive to social meanings . . . A given society is just if its substantive life is lived . . . in a way faithful to the shared understandings of the members." Walzer, *Spheres of Justice*, pp. 312–313. Walzer allows, however, that prevailing practices of rights can be criticized from the standpoint of alternative interpretations of a society's shared understandings. Ibid., pp. 84–91.

11. Much of the debate about liberal political philosophy in the last decade has focused on the "communitarian" critique of liberalism, or, more broadly, on the challenge to the priority of the right over the good. The best overall account of this debate is Stephen Mulhall and Adam Swift, *Liberals and Communitarians* (1992). Edited volumes on the subject include *Communitarians and Individualism* (Shlomo Avineri and Avner de-Shalit, eds., 1992); *Liberalism and Its Critics* (Michael J. Sandel, ed., 1984); *Liberalism and the Good* (R. Bruce Douglass, Gerald M. Mara, and Henry S. Richardson, eds., 1990); *Liberalism and the Moral Life* (Nancy L. Rosenblum, ed., 1989); and *Universalism vs. Communitarianism* (David Rasmussen, ed., 1990). Notable book-length works include Daniel Bell, *Communitarianism and Its Critics* (1993); Will Kymlicka, *Liberalism, Community, and Culture* (1989); Charles E. Larmore, *Patterns of Moral Complexity* (1987); and Stephen Macedo, *Liberal Virtues: Citizenship, Virtue, and Community in Liberal Constitutionalism* (1990). The vast literature on the subject includes among others: Jeremy Waldron, "Particular Values and Critical Morality," in *Liberal Rights,* 168 (1993); C. Edwin Baker, "Sandel on Rawls," *U. Pa. L. Rev.,* 133, p. 895 (1985); Sheyla Benhabib, "Autonomy, Modernity and Community: Communitarianism and Critical Social Theory in Dialogue," in *Zwischenbetrachtungen im Prozess der Aufklaerung,* p. 373 (Axel Honneth, Thomas McCarthy, Claus Offe, and Albrecht Welmer, eds., 1989); Allen E. Buchanan, "Assessing the Communitarian Critique of Liberalism," *Ethics,* 99, p. 852 (1989); Gerald Doppelt, "Is Rawls's Kantian Liberalism Coherent and Defensible?" *Ethics,* 99, p. 815 (1989); Stephen A. Gardbaum, "Law, Politics, and the Claims of Community," *Mich. L. Rev.* 90, p. 685 (1992); Emily R. Gill, "Goods, Virtues, and the Constitution of the Self," in *Liberals on Liberalism,* p. 111 (Alfonso J. Damico, ed., 1986); Amy Gutmann, "Communitarian Critics of Liberalism," *Phil. and Pub. Aff.,* 14, p. 308 (1985); H. N. Hirsch, "The Threnody of Liberalism," *Pol. Theory,* 14, p. 423 (1986); Will Kymlicka, "Liberalism and Communitarianism," *Can.*

*J. Phil.*, 18, p. 181 (1988); Will Kymlicka, "Rawls on Teleology and Deontology," *Phil. and Pub. Aff.*, 17, p. 173 (1988); Christopher Lasch, "The Communitarian Critique of Liberalism," *Soundings*, 69, p. 60 (1986); David Miller, "In What Sense Must Socialism Be Communitarian?" *Soc. Phil. and Pol.*, 6, p. 57 (1989); Chantal Mouffe, "American Liberalism and Its Critics: Rawls, Taylor, Sandel, and Walzer," *Praxis Int'l*, 8, p. 193 (1988); Patrick Neal, "A Liberal Theory of the Good?" *Can. J. Phil.*, 17, p. 567 (1987); Jeffrey Paul and Fred D. Miller, Jr., "Communitarian and Liberal Theories of the Good," *Rev. Metaphysics*, 43, p. 803 (1990); Milton C. Regan, Jr., "Community and Justice in Constitutional Theory," *Wis. L. Rev.*, 1985, p. 1073; Richard Rorty, "The Priority of Democracy to Philosophy," in *The Virginia Statute of Religious Freedom*, pp. 257–282 (Merrill D. Peterson and Robert C. Vaughan, eds., 1988); George Sher, "Three Grades of Social Involvement," *Phil. and Pub. Aff.*, 18, p. 133 (1989); Tom Sorell, "Self, Society, and Kantian Impersonality," *Monist*, 74, p. 30 (1991); Symposium, "Law, Community, and Moral Reasoning," *Cal. L. Rev.*, 77, p. 475 (1989); Charles Taylor, "Cross-Purposes: The Liberal-Communitarian Debate," in *Liberalism and the Moral Life* (Rosenblum, ed.); Robert B. Thigpen and Lyle A. Downing, "Liberalism and the Communitarian Critique," *Am. J. Pol. Sci.*, 31, p. 637 (1987); John Tomasi, "Individual Rights and Community Virtues," *Ethics*, 101, p. 521 (1991); John R. Wallach, "Liberals, Communitarians, and the Tasks of Political Theory," *Pol. Theory*, 15, p. 581 (1987); Michael Walzer, "The Communitarian Critique of Liberalism," *Pol. Theory*, 18, p. 6 (1990); Iris M. Young, "The Ideal of Community and the Politics of Difference," *Soc. Theory and Prac.*, 12, p. 1 (1986); and Joel Feinberg, "Liberalism, Community and Tradition," *Tikkun*, May–June 1988, p. 38. Prior to *Political Liberalism*, Rawls addressed these issues in a number of essays, including "The Idea of an Overlapping Consensus," *Oxford J. Legal Stud.*, 7, p. 1 (1987); "Justice as Fairness: Political Not Metaphysical," *Phil. and Pub. Aff.*, 14, p. 223 (1985); and "The Priority of Right and Ideas of the Good," *Phil. and Pub. Aff.*, 17, p. 251 (1987). In "Political Liberalism," however, he states: "The changes in the later essays are sometimes said to be replies to criticisms raised by communitarians and others. I don't believe there is a basis for saying this" (p. xvii).

12. Rawls, *A Theory of Justice*, p. 560.

13. Ibid., p. 561.

14. Ibid., pp. 574–75.

15. The objection to the conception of the person presented in *A Theory of Justice* does not depend on failing to see the original position as a device of representation. It can be stated wholly in terms of the conception of the person presented in Part III of *A Theory of Justice*, which Rawls now recasts as a political conception. Not only critics, but also defenders of Rawls's liberalism interpreted *A Theory of Justice* as affirming a Kantian conception of the person. See, e.g., Larmore, *Patterns of Moral Complexity*, pp. 118–130.

16. See MacIntyre, *After Virtue*, pp. 190–209; MacIntyre, *Is Patriotism a Virtue?*, p. 8, passim; Sandel, *Liberalism and the Limits of Justice*, pp. 175–183; Taylor, *Sources of the Self*, p. 508.

17. For contemporary examples of comprehensive liberalism, see George Kateb, *The Inner Ocean: Individualism and Democratic Culture* (1992); and Joseph Raz, *The Morality of Freedom* (1986). Ronald Dworkin describes his view as a version of comprehensive liberalism in "Foundations of Liberal Equality," in *The Tanner Lectures on Human Values*, vol. 11, p. 1 (Grethe B. Peterson, ed., 1990).

18. See Rawls, *A Theory of Justice*, pp. 11–12.

19. Ibid., p. 560.

20. Ibid.

21. Ibid., p. 561.

22. The notion that we should regard our moral and religious duties as "self-authenticating from a political point of view" (p. 33) accords with Rawls's statement that "from the standpoint of justice as fairness, these [moral and religious] obligations are self-imposed" (*A Theory of Justice*, p. 206). But it is not clear what the justification can be on such a view for according religious beliefs or claims of conscience a special respect not accorded other preferences that people may hold with equal or greater intensity. See ibid., pp. 205–211.

23. John Rawls, "Kantian Constructivism in Moral Theory: Rational and Full Autonomy," *J. Phil.*, 77, pp. 515, 519 (1980).

24. Rorty, "The Priority of Democracy to Philosophy," pp. 257, 262.

25. Ibid., p. 265.

26. Ibid., p. 268.

27. Ibid., p. 264.

28. Thomas Hobbes, who can be interpreted as advancing a political con-

ception of justice, ensured the priority of his political conception with respect to claims arising from contending moral and religious conceptions by denying the truth of those conceptions. See Thomas Hobbes, *Leviathan*, pp. 168–183 (C. B. Macpherson, ed., Penguin Books, 1985) (1651).

29. Rawls seems to take this view in a footnote on abortion. But he does not explain why political values should prevail even if the Catholic doctrine were true (p. 243 n.32).

30. *Created Equal? The Complete Lincoln Douglas Debates of 1858*, pp. 369, 374 (Paul M. Angle, ed., 1958) [hereafter cited as *Created Equal?*].

31. Ibid., p. 390.

32. Ibid.

33. Ibid., p. 392.

34. Ibid.

35. Ibid., pp. 388–389.

36. 347 U.S. 483 (1954).

37. Voting Rights Act of 1965, 42 U.S.C. §§1971, 1973 (1988).

38. See *Created Equal?*, p. 374.

39. See U.S. Constitution, art. I, §2, cl. 3.

40. See ibid., art I, §9, cl. 1.

41. See ibid., art IV, §2, cl. 3.

42. Scott v. Sandford, 60 U.S. (19 How.) 393 (1857).

43. See ibid., pp. 404–405.

44. See Milton Friedman, *Capitalism and Freedom*, p. 200 (1962); Milton Friedman and Rose Friedman, *Free to Choose*, pp. 134–136 (1980); Hayek, *The Constitution of Liberty*, pp. 85–86, 99–100; Nozick, *Anarchy, State, and Utopia*, pp. 149, 167–174.

45. Although Rawls does not state this view explicitly, it is necessary in order to make sense of the "fact of reasonable pluralism" and the role it plays in supporting the priority of the right. He notes that reasonable disagreements may arise over what policies fulfill the difference principle, but adds, "this is not a difference about what are the correct principles but simply a difference in the difficulty of seeing whether the principles are achieved" (p. 230).

46. See Rawls, *A Theory of Justice*, pp. 72–75, 100–107, 136–142, 310–315.

47. See ibid., pp. 20–21, 48–51, 120, 577–587.

48. In this paragraph I draw on some of the arguments for and against the

morality of homosexuality that appear in John Finnis and Martha Nussbaum, "Is Homosexual Conduct Wrong?: A Philosophical Exchange," *New Republic,* Nov. 15, 1993, pp. 12–13; Stephen Macedo, "The New Natural Lawyers," *Harvard Crimson,* Oct. 29, 1993, p. 2; and Harvey C. Mansfield, "Saving Liberalism From Liberals," *Harvard Crimson,* Nov. 8, 1993, p. 2.

49. An alternative line of reply might undertake to defend promiscuity and to deny that the goods of love and responsibility are necessary to the moral worth of sexuality. From this point of view, the line of argument I suggest mistakenly seeks to defend the moral legitimacy of homosexuality by way of an analogy with heterosexuality. See Bonnie Honig, *Political Theory and the Displacement of Politics,* pp. 186–195 (1993).

50. It is possible to argue for certain gay rights on grounds that neither affirm nor deny the morality of homosexuality. The question here is whether government is justified in supporting laws or policies (such as gay marriage, for example) on grounds that affirm the moral legitimacy of homosexuality.

51. Rawls states that the limits of public reason apply to all discussions involving constitutional essentials and basic justice. As for other political questions, he writes that "it is usually highly desirable to settle political questions by invoking the values of public reason. Yet this may not always be so" (pp. 214–215).

52. This idea is repeated at several other points (pp. 215, 224, 254).

53. 478 U.S. 186 (1986).

54. See Michael J. Sandel, "Moral Argument and Liberal Toleration: Abortion and Homosexuality," *Cal. L. Rev.,* 77, pp. 521, 534–538 (1989).

55. See Eric Foner, *Politics and Ideology in the Age of the Civil War,* p. 72 (1980); Aileen S. Kraditor, *Means and Ends in American Abolitionism,* pp. 78, 91–92 (1967); James M. McPherson, *Battle Cry of Freedom: The Civil War Era,* pp. 7–8 (1988).

56. I elaborate this claim in Sandel, *Democracy's Discontent* (Harvard University Press, 1996).

### 30. The Limits of Communitarianism

1. See Alasdair MacIntyre, *After Virtue* (Notre Dame: University of Notre Dame Press, 1981).

2. See Charles Taylor, *Philosophical Papers*, vol. I: *Human Agency and Language*; vol. II: *Philosophy and the Human Sciences* (Cambridge: Cambridge University Press, 1985); and Taylor, *Sources of the Self: The Making of Modern Identity* (Cambridge, Mass.: Harvard University Press, 1989).

3. See Michael Walzer, *Spheres of Justice: A Defense of Pluralism and Equality* (New York: Basic Books, 1983).

4. *The Politics of Aristotle*, 1323a14, ed. and trans. Ernest Barker (London: Oxford University Press, 1958), p. 279.

5. The phrase is from Wallace v. Jaffree, 472 U.S. 38, 52–53 (1985): "Religious beliefs worthy of respect are the product of free and voluntary choice by the faithful."

6. The phrase is from Employment Division v. Smith, 494 U.S. 872, 886 (1990).

7. See Goldman v. Weinberger, 475 U.S. 503 (1986).

8. See Employment Division v. Smith, 494 U.S. 872 (1990).

9. See Thornton v. Caldor, Inc., 474 U.S. 703 (1985).

10. See Collin v. Smith, 447 F. Supp. 676 (1978); Collin v. Smith, 578 F.2d 1198 (1978).

11. See Beauharnais v. Illinois, 343 U.S. 250 (1952).

12. Williams v. Wallace, 240 F. Supp. 100, 108, 106 (1965).

## CREDITS

Chapter 1: Originally published in *The Atlantic Monthly,* vol. 227, March 1996; based on Michael J. Sandel, *Democracy's Discontent* (Harvard University Press, 1996).

Chapter 2: Originally published in *The New Republic,* February 22, 1988.

Chapter 3: Originally published in *The New Republic,* September 2, 1996.

Chapter 4: Originally published in *The New Republic,* October 14, 1996.

Chapter 5: Originally published in *The New York Times,* December 29, 1996.

Chapter 6: Originally published in *The New Republic,* October 26, 1998.

Chapter 7: From a talk presented at the John F. Kennedy Library, 2000, drawn from Michael J. Sandel, *Democracy's Discontent* (Harvard University Press, 1996).

Chapter 8: Originally published in *The New Republic,* March 10, 1997.

Chapter 9: Originally published in *The New Republic,* September 1, 1997.

Chapter 10: Originally published in *The New Republic,* January 19, 1998.

Chapter 11: Originally published in *The New Republic,* May 25, 1998.

Chapter 12: Originally published in *The New Republic,* April 13, 1998.

Chapter 13: Originally published in *The New Republic,* May 26, 1997.

Chapter 14: Originally published in *The New York Times,* December 15, 1997.

Chapter 15: Originally published in *The New Republic,* December 23, 1996.

Chapter 16: Originally published in *The New Republic,* December 1, 1997.

Chapter 17: Originally published in *The New Republic,* July 7, 1997.

Chapter 18: Originally published in *The New Republic,* March 2, 1998.

Chapter 19: Originally published in *The New Republic,* April 14, 1997.

Chapter 20: Originally published in the *New England Journal of Medicine,* July 15, 2004.

Chapter 21: Earlier versions of this chapter appeared in the *California Law Review,* vol. 77, 1989, pp. 521–538, and in Michael J. Sandel, *Democracy's Discontent* (Harvard University Press, 1996).

Chapter 22: Originally published in *The New Republic,* May 7, 1984.

Chapter 23: Originally published in *Political Theory,* vol. 12, no. 1, February 1984, pp. 81–96.

Chapter 24: Originally published in *The New York Times,* April 24, 1983.

Chapter 25: Originally published in *Dissent,* Summer 1986, reprinted with permission.

Chapter 26: Originally published in *The New York Review of Books,* vol. 43, no. 8, May 9, 1996.

Chapter 27: Originally published in *Judaism and Modernity: The Religious Philosophy of David Hartman,* ed. Jonathan W. Malino, pp. 121–132, © Ashgate, 2004.

Chapter 28: Originally published in the *Harvard Law Review,* vol. 107, no. 7, May 1994, pp. 1765–1794.

Chapter 29: Originally published in *The New Republic,* December 16, 2002.

Chapter 30: Originally published in Michael J. Sandel, *Liberalism and the Limits of Justice,* 2nd edition, pp. ix–xvi, © Cambridge University Press, 1998. Reprinted with permission.

# INDEX